SOUL OF AFRICA

SOUL OF AFRICA

Magical Rites and Traditions

Photographs by Henning Christoph
Text by Klaus E. Müller
and Ute Ritz-Müller

KÖNEMANN

© 1999 Könemann Verlagsgesellschaft mbH
Bonner Str. 126, D-50968 Cologne

Publishing and Art Direction: Peter Feierabend
Project Manager: Ute Edda Hammer
Assistants: Kerstin Ludolph, Anna Bechinie
Layout: Christian Maiwurm, Carmen Strzelecki
Cartography: Studio für Landkartentechnik, Norderstedt
Graphics: Rolli Arts, Essen
Production Manager: Detlev Schaper
Production: Mark Voges
Lithography: niemann & steggemann, Oldenburg

Original title: *Soul of Africa. Magie eines Kontinents*

© Copyright 2000 for the English edition
Könemann Verlagsgesellschaft mbH

Translation from German: Amanda Riddick, Neil and Ting Morris and Sabine Troelsch
Editing: Lucilla Watson for Book Creation Services, Ltd.
Typesetting: Gene Ferber for Book Creation Services, Ltd.
Project Management: Tami Rex for Book Creation Services, Ltd.
Project Coordination: Bettina Kaufmann, Kristin Zeier
Production: Ursula Schümer
Printing and Binding: Imprimerie Jean Lamour, Maxéville
Printed in France

ISBN 3-8290-2716-8
10 9 8 7 6 5 4 3 2 1

Table of contents

Following pages:
A map of Africa framed by illustrations.
Map by Victor Levasseur, c. 1840, 11 ½ x 17 inches. Illustrations by Raimond Bonheur, Paris.
Hand-colored etching by Laguillermie.

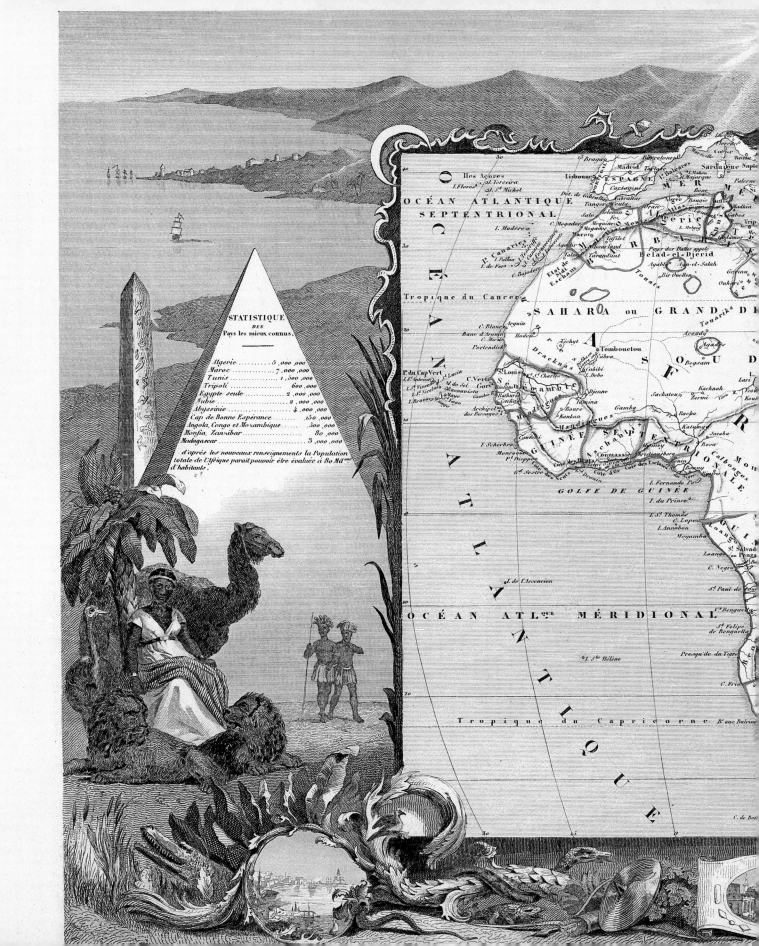

STATISTIQUE
DES
Pays les mieux connus.

Algerie	5,000,000
Maroc	7,000,000
Tunis	1,500,000
Tripoli	600,000
Egypte seule	2,000,000
Nubie	2,000,000
Abyssinie	4,000,000
Cap de Bonne Espérance	150,000
Angola, Congo et Mozambique	500,000
Monfia, Zanzibar	80,000
Madagascar	3,000,000

d'après les nouveaux renseignements la Population
totale de l'Afrique parait pouvoir être évaluée à 80 Mil.ons
d'habitants.

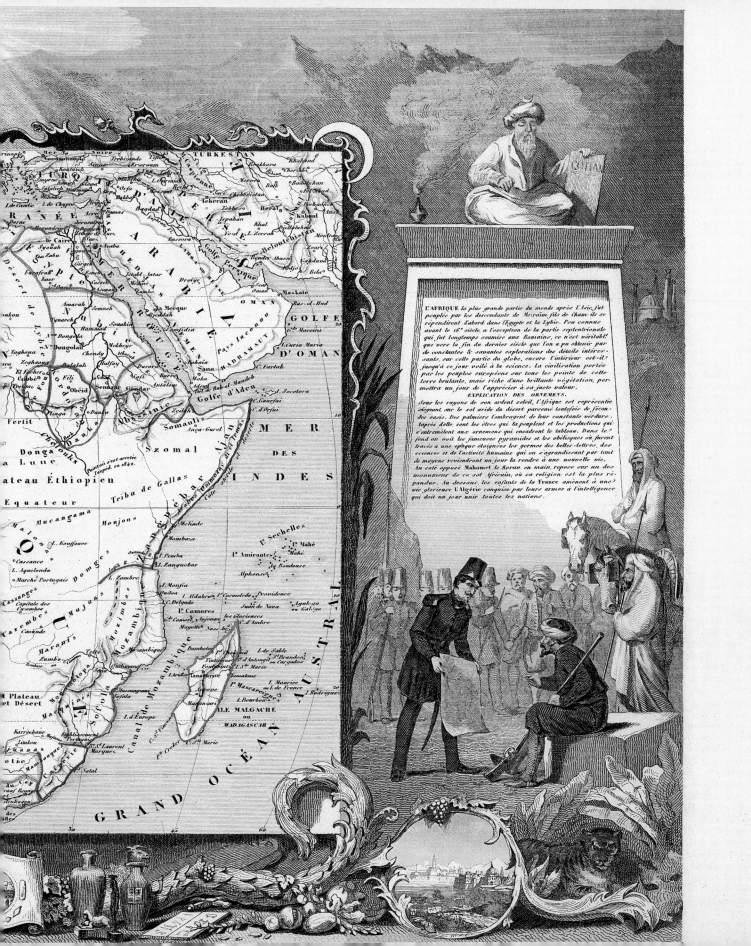

Family, relatives, and community

We take for granted that most of us grow up in a family. Nevertheless the rate of divorce in modern Western societies is increasing dramatically, and more and more families are falling apart after only a few years. It used to be different in the old rural communities. The family represented a truly "sacred" and also universal institution. Ethnological research has found no culture where the family does not form the core of every social community.

There had to be pressing reasons for this. The most important was obviously the continuation of the group. Without successive generations small village communities would not have been able to survive. The issue was not so much to make sure that enough children were born but that they were raised in a safe environment and that they were sufficiently prepared for their future tasks. In particular, it had to be absolutely clear who was responsible for this. In current Western societies this is primarily

the responsibility of parents because it is assumed that both mother and father contribute equally to the formation of their children in equal parts.

It was precisely this that in earlier, more "traditional" societies, including those of Africa, was seen quite differently. According to old but universally accepted interpretations, the basic substances necessary for creating the fetus are the father's sperm and the mother's menstrual blood, which through repeated intercourse is kept inside the mother's body; this is also why, after conception, menstruation stops. The blood forms the more liquid and the softer, and thus more transient, parts of the body, while the sperm forms the harder, more stable parts such as bones, teeth, nails, and hair.

But a child only really starts life when it gains its soul. This happens in two ways, as according to old beliefs, a human being has two kinds of soul. One is the "life soul," which is responsible purely for the maintenance of the organic functioning of the body and which is transmitted immediately to the fetus by the sperm. The other is the "free soul," independent of the body and immortal, which gives a human being consciousness, the ability to think, and the power of will and judgment. This is then transmitted gradually from outside the body but also from the father. It was assumed that the father received the child's soul in a dream or in nature, by going past a particular refuge of children's souls – this could be a puddle, pond, group of rocks or particular trees – and transmitted it to his wife during the next occurrence of intercourse.

In this respect, therefore, fathers play the biggest part in conception. From them comes the skeleton, which means the figure, strength, and consciousness. It is for this reason that the rule of patrilineal origin exists in most traditional societies. Children are really "related by blood" only to their father and his ancestors, and to members of the family on their father's side, which is why we also say "related through the bones."

In about 15 percent of known cases the other possibility – of maternal, that is, matrilineal ancestry – exists. This is also the case in some parts of Africa. In these instances, the life soul carried in the mother's blood is the dominant factor, and the free soul is transmitted purely by physical proximity or touch from the mother's brother or often a male ancestor – members of her family albeit male ones.

Even so, matrilineal, or "matrilegal," societies differ from patrilineal, or "patrilegal," ones in some important ways, for instance in the relation of family members to each other. There is a closer relationship between a mother's brother and her children – blood relations – than between them and their physical father. They belong to their mother's family. Therefore their uncle is responsible for their upbringing, in particular that of his nephews, for whom he is a kind of guardian. Rules of inheritance are also dictated by this. Following the death of the mother, entitlement to her inheritance goes first to her eldest brother, then to her sons (his nephews) and their sisters. Only in Angola is the mother's (eldest) sister the preferred heir. On marriage, daughters remain in the area of their mother's family; the man moves in, but not always. Often his main place of residence is that of his own family, and only he comes to visit his wife and children, which is why this is often described as a "visit marriage."

In Africa matrilegal societies are also distinguished by a range of particular cultural conventions. For instance, there are distinctively collective coming-of-age rituals for girls, which otherwise would be carried out individually. During these rituals – and also on other occasions – the strengthening of female fertility is particularly emphasized. Sculpted images of breasts decorate doors, drums, and even furnaces. Only female ancestors are made into idols. Also, obssessional cults appear noticeably

Left: A Turfinu family, who live in pile dwellings. The figures of twins in the foreground indicate that a pair of twins in the family have died and thus become the family's guardian gods. The family treats them as if they were living, feeding and powdering them, for example.

A family (Habbaniya, group of the Uled Hemat, Darfur) in front of their dome-shaped straw hut. Photograph c. 1930.

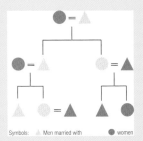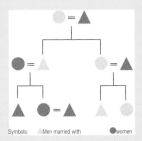

Diagrams showing matrilineal and patrilineal order of descent. In the first instance (left), blood relations are passed through the mother, in the second (right) through the father.

more often than in patrilegal societies. Women, in particular the wives of chiefs, possess far greater freedom and more rights, but they nonetheless never have unlimited power over the younger members of their family. The eldest brother remains the ultimate and highest holder of power and is therefore the real head of the family.

The matrilegal societies of Africa show a distinctive spread. There is a particularly dense incidence of these in a broad belt running from Angola, in the west, across central East Africa to the coasts of Mozambique and Tanzania in the east, extending northward all the way to the southern Republic of Congo. A second grouping in West Africa reaches from the Gabon, in the south, across parts of Cameroon (Duala) to Upper Guinea. Its main area of concentration lies in Ghana and in Ivory Coast (Kru, Baule, Agni Ashanti, Fante, among others). In the north an old matrilegal culture still exists among the Berbers and their Tuareg descendants. There are also isolated instances of societies with matrilineal descendancy in other areas, such as the Nuba in Kordofan (Republic of Sudan).

This area is affected by its close proximity to the territory of African kingdoms. These also often show specifically matriarchal characteristics, even when the ruling elite differs ethnically from the long established population. Particularly typical of these societies is the elevated position of the queen's mother (whose position can also be taken by the oldest woman in a high-ranking aristocratic family (as in Loango), the king's sister, the queen herself, or her eldest daughter. They have their own residences and can take on particular administrative tasks, such as acting as judge, and even responsibilities of rule (as with the Kuba and

Among other things the Dogon are well known for their particularly good onions. Here Dogon women are carrying them to market.

A Kirdi village, with the pointed roofs particularly typical of northern Cameroon. The village is surrounded by terraced fields belonging to individual inhabitants.

Luba in the Congo area, among others). Sometimes accession to the throne also runs along matriarchal lines in that the position of ruler does not pass to the king's eldest son but to his sister's son. Ideally, son and nephew are one and the same person, as it was common for the king to take his own sister for his wife.

In both matrilineal and patrilineal systems of succession it is important that blood relations be unilinear – through a single line, either only through the father and his family or through the mother and her relatives. This means that the children belong only to one clan, in the more frequent case to the father and his family. Therefore the father, in the position of priority in the family, holds the main responsibility for their upbringing.

This, however, mostly concerns sons, for they are the ones who, like their paternal ancestors, will remain in their home village. According to legend the originator of their clan founded or "created" the village so that it now "belongs" to his descendants. From this ancient point of view, one has a legitimate claim to everything one produces, manufactures, discovers, and invents as well as to the ground beneath one's feet. Therefore the village and its surrounding fields are a rightful possession of the local clan. As the members of that clan have lived there for the longest time, they also know their surroundings better than others, including the spirits who care for hunted wild animals and grant fertility to the earth, or who live out in the bush in springs, ponds, caves, or undergrowth and lead careless people to ruin. Sons have to learn all this, the long handed-down knowledge and the culture of their group, from their fathers and older relatives. Girls in a patrilineal society, by contrast, leave their home village and move in with their husband's family.

In many cases the members of one particular clan or a subgroup of the clan (a so-called lineage or subclan) make up the majority of a village's population, which on average, comprises between 50 and 150 people. This means that there are insufficient numbers of prospective marriage partners of the same age within the community; the limits of the incest taboo would also soon be reached. The solution to the problem of, on one hand, staying as closely as possible within the circle of one's own family and, on the other, of avoiding marriages between close relatives is the age-old tradition of exogamy ("outward marriage") within the limits of the tribe (tribal endogamy). Two or more lineages, subclans, or clans tend to

13

choose their marriage partners from among each other, with the girls, as already mentioned, moving to the home village of their husband (virilocality).

The wives are thus in a sense "strangers" in the families of their husbands. At the same time it is expected of them that they bring future sons and keepers of the clan into the world. This explains the often very complicated and long drawn-out wedding ceremonies. Analysis of the structure of these ceremonies reveals that they are basically adoption rituals by which the "alien" young woman is turned into a "semi-blood relative." Therefore, a marriage is really only fully contracted when the first child is born, and the relationship is bound tighter with each further birth – particularly if the woman gives birth to many sons.

Marriages are initially not based on attraction, especially in the past, when the future partners hardly knew each other.

A potter in Burkina Faso with earthenware beer jugs, in which African millet beer is served.

A Kirdi woman wearing traditional clothing, a leaf tied to her body. The calabash is used to carry millet.

However, their parents, in particular their mothers, begin early to look for suitable partners within the ascribed limits. Outward appearances matter less here than diligence, dexterity, reliability, and respect for the family of origin. Only attributes and virtues of this nature are the sort of reliable criteria which will guarantee the maintenance of the family and ultimately the community's survival. Since attraction alone is given little importance, divorce in rural areas is quite rare. This is especially because the two partners are supported by a wide network of many relationships and relations whose interests would be unpleasantly challenged by such a break. Everyone keeps a watchful eye on the couple, admonishing, counseling, and mediating in serious cases to the last possible resort.

Should separation really occur, there must be serious reasons for it. These could be continuous cruelty by the husband, adultery, serious abandoning of duties, and suspected black magic and witchcraft. The most important reason is a woman's infertility. After all, according to the theories of conception described above, the reasons for childlessness are not to be sought in the man. Since his part is especially the transmission of the free soul, one must therefore assume that the soul has a strong reason for not wanting to come near the mother.

Connection by marriage involves two types of relations: on the one hand, consanguine origin, or blood relation, and on the other, relation by affinity, the marriage relations. The idea of distance that nevertheless exists between them is emphasized in many languages in such words as "mother-in-law" and "father-in-law," where the terms from the family of origin are applied to the in-laws, so that the members of that family, in fact, become "quasi-blood relatives."

Relations become closer if the husband later enters into one or more other marital relationships, especially as not infrequently he chooses the sisters of his first wife. In such cases one speaks of sisterly polygamy, a "many-women-marriage with sisters." African families can be monogamous or polygamous. This depends not only on the man's wealth, but also on the type of field-farming. If the women are more involved in this work, then a family with several wives will do better. However, in this case it is customary for each wife to live in her own hut with her children. The husband visits and stays the night at each one according to a strictly regulated cycle.

Thus a single household can expand to become a farm. If the sons remain living with their father, as is often the custom in

Africa, then a large family of usually three generations – grandparents, parents, uncles, aunts, nephews, nieces, and so on down to the grandchildren – will live together in an appropriately wide-ranging area with several huts and a central space for gatherings and religious celebrations, all within one encircling wall.

Nevertheless, all members of the family are aware of and adhere to the distances between the various degrees of relation, dictated by sexes and age. A young wife in particular must observe a number of rules regarding her behavior, style of greetings and address, and much more, when dealing with her husband and his siblings, her mother-in-law, her father-in-law, her grandparents-in-law, and so on. The more children she bears, bringing her closer to her husband's family as parts of both families are united within them, the less strict these behavioral rules become. As is the case with the Fulbe, she may now eat with

her mother-in-law and behave with less reserve toward her, but nevertheless physical contact between them remains taboo. The younger woman must speak more softly and must also observe other particular forms of politeness. Hardly anything changes in her behavior towards her father-in-law. Addressing him directly, for instance, would be a severe breach of customs.

This is certainly a way of preventing conflict in a space where many live closely together. Many other regulations regarding domestic life serve the same purpose. In monogamous families, the hut (which normally consists only of one room) is divided into two spaces: one for the woman and the younger children, the other for the man and the sons from the age of about five. The head of the family has a place of honor behind the fire, facing toward the entrance and out into the village. On farms

Fulbe women in the market in Djenne (Mali). The market is a woman's place.

A Kirdi woman milling millet, Africa's staple food, which is used in many different dishes.

Only few tribes eat pork. Pigs are used mostly for keeping villages clean (as here in Zambia), as they eat all refuse. However, the animals are also prone to infestations of worms.

with large families the hut of the oldest family member or the head of the family is usually situated at the center, close to the communal space.

Different types of work and responsibilities are also assigned strictly by sex and age. The main responsibility of women is housework. Besides looking after the younger children, this includes cleaning and maintenance, collecting water and firewood, preparing food, and often also monitoring food supplies. In addition, there is the care of domestic animals, which in traditional agricultural societies with low-level farming are usually few: chickens, goats, pigs and, in drier environments, also sheep. The women also make the implements and other items that they use in their work – particularly pots and textiles – and very often build the hut for a small family.

Men's tasks include all larger and public building work (wells, roads, bridges, walls, huts for large families or for gatherings, mosques), the manufacture of all the tools and weapons that they use, and the care of cattle, which are sometimes kept in small numbers. The men also receive guests, assume functions in the community and act as members of communal and elders' councils, and with increasing age take up religious roles.

Although they have separate roles to play, both sexes take part in agricultural work. Usually the men prepare the ground for sowing by breaking it up, by hand or using a stick or pickax; this is tough, demanding work in a savanna or steppe at the end of the dry season. Until recently plows were known only in northern and northeastern Africa, and in the colonized areas. Practically all other work in the fields falls to the women. They sow and plant small cuttings, rake the fields several times over, and finally bring in the harvest. They often also go into the bush and woods to gather edible roots, wild plants and herbs, berries, insects, and small animals such as snails, frogs, and lizards. These count as a desirable addition to the diet, as they provide a high level of vitamins or nutrients, and frogs and lizards are rich in animal protein and fat.

Overall, the men are assigned the riskier tasks which require greater strength in the short term, while the women carry out work that is less dangerous and requires less concentrated but more prolonged effort. This makes the load appear equally distributed. However, it is the women who work longer and harder and who also contribute most to providing for the family. As soon as they are able to, children are also drawn in to work. In contrast, with increasing age, older men take on more and more intellectual and spiritual or mental tasks. They plan and organize family and community projects, dispense advice, mediate in arguments, guard the upholding of traditions, take responsibility for the cult of the ancestors, and represent

A Dogon blacksmith at work. Apart from being metalworkers they are also responsible for carving religious sculptures.

A Senoufu village in Ivory Coast, where several men have teamed up to build a new house out of clay bricks.

family and community at meetings and negotiations with neighboring groups. This must not be seen merely as a sort of well-meaning care for the elderly. In societies which used to change little over centuries, older people were seen as superior to those who were younger because of their experience in every regard and so were closer to the ancestors – all good

reasons for making them invaluable and according them the greatest respect that they deserve.

However, age is not only a matter of considerable years. Generally anyone may expect respect and obedience from those younger than himself, while the older one is duty-bound to be helpful and generous toward the young. This applies as much to children who are only one or two years apart in age as to the eldest people and others in the community. It is one of the basics of politeness which is impressed on children at an early age. The process of upbringing itself is rather discreet, taking forms like patient reminders, descriptive gestures, warning glances, teasing, an occasional slap, which only rarely turns into a proper beating, and above all the parent's own example.

Africans have a strong sense of tact and treat each other with the utmost consideration. For example, well-behaved children would never open their mouths while anyone older is speaking, particularly adults. For this reason Westerners are often regarded as highly ill-mannered – of course, this behavior is the subject of many jokes once they are out of earshot.

Good manners are no less an indispensable precondition for living in close proximity without conflict as are the clearly defined assignment of duties and powers. This has an important additional function: as everyone is responsible for something different, everyone is also dependent on each other. Ethnologists speak of the principle of reciprocity, by which everyone is obliged to return a gift with a gift of the same value, whether immediately or over a longer period of time. The closer people live together or the closer they are related, particularly in the case of blood relatives within the family, this counts all the more. For instance, brothers carry greater responsibility for their sisters than

At communal gatherings a highly nutritious millet beer is served, which is stored in clay pots and then drunk out of halved gourds.

do husbands for their wives; often the sibling relationship is closer than the marital one.

In this way a conscious solidarity is formed between relatives and in particular family members, the intensity of which goes beyond a Westerner's understanding. One is there for the others, absolutely and at any price – or at least one should be. The shared hut, the house, are areas of real safety, togetherness, and community, with the hearth at the center as a symbol of family life; the hearth is where food for all is prepared every day, it gives out light as well as warmth, and around its fire, which should never go out, the family comes together in a close gathering.

Like the family in their home, relatives tend to live in one village, or, in the case of larger settlements, in one street or area. While marriages and any ensuing relationships through marriage can be dissolved, blood ties are forever. It is not only the shared traditions, customs, language, and the whole culture that serve as an expression of these ties; it is also believed that members are the same in being. The joy or pain experienced by one is immediately transmitted to all the others. When food is in short supply, one helps the other out. Orphans are adopted by others in the family. The sick and the old are not left to fend for themselves. There have been several reports of "crisis telepathy" between very close relatives: for instance, a father can dream, "see," or feel that his son is in danger. All form a higher overall organism in which experiences immediately take root and multiply. The individual is in a highly sensitive reciprocal relationship to all others, so that, in the words of an ethnologist describing the Iraqw of Tanzania, "the good as well as bad actions of any member immediately pulls the whole group into the shared experience," all of them therefore forming a "morally closed body."

Irritation, jealousy, and hatred can easily turn into divisive arguments and are therefore strictly taboo between relatives and even more so between family members. The Zande in the south of the Republic of Sudan say that "witchcraft follows in the footsteps of malice." Jealousy in particular is seen as the root of all evil. To prevent such problems from even beginning, there is a clear rule to maintain harmony and peace. Undoubtedly it is an ideal, but everyone is aware of its absolute necessity. The Boran in southern Ethiopia, for instance, openly describe this as a "sacred duty" and bring up at every opportunity the "peace of the Boran" as a constant appeal. At a higher level – at meetings of the councils of elders, for instance – this sense of unity can practically turn into an incantation as the councilors, among the Iraqw, for example, chant in unison at the beginning of each meeting "we are one, we are of one opinion, we love each other."

It is particularly in times of crisis that this must prove itself. At births, after circumcisions, in serious cases of illness, or during other emergencies, relatives must not be at odds, much less argue or break a taboo. The latter in particular could carry terrible consequences, as this would damage the existing order and therefore make demands on the ancestral authority. African communities feel strongly that a group consists not only of the living generations but also of those who have died – their ancestors beneath the ground. Through blood ties the two are inseparably bound together to form a single, tight social organism. Its "heart" continues to beat always, as the souls of the departed, continuously circling between this world and that beyond, will one day return, usually after the third or fourth generation, to their family through reincarnation. Thus, as the highest elders, the dead do not only enjoy greater reverence than the elders on earth, but are also the object of a cult which is often

Babies are often left in the care of their siblings so that the mother can go about her business without disruption.

the basis for African religiousness. Ultimately, it is the ancestors who are responsible for guarding the traditions that they once experienced and maintained. Therefore, if someone commits an offense that goes unnoticed among the living, the ancestors intervene, striking the sinner – or perhaps a relative, since they are all "one body," so that retribution could fall on them all – with sickness, a disaster, or a bad harvest.

Only on particular occasions, such as when important decisions affecting the whole village are made, are the elders allowed to enter the abode of the *hogon* (religious leader), which, as the hogon's most sacred place, is otherwise closed to human beings. A hogon is also bound to certain rituals and duties. For instance, he is not allowed to wash with water but must lay down in a pit of snakes, whose movements cleanse him.

Feasts and celebrations – ritual anarchy

Feasts are community events. At least two participants are required. However, in African societies celebrations take place in a larger circle: within the family, among relatives, or involving the whole village. The occasion must not necessarily be a happy one, but it must be special and ceremonial. This is what makes feasts different from the everyday.

Generally, celebrations mark important life stages or seasonal events: they take place at the birth of a child, soon after its naming, and at the end of puberty (initiation). Later will follow the wedding, perhaps an official appointment and finally the funeral, as well as the memorial celebrations of the dead at regular intervals. In all these instances the life stage is connected with a change in status. A dead soul reincarnates itself and transforms from an ancestor into a human being; a woman into a mother, the husband into a father, an adolescent into an adult; unmarried people enter wedlock, a living person departs to join his or her ancestors.

The whole society is affected by seasonal changes, which in Africa particularly means those between the wet and dry seasons, as these are fundamental to farming. Farming begins toward the end of the dry season, in anticipation of the first rains; it is marked by the ceremonial beginning of working the field and by sowing rituals. At the end of the rainy season there is a harvest celebration. In hunter-gatherer societies the equivalent would be

The Latuka performing a death dance. Drawing after E. Ade, after Baker, Albert Nianza, Costenoble. From: *Die Völker der Erde*, Würzburg and Vienna, 1891.

the return of certain migrating birds, the beginning of a particular hunting season and the fruiting of important wild plants (nuts, seeds, berries). With nomadic herdsmen it is driving the herd out to pasture and its return.

Celebrations thus mark a kind of pause between phases of living, being, and doing. It is a change from one phase to the next; however, those experiencing the change remain for a short while in an insecure limbo where the rules of the former stage – for instance, that of childhood – no longer really apply, but where those of the next stage – that of being an adult – are not truly valid either. It is precisely this hiatus that is treated both as risky and as a way of influencing the next stage. Celebrations, with their defined dramaturgy and sequence of ritual, take all of this into account.

Basically, a feast always consists of three steps, which, depending on the meaning of events, may sometimes be very short, may sometimes be carried out to their full extent, and sometimes take place with a decadent richness of form. In the last instance the whole process mirrors a human life in order to give the event greater dramatic impact. The celebrants "die" (for instance, as unmarrieds), pass through a phase of "being dead" and transformation, and are finally "resurrected to a new life" as a married couple. At these celebrations attendance by all members of the community is vital so that the participants or the whole

Sharpening the teeth, preparations for a wedding among the Mandigo. From: *Westafrika. Vom Senegal bis Benguela*, Leipzig, 1878.

community experiences the transformation, the ritual rebirth, as one body, without a gap or a weak point which could admit destructive influences.

The beginning, the "dying," is marked by particular rules of abstinence (such as sexual abstinence) and fasting. In the case of weddings the bride and groom go into hiding so that they can no longer be seen: they are "dead" until, wearing the clothing and ornaments that mark their new status, they re-enter the community. Only then, with the beginning of the wedding ritual, a shared meal, and the inclusion of all does the celebration's high point really occur.

Celebrations temporarily take life out of the regulated routine of the everyday. One of the most marked dramatic devices of celebrations is therefore their sharp contrast, the "turning inside out," of the everyday. Nobody works; instead everyone devotes themselves to enjoyment, puts on clothes which are not everyday but a special kind of celebration dress; everyone eats and drinks more than circumstances would normally allow, and entertains themselves with music, dancing, singing, and games. The "inside-out" is even more emphasized by the sexes' change-over of clothes and roles as well as a general air of permissiveness that often also temporarily invalidates all rules of politeness as well as sexual taboos. The ethnological term for this is "ritual anarchy."

Notwithstanding these regulated irregularities, so to speak, the cult of ancestry is the iron core of all important feasts. As the different phases unfold, they allow not only the bonds of regulation to be loosened, sometimes even dissolved for a short time, but also the opening of the living world to the beyond. It is believed that spirits, gods, but above all ancestors can gain entry to the larger feasts. Often they are helped by letting their idols or mask wearers appear so that they have a place for the duration for their visit where they can receive fitting respect and adoration. It is proper to praise them and to commemorate them in songs, to thank them for the harvest blessing, to serve them sacrificial food, and dine together with them. The latter is the zenith of the most important feasts, the harvest, or "new year" celebrations. Usually, a sacred meal is made out of the harvested produce – bread is baked, a porridge is prepared, beer is brewed from the grains – which the oldest of the group eat in the presence of the others and, it is believed, together with the ancestors. Only after this may everybody avail themselves of the new harvest. And, as much still seems "open" before the next phase is entered, it is also part of the celebratory cult to carry out strengthening rituals, particularly those which will bring health and fertility. People try to influence the future by making promises to each other, in some cases by solemnly vowing to improve, or, not least importantly, by using the "window into the beyond" – consulting oracles, visualizing or dreaming the future, and having their fortune told by seers.

The function of celebrations is once again to strengthen through ritual the order that has been seemingly loosened and therefore endangered during shifts between phases. After the ancestors' attendance, the dressing up, and the turbulent permissiveness, the everyday returns – but under improved conditions. The huts, the tools, the animals, and the people have undergone a thorough cleansing. Differences have been settled, misdemeanors admitted to and atoned for – for instance, through sacrifices – and both fertility and vitality renewed. Everyone has done this together and lived through something that their unity and solidarity have not only made an immediate and unavoidable experience but also have made clear: what can be achieved by working together.

Disciples of Legba at the consecration ceremony of a figure of the god. Legba, a trickster, has a mischievous and educational character.

Through dramatized heightening, celebrations demonstrate both the existence and the meaning of the overall order. They prove that if all work in unity and as a community, this order can not only withstand any possible upheavals, but also that it can emerge even stronger afterward. Celebrations bring trust and strengthen confidence. As the nostalgically reminiscing village eldest of the Kossi in Cameroon once said to an ethnologist, the annual celebration of harvest and ancestry "used to be our religion."

The power of the chieftains

In the kingdom of Akuapem, the old year ends and the new year begins with the *odwira* ("cleansing"). Only after the conclusion of this celebration, which takes place in September every year, is it permissible to eat the new yams, the traditional food of the Akan. The inhabitants of Akuapem say, "We wash before we eat."

Mirroring the underlying ideology, odwira is considered as timeless and unalterable as the royal ancestors, their blackened stools, and the king himself. Odwira celebrates the unbroken continuity of the realm, the monarchy, and the power

On odwira Friday messengers run through the streets of Aburi and call upon the royal officials to appear at court. Aburi is one of the cities of the Akuapem kingdom which broke away in 1994 and now no longer recognizes the king's authority.

structures that it has developed. At the same time reality paints a different picture. Since Akuapem's foundation (around 1730) several sections have fought for control. Apart from conflicts within the dynasty, separatist tendencies by single villages or areas have now and again threatened the kingdom's unity. The origin of these tensions lies also in historical events, which are interpreted and presented differently by different groups. However, it means that the legitimacy of the ruling position of the king, who resides in Akuropon, is permanently open to question. During colonial times the efforts of the British appeasement policy protected easily damaged power structures. However, in more recent times there has been much unrest. Conflict reached a peak in 1994 as revolts and open resistance to the king broke out in several places. Since then, no representative from these breakaway communities has come to the odwira in the capital. Instead they have their own celebrations, emphasizing their own power and independence.

Officially, however, Akuapem only has a religious king. He is the link between ancestors, the living and the as yet unborn. As an ideal, he embodies the country's unity and singlemindedness. He stands at the center of the odwira celebrations, which renew him as well as the whole kingdom. In Akuropon these celebrations last more than two months, reaching their high point in one eventful week. During this time the kingdom and its history are, so to speak, broken up into separate events and then put back together again. The king suffers a symbolic death from which he rises full of new life.

On the Wednesday preceding the week of the festival the blackened stools of the royal ancestors are set aside to "rest" until the beginning of odwira week. From now there is an immediate ban on drumming – and therefore on any funeral celebrations – as well as on the eating of yams. On the Monday morning of the festival week royal servants clean the path to the place where the royal ancestors' bones are kept, thereby preparing the

The "soul child" wears a headdress made of eagle feathers, leopard skin, and small pieces of crocodile skin which are all held together by gold wire. It is decorated at the front by gilded rams' horns. The child lives in the palace and is supposed to protect the king from any danger. The child tastes the king's food before he is served, and in the past also had to follow the king into death.

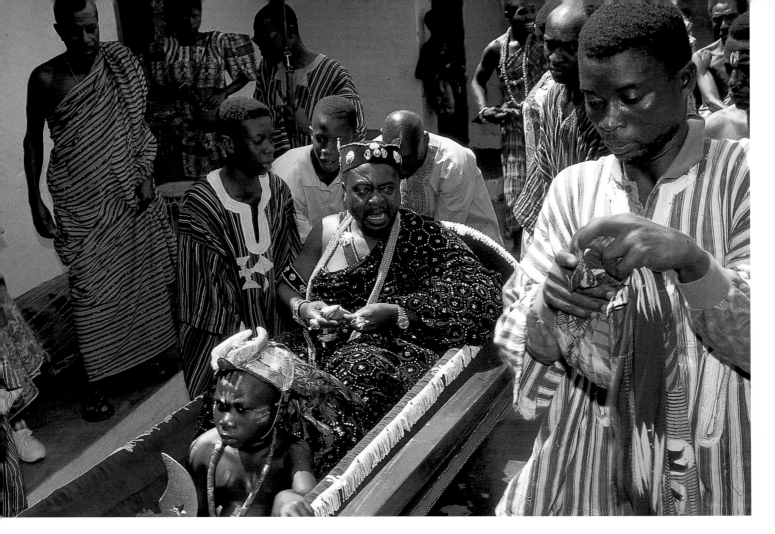

The king, protected by a circular screen, is accompanied by his dignitaries. Women praise his name while servants carry gold rods decorated with golden amulets. Everything surrounding the king embodies his majestic reign. Even "the leaves on the trees tremble" before such might.

Previous pages: The procession of king, queen, and chieftains on the odwira festival's last day through the now cleansed city of Aburi.

way for their entry into the city. On Tuesday the new yams are displayed. The "white" stools on which the king and his advisers sit are washed early in the morning.

After this the city's elders process to the royal mausoleum, accompanied by two drummers. There the Banmuhene, the First Guard of the Graves, takes some earth from the ancestral graves and leads the visitors back to the city. On their way they sing war songs and make brief halts at historically important sites. As soon as they reach Akuropon the ban on drumming ceases, and the beats loudly announce the arrival of odwira time. Kept apart in his residence the king now undergoes a most effective and dramatic ritual. Wearing mourning clothes he retreats behind a cloth screen, where the Banhumene rubs earth from the graves all over him so that the living king is accepted by the ancestors. Soon after the king publicly presents himself in all his splendor and with renewed powers. From this time on the ancestors rule the city and the royal

residence. The usual order is no longer valid: when the king is between life and death, his realm too becomes unsteady.

The new year starts on odwira-Wednesday. It is a day of mourning, and loud drumming and wailing can be heard all over the city. Life on this Wednesday is the opposite from the everyday: people fast but drink at the same time; the women sing bawdy songs and sexual liberties are allowed; anarchy has come to Akuropon. The king appears not as a mild and benevolent ruler but in the role of his conquering ancestors, as a frightening warrior decorated with numerous amulets. After midnight a procession of young men takes the blackened ancestors' stools to the river, where they are cleaned, freed from all the "dirt" that has settled on them over the last year.

While Wednesday is a day of gloom and death, Thursday sees the return to life. Early in the morning several sheep, Akan symbols of peace, are slaughtered. The meat and oto-yams together make up the feast. For this, the yams are not cooked as usual, as a kind of white porridge but instead are mashed and prepared both with and without palm oil – "red" and "white." Oto is seen as the food of the gods, ancestors, and souls (*kra*). The blackened ancestral stools are once again put out, and the living eat for the ancestors too.

Akuropon stays closed for the following night, when secret rituals honoring the gods take place. Angry spirits of the dead are appeased so that from now on ancestors and the living can again exist side by side. On Friday all the king's officials must appear at court. During their preparations the king is quietly taken from the palace to the edge of town, from where he processes back into the city in a splendid display of gleaming wealth and power. He ends his journey by stepping from the palace onto a raised platform. Peace is re-established, and all those present wish each other the best for the new year. By their attendance, subordinate princes and village chiefs renew the oath of loyalty that they made at their appointment to office. Then they swore that they would come whenever the king called them, "whether rain or shine," a promise which is no longer kept by everyone today.

On the last day of the odwira festival the king's stool, which is filled with gold, is carried through Aburi. The display of gold is grounded in the tradition of presenting all his wealth on this day.

A view of crowded Aburi as the king, queen and chieftains make their way through its streets. Umbrellas always signify rulers or kings, who are carried through the city.

Thanksgiving to the city god of Atito

A priestess of the city god of Atito painted for celebration. The white clay (*kaolin*) represents her ritual purity, a condition for making contact with the deity. The city god was adopted as a patron particularly by the fishermen, as he was discovered in a tree trunk which was lying in the water.

The Anlo-Ewe inhabit the far southwest of the Ewe region, which extends from southeastern Ghana across southern Togo to southern Benin. From their original home in the bend on the Niger, the Anlo brought various gods, who were joined by older local deities in the new homeland. Living on mountains and steep cliffs, and in canyons and caves, these *trowo* (deities) play an important part in life. Mawu-Lisa, the distant god of the sky, created them to help humans. Since then they have been close to people, working as mediators between humans and the sky god. Tirelessly they make sure that his commandments are obeyed, and they punish transgressions with drought or devastating storms, with sickness or sudden death. However, they also reward loyalty in individuals, families, villages, and towns, who owe their health and prosperity to the trowo's care. The trowo call particular people into their service through revelations and through them communicate their wishes and orders. These people, their priests and priestesses, are in constant contact with them, while the general public turns to them only in times of urgent need. As family or clan deities, they protect single families as well as small family and neighbor communities who give their thanks in a large annual celebration.

The city god of Atito resides in an old tree trunk. The tree was once found in a nearby lagoon and was nearly used as firewood, but the deities (trowo) spoke through their priests, "This tree is the city's father, he is an important god (tro) who must be obeyed." As he had been lying in the water he was adopted as a patron particularly by the fishermen. They made sacrifices to him on the banks of the lagoon or directly on the tree trunk by pouring blood over him and serving him with mashed corn and brandy. The attending priest

would say the following, "Your children have not caught any more fish and have therefore gotten these things for you. Here are the gifts they have brought you! When they go into the yonder with the fish, may the yonder be good to them!" Then he would sprinkle the nets with a medicine, and usually the god would reward this attention with a good catch.

The thanksgiving festival for the city god takes place on the Tuesday after Easter, as Tuesday is usually a day off for Ghanaian fishermen. All those whose prayers have been answered by the deity over the year gather to fulfill their side of the deal. Accompanied by loud drumming a crowd of people processes towards the god's residence. An iron rattle, the so-called divine bell (*awaga*) summons the god to be present. His priest welcomes him with a sacrificial drink and in quick succession slaughters the many animals brought in for sacrifice.

A drummer calls all those who over the past year have made a request of the god of Atito and have promised a sacrifice in return. Now is the time to fulfill that promise.

A follower of the city god of Atito wearing a crown and necklace that she made herself from whisky bottle tops. The celebrations always take place on the Tuesday after Easter, as Tuesday is usually a day off for Ghanaian fishermen.

29

Those who have promised a sacrifice hand their gift to the priest, who quickly slaughters the many chickens and goats that have been brought in. Goats which often wander beyond the village boundaries to feed in the bush are the favorite sacrificial animal for nature deities, while sheep grazing within the village tend to be kept for ancestors.

A priest pouring out the blood of sacrificial animals.

The celebrations end with a great communal meal, at the end of which the priest gives the deity's blessing to all those present. In earlier days he made a visible representation of the promised salvation by rubbing a mud paste on the foreheads and temples of the worshipers. The return into the city is again accompanied by loud drumming, and the cry "Life, yes, life!" can be heard over and over again. The celebration strengthens not only the links within the community but also brings hope and confidence for the future. However, due to external influences which have loosened family and neighborly bonds, the introduction of other, alien deities, and the spread of Christianity, the city god of Atito no longer enjoys the community's undivided attention.

When the god has had enough blood, meat, and porridge, he will possess one of those present. Hermaphrodites seem to be particularly susceptible to possession, as their dual sexuality brings them naturally closer to the often androgynous gods.

Ewe priestesses dance around a man possessed by the city god.

Jeering at hunger

The Ga too have not forgotten their history. Their main festival *homowo*, "jeering at hunger," is today celebrated all over the Ga region. It is a reminder of the first meager meal eaten by the ancestors on their arrival in their new homeland. Then, all resources were in short supply, whereas now everyone has plenty of *kpokpoi* to eat. The word kpokpoi consists of two parts, *kpo*, "a whole part" – for instance a piece of cloth four yards long – and *kpee*, "a large assembly." The term describes both the coming together of family and clan members as well as the festival food itself.

When the ancestors had prepared their first meal in their new homeland from millet, they first sacrificed a little of it to the gods to thank them for a safe journey. They planted the remaining grain in the as yet unfamiliar ground. The Ga kept up the cultivation of millet until they felt at home in their new surroundings. Then corn became their basic foodstuff.

The populations of the Ga cities – which include Accra, Osu, Labadi, Teshi, and Tema – consist of various groups that arrived at different times, so that the times and processes of rituals also differ. However, they all have in common two things: a ban on noise, particularly drumming before the festival, which would indicate a funeral celebration, and the cleaning houses and paths for the expected streams of visitors.

The week of the festival itself represents only the peak of a series of rituals which start in Gamashi (Accra) with the "holy year" in April or May. Homowo is their crowning finale, when a different custom is observed every day. On Tuesday all those who inhabit the small areas behind the coastal towns return to their home town (*mantease*). The *soobi* ("people who arrive on a Tuesday") bring much with them. In earlier times they carried heavy baskets of fruit on their heads. They entered the city in noisy processions, cheerful and relaxed. These days they travel in bush taxis or in a convoy of splendidly decorated "mami-trucks." Part of homowo, when all family members should return home, is a ritual exchange of gifts. One of these exchanges is between urban and rural dwellers, who exchange agricultural produce and fish; the other is between people whose relationships are usually tense. Thus newlywed women must bring firewood to their mother-in-law three times. In turn the latter will later respond to this sign of submission with a piece of clothing or jewelry, often also with a small amount of money. Men give their fathers-in-law a short piece of wood. These serve to fuel small celebratory fires in the courtyards, so that the dead souls which have come with the soobi can warm themselves and rest.

On Friday the old women of the various families set out in the early hours of the morning to dig for red clay (*akpade*). With this they paint the two side gates of each estate through which the dead were earlier carried. The color red protects the residents from death and bad luck. On the night leading up to Saturday, the eve of the real celebration, a gun is fired at midnight as a sign that no one may enter the city anymore. The night is short anyway: in every household the preparation of kpokpoi begins around 3 am or 4 am Meanwhile, the young have fun. Particularly in earlier times this part of the celebrations was marked by sexual freedoms which are meant magically to stimulate fertility. On Saturday

Dressed in white, the First Priest (*wulomo*) offers his god a sacrificial drink at his shrine (*gbatsu*). White stands for purity, peace, and harmony and shows the deity's well-meaning nature. The former headdress, a pot-shaped grass hat, has been replaced by a white turban. The long necklace and other jewelry are made of white shells (*abodi*) from the Volta river and of round, black, hard seeds (*ayiglibi*).

The homowo feast serves to jeer at hunger. Rich foods are prepared to fly in the face of hunger.

The priest is the first to receive some of the food, so that he can offer it to the deity whose protection against famine is hoped for.

morning, around 7 am, when the food is ready, shrines everywhere in the city are sprinkled with it. The gods eat before the ancestors and the living people. Then kpokpoi, palm-oil soup, and rum are spilled in and outside the houses for the dead, thereby inviting the ancestors too. They are asked to protect their families from bad luck and sickness in the coming year. Only after the ancestors have been taken care of do the living themselves eat, always in the house of their father. They eat up the old maize, as nothing from the year just gone must be carried over into the new.

Everyone is up early on Sunday morning. People visit each other and exchange homowo

greetings, and there is a lively coming-and-going in all houses. Those who did not speak to each other over the past year take the opportunity to make peace with their relatives, neighbors, and friends. What was kept quiet is now openly talked about. Even offenses such as theft and adultery are forgiven. Everything is ready for a new beginning. To show their joy and unity people shake hands, drink together, and celebrate late into the night. Today the feast's high point is a durbar, which provides those in authority with a forum for making public announcements and broadcasting their political views. This ends the homowo week in Ga-mashi.

The spread of Christianity among the Ga has had a marked influence on homowo. It is no longer always seen as an expression of backward paganism; indeed, some churches have timed their harvest celebration to coincide with the final homowo celebration. However, the sacred functions carried out by the priests, and therefore the festival's religious meaning have retreated into the background. Instead the celebrations have become more and more commercialized – and politicized.

The chieftains of Jamestown during their festive procession through the streets on the day of the homowo festival.

Ground corn is strewn in and outside houses. In contrast to the priests' ritual white clothes, red clothes expressing not peace and harmony but aggression and an unrelenting spirit are often worn on this occasion to show that war on hunger has been declared.

Setting off into the new year

A woman dances with a doll as part of the re-enactment of the Ewe's flight from Togo.

Above right: The numerous celebrations around the hogbetsoto offer both "old" and "new" leaders, traditional rulers and modern politicians an opportunity to meet and exchange opinions.

Festively decorated and painted Anlo-Ewe girls at the hogbetsoto celebration (the commemoration of the Ewe leaving Togo).

Great attention is paid to hogbetsoto, a celebration by the residents of Anlo on the first Saturday of November each year. They honor a historical event which represents unity and is therefore meant to strengthen identity, which is why political authorities have declared it a state occasion. The focus of the festivities is a re-enactment of the flight from Notsie, an old town between the Haho and Zio rivers, in what is now Togo, where the ancestors used to lead a happy life.

Just and clever kings who were also First Priests made good use of their advisers and caused the city to flourish. This changed toward the middle of the 17th century, when the unscrupulous and cruel tyrant Agokoli came to power. He terrorized his subjects and ordered the elders to be killed. As a result most city residents decided to leave. The women were ordered to pour out all water over the thick city walls, as these were made of unburned clay bricks which would be slowly softened by the water. On the the afternoon before the flight the men began drumming as a sign for the women to gather up their possessions. At midnight, when the drumming reached its peak, the leaders of the various groups gathered by the wall. One of them uttered a prayer and then thrust his dagger into the

wall with the words "Oh God, open for us!" Others followed until the softened mud could no longer withstand the pressure. The wall collapsed, leaving open the way to freedom. This historical event is revived in the people's memory every year. Its immense significance is shown by the elaborate and careful planning for the festival as well as by the number of celebratory acts, which reach their peak in the public appearance of the ruler (awoamefia). The time between August and October is one of cleaning. In every Anlo village and city all "dirt" is removed from houses, streets, and shrines, according to an exact sequence. All dirt is collected at a roadside location which is dedicated to the particular city god. The village inhabitants pray to him to take all misfortune, in particular plagues, with him. After this, young men and women carry the waste to the edge of the village that is next in turn for the ceremony.

In the past, the town's leading fortune-tellers would then be consulted. They would communicate which sacrifices would appease the gods and which impending disasters they could prevent, and carried out the necessary rituals. During the next seven days there would be a strict ban on drumming and dancing. Today, when the danger of epidemics has been mostly eradicated, the overall cleaning ceremony is been limited to one day.

In the middle of the festival week numerous public appearances and addresses are given by

Anlo-Ewe priests at the beginning of a sacrificial ceremony bringing the festival to a close.

"experts" as well as by the region's leading figures, in particular the ruler. The latter tirelessly emphasizes the meaning and values of Anlo culture and at the same time demands the setting up and maintenance of a variety of development projects. There is no contradiction between the two, as both build upon community and cooperation.

Above all it is important to teach traditional values to the young people.

A celebration of peace and harmony forms the ritual core of the festival and takes place on a historical site between Thursday night and Friday morning.

For this the leading priests and warlords of the city gather in the old part of the palace (*agowowonu*).

An Ewe-chief with his tribe at the hogbetsoto festival in Anlo. The girls wear necklaces to show they are adept at voodoo. An old war drum stands in the front, decorated with a skull and bones.

A musician blowing an ivory horn to announce the arrival of the chieftains.

One of the performers, dressed in traditional clothing and bedecked with old beads.

This is where the ancestor Togbui Wenga performed the ritual of founding the city. His successor, the king, appears on this occasion as the embodiment of the god Nyigbla, who was brought with the ruler's own ancestors from Notsie. This deity was the most important in Anlo and the patron of Anloga. As the king appears he is greeted with traditional cries, drumming and warring songs. He opens the ceremony by handing water and a bottle of rum to two of his elders. This sacrificial drink for the ancestors is meant to bring in the founding fathers, who will bless the hogbetsoto. The elders gather plants in the courtyard and pile them up in a heap. Then the ruler begins to make all sorts of complaints against his warlords. They reply with accusations against him. After every complaint the women utter ritual shouts, and the plants are turned over so that all complaints are "buried beneath them."

Finally, the two chosen elders say a prayer over the heap of plants and put them into a ceremonial bowl (*afianu*). Then they pour water over it and mix everything well before sprinkling the water over the old part of the palace. Now all others present can voice their dissatisfaction. Only when everything is cleansed is the holy water poured into the jugs of Anlo's 15 clans so that it can be sprinkled around their houses too.

The reconciliation ceremony ends with a communal meal (*hanududu*). The next day, at midnight, the wheel of history is turned back to commemorate the "origin." The old court is used once again, this time by a dance ensemble re-enacting the exodus from Notsie, performing the flight's important episodes, with the tearing down of the wall as the high point.

Right: In the old court of the Ewe royal palace members of a dance ensemble reenact the most important event in Anlo history: the ancestors' flight from the walled town of Notsie.

Center: Re-enacting the flight from the tyrannical king Agokoli in Togo to Ghana. The history of the Ewe is passed on through oral tradition.

Below: In contrast to the peaceful ideals of the hogbetsoto festival, the war drum, decorated with the long bones and skulls of enemy leaders, is a reminder of the time when the Anlo conquered neighboring groups to establish power in their new home. When the enemy's bones were taken their power was also won.

A great durbar takes place on Saturday, for which visitors from a wide area stream into Anloga. The main square, decorated with banners, can hardly accommodate the masses of people wearing splendid clothes. Numerous groups of drummers and dancers provide entertainment, while cannon blasts announce the beginning of the royal procession. Carried on his litter, and flanked by warlords and city elders, the king arrives at the festival. As soon as he descends from his litter Anlo's anthem is played. He sits down on one podium, while opposite there is another for a guest of honor. Usually the head of state is invited. When the president – or another government official – arrives, the Ghanaian national anthem is played. The elders offer the ancestors a sacrificial drink, while a representative of the Christian churches says a prayer. The ruler reads out a speech emphasizing last year's achievements in the development of the region. He then sets out the plans for the coming year and encourages active participation from the population. The guest of honor replies with an address from the government.

When the official part of the ceremony is over, the visitors have plenty of opportunity to celebrate. A great ball is held for the younger people. On Sunday of the following week a great nondenominational service is held, led by representatives of the various main churches. During the service the city dwellers pray to God for future prosperity and peace for Anlo and for all of Ghana.

Initiation – the ritual of being born again

Every change in status, whether the passage from adolescence into adulthood or from being single to married, presents a village community with a particular problem. It is a process that leads through a phase of social insecurity and it has to succeed because so much depends on the ability of those who have assumed a new role to cope fully with their new tasks. Its failure even in one or two cases is enough to threaten the survival of a small community.

Particularly critical is the situation of adolescents about to make the transition into the adult world. Adults are the pillars of society and they must therefore be able to carry out their duties and fulfill responsibilities reliably. The greatest of these is the education of children. The processes of initiation described below are simply the official conclusion of this process.

Nature herself, moreover, dramatically marks these changes. Puberty gives boys the ability to procreate and girls to conceive, so that both are fertile, an essential condition for reproduction. While education is concerned with teaching economic and social survival skills, puberty secures the biological existence of the group. Both are elementary concerns to all, and it must be in their interest to accompany, control and steer the changes in such a way that those adolescents indeed become reliable and responsible adults. Nothing can be left to chance. It is for this reason that even today many rural communities insist on carrying out the whole process of entry into adulthood in a strictly ritualized manner.

This takes place in the context of initiations, a term originating in the Latin word *initiatio* (from *initiare*, meaning "to begin" or "to introduce"). In many cases these are particularly described as "maturity initiations" or "youth initiations." The general aim of this ritual is to transform adolescents into adults, and it can be performed on individually or collectively. As described in the introduction to the chapter *Feasts and celebrations* (page 20), the transferal process typically has three phases: separation, transformation, and reassimilation. However, in this case it is seen as a ritual new birth. The initiates "die" as adolescents, spend some time as "dead" in the underworld with the ancestors, and finally "come back to life" as "new" adult human beings.

In some parts of Africa, there are initiations even today for both sexes, individually and collectively. Individual initiations of boys are typical of hunter-gatherer societies, and in Africa this applies to Bushman and pygmy societies (in the central rainforests). There are two particularly important points to these hunter initiations. The initiate has to perform a kind of masterpiece by killing a large animal under the supervision of elders. Then, through magic, a sort of family relationship with the animal is created. With the Bushmen, for instance, powder made from

The initiation of an African fetish priest. An engraving from: *Fetishism and Fetich Worshipers*, New York, Cincinnati, St. Louis, 1885.

the burned flesh of the most important hunted animals is rubbed into incisions made between the boy's eyes and on his upper arms so that he can see the animals from far away and can hit them with his arrows. Alternatively, he and his weapon may be covered in the blood, often from the heart, of the animal killed in the trial hunt, which establishes them as "blood brothers." The conclusion is a celebratory meal made from the prey's meat which is attended by all members of the group.

Individual initiations for girls take place in almost all traditional cultures; indeed, they are the most usual form of female initiation. They take place at the onset of puberty, that is, at a girl's first period. The girls are first kept away ("dying"), then they spend a few days in a shed behind the house or in a hut at the edge of the village specially designated for this purpose ("in the underworld"). Here, as "dead" and painted white, they must fast, sit or lie for a time without moving or showing any emotion,

When boys become men: adolescents in self-made costumes. Two "new" men after their initiation ceremony, in a photograph taken in about 1930.

they must neglect bodily care, and have no contact with anyone but their mothers or older women. Their visitors ("the ancestors") instruct them mainly in questions of feminine hygiene, aspects of sexuality, and methods of contraception and abortion. The purpose of this is above all to make the girls aware of the significance of their tasks as wives and mothers; that is, to impress on them their moral and social responsibilities. Toward the end the behavioral limits are loosened. The girls being initiated awake from their "sleepy" inactivity and take up typically female tasks, such as spinning. The consumption of certain foods, sometimes even fattening-up diets, serve to enhance their fertility. Again, it all ends with a great feast, in this case more within the family or with close relatives. For this

41

occasion the "newborns" not only wear the clothes and jewelry of adult women but often also take on a new name, while also behaving appropriately, receiving presents from everybody, and being feted. Now they are allowed to get married.

The most common classic form of coming-of-age rituals is the collective initiation of boys. The reason for this lies in the fact, already mentioned, that the great majority of all traditional societies are organized along patriarchal lines. While girls marry "out," boys remain in their village: they are therefore the group's future carriers of responsibility.

Again, the initiation begins with separation ("dying"). Some time after the onset of puberty the boys are torn away from their mothers by older, often masked men (the "ancestors") in a kind of kidnap situation and taken to a resting place in the bush, outside the settlement. As the "dead," they shed their clothing and often also their name, are painted with white paste, are hardly allowed to move, and must speak only when absolutely essential, and even then in a whisper. They stop their bodily care and have to fast and observe various other rules of abstinence.

A few days after their entry into "the land of the dead," the core of the ritual – their transformation – takes place. First comes the physical transformation, starting perhaps with circumcision so that the establishment of sexual differences may be physically completed. Up to puberty, children are usually regarded as bisexual. To turn them into complete men (or women), this "corrective" measure is necessary. With girls the clitoris is seen as the male, with boys the foreskin as the female, vestige of the bisexual phase of childhood. The removal of both – in the case of girls the excision, which tends to take place only in the less frequent female collective initiations – therefore completes the physical process of maturing and ensures that both sexes are henceforth able to reproduce successfully. Other physical changes, such as scarring or piercing earlobes, lips, or noses for the attachment of adult jewelry serve the purpose of permanently marking the initiates with the signs of their ethnic origins; by these signs they will, after their death, recognize their ancestors.

Disguise is an expression of the transferal phase between death and life that initiates undergo through their ritual transformation. Photograph c. 1930.

At the beginning of this physical transformation they are, as the Kaguru of Tanzania put it, like "hungry chicks who have just hatched." This is also too how they are fed by the elders who look after them – like newborns, with "baby food" such as porridge, soup, and a little millet beer. As they gradually regain strength they must undergo measures to strengthen their fertility, such as a beating with the stems of powerful plants, and withstand other forms of mistreatment and trials of their courage to establish their physical and moral powers of resistance. Transformed within a short time from "babies" into strong young men, they are finally rendered fit to receive specific instructions. The latter are not primarily concerned with practical education, for the initiates are already familiar with the skills that they must master as adults. The focus lies rather on the morally correct social behavior that is expected of responsible adults. Finally, as the climax of this period of instruction, comes initiation into the group's religious traditions: the creation myths, sacred songs, rituals, dances, and the meaning of certain cult objects (such as relics, musical instruments, and sacrificial knives) and above all of the masks in which the ancestors appear.

The third phase, that of returning, begins with thorough cleansing. Then the initiates are painted anew, with red, the color of life, the strongest; they put on adult clothing and return, often after destroying the bush camp, to the village. As "newborns" they often find it difficult to find their bearings. They seem to have forgotten everything that was familiar to them in their earlier life and must learn again who their relatives are, how to move, eat politely, talk, and so on. As always, a great communal feast is the crowning conclusion.

Less frequently, in societies organized along matriarchal lines, where girls remain in their home village, there are collective initiations for them, particularly in the Zambezi-Angola region and in parts of West Africa. The fundamental aspects as well as the formal procedures are basically the same as those in boys' initiations. However, after the excision, possibly even more importance is given to strengthening powers of fertility, the ability to conceive. Otherwise there is the same concern with awakening the initiates' sense of social responsibility in carrying out their future tasks.

Initiations were a kind of forerunner of the later public schools. In summary, the following four main goals can be identified:

– firstly, the provision of accompanied support and controlled supervision of the physical process of transformation and maturing by responsible representatives of society (the elders), in particular to complete the sexual differentiation and secure the ability to procreate or conceive;

– secondly, the dramatic reinforcement of cultural and moral core values, which are again impressed upon the initiates in a concentrated way;

– thirdly, the official conclusion of the educational phase and public recognition of its success; and

– finally, the magical-ritual perfection of the physical and educational maturing process through the ritual of rebirthing and therefore the guarantee of the overall order of life, which presumably also stands for life in the future.

Similar initiations take place on other comparable occasions – for instance, taking up an important religious or political post, joining a secret society, moving up into a higher status, or the enthroning of a new king.

As part of her initiation ceremony, a girl is rubbed with ointment by splendidly decorated women. Photograph c. 1930.

Left: Krobo girls on their way through the village of Kordiabe. Their appearance shows that they have successfully passed the examination on the sacred dipo-rock (*dipo* means "initiation of girls"), which is part of the initiation ceremony. During this test the girls have to sit down three times on the rock. If the girl has already conceived, the consequence could be the death of a relative. If nobody falls over dead, it is proved that the girls have not conceived before time and have not therefore become "women" against the rules.

Becoming a woman

Opposite page: The initiates are seated on "stools of honor" and are given presents by relatives. The cylindrical straw hats that they are wearing symbolize their purity, which is a precondition for their future identity as complete women. In earlier days girls wore these hats for a whole year.

In the area in southeastern Ghana where the Krobo originally came from, on the mountain Klonyo or Klon-wen, there was a sacred rock which the elders addressed as *Yomo o* ("honorable old lady") or simply as *Nana* ("grandmother"). It is said to have constantly grown with the number of initiates who have sat on it. However, if there was a pregnant girl among them it buried them all beneath itself.

The mountain, over 1,000 feet high, was a sacred place for the Krobo. This is where they held the coming-of-age ceremonies for young girls, where they buried their dead and served their gods – until it reached the ears of the British colonial administration that human sacrifices were carried out on the mountain. In 1892 the governor forbade the Krobo to take part in any such "fetish celebrations," and within three days they had to remove all their possessions from the mountain.

Hausa soldiers supervised this process and made sure that all settlements and shrines on the mountain were destroyed. Initiation ceremonies were also forbidden so that, from then on, these could only be carried out in secret.

In spite of colonial rule and the spread of Christianity, the Krobo were able to continue the initiation of girls, albeit in simpler and briefer form. This takes place annually between February and May, whereas it could last for up to twelve months and longer on the mountain. Every girl is allowed to attend, as long as she does not become pregnant beforehand or has already given birth. In this case she can no longer be initiated and is despised for the rest of her life. It is also highly unlikely that she will ever marry, as only a girl who has undergone the initiation ceremony can be a Krobo woman in the full sense, and partner to a Krobo man.

Girls seen from the back in the first phase of their initiation, when they are seated on their "stools of honor." Only after initiation can girls fully become a man's partner, that is, marry. The initiation itself lasts several weeks.

The celebrations take place not in a bush camp but right in the village, with the whole population participating. It is led by older women and priestesses, but also priests. On a Thursday, the sacred day of Kloweki, the most important goddess to whom the initiation of girls is always dedicated, the candidates first undergo a change in clothes and hairstyle. The main ceremonies themselves begin on a Saturday with a bath in the stream. The girls walk there in single file, covered only by a bright red loincloth. Village inhabitants can hand them clothes for washing. They return to the village quietly and without speaking to anyone. They are greeted in their family estates with dance and music, and every family gives a festive "farewell meal." On the same evening the head of the family, in the presence of relatives on both the father's and the mother's side, makes a sacrifice of a castrated black goat. If there are several girls ready for initiation, he will sacrifice the corresponding number of animals. Before he cuts the goat's throat, he touches the ground with the animal's head, then the initiate's head, the girl grasping both horns and pushing it away. Through this she shows that she

Initiates in their bright red loincloths at the *dipo* (initiation) dance after their trial on the rock.

The girls assemble in a row in preparation for the dance.

wants to banish all bad thoughts from her head. When this has been done three times before the animal is slaughtered.

A few days later, once again on a Saturday, the celebrations approach their climax. Toward evening the initiates make their way either to the estate of the village chief or the priest, with a leaf in their mouth as a sign that they are not allowed to speak. There they are sprinkled with sacred water, and prayers are said are for them. Sprinkling sacred water on the way, one of the priest's assistants (labia) leads them to the sacred grove, accompanied by happy singing and loud drumming. Here, hidden in the shrubs beneath the trees, lies the sacred rock. In commemoration of the original shrine on the mountain, dipo rocks have multiplied almost infinitely. Nearly every family has its own. On these the most important, if very simple, initiation ceremony takes place. The Krobo still insist that only when a girl has sat on the sacred rock may she consider sexual intercourse and marriage.

While young men fire off guns at a respectful distance, the woman leading the ceremonies (yomowo) makes the girls sit down on the rock three times in succession. She speaks these words, "Sit down, stand up! I make you a Krobo woman!" Should a girl who has already conceived and has therefore become a woman without going through the rituals dare to sit on the sacred rock, it could lead to the death of relatives or even of the yomowo. But if nobody falls over dead immediately, the initiates are given a triumphal reception in the village. Gun salvoes and joyful dances confirm that the girls have passed the test. They are given a cylindrical straw hat to wear, normally worn only by priests. As a special treat they are served a goat's head, which is usually reserved for the head of the family.

Only in the following week does the actual training take place. The initiates gather in a special hut and are isolated from the outside world for the duration of the teaching. Teaching and preparing the girls for their future duties and tasks as women, wives, and mothers used to a duty of the priestesses of the goddess Kloweki. One of the special taboos and ways of behavior that must be observed during this time of seclusion is that the girls may only eat

At the final celebration the girls publicly present themselves "like queens," with fine hairstyles, splendid clothing, and richly bedecked with beads and red parrot feathers. This celebration also marks the end of the training that has prepared the girls for their future duties and tasks as women, wives, and mothers.

Left: A Krobo girl at the final celebration. The strings of beads wound around her neck, upper body, hips, upper arms, wrists, and legs are old family possessions or are lent especially for this day.

Right: The girls' dance, which can last well into the night, is accompanied by the women singing. One of their so-called ha-songs goes, "These are beautiful things, you know, we have lovely things before our eyes."

Below right: At the final celebration the girls can be admired in their full splendor. In the past, marriage arrangements began then. Today the girls are often still too young and also more frequently choose their partners themselves.

"old," traditionally Krobo foods (mostly mashed millet and corn) and not those adopted from the neighboring Akan. In the past the initiates spent much time on the mountain singing, dancing, and playing. They had no duties and were well looked after by their families. The easy life and good food made them appear well fed and therefore in the eyes of the Krobo particularly pretty when they came down from the mountain.

At the final ceremony (*yi fomi*, "washing of the head") the yomowo removes the hats from the girls' heads and draws three red lines with wood on the crown and both sides of their heads. Then she lays three leaves on their heads and covers them briefly with the hats. Then their hair is washed and beautifully dressed. On the same day, the girls make their public appearance, splendidly dressed and richly bejeweled, and show off their dancing skills. The entire family, both paternal and maternal, neighbors, and friends admire her "perfect" appearance and celebrate her beauty until late into the night. The next day dietary restrictions are lifted. In the past marriage arrangements could then begin. Today the girls are mostly too young for marriage, and are increasingly choosing their partners themselves.

Prepared for the sexual soul

Circumcised Dogon youths in front of the famous overhanging cliff in Songo. The painting shows mostly religious motifs relating to the cosmos and life in its many different forms.

Right: Circumcised Dogon girls in Mopti (Mali).

"It all came quite unexpectedly. One morning mother told father that she wanted to go and have Egnelu circumcised. Together with girls of the same age and their mothers they left the village, joined on the way by a matron. Then everything happened very quickly. Egnelu suffered a terrible pain, and only her mother's strong grip prevented her from rearing up. A hand covering her mouth made it impossible for her to utter any sound. Silently and numbed she had to endure the operation. Even so

tears ran down her face when the old woman began to burn out her wound with oil. After the operation the girls were fed. Indeed, the meal was the only pleasant thing about this otherwise horrible event. During the whole time they spent at the bush camp the girls were served selective and particularly rich foods: rice with meat sauce, millet porridge with sugar, and, Egnelu's favorite dish, rice donuts with honey. Even so, she could not sleep at all during the first night. The pain was too strong, and fierce stabs

The "circumcision master" of Songo with a giant circular rattle. Traditionally, the circumcision of boys is carried out by blacksmiths, who enjoy a special position among the Dogon, as in many other parts of Africa.

Newly circumcised Dogon boys with rattles at a market exit, where they expect a present from passers-by. Anyone who does not part with a little money or food is open to ridicule from the boys.

went through her abdomen. She tried to remember that her older sisters, indeed all the women in the village, had endured much the same – and that next year it would be the boys' turn. She stayed in the bush camp for ten days, during which the girls learned how to deseed cotton and spin it.

On Egnelu's return to her part of the village her mother sent her to the house of a female elder. Here she heard many tales. Every evening her friends would also come to listen to the old woman's stories which seemingly took them into another world. At the same time they learned of the hard duties of a Dogon woman, and she suddenly realized that she had been betrothed since birth. Although her mother had often spoken of a particular boy as her husband, she had always thought of this as a joke." (A Dogon woman recalling her circumcision, recorded by the French ethnologist Nadine Wanono.)

Girls are indeed fit to marry only after circumcision. Even if they are not yet menstruating at the time of being excised (which is often the case today, as circumcision takes place increasingly early) they are then regarded as women, with all the rights and obligations of a woman. Circumcision enables children to take on their "proper" male or female physical and sexual soul. It transforms these "sexless" beings into definite, complete members of society who can marry and will be responsible for the family's future.

While in earlier days boys had to endure the operation between the ages of 11 and 17, today it takes place when they are between 8 and 12 years old. Traditionally, the circumcision of boys is carried out by blacksmiths, whose original ancestor is seen as the one who brought culture. He gave the Dogon the grains and made the tools essential for cultivation, such as the hoe, the ax, and the scythe.

Today he is often assisted by a paramedic, or a doctor stationed in Sanga is consulted. However, even then the operation is followed by a time of initiation which all those circumcised at the same time spend together in seclusion. From then on they form an "age class" whose members have obligations toward each other for the rest of their lives.

If the circumcision is collective, the boys leave the village together and make their way into the bush. They are accompanied by their fathers, who stand behind them and hold them tight. They strengthen their backs, so to speak, because the circumcision is a test of their courage: the boys must not show any sign of pain or indeed move at all. They must endure the operation with no expression on their faces. If a paramedic is present, he will see to their wounds to prevent continued bleeding. The boys put on uniform clothing and spend several days in the bush camp until the wound has healed. They are supplied with appetizing and particularly nutritious food by the female members of their family, and spend their time playing and singing. On market days they stand with their rattles at market exits, which all visitors must pass. Everyone can recognize them by their clothing and knows that a gift is expected. Most people give them some food or a few coins, which is meant to bring good luck. Anyone who gives nothing is open to their ridicule and is accused of meanness in songs.

As described in Egnelu's story, 10-to-17-year-old girls and boys used to be circumcised in alternating years. Today the girls are much younger (six to eight), and their excision is no longer carried out in groups but takes place in secret, as it is now illegal. However, a legal ban and several educational campaigns have so far failed to stop this extremely painful practice.

Newly circumcised Dogon boys in uniform circumcision gowns.

Appointed a seer in a dream

Numerous postulants have assembled outside the house where the great sacrificial feast (*buur*, the seers' initiation) takes place.

Part of a shrine with figures made of mud and wood, shrine pots, and pumpkin gourds. The two figures with outstretched arms block the entrance to invisible enemies.

"Once upon a time people lived in happiness. God fed them with meat, and they did not have to work. They knew neither sickness nor early death – people died only with old age. There was neither conflict nor war, for the people obeyed God, who had commanded: 'Do not steal, do not take away each other's women, do not kill each other or threaten each other; stay united!' But as people multiplied, the men needed women, and so they began to take away each other's women. Conflict and war were the inevitable consequences. So God took away meat from the people and instead gave them the hoe with which they could dig for roots. In addition he sent them sickness and early death. But before he finally retreated from them, he gave them the guardians (*thila*) to stand by their side from now on." (Piet Meyer)

These guardians still perform their function today. As instructed by the far-away god, their concern is that the village inhabitants lead a life together that observes tradition and maintains harmony. They have also passed on various goods and ceremonies to the Lobi, pointed out effective ways of healing, and protect them from misfortune – as long as the people obey their orders and commandments and keep them well disposed toward them with sacrifices. Seers (*buur*) act as mediators between the guardians and the villagers, voicing the guardians' wishes and orders.

Ever so often it happens that a villager will come across something unusual in the bush, perhaps a piece of iron, small wooden figures, oddly shaped rocks or pieces of wood, which a seer will identify as the embodiment of a guardian

The celebration is led by a seer-priest (*buur-kontin*). Inside the house the elders sacrifice numerous domestic animals at various shrines, particularly chickens, but also goats and sheep. These gifts are meant to please the guardians (*thila*) and make them work harder for the well-being of the estate's residents.

One chicken is slaughtered for every postulant – 85 in total!

Following pages: All those who have obeyed the calling from their guardian (*wathil*) and have taken part in particular ceremonies at the sacrificial feast have accepted their vocation as seers, the initiation of which follows the celebration. This is visually expressed through the artful application of white paint, which signifies the ritual death of the postulants.

The calling to become a seer comes in a dream. The guardian tells his owner and other family members of different ages to become fortune-tellers.

Apart from food, banknotes are also a customary gift before the postulants enter the spirit world.

Above right: At the end of the celebration the postulants leave the village and spend a month in the spirit world – in the bush outside the settlement.

Below right: During the month following the ceremony the postulant must decide whether he really wants to become a seer. The decision is not easy, as the position both demands energy and is time-consuming. If a seer is to give advice to four or five clients a day, at the most twenty, he has to neglect working in the field. As it is impossible to make an adequate living from fortune-telling alone, many who are chosen prefer to stay with farming.

The postulants sit in a row with great baskets in front of them. The celebration guests fill these with food, especially millet and corn, as provisions for the month-long stay in the bush.

(wathil). Should the lucky finder be the head of a family not only he but the whole family enjoys the guardian's protection. However, certain conditions must be met beforehand. In particular, the owner must obey the guardian's call and give a great feast (buur). There are several variations to this: a celebration can last two days or extend over several weeks. It takes place before the start of the rainy season – March, April, or May – in the house of the individual who made the find. The purpose of the celebration is to bring the family's concerns and needs to the guardian's attention.

However, buur are also "real" celebrations. Visitors come from all over to dance to the sound of xylophones and drums, and to eat, drink, and party to the extreme. The feast's success is not least measured by the number of guests attending: the more visitors, the better. The guardian who has demanded the buur, feels honored and

will in future take even greater care of the family.

The celebration is also always connected with a calling to become a seer. Before the start of the celebration the guardian will appear in a dream to his owner as well as other family members of varying ages and tell them to become seers. The buur is only the first step on the way towards this; the real test comes after the celebration is over.

The visual expression of the initiation of those called is the application of white paint to show the postulants' "death." During the time that they spend in the bush – that is, in the "spirit world" – the postulants must decide whether they really want to take up the position of seer. This is not easy. Only few follow the guardian's calling, as fortune-telling not only takes a lot of energy but is also very time-consuming. Those advising four or five clients a day, at the most 20, must neglect their work in the field. However, honest fortune-telling is far from lucrative. Nobody could live on it alone, and so many prefer to stay with farming.

It was 14 years ago that the Lobi of Ghana last celebrated buur, not least because Muslims are opposed to it. Life has become hard. Many people believe that the guardians have punished them for this neglect with the disastrous droughts of recent years and the consequent bad harvests. But the way things develop can hardly be stopped: the buur of 14 years ago was probably the last one to take place in that region.

Wedding night with Mami Wata

Near the Adomi bridge (Volta region, Ghana), followers of Mami Wata, goddess the sea and water, have gathered for the initiation of a new member. The central part of the initiation ritual is a bathe in the river.

Mami Wata greatly appreciates the novice's attire, a pair of spectacles standing as a sign that he will see clearly from now on, as he is led to the shrine. Together with other believers he walks around an idol in the courtyard, a statue with seven heads, similar to depictions of Indian deities. Indian influences on the cult of Mami Wata are obvious.

The central part of this initiation ritual is the immersion in Mami Wata's element – the sea for those living on the coast, the river for the Ewe living in the Volta region. Mami Wata is a "modern" water goddess. She presumably follows the model of the mermaid figure fixed to the bow of European galleons. A long-haired mermaid, Mami Wata appears in several guises: sometimes naked, sometimes bedecked in jewelry, sometimes with a lower body ending in a fishtail. The Ewe acknowledged the idea of "water people" (loklovi) living in rivers long before the introduction of the Mami Wata cult. However, these spirits did not receive cult-like adoration, nor could they provide any help towards wealth. According to local beliefs there were also people who lived at the bottom of the ocean, emerging on market days and visiting

the market. However, the connection between the sea, wealth, and European consumer goods that now marks the cult of Mami Wata was only very vague then.

Mami Wata appears in dreams as a supernaturally beautiful woman with long hair and light skin, often with shimmering snakes draped around her. Some people are grabbed by her: she tries to pull anyone she can get hold of down into her underwater world. Many of those who are taken against their will run into the water when they hear her beautiful voice. Possession, a trance that girls often fall into, men less so, also announces itself in dreams or through sickness and depression. Those who are called by the deity in this way seek the help of the local priest. If the oracle confirms that the vision is true, those affected by it must offer

sacrifices, undergo a ritual cleansing, and be initiated into the cult.

Accompanied by the priest and older believers, the novice makes his way to the Volta River at night. Facing the water he steps into the river, is immersed several times, and is then symbolically cleansed with the blood of a black dove, soap, and selected herbs. He is then "washed" again, this time with a white dove's blood. Now all evil is finally removed and he is ritually cleansed. Then he is luxuriously washed: powdered, perfumed and generally made up as Mami Wata likes best. His outer appearance also changes to show the abandonment of his former life. His head is shaved and sometimes he is given a new name. He receives a white gown which he wears for the entire time of initiation. Thus prepared, he makes his way to the shrine. Further

The novice is immersed several times and then "washed" with the blood of a black dove, soap, and selected herbs. This cleansing wipes away all evil clinging to him. This is symbolically expressed by throwing the dove into the river which carries it away.

The congregation kneels in front of the goddess's altar in the shrine. The priest, Abidjan Mami Wata, says a prayer for the novices.

The priest then returns to the banks of the river to be close to the goddess, where he spends the next eight days in a small, basic hut. The "wedding" with Mami Wata takes place during this time.

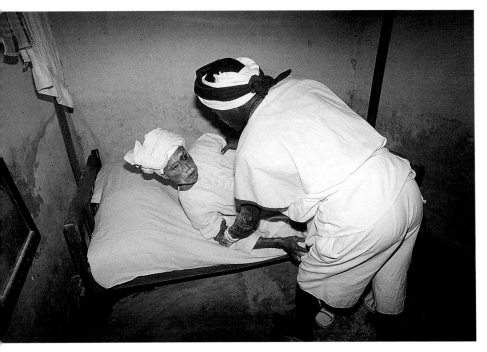

rituals are carried out there before he returns to the banks of the river to be close to the goddess. He now spends some time in severe isolation and darkness. He must not see the sunlight under any circumstances and is more asleep than awake. During this the goddess appears to him again and again. Eight days later he is taken back to the shrine, where he is gradually initiated into the various secrets of the cult. Only then, as a full member of the Mami Wata community, does he leave the protected area of the shrine. He now has a higher reputation, for everyone knows that he now possesses magical powers far greater than those of ordinary people. He has suffered a ritual death, spent some time in the land of the gods and has returned to life as "another."

The cult of Mami Wata is assumed to have its origins in the Cross River area in Nigeria and is today also practiced in the coastal regions of Togo, Benin, and Ghana in much the same way. The Ewe first took it up in the 1950s, since when they have integrated the figure of Mami Wata into their spiritual world and the older system of vodun convents. Her followers form cult groups with priests and particular shrines where they make sacrifices to the goddess. However, her followers do not define themselves by belonging to a particular family or local community, as is the case with clan or city deities, but come from widely varying groups and social classes. Anyone revering Mami Wata counts on special favors by expecting from the goddess strong support in his higher social position, and hoping for material blessings as well as for status and power. This explains why luxury goods from Europe – for instance, plastic dolls, baby powder, porcelain, perfume, and bottles of liquor – are so important in the cult's dealings. In particular mirrors, which represent the water's surface, the border between the underwater world and land, are an essential requisite on altars dedicated to Mami Wata.

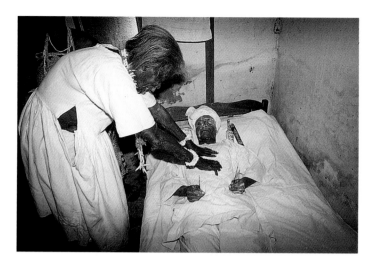

Above: The priest says a final prayer, then the novice sinks into a deep sleep.

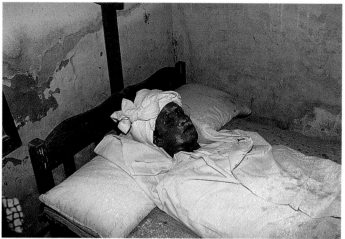

In his dream he travels to Mami Wata's domain, "marries" the goddess, and will from now on live and serve her according to her mmandments.

Below: The goddess's presence manifests itself in her followers' possessional trance happening outside the cult's hut.

Building in harmony with nature

The earth is not just a field and a sacred being, it also provides regions that have little wood or stone at hand with the main building material. Mud, of which there is plenty in the savannas of western Africa, is, however, not a particularly resistant material: extreme temperatures as well as strong rains can wear it down.

The gender-specific division of labor also applies to building. Putting up walls, which requires great strength, is the men's work. The women apply the plaster and in many places are also responsible for painting the walls. The "good," in the form of friendly people, helpful ancestors, and spirits bringing good fortune, are imagined to live within the estate's walls. The inside feels safe, while misfortune lurks outside, always ready to slip in through gaps or holes in the physical or the social structure of the community and attack it. Only the communities of family and village provide support, protection, and safety.

The solidarity necessary to a community is clearly expressed in traditional types of residence. When possible, young men do not build separate houses but extend the building of their father, their uncle, or their grandfather, like another honeycomb

Makololo building a hut. The circular, peaked roofs are put together on the ground and then lifted onto the base structure of the hut.

Engraving from: *Die Völker der Erde*, Würzburg and Vienna, 1891.

in a beehive. In the past every such house was its own social, economic, and ritual unit. This was where the extended family of all the founder's male descendants and their wives and children lived. Usually the men stayed in the place of their birth, while the wives married in (exogamy) to their husband's family.

These complexes are a small world in themselves in which everyone has an assigned place. The house of the oldest man, who is also head of the estate and therefore of the community, always lies in the best position, to the right of or opposite the entrance. In a building with several floors it is at the top, and if it is a large estate, it will be again near the entrance. Altogether the gate area carries great ritual and social importance, as this is where greetings, communal discussions, and even funeral celebrations take place. The first woman's residence, however, lies close to the shrine, at the center, or at the back of the estate. The houses of widows, younger sons and brothers are less prominently positioned. Unmarried young men used to be responsible for defending the property, so their houses stood left of the entrance. In some estates the residences and courts lie in a circle around a communal farm containing storage space and barns where the animals are kept at night.

Social events involving the arrival or departure of family members – such as deaths, marriages, divorces, and births – change the familiar structure of authority and therefore also that of the estate. Recently there have been additional developments. Initially they were comparatively minor, concerning merely the type and material used for building. In many places mud was replaced by the more weather-resistant concrete, which is stronger but does not allow air to circulate. Instead of flat mud

roofs, roofs made of straw or even corrugated iron were used which provided better protection against precipitation.

A more decisive factor in the decay of the traditional estates is the change in methods of work. While all residents of the estate once worked in the fields together and earnings were shared, Western influences and a financial economy have resulted in growing economic independence and the development of individualism and privatization. This led to the loosening of family bonds: the sons and brothers of the head of the estate no longer want his leadership and start their own farms, whose building forms and structures are clearly less elaborate. In addition there is a high rate of emigration from rural areas.

Kirdi village with houses and millet stores. The storehouses can be recognized by their round and somewhat smaller shape.

Young men in particular are attracted to cities or large agricultural businesses where they hope to improve their standard of living. However, despite this displacement the ritual link to people's place of origin still remains. Everybody returns for funerals and annual commemorations, when the head of the family represents the community in offering sacrifices to the ancestors and the gods.

Nankanse – sacred animals on mud

Rich ornamentation gives the houses of the Nankanse great appeal. Animal figures, mostly in relief, decorate the houses of high-ranking women, but murals are also seen on men's houses, on the walls of courtyards, and on storage buildings.

One of the most beautiful and at the same time most expressive settlements on the border between Ghana and Burkina Faso is the Nankanse village of Sirigou. In the rainy season its houses lie hidden between high millet stalks. Like castles without windows and with only one entrance, they seem to defy all threats from without. Single round and square houses, granaries, warehouses, and stables are gathered together within a tight complex encircled by a wall. All buildings are connected by this outer wall. The entrances to the estates, arranged in an oval or a circle, face west and are flanked on both sides by barns. Low walls keep chickens and goats away from the cleanly swept areas and separate the narrow courtyards. The living area is reached through the farmyard, where the estate owner's tall granaries stand. Only since raids by other groups have stopped has it been considered safe for some of the storage buildings to stand outside the estate.

Among the Nankanse the head of the estate resides in a rectangular house to the right of the entrance, with a flat roof, a porch, stairs, and an attached circular building where his second wife lives. Here, near the entrance, are the areas reserved for men as well as the ancestral shrines. The barns and farmyards are part of this too; domestic animals have an important part to play as sacrificial offerings and bridal gifts. Bordering these are the tall granaries, and beyond lie the women's quarters. Most buildings belong to the women. Usually each one has her own small property which is separated from her neighbor's house by a low wall. Each of the women's living complexes consists of a bedroom, a storage room, a small kitchen with a roof for the rainy season, an eating area, an outside kitchen for the dry season, and sometimes a smaller storage room which doubles up as a guestroom.

Geometric patterns decorate the houses of women of important rank, such as the first wife and the estate-owner's mother. These patterns are usually created by older women who still know the

E. Aburiporeh in the entrance to her house. Every woman has her own storage containers in which she keeps pots, calabash eating bowls, and personal possessions.

The snakes and lizards, depicted in low relief on the earth walls, are meant to bring fertility and guard against enemies. They are often placed above shrines at which the head of the family will offer sacrifices to family or personal deities in times of sickness or other crisis. For a number of clans the lizard or the crocodile is a sacred animal that is neither killed nor eaten. This is in thanks for the animal having done the original ancestor and clan founder a valuable favor, such as showing him a watering hole or offering him some other help.

A Nankanse kitchen with various cooking pots, cooking implements, and storage vessels.

meaning of most pictorial and decorative elements. They include the crook of the estate's eldest, the drum shaped like a sand-glass (*donno*), used for ritual occasions, or particular women's cloth or tattoo patterns. As these elements have become increasingly rare, they are today replaced by symbols, such as chevrons, which are intended to secure protection and bring good fortune to the house's residents. Several cross-connected chevrons depict the wings of a bat, an animal which eats insects and which is therefore desirable to have near the house. A simple peak, or one consisting of three parts, represents a chicken's foot. Chickens and chicken huts belong to the domain of women, who are the real rulers of house and home. This is expressed by chevrons depicting a calabash net (*zalenga*) and thus indicating an ordered household. A triangle pointing downward is a sign giving protection from misfortune. It stands for the pieces of a broken calabash and for loss, as on the death of a woman some of her possessions are broken on the path to her father's estate. A "happier" sign is the triangle pointing upward, a symbol of the female sex and fertility in general. A double peak stands for the wings of a goshawk; the sign is intended to stop the bird from stealing the chickens in the women's yards.

Unstoppable developments have resulted in an ever-decreasing application of decorations, which are now limited to certain easily reached areas such as pedestals, railings, and the estate's borders. Abstract patterns are giving way to more representational displays.

Left: Triangles are a common form of decoration. Pointing downward, they represent the broken pieces of a calabash, and are there to keep away death. Pointing upward they symbolize the female sex and, with that, fertility, which is intended to benefit the residents as well as the crops and the farm animals.

Top: Chevrons depicting a calabash net (*zalenga*) frequently decorate houses and the inner walls of courtyards. They show that the women are the real rulers of house and home. The smaller chevrons (a fishing net) are meant to guarantee rich pickings for the women.

Above: Strong rainfall necessitates repair work. Here Akaaba Adomgo is working on the stairway to the roof. Following the European example, solid carved steps have in many places replaced the older forked posts. In the past the roofs, built in terraces and used as defenses, could only be reached via these "climbing trees."

Dogon – living at the foot of the table mountain

The architecture of the Dogon follows mythical structures in a thoroughly thought-out way. It took French ethnologist Marcel Griaule (1898–1956) more than 50 years to understand and record the Dogon's highly complex conception of the universe. Although aspects of his work are open to doubt, it is to him that we owe insights into a fascinating view of the universe that is of far greater magnitude than all previously established links between myth and architecture. The Dogon's conception of both the universe and humanity, passed down in mythology, finds its concrete expression in the arrangements of their villages and houses. Basic architectural structures that, modeled on the human body, take anthropomorphic form can also be found in various types of house south of the Sahara, although they are less elaborate than those of the Dogon. The underlying idea focuses not so much on the individual and as on the couple, which through its bond guarantees fertility and therefore the survival of the community.

According to the Dogon conception of the universe, the earth is part of an overall cosmic system consisting of 14 disk-shaped worlds. The earth itself is the seventh and the highest of the lower worlds. Its edge is encircled by a snake who stops the water of the surrounding ocean from flooding the earth. All the disks – each a world of its own – rotate around a cosmic pole (amma dyi), which is architecturally represented by the central pole of the house holding up the roof.

According to Dogon mythology, the Dogon originally came from the (geographically undefined) "land of the Mande." The oldest man alive there, the lebe, was a descendant of the eighth nommo. The eight nommo, who had come from heaven, were made by Amma himself, the creator god. At that time people did not die but changed into snakes. When the lebe's body lay in the grave, ready for the transformation, the seventh nommo swallowed his head. As a result both their souls bonded and together formed a ninth power, the hogon, who from then on became the spiritual leader of the Dogon in the shape of the oldest man alive. Consequently, the people multiplied and land space became tight. The Dogon decided to emigrate; they opened the lebe's grave to take his bones with them only to find that he had changed into a snake. In this form he, the first hogon, led them to the area where they later settled, the inaccessible rocky landscape of the Bandiagara plateau south of the bend on the Niger. The lebe symbolizes the earth and is paid homage to at special altars in the villages. The hogon stands at the top of the cult of the lebe. He takes care of the altars, passes down the myths, and calls the village residents to the most important ceremonies. His house lies on a desirable site and is built and maintained by the general population. Other than that the central building in the settlements is the rectangular men's house (toguna). The rows of stone or wooden support stakes hold up a gable roof whose wooden rafters are covered with millet straw. On the foundation of a settlement the men's house is the first to be put up, in exact replication of the original mythical form in which the first eight ancestors gathered together. Dedicated to each of them are three forking posts, which are arranged in a spiral as a symbol of the mythological snake.

Left: The men's assembly house (toguna). All grown (circumcised) men gather in the toguna, and the elders' council meets here. The Dogon believe that after sunset the ancestors come here too.

The Dogon village of Hombori. Until the French invasion of Mali the Dogon built their settlements into the Falaise of Bandiagara, a bizarrely shaped cliff 125 miles long and 1,300 feet high. Their fields lay south of the inaccessible cliffs and scree, but in uncertain times they kept away from the area.

Among the motifs in the carved reliefs are pairs of breasts, various masks, female figures with full breasts, ancient heroic couples, and sometimes even sandals. The latter represent footprints made by the iron footwear worn by the ancestral blacksmith, cultural hero of the Dogon. Using a wooden stick he stole a piece of the sun in the shape of glowing coal and red-hot iron from the first male nommo. He then fled to a grain store shaped like the base of a pyramid and traveled down toward earth in it along a rainbow. The store contained not only the ancestors or the original forms of all humans, animals, and plants, but also the original forms of

minerals and various working methods. During this particular journey the blacksmith-nommo was standing on his roof. The first female nommo threw a roll of thunder, then a bolt of lightning after the thief. The latter hit the grain store's roof, but the ancestral blacksmith held up part of a fan to shield himself and was not injured. Through the stolen coal the fan's skin was loaded with solar energy. The first male nommo then also hurled a bolt of lightning at him, and this set the store alight, but the blacksmith quickly managed to put out the fire.

Finally the store hit the ground hard, and its contents – humans, animals, plants, and minerals –

Dogon storehouses. Storehouses are a family's most important possession. The elaborate relief decoration is intended either to encourage fertility and growth or to give magical protection.

Entrance door, with a "climbing tree" in the corner. Doors not only have a practical function but also act as a magical defense, hence the elaborate relief decoration. Frequent depictions include rows of ancestors, the original twin couple (*nommo*) and their ancestors who later populated the earth, breasts, and a horse and rider, who represents the first *hogon* (religious leader).

Storehouse door with lock. Since colonial times Islam has advanced in Dogon country. Muslims are, rightly or wrongly, accused of stealing many of the artfully decorated wooden poles, storehouse doors, and locks and selling them to traders. In any case the decay of Dogon art is visible.

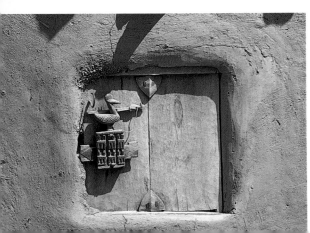

Storehouse door with lock, considered to have magical powers of defense. Many such doors bear decorations. Some of these relate to the Dogon myth of origin particular to the nommo couple. However, standing or sitting human figures are also depicted. The "sun lizard," representative of the foreskin on the penis (considered to be a female attribute), is often shown.

The Dogon village of Ireli. The Dogon use mostly mud as a
building material. Only the foundations are of stone, while
the beams, floors, and ceilings are made of wood, which,
probably because of its scarcity, is considered a sacred material.

spread themselves all over the earth. During this impact the blacksmith-nommo was holding his hammer and anvil in his hand, and his limbs thus broke at the elbow and the knee. He thereby received the joints that later passed to all human beings. Many cultural traditions find their origins with him, as he led the eighth nommo's descendants in civilizing the world.

The men's house represents the eight original ancestors; it is a sacred, powerful place and, like the village altars, is regularly offered sacrifices. Connecting the various altars of the village in a particular way produces the basic outline of a human body.

Following the Dogon interpretation, residential houses represent a person lying on his or her back. The entrance hall leads through to the inner courtyard, which is lined by barns, storehouses, and the living area. The lower floor is the earth and with her, the lebe come back to life; the rectangular overhanging roof terrace is the sky, and the upper floor's ceiling is the space between heaven and the earth. Four smaller, also rectangular terraces at the sides of the main terrace stand for the four points of the compass. The same goes for the stove, whose fire comes from the fire once stolen by the blacksmith and which is therefore of heavenly origin. If the house is rightly arranged to face northward, the pot on the stove will also do so, while the stones around the stove will point east and west. The wall, the back of the stove, faces south.

The interior of the house, with its various rooms, reflects the human "caves" of this world. The entrance hall, the landlord's quarters, is a double representation of a man, the door opening outward symbolizing his sex. Rooms and storage space are likened to his wife, lying on her back with open arms, ready for the act of love. The space behind, which contains the stove and which is lit from a window in the roof terrace, is the woman's breathing breast; it is covered by the ceiling, the man's body, with the beams as the bones. The four stakes on which the house rests represent the

The layout of a Dogon village, following a drawing by Marcel Griaule. The arrangement of villages forms the outline of a person, the original ancestor, lying on his or her back. The forge and the men's house make up the head.

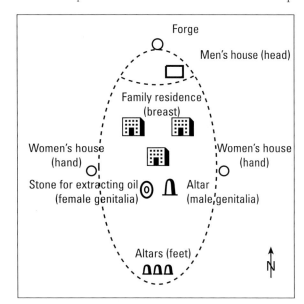

Forge

Men's house (head)

Family residence (breast)

Women's house (hand)

Women's house (hand)

Stone for extracting oil (female genitalia)

Altar (male genitalia)

Altars (feet)

N

couple's arms. The little earth platform that serves as the bed is oriented north to south; the couple lie with their heads to the north, just as the front of the house, its "face," looks in this direction. In this type of house, built in the image of a human being, the married couple itself, the guarantee of the family's fertility and reproduction, is at the center.

The estate's oldest resident always lives in a larger house whose decorated facade is symmetrical in relation to the central axis. The door, set in the center, opens onto the main grain store. Several niches for sacrifices to the ancestors are carved into the facade. Their number is always divisible by eight, the number of the original ancestors. The cone-shaped towers at the top of the terraces also number eight or a multiple thereof. The ten pillars supporting the house however symbolize the fingers of both hands.

Like the houses, Dogon villages are also arranged so as to depict the body of a man, the original ancestor, lying on his back. A village is marked out by eight stones representing his descendants, four women and four men. Within this dotted outline, the smith's forge, the men's house, or assembly house (*toguna*), and the village square make up the head. The women's huts, to east and west, depict the hands; the family houses at the center the breasts; the oil stone and founding altar the female and male genitals respectively, and the altars to the south the feet. The dead are laid to rest in niche graves high up in the cliff outside the village. These niches are echoed by the sacrificial niches in the facades of the elders' houses.

Groundplan of a Dogon house. Following the Dogon interpretation, a residential house represents a person lying on his or her back. The different areas correspond to the man, the woman, or the couple.

Caves above the Dogon's millet storehouses. The high caves once inhabited by the now extinct Telle are today used by the Dogon as graves.

Tofinu – lake villages on stilts

The Tofinu, the "water people," have a completely different way of life from that of the Dogon, but they just as perfectly adapted to their environment on Lake Nokwe (Lac Nokoué) in Benin. Attempting to flee the armed conflicts in their homeland (first Ketu in what is now Nigeria, then Tado in today's Togo), their ancestors reached the swampy regions near the coast probably in the 17th or 18th century. Only in the second half of the 19th century did the Tofinu begin their life on water, where they found safety from slave-hunters and colonial armies, and were also less plagued by mosquitoes.

Within view of Lake Nokwe, which, extending over 60 square miles (including a connected lagoon), reaches as far as Porto Novo, but which is only about six feet deep at most, lies Benin's capital, Cotonou. Nokwe can be translated as "the mother's house." According to legend, the lake was created by the tears of a female slave. The girl, who suffered greatly under the cruel abuses of a king, collected her tears in a calabash. When the calabash was full she overturned it and drowned herself in the pool of water. The pool expanded further and further so that in future it would offer all a refuge from persecution.

During the annual flood animals must be moved by boat to somewhere that is still dry.

The women on Ganvié's floating market are ready to trade in anything which will attract buyers.

When the flood arrives in August people and animals move closer together on the shrinking sandbanks.

The people on the lake live from catching fish and shellfish. Boys receive a small net from their father so that they can learn to make a living for themselves. Older brothers teach them how to handle boats and fishing rods. The women trade in fish, which they offer alongside vegetables, medicinal herbs, and firewood on their little canoes in the floating market of Ganvié. The firewood they obtain on land with the earnings that they make from dried fish. In recent times things have deteriorated on the lake. Many of the colorful vegetable boats have been replaced by motorboats. These are loaded with fuel smuggled in from Nigeria, crates of beer and cola drinks, gray plastic buckets of drinking water, transistor radios, and other current products, as well as masks and T-shirts to sell to tourists, and these all pollute the lake.

However, that is not the only reason for the shrinking catches and the subsequent departure of many Tofinu for neighboring Nigeria. The real cause of the decreasing catches of fish is the growing amount of salt in the lagoon. In 1885, to protect Cotonou from floods, the French governor ordered the land separating the lake from the open sea to be dug through. Up to 1959 the lake's water level was regulated by a sluice gate. Since then, however, this has been so defective that seawater comes with every incoming tide. The erection of a raised harbor in Cotonou has finally completed the program of destruction. The diverted tide has already created a wide channel in the tongue of land. The changing nature of the water brings in salt water during the dry season, which has led not only to changes in the types of fish in the lake, but also to a decrease in their numbers. The fish simply cannot withstand the stress of the constantly changing water.

During the rainy season the seawater rises to just below the floors of the houses. Stronger rainfalls also endanger the houses, which traditionally consist only of plant material – a skeleton of stakes and poles, and walls of vertically or horizontally arranged palm fronds covered with straw. These allow air to circulate freely and kitchen smoke to escape quickly. The saddle roofs, made of straw, are constructed on site. Three stakes, supported by forked poles, hold the roof truss. Attached to it are the rafters. Between these are thin, horizontally placed wooden rods which support the roof's covering. The truss is usually open on the underside.

The Tofinu breed their own fish. They erect woven fences in the mud. In these "fields" (*akaja*) they fatten up fish and crabs which are "harvested" six or seven months later with a net. Here a boy is casting his net.

Although Ganvié, often hailed as Little Venice, is Benin's greatest tourist attraction, it has increasingly been neglected. Many of the buildings that were intact in the 1970s have now collapsed, the stakes are bent, and the roofs have rotted through. Most of the old houses have not been restored but have simply been abandoned. In their place have come new houses, with roofs of corrugated iron and wooden walls. This has removed much of the village's earlier charm.

More depressing, however, are the deteriorating conditions for the lake's inhabitants. The population is growing steadily, and if the black pigs did not eat the refuse, Tofinu villages could no longer deal with all the waste. Particularly during the time of floods, from August to November, diseases, especially diphtheria, typhoid, and cholera, appear, and medical care is minimal. There is hardly any prospect of change; only the state profits from the flourishing tourist trade.

Morning call in front of the village school of So Tchanhoué. During 1975 a mission was set up here which gives medical advice to the Tofinu, helps with the supply of clean drinking water, and works for the education of the lake's residents.

African cultures

Geopolitical conditions

Africa's cultural history has generally been defined by the geoclimatic conditions of the continent, especially by its particular position in relation to its neighbors. With two thirds of the continent surrounded by ocean, Africa has close connections to the outside world via sea or land (Egypt) only in the north and northeast. The bordering regions of the Mediterranean, from Spain to southern Arabia, have historically always been areas in which the most turbulent historical movements have taken place. This is where agriculture as well as the farming of animals began, and where the oldest civilizations, and not least four "world religions" (Judaism, Zoroastrianism, Christianity, and Islam), have their origins.

Early influences from the western Mediterranean came via North Africa and the Sahara (which in prehistoric times was a blooming, partly densely populated savanna), and through the Sudan, finally reaching the borders of the rainforests to the south. Later, ancient Oriental, Egyptian, and Arabic-Islamic influences arriving overland from the northeast left their mark in the cultural development of the continent. On the classic trade routes they pushed forward through the Sudan to the west and via East Africa to the south. Since the early Middle Ages, cultural impulses from India too reached the central part of East Africa through trade across the ocean, albeit on a smaller scale.

However, since connections were both infrequent and always dangerous, these influxes tended to be grafted on to the existing cultural stock rather than change it fundamentally. Also, large parts of Africa, namely the arid lands and deserts in the south (the Kalahari) and north (the Sahara), as well as the tropical rainforest in the center, remained impenetrable until recent times. Old traditions therefore had a greater chance being maintained in just these isolated areas and bordering land; changes were much more significant in the northern, northeastern, and eastern coastal areas and in the hinterland (Ethiopia) as well as in the Sudan and East Africa. However, even there the ancient heritage, except in areas which have converted to Islam (eastern and central Sudan), has remained the main and most strongly influential force.

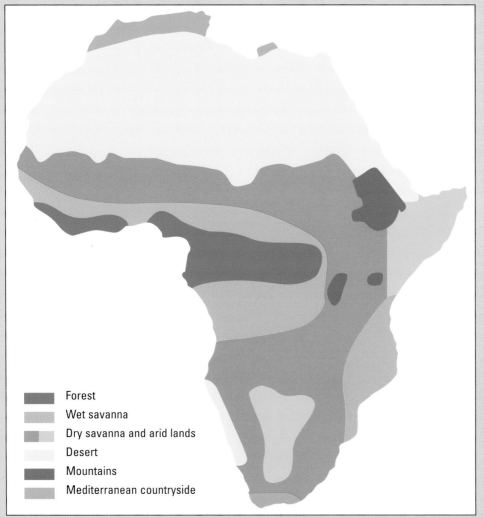

Forest
Wet savanna
Dry savanna and arid lands
Desert
Mountains
Mediterranean countryside

Among the traditional cultures of Africa four standard types can be identified: hunter-gatherer societies; agrarian culture; nomadic herdsmen; and royal, or high, cultures.

These are described below in the so-called "ethnological present tense," although many of the attributes described have probably fallen victim to the ongoing changes of recent times.

Opposite page and below: Maps showing in relatively simplified terms the division of Africa into geographical and economic zones, as well as cultural areas, revealing near-congruence between the three. Six major types of environment are significant to cultural and historical developments: 1) the rainforest, the evergreen center; concentrically around it 2) the wet savanna near the rainforests; 3) the dry savannas, merging into 4) the arid lands and deserts, such as the Sahel in the north and the Kalahari and the Namib in the south; 5) zones with a mild climate in the extreme north and south; 6) the mountainous regions of northeastern and eastern Africa.

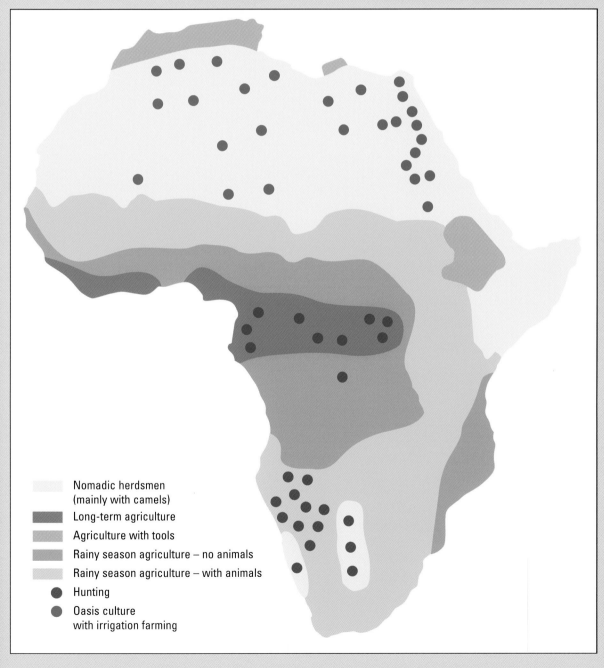

Nomadic herdsmen
(mainly with camels)

Long-term agriculture

Agriculture with tools

Rainy season agriculture – no animals

Rainy season agriculture – with animals

● Hunting

● Oasis culture
with irrigation farming

King Toffa, a popular ruler of the West African kingdom of Dahomey at the end of the 19th century. He was held in particularly high regard by his subjects because of his princely feasts, at which champagne flowed and he appeared in golden costumes. From: *Malerische Studien*, Neuchâtel, undated.

Royal cultures

From the great early cultures of the western and particularly the eastern Mediterranean, monarchies in Africa – and also in other parts of the world – emerged as a form of state on the secondary level of high civilization. Through trade links, and sometimes also through longer term connections, ideas and cultural values from the high civilizations reached even traditional societies in more isolated areas that were further away from the main trade routes. In these areas the economy was limited to the cultivation of roots, shrubs, and trees, and storage of produce on a large scale was therefore impossible. In a circumscribed space, greater population density, the building of towns, a developed artisanship, and standing armies were beyond consideration. Power politics played only a subordinate role. What developed

was the phenomenon of the "religious monarchy." The old "earth lord," or religious chieftain, assumed a new importance and let courtly pomp and circumstance unfold, so that his position took on somewhat grander dimensions. However, the religious aspect of his positions remained dominant.

The ruler, who usually controls only a small territory, is seen as the representative on earth of the heavenly god and therefore also possesses corresponding supernatural powers. He is regarded as the bearer of the life and fertility of the land, of vegetation, animals, and people; with his life and the way he leads it he guarantees his subjects' well-being. His authority as a ruler is secondary to his responsibilities. This is an enormous strain. As the embodiment of the guarantee for his subjects' well-being, he must always be vital, strong, and healthy, which also implies that he should have no physical handicaps, such as blindness or deafness, nor any other disability.

Whatever he does is representative of the people whose existence he embodies and guarantees. His behavior therefore possesses a higher and symbolic meaning and must never be dictated by whim. This carries several consequences, not all of which are comfortable for the king. His people lay down so many rules of behavior and cautionary procedures, all of which must be painstakingly observed, that he is basically not so much the ruler as the prisoner of his own subjects. Often he is allowed neither to leave his residence nor to accept or use any goods made outside his realm. The radiance of his power would only be dangerous for others, so that contact, whether by touching or even just by looking at him, is often avoided by all but his closest relatives and highest dignitaries. For this reason religious kings make rare public appearances and at audiences often wear veils or sit behind curtains so as to remain unseen.

Every transgression, every step outside the magical circle of his religious existence would endanger those in his care.

One of King Toffa's ministers. As a sign of his position he wears a tiara with his own hair woven through it. From: *Malerische Studien*, Neuchâtel, undated.

To show that it is identical to "the world," every kingdom is divided into four regions corresponding to the points of the compass. The roads to each region lead from the center through four palace gates, then through four city gates. Every newly enthroned king claims ownership of his land by shooting an arrow in each of the four directions and then traveling to all four regions to let himself be adored. The princely governors of the regions are also the four arch-officials among the highest ranking ministers and advisors of the king at court.

Not only the religious kingdoms of the Sudan, but also those more remote kingdoms in the Congo region and in central

Left: Sultan Njoya in front of the reception hall of the palace. Cameroon (1910).

A Yoruba chieftain. During important ceremonies the face is customarily veiled with special decorations so that it is not shown to the common people. It is also not customary to address chieftains or kings directly.

Only if the king strictly observes the rules are fertility and life guaranteed and everyone can rest assured that there will be sufficient rain and plentiful harvests as well as protection from misfortune. For example, about the king of the Mbum in central Cameroon an observer reported in about around 1930, "He is the keeper of life and the flourishing of everything …. The king is the keeper of the seed. All the corn harvested on the king's field is piled up in a large corn store near the rain-and-grain altar. At sowing time all the farmers come to receive the seed, which is full of magical power because it belongs to the king. Every farmer receives a little of the seed, takes it home, and plants it on the same day."

Numerous wives, children, and visible wealth are proof of the king's vitality and power. It is practically a social requirement of the king to be as rich as possible, to have an army of slaves and servants at his beck and call, to lead an ostentatious life, to show off as much luxury as possible – matching up to the shining courts of the gods. The earthly kingdom mirrors on a microcosmic scale the macrocosmic heavens, just as the king stands for the heavenly god. Therefore one's own realm always lies at the center of the world, and he deserves his superiority over all those around. It is in the center where the king has his official seat, where the eternal fire burns that can only be put out after the death of a ruler. It is here that the royal insignia and symbols in which the rulers' power and majesty are concentrated and maintained are kept.

An Ashanti chieftain wearing a crown and chain as ceremonial jewelry.

eastern and southeastern Africa, are marked by a highly civilized, rich, and luxurious court culture. In the past they usually controlled important markets and trade routes. At the African courts, artisanship, arts, dance, and music blossomed as nowhere else. Everything could be found there: refined methods of dyeing, embroidery, appliqué, silversmithing and goldsmithing, tin casting, handiwork with bronze, glass, or beads, precious clothing, and fine jewelry, as well impressive parade armor, musicians playing a wide variety of instruments, the highly developed art of carving reliefs (in Benin and Dahomey), bards, and court chroniclers. All this of course contributed to the brilliance, etiquette, and majesty of African court life, and still does so today, if on a more modest scale.

This sparkling display disappears in a moment when the king dies. In earlier days this process was hastened. If there were droughts, disease among plants or animals, attacks by swarms of locusts, or a downturn in fortunes of war, it became clear that the king had either done something wrong or that his powers were fading. "The land began to mutter," the proverb went. Then the highest dignitaries, judges, and elders of the various clans would meet and discuss, whether the king was still able to carry out his responsibilities. A serious disturbance of order was seen as a sign from heaven to depose the ruler, exile him, or, as was often the case, even ritually murder him. This had to be done, for, as the Katla, a subgroup of the Nuba in Kordofan, reasoned, "otherwise no rain would fall and nothing would grow."

Once the king has died general anarchy breaks out. The pillar carrying the firmament has cracked and the ground has become shaky. Normally valid rules no longer apply, and life is turned upside-down. Practically everything is allowed. Only when the new king has been chosen and appointed to office does the old traditional order return and the people's sense of faith and hope are restored.

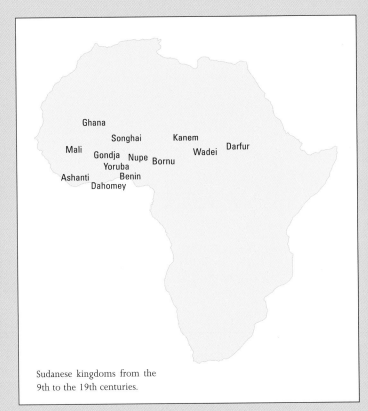

Sudanese kingdoms from the 9th to the 19th centuries.

An asantehene (king of the Asante), surrounded by his court. As a sign of power, a screen has been placed over his head.

84

Hunter-gatherer societies

For about two and a half million years from the beginning of their existence, humans lived literally hand to mouth. They gathered, caught, or hunted whichever plants, fruits, and animals nature offered. With the development of agriculture and the great early civilizations the original hunter-gatherer peoples increasingly lost ground. By the time of Christ's birth they had already forfeited about half of their living space, during the time of great explorations they occupied just 15 percent of the earth's surface, and today, except for a few decreasing numbers who have retreated to remote and inaccessible areas, they have nearly completely disappeared.

In Africa today, only the only hunter-gatherers are the Bushmen (who call themselves the San) of the Kalahari in southern Africa, the rainforest pygmies (the Mbuti, Akka, Efe, and others in the east; the Central African pygmies; and in the west the Baka in Cameroon and the Gabon pygmies), the Hazda, and smaller related splinter groups on the dry savannas of central East Africa. The San and the Hadza are the last survivors of a savanna hunter culture that once spread over large areas of northern, eastern, and southern Africa and whose origins, also documented in rock paintings, reach back into prehistory. Both groups, as well as the pygmies, differ markedly in appearance from the dark-skinned farming populations of Africa. They have a definitely paler, nearly yellow skin and are quite small (pygmies reach an average height of four feet three inches to five feet, the San five feet); San women display remarkably plump buttocks, and both sexes have tuftlike head hair. Although certain cultural attributes indicate that the ancestors of the San, the Hadza, and the pygmies had contact with each other, they do appear to be of different physical origin.

All African hunter-gatherer societies are of a nonspecialized type. In contrast to societies who depend mainly on fishing, the gathering of wild grain, grass seeds, nuts or acorns, or hunting a particular animal (such as sea mammals, bison, and wild cattle), nonspecialized hunter-gatherers live according to the seasonal offerings of their environment, from gathering and sometimes fishing as well as from hunting, without concentrating on any single one of these methods.

The advantages of this approach are not to be underestimated. If there is there is no luck in hunting, there is always the possibility of increasing dependence on gathering, which on a purely quantitative basis in any case provides the most part of the food.

However, this means that nonspecialized hunter-gatherer societies lead an unsettled nomadic life. Plants, fruits, mushrooms, and nuts ripen at different times, and rarely in large quantities. Population density is therefore low. People live in groups of about

A San hunter with spear and camouflage. Photograph c. 1930.

25 to 50, each group consisting of eight to ten small, usually monogamous families spread over a large territory. Connections are not particularly close. All members of the group have almost equal rights, which is why these communities are also known as egalitarian societies. Should there be social or marital conflict, the problem is resolved by one of the adversaries temporarily moving into a neighboring group until acrimony has abated.

Some inequalities nevertheless exist. The mainstay of such settler communities is usually patrilineal origin and heritage, which means that the hunter-gatherers' territories, including their sources of food and raw materials, are controlled by the men. It is also the men who are in charge of contact with the outside world, whether with other human beings or with spirits. An older man possessing greater experience, communication skills, and hunting success than others usually commands particular authority and occupies a kind of leadership position. As soon as his abilities weaken and his advice becomes increasingly unreliable, he forfeits this position without disruption and with no formal appointment or discussion another will take his place.

San hunters taking a rest with their dogs in the Kalahari Desert. A hunt can last from several days to some weeks.

fashion those tools that they need for their own work. Women are also responsible for specifically "domestic" tasks. They build simple shelters – protective roofs or small huts out of branches – look after babies and small children, collect water and firewood, and prepare meals.

This strict division of duties fulfills an important function by making the sexes interdependent. If there is no luck in hunting, everyone can live on the foods gathered by the women – and vice versa. Overall, sharing resources is of fundamental importance. Meat is distributed among all members of the community, albeit in different quantities according to relation and age, so that even those families whose men were unsuccessful in the hunt can enjoy a little meat. Moreover, members of the community who are in trouble will be helped by being given tools, weapons, and food; those who are sick or old will be taken care of and orphans taken into the family.

Tasks are divided basically along lines of gender. The women are required to gather vegetarian food (leaves, herbs, mushrooms, berries, fruits, roots, nuts, and so on) as well as larvae, caterpillars, and insects, and to catch turtles, frogs, and other small animals. The men meanwhile are in charge of hunting. Where circumstances permit community hunting, including children, takes place. Otherwise men and women each

On the hunt, a San hunter adopts a bent position similar to the silent stalking approach of predatory animals

A group of pygmies at an evening gathering around the fire after a day's hunting.

Among the San it is also customary to "lend" tools and jewelry for equivalent returns. Some of these objects circulate for years. Again, this is a kind of insurance against the attraction of leaving that often occurs in such a loosely bound community. These are attempts to establish ties at least between individuals so that the community remains a whole and is able to survive.

Although over the last few centuries African hunter-gatherer societies have been pushed into sometimes quite hostile areas, they usually have an ample supply of food because of their particular way of life. The basic foodstuff of the San in Botswana is the mongongo nut (Ricinodendron rautanenii Schinz), which grows in abundance and contains five times as many calories and ten times as much protein as is found in comparable grains. The supply is so great that every year thousands of pounds of the nuts remain unused. To complement 84 other sorts of edible wild plants are in plentiful supply, so that even in years of drought there is no shortage of food and even those unable to work, the old, and the sick can be easily

supported. The situation is even more advantageous for the Hadza in Tanzania. Their area of settlement may be a rocky and dry steppe, but it offers many different animals for hunting as well as a wide variety of vegetables, berries, fruits, roots, and the like.

In addition to this, there is the often underestimated consumption of small animals such as birds, lizards, frogs, turtles, snails, and insects. Caterpillars, butterflies, and larvae, and to an even greater degree termites and locusts, have an impressive fat content. Land snails, which in the area of the pygmies grow to about the size of a fist, provide animal protein, as do wild animals, while plants and wild honey supply the necessary carbohydrates. Research has shown that not

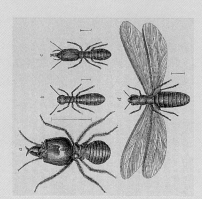

a) Bashikuay, after an illustration by Du Chaillu.
b) – d) Termites: b) worker, larval stage; c) soldier; d) adult insect. From: *Westafrika. Vom Senegal bis Benguela*, Leipzig, 1878.

only do African hunter-gatherer societies have plenty to live on, precisely because of the balanced combination of foods in their diet, but that their diet meets all requirements in terms of vitamins and other nutrients. Their overall health is therefore excellent and much better than that of their agricultural neighbors who not infrequently suffer from famine, usually just before the next harvest. In ethnology these types of nonspecialized hunter-gatherer societies are termed affluent societies.

However, this refers only to food. Their material ownership is very modest in comparison, a circumstance that can be explained by their nomadic lifestyle. Only things that can be carried over long distances on foot to the next temporary encampment, which of course also includes small children, can be taken along. Therefore only the bare essentials are used: a bow and arrow for hunting, spears (among the San); containers made of leaves (among the pygmies) or leather; and digging sticks to pierce the

Pygmy hunters near Wamba. They are highly skilled in setting up traps and catch smaller animals in nets.

hard desert ground and ease the search for roots. The San attach a stone on the digging stick so as increase its weight, while the pygmies have wooden mortars to break up meat and fruit.

Ethnology has a rule that the poorer the material ownership, the richer the imaginary world. The imaginary world of hunter-and-gatherer societies is populated mostly by animals. As hunting animals requires as much experience and dexterity as courage and skill, animals are a rich source of material for myths, stories, and fables. Animals are also considered to be closer to humans than plants: it is assumed that they are related. During the initiation of hunters, already mentioned in the discussion of initiations, this relationship is always strengthened anew by covering young men with the blood of the first animal they kill, or by rubbing the animal's ashes into cuts on the upper arm and between the eyes as a kind of "vaccination." According to the San's myths, today's people were once animals and took their current appearance only through a process of transformation at the end of ancient time, while the animals themselves underwent the process in reverse. Some people today are still able to change into animals, just as some animals can become humans. Hunters

In all cases the heavenly god carries clear signs of also being lord of the animals, a spirit well known to all hunter-gatherer societies. He is responsible for the maintenance of wild animals and has the final decision over which animal can be killed where and when by a hunter. Related spirits are often also recognized as existing either on the same level as the heavenly god or at an inferior one. For the Gabon pygmies, for example, this is a giant elephant. It is also believed that the world is full of various desert and bush spirits, some helpful, some malicious.

The importance of ancestors is negligible, however. In small nomadic groups whose consistency changes so frequently, one soon loses sight of graves, and memories of the dead fade quickly. The Mbuti believe that Tore, the heavenly god, takes people after their death. The San, who have a clear night sky above them nearly all the year round, believe that the dead move far away to the sky. When the living sit together in the evening, they can see the dead's campfires as the countless stars above.

Since living together throws up few problems, and there is the possibility of physically avoiding them, hunter-gatherer societies are marked by a paucity of rituals strengthening social bonds. Births, marriages, or funerals happen without much ceremony. Weddings may simply consist of parents and the marriage couple exchanging small presents and the couple then moving into their own hut. Everything is unforced and relaxed, free of severity, intolerance, and dogmatism. Even the belief in magic is limited. As always, magic does play a certain role, though only a small one in critical situations such as sickness, protection against malicious influences, and the strengthening of fertility, health, and energy. The hunt is therefore the event that attracts the greater instance of ritual.

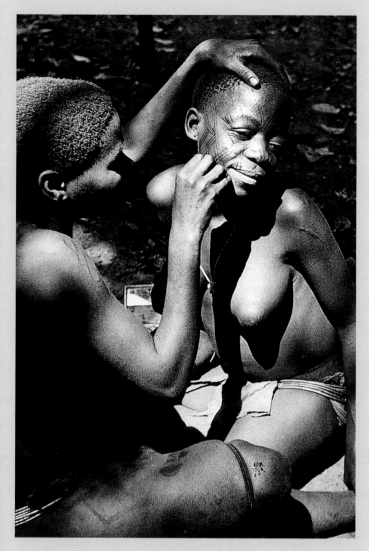

This young woman's face is being decorated with scars.

have guardian spirits in the shape of animals who help them in the hunt.

The San, Hadza, and pygmies only really believe in one heavenly god, whose appearance differs according to the environment in which these people live. To the Mbuti, pygmies of the eastern rainforest, he is manifest as the god of thunderstorms. Like themselves he dwells in a simple hut, has a family, and lives from hunting. Before the hunt one prays to him, "Grandfather, great father, I am now going into the forest, provide me with an animal, let me kill an animal!" If the hunter has observed the rules, neither broken a taboo nor sought a fight, nor thrown away food thoughtlessly, the god is merciful. Otherwise, he punishes the guilty with falling trees, attacks by wild animals, sickness, or no hunting success. For the hunters of the steppe, such as the Hadza, the same role is played by the sun.

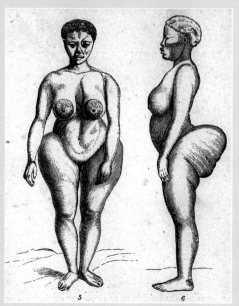

This etching shows a so-called "fatty behind" which is found only in Africa. It functions as a food store. In this way San women are able to go long distances without food or water. By the end of a journey the behind collapses in on itself.

Nature is a playground for this group of pygmy children. While some are skillfully climbing the trees, others are watching or beginning to follow them.

However, even life in African hunter-gatherer societies is not without its dark side. People suffer accidents, become sick, or fall victim to sudden drought, which causes water evaporate, dries up foods for gathering, and drives hunted prey away. It appears to be one of nature's moods, and behind it is the trickster, a godlike power typical of nearly all the world's hunter-gatherer societies. From the very beginning he has existed alongside the heavenly god and is an unreliable, moody spirit who is always ready to play nasty tricks, less so to bestow blessings. He possesses wit, but all too often this is aimed at making cruel fun of others; he tends to mad escapades of all kinds, but at the same time he is thoughtless, even stupid enough to fall into others' traps. Already at creation he spoilt God's handiwork so that people became weak and mortal. Since then he seeks entertainment by causing mischief and damage to people and deriving pleasure from their misery. Of course he also appears in the guise of animals, one in particular. The San see him as a praying mantis, caterpillar, or beetle. He is the real hero of the myths, tales, jokes, and fables. Although they are often enough the trickster's victims, people enjoy these greatly. In general a carefree, cheerful nature is typical of hunter-gatherer societies living in conditions such as those in Africa, and they love to amuse themselves and laugh a lot.

The conditions of their lifestyle predispose them to his attitude. According to research, the San and Hadza have to work fewer than two hours a day in order to secure a living. Thus they have plenty of free time in which to develop their imagination, and they while away the hours with play, dance, song, discussion, and storytelling. We can assume that life was like this everywhere during the many thousands of years before the development of agriculture. But this era, the longest in human history, is inevitably bound to end.

A group of San in the Kalahari Desert resting in the shade of a tree.

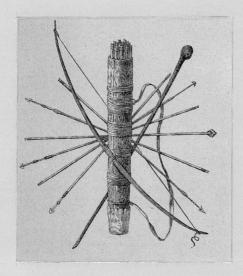

San weaponry. From: *Die Völker der Erde*, Würzburg and Vienna, 1891.

Agrarian cultures

The discovery of agriculture, which occurred between 10,000 and 7,000 BC, brought about a true revolution in the cultural history of mankind. These developments apparently occurred independently in several places around the world, and clearly adapted much from the practice of gathering plants. Put another way, this revolution represented a specialization in the tending and use of certain particularly fruitful edible plants. The main field tools used in early agriculture, and which indeed are still used in many parts of the world, including Africa, were the digger or planting implement, a variation on the gatherer's digging stick, the shovel, and the ax. Therefore this type of agriculture is also described as "digging-" or "ax-farming."

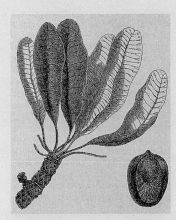

Leaves and nut of the shea-butter tree (Bassia Parkii).

Fruit and flower of the baobab tree (Adansonia digitata).

However, it is more usual to speak of "plant agriculture" or "planter cultures," as in the main bulbous, bush, tree, and vegetable plants are cultivated, as well as large-corned millet (such as sorghum) in savanna areas. Farming these does not involve sowing but the planting of bulbs, shoots, and cuttings. Grains and pulses such as millet, beans, and peas are planted by the planter digging a small hole in the ground with his bare toe or a digger and throwing a few grains or seeds into the hole before filling it in again.

"Farmer cultures," by contrast, are based on a more intensive method of farming; the main crops are cereals (barley, wheat, rice, and maize) and small and large domestic animals are raised. Fertilization with manure is practiced, as well as irrigation if necessary, and most

Manioc branch (Jatropha Manihot).

importantly, hoes, rakes, threshers, and other traction tools are used. Farmer cultures developed only c. 4,000 BC in Asia, with the rise of the ancient cultures of the Near East and, a little later, in Mesoamerica. In Africa they were to be found only in the hinterland of the northern coast (the Mahgreb), the northeast (along the Nile and in Ethiopia), and around the larger desert oases.

African plant farming can be roughly divided into two types: long-term farming in the tropical rainforests, and seasonal farming in the savannas and steppes, where the difference between the rainy and dry seasons is more marked. Farming methods depend on climate zones and vegetation, both of which are clearly demarcated. The equatorial rainforest is surrounded first by the wet, then surrounded by dry savanna, and grasslands with forests lining the rivers flowing through them. Beyond these are the wet and dry steppes, with increasingly fewer trees and where field farming becomes increasingly unviable. The steppes merge into deserts in the south (the Kalahari and Namib), the northeast (Somalia), and the north (the Sahara). While these deserts to the south and east are inhabited partly by hunter-gatherers (see pages 85–91), they are mostly, however, inhabited by nomadic herdsmen.

Long-term farming is concerned with the cultivation primarily of bananas, the basic foodstuff in the rainforest, as well as several root vegetables and tubers (taro, manioc, and yams) and the produce of trees (coconut and oil palms). Small farm animals – pigs, goats, and chickens – are raised and the diet is supplemented by fishing. The situation is much the same in the wet savannas. However, there is more cultivation of millet and vegetables (pulses, melons, and cucumbers), and less animal

Palm oil extraction by the Niger.
All illustrations on this page are from: *Westafrika. Vom Senegal bis Benguela*, Leipzig, 1878.

farming. Both in the rainforest and in the wet savannas slash-and-burn agriculture is the usual method. In the drylands and the steppes only millet and vegetables (in particular beans) are planted. Here, however, animal farming assumes a place of equal importance to plant agriculture. Sheep and cattle are kept along with chickens, pigs, and goats. Slash-and-burn agriculture is increasingly being replaced by crop rotation. However, diggers and axes remain the principal tools.

Contrary to widespread opinion, agriculture has not improved life. Dependence on a particular place and specialization in a few crops make this type of economy more vulnerable to crises. If ground water dries up, if there is too little rainfall, or if the plants fall victim to disease or attack from insects, the threat is immediate. While bush and bulb plants cannot be stored, grains like millet can be kept. However, the harvest usually falls short and there is only enough for eight or nine months, which means that the following weeks to the next harvest can be quite sparse. The unbalanced vegetarian diet also carries some risks. At best it provides sufficient levels of carbohydrate (for instance, sugar, starch, and fiber).

Dogon women in Mali carrying buckets of water back to their village. Fetching water is traditionally a woman's task.

Quantitatively this diet is adequate in that it provides enough energy but it is insufficient in qualitative terms, as there is a lack particularly of animal protein. Animal protein is important in the human diet because it has particular metabolic functions and higher biological value than vegetables. The main sources of animal protein are meat, fish, milk, cheese, and eggs. Vegetable protein, of lesser value in nutritional-physiological terms, is present only in small quantities in the cultivated tropical plants (yams, taro, bananas), but in noticeably higher ones in millet, with the highest percentage in peas and beans. People in planter cultures therefore always suffer from a lack of protein. This is compounded by traditional taboos. In some societies the consumption of fish, chicken, and eggs, and often also of milk, is forbidden, as these are seen as a type of excrement. Others, such as the Bemba in Zimbabwe, for instance, eat no raw foods because that would be eating like animals. Also, plants are dried in the sun and thereby lose their vitamin C content.

Women in Katete (Zambia) at work in the fields. If there are no older siblings available to babysit, the baby comes along.

Not all societies consider work in the fields to be a woman's job. Men often work in the fields, while the women are responsible for selling produce in the market.

A Dogon woman carries the harvest home on her head.

The situation is best for groups who also or mainly plant millet and keep more animals. The latter, however, bring improvements only in the temperate areas of the dry savannas which are free of tsetse fly. However, even plant farmers have probably always sought some dietary balance by consuming the meat of wild animals, hunting when the opportunity arises (mostly in eastern and western Africa) and especially by gathering insects, snails, frogs, and other small animals as well as wild plants, herbs, mushrooms, berries, and nuts. Less well known is the fact that the consumption of mineral-rich earth and clay provides important complementary nutritives, in Africa particularly in the rainforests. Analyses have shown that earth contains calcium, magnesium, iron, selenium, and phosphorus.

As in hunter-gatherer societies the women in agrarian societies gather foods while the men go hunting. However, they both work in the fields, although the work is divided into different tasks. In some societies it is the women who plant or sow and harvest, in others the men, while in some both do this work together. Hoeing and breaking up the ground, especially in dry regions where the earth is hard, is nearly always done by men, and the laborious raking which requires constant bending is done by women. Men also carry out all large-scale construction work (erecting walls, carrying building material, building houses and storehouses) and the manufacture of tools from wood, gut, skin, and iron. The women meanwhile are responsible for looking after children, collecting water and firewood, and the customary domestic tasks, which now often include brewing beer (usually from millet). Women's handiwork involves weaving baskets and mats, spinning and weaving cloth, and especially making pottery, in short, manufacturing all that they would need for their work.

Agriculture has therefore dramatically increased the workload for both sexes, but other things have changed for the worse, despite initial appearances to the contrary. With working the fields came a greater need for permanent settlements, which led to the erection of more solid, larger buildings and therefore a greater need for tools and furnishings, and frequently also a more artful, elaborate decoration of the properties and the technologies required for this. In the rainforests most settlements are along one or two streets; otherwise they are either circular in shape (often in the savannas and steppes) or scattered settlements and estate hamlets (as in western Sudan).

A characteristic of African agrarian cultures is the cylindrical hut with a conical roof. Inside there are utilitarian and domestic furniture and beds made of palm leaves or posts. Clothing remains sparse. Only a few decades ago both sexes went naked or merely covered their genitals with bunches of leaves or aprons made from rolled palm or gut string material, leather, or cotton (in the savannas). Jewelry, worn mainly by women, was limited to bands around the arm, leg, and neck, snail shell necklaces and studs through nose and lips. In parts of East Africa the latter have been expanded to the size of plates.

Life together in an agrarian society was more complex and therefore more problematic. A greater number of people shared more restricted spaces and were immediately dependent on each other, without having the possibility of getting out of each other's way in case of conflict, since abandoning the village and the fields would mean giving up the foundations of existence. Social tensions therefore became greater in agrarian cultures. Differentiated social orientation systems were needed to control them, and this led to the strengthening of social organization along family and community lines.

Still managing to live in impressive harmony, agrarian societies typical of the old Africa can today be found away from the great continental trading routes in the remote hills of the Sudan from Kordofan to Senegal, in the northern Congo forest regions, and in central East Africa. The inhabitants of a single village usually comprise one clan or subclan, which is usually organized along patrilineal lines. The clan's or subclan's eldest takes a leading position, but he remains dependent on the council of elders, which consists of all heads of families. The social fabric is generally still an egalitarian, democratic one. Often, as in western Sudan, the village head is also the "lord on earth" and acts as the main priest. In savannas and steppes most families are large ones; sons (brothers) remain with the paternal family, so that all live together in one estate similar to a castle, as in western Sudan. As the women carry the main burden in working the fields, men who are sufficiently wealthy may find it worthwhile to marry more than one woman.

These more complex forms of social organization in turn required a greater number of control mechanisms to guarantee the necessary level of cooperation and maintain the society's ability to perform and survive. Gradually councils of elders, officials, sometimes men's associations and secret societies with special authorities gained more power. Breaks and transgressions

Laborious work with the simplest tools for a usually meager harvest: two Dogon men at work on a millet field in Mali.

began to disrupt the basic egalitarian social order, and power and privilege was concentrated in the hands of few. This needed to be legitimized by higher authorities, and the result was an accordingly differentiated and dogmatic faith, with a high level of bonding rituals, cults, and celebrations.

The core of the religions of African agrarian societies is worship of the ancestors and of the earth, the latter often taking the form of a goddess. Both beliefs could only evolve in conditions of settled life. The ancestors guarantee the fertility of the ground, animals, and human beings, and strictly watch over the order that they carried with them in the past and passed to those alive now.

The ancestors' representatives on earth are the old men, especially the elders of families and clans, but most notably the eldest of the elders, the "lord on earth." Within the family or the whole village they are responsible for the cults of the ancestors and of the earth, meaning that they voice the prayers, whether in request or in thanks, and offer up the sacrifices. Sacrificial animals are usually black, the color of the earth as well as the rainclouds, if rain is what is asked for, for the ancestors rule over the clouds, too.

Apart from agrarian rites, especially fertility rituals at the times of sowing and planting, the main ceremony is the harvest celebration. In the presence of the ancestors, who have been invited as guests, the elders enjoy a religious meal of porridge or bread and beer from the first harvested produce. Only then are all free to use the fruits of the harvest. The ancestors receive thanks, are entertained with song, dance, and games, and, finally, are given a ceremonial farewell with plenty of sacrificial offerings. In previous times people were often sacrificed too, in order to revitalize the exhausted earth with their flesh and blood. The Asante (in Ghana) let the blood run straight into the holes left where the yams had been harvested.

The earth, edible plants, and people are closely connected to each other. The original ancestors either stepped out of the earth, grew out of her like plants, or were modeled out of her by the creator and filled with a vitality (fertility) that has been reproduced over generations and passed down to the human beings that are alive now. This fertility is taken back down into the earth by the dead, where it gathers again in the growing plants that later generations live on. It is constantly circulating, pulsating through the earth and through people, the dead and the living, forming them into a single and timeless social organism. It is precisely for this reason that any deviation from the norm, any transgression against tradition must be understood as a threat to existence, and this is why these issues are so sensitive in a way completely unknown to hunter-gatherer societies. A child falling sick, animals damaging plants, an accident, and so on, all require interpretation, as they could be a sign or warning, or already the

The locust.
From: *Land und Leute von Abessinien*, Leipzig, 1869.

punishment from the ancestors for an unknown transgression. It could also be due to the sorcery of someone malicious, or the result of witchcraft. In agrarian cultures, where peaceful cooperation and solidarity are essential but where social tensions and conflicts are also likely to increase, disagreements and fears are expressed in a stronger belief in magic and fear of witches and spirits. A wide variety of fortune-telling practices seeks to counter this superstition: everyone is looking for reassurance and wants to know the reason behind this or that unusual event, what behavior should be adapted to calm angry spirits, and how to avoid risks.

Life has become more complicated and less transparent. However, the institutions set up as a counterbalance – in particular the cult of the ancestors, the extended family systems, and the controlling authority of the council of elders – still make people's lives worthwhile and, on the whole, easygoing. The majority of agrarian societies are autonomous, responsible to no one but their ancestors and their elders. They belong to no kingdom or state. They are their own world.

Nomadic herdsmen cultures

For regionally varying reasons, mostly related to climate, economy, or overpopulation, single groups began to abandon agriculture in favor of animal farming, first in 3,000 BC and repeatedly in later times. Instead of a few animals, large herds were kept. The process of change came in stages, plant and animal farming coexisting albeit in changing proportions. Some groups maintained this formula. However, the precondition for it was on the one hand the existence of sufficient grazing areas and on the other that these areas, such as dry steppes or mountainous regions, were unsuitable for agriculture.

Depending on the surrounding conditions, people chose different animals for their nomadic economy: sheep and goats, horses, yaks, water buffalos, or camels. Nomads mostly specializing in cattle herding are found less frequently. This is because cattle need much care: they require good pasture and have the highest water consumption of all domesticated animals (over six gallons each a day). Even if the pasture is lush they must be led to drink nearly every day. Apart from a few groups in southern Arabia and, in earlier days, the Yakuts of Siberia, this special type of nomadic pastoralism is found only among African

Millet straw is carefully bound together to make a roof for a hut.

people. It also seems to be very ancient here, possibly reaching back to 4,000 BC, as suggested by rock paintings in the Sahara, all was once a flourishing savanna.

Everywhere, including southern Arabia, the cattle originally kept were longhorn cattle (Bos africanus), but later, since about the beginning of the early Middle Ages, Brahman cattle (Bos zebu) became the most frequent and still dominates today. Large herds of cattle (bos brachycerus, bos longifrons) could be found in parts of the Sudan and northeastern Africa, presumably also brought thousands of years ago from the Mediterranean, but today this type lives only in White Africa and sometimes in Egypt and Nubia. The cattle are kept usually with sheep, but also, in smaller numbers, goats, as well as donkeys, horses, and camels as pack animals. African nomadic cattle herding differs from other nomadic economies in that agriculture plays an important part. However, the herdsmen tend quite literally to farm this task out to other, agrarian communities.

Often competing with agriculture, African nomadic cattle herding is spread mostly in the dry savannas, where the tsetse fly, requiring high humidity, cannot survive. The tsetse fly does not only carry sleeping sickness but also transmits the tsetse disease, which can be fatal to cattle and horses. Typical nomadic groups include the Fulbe, Selim, and Baggara in the Sudan; the

Nomads who specialize in raising cattle, such as the Masai, are rare, as cattle need large amounts of water and good pasture.

Hadendoa, Boran, some of the Somal, and Afar, in the northeast; the Samburu, Nandi, Jie, Dodoth, Karamojong, Kipsigi, Masai, Hima, and Tutsi in central eastern Africa; and the Herero, Himba, and Hottentots in the southwest. Other fully nomadic groups are the camel-herding nomads in desert areas, such as the Tuareg and Bedouins in the Sahara and in the eastern Sudan, as well as the Ababde, Bischarin, Somal, Afar, Beni Amer, Kababisch, Meidob, and Rendille in northeastern Africa. Only camels are able to feed on sparse desert vegetation all the year round and to take in 34 gallons or more at once, after which they can go for several days without drinking and even longer without feeding, even in extreme temperatures.

The existence of camel herding in North Africa is known to date back to at least 100 BC. About 400 years later the nomads who rode the camels already presented a real threat to the Roman provinces in Africa. Ethnically these nomads could only have been the Berber, the ancestors of today's Tuareg. However, nomadic camel-herding only really extended into the desert after the arrival of Bedouins as part of the expansion of Islam, first in the 7th century and then in the 11th and 12th centuries. The destruction caused was so great that in many areas agriculture ceased altogether, the land turned into steppe, and seminomads as well as agricultural farmers were forced to turn to full-time nomadism.

Nomadic herdsmen live mostly on the milk that their animals give. The animals are milked several times a day. In times of need, the Tuareg can live solely on camel's milk for weeks, even months, requiring one to two gallons every day. Camels give large amounts of milk. Over 15 to 18 months of lactation a camel gives up to 650 gallons on average, by contrast to a cow, which lactates for eight to ten months and produces about 65–100 gallons. Frequently means of increasing productivity are also used, such as keeping the young away from the mother at an early stage, blowing into the cow's vagina, or inserting certain plants or even an arm to stimulate milk production. If a young animal dies, it is stuffed with grass, straw, and other material, some of its urine is rubbed on it, and this "milking doll" placed next to its mother during milking times. The Kipsigi in Kenya are more sophisticated. They play their cows seductive tunes on the flute to make them more productive.

However, African nomads hardly ever process the milk further. Camel and cattle herdsmen enjoy it both sweetened and soured. The latter also make butter, but use it only for rubbing into skin and hair or for pelts or leatherwork. Nomads, especially the cattle herdsmen of northeastern and eastern Africa, live not only on the milk but also the blood of their animals. For this a tourniquet is tied around the main neck vein. The swollen blood vessel above the tie is opened by shooting an arrow at close range, and the blood is collected in a bowl. This does not happen regularly, but some groups do this once every four weeks; seven to eight pints is taken from male animals, three to five from females. Very rarely sheep and goats are also used, as with the Masai, Samburu, Karamojong, and Turkana. Usually cattle herdsmen keep no small animals. The Tuareg, Bedouins, and some Somal groups bleed camels, but certainly the former only do this as an emergency measure when there is a lack of water and milk, during long treks through the desert, for instance.

Meat makes up a relatively small part in the diet. If available, sheep and goats are slaughtered, but cattle and camels are killed only for celebrations and rituals. Camel meat and beef may count as a delicacy, but as the number of animals determines a family's reputation, and large domestic animals are highly prestigious, parting with any one of them is very hard. If this is absolutely necessary, people choose an injured, sick, or old animal.

The number of cattle of high value determines a family's reputation, so people take great care of their animals.

Masai by their huts, basic wooden structures covered in mud. When the group moves on the huts are eroded by the weather. New ones are put up at the next settlement.

threatened, especially as trading also becomes almost impossible. For just this reason nomads often seek a forced "alliance" with agrarians, as in areas in East Africa, where the Tutsi and Hima subjugated the local population, established kingdoms, and formed (unloved) aristocratic ruling classes. Others also increased their income by taxing and controlling caravan trading, as in the Sahara.

It might be assumed that in terms of nutrition, camel and cattle herdsmen are better off than agrarians. Not only do their animals convert the area's scant vegetation, which provides only carbohydrates, into protein, fat, and meat, they are also able to convert the water they drink – which may be rich in soda, calcium, and magnesium salts, sulphate, carbonate, hydrogen sulfide, and other minerals, gases, and salts but which is practically undrinkable by humans

The nomads' diet would therefore be restricted if they did not make use of other sources of food. As already mentioned, cattle herdsmen are usually also agriculturists. At the start of the rainy season they sow a few millet seeds at a particularly appropriate place, and arrange their future journey so that they will pass by again at harvest time. Hunting small animals and gathering wild vegetables, berries, grass seeds, birds' eggs, and honey play a not unimportant part. Other goods, especially fruit, vegetables, and work tools, are obtained by bartering with their own products, such as milk, butter, blankets, leather goods, and recently also items for tourists.

Gathering, working in the fields, domestic tasks, processing skins and furs, weaving mats and materials, and the care of small animals are women's tasks. Men are responsible for hunting, trading, and in former times warfare, but most especially for care of cattle and camels, which sometimes assume a near-religious significance. Sometimes, as with cattle-herding nomads in eastern Africa (for example, the Masai, Nandi, Samburu, Suk, and Turkana) and the Fulbe in the Sudan, women also play a part in looking after larger animals, and in some cases are even involved in the milking.

Nomad economies are anything but risk-free. The animals provide the basis for their diet. If many succumb to disease, if there is a drought, of if many people, particularly young men, become victims of warfare, the group's existence is immediately

– into nutritious milk. There should be enough fat and animal protein in the diet, but in fact this is only partly true, as much milk but little meat is consumed. Even so, camel's and cow's milk contain between three and five percent fat, about three and a half percent protein, and about three to three and a half percent lactose, and is also rich in vitamin C. The meat of wild animals provides some counterbalance, while the gathered plants and the bartered grain and vegetables provide the necessary amount of carbohydrates. Generally nomads are therefore a little better nourished than plant farmers, although this advantage can be exaggerated in that the high level of vulnerability of their economic methods often results in acute crises.

Although the nomadic way of life limits the amount of material possessions, nomads have more possessions than hunter-gatherers because there are pack animals at hand. Shelters are lightweight and quick to assemble and dismantle: most camel-herding nomads have tents, while cattle herdsmen prefer beehive-shaped huts covered with branches, mats, or furs. Their sparse possessions consist of light and unbreakable materials made by the people themselves: mats and blankets; vessels fashioned from calabashes, animal bladders, or leather; wooden or bone tools; and drinking horns. Apart from the camel-herding nomads in northern and northeastern Africa, the men wear leather capes, sometimes tied over one shoulder so that the other stays free, and a leather loincloth (unless they go completely naked); the women wear leather aprons, which are sometimes decorated with beads.

Apart from the matrilineal Tuareg, who owe this social system to their Berber heritage, African nomadic herdsmen are organized along patrilineal lines. Grazing territories, waterholes and wells, and animals therefore belong to, and are controlled by, the men in the group, which is why women are generally kept away from the large animals (apart from the exceptions in some East African and Sudanese communities, mentioned above). To keep property issues absolutely unambiguous special emphasis is placed on genealogy. Everybody knows the families' histories, and they are a popular subject of discussions, stories, and songs. Marital fidelity ranks high, as a "wrong step" would "contaminate" the genealogy. Otherwise nomadic herdsmen societies can be described as generally egalitarian. Only the eldest men carry some social superiority. If there are leaders, they usually have no executive powers, at least not in times of peace, and all their decisions depend on the agreement of the elders. If they lose the group's trust they can be voted out.

Again much like hunters-and-gatherers, nomadic herdsmen societies seem to be uninterested in religious aspects of life. Apart from the camel herdsmen, who are nearly all Muslim (but who, like the Bedouins, do not very strictly observe Islamic canons), African cattle herdsmen tend to look to the starry sky. Sky and thunderstorm deities figure to some extent, but images of the dead and the beyond are few. At best they form part of hierarchical societies in which the gods of the conquered people live as masters of the dead in the underworld, while the ancestors of the ruling dynasty live as heavenly heroes and courtiers of the highest god. Births, weddings, funerals, and other important life events are celebrated only with the minimum of ritual.

Only the cattle, which the men deal with every day and all year round, which are the lifeblood of all, and which constitute their property and define their reputation, receive rapturous, almost religious attention. A rich vocabulary makes it possible to differentiate animals exactly by height, strength, coloring, markings, and other attributes. Songs in praise of favorite cows are composed and performed in public. The most important social relationships – family and sexual – are expressed in terms of cattle. Girls fall in love with "bulls"; a married woman's lover "caresses the favorite animal" of the cheated husband. In ethnology this is called a "bovine idiom," a language taking definitions and images from the world of cattle.

As the culture's semireligious core, the animals must only come into contact with material that has been made within the

Masai warriors at a war dance...

... where they prove their strength by the height of their jumps.

group and passed down for generations so that they are not contaminated. Milk containers may not be made of clay or metal; butter can only be churned in calabashes or fur bags. Cattle urine is used for cleansing and healing, butter as an ointment, and dried dung as fuel for the evening's fire, where everyone inhales the smoke. Myths tell of the joint origin of humans and cattle, and chieftains are buried in cattle skins.

Unlike other nomadic herdsmen, some African herdsmen hold collective initiations ceremonies for boys. The reason for this may be that these particular tribes are still "pagan," while most other nomads are now Hindus, Buddhists, Christians, or Muslims. The initiation rite is again a particularly typical expression of their lifestyle, as it aims to build a magical link between the young men and the cattle.

Among the Karamojong in northeastern Uganda it has three stages. The boys are isolated in a specially designated ceremonial place, where they each have to kill a cow by plunging a spear into its side. They then cut up the cow in a particular prescribed way. The elders receive a small part of the meat for immediate consumption; the rest is piled up in the middle of the site. Only the stomachs are laid out separately. The eldest of the men present slices them open with his spear so that the chymus (half-digested fodder) is visible. He rubs this onto the initiates' heads, shoulders, chests, and bellies, murmuring the blessing "May you fare well. Grow old. Gain a wealth of cattle. Become a member of the elders!" In the next stage, the initiation leader lifts the front legs of each cattle and calls the boy who killed that particular animal. He steps forward, gnaws at the hooves and then spits the fragments on his chest. After songs praying for the initiates' welfare, the group, and their herds, a celebratory meal takes place. The initiates prepare the meat and pass it to the elders, who are really the only ones entitled to eat it but who now give everyone, including the initiates, some of it.

In the last stage, which takes within the family place two or three weeks later, the boys go into the calves' stable. There their mothers kneel before them, push a handful of butter into their mouths and rub the back of the boy's necks and those of any friends present with some more butter. The back of the neck here represents the hump of the zebu, which is seen as the animal's source of vitality. Now the initiate has become a grown man. He has the right to enter sacred sites, to sacrifice cattle, eat of their meat and drink their blood, and to participate in all the group's discussions. He has become a part of the magic bond, the age-old relational link between cattle and human, which alone is the guarantee of the group's survival.

Masai woman with jewelry on her arms and legs, driving wooden poles into the earth for the cattle to be tied to.

Warrior herdsmen

In densely populated areas which could often be used for agriculture, nomads frequently had first to conquer their territory and then constantly defend it. It therefore made sense to raise young men as warriors so that there would always be fighting groups when and as necessary. This explains why many now peaceful nomadic peoples still maintain a warrior tradition, and why for instance it is still customary to put young men, usually after initiation, through a warlike phase with the appropriate clothing, painting, weaponry, and behavior – for instance, among the Masai, who overact a little for the benefit of tourists.

This was particularly the case for groups living in the Sudan, an area that has seen many population movements and conquering wars throughout history. The Fulbe (also known as the Peulh or Fulbeani) were particularly involved: as late as the 19th century they entered the steppe regions of northern Cameroon and, thanks to their strong cavalry, established dozens of kingdoms there. Although today they make up only 35 percent of the population, their influence on language and culture is considerable. The horse has remained the status symbol of the ruling upper class. On ceremonial occasions the Fulbe revive their warrior traditions and reenact important moments in their history in dramatic performances on horseback, showing off their power most effectively in highly impressive and colorful displays.

The Fulbe are also important as imperial conquerors in other parts of West Africa. They are first mentioned simply as nomadic

A Masai warrior with bow and arrow. It was particularly important for the nomads to bring up their young men as warriors, as in densely populated areas they would have to first conquer and then constantly defend their territories. This is why many now peaceful nomadic tribes still maintain a warrior tradition.

A group of Lumbwa warriors set out on lion hunt. They wear ritual jewelry to express their respect for the lions.

Hunters deep in the bush make their way through the high grass, for which their shields are of great help.

herdsmen in the valley of the Senegal in western Guinea. From there they spread eastward to what is now southern Nigeria. Today they inhabit the area between the Senegal River and the Central African Republic, being particularly concentrated in Niger, Senegal, Guinea, Mali, Cameroon, and Nigeria. While part of the Fulbe, the Bororo, remained nomadic herdsmen, the "city Fulbe" rose to be the rulers of several kingdoms.

The warrior ethos undoubtedly has an important place in the historical tradition and value system of the Fulbe. The Bororo practice using weapons from an early age and carry out a training course that reaches its life-threatening peak in the initiation ceremony. The young men's self-discipline and courage decide their future reputation in their community. Even so, the nomadic Fulbe have not developed as full warrior herdsmen as in Asia. This may be due to the conditions of the savannas of western Africa, which lack wide open spaces. All the land south of the Sahel is densely populated, and the Fulbe have found niches only as minorities in their host countries. Often it has made more sense to use cunning rather than violence.

Early on in this process some groups settled as agrarian farmers or went over to trading or some other business.

103

Fulbe in full warrior dress. Both horse and rider are richly caparisoned and well armed with Islamic "magic means" to protect against death and injury and to favor the victory of the "faithful" over the "infidel."

Fulbe warriors at fighting tournaments at an annual festival in northern Cameroon.

Fulbe warriors seek to impress their audience
with their riding skills.

Increasingly urbanized, these "city
Fulbe" adopted Islam in the 12th
century. As scholars of the Koran and as
merchants, they had become
influential figures and came into
contact with the early West African
rulers and their courts. The Moorish
geographer al-Bakri (1040–94)
studied the meaning of the horse in
the cults of Sudanese kingdoms of his
time. It probably came into the
ownership of the rulers. It is likely that
the Fulbe developed their aggressive
political belligerence only after they
became familiar with the conditions of
their new environment. Even today the
horse is hardly found among Fulbe
herdsmen, while for the dynastic
Fulbe it possesses the greatest value as
an aristocratic status symbol and a manifestation of wealth,
sophistication, and power, still embodying the feudal world that
came into bloom in West Africa in the 19th century.

The conquering wars of the Fulbe received much of their
impulse from Islam. Again, its adherents were not so much to be
found among the Fulbe herdsmen as in the urban elites, who
knew how to unite the goals of religion and power-politics.
While the main contingent of these "defenders of the faith" were
seminomadic Fulbe warriors, the key to negotiations lay with the
educated leaders in the cities, trained both ideologically and in
warfare. They often possessed so much charisma that they were
able to mobilize the discontented masses at any moment: just
such a man was the famous Islamic scholar Uthman dan Fodio,
who led a successful campaign against the Hausa rulers in the
early 19th century and founded the powerful kingdom of Sokoto
in what is today northern Nigeria. The Fulbe's rapid victories
came about thanks to their cavalries, which played key roles in
so many armies of West African rulers that the power of a
kingdom was determined by how many cavalry units it could
bring onto the field.

Thus supported, the Fulbe waged their wars against the
"infidel". One important target was the taking of slaves: the
ethics of Islam did not conflict with the commercial interests of
the "faith warriors." This becomes particularly clear in the eastern
areas, where the Fulbe waged their holy war (jihad) to overthrow
the "unbelieving tribes" with the actual purpose of making
material gains, moving away from the official ideal of spreading
the faith. On what remained of the "pagan" cultures they

Musicians provide the ceremony with some accompaniment.

constructed new, centralized systems of rule. Some indigenous
groups managed to flee the domination of outsiders. The
conquered "infidel" had the opportunity of becoming
assimilated into the ruling Fulbe community by converting to
Islam, but the majority were subjugated and some transferred as
slaves to the urban Fulbe settlements.

Law and judgement

Premodern village societies could in the long term live together only if all were prepared to cooperate peacefully and for the common good. This assumed that they not only observed the rules, but that they also agreed unconditionally with the norms and values underlying these rules.

However, this altruism could not be taken for granted. It was always necessary for there to be ways and means of preventing possible transgressions through effective controls and of punishing offenses, in serious cases by physical force. This was "common law," as opposed to the civil law, which is still in force in rural areas of the Third World today, below the state law. Its function is mainly to set out clearly what is permitted and what is not, to uphold public order, including in relations with ancestors, spirits, and deities, and to provide solutions to conflicts originating in transgressions. Common law provides a series of measures, progressively more severe in relation to the gravity of the offense.

One control that is both in force at all times and fundamental is public opinion. In a rural community everyone is almost always under the gaze of others – in the family, in the village, and in the fields. Therefore everyone endeavors not to do anything which could meet with disapproval or suspicion or could make them unpopular. If one were to attract attention through strange behavior, one could easily become "talked about," and would possibly be isolated. The Nyakyusa in Tanzania even say that someone causing others offense runs the risk of becoming sick, because the others will begin to talk, and the offender could catch cold from the "cold breath of their rumors."

If this measure does not work, the next step is public mockery. People gossip, tell stories to ridicule the particular person, write satirical poems or songs about them, even caricature them at communal celebrations. This literally brings the victim down. Their reputation suffers, even if only temporarily, as does their chance of assuming a higher position of importance in society.

Rumors and mockery are a type of reprimand known in every common law – up to the European carnival. Their real effectiveness lies in the fact that the "talked about" are not only temporarily shut out, but also find themselves severely isolated from the community. If this does not resolve the situation, the individual concerned is advised to leave the village together with his family. Should he ignore this, the noose is tightened further. Nobody pays attention to him and his family anymore, nobody greets them, helps them, or invites them. It is as if they did not exist, and in a traditional community this means that the foundations of life have been taken away. The final step is exile or deportation, a kind of excommunication, which certainly in the past was like an execution, as the exiles were lawless, "free as a bird," but at the same time could not find acceptance anywhere else, much less receive land for cultivation. They would not have been able to survive on their own in the wilderness.

Particularly severe offenses usually include adultery, rape, incest, theft, sorcery causing damage, witchcraft, murder, and transgressions against the ancestors and the gods. These are dealt with by the local courts, consisting of the elders and the village chief. As everywhere in the world, appearances, examination of accuser and defendant, witness statements, circumstantial as well as immediate evidence, the oaths of those questioned, and last but not least the judges' experience are all used in reaching a verdict. The judges often make their decisions on the basis of earlier verdicts in similar cases, that is, on precedence.

If, because of contradicting evidence, difficulties arise in reaching a verdict, higher authorities are called upon: that is, "God's judgment" – trial by ordeal, poison, fire, or water –

Dance of the executioners in Kumase (Ashanti, Gold Coast).
From: *Im Lande des Fetischs*, Basel, 1890.

is used. In the first the delinquent is pronounced guilty if he dies of the poison administered to him; in the final case the offender is thrown into the water with his limbs tied and, if he does not sink, he has spoken the truth. During an ordeal by fire the accused must walk through fire or touch a glowing metal object; if he is unhurt, he is innocent.

In differentiated societies such as the West African kingdoms, the councils of elders are replaced by institutional courts whose members – village and clan chiefs with their aides, also full-time judges – are elected by the people or appointed by the king, who in some cases takes the position of judge or chairman.

The measure of punishment usually follows the principle of the ius talionis, the law which prescribes "an eye for an eye, a tooth for a tooth, a hand for a hand," as also written in the Bible (Deuteronomy, chapter 21, verses 24–25). Transgressions where the sinners remain unknown do not go unpunished; quite the opposite, they are hit with the full force of the ancestors' or the gods' judgment. They or one of their family may be carried off by disease, their harvest could wither, misfortune may dog them, they may suffer a fatal accident, or be struck by lightning.

Vigilant yet merciless public supervision plays a major role in the very low crime rate in traditional societies, at least in the past. Everyone had to be able to rely on each other; families and neighbors build their relationships on solidarity and trust. Conditions are totally different when applied to those "not

Gathering of chieftains from various tribes for a judicial hearing. The assembled are festively dressed. Some, aiming to be particularly elegant, have imitated the style of colonial rulers. Photo c. 1920.

belonging." The norm is what is "normal," and this counts as identical with one's own life order. This also means that the judicial area of a group is always the same as its territory. Beyond its borders lies a state of lawlessness. All those living there or who have been banished there are no longer accepted as human beings in the full sense of the term. They are "barbaric" and, as already mentioned, "free as a bird," (lawless) so that theft, robbery, even murder committed against them is regarded less as an offense and sometimes even a deed of glory – a view that has found adherents in the old civilizations as well as in more recent times in modern industrial society.

In the name of the ancestors

In Ashanti the king (the asantehene) is also the highest judge. On certain days of the week he, together with his elders and dignitaries, holds legal court. For this occasion servants carry chairs with brass fittings (asipim) into the royal reception hall. These chairs serve as representational seats for the country's notables during judicial hearings.

Directly or indirectly, responsibility for good harvests, the changing of the seasons, safety from natural catastrophes, attacks from wild animals, for sickness, and even for death lay with people, in that it was up to them to observe the old traditions, or not. In premodern agrarian societies the dead are regarded as the prime keepers of lawful order. The ancestors "attend" all judicial dealings, which traditionally are conducted by heads of families, village chiefs, lords, and kings. As elders and people of superior rank, they have the ultimate power to decide on how any possible transgressions by their descendants should be dealt with.

The first point of contact is always the accused's immediate superior. In conflicts between members of different families, it could also be the heads of both. If the dispute cannot be settled it is passed on to the next highest authority. Depending on the gravity of the offense the offender could be brought before each of the judiciary hearings. In the past, the king of the Asante was the final judge in all judicial dealings. He alone could decide on life or death, but obviously called on his legal council for advice. If he imposed a death penalty, those sentenced to death were killed at a special place of execution by the royal executioners. They

were bludgeoned or strangled to death so that their blood would not defile the earth. Their corpses were buried there and then without any ceremony. Similar in severity to execution was a verdict of exile. It made the offender "free as a bird," so that anyone could lay a hand on them without punishment.

Today the traditional courts deal only with transgressions against decency and heritage. A frequent offense of this kind is adultery, where not only intercourse but also the "indecent" touching of noses, ears, breasts, or any other delicate part of the body, as well as tickling the palm of the hand, are considered punishable. Intercourse in the bush or on the floor is regarded as damaging to the whole community, as it disturbs the spirits or defiles and angers the earth.

Even more frequent are conflicts within the family or between neighbors, often concerning the use of land. Serious offenders, however, are handed over to the police and are therefore dealt with by the state judiciary.

Society is still vigilant in ensuring that there are no disagreements between people and supernatural powers, especially that the wrath of the gods is not called forth thoughtlessly. In this respect Christians and Muslims especially, who no longer feel bound to the rules of the "old" religion, come into conflict with the code of traditional norms. Often they neglect to offer sacrifices to the (nature) spirits omnipresent in Ashanti and therefore expose the whole community to danger. For instance, in Kumawu, a princedom belonging to Ashanti, Muslims had built a dam without seeking the prior permission of the river deity (or her priests). The transgressors were called before the state council, and together they worked on finding a solution agreeable to all. The judgment, true to the spirit of Solomon, ordered a sheep to be sacrificed to the river deity as a peace offering. The Muslims' refusal to carry out the sacrifice themselves was accepted, but they were liable for the costs. Thus peace was restored again.

Like the asantehene, the judges on either side of him wear black togas. Their right shoulders are uncovered, so that they are dressed exactly as when they step before the blackened stools of the ancestors in the "stool house."

The four accused await their trial. The seriousness of the occasion requires them to wear black mourning clothes and to leave their upper bodies uncovered as a sign of humility.

Adultery:
she cooked for another man

Followers of the water goddess Mami Wata must observe strict moral rules. In the event of adultery (which includes even simply cooking for another man) Mami Wata takes possession of her initiates and lends them her voice so that they can confess publicly. If during a ceremony an initiate accuses herself of adultery by the shrine near the Adomi bridge, she must be thoroughly ritually cleansed.

Adultery is one of the most common transgressions in the life of a society, a severe violation of the order laid down by the gods and lived out by the ancestors, because it upsets the regulations of descent and heritage. This is particularly serious if wives of the king are involved. In the past they were kept away from all men, under the strict supervision of eunuchs. This even applied to the children. Among the Mosi, the king's (the Naba's) eldest son had to leave the royal residence at the age of three, his younger brothers following him when they were seven or eight. Ideally the Naba was to be the only man in the house. Even so the faithfulness of the royal wives was checked once a year by a specialist who was a eunuch and according to etiquette the king's "first wife." For this he used a calabash filled with water and particular plants, in which he was able to see the adulteress and her partner. There was no mercy at all for either of them; they were both immediately executed behind the palace.

Normally adultery committed by the man seldom has serious consequences. Should the seducer be uncovered he gives the husband a certain amount of money and pays for a sacrificial animal to soothe the gods – and that is the end of the matter. Things are not so easy for the woman. Even if her transgression remains undiscovered, its consequences often appear at the next time she gives birth. Sharp, long-lasting labor pains arouse initial suspicions. The ancestors are "pointing the finger," so to speak. Complications at a birth is classic evidence for marital infidelity. Only a confession can help, during which the woman says

something like, "I am a disgrace to my family, to all women, to all of humanity. Guilt lies heavy on me. I had an affair with one of my husband's cousins when I was already pregnant by a driver. I don't even know exactly who the father of my child is!"

Not every woman who experiences a difficult labor has committed actual adultery. It is enough just to have considered it or to have been faithless in a dream. As soon as she admits to this she feels better and the complications disappear. However, if she keeps it hidden away and refuses a public confession, she may – in the worst case – die in childbirth.

In the cities and the suburbs, where traditional family and economic structures have broken down or are in the process of doing so, many of the old ideas are seen as outdated. Some cults incorporate new ideas, others cults are totally new. An important function of all these new cults is still to ensure morality and order, and they play an important part in detecting and controlling antisocial tendencies. Cult followers adhere strictly to the service of their deity. If they err, the deity will take away her protection. And woe to those who are guilty of a

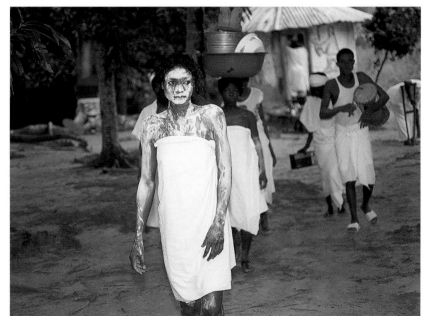

Top: As a sign of death, from which the adulteress will rise again after cleansing, she is dressed in white by the priest and covered in powder of the same color.

Thus attired, the adulteress sets out on her walk through the village. She is accompanied by a drummer and other cult followers on this journey of atonement, where she is publicly presented.

Instead of the usual white clay, followers of Mami Wata use talcum powder. The use of foreign goods in the cult is explained by the foreign nature of the goddess herself, who seems to attract particularly those who have problems with their own identity and are caught between two worlds, between the African way of life and the European one.

more serious offense! Many, especially older men, lead women to the cult so that they will be kept away from temptation. As thanks for guarding over the women's virtue the deity receives an annual sacrificial gift. However, women do not have the right to entrust their husbands' fidelity to a higher power in a similar way.

The cult of Mami Wata also serves to uphold order, and the goddess passes severe judgment on those followers who behave asocially. She also judges those women brought to her shrine by husbands accusing them of adultery. This needs little proof: in most African societies cooking for a man other than one's husband counts as evidence of infidelity. In Twi, the language of the Akan, as in many societies around the world, sexual intercourse is described in the words, "the man eats the woman" (*obarima di obaa*) and adultery as "eating

someone's wife" (*obi ye*). A woman cooking for a man who is not her father, brother, or some other close male relative, must be married to him, that is, sharing his bed.

Cooking, and no more, is a less severe transgression; in such cases Mami Wata usually deems it sufficient to order the culprit's head to be shaved and to whip her symbolically with a twig. Sanctions for genuine adultery are far more severe.

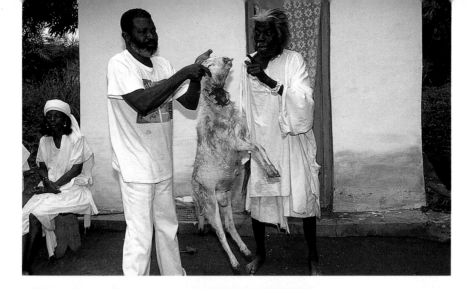

To make it up to the goddess the adulteress must donate a ram, which is sacrificed by Mami Wata's priest. He asks her to accept the sacrifice, to guard over the woman better in future, and also to protect her from immoral thoughts and deeds.

Mami Wata then speaks through the mouth of a possessed woman and gives instructions as to what exactly must be done to atone for the guilt. Mami Wata thereby does what similar older rites in cultures before her promised: cleansing, reformation, and reassimilation into the community.

After passing on Mami Wata's messages, her medium finally collapses exhausted on the ground.

Shango the lightning god punishes thieves

A priest of the lightning god Shango, who also protects justice, wearing a red cap. In his mouth is a red parrot feather, a sign of Shango's power and reserve and an insurance of secrecy. The priest summons the god with a double bell.

Stools, a typical symbol of authority, are carried to the place of ceremony. "Enthroned" on them are the *achina kpon*, objects symbolizing Shango's burning stones and his thunderbolts and displaying his great power.

At the same time statues of the goddess Oya, Shango's favorite wife, and her favorite objects (dolls, perfume, and other items) are displayed in the adjacent shrine of Mami Wata.

Deities too are guardians of the law and can expose sinners – deadly sorcerers, thieves, or perjurers – by bringing disease, in some cases even death, or causing conflict and "thunderstorms." Thunder, which among the Yoruba is personified by the god Ara, is paradoxically only an announcer of lightning, and his grumblings are not dangerous: as the Mosi say, "no tree has yet fallen from thunder alone." His "successor," lightning, is far more feared; it is the "rain's knife" and a deadly weapon. Lightning is the manifestation of the heavenly god's omnipotence, or that of another powerful deity, who with this "bad death" punishes all who have stolen grain from a field store or plucked fruit from the trees of others.

Death by lightning counts as punishment for theft or perjury. The injured party must turn to the village eldest or a certain priest, depending on the social order: they possess the means of summoning lightning as a ray of judgment. Lightning knows his target exactly: he picks out the guilty, literally brands them, and so makes their transgression obvious to all. Sometimes he even returns the stolen goods, which may be found on or near the burned corpse.

This shameful death even has a special place among the list of "bad deaths," as the remains of those punished by lightning are thought to exude threatening energies endangering all those who do not know how to deal with them. Only specialists, that is, those who can call up lightning, have the necessary antidote, allowing them to approach the corpse without fear of danger and to bury him without ceremony. Such victims of lightning are only despised. Even their property is considered to be infected, which is why it once would pass straight to the specialists.

In societies with polytheistic beliefs, such as the Yoruba, Fon, and Ewe, the lightning gods and their cult followers are high up in the hierarchy. Hevioso, the lightning god of the Ewe and originally a city god of Xevié (situated about

A novice dances round a tree dedicated to Shango and decorated in his colors, bone-white and blood-red. The colors symbolize his embodiment of both peace and violence. A novice of Shango's is really a temple slave. If she was once healed by the Shango priest and her family was unable to provide the sacrificial goat, the girl must stay in the temple until she is redeemed by the sacrificial gift. The loincloth is still snow-white, showing that the novice has not been in the temple long. As a sign of humility the novices are not allowed to wash the cloths, so that these indicate the length of stay from these. Some novices leave the temple as priestesses.

Following pages: A priest dressed in white dances on the night before the tribunal – again with a red parrot feather in his mouth. On his back he is carrying the *achina kpon*, a heavy burden which the priests put on their shoulders before they become possessed by their god.

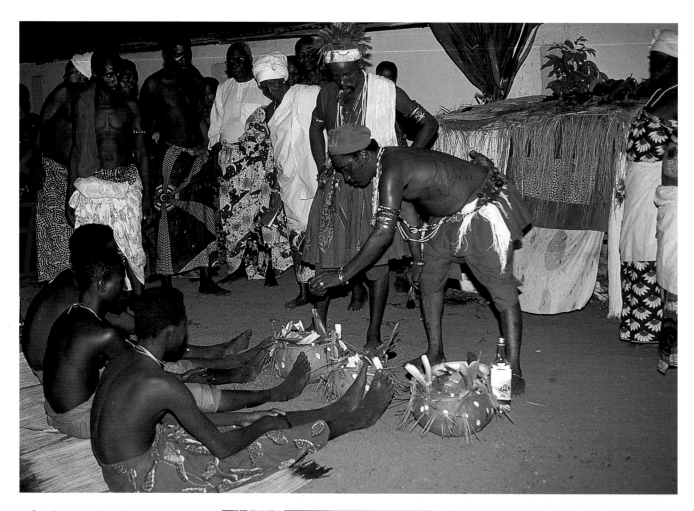

Before the priests begin the ceremony, pots filled with sacred water and herbs are placed in front of the boys and are later used for cleansing them.

The atonement ceremony starts with each of the boys, following the priest's instructions, individually touching the goat that they stole with their mouths. This is a sign of humility. Afterward the animal is slaughtered and its blood poured over all the objects dedicated to Shango.

halfway between Allada and Ouidah in the former kingdom of Dahomey), possesses great powers and has numerous followers. During thunder he tends to possess the faithful and make them dance. He is regarded as the owner of the sky and as the supreme judge. Really he is a fertility god: the rain, which is considered as cleansing as well as bringing life, is said to be his sperm. He is also able to summon up searing heat, kill people in anger and destroy their houses.

The Fon too honor Hevioso, who carries the additional name Agbolesu ("great ram") after his sacred animal. His cult was probably introduced by the mother of King Tegbesu (reigned c. 1740–74). In Xevié he replaced the older thunder god Só (Sogbo). There were many thunder gods in Dahomey before him, which made it difficult to know which one had caused a person's death. An autopsy had to be carried out by authorized priests.

Hevioso is in many ways similar to Shango, the thunder-and-lightning god of the Yoruba. However, Shango is one of the earth gods, not the sky gods. He has many followers among the Yoruba. His cult plays an important role in enthroning the king of Oyo, an old Yoruba center. There is much that links Shango with the king. For instance, if a stroke of lightning is followed by a roll of thunder, it is custom to shout out "Welcome, your majesty, long live the king!" As divine supervisor Shango lives above the firmaments. It is imagined that he keeps a number of horses in his great palace behind bronze doors and keeps himself amused with hunting and fishing. His brother Ogun, the god of iron and war, makes chains of fire (lightning) for him, which he uses to kill his enemies. Shango is also responsible for hurling what are known as thunder flints, small, polished, prehistoric ax blades. A house destroyed by lightning was a sign that its inhabitants were guilty of something. Shango's priests would then carry out extensive cleansing ceremonies. Even the local lord had to attend to pay the tribute due to Shango; the only exception was the uppermost ruler, the Alafin ("lord of the manor") of Oyo. One of the priests' important tasks was finding the thunder flint, which was always found in the ground nearby.

Although the form of his cult may have changed, Shango continues to guard morality and grumbles in the clouds when people's offenses anger him. He particularly punishes adulterers, liars, and thieves. His wife Oya, goddess of the Niger and its tributaries, supports him by sending dangerous storms which uproot trees and shatter houses.

Shango is a punishing god but also a just one. In Cotonou a goat that had been tied to one of his shrines was stolen. It had been offered by a girl "marked" by him. Culpability for her fate lay with her older sister, who had accepted money from a man, traditionally interpreted as a promise of marriage. However, this promise was never honored. When the young woman refused to return the money, the man, deprived of both money and wife, turned to Shango's priests to ask the god for justice to be done. The god responded accordingly by killing the young woman with a bolt of lightning.

When she tried to lift the corpse, the younger sister came into contact with evil, and Shango marked her right arm with his sign. To take the evil away from her, the priests intended to carry out a cleansing ceremony, and the goat was meant for just this purpose. However, three young brothers stole the animal, intending to sell it at market, but they were caught and led to the shrine. Their redemption came at great cost to their mother. The priests demanded not only a higher price for the goat but also several other sacrificial gifts. However, had she not bought her sons' freedom, the loss would have been much more painful, as Shango would have killed the boys for their offense.

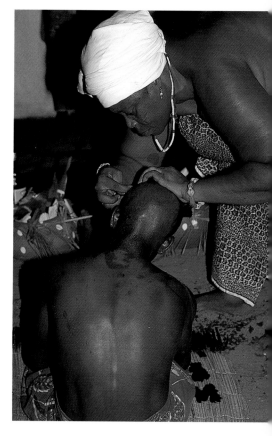

By having their hair cut by a priestess the boys also shed their guilt. For full reconciliation the offenders' mother must donate several sacrificial offerings. Only then is Shango appeased, and the boys can be safe from his wrath, as long as they do not err again.

Shango myths

The god Shango and the three goddesses of the Yomba. From: *Fetichism and Fetich Worshipers*, New York, Cincinnati, St. Louis, 1885.

According to legend Shango ruled as the fourth king in Oyo, in what is today western Nigeria. The years that he was in power were seven, a mystical number. His reign was exciting, and many successful war campaigns were attributed to him. However, he owed his successes not only to his heroic courage but also to special magical gifts: he could breathe fire and smoke out of his mouth and nostrils, which made his enemies flee and his subjects fear him. Another of his magical powers was the ability to summon up lightning.

One day, accompanied by his loyal servants, he climbed the hill, at the foot of which lay his palace. On the way he suddenly became convinced that he had to test his lightning medicine, as it might have become damp and he feared for its reliability. Sure of his fears he directed the lightning toward his palace. However, the medicine had lost none of its effectiveness: a storm started up, and bolts of lightning shot from the sky, turning the palace into a raging fire. Most of his wives and all his children fell victim to the flames. With a broken heart Shango resigned. He left Oyo to seek refuge with Elempe, his maternal grandfather, in northerly Nupe. His subjects tried every way of persuading him to return, not even stopping at the use of force. However, Shango held his sword out against anyone attacking him. They promised to replace his lost wives so that he could have children again, but nothing could change his mind. He set out with a few loyal followers, including his favorite wife Oya, but soon his companions regretted their decision and went back. Even Oya, his true one, lost courage when they reached her hometown, Ira.

Although Shango did not want to continue on his own, his honor prevented him from turning back. He therefore decided to end his life. There are several versions of the way in which he went

not need such things, unless he wants to harm people in his immediate surroundings.

Whatever the genuine sequence of events, Shango's tragic end caused his loyal companions to panic. According to the first version, his slaves also committed suicide, as did Oya when she heard of her husband's death. However, in the version portraying Shango as a brutal tyrant, his courtiers went to the land of the Bariba (after Borgu) to be instructed in the manufacture of certain medicines. With the help of these they could direct lightning at the houses of their enemies. On their return, the number of those struck dead by lightning increased, and they soon fell under suspicion, but in self-defense they attributed the catastrophes to the dead king who was taking revenge for the injustices he had suffered. Sacrifices would be necessary to appease him. These first courtiers of Shango and their descendants make up Shango's priesthood, the magba.

Representation of the Shango, god of thunderstorms, holding his attributes, an ax and a bowl.

through with his decision. In one legendary transfiguration he does not die an ordinary death but enters the ground. When he sat under a shea-butter tree, thunder and lightning suddenly made the earth tremble and he sank into it. According to a less spectacular version he climbed a cotton tree (Ceiba petandra) and hanged himself. Certainly his demise ended the earthly works of this important king who is said to have ruled over the realm of the Yoruba, including the old Benin, Dahomey, and Popo. After his death his loyal friends elevated him to the position of god of thunder and lightning.

In yet another interpretation Shango was deposed and exiled from the country, as he was an extremely cruel, corrupt, and unjust king, whose path was littered with thefts, murders, wars, and other acts of violence. He laughed at the elders and made fun of the priests – there was no one with whom he did not make himself unpopular. When the situation became unbearable, his courtiers sent him a pumpkin gourd with parrot eggs, as a sign that he was no longer wanted, but that he could choose his own way of death. Shango therefore chose death in exile and hanged himself in Koso, hence his added name Oba Koso ("king of Koso").

This version is quite plausible, for even today the Yoruba are still hostile toward kings who possess deadly magical powers. A good ruler does

A bo, which among the Fon is used to protect innocent people from the wrath of the thunder god Shango. It is also used to cleanse those who have been hit by the "African pistol" (invisible arrows or bullets aimed by sorcerers at their victims). Made of human bones, this is a particularly powerful example.

The invisible world

Religious ideas

The cult of the ancestors can be regarded as the basis of African religiousness. All African peoples have a vital interest in living harmoniously with their powerful though departed relatives. Before making important decisions they ask their advice in prayers and receive answers through a sign or in a dream. The ancestors are asked for help in emergencies. Sometimes they also warn their descendants of looming danger.

The ancestors are regularly offered sacrificial food and drink, and people share meals with them just as if they were alive. They are believed to be present at large celebrations; everyone eats with them, as is customary among the family, again to strengthen mutual links. As they are the nearest to them, it is the elders who bear immediate responsibility for the ancestors. But also, as is

often the case, in West Africa, this responsibility may fall to the "lord on earth," the most senior of the elders, that is, of the local "founders' clan."

The dead carry particular responsibility for the fertility of the land, especially since they have such close connections with the earth. Fertile fields are vital to agrarian peoples. Apart from the ancestors, the earth itself and water (springs and rivers) are essential for the growth of plants, especially in dry areas – and the sky from which the rain falls is also of great importance. Often, although not always, the earth is embodied as a goddess, and the sky as a god. Both of them generally form a "world-parent couple," celebrating their marriage in the spring every year, at the beginning of the rainy season. Accordingly, the first rainfall is understood to be the sky god's sperm and is considered to be particularly fertile.

However, the main responsibility for the strong growth of edible plants lies with the people themselves. Transgressions against heritage, neglect of the ancestors, and disrespect toward the earth would upset the necessary balance between people and their environment, leading to disaster, social unrest, and above all serious harvest losses. Again, the ancestors, as the group's representatives in the world beyond, have an important part to play. Just as they punish an offense by their earthly relatives, they also mediate between the living and the earth by putting in good words and passing the living's prayers and sacrifices on to the earth. Sometimes, as with the Ibo in Nigeria, the ancestors are therefore also described as "servants of the earth."

As already mentioned, maintaining both cults among the living is the obligation of the eldest within the family, and the overall lord of the earth, or "owner of the land," as he is sometimes known, for instance in parts of eastern and western Sudan. His mainly priestly duties consist principally of carrying out cleansing rituals after any transgression, which lies like a

Above: A sacred grove with "idols and fetishes," drawn by an anonymous artist. From: *Les Missions catholiques*, 1875.

Left: Asen (ancestor altars), on which sacrifices to the ancestors are made. The chameleon on one side of the asen is a symbol of Lisa, the male side of the vodun deity Mawu-Lisa.

Opposite page: Rainmakers of the Lotuko (of Uganda/Sudan) preparing rain magic by mixing the contents of a black goat's stomach with millet beer and earth. The pots contain quartz crystals, which play an important part in rain magic with peoples all over the world.

123

poisonous cloud over the country; opening or fully performing all important agrarian rituals, as at the beginning of sowing and harvesting; and offering collective sacrifices to the ancestors and the earth, as well as a variety of magical fertility practices which everyone carries out in their fields. Apart from the daily familiar gifts of food and drink, the sacrifices are mostly animals, and in the past also humans. While the blood is poured over the altar or a particular place in the field, the meat is eaten by all those present, as long as there is no conflict between them. In cases where conflict exists, the parties in question would first have to settle their differences in order to gain admission to the sacrificial meal.

However, separate specialists, the rainmakers, are responsible for the rain. They possess specific magical knowledge, special talent, and an element of meteorological experience, all of which enable them to pray to God himself for rain or to summon the tardy rainfall by magic. By the same methods rainmakers can stop too much precipitation, which can also cause great disasters.

Here, "God" means the god of the heavens, known and admired by nearly all African peoples: "The Big One In The Sky" (*Njadenga*) or simply "The One Up There" (*Wokumusoro*), as he is called by the Shona in Mozambique as well as by many other tribes. He airs his anger by thundering, while lightning is the weapon he uses to strike serious offenders and frighten others as a warning. In some cases, as is the case with the Thongo in South Africa, the rain is worshiped as his son, and therefore as a separate deity.

African peoples also see the world as governed by a limited number of "area deities" – powers inferior to the "highest of all" in heaven, who rule over certain rivers or mountains, the sea or the forest, wild animals or war, the sun and the moon. Armies of gods comparable to the divine worlds of the Egyptians, Babylonians, or Romans really only figure in the old civilizations in western Sudan. However, the Yoruba in Nigeria adore 1,700 deities (the Orisha)!

As everywhere in the world, spirits are closer to people than the gods are, and contact with them is unavoidable, if not always desired. On the one hand there are the friendlier ones, well disposed toward humans. They are the local guardian spirits of a family, or village, and they have practically the same tasks as the ancestors; indeed, the difference between the spirits and the ancestors is often blurred. They also communicate through visions and dreams, through signs and through possession; they mediate between mortals and gods, and take care of the well-being of their charges, for which they in return receive adoration and sacrifices. If anyone neglects this, the spirits promptly punish the errant individual with sickness, bad luck, bad harvests, and other misfortune. In Islamic countries, these spirits have, not infrequently, turned into Muslim saints.

These civilized spirits of the pure, sophisticated world of humans stand in sharp contrast to the much greater numbers of wild, uncultivated bush spirits. These are as unpredictable and deceitful as their environment, and always try to harm those who dare to come near them. They live in gloomy caves, deep springs, rivers, and swamps, in undergrowth, on sparse mountains or in searing, hostile deserts, and are able to assume any guise. But whenever they let their mask drop, they are as ugly as they are terrifying. At least one can keep out of their way, and there are ways of protecting oneself against them.

This protection from spirits is conditioned not least by the omnipresent "belief in power." Whatever seems in any way unusual or shows itself to be effective in a special manner – the "eating" fire, a raging whirlpool, bizarrely shaped roots or rocks, a crystal, hard stone, old trees with strong wood, poisonous or healing plants – possesses exceptional powers, according not only to African but also to universal beliefs. This power can be used, and the more so, the greater one's own abilities. People who are especially strong, healthy, and fertile owe this to their

A magic belt to protect hunters (Fon, Benin). It combines several powerful materials (including parts of a bird, cowry shells, and "medicines") to strengthen resistance. The mirror warns the hunter of dangers.

A priest of water goddess Mami Wata and her altar.

great measure of vital energy. If such individuals are older and possess much experience, they will also know better than others how – that is, where, when, and by what means – to harness the powers to be found in nature, whether for good or bad, whether to bring happiness or harm.

Three Asante women accused of being witches kneel in humiliation next to a pile of witch-stones to honor the priest walking past. Afterward, following rituals exorcising witches, they have to kneel on the stones.

Soul of Africa

Some people, like the Chinese, the Greeks, the English, or the Germans, are famous for their philosophers; others never seem to produce any. Yet, no nation is more intelligent than another: the only differences are between individuals.

In Europe, philosophy began with the Ancient Greeks, originating with the so-called pre-Socratic thinkers who preceded Socrates (469–399 BC), among them Thales of Miletus (c. 624–546 BC) and Empedocles (c. 494–434 BC). They considered questions that anyone could have asked themselves, because they had to do with everyday experience and observation, such as how the earth began and assumed its current form; whether and to what extent animals and humans have common origins; whether a river always remains the same even though its waters flow by continuously; whether what we think we see is really so or only appears to be so; and how thoughts and

images come into being. By the time of Plato (c. 427–347 BC), Socrates' most important student, philosophy was understood as the struggle toward the discovery of concrete cognition. *Sophia*, or "wisdom," a widely used word at the time, referred less abstract, say mathematical understanding, than to material, working knowledge.

The situation was no different in cultures without writing. People could survive and flourish only if they had a solid understanding of how to make tools, hunt, and work the fields, of the working of the weather or the effectiveness of healing plants, or of the behavior of humans, animals, spirits, and gods. This in turn required the ability to link one to the other, to make connections between various phenomena – between water and growth, health and fertility, or peaceful cooperation and success, for instance. Further associations led to greater, finally all-embracing systems of viewing life and the universe. Experience passed down through the centuries, supported or called into question every day and corrected as appropriate, ensured the reliability of these philosophies, in ethnological terms labeled "elementary," "naive-realistic," "people" philosophies, or "natural philosophies." These were "schools"; however, they were less about teaching than about the young observing and imitating the life of the old. These are described as "implicit philosophies," because their values with respect to behavior, action, upbringing, morality, and so on would have to become obvious before they could even be expressed in unambiguous formulas. For instance, according to English ethnologist Edward Evans-Pritchard, the belief in witchcraft contains "elements of a natural and moral philosophy." To bring out these "coded" thoughts, to "make them explicit," is what African philosopher Theophilus Okere understands as the precondition for the development of African philosophy in the real sense.

Myths, fairy tales, proverbs, phrases, stories of the ancestors' exemplary deeds, customs, and moral rules – in short, really the whole of tradition – are typical ways in which knowledge is passed on. As most of this in turn depends on and develops out of experience – in social situations and especially in cases of conflict – one could speak of "worldly wisdom," which is what philosophy originally meant, too. In village societies this wisdom is shared, mostly by the older adults, but there are often individuals who are wiser than the others because they have a particular leaning toward speculation and have thought more about things. In problematic situations they are consulted for advice, even by the powerful – just as in ancient Greece. A famous example is the Dogon man, Ogotemmêli, the main supplier of information and teacher of French ethnologist Marcel Griaule (1898–1956).

Opposite page: Shango priests and followers in the Zebu quarter of Porto Novo, Benin.

Below: In 1955 African photographer Dossa Z. Cosme portrayed this group of priests and their followers before their "Ceremonie du Fetiche Gbeloko, Quartier Zebu Aga," Zubu quarter of Porto Novo, Benin.

Possibly there was a tradition of philosophy there. It emerged from the long discussions that Griaule had with Ogotommêli that the world view of the Dogon – and indeed that of their neighbors (the Bambara, Malinke, Kurumba, and others), as Griaule's colleagues discovered – is a highly complex, most impressive structure of thought. Ordered according to firm principles, arising from the material, passing via the symbolic to abstract, "pure" ideas, everything within this structure is bound together into one meaningful whole that can easily hold its own in comparison with pre-Socratic philosophies of nature, partly even with Platonic thinking (the school of ideas). Griaule himself sometimes spoke of *sophia* (wisdom), sometimes of ontology ("the nature of being"), sometimes of "practical and theoretical metaphysics." Some of these will be mentioned here again later.

Belgian Franciscan monk and missionary Placide Tempels (b. 1906) had gathered similar impressions among the Bantu-speaking Bemba (in Zambia) and Luba (in the Democratic Republic of Congo) in the 1930s and 1940s. He regarded their belief in energy as the key element of their imaginary world or, to be precise, the force of life (*force vitale*). This runs through everything, although in different degrees of concentration, the least in purely material things, more in plants, in increasing measures in animals and humans, and its highest potency in God.

To the book explaining all this Tempels gave the misleading title *Bantu Philosophy* (*La philosophie bantoue*, published in 1945). On one hand he referred only to two groups; on the other, "Bantu" does not describe a cultural or ethnic community but one merely connected by language.

Even so, the book had an inspirational effect, especially on African thinkers, who praised it as a pioneering work. It was the blueprint for what is today termed ethnophilosophy, the attempt to extract the philosophical conviction and ideas from ethnic traditional and religious material through analysis and interpretation. Just after Tempels, Alexis Kagame tried to determine Rwandan groups' conception of existence (ontology) from interpretations of their use of language, proverbs, and customs. Leo Apostel noted fundamental agreement between the conceptions of power held by the Luba and the Dogon, and characterized the latter's world view as "pluralistic energetism" because of its high degree of differentiation. Indeed, he saw "pluralistic-energetic ontology" as the real basis of African philosophy. Others came to similar conclusions. Some, such as Stephen Okafor, also regard the sense of community (*corporalité* in French, commensality in English) as a fundamental category in African philosophy.

However, this theory was by no means undisputed. Adherents of so-called critical philosophy (such as Paulin J. Hountondji, F. Eboussi-Boulaga, and Marcian Towa) decisively support the point of view that there is only one, real philosophy – not a Greek, German, or African one – but this has not met with much acceptance. Ethnophilosophy still retains its enthusiastic supporters, and no doubt for legitimate reasons. Between the defenders of the two opposed extremes, an

Hunters of the Latuko tribe have killed a mighty buffalo, but before they cut it into pieces, they must observe the appropriate rituals. They show their killed "enemy" due respect, approaching him with great caution to appease the spirits, otherwise luck will desert them on the next hunt. This photograph, taken c. 1930, was released for publication under the title *The Primitive Latukos* by a press agency in 1952.

A Lungwara witchdoctor and members of the tribe. Wearing antelope head decoration, they approach the enemy in a ceremonial dance. Photograph c. 1930.

increasing number of authors take a mediating position. Kwasi Wiredu, Theophilus Okere, J. O. Sodipo, to name but some, are of the opinion that traditional systems of ideas as well as very specific concepts, such as the belief in causality or energy, or the understanding of time or personality, are indeed suitable material for critical philosophy and subjects for targeted field study. However, African philosophy should not be lost in the study of traditional wisdoms alone, because then, as Wiredu points out, disciplines such as symbolic logic or the philosophy of mathematics would have no place within it or would even be dismissed as "un-African."

Ethnophilosophy will maintain its importance, even if only for reasons of self-determination. Just like others, African people are interested in what makes their way of thinking special, and what their specific achievement and contribution to the cultural and intellectual history of humanity is. What is still contentious is the primary goal: whether to study single ideological systems or to work out at least the basic foundations of pan-African philosophy.

Whichever direction developments take, using experience as a guide, thinking in social terms (particularly the high values of social mores), connecting all being and happening to one's own history through the ancestors, and last but not least maintaining one's own spirituality, all stand out as fundamental features of traditional African thinking. African spirituality has nothing in common with the Buddhist, Islamic, or Christian sense; it is a specific feeling for something occurring just behind the numerous visible manifestations and indicated more by suggestion. Delight in dealing with words, always with much humor, which makes seemingly hard facts fall apart and leaves everything, even the rules of society, floating in mid-air, a constant balancing between spontaneity and thoughtfulness, seriousness and serenely looking for an underlying deeper meaning, a sense of obligation and relaxed generosity – this is the soul of Africa.

Living nature

For modern people, particularly town-dwellers, "nature" has an almost exclusively positive meaning. Nature provides a contrast to an environment built of concrete, to the noise of traffic, to polluted air, and to the hectic pace of everyday work. Those who have the opportunity of getting out "into the country" at the weekend and during their vacations, enjoy the beauty of what seems to be untouched, or at least create a small, artificial piece of nature in their own back yard. Glancing back through history, China and India are two good examples of countries that highly regarded and idealized nature. The Garden of Eden too has always been a symbol of nature, and poets praised life in the country as a peaceful, carefree, and happy idyll.

Those living in the country see it differently, having lived in and with nature. The way that nature has been viewed and interpreted has depended greatly on the society, whether people lived as, say, hunter-gatherers or as agriculturalists. Terms such as "beautiful" or "restful" played no part whatsoever in these people's concept of nature: nature was the usual everyday world. In addition there was a sharp contrast between the natural world that was lived in and exploited, or "civilized," and the wild, "uncivilized," untouched world beyond. Usually people differentiated between three areas: the familiar, closer areas around the camp or settlement; the surrounding territory, for gathering and hunting or for cultivation; and the unfamiliar bush, the alien world and wilderness. Everyone felt safe and "at home" in the innermost zone, less so in the middle zone; the outer zone one tried to avoid altogether, as it was dangerous and full of incalculable risks. However, it seemed an obligation of civilization to make parts of the wilderness accessible, to turn nature into cultured land.

Landscape on the Prince's Isles on the Gulf of Guinea. An engraving from: *Westafrika.Vom Senegal bis Benguela*, Leipzig, 1878.

Forest and bush, however, also have their positive aspects. They are great sources of clay for making pottery, of valuable minerals, wood, wild honey, and medicinal herbs. Of course, people who make their living from these things are always considered a little scary, as were the herb-collecting women in Europe, who were often enough suspected of witchcraft, along with shepherds and coal burners; in Africa the equivalent members of society were the healers who gather their medicines in the bush, and hunters in agrarian societies. Such people will only be successful if they first ask permission of the animal and forest spirits. Their expeditions into the unknown earn them special respect.

In West Africa it is believed that these people possess strange magical powers, understand the language of animals and trees, and are even able to become invisible, for how else could they escape all of nature's dangers unharmed? However, sometimes they too become the victims of the horrors that they encounter. Eerie, terrifying appearances who seem to have come out of nowhere can take any shape right in front of them and rob them of their senses. The Gurma in northern Togo believe that such an experience can make them lose their mind. Hunters who return many times unharmed therefore enjoy even greater admiration; they are respected like great warriors. As American ethnologist Thomas Beidelman discovered among the Kaguru in northern Tanzania, the successful hunt is "an expression of having control over the wilderness, and, as with many East African peoples, is equal to especially successful, heroic leadership."

In contrast, a man or a woman on familiar ground impresses others by being skilled at their work, and calm, helpful, experienced, and wise. Home ground is still nature, too, but has, since creation, been taken into the culture, meaning that it is

A sacred mountain in northern Cameroon.

A sacred tree near Hlepehoné, Benin.

civilized and appeased. The ancestors have been resting in its depths since the dawn of time. The earth is sacred: she provides the food that people live on. Indeed, many African peoples, such as the Lyela in southern Burkina Faso, are convinced that she maintains and guards over the order of life, and also that she punishes transgressions with infertility, drought, bad harvests, sickness, and death.

There is more to field and bush than their immediately apparent forms and attributes. Behind the "refuge of appearances" hide the structures of another, transcendent world. This world and the beyond merge fluently with nature. Surprising events, a stumble or a slip, a lucky find, and suchlike can be signs from spirits or reminders of encounters with them. As already discussed, this depends on their closeness to the human world. Kitchen, house, and field spirits are benevolent as long as people treat them with appropriate respect

and friendliness; like the ancestors, they warn people of dangers, protect them, and help them in difficult situations. Bush spirits, however, are marked by unpredictability, deceit, and malice, especially when one comes near them, disturbs them in their sleep, or even unknowingly kicks them. This can be avoided in most, although not all, cases, because people know the preferred places of "nature spirits." They should always be expected at springs and wells, at junctions, in caves, in the thick of the forest, on rocky slopes, in deserts, and in high, bare mountain regions. These are all points of contact with the other world, where the spirits "come over here from there," usually at night, at "spirit time." People can have visions there, and see into the future, but also meet with death, just as it pleases the bush spirits.

Spirits can take on a variety of forms, moving freely, or being attached to, even subsumed within, certain places or particular plants. Slow-growing, old, large trees in particular, such as the baobab tree (Adansonia digitata), are just such an example. They have a soul, feel joy and sorrow, and become angry when humans give them occasion to feel that way. Basically, the entire environment is humanized. Spirits live alone, in families, or in groups. Long, narrow, and sharp objects, everything right-sided, the waxing moon, lightning, thunder, and rain from the north, which encourages growth, are considered "male" by bushmen, for instance. Short, round, blunt things, everything left-sided, the waning moon, drizzle and short showers from the south, destructive natural phenomena, and materials made from the small particles, such as powder or sand, are seen as "female." Heaven and earth are the perfect marriage partners.

Nature lives with people. She provides them with raw materials for the manufacture of goods, she feeds them, speaks to them in signs (omina) and influences their existence, as does the moon. Fertility ceremonies or those promoting a person to a higher status are carried out when the moon is waxing, as for instance among the Swazi in South Africa, and opening rituals during new moon. Offenses also have an effect on the environment. Sexual transgressions, in particular incest, and theft, murder, or irreligious, heretic behavior bring on droughts or floods, make springs dry up, and cause hunting prey to leave.

A fetish tree.
From: *Fetichism and Fetich Worshipers*, New York, Cincinnati, St. Louis, 1885.

Leading a blameless life that conforms to the rules therefore contributes to the support of nature. Special authorities such as the "lords of the earth" ensure that no offenses are committed against the order and rules set by the earth. Altogether people treat their environment with great care, watch their step, and are frugal in their use of resources such as water, plants, and wild animals. The bushmen, for instance, consider it a great sin to exploit these fully, killing more animals than are needed for food, or collecting the whole of a wild plant so that nothing is left for regeneration; this sin can only result in punishment from God.

Moreover, the earth is always the land of the ancestors. Within the settlement and in the fields everyone walks over the skulls of long-gone generations whose graves have left no trace. Certain points in the landscape tell of important events in creation; others are connected with special occasions – an ancestor's vision, a miracle, a victory over previous inhabitants, or even a crime. The environment keeps the memories which make a people's history come alive. Whenever anyone reaches a historically important site, they tell younger people what happened there once.

Much has changed since colonial times. Then, many of the old traditions were affected, and the reaction was one of anxiety, fear even, that along with the traditional order the ability to survive was also under threat. As changes were often extreme, they cannot be blamed entirely on the society's own wrongdoing, and can therefore also not be reversed by the society's efforts alone. The reason for the decay must lie with the foreigners, the Europeans, who interfered on too large a scale and with no consideration for the old order passed down from the ancestors. Like many African peoples, the Tugen in Kenya suffer from increasing drought. Their explanation is that the British stole their rain god (Ilat) and "abducted him to England, where rain has fallen abundantly since, where fields and meadows are green, and the people and animals are fat, while the Tugen mountains are dry and the people must starve."

Time

Time is particularly obvious when we glance at our watches or use public transportation. However, this is only a small part of what the experience of time really means. In earlier civilizations there were neither watches nor buses and trains, but people nevertheless had comparable methods of measuring time. Otherwise it would not have been possible to complete tasks within a given time span, nor, more particularly, to carry out these tasks in synchronization with the activities of others without disharmony in the process of working together.

For instance, a typical day for the Nkole in Uganda, who live mostly from herding cattle, begins with milking the cows (at about 6 am); other important events are a break both for humans and animals (about 12 noon); fetching water (about 1 pm); the time when the animals leave the drinking trough and return to grazing (about 3 pm); and so on. For greater precision, these particular event-bound times can be connected with the movement of the sun, particularly at the moments when the first rays in the morning and the last rays in the evening touch certain points on the horizon; with the absence of shadows at noon; or when the light falls through gaps in the roof and lights up certain places in the house. Such points of reference change through the year, eventually returning to their original place. They mark lines in space which represent periods of time. For agrarian peoples their greatest importance is of course related to work in the fields, especially the times for sowing and harvesting. Both of these represent the beginning and the end of two

seasons, which in many parts of Africa are further sharply divided by the onset or ceasing of rain. The rainy season is summer, the dry season winter.

A further subdivision of these larger phases is the appearance and orbit of the moon. The time between two new moons is one month, each month again divided into two by the waxing and waning of the moon, the halfway stage being marked by the full moon. The whole process gains even more precision and clarity when the "clocks" of sun and moon are correlated with events in nature that are typical of a particular time phase, for instance, the reappearance of particular birds, the blooming of flowers, bushes, and trees, the ripening of their fruits, or the rising and setting of certain constellations.

There is a further aspect. The inner, omnipresent axis of orientation in the experience of time is each individual's own life, and for the community it may be the king's time in office. Again, both are marked by particular events: birth, naming ceremonies, teething, puberty (initiation), marriage, first motherhood or fatherhood, an official appointment (enthronement), death.

Time in rural African societies is therefore experienced very much in concrete terms, and not as unitary but as multidimensional. It is defined by personal as well as community life, it is linked to natural events and daily work, and it connects life, space, and society; in short, it is a constant experience of "nature – space – time." Therefore, in order to be a reliable tool or orientation, time requires ritual to anchor it down. If a part of the interconnected systems measuring time were wrenched out, the whole would start to collapse. For this reason rituals (celebrations) are always performed at the most important events

in life – the start of a new life stage, the beginning and end of an agricultural phase, "new year," and so on. Rituals bring a framework to society and nature by imposing a cycle upon them so that the people do not deviate from what they should do during any given period. The "between-times," or the times between rituals, when the ruling order is relaxed, offer people more room for creativity than during the period of strictly ordered rituals, and this can have positive effects on the

Time is experienced in a concrete way, as it is bound to daily tasks, for instance.

For tribes that live from cattle farming the orientation of time is based on the activities specifically linked to the herds. Here the cattle are being led to drink.

phase to come. Therefore celebrations of birth, initiations, weddings, sowing, and the new year always have at their core rituals of bonding, fertility, and strengthening.

The overall impression is that, unlike Western industrial societies, rural African societies have a cyclical understanding of time. To a large extent this is true, though it is in fact no different from Western notions of time. All important processes and experiences repeat themselves daily, monthly, or annually. People are born, grow up, get married, have children of their own, and die. They commit a sin, fall ill as a punishment, undergo atonement, and find their place again in society. We also help to make time cyclical by having birthday parties, marking feats and holding periodical commemoration ceremonies, celebrating jubilees, centenaries, and many other similar anniversaries.

In reality all human societies have a cyclical as well as a linear conception of time. Both are always combined; it is merely the ratio between them that differs. Like us, Africans regard both short-term and cosmic events as linear: for instance, the phases spanning defined life periods of, for example, the manufacture of a tool and its use in sowing or harvesting, or the span of time from the creation of the world and of the first human being – which always means the ancestors of the group – to the present. They combine linear and cyclical time-systems, but prefer the latter because they better meet the requirement of rural life as well as being easier to keep track of, control, predict, and synchronize than those conditioned by the needs of industrial production and urban life.

The extreme case of linear measurement is the duration of a dynasty's rule. To make the population believe that they are the righteous rulers of the land, kings must pretend that their family has always been in power, and that their original ancestor came from the local population, or, better still, was fathered by a local hero or even by God. Long genealogies without gaps are essential; they are recited by bards at the great annual celebrations and sometimes recorded by court chroniclers. Similarly the order of the royal stools among the Akan is the material representation of the dynasty's genealogy.

From all this it follows that African societies not only live by several (sometimes combined) time systems, but that they also

ascribe different qualities to them. Apart from periods of peace, war, and catastrophe, or times filled with activity or devoid of events, times such as pregnancy and the weeks after the birth carry a meaning different from a stay in an initiation camp or a celebration lasting several days. The first half of the day, defined by the rising, "strengthening" sun, and the time of the waxing moon are regarded as beneficial; phases of "going down" are considered potentially dangerous. The light of day and the times of farming stand in contrast to the night and the dry season (winter); these are "ghost" times, when it is best not to stray too far from the house and village. A special quality is given to the times of transferring, when not only the ancestors make appearances in dreams or as guests at celebrations, but the less welcome spirits also roam.

The future is – or certainly was – not considered to be very important. It appears "flat," as it is predictable only in the short term. Its horizon reaches as far as the concrete planning of activities which unavoidably goes beyond the present – up to initiation, the next harvest, or one's own death. The possible futures of grandchildren or one's own rebirth after three or four generations are but shadowy outlines.

Finally, historical time, which is so important to modern nation states, plays a minimal role in rural communities. It is assimilated into the three phases of time: the time of creation, in which the current order was established; the present, alive and experienced; and the past, or "ancestor time," in between. The past is the least interesting, as it is assumed that the ancestors' lives were no different from those of their present descendants, and that nothing remarkable could have happened in the meantime, for otherwise it would not be possible to continue to exist. In this case too the experience of time is "flat": it usually reaches back no more than three generations.

Along the immovable cosmic axis of time, which is a linear link between original time and the present, life moves along its cyclical tracks, supported by shorter vertical paths which also hold it on its correct levels. This conception of time is clearly a great guarantee of orientation and reliability, essential to all agrarian societies.

The movements of the sun and moon precisely define periods of time. Time also connects life, space, and society and becomes an experience of "nature – space – time."

Africa's secret powers

Many people, including such specialists as medieval historians and ethnologists, are not clear as to the exact difference between witchcraft and sorcery (magic). However, these are two fundamentally different things, although they can have similar results. In most languages, especially non-European languages, therefore, the two phenomena are expressed in terms that have nothing in common with each other. In European languages the absence of differentiation between witchcraft and sorcery is obvious in the uncertain use of the terms that describe them. In German "witchcraft" also means "sorcery," but in English the word for the first concept is "witchcraft" (literally, the power of witches), and for the second "magic," "sorcery," "enchantment," and also again "witchcraft." In French witchcraft is referred to as *sorcellerie*, *magie*, or *charme*, and sorcery as *magie* or again as *sorcellerie*.

Because of the common use of such imprecise definitions, ethnologists found it hard to deal appropriately with these phenomena when they encountered them among the peoples they visited, and often unknowingly recorded their misunderstandings in their reports. No notice was taken by those back home, who were also not clear as to the differences. However, in African societies people understand the two as separate entities, even today.

One of the witch-priest's assistants falls in a trance and calls on "God" to support the exorcism of the witch that is about to take place.

Witchcraft

The belief in witches is manifest everywhere in the world, but only among settled societies. Inherent in that belief is the idea that certain people – usually women – possess a specific power which enables them, even drives them, to separate their "free soul" from their sleeping body at night and send it on its journeys. Their intention is always evil. Witches are seen as the bringers of death, disease, and material loss. Their desires are at odds with all social values, such as helpfulness and solidarity. Witches uproot trees, rage through storms, unleash disfiguring diseases such as leprosy or scabies, and make people blind, lame, deaf, mute, impotent, or infertile by "eating" the relevant organ or turning women's wombs around in their bodies. They tempt people into theft, wastefulness, and drinking. In other words, any inexplicable misfortune is credited to them.

Unlike sorcerers, witches tend to have no understandable motive for their misdemeanors. Only in the rarest cases do they kill or damage people who have done them wrong. They attack mostly blood relatives, even their own offspring. No wonder witchcraft spreads terror! Male witches are even more frightening than female ones. However, they are often able to gain control of their destructive powers, even turning them to good, hunting down other witches and making them harmless. This requires the exorcism of their witchcraft.

The special power of witchcraft can take someone against their express will and without their knowledge. However, it always causes the affected person to act against their human nature, changing them into a dangerous being who attacks the community at its core. A witch's destructive actions mark them out as a denizen of the nonworld, a nonhuman, a monster. In the past, anyone found to be a witch was burned to death, strangled (so that the earth would not be contaminated by his or her blood), or chased from the village with burning torches.

A witch who senses the end of her life approaching can transfer her powers to any object, or lock it in a pot, calabash, seashell, pearl, or coin, an amulet, or a piece of cloth. Whichever of her descendants inherits this "container" is also given the power of witchcraft. Some find it simply by thoughtlessly picking up a coin from the floor, and others obtain it as part of a meal that is eaten, while there are those who seek it out intentionally.

Not all witchcraft is equally strong. The most terrifying is that of witches who received their powers while still in the womb and who were born already evil. Exorcism rarely works in such cases. The Asante say, "With them it is like plucking a live chicken. Just as you have torn out the feathers, they start growing back again."

Witches can split themselves into two. At night, when one part, the body, lies fast asleep, the other leaves it as a witch to do wicked deeds in the dark. According to the Gonja of Ghana, the witch takes the form of an animal; the Kaguru in Tanzania believe that the witch accompanies nocturnal creatures, such as owls or hyenas. Whatever the form, the witch's soul attacks those who are sleeping and sucks out their vital energies (the life soul). This can continue for days, weeks, even months. It becomes apparent in the victims' sudden decline and lasting weakness.

It is not only the activities but also the appearance and behavior of witches that is as if turned on its head. Everything about witches is "upside down"; they go out at night like ghosts, walk with their legs pointing upward, but are also able to fly. Then they gather like birds of the night on high trees, from where their eyes blink red in the dark. They are naked, eat human flesh, and have orgies with animals. Witches also tend to gather every year at a special place, such as a mountain, where they sacrifice humans, especially children, eat their flesh, and perform orgiastic dances.

According to the Asante, witches gather for a "witches' sabbath" at the edge of the village. Within the organization, however, they keep to the model of ordinary society: they form cooperative links, with the same hierarchies as in political life. At the head of their "antisociety" stand the kings and "queen mother," below them the elders, speakers, executioners, messengers, butchers, and cooks – in fact, all the officials and servants that one would find at any court. Women too can rise to leading positions as long as they possess extremely strong powers that enable them to change at night into men with long flowing beards. Their leisure activities have quite a lot in common with those of the village community: they appreciate rich meals with plenty of meat and also enjoy other fleshy delicacies, and they are enthusiastic dancers and football players – using a human skull as a ball!

Whenever there is a celebration in the village, witches also give out invitations to their banquet. Each time, a different witch provides the sacrificial "animal" that is to be eaten by all at the feast. Usually it is the witch's own child or another close relative. The witches suck out his or her soul, change it into a sheep, and tie it to a pole or a tree. The body falls sick and feels weak and miserable. However, a rescue attempt is still possible at this stage,

The assistant of the witch-priest, also known as the witchdoctor, dances himself into a trance in front of the drums. Drums are important instruments for sinking into a trance because of their trance-inducing rhythms.

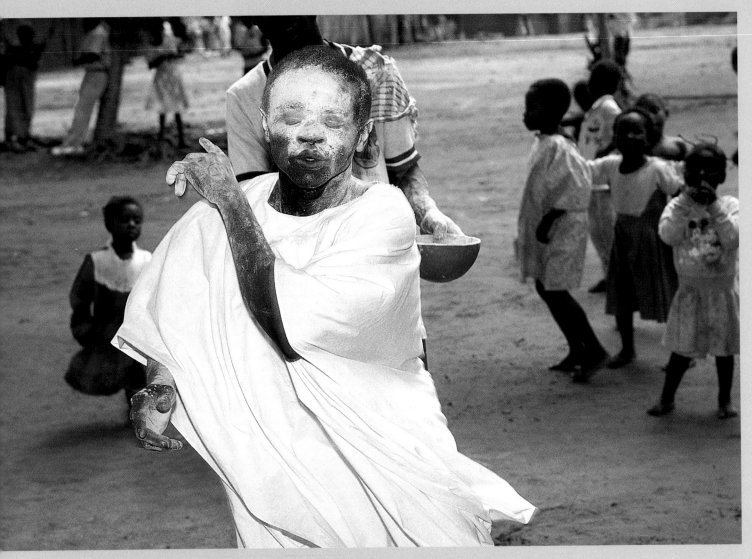

The witchdoctor's assistant dances, totally sunk into a trance. As a sign of his ritual purity, he covers himself in powdered white clay. The power of witches to separate their free soul from their body at night is used only to bring evil. Witches are seen as the bringers of death, disease, and material loss.

if a specialist manages to bring back the soul unharmed. If the witches have already eaten a piece of the meat, the victim may recover but the affected part of the body is disabled for life, for instance, a stiff leg or limp arm. The moment that the "sacrificial lamb" has been carved up, and the flesh distributed and eaten according to precisely established rules, the person dies without any possibility of revival.

Like the village community, these witches have a common shrine, usually in the form of a plot blackened by blood. It is regarded as the basis of their existence as a group and is kept hidden in the thick branches of a high tree or buried in its roots. If the shrine is lost or discovered, the witches' community breaks

up. The personal powers of witchcraft are also contained in objects carried near the body or in black pots. In addition, witches have at their service a variety of helping spirits in the shape of animals, usually snakes, beasts of prey, and night birds, on whose backs they rise or fly and who protect them from being discovered.

Although only witches can recognize each other, there are certain external signs, which may give them away. For instance, thick growths of hair, especially on the chin, gaps between teeth, and reddish eyes – conditions suffered especially by women after the menopause – all arouse suspicion. Favoring certain dishes, in particular the red palm oil soup typical of West Africa, can also set off distrust. Other signs are taciturnity, reserve, and stuttering, as well as generally unsociable and solitary behavior. Apart from these outsiders on the fringe, suspicion can also fall on anyone who suddenly and for no apparent reason, that is, "by their own power," enjoys social or economic success. If this person displays

At the beginning of the ceremony in which the witches' powers are exorcised the three possessed women sink to the ground next to the witch-hill, a pile of magical stones.

generosity toward their relatives so that their own fortune shrinks again, suspicion vanishes too. However, should they seek to keep the money for themselves, suspicions are confirmed. Everyone secretly agrees that this person is a witch and from now on holds them responsible for any deaths in the family. They "sacrificed" relatives for their own purposes, and thereby gained riches at their cost. This is also the origin of the Asante proverb, "Where there is wealth there is death."

Witches' power is inherited in different ways, too. In patrilineal societies, it passes directly from the mother to the daughters. Sometimes witchcraft appears in several members of a family or clan, like an inherited disease. Since witches do their worst without being conscious of it when they are awake, it can happen that a woman suspected of being a witch on grounds of evidence can come to believe it herself.

Of course, not everyone is able to identify witches as such. This requires either experienced fortune-tellers, who consult the oracle as soon as someone falls ill in a suspect manner, or witchdoctors, who, like criminologists, not only know how to expose the suspects but also possess the required medical understanding to heal the victims. In less frequent cases, such as among the Nupe in northern Nigeria, witchhunting may be the responsibility of a men's secret society. However, if no definite proof can be found, nothing can be done but wait for the suspected witch to die. If during the ensuing autopsy certain substances in the bowel or noticeable growths inside the body are found, the suspicion is confirmed. The abnormality may not have been part of the suspect's outer appearance, but it has clearly marked the body internally.

Witchcraft is to this day a phenomenon that has not been satisfactorily explained. Certain isolated elements, such as the annual orgies with child sacrifices and cannibalistic meals, particularly perplex researchers, as these ideas are held around the world, although no historical link is likely: certainly it could never be proven.

The witch-priest, or witchdoctor, appears. As a declaration of war against the witches, he stabs the air with a knife on his way to the dancing grounds and strews white chalk powder before him.

The witch-priest is ready for the fight against the evil powers. As there are usually no motives for the harm witches cause, they are greatly feared, and the exorcism of these powers is also very important for close relatives.

Magic

By comparison to witchcraft, magic is far more accessible, as it is not a special innate power but principally a technique for dealing with things, which can be learned by anyone. Unlike in witchcraft, the powers of magic can be used for good as well as evil.

Magic powers can be found in minerals, rock formations, plants, animals, and human beings – in fact, everywhere in nature. They are fundamentally neither good nor bad, only of varying strengths, and can be activated on command by someone putting them together in the right way, choosing the right place, and casting the correct spells. Thus magical means or medicines of different types and intensities are made out of impersonal powers. If these powers are locked into certain objects – such as pots, figurines, horns, or bottles – and brought to life with blood

The ceremony has increased in intensity: in a state of wild ecstasy the priest has bitten the head off a cockerel and dances with it in his mouth.

The priest once again listens to the drums to make him sink deeper into the trance, so that the deity can advise him on how to proceed.

sacrifices, they gain in effectiveness and can be used magically. However, magic medicines must be refreshed regularly, that is, exchanged for unused ones.

Every medicine and every magical means have its own rules for use. If it is damaged, its effectiveness is lessened or is even fully destroyed. The relevant knowledge, the recipes, and the medicines are passed down within families from father to son. Much magic can also be bought. However, such a step must be carefully considered, as mistakes in using the magic can cause it to backfire on the owner, who often pays for the desired effect with other drawbacks. For instance, magic promising wealth and success can have negative effects on fertility or be harmful in some other way.

Also, successful magic makes specific demands on the user, such as certain powers of concentration. Great physical exertion, even sexual intercourse, is therefore avoided before a magic act. Particular energizing food, drink, or medicine can also add positive strength. The means used should also be at their most effective – such as one's own vision, particular proven formulas and songs, energizing animal organs, human bones, or a fetish object. The choice of place and time is equally important. Places that are passages to the underworld or to the heavens above and which attract energy from the beyond, such as caves, springs, junctions, shrines, or mountain peaks, and times of change, such as sunrise, midnight, or new year, when a small opening between this world and the beyond appears, can give an additional boost of power to magic.

Generally there are two main types of magic: magic by contact and magic by analogy or image. Magic by contact involves influencing someone through direct and indirect contact, the latter transmitted by a carrier, such as the laying on of hands, casting a glance, calling, or rubbing, "vaccinating" with or eating certain substances. Magic can work on names (which are part of a person's whole identity) as well as on materials and objects containing the vital energy of the intended receiver of the magic. These could be scraps from a piece of clothing he or she has worn for a long time, or a tool he or she has often handled, as both of these contain sweat (a carrier of a high charge of vitality). After they have had a spell cast over them or have been treated in some other way, such "carriers of soul material" are placed as unobtrusively as possible near the particular person, so that the magic can work to its full effect.

Magic by analogy, on the other hand, is used for exerting influence over long distances: the witch outlines or displays in mimicry what he or she wishes to effect. The best-known example of this is the use of voodoo dolls, images of the person one intends to harm; by sticking a pin in the doll near the heart or breaking off the head, the person is hurt. While doing this it is essential to concentrate fully on the victim so that the link to the recipient of the magic by missile, as it were, is fully established in

the sorcerer's thoughts. In support, appropriate spells are often used to express verbally the desired result.

Damaging magic is particularly feared. If someone learns that another wishes them harm, they are plagued by uneasy thoughts and feelings, sleep badly, and perhaps even become sick.

Magic can also be used as a defense against the magic of another, whether for good or bad purposes. The intention is the decisive factor in the process, the power itself remaining neutral. There are four elementary principles, which form the foundation of all magical actions: the intention to link (to tie together, to bond), as in marriage rituals; the intention to separate (or to dissolve), by symbolically cutting through something, opening something locked, crossing a line, or stepping over someone (who is usually asleep); the intention to strengthen something, such as growth, health, or the fertility of plants, animals, and humans; and finally, the intention to weaken or destroy, for instance through the evil eye, which can cause disease or bestow a curse, by throwing an object belonging to someone else into a river, which carries away the object forever and therefore deprives someone of a part of their health, or in extreme cases, by casting a death spell.

Weak people, such as children and the sick, possess few magical powers, while chiefs and kings possess the most, which they are expected to use only for the good of their subjects. Chiefs and kings therefore also open important community rituals – for instance, when sowing and harvesting. However, strong people of

evil character present a threat to society, as their hate and jealousy drive them to harm others – not openly, for that would do them no good, but secretly, through magic. If they are discovered, they may face the death penalty – no different from Article 109 of the Order of Punishing Laws decreed by the Holy Roman Emperor Charles V of 1532, which was at least formally valid until the end of the 18th century. If evil magic were to gain the upper hand, the existence of every society would be threatened.

Mahama Samyine, a fortune-teller from the village of Sombo, also sells magic powers. He throws two cowry shells into a calabash filled with water to see whether he can sell this power to the client. To the right of the bowl is a fetish bag with unknown contents on which sacrificial blood is poured ever so often.

As proof of his magical powers Mahama speaks a formula and then places a chicken on the fetish bag. In about three minutes the chicken dies without any visible use of violence: the sorcerer's power has taken away its blood.

Mahama sells white and black magic. Most clients come for black magic to injure others, less so to protect themselves.

Mahama reaches for the chicken to cut its throat.

Selling magic potions

Country folk from remote regions are often said to possess special magical powers. This is the opinion that the more sophisticated southerners in Ghana have of what they see as the rather backward inhabitants of the northern parts. Many seek out these people for help with their problems.

One sorcerer in Ghana who has many clients from the south is Mahama Samyine, who lives in a village near the city of Wa. He belongs to the Dagarti tribe, who live in the extreme northwest of Ghana. Mahama also has a sideline in fortune-telling, but he has at the same time gained a reputation as a powerful sorcerer or ju-ju man (from the French joujou, "toy") who knows how to deal with both white and black magic. For the symbolic fee of three cowry shells or three cedis (a coin in the Ghanaian currency) and a bottle of gin he will provide magic means to anyone who asks. Every potion or method has its fixed price. Anyone paying more or less than that price reduces the magic's effectiveness. Paradoxical as it may seem, often a particularly potent magic can be acquired for a relatively small amount.

The visitors from southern Ghana are particularly interested in defenses against enemies as well as ways of harming them in turn. Mahama is also a healer. He mainly treats injuries caused by magic or witchcraft and even offers prophylactic measures, but these are more expensive than his other medicines. In such a case the client must pay extra for sacrificial offerings, including a black hen and a black ram. In spite of the cost, ever more people seek his help. Ensuing success has a visible effect: Mahama's trade in magic means is doing much better than his fortune-telling.

This flourishing business is not restricted to northern Ghana. Skilled sorcerers can also be found among the Nzima, a small tribe from southern Ghana who settled in Ivory Coast. Indeed, one of them, Kwame Nkrumah, became the first prime minister and later president of Ghana (until 1966). The Nzima too trade in magic means.

Mahama cuts open the chicken's throat and shows that there is practically no blood coming out. This lack of blood proves that the powers of magic or witchcraft have sucked away the chicken's blood on an astral plane invisible to us, whereupon it died. Witches often work on this plane. If people die or become sick, a witch may have sucked their blood or eaten one of their organs on this level.

Germain, the sorcerer

Life in the cities has also changed the practice of magic: like life, it has become more diverse and differentiated. In large cities such as Cotonou (Benin) with about 600,000 inhabitants and enormous buildings, the fear of black magic is rampant. Many are prepared to spend large parts of their savings on protecting themselves, getting back at their enemies, or achieving success in love, at work, or at school.

The first port of call is Germain Bamenou. During the day he carves "airport art," wooden objects which are offered to gullible tourists as traditional art, but once the sun has gone down, he changes into a sorcerer (*bokonon*). His services range from providing protection from attacks by witches and harmful magic to treating women for hemorrhoids and infertility. These days he need only visit the great magic market of Cotonou to

For sorcery to succeed the pronouncement of the correct magic spell is crucial – without it there would be no effect. Here the sorcerer Germain speaks to the skull of a dog which he has filled with different herbs, tree bark, and splintered animal bones.

Binding the dog's skull stands for what is known as nestling magic: Germain tries to tie his client's debtor down. The dog is used because it is a fast animal and can therefore hunt down the debtor.

obtain his "medical" equipment – animal skulls and claws, bird talons, snakes, numerous plants, and much more.

On request Germain will also act as debt collector, for instance in the case of a businessman who has been unable to recover the money owed to him by his partner. For this Germain pulls several herbs out of his leather bag, puts them into his client's mouth, and hands him some brandy to drink it all down. He then throws some cowry shells: the oracle will verify the story and tell him whether the magic will be successful. If, as always, the answer is positive, he starts his work. He is supported by various bearers of power (fetishes, or bo and bocio), whose favor he seeks with a sacrifice of gin and blood. To finish the night's ritual Germain also hands his client some gin and blood in an encrusted black sacrificial calabash and promises that the magic will work quickly. Germain never loses out: his client not only has to pay for the sacrificial gifts, he must also hand over ten percent of the money owed – provided the debtor pays up.

Germain places the dog's skull in the open front door. This way the "dog" can pick up the scent and begin to "hunt" down the debtor.

Germain lets some chicken blood drip onto the dog's skull to start the magic working. A goat is also slaughtered for this reason.

Germain keeps his fetishes in a basket. Sacrifices are also made to them so that they do not cause harm out of jealousy.

The powers gathered in the dog's skull are activated by the blood poured over it. In his dreams, the debtor will be chased and tormented by wild animals. This will make him think about possible reasons for it, until he remembers his creditor. One day he will no longer be able to stand the torment and he will repay his debts.

Following pages: The magic dog's skull will ensure that the debtor will continually have nightmares about being chased by wild dogs.

149

Myth of the origin of magical cures

Legba, the youngest but especially gifted child of the androgynous creator god, is regarded as the first magician. At that time the gods received no sacrificial victims, which meant that they were constantly hungry. So Legba created a snake, put it on the well-trodden path to market and told it to bite passers-by. Then he demanded of them, "Give me something and I will cure you." In this way he lived well.

One day he met a shrewd man named Awe, who pointed to the snake and asked, "What is this thing that bites people?" Legba answered, "That is a bo. If you bring me two chickens, eight cowries, and some straw, I will show you how to make one." Awe did so, and Legba led him away from the path and showed him how to make a bo. Then he told him to throw a creeper plant on the ground, and thanks to the bo this turned into a snake before his very eyes and bit people. As well as magic, Legba also gave him medicine to cure snakebites, for as the saying goes, "If God gives you sickness, he also gives you medicine."

Over a period of time Awe received a great deal more bo from Legba, whom he always then turned to when he needed a magic spell for someone. Indoors and well away from prying eyes, they would make the right bo together. Legba remained a deity (vodun), and Awe became a magician (bokonon) in command of both white and black magic. People rewarded him quite generously for his services.

Awe soon became arrogant, however, and he even believed that he could compete with Mawu. Annoyed by this, Mawu decided, "People are bad, and from now on any person who does evil will die." This was how death (ku) came into the world, and Awe could do nothing about it. He continued to take care of the sick, but when death came, he could only give way to it.

People have to thank Legba for many remedies, which cure headaches, colic, diarrhea, leprosy, eye complaints, and rheumatism. He also taught them magic spells to protect themselves from wounds in wartime or accidents when traveling. As well as Legba, two other deities are considered to be well versed in the production of magical cures. Da (embodied in the snake and associated with rainbows, who himself is regarded as a giant, primeval python) specializes in spells which bring wealth, prestige, and success; while the earth and smallpox god Sakpata has command over an enormous number of remedies.

Today, however, people receive scarcely any magic potions from the gods. Rather, they receive them from bush spirits (aziza), whose skills were given to them by Mawu. Hunters, especially, can meet them, and if they succeed in winning their goodwill, can learn from them how to produce effective hunting spells. Bush spirits can also help with childlessness, for in addition to hunting magic they are especially familiar with fertility spells.

A "medicine bottle" of the Fon (of Benin), richly decorated with beads and cowry shells, such as is often found in the possession of healers and vodun priests. The container is of secondary significance; more important is the magic substance that it contains.

A figure of Legba with cowry shells for eyes. Legba is a son of the principal vodun deity Mawu-Lisa. Before any other god is spoken to or petitioned, Legba must first be contacted, since otherwise he could get in the way of human endeavors.

Fetishes of Legba are commonly found at the edge of villages which they are supposed to protect. This horned Legba is almost 6 feet tall. The chain around his neck is made of parts of animal skulls. Once a Legba had been put up, humans had to be sacrificed to it for a long time. Human bones can be found beneath this very old example.

The warrior god Koku searches for witches

Some 30 calabashes wound in cloth are stored at the shrine of the warrior god Koku, who fights against witches. The calabashes contain various powerful substances or "medicines." A follower of Koku sits on one of the calabashes in order to transfer its power to himself. During rituals Koku's warriors wear skirts of raffia or straw, demonstrating clearly that this god is in tune with nature.

Like the whole goro-vodun pantheon, the Ewe god Koku is of more recent origin. During colonial times the goro-vodun cult had many followers among various ethnic and linguistic groups along the coast of Ghana, Togo, and Benin. Centers of cult worship for these new gods are found today in almost all Ewe settlements, such as Gbezedzekope, in Ghana.

Unlike the older nature deities (*voduwo* or *trowo*), the new gods are not bound to their followers by family ties. Rather they are the focus of "medicine cults" which represent gods and exist in a multitude of copies. They are "bought" or "tied"

humans (*amefeflewo*), that is slaves, who protect and cure their owners in return for their support. The reputation of these cults rests primarily on protection from witches and malicious magicians. Just like the old deities, they also commit their followers to particular moral patterns of behavior.

The ethnic variety of the inhabitants of Ewe settlements ensures that Koku's characteristics are made up of traditions and ideas of the most varied origin. Like all "medicine cults" he draws his special power from a combination of active substances which are collected at quite specific places, frequently in cemeteries. Which of the

Left and below: When they are in a trance Koku's followers inflict injuries on each other, thereby demonstrating the great strength and immunity which protects them against witches. Drummers are always connected to the cult. They stimulate the induction of a trance by changing the rhythm of the drums, getting faster all the time, or by gradually increasing their volume.

Following pages: Koku's followers light gunpowder and inhale the smoke. The heat of the fire makes their blood seethe. Breathing gunpowder also serves to give them renewed energy for the ceremony.

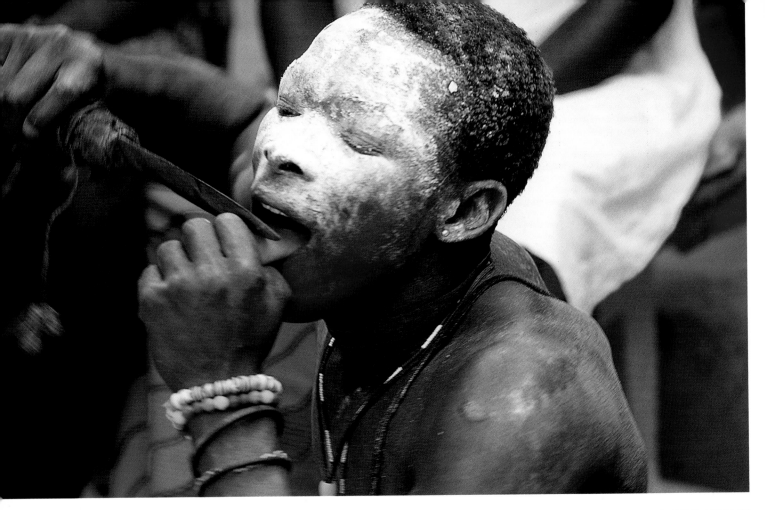

A Koku initiate cuts his tongue as a sign of his strength.

Two initiates are exhausted after the ceremony.

A follower of Koku hangs from a tree by his feet, imitating the behavior of the witches, who have "turned their nature upside down." Beneath him two owls (birds of witchcraft) are hanging in the same position.

substances are used in which combination for what purpose remains a secret of the cult. In order to make their "free" powers tangible and manipulable, the substances are captured by certain objects, which thus take on the meaning of their "body," their "skin," or their "house." Since people can be possessed by them as they could be by the old gods, they are also called vodun.

Koku is a bloodthirsty god. He causes his entranced followers to injure each other with knives, pieces of glass, or scissors. Earlier warriors prepared themselves for battle in a similar way: by taking "protective medicines," making threatening gestures and simulating battle, they wound themselves up into a state of rage and uncontrollable savagery, in order to be able to stand up to any enemy. The opponents of the new war-god are not strangers, however; they come from their own ranks. Koku's rage is directed toward witches and magicians who may be able to deceive their own family and neighbors, but not him. Without having to intervene himself, Koku gives his followers the immense powers which enable them to expose and fight black magicians and witches. This conferring of power is the main purpose of the meetings of the cult community.

The Ewe are known for not blindly adhering to old traditions. For a long time there has existed a lively exchange between them and people of the northern regions; theatrical performances in costumes from those regions form part of their religious practice.

Ama, the fourteen-year-old witch

Above: The right time for the purification and reconciliation ceremony is determined by the Fa oracle. For this, a priest's helper throws cowries on the ground. As the answer is positive, he immediately goes to get the required goods from the nearby market: kola nuts, a cockerel, a bottle of gin, and a young dog.

Right: The ceremony can begin. A liquid offering poured on the ground is intended to make the ancestors feel conciliatory toward the girl. Then the priest uses a rattle to summon his god.

Opposite page: Ama, who considers herself to be a witch, offers Alafia, god of reconciliation, a kola nut. The nut is sacred and is seen as food for the gods.

Goro-vodun is a more recent "medicine cult," which may only have been widespread in Ewe settlements since the 1940s. Today the cult's "medicines" are seen as belonging to protective deities who act independently and who have set themselves the task of taking energetic action against any form of resentment or bitterness.

The secret powers of the kola nut (or *goro* in the language of the Fon) lie at the center of goro-vodun. This takes up an old tradition; the stimulating effect of the kola nuts plays an important part in the religious and social life of many West African societies. Guests receive them as a sign of particularly high esteem; princes and village chiefs honor highly regarded followers with them. In earlier times they were rarely consumed; they were regarded as luxury goods which were normally used only as ritual gifts at name-giving ceremonies, weddings, and burials. The nuts still stand for closeness and friendship. Since each shell contains two seeds, sharing and eating a nut together signify an unreserved expression of trust between people. This also makes

them an ideal gift for the gods, and especially for the Hausa god Tonou Deka Alafia.

His simple shrine (*hukpa* or *hukpe*) lies in Ashaiman, a fishing town between Accra, the capital of Ghana and the country's chief port, Tema. The center of cult worship consists of nothing more than a small area surrounded by white clay walls. In the middle is a plain altar, at which blood and kola nuts are offered. Alafia is regarded as the god (*kpa* or *kpe*) of peace and reconciliation. His current priest (*hunon*, literally "mother of spirits or gods"; *hu* also means "blood"), Klutse Aliso Kodzo, has many followers among the decidedly mixed population of the town. He has various tasks: he heals people with herbs (*amasi*, medicinal plants), tells fortunes by means of the Fa oracle, and promises protection from misfortune and witchcraft. He also frees confessed witches from blame if they come to him of their own accord or are brought by their relatives.

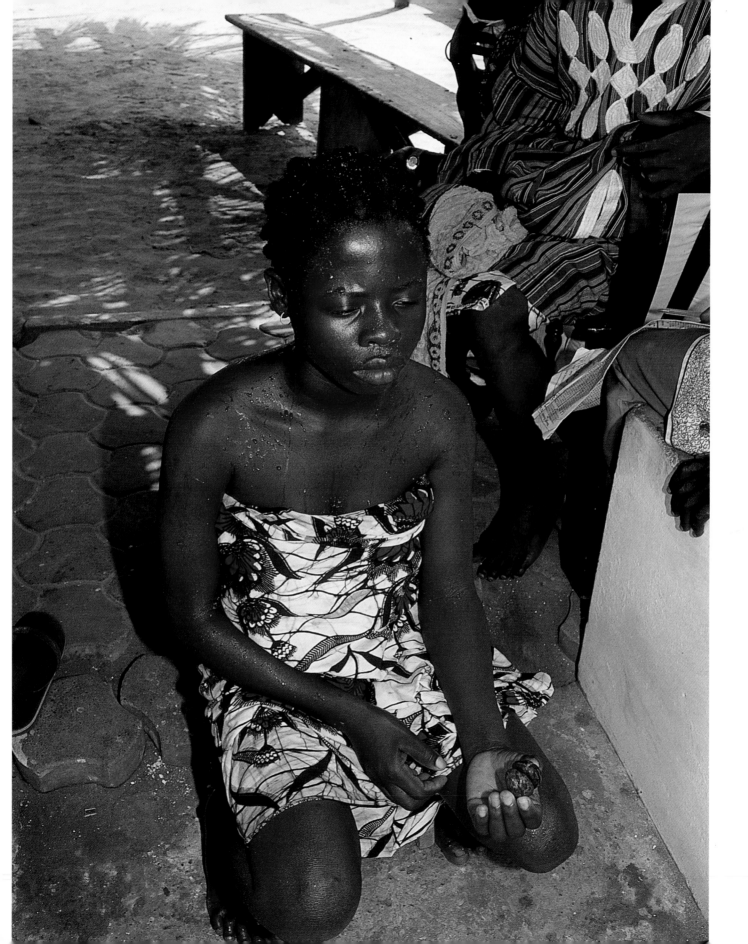

The priest washes and massages the girl with various herbs to take the witchcraft out of her.

The gods are offered whatever will bring them strength and life. In the case of Alafia it is dogs. This shows that he is a stranger from the north, for the people of the south do not usually "eat" dogs. The dog's soul makes its way as a kind of messenger to the other world in order to ask for support in the casting out of witchcraft.

Fourteen-year-old Ama is brought by her mother, who has accused her of being a witch. Ama declined to make a written confession: goro-vodun is a religion of public and private confessions; everything "which one has in one's stomach" can be unburdened here, so that the sting is taken out of bad feelings, death wishes, and jealousy. Ama's confession reveals not only her life story but discloses her hidden desires and secret thoughts.

She accuses herself of a whole series of offenses. These include such witchlike features as a special liking for human flesh and palm-oil soup, as well as belonging to a group of witches who particularly like consuming young children. Her hostility was aimed especially at her relatives, to whom she continually brought misfortune. This usually revolved around money, which causes splits in many families today. Ama's resentment was directed particularly at her father, who absolutely refused to allow her her wish to become a dressmaker. In a society in which most clothes are made by hand, dressmaking is a very sound trade.

Ama made no secret of her anger: she became rebellious, insulted her father, cooked for him when she was in an impure state (that is, during menstruation), and wished she could "pierce his eyes with a stick." As she felt constrained, she also begrudged her sisters any success: she led them into extravagance by encouraging them to waste their money on useless things instead of using it profitably. She repeatedly borrowed money without paying it back. If she was refused money, she simply took it. As well as stealing, she lied and played sexual games. Whenever something fortunate

The dog's blood is poured over the cult object of the god, which is surrounded by countless kola nuts.

The dog's body is buried near the cult center. It is impressed upon the dog's soul that it must watch over the girl from now on. Then the priest places kola nuts on the carcass and sacrifices a cockerel in order to placate evil spirits.

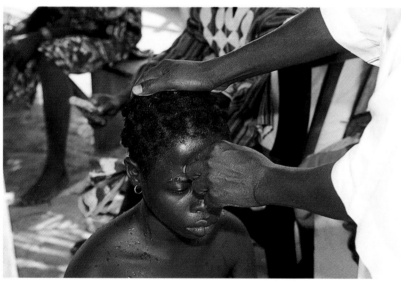

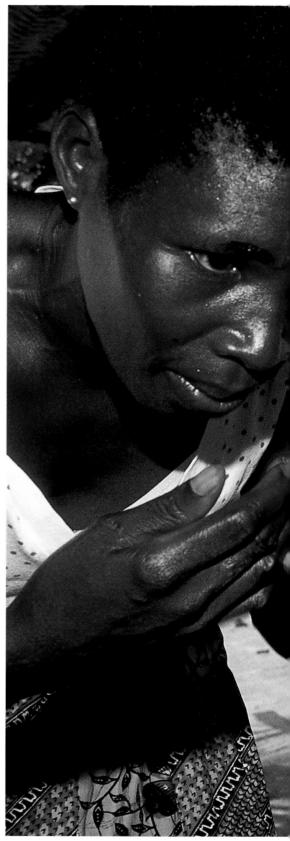

At the end of the ceremony the priest presses a nut against the girl's forehead. This is to take away all the bad thoughts that are in her head.

happened to anyone else, she involved herself and made sure that things were ruined.

The root of all the evil and the cause of all her misdeeds was money. This needed to be dealt with, and Ama's confession was the first step. With the help of Alafia, the ritual that followed was intended to free the girl from witchcraft.

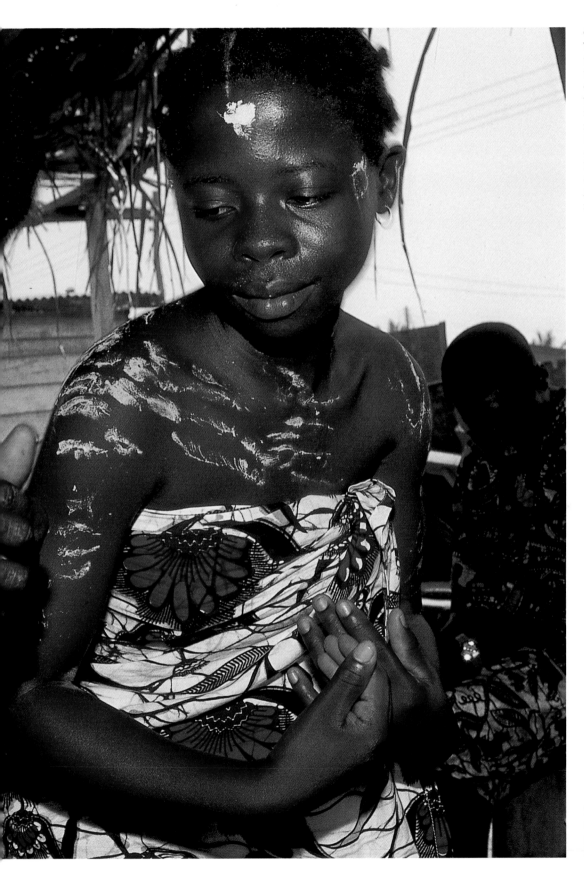

Opposite page, above:
The girl's mother commands the bewitched animals, in this case snakes, to come out of her body through the vagina. Once she has been freed from witchcraft, her mother first washes her and then the priest rubs her down with ground kola nuts. He then gives her a nut to chew so that she absorbs Aláfia, the god of peace and reconciliation.

In grateful recognition of the completed cure mother and daughter dance in front of the kola-nut temple.

Fetish –
the concept and its problems

A nail fetish, widespread among the Bakongo. It is used mainly to cause damage in destructive, avenging magic.

Opposite page:
Three Fon *bocios*; the word is made up of "power" (*bo*) and carcass (*cios*), meaning that the power has been translated into figures. A *bocio* can be used for both good and evil.

The term "fetish" was one of the most problematic concepts for 19th-century European explorers in Africa. The word comes from the Portuguese and among seafarers and traders it had long referred to carved objects and figures. In Portuguese the term *feitico* (an object made by a magician by means of magical arts) has a neutral meaning in the sense of "charm" or "amulet." Its meaning changed to refer specifically to images worshiped in early, especially African cultures. Some ethnologists and religious historians saw it as the quintessence of the oldest stage in human-religious cultural development: according to this belief, objects which contained a spirit stood at the heart of fetishism, or a belief in fetishes.

French historian and parliamentary president Charles de Brosses (1709–77) published a book on the subject in 1760 entitled *Cult of the Fetish Gods*. Referring to the reports of Portuguese and French mariners, he wrote, "The Negroes of the west coast of Africa have certain deities as objects of worship, which the Europeans call fetishes. These sacred fetishes are nothing more than the first earthly thing that a nation or an individual arbitrarily chose to be consecrated by priests; it could be a tree, a mountain, a sea, a piece of wood, a lion's tail, a pebble, a shell, salt, a fish, a plant, a flower, an animal or a particular species such as a cow, goat, elephant, sheep; it could be anything you can think of. They are all deities to the Negroes, who dedicate a strong, sacred cult to them, who swear by them, who offer sacrifices to them, who carry them on processions (if they are suitable), who carry them with all due reverence, and who turn to them for advice on all important matters." According to de Brosses and others, "the Negro" seldom differentiates between the spirit and the sensory object; both represent a whole for him, the "fetish."

It was thought that these sacred objects were worshiped by African peoples because anything unforeseen aroused fear in their souls and, since

A Fon *bocio* (guardian figure) of Legba. The power of the vodun deity Legba lives in him; this messenger of the gods and intermediary is called upon when the gods are asked for special privileges or favors. He is usually the first to receive a small sacrifice. The enormous penis shows his masculine potency.

they could not differentiate between cause and effect, they regarded certain objects as the powers that cause things to happen; they then invoked them and offered sacrifices to them. The colonial peoples of Africa gained the reputation for being "stupid, amoral fetishists" who worshiped trees, animals, and stones. Travelers, missionaries, and colonialists, who at best had only a superficial idea of African cultures, took up the expression as being meaningless but useful. Fetishism was set alongside witchcraft and superstition. It was associated with any object which had anything to do with magic or cult ideas and practices; this might be a sculpture of a traditional hero or royal insignia, an ancestral statue, or a piece of fortune-telling apparatus. The local people were seen in the same way, so that Europeans referred to fetish huts, fetish services, fetish priests, fetish ceremonies, fetish people, protective fetishes, and so on. The "history of the fetish" draws on a misunderstanding on the part of Western civilization; the use of the term is avoided in more recent ethnological and religious literature. It is considered to be not only old-fashioned but also offensive.

Among the most famous objects to be labeled "fetishes" are the nkisi, or nail fetishes, of the Loango coast and lower Congo, as well as a series of Fon figures of modern southern Benin.

The people of the latter region typically believe in vodun, mysterious powers which guide the events of the world and the fate of humans. Their power lives in "guardian figures" (*bocio*), which come to people's assistance, lending them vitality and causing changes. They are not portrayals or symbols of the "gods" (*vodun*), however; they are closely associated with them, concentrating their power and acting as a philosophy of life and nature. One can hope to obtain healing and help from them when in need, as well as the fulfillment of one's desires. They help to overcome many serious problems, and as such are objects of hope and trust, like saints to rural European peoples.

Left: Fon *bocio* of Kpobla, who is supposed to stop an enemy. This function is symbolized by the chains and locks on the figures.

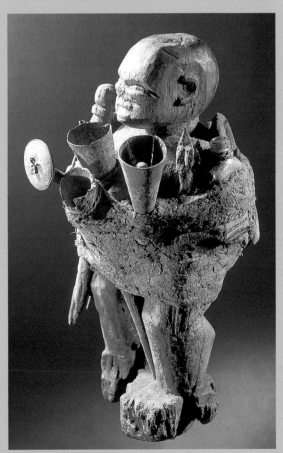

Far left: A Ewe representation of the water goddess Mami Wata; her love of jewelry and beautiful things is shown by the necklaces on the figure.

Left: As well as the representational bo, the Fon also have figurative portrayals for example the *bocio* ("authorized carcass"), to which additional containers are often attached, especially around the navel.

Far left: A bocio, with a metal sculpture (*asen*) on its head. The Fon use this figure to honor their dead parents and relatives and to offer sacrifices. Since ancestors contribute greatly to the fertility of their descendants, the figure acts as a remedy for impotence.

The dead are awake,
when the living are asleep

"Death is the fruit of life, life is the fruit of death" goes a saying of the Dyula of Senegal. When a human being has to leave the world one day, it is because he has lived, eaten, drunk, slept, worked, and rested, because he has tilled his fields, danced, celebrated, and above all because he has produced children. In many myths death appears as the price to be paid for living life to the full. It is seen as the necessary prerequisite for the regeneration of man, nature, and cosmic energy. Without it there would be an eternal standstill. Life is a constant flow of forces and forms, it is movement and rest, circulation and activity. Looked at in this way, death is justified by life itself.

Death is always seen as somehow strange, however, as an external power which intervenes in the life of society. Seen as the epitome of destruction, as the essence of evil, it represents the exact opposite of the divine order of creation. There are myths in

At the funeral of her child a mother is overcome by grief and sinks to the ground before the coffin.

all parts of Africa which mention that death was not originally in the world. Humans are created immortal, and succumb to death through the fault of a messenger, generally an animal, who either brings his message too late or mixes it up. In this way man receives a message of death instead of the intended promise of eternal life. Or death, which existed in the background of the universe from the very beginning without God's knowledge, sneakily makes its way among human beings. According to the tradition of the Krobo, "Previously spider was the wisest man on earth. When bird disputed his position as adviser to the chiefs, the leader decided to test the wisdom of both. Knowing full well that there were numerous obstacles on the way, he sent them with a message. Spider carried his wisdom in a bag. After bird and spider had set off together, it was not long before they came to a place where a mighty tree trunk barred the way. Bird overcame the obstacle easily, but spider had difficulty climbing over the trunk. Then bird came back and offered to carry spider's bag. He flew with it high up in the air, far away to a place where death lived, handed him the bag and received another one instead. He then went back to spider, and both continued on their journey. Their path was soon blocked by a huge rock. Bird flew over it without any trouble, but spider could not climb over the rock however hard he tried. Bird came back again. 'Hit the rock with your bag,' he told spider, 'then your wisdom will appear and lead you.' Spider followed the advice and struck his bag against the rock with force. Then death came out of the bag and spread throughout the whole world."

As in this story, many African traditions are based on a trickster figure who is responsible for releasing the nocturnal being of death from his hiding place in the underworld or the other world.

Life and death are not the same for everyone. The world is often portrayed as being like a market, where all sorts of different traders meet to offer, sell, and buy all sorts of goods. Everyone must try to get the most they can out of life. A good life is distinguished by being successfully mastered and lasting a long time. Only the death of an old person who has fulfilled his duties toward the community and been called to God, as they say, has a beneficent effect on his descendants. Those who pass on after a fulfilled life live on in the kingdom of the dead, where they are surrounded

A grave is dug for the child's coffin. Child mortality is very high throughout Africa, in particular among children below the age of five. Almost all of them die of malaria. If children survive to the age of five, however, it is much less likely that they will die of malaria.

by those who died before them and go on leading a life similar to that on earth, except that everything there is reversed.

In the kingdom of the dead everything is inverted in relation to the world of the living, so that things are the other way around. When it is day on earth, it is night in the kingdom of the dead, and when it rains on earth, it is dry there. The dead are awake when the living are asleep. There the sun rises in the west and sets in the east. The right side corresponds to the left on earth. The dead enter their houses from the back and walk on their heads, with the soles of the feet against the underside of the earth. Rooftops and treetops point "downwards." A Zulu woman expressed this to a European by pointing to the upturned palm of her hand and saying, "This is how we live"; then she turned her hand over so that the back was pointing upwards and said, "That is how our ancestors live."

The mourners crouch reverently around the grave.

171

Entering the kingdom of the dead

These fantastic coffins are produced in Teshi, near Accra. Each one has a special connection with the dead person. The fish- and crab-shaped coffins were probably made for fishermen. The coffin in the center, in the form of a chicken spreading its wings, is for a mother who had many children and always looked after them well, like a hen with her chicks.

Every death causes distress. Children lose their father or mother, spouses lose their partners, or a family loses its main support in the struggle for survival. A group might lose a member who is cherished for his experience, knowledge, and kindness, and in the case of a king people lose the "supporting column" that held together their microcosm and macrocosm. Those left behind react to their loss with strong emotions, which frequently include anger. Death causes chaos and turns the life of the community upside down. Ties are severed, urgent business remains undone, important religious rites can no longer be carried out; in short, the existing order is in danger of breaking down.

From the time of death until the funeral nothing runs as normal. Work and everyday activities are forgotten, as if they too had been touched by the hand of death. Precautions have to be taken in order to counter this threat, and countless rules must be followed. Death touches everyone, and people worry that dying could spread. Society concentrates on trying to drive death out as quickly as possible. Those left behind have the task of performing the necessary rites. Without these the departed, or his soul, will not be able to pass into the kingdom of the dead and be received by the ancestors.

Funeral ceremonies are great social events. Family members travel from near and far to mourn the deceased and to demonstrate family solidarity. Although death severs ties, it also strengthens bonds among the bereaved. For relatives, neighbors, and friends paying their last respects to the departed is a natural duty.

A coffin in the form of a lion is completed in the workshop. The lion, who is king of beasts, shows that this coffin is for a chief.

The significance accorded to an individual death depends very much on the age and status of the deceased. The course and extent of the ceremonies are determined by whether the deceased was a child, man, or woman, was young or old, or an ordinary individual or important personality. Less is made of the death of a small child who was only at the very beginning of its human existence, and children are often buried without great ceremony within a few hours of their death. People believe that children will soon be reincarnated, and if the parents behave properly, the children will remain in this world. The death of an older child is regarded as more painful and is appropriately mourned, but still not with the same amount of ceremony as is generally given to the death of an adult. Large-scale ceremonies only take place for adults of a suitable age, status, and reputation.

The manner of death also plays a part. Those who die in an unusual way suffer a "bad death" – such as being struck by lightning, being killed by a bird of prey, or dying from certain illnesses such as leprosy or smallpox, or as the result of murder, suicide, or an accident – and are accorded few or no or rites. The suddenness and severity of the blow are often seen as an indication that death must have been caused by serious misconduct on the part of the particular individual. Those who suffer a bad death are generally disposed of as quickly as possible and with no great trouble. They are neither mourned, at least not officially, nor given a ceremonial funeral. Today they are usually buried quickly and quietly at the edge of the cemetery; it used to be common simply to cast their body into the bush or give it a very shallow grave. Since they were banished from the environs of the village, they were also excommunicated in death: their souls never return.

Only those who are buried according to traditional rules find their way into the kingdom of the dead. They are buried within the settlement,

This unusual coffin, in the form of a car, is being made for a taxi driver. He probably did not drive a Mercedes in life, but no doubt this was his dream.

The license plate of the car-coffin reads "Rest in peace."

An unfinished crab-shaped coffin for a fisherman. Once the shape has been made, there is no limit to the fantastic patterns and colors that can be painted on.

This lobster-shaped coffin has already been painted; all it needs now are a few additional feelers.

appropriate for his age, and in many societies for his trade or status. This labor of love is usually carried out by old women. Since they themselves are close to the threshold of death, the miasma of decomposition given off by every corpse cannot harm them. The so-called "corpse cosmetics" are applied without any great fuss in the close family circle.

The body is then usually laid out in the dead person's house. He is allowed to share in the mourning, and relatives, neighbors, and friends are given the opportunity to say their goodbyes. The house is open to visitors. Loud lamenting begins, and the deceased's praises are sung in songs about life and death. If he was a member of an exclusive community, such as a secret or masked society, or a hunters' or craftsmen's guild, other members honor him by appearing in special masks or costumes.

If the funeral is to be carried out with great ceremony, mourners lament and sing to the beating of drums until late into the night. When they are exhausted, mourners leave the room in order to refresh themselves and rest for a short while. New visitors arrive all the time, and none come empty-handed. The value of gifts depends on the givers' relationship to the deceased. Gifts used to be prescribed for different levels of relatives: classic gifts consist of a certain number of chickens or cattle, large cotton cloths sewn together from strips

often directly beneath their house, in the courtyard, in front of the farmstead, or in a nearby family field.

Taking leave of a respectable dead person, especially if he reached old age, is a lengthy process with several phases. The first step is to prepare the body for a burial befitting the deceased's station. The body is carefully washed, sometimes also painted, and rubbed with fragrant essences. Toenails and fingernails are cut, and the hair is tidied or shaved off. Then he is usually dressed in his best clothes, sometimes with jewelry and holding goods

of material, a specific amount of shell-money (cowries, or the shells of the small sea mollusk Cypraea annulus), or a bottle of high-proof alcohol. Today people often give banknotes. Relatives and friends touch the body for a last time, always with the left hand. Someone makes a short speech, saying farewell to the dead person and requesting him to stand by those who survive him by giving them a long life, health, and fertility.

Most funerals, however, are quite modest affairs and take place within a circle of close relatives. Neighbors and friends make a short appearance. During the vigil by the corpse a grave is dug. The burial, which is attended mainly by men, takes place after dark during the evening of the day of death, or at the latest on the next day. In earlier times the bodies of important people were laid out for several days. Since the corpse began to decompose rapidly, because of climatic conditions, certain preservation methods were used. Camphor, obtained from the wood of the Cinnamonum camphora tree, was widely used. This white, translucent substance is soluble in alcohol, and a rum-camphor solution inhibited the process of decomposition. The camphor was poured into body orifices and rubbed into the skin, but not on the face. Modern cooling techniques, especially in towns and cities, allow the burial to be postponed for a few days, making it possible for faraway relatives to attend.

In rural areas, however, the burial must take place shortly after death. A large farewell ceremony is planned for a later date and may take place months or even years afterward. Until then the dead person continues to exist among the living, so that a widow or widower must remain faithful to their spouse, and a dignitary's term of office is not officially over.

Relatives and friends are notified of the ceremony well in advance, so that no one can miss the event without a very good excuse. Because of the high costs involved, families usually choose to hold the memorial service after the harvest season. Then there is sufficient food for all the guests. Sacrificial animals are fattened so that the deceased can take their essences to the ancestors as a gift. Once the harvest has been brought in, villagers also have more time for celebration. Since there has probably been a death in almost every household in the meantime, the villagers travel from one ceremony to the next. They can at last bid farewell to the deceased to the sound of beating drums, the rattle of calabashes, and rifle shots. Since the deceased has been buried for some time, he is often represented by an item of clothing, and sometimes people wear some of his clothes, so that he is still in a sense present at the ceremony.

Dancing forms an essential element of the memorial ceremony. It rouses the mourners from apathy and leads them back to normality. Music and singing serve to honor the dead, and in urban regions the music is often played by modern steel bands. Everywhere guests are looked after most generously. They are offered lemonade, beer, and palm wine, as well as rum, gin, and whisky. The

greater the range on offer, the happier the event as far as the deceased is concerned, for the extravagance brings him honor not only among the living but also among ancestors in the afterlife. The relatives of the deceased therefore spare no cost in making this event unforgettable for all those present. Afterwards the deceased belongs to the community of ancestors, and in future he will be honored along with them at least once a year.

This beautifully decorated eagle has been made for a chief, since the eagle is regarded as the king of the skies.

Honoring the dead

Death spares no one, but departure from this life is different for everyone. Among the Asante the extent and splendor of their funeral ceremonies depend on the wealth and standing of the family of the deceased. In earlier times the king's mortal remains received special treatment, and many followed the asantehene into death. Some did this willingly: women and courtiers regarded it as an honor to be allowed to accompany the king into the next world and serve him further there. Others had no choice at all: prisoners of war and those branded as criminals made up the main contingent of his other-worldly followers. Others also lost their lives: the *aberafo*, or royal executioners, went into a murderous frenzy and seized anyone careless enough to cross their path.

Meanwhile *asokwafo* (ivory-horn players and gravediggers) took the king's body to a holy place before the gates of Kumasi, the *Asonyeso* ("dripping place") or *Barim Kese* ("large cemetery"). There the asantehene's body was laid in a coffin made from the taproots of the kapok tree which rested on supports over a pit. As the body decomposed, its fluids dripped through holes in

The mourning clothes of the Asante are in dark colors, in contrast to their bright festival robes and white ritual costume. The mourning bands (*abade*) around the head are to stop evil spirits, and therefore grief, ruling their thoughts.

The family of a rich man from Kumasi make a public show of their wealth at his funeral. His widows and children wear valuable gold jewelry.

A little girl dances to the drumbeat for the funeral guests.

The appearance of girls at the funeral shows the continuity of life, comforting the mourners and helping to remove death's sting. Dancing sets the seal on the community's return to normality: moving means sharing in life.

the bottom of the coffin into the pit. Guards watched over the coffin day and night, throwing earth into the pit and driving flies away with fans. The corpse could be removed only after 80 days. If there was still any flesh left on the bones, it was scraped off by the asokwafo. Then they rubbed the royal bones with buffalo fat and hung on them the talismans (suman) which had protected the asantehene while he was alive. The long bones were bound together at the joints by thin gold wire.

On the first anniversary of the king's death, the asokwafo carried his skeleton in a hexagonal coffin from Barim Kese to the royal mausoleum at Bantama, the final resting place of the rulers of the Asante. At that time Bantama, which the British destroyed after the final Asante uprising in 1895, lay outside Kumasi. The ruling asantehene had to ensure that the skeletons of his predecessors were well looked after. They had their own courtiers, including cooks. Eunuchs watched over them. The

rule that the king must not come into direct contact with the earth was upheld even after death.

Ordinary mortals are simply laid underground. Their simple burial usually takes place shortly after death. Lesser rites take place on the eighth, fifteenth, fortieth, and eightieth days after death, as well as on the anniversary. The final ceremony is often held on one of these days. Those who can afford it hold an extravagant event on this occasion. Although the ceremony's focal point is the deceased, it also returns the mourners to normality. The mourners lament for a last time, "Agya e! pue!" ("Oh father, alas!"). A rifle salute is also fired.

A large number of visitors, easily recognizable in their dark red, black, or orange clothes, arrive to pay their last respects. Costumes and jewelry play an important role in Ashanti by making stages in people's lives and important rites of passage clearly visible to all. The clothes worn by relatives and guests at a funeral express their relationship to the deceased.

Top: Men and women dance separately at funeral ceremonies. Young girls stand in the foreground. In the matrilineal Ashanti society only women can pass on blood, so that girls carry hope for the continuance of the family.

Above: A prince's bodyguard at a funeral ceremony in Konongo. The leopard's head symbolizes power.

Daily's coffin: a folded newspaper

A coffin in the shape of a folded edition of the *Daily Graphic* for Ernest Tagoe, called Daily by his family and friends. Daily himself could not read, but he came by his nickname by getting his son to read the *Daily Graphic* to him every day; then he would tell all the news to his neighbors, thus becoming their edition of the Daily.

The purpose of extravagant burials and funeral ceremonies is to strengthen contact with the dead, and relatives of the dead spare no efforts in achieving this. In recent times the Ga of coastal Ghana have buried their dead in unusual, brilliantly decorated "fantasy coffins." The usual rectangular wooden boxes were introduced into Ghana a long time ago by Europeans, and were seen as a privilege of important people. The unusual variations came into fashion toward the end of the 1960s. They are produced by a small group of carpenters in Teshie, near Accra. Their aim is to emphasize the individuality of the deceased and to represent special facets of their life.

The coffins are not cheap, but many people are more than ready to pay for a final token of love for their beloved deceased. Depending on the design, type of wood used, and artistic freedom, a fantasy coffin costs around US $400, the average yearly income of a Ghanaian. Other expenses have to be added, and this is beyond the reach of most people. Funeral guests contribute as far as they are able, but

this only covers a fraction of the cost. Funeral celebrations have pushed many people to the very edge of ruin. Yet, no one has any intention of curbing their expenditure: after all, the most terrible debts are preferable to insulting the dead.

Cabinetmaker Kane Kwei had the idea of sending people on their final journey in fantasy coffins in the 1960s. He carved the first examples in the shape of fish and boats for his own relatives. They caused great amazement but were also hugely admired. He was congratulated and toasted with enormous quantities of palm wine, and talk of his abilities soon spread. Before long he was receiving commissions from outside Ghana. His four sons and several apprentices learned from him, so that after his death in 1978 his work could continue. The coffins are in great demand; many see great value in a prestigious coffin that will make the

deceased stand out from the masses. The bereaved also hope that such a coffin will secure an appropriate position for the deceased among their ancestors.

There is no limit to the fantasy element of the coffins. Most of the chosen designs are linked to the life of the deceased: devoted mothers receive coffins in the shape of a hen, while important men receive an eagle. A coffin in the shape of a cocoa bean or an onion honors a successful farmer. Boat or fish shapes are favorite designs for fishermen and for women who sell fish. Those who choose houses, automobiles, or airplanes often send the deceased on their final journey in something which they could only dream of when they were alive. Even if they did possess such a thing in life, the coffin design is usually much more luxurious. A simple canoe becomes a wonderful ship, a modest

Daily is laid out with dignity on a bed which his son borrowed for the purpose. He is dressed in white, the color of purity and death. In order to honor his services as a fisherman, the mourners are holding a fishing net and wishing the deceased a good catch in the next world.

Above and below: When the coffin was finally ready, though the paint was not totally dry, young men squeezed the body into the narrow opening. Once the coffin lid was closed, the deceased began his final journey.

Below: Daily's wife and son support each other in their grief.

small car becomes a luxury limousine, and an ordinary house becomes an impressive villa. All this springs from the wish to improve the deceased's position in the next world and to make a good impression on other people as well as the ancestors.

The coffin makers showed their great skill in the design that was made for Ernest Tagoe, a fisherman who died at the age of 72. Ernest could not read or write himself, and every day he had his son read to him from Ghana's leading newspaper, the *Daily Graphic*. Once he had learned the latest news, he would go from house to house to discuss events with friends and neighbors. This earned him the nickname Daily.

Daily lived and died in Jamestown, an old, noisy district of Accra that is inhabited mainly by Ga. When he died, his son wanted to secure a respectable position among the ancestors. He borrowed white sheets and a magnificent bed, on which Daily's body was laid out for several days. Meanwhile the carpenters of Teshie were working frantically to produce the coffin that had just been ordered for Daily. The commissioned design of the coffin was in the shape of a folded newspaper. In the meantime the family kept vigil by the body. Relatives, neighbors, and friends stood around the bed and struck it lightly with their left hands.

When the coffin was ready and Daily's body had been squeezed in, young men argued over the right to carry it to the burial ground. This part of the ritual is regarded as showing a special honor towards the deceased, who will repay the favor in due course from his position in the next world. As soon as the coffin was closed, four strong young men, fortified even further by gin, lifted it onto their heads. Instead of marching in a dignified way, they ran with the coffin through the narrow streets. They were soon in a sweat, and every so often they staggered to a halt so that relatives and friends could say a final farewell to the dead man. When everyone far and wide had been informed of Daily's departure, the bearers made a number of detours so that the deceased's soul would lose its bearings. This meant that the soul could not find its way back and so was forced to make its way to the kingdom of the dead, doing no further harm to the living. The bearers covered most of the ten miles to the cemetery at a running pace, and the funeral procession had trouble keeping up with them. The coffin was spun around many times, and it came to

rest only when they reached the cemetery. The coffin was carefully lowered into the grave, a final offering was made, and then the mourners made their way back without further ceremony.

Daily was only properly established in the kingdom of the dead, however, after a further series of small commemorative ceremonies had been held for him. Rather like the incorporation of a child into human society, introduction into the ancestral community is a lengthy process. Daily's chances are good: his unusual coffin and the extravagant trouble that was taken with his body showed the ancestors how much he had achieved on earth and the reputation that he enjoyed. They will surely make a suitable place for him among their ranks.

Above left: A chicken is sacrificed over the coffin so that the gods will be with the deceased and can bless him.

Above: The coffin is carried from door to door, so that friends and relatives can pay their last respects.

After being carried through the streets of Jamestown at the head of the funeral procession, the unusual, artistically made coffin is lowered into the grave.

The hunters mourn

Social differences remain beyond death, which by no means makes everyone equal. Some professions or specialisms, such as fortune-telling or metal-working, have special rites. Hunters are another group with their own special position. They are often cult heroes who founded new villages and turned natural land into cultivated areas.

Their world is the bush – the wild country beyond the open farmland which is always thought of as threatening. Strange things happen there, especially at the culminating times of midday and midnight: animals, trees, and even stones change shape, deceive, and fool people, even endangering their lives. That is why nobody willingly leaves the domestic safety of their village and cultivated land.

Hunters have to roam this eerie wilderness, however. Hunting is a risky business. One can easily get lost in the dense undergrowth. Wherever he goes, the hunter has to be prepared for attacks by wild animals, and even greater dangers lie in wait for him: the bush is the home of countless spirits which do not necessarily feel friendly toward those who want to kill. A hunter is always in danger, and the slightest carelessness will cost him his life. If he survives to become an old man, he deserves to be treated with respect and reverence. It was only because he possessed special knowledge that he was able to outwit animals and bush spirits. But such knowledge cannot be acquired unaided; assistance from beyond is always required, which is why hunters are reputed to have a particularly good relationship with the creatures of the wilderness.

At times the bush spirits reveal themselves to the hunters and offer to be their protectors, guarding the family, clan, or village and offering

In Kankalaba, a village in southwestern Burkina Faso near the border with Ivory Coast, the burial ceremony of a dead hunter takes place. The elders of the hunting society occupy the seats of honor. In front of them stands a buffalo skull with splendid horns, a hunting trophy of one of the most dangerous wild animals.

Every mask has its mythological origin or "story of discovery," which is usually passed on within the family or larger cult community. Hunters especially have in many places formed such societies where this knowledge is strictly guarded. This also applies to the Senoufu, who belong to culturally very different population groups in the north of Ivory Coast, southeastern Mali and southwestern Burkina Faso. They are familiar with highly developed cult associations and hunters' societies, which are present in almost every village. The reason that so little is known about this is because the Senoufu people treat the subject with great discretion.

Like members of other secret societies, hunters also use a secret language. When they return to the village after a successful hunting trip, their own orchestra welcomes them with music. Usually there is also dancing. Hunters are inconspicuously dressed in camouflage colors. Their hunting clothes are often decorated with charms and talismans. The roots of certain plants, animal skins, claws, teeth, leather thongs, iron wheels, and rings on their arms and legs fend off disaster and lend power.

When one of their members dies, hunting societies have important functions, which help to separate the soul from the body and to recreate the separation of the worlds of the living which death has momentarily blurred. As people who cross the boundaries of wilderness and village, nature and culture, they are ideally suited for this. At the funeral of one of their fellow hunters, they adopt the role of guards who control and guarantee that all the rites for the deceased are conducted according to the rules for which they bear testimony to the ancestors. They also help to drive out the forces of evil which every death releases. The climax of a hunter's funeral is the destruction of his weapons. This is the task of his relatives and friends. At both the funeral and the memorial ceremony the hunters are accompanied by different groups of musicians, mainly from the village itself or from the locality, who accompany the stories which are recited and the songs that are sung by the hunting society's elders at the burial. These mainly

During the ceremony various masks appear: Kafieni, a bush spirit; Zachaya, the warthog; and Nionhon, the antelope. The younger members of the hunting society are hidden behind the masks, which are worn like helmets, and beneath the woven costumes (made of Hibiscus cannabinus or Cannabinus indica).

fertility, health, and prosperity if they are properly venerated. But animals and bush spirits can only become cult figures once they have been captured in an object or a replica that has been made of them, in clay or wood, or in the form of a mask. Then they become closely related to the ancestors, which is demonstrated by the fact that masks are also worn at sacrifices at ancestral shrines and at memorial ceremonies.

Exhausted from the dancing, antelope and warthog take a short break.

relate to the hunter's world – the bush. Animals with their individual characteristics play a leading role alongside miraculous experiences with the spirits of the bush. Usually the society members are dressed in their hunting clothes, shouldering arms. Others, as a special honor to their departed friend, come in the guise of an animal.

If the necessary means are available, the memorial ceremony takes place as soon as possible after the burial. But as this is rarely the case, it often takes some time before they finally say farewell to the dead man. Now the masks help to separate his soul from this world for ever. Only then will it gain admission among the ancestors. The helmet-like animal masks of the Senufo impressively illustrate how frightening, wild, and dangerous the animals of the bush are to humans; at the same time, they are useful for familiarizing people with the animals. Essential elements of the masks are horns, tusks, double rows of teeth, leaves, and parts of plants which show dramatically the concentrated aggression, readiness to fight, danger, risk of death, and ferocity of the inhabitants of the bush. To a rhythm dictated by the musicians on their wooden, beaker-shaped calabash drums, every mask wearer dances for about five minutes, imitating in stylized movements the behavior of the particular animal. Despite its stocky and powerful body a warthog moves with remarkable agility, swirling up clouds of dust as it dances across the ground. A broad snout, big wartlike folds of skin under the eyes, canine teeth curving upward in upper and lower jaws mark out this dangerous animal. The tusks are obviously the dominant feature of this mask; they symbolize the blind, violent rage of a boar and its unpredictable, destructive nature. This mask is in every respect the opposite of the ideal of social behavior which urges restraint and consideration, the very qualities that constitute culture and civilization.

This antiworld is also embodied in the mask of a bush spirit. Though he looks more like the villagers than the animals, he is not a human being. His dancer cowers on his knees as he moves about. Due to their small build and moodiness, bush

spirits are very similar to small children. By nature still alien and savage, they must first be tamed before they can be integrated into society.

Thus all the masks represent different aspects of the bush, which can be dangerous for the villagers but from which they also profit in terms of food, raw materials, knowledge, and children.

Bush spirit, antelope, and warthog cower before the hunters, who point their rifles at them in this representation of a hunt in honor of the deceased.

Blood for the ancestral stools

Death marks a turning point, but it is only a part of a continual process. The deceased continue their lives as ancestors in the next world. In their new role of "chief elder" they are responsible for the well-being of their descendants.

Not every dead person gains entry into the ancestral world. As already mentioned, this happens only to those who have led a flawless life; that is, to those who have reached an old age and an elevated status, who had a wealth of goods, and can look back on numerous descendants. Death acts in a certain way as a measure of the correct lifestyle: those who die without a proper, honorable burial are damned to wander restlessly between worlds. These unsatisfied souls strive to avenge themselves on the living, causing them harm whenever and wherever they can. They are condemned to be forgotten and the community wants nothing more to do with them. The places where they dwell are carefully avoided.

The attitude toward the respectable dead is entirely different. Here the relationship remains a mutual one beyond the grave: the descendants provide their forefathers with everything they need in the kingdom of the dead. In return the dead bestow blessing, health, long life, happiness, success, and most importantly children.

Although the dead have left the world, they are still connected to it: so long as they are remembered, they are still alive, which means that they are still part of the group and maintain contact with it. They are usually remembered at daily mealtimes, and a small amount of food and drink is usually set aside for them. They receive the first portion of all food. When anyone is in trouble or has worries, they turn to the ancestors in the certain knowledge that they will help. The ancestors often appear in their descendants' dreams, giving advice, offering helpful hints, or warnings of danger.

The ancestors are generally thought of as benevolent, caring, and helpful. They play a lively part in the fates of their descendants, observing

The chief's power is not valid in the stool house. Those who enter the house first take off their shoes and arrange their dark-colored robe so that the right shoulder is bare, as a sign of humility. A simple, old robe is usually worn, since it would be poor manners to show any splendor in one's appearance before someone of higher status. Nana Obei reverently pours a liquid sacrifice over one of the stools.

happenings on earth so that they can intervene at any time to help, correct, or when necessary punish. They strive to uphold the social order in which they lived their own exemplary life. Violations of tradition or common custom are repugnant to them. They react to any such violations by withdrawing their protection from wrongdoers or, depending on the severity of the offense, by afflicting them with small misfortunes, illness, sterility, miscarriages, early death, poor harvests, cattle disease, or climatic disasters.

The ancestors play a fundamental role in the existence of the living, which is crucial for the survival and preservation of society. It is not surprising, therefore, that people make such an effort to maintain good relations with them and to give them no cause to be annoyed. The living inform their ancestors about minor incidents and trivial plans, as well as discovering their will through fortune-tellers and oracles.

In addition to larger or smaller daily signs of attention, prayers of supplication, and sacrificial offerings, ancestors are commemorated in a major way once a year, usually after the harvest has been brought in. At this "All Souls' Festival" villagers express their wishes for the coming year, thank the ancestors for their support and assistance, and ask for their blessing for the future. Animals are sacrificed so that the recipients may fortify themselves with the vital energy contained in the blood. The sacrifices take place on graves or on special altars that often take the form of clay cones.

In many societies people also dedicate extremely artistic objects to their ancestors. The souls of the dead enter these ancestral altars after prayers and sacrifices. The annual festivals constitute a constant act of remembrance, demonstrating the great respect and high esteem accorded to the dead. They end with the communal sacrificial meal, at which the living and the dead are united in a form of holy communion.

The village chief and his servant, who has completely bared his torso, are accompanied by an old woman. She is probably the sister or aunt of the chief. Old women are regarded as the best experts and guardians of family genealogy.

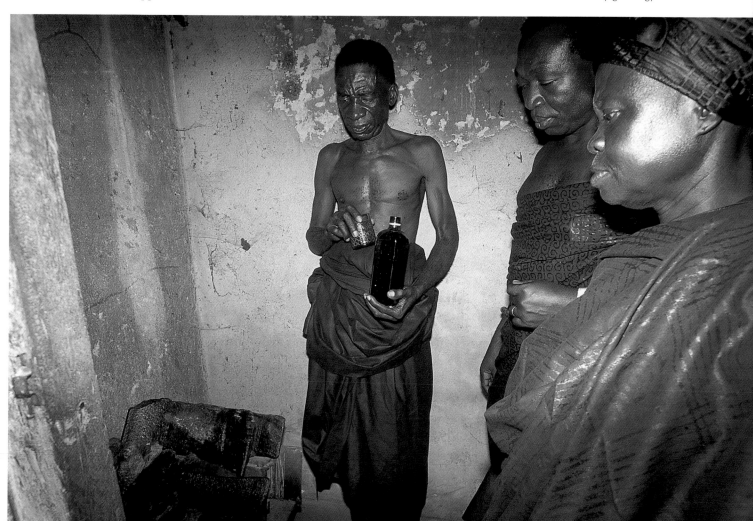

Asen – altars for the ancestors

KPO DOKPO MA HU ASS

In Abomey, the former capital of the kingdom of Dahomey, a member of the Lammadoucelo metalworking family opens the door of the house where the asen are kept. The asen are metal sculptures through which the relationship with the ancestors is maintained. The skulls and jawbones hanging over the door belonged to animals which were sacrificed to the ancestors.

"There are no secrets between a person and his stool" – the Asante and other Akan-speakers believe that something passes from an owner's being to his stool. A stool gives its owner everyday comfort and offers him the opportunity to rest. When it is not in use, the stool is put to one side so that the bad souls (sunsum bone) of people or other living beings who died a violent or bad death and who can find no rest do not take possession of it.

A stool accompanies an Asante from his entry into society until his death. It is the first gift from a father to his son, and is just as important in the puberty ceremonies of young girls and as the gift of a newly married husband to his wife. Dead bodies are washed over stools before being laid out. Since stools play a role at all the important rites of passage and critical life stages, their significance goes well beyond their use as an item of practical use. A person's attachment to his stool even lasts after death when the "white" stool of the living is "blackened" and thereby turned into an ancestral stool.

Such recognition is not given to everyone when they die, however. The honor is bestowed upon outstanding personalities: at the head are the king and the "queen mother," then princes and their co-regents, important clan elders, leading priests, and in earlier times important commanders. Since their stools are signs of authority and symbols of power, they are not only associated with individuals but with a whole family, cult community or, in the case of the king and princes, with their sacred office. As leaders they represent a larger community for whose well-being they use all their powers.

They can only bring about blessing, however, if they have led an exemplary life. Only those who produced offspring, were not relieved of their office, and died a good death are remembered. A premature or sudden death – with the exception of death on the battlefield – is regarded as being a dishonorable, bad death. The souls of these unfortunates have not earned the right to be immortalized in blackened chairs, which take on the importance of a family heirloom (agyapadie).

One of the duties of a newly appointed prince is to blacken the personal stool of his predecessor and to have it placed with the stools of previous incumbents in a dark, windowless room or building within the palace. He must look after them carefully and make sure that they receive regular food. In the stool house (nkonnwafieso) the stools stand on a wooden or clay bench under a heavy blanket or a handwoven coarse, woolen cloth (nsaa). In front of them stand earthenware pots which contain everything that it is believed the dead need in the next world. Years ago it was also the practice to put metal vessels containing gold dust or gold nuggets in front of the stools of important kings.

The blackened stools are stored in genealogical sequence. Some are held in higher regard than others, because they belonged to rulers who rendered outstanding services to their country and their people. Men's and women's stools are usually stored separately. If both are in the same room, women's stools (ahemmea) stand on the left, with those of princes on the right.

On the day chosen for the blackening ceremony all officials subordinate to the prince come to court. It is a sad occasion, for the ceremony brings the transience of life before everyone's eyes and reminds the prince especially of his own fate.

All the ancestral stools are carried out of the stool house to the open hall of the palace. The recently deceased's white stool is placed among them. The living relationship between a stool and its dead owner is often strengthened by putting a tuft of his hair or some fingernails or toenails in a hole in the central column of the stool. Many stools had brass clasps attached to them, in order to bind souls to the stools. Specially fitted bells served to call up the ancestors.

First the prince pours a sacrifice of palm wine over the stools and asks for the ancestors' blessing. He starts with the oldest stool and ends with the most recent. Then the first stool-bearer and his assistants break some raw eggs, which they mix in a calabash or clay pot with soot from the hearth and cobwebs from the kitchen. The spider appears in many folktales. As a trickster figure the spider (Anansi) outwits humans and animals. Its web therefore stands for the cleverness and wisdom of the ancestors. As an insect trap the web also symbolizes the far-reaching arm of the regent, who represents the power of the ancestors on earth. Eggs must be handled carefully so as not to break their thin shell, and they therefore symbolize the saying "Power is an egg," meaning that it must be treated with care. Since it has no bones, the egg also stands for peace and shows the conciliatory nature of the ancestors and their stools.

The collection of animal skulls and jawbones shows how many were sacrificed to the ancestors. This was done to pacify the ancestors and gain their protection.

Shoes are removed before entering the room with the sculptures. Men bare their torso, women their shoulders. The family elder calls the ancestors, sometimes with an offering of beer, spirits, or soft drinks. Then the elder directs the ceremony in which all the family's problems are presented to the ancestors. Young family members remain outside the door.

The stool is finally coated with the mixture of soot, eggs, and sometimes gunpowder, which blackens it. Black is a sign of power and time, standing for changes, for death and rebirth, and for the power of the ancestors and the empire; in other words, it stands for history, tradition, and remembrance.

Next a ram is killed. Its blood flows first over the stool to be dedicated, and then over all the other stools, giving them an even darker color. Until the beginning of the 20th century many stools were dedicated with the blood of an important male relative. The fat of the sacrificed ram is also smeared over the stool. Then the ancestors are asked for their blessing. After this the new stool belongs with all the old ones in the stool house.

The places where the ancestral stools are kept are sacred. Only certain people may enter the stool house. They are primarily people who serve the empire and the prince: stool-bearers, important house servants, and speakers. Europeans are not usually allowed entry, as well as people with physical disabilities, which used to include those

who had been circumcised. Menstruating women are also not allowed to enter the "pure" (konkron) stool house. Neither are warriors, especially the kurontihene, or leader of the advance guard. His presence in the stool house would remind the ancestors of previous battles and disturb their peace.

It is the duty of the prince to commemorate his forefathers on bad days (nnabone). The two most important days of each adaduanan (literally a 40-day cycle, but which can in fact last up to 42 or 43 days) are considered to be particularly bad. They fall on a Wednesday or a Sunday. On both days people concentrate on their inner thoughts and try to placate those who once held power with a commemorative ceremony (adae). The ancestors are offered food and drink, especially rum and spirits. Their names and deeds are remembered, as they are asked for help and privileges.

The ritual calendar ends with the ninth akwasidae, the adae kese (large adae), or odwira, the climax of the year. This was once a saturnalian festival which gave all who took part – the king, princes, village chiefs, subjects, ancestors, and deities – the opportunity to strengthen their ties with each other. It was, and still is, the time to remember past battles, as well as former fame and glory; reason enough to honor the dead with particularly extravagant offerings, and to bury all resentment and family disputes.

The conciliatory aspect of the ancestors remains to this day. In previous times they had other, less peaceful duties: they were often asked for active support in war. Their stools were taken out of their house before important battles, to stand by the warriors. If there was a threat of defeat, a final, desperate call for help was made. A taboo was broken in order to stir up the ancestors' anger: warriors stood on the stools to desecrate them.

The blackened stools are at the core of Ashanti ancestor worship. They are taken on processions, for kings and princes are not only greatly revered in life. Reverence survives death, because its power continues in the next world (asamando). With their stools descendants assure their ancestors of a place in the world. Ancestor worship primarily concerns the descendants, who otherwise would not be allowed to come into contact with death, for fear that they would lose their vital energy. No one dies in the palace; a prince would never visit a cemetery, except in extraordinary circumstances. Common ancestor worship at the graveside was made tolerable for the Ashanti elite by the reverence of stools. Coming into contact with the stools held no danger for the princes. In this way they retained control over the cult of ancestor worship, which represented considerable power in their hands.

The Fon worship their ancestors in their own special way. They commemorate their dead in asen, altars or metal sculptures (mostly made of iron) which dead spirits enter on certain occasions. Anchored in the ground by an iron rod, the asen "grows" upward: it widens to a plinth topped by a flat, round platform at the top. This is reminiscent of a calabash, and the Fon have a saying: "An asen is like a calabash, in which the dead are offered water and food." Old people still use the word sinnuká ("water calabash") when referring to an asen.

According to tradition, the asen came originally from Allada, where a people related to the Yoruba once held power. It is said that they went from there to Abomey, the capital of Dahomey.

For a long time the use of asen was monopolized by the monarchy. Royal patronage ended with the exile of the last ruler in 1900, and metalworkers had to look for new clients. In order to uphold royal prestige and to honor their forefathers properly, the eight district chiefs, who were all descendants of the former ruler, put in orders for asen. At about the same time asen with decorated platforms came into fashion with wealthy citizens, and this art form flourished at the beginning of the 20th century. A royal privilege was democratized, and today asen are widespread among all classes of society. Tin versions are affordable for almost everyone and are for sale in many markets.

There used to be a monopoly whereby only certain families were allowed to produce asen. This is no longer the case, and today they are made in metal workshops in various towns in southern Benin. Many of the products are true masterpieces. The artists sign them on the base (gó), or sometimes put their own unique stamp on the pendants hanging from the platform. This gives the artist a wide choice of designs. When an asen is made for a high-ranking person, the artist remains in the background and allows motifs reminiscent of the deceased to dominate. Today, many of the personal pendant designs have become so popular that they are no longer an indication of one particular metalworker.

Ogun (or Gu), the god of iron, watches over the production of asen. He is an energetic god who also incorporates the heat of the fire. Iron weapons also possess his strength, which gives them the power to wound or even to kill. Ogun's characteristics do not seem altogether compatible with the peaceful character of the ancestors. That is why iron must be cooled before a dead spirit can enter an asen, so that Ogun's heat has been removed. The client tries to placate Ogun by bringing various things to the workshop – gin, money, kola nuts, or malaguetta pepper. Once the craftsman has discovered Ogun's wishes by means of a kola-nut oracle, he puts three of the leaves that are sacred to the god into a calabash filled with water. He uses this to cool the asen, and at the same time he pacifies Ogun with gin and money. When this ceremony has been completed and Ogun is no longer in the metal, the asen is ready to receive the spirit of the deceased. At the climax of the memorial ceremony, the asen is erected and dedicated to the ancestor.

The history or special achievements of the deceased are represented on the platforms of the ancestral altars. Families turn to their ancestors on all important occasions. A newborn child is always presented to its forefathers. Marriages and seeds must also be blessed by the ancestors at large ceremonies with rich offerings. Between times the ancestors must also be looked after so that they do not get angry.

The dead have been taken away from the world, but they are not unreachable. The Fon's asen not only act as a worthy memorial to their dead, but also as a place to which their souls can return and participate in the life of the community. In this way the asen demonstrate the family's unity and closeness beyond the grave. They form tangible links between the living and the dead, and show how much they depend on each other. They remind the living of their duties toward their ancestors, acting as symbols of their devotion and personal monuments to the dead. Families often do not have the means to acknowledge all their dead in this way. Many ancestors are therefore remembered collectively.

The asen are erected within the context of a particularly extravagant ceremony. This requires a great deal of preparation and usually takes place a long time after the burial, sometimes after one or even several years. The bereaved are further required to remember the deceased in future, and he or she should receive offerings at least once a year. The ceremonies are reminiscent of the courtly occasions of precolonial times, but they vary in extravagance. While most are fairly modest, some ceremonies are veritable feasts. This can take up a great deal of the available resources and plunge families into debt. In principle every family member has a duty to contribute a share of the costs. Even so, many families cannot afford to honor their dead to the same degree every year. Many families choose to save up and then, perhaps every sixth or seventh year, have a truly magnificent ceremony.

In the meantime the dead are provided with essentials. After all, everyday life gives ample opportunity for needing to seek their help and advice. Their support is always sought in critical situations. Every newborn baby is presented to the ancestors, while marriages and wives' fertility are dependent on them. They are asked to bless seed before it is sown, and in return they receive the first fruits of every harvest. They are also asked for their protection and support regarding ventures with an uncertain outcome, such as an intended journey or imminent examinations, and they are promised gifts should the supplicant be successful. If there are signs that the ancestors are unhappy, such as illness, sudden deaths, or catastrophic harvests, attempts are made to placate them. If there is no rainfall for some time, water is sprinkled over the asen in a special ritual called ahanliba, in order to encourage the ancestors to use their influence with the god of the heavens to make rain.

The Fon honor their dead parents and relatives with the asen. Iron, steel, or brass portrayals of people, animals, and plants are placed on the platforms to commemorate the person for whom the asen was created. Wood carvings, fragments of bones and cloth, and even special items such as bottle tops and coins form additional decoration. All these individual elements combine to make the asen a complete work of art. In earlier times they were made only for influential personalities, but today the Fon honor their dead mothers and fathers with their asen.

The sculptures "speak" in rich, often subtle pictures, passing on messages in which various forms of the optical discourse are combined. As well as the deceased, the donor or donors of the asen are often represented. In addition, the sculptures demonstrate the central values of Fon culture, alluding to certain deities, sayings, songs, and plays on words. Each of these various elements can possess several meanings and lead to different interpretations. Without any explanation the symbolism of the asen is often difficult to understand, especially if sayings and plays on words are involved. The Fon themselves say that the sculptures' symbolism is often understood by only two people – the producer of the asen and the person who ordered it. Nevertheless, some general characteristics may be determined.

The round platform at the top of the asen is usually adorned with various figures made of iron, brass, or wood. They reproduce the honor of the dead and emphasize the unity of the extended family. If the deceased himself is a part of the ensemble, he takes up a central position on the platform. He can be recognized by the fact that he will be engaged in a typical activity, such as weaving. Another asen might show a particular religious connection, so that the deceased is shown as devoted to the storm god Hevioso and his cult. As a rule the deceased are presented on the asen as figures of authority, such as considerate family or village elders. Dressed as princes, they are raised to

The oldest women in the family offer the food and drink to the ancestors while they present their problems to them.

Only ancestors who have led an exemplary life are able to confer blessings later. For this reason only those who left behind offspring and died a good death are remembered.

the stature of rulers by the Fon, and on many asen the dead person is shown seated on a stool.

The donor is also often represented. He stands or kneels before the deceased, showing humility and great respect. At the same time many asen demonstrate the wealth and socio-economic status of the donor. Further clues are given by the clothing: the deceased wears his robe over the left shoulder, while the donor is stripped to the waist. Hairstyle is also important: shaved heads belong to the bereaved, while the deceased often wears a hat, which acts as a status symbol. The asen themselves are often reminiscent of large hats.

Numerous symbols are more difficult to interpret. A calabash with a lid often forms the central motif of many sculptures. This stands for the separate provinces of the living and the dead, which nevertheless touch and complement each other – like the two halves of a calabash. In addition to its profane function, the calabash possesses a symbolic meaning. It is used to offer water to visitors, people eat from it together, it is an essential ritual vessel, and the most important metaphor for the relationship between the living and the dead. Its symbolism goes even further: the calabash represents the universe, which is also made up of two halves and yet forms a whole. It is associated with the two creators Mawu-Lisa, who are also complementary to each other. The female Mawu principle incorporates fertility, rest, joy, the night, and the moon, while the male aspect of Lisa incorporates power, work, the day, and the sun. Thus the two halves of the calabash embrace the whole of human life, nature, and the cosmos.

The cross is often represented as a symbol of Mawu, which may possibly go back to Christian influences. Pictures of the sun, moon, chameleon – a sign of Lisa as well as of thoughtfulness and happiness – and the (rainbow) snake, which stands for wealth among other things, are also common. Representations of sacrificial animals show which of them accompanied the deceased to the next

The ancestors receive offerings of water, alcohol, blood, and food, especially beans, all served in small calabashes. Without being seen, they take in the spiritual essence of the gifts.

Asen are not only memorials to the dead. They are also places to which their souls can return and participate in the life of the community. In this way the asen demonstrate the unity and closeness of families beyond the grave.

world, and which were offered to him in his position as an ancestor. A cord woven into a Y-shape symbolizes continuity, and the open end means that it is the duty of the living to ensure the continuation of the family.

Plays on words usually refer to the person for whom the asen was produced. A man from Abomey, for example, decorated the metal sculpture for his mother with a fish and a grinding stone. In the language of the Fon the word for fish is hué, and for grinding or crushing it is li. Together they form the mother's family name, which was Huelinu.

Sayings and proverbs, on the other hand, usually express the relationship between the living and the dead. For example, an asen platform might show a dog standing expectantly before its master with something that it has caught in its mouth. The saying referred to is "A dog shows its prey to its owner first," which means that the living must share their wealth with the dead.

After the ancestors have received their offerings and heard their relatives' concerns, the oldest woman of the family sprays the asen with a mouthful of beer before leaving.

Twins, moody companions

Newly carved figures of twins who have recently died undergo a protective ceremony. The priest draws a protective circle around the figures.

African people considered their mythical primeval being to have been bisexual; heaven and earth were thus thought of as divine twins. Among the Yoruba, for example, the twins Obatala (heaven) and Ododua (earth) rank beneath the vaguely imagined supreme god Olorun (or Olodumare). According to popular belief the twins are likened to the two halves of a calabash, closely lying on top of each other. In primeval times a clear separation of shapes did not yet exist, with male and female components blending smoothly into one another. Twin beings therefore mark the beginning, at the same time embodying the peak of creation.

Another common belief is the idea of two fathers of twins, one earthly and the other spiritual, the younger twin having been fathered by the power of the spirits. He is often regarded as the first-born child. As the younger generally has to run errands for the older twin, he is thought to have been sent out first by his sibling, to check whether it is worth entering life at all.

There is also the belief that both children owe their life to the influences of evil spirits, and for that reason they were once killed at birth. In some places twins are still associated with bush spirits,

Twin births are not a rarity. If anything, they are quite frequent, yet such children are not regarded as normal: twins are considered to be a bisexual unity. The Bambara (Bamana) of Mali believe that Faro, the "master of the waters," gives twins to people. While Faro imparts to "normal" children the spiritual substances of relatives who have recently passed away, the soul, or "double" (dya), of twins never leaves the waters, but always remains with Faro and is for that reason free from danger and impurity. Each twin is the "double" of the other, and in so being form a kind of replica of Faro. Their birth is therefore a blessing and intended only for the privileged.

The Bambara and Dogon in Mali, the Luba-Lulua in southern Congo, and other

In the protective circle, the twin figures are also given offerings.

198

A follower of vodun (from the Mono region, Benin) with twin figures. Dead twins become small deities who have to be well cared for because they are known for their moodiness. These skillfully made dolls, images of the twins, have to be looked after by their relatives from now on. In exchange, they offer to protect their family.

A mother with her children and twin figures (from the Mono region, Benin). Twin dolls have to be cared for and taken everywhere, just like living children. The twins are not necessarily her own children; they might well be a grandfather's or an aunt's twin brother.

which also appear in pairs. Female bush spirits are said to give birth only to twins. That is why among the Mosi and Bisa twins are given the names of bush spirits: Kinkirsi or Kirgar.

Understandably, caution is advisable when dealing with twins or with bush spirits. Both are regarded as moody and capricious beings who demand one's whole attention and whose wishes have to be fulfilled immediately. Most importantly, twins have to be treated equally; for example, they should be given equal portions of food and identical clothing. After all, it needs very little to turn the children against their parents. If they feel neglected, twins will quickly leave this world again, which explains why one of the children and often both die soon after birth.

In the past the gender of the twins often determined their future fate. In Ashanti, according to a 17th-century report, only children of the same sex were raised. Alternatively, one was allowed to live, while the other was killed. Later, pairs of twins were presented at court and entrusted to the

A schoolboy (in Cotonou, Benin) carries the figure of his dead twin brother in his shirt pocket so that his brother can take part in everything. When the schoolboy has lunch, he puts the twin figure on the table and gives him something to eat too.

king. He took all boys into service as courtiers and all girls as his wives. That way it was felt that equal treatment appropriate to their origins had been secured.

If twins were born into the family of the Asantehene, however, this was terrible. They had to be killed immediately, because they constituted part of all that was hateful to the "golden stool." This was based on fear for the maintenance of the empire's unity: twins have identical rights to the throne and should therefore share power. But how could two rulers reign at the same time? Apart from the usual rivalries and squabbles about the throne, their survival might easily lead to a split in the empire.

The example of the Tenkodogo of the Mosi empire proves that this was not a purely hypothetical problem. There toward the end of the 19th century twin brothers caused civil war; many people lost their lives and the war brought great suffering to the population. In order to stop anything similar happening again, a powerful magic spell was supposed to have been buried; in the case of a twin birth, it would cause the immediate death of one of the children.

In other rather more democratic societies ruled by councils of elders, twins of the same sex were also often viewed with suspicion. If twins of different sexes are born to the Senoufu, the relationship is regarded as well balanced. If twins of the same sex are born, it is interpreted as a one-sided and dangerous dominance. Therefore, twin

births used to be seen as a great misfortune in many places. But, as mentioned above, the view that twins are regarded as more valuable because they are unusual is also common. As at least one twin has a spirit for a father, twins are seen to have been endowed with special gifts and are greeted at birth as a sign of great blessing, particularly involving raised fertility. They are considered to be a precious gift for the whole family, to whom they can give nothing but health, prosperity, and protection from sickness and death. Nevertheless, twins are able to use their supernatural powers for good as well as for evil and bring about happiness as well as unhappiness. Much depends on what happened in the family before the twins were born. To make sure, the Gulmanceba in Burkina Faso consult a fortune-teller, who is supposed to ascertain whether the children are good, or human, twins or bush spirits.

Because they weigh little at birth and thus more prone to illness, twins are usually shown off in public later than other children. If one of them dies before this happens, he is returned to his place of origin, which is usually the bush or the edge of a stretch of water. The twin who goes first returns to nature without ceremony or fuss: he is buried outside the village or, according to Mosi tradition, under a termite hill.

If both children should survive these critical early years, their mother takes them to market. It is believed that by now their soul is sufficiently strongly linked to the body that it will not escape at the slightest irritation. The walk to market, which is always brimming with strangers, is a sort of test to find out whether the children will stay or after a fleeting visit want to turn round and go back.

Everybody they meet on this day gives them presents; this is an effort to entice them to stay by showing a high regard for them.

If twins are to be of any benefit, they must be housed and looked after particularly well. They must be given the best food, drink, and clothes. One tries to spoil them in every possibly way, in order for them to display their abilities for the benefit of the family, rather than making them feel so neglected that they might do harm.

Among some groups, such as the Yoruba in Nigeria, the Ewe in Togo, and the Fon in Benin, a real twin cult has sprung up. Twins are regarded as the chosen ones of the spirit powers. Their amazing closeness, which is believed to survive even death, is stressed. The Yoruba believe that twins have a joint soul. If one dies, the other twin is also threatened with death. Their soul has lost its equilibrium and sways between this world and the next. The dead twin determinedly tries to pull the survivor over to him as soon as possible.

That has to be opposed. Not only do the parents put more effort then ever into the surviving child, they also try to keep the dead one in their midst. If a twin dies before he is seven, the Yoruba commission a carver to make a small ten-inch figure, a so-called ere ibeji ("copy of the twin"). This figure then replaces the dead child. A babalawo ("father of secrets"), a priest of the oracle deity Orunmila, arranges for the twin's soul to enter the ibeji. The figure makes sure that the twins do not remain apart and serves as an earthly home or holder of the soul, which continues to exist in the ibeji. On special occasions, especially at festivals, mothers cradle their "child" in their arms and dance with it as if it were still alive. At other times they cherish, look after, feed, and dress the "child." From a certain age the surviving child takes on the care of his dead twin. Should both children die and there is no separation of the twin soul, the mother has figures carved for both children. She takes care of the ibeji as if they

201

were alive. They are placed on the altar of the family deity (*orisha*), where great respect is paid to them, and they are included in the cult of the gods.

The custom of making a sacred home for twin souls while they are still alive is common in West Africa. Among the Ashanti and the Fon earthenware pots with two interconnected divisions are most commonly used. If the children are of the same sex, the openings point in the same direction; if they are a boy and a girl, the openings point in opposite directions. The Mosi and Bisa build small mud houses (*kinkirs-roogo*), with two rooms for their twins. Here families come for advice when they have problems, offer sacrifices at different festivals, and ask the twins for their blessing. Although they do not rank in status above the ancestors, they in a sense precede them. Their goodwill ensures the fertility of fields and people, and guarantees the continuation of the community.

The Ga also welcome a twin birth as a very happy event. The twins' mother considers herself much envied and from then on must never show any signs of grief. Like the priests and priestesses of various deities, she puts on white clothes – a sign of new birth and spiritual purity – which is also the reason for dressing the twins in white. Twins have

everything in common. They share their presents and react, so it is believed, in identical fashion. A neglected twin falls ill and will only respond to a cure when he has become reconciled and been satisfied. Once they are adults, twins are almost encouraged to marry two brothers or sisters, which is quite unusual. This deviation from the norm seems legitimate, because twins are of superhuman origin and sibling marriages are common among the gods. People once believed that twins were animated by the spirit of a bush cow (*wuo*), which is regarded not only as unpredictable but also as particularly "wild." Today they are associated more with certain nature deities.

When the twins are a week old a name-giving ceremony takes place, at which each child is given a small earthenware pot. Both containers, filled with herbs, rum diluted with water, cowry shells, and money, are buried side by side on a mud platform outside the mother's hut. Afterwards the blood of sacrificed hens is poured over them. At the same time fibers of the nyanya plant are wound round the children's wrists and ankles to "tie" their soul and strengthen it. A wooden bowl containing water, rum, the leaves of various plants, and the point of an iron ax is carried into the middle of the courtyard. Around it kneel the children's parents, as well as all those present who are either twins themselves or parents of twins. One after another they take a mouthful of the liquid and then spit it out again. Finally they wash and clean their own and their children's faces with it.

Among the Ga, as in many West African societies, the names that the twins are given have already been decided on at birth. Girls are called Akwele and Akuokor, boys Oko and Akwele. If it is a boy and a girl, the boy is named Oko and the girl Akwele. With that the names of any children born later have also been fixed. The next one will be called Tawiah; if it is a boy the suffix nuu will be added, and if a girl yoo. Tawiah is followed by Ago, Abam-Kofi, and then Nyankoma-Ago, which means that for the Ga a twin birth affects many other children.

Once the twins are a few months old, the parents may feel justified in hoping that they really want to "stay." Then their earthenware pots – which, like them, remain fragile – are exchanged for a pair of horns, supposedly from a wild bush cow. These are placed on a white cotton cloth. They

If an animal is sacrificed at a ceremony, twin pots (the twin figures' dishes) are placed close by so that some of the sacrificial blood reaches them.

An altar for twin figures (Mono region, Benin). The earthenware pots are filled with sacrificial blood in front of the twin figures.

are from then on the twins' most valuable possession. A twin who feels that he has been hurt by somebody can kill him by picking up the horns, beating them against each other, and calling out the name of the offender. If a twin dies in the village or its environs, everyone who hears about it falls under the spell of the spirit of the bush cow. The possessed run about wildly, roar, butt, and lash out all around them. After a few hours of going berserk, they are finally overcome by total exhaustion.

At least, this is how it used to be. As the Ga are not a homogenous community and as coastal inhabitants were subject to very different influences, small local variations always existed. Not least among the influences was the spread of Christianity, which contributed to the decline of "heathen" customs.

Today it is very rare for twins to be bathed in plant water, or for clay and fragrant herb paste to be rubbed into them before they are presented in public. But where certain customs are still upheld, the head of the family sacrifices a cock, which is eaten with mashed yams as a communal meal. After the meal and before washing their hands, everyone touches the children's bodies with the hand they ate with. Afterward the twins are washed in the rich broth with pieces of yam and specks of fat floating in it. The father has reserved cattle horns for each child, into which their soul now enters. The horns become an altar where prayers are said and help is sought. The spirit of the twins has the power to fend off disaster. It can bring unhappiness, ruin, and even death to the jealous and malevolent.

The veneration of twins is common practice as part of the homowo celebration at the beginning of the traditional new year, when there is a twin festival. The Ga in the greater Accra area (Ga-mashi) cleanse their twins on the Friday before the festivities. The pairs of horns are brought out of the house for that purpose and placed on a white cotton cloth for public display. Coins are arranged all around, and in the old days nyanya leaves were also used. A special sacred meal of mashed yams with red-palm oil is prepared. Boiled eggs are added to the golden-colored dish, which is then poured into a small calabash. The twins themselves, if they are old enough, pour it over the horns along with rum. The next morning the head of the family kills a goat and washes the horns in its blood, to give them more strength for the following year. In the past they were often also painted with red and white stripes as a sign of the conflicting nature which could bring both danger and blessing.

The twins also have to be cleaned of the "dirt" which has accumulated on them within a year. On the morning of the celebration, parents and twins rise early to collect certain plants, which are then soaked in water, and sacrificial blood; these are used to wash the twins' bodies and most importantly their faces. Now much "cleaner," they and especially their faces are painted with white chalk. Dressed also in white and thus visible to the whole world, they enter the new year in a state of purity. The water with the previous year's dirt, however,

On the day before the homowo festival (a major event lasting several weeks), a general purification ceremony takes place in Jamestown. Every family with twins sets up a form of altar on a table. The two horns containing the twins' powers, or "souls," are placed on the table. The horns receive coins, eggs, and other food as offerings.

has to be removed from the village before sunset. To achieve this, a procession moves to the twin's assumed place of origin. It is a specific place in the bush, usually on the shore around a certain lagoon or a place at the river. When the procession reaches the spot, the water is poured out. Finally, a priestess makes a liquid offering.

The twin festival was once closely linked to the yam cult. This is why it is celebrated most in bush villages further away from the coast, where the yam is a staple food. Here the celebration becomes a general ritual of thanksgiving. Everybody who possesses an effective "medicine" which promises success when hunting, fishing, or trading and protects them from witchcraft expresses their gratitude. Everybody who believes that they are in some way blessed celebrates in his or her own way on twin day, yeleyeli; they offer thanks for the help given and ask for the same favor to be bestowed on their family and the village community in the coming year.

The twins are washed with water that has been mixed with sacrificial blood and various plants.

On their own special day the twins are painted with white chalk, a symbol of purity and rebirth.

Painted white and dressed in white, the twins walk through the streets of Jamestown.

Mothers carry heavy enamel bowls filled with the twins' bath water on their heads to the site of ancestor worship.

The bath water contains all the disasters that have been washed off the twins.

During the ceremony the forces of disaster may enter the mothers carrying the water, and they then go into a trance.

A mother almost falls to the ground in a trance. Two young men rush to help her and hold her up.

The healers –
body, mind, and soul

According to an old universal belief that persists in many rural parts of the world, there is a compelling link between illness and bad behavior – namely, that a sense of responsibility, or the soul, is involved. In modern parlance this would be referred to as psychosomatic illness.

According to the traditional view, a human being is made up of a body, a mind, and a soul. The first two form a close functional association, which comes into existence immediately upon procreation: as mentioned in the chapter on family, relatives, and community (pages 10–19), the fetus is formed immediately after conception from "stanched" menstrual blood and the father's sperm, a high condensate of vital energy. The vital soul, or mind, gives the body its ability to move and controls its organic functional ability. It is therefore especially concentrated in everything that moves and, as a result, develops warmth: constantly circulating blood, the organs which are rich in blood (the heart, liver, and kidneys), as well as breath, feet, hands, and sexual organs. Since intense emotions and physical movement cause excretion, sweat, sperm, tears, loving or hate-filled looks and words, and spit (caused by chewing) are all thought to be filled with vital energy. All the things which are more resistant, such as nails and hair (which also grow throughout life and therefore show movement), and especially teeth and bones, are thought to have a great deal of vital energy. All these substances and parts of the body are often used in magic.

It is the soul, which is independent of the body, that gives the human being life in the true sense, since it bestows consciousness, imagination, and willpower. This happens after the third month of pregnancy, when the fetus first starts to move: from then on the ability to move receives specific impulses. The soul represents the spiritual element in man; it usually has to do with an ancestor who wants to be reincarnated. Since it is independent of the body and the mind, their relationship is never complete. In situations of weakness, when the organism is deactivated or at rest, as during sleep, the soul can easily slip out of its physical "container." In the former case, the person is then in mortal danger; in the latter, he dreams, perceiving whatever the soul sees and experiences during its nocturnal wanderings. There is always a certain risk in this.

A person is healthy if his body, mind, and soul are closely connected, as is usually the case with adults in their prime when they have no worries and can go calmly about their business. This is rarely the situation, though. Discord is usually caused by differences of opinion, careless mistakes, or violations of duty or rules. These stir up people's feelings and lead to indisposition. But that is not all. Since everyone is dependent on others, it harms the equilibrium of the community when an individual is disturbed. This leads to the view that an illness affects those who are close to that particular person. The well-being of the individual is connected to that of everyone else. People can be healthy only if everyone is healthy, which is why people such as the Lele in the Democratic Republic of the Congo (formerly Zaire) believe that there is a close mutual relationship between the individual and the condition of the village. It is only when there are harmonious, undisturbed relationships between everyone and when the whole society is intact that there is a prospect of health.

Illnesses and accidents are caused primarily by personal or collective guilt. If someone has lied, cheated, or stolen, committed incest or adultery, or has had relations with a minor, or even neglected to make a sacrifice to his ancestors or the gods, those on the other side take action against the guilty party in order to uphold the threatened order. They strike sinners with illness, infertility, or some other misfortune. If they take less severe measures, perhaps simply issuing a warning, this nevertheless weakens the victim. Their "bad conscience" makes them more sensitive and liable to harmful influences from their surroundings. This explains why some but not all endangered individuals fall victim to infectious disease. The South African ethnologist, Monica Wilson, discussed this question with a primary-school teacher in Pondo (Transkei), and was told: "I know that typhus is transmitted by lice, but who sent the particular infected louse, and why did it bite A and not his brother B?" It is the same with malaria. When illness strikes the family of a farmstead, it surely must have been sent by someone for some reason.

Illness generally comes about in one of three ways: through damage to the body, mind, or soul. In the first two cases the problems affect both because of the close functional connection between body and mind: an injury leads to blood loss, which then weakens physical performance. The following are the most likely causes of illness or an accident.
– Contamination, caused by looking at, touching, or consuming things, substances, or persons with whom the affected person

A Lobi fortune-teller in his hut with fetishes and sacrificed animals.

should not have had any contact; this includes imported goods and foodstuffs, as well as strangers.

– "Natural causes," according to Western medicine; for example, a wrong diet, an attack of worms, breathing polluted, toxic air, as well as genetic disorders.

– The uneasy feelings of others, such as resentment, envy, and hatred, which often lead to open disputes, "make the village ill," and have a hidden effect on willpower. An observer expressed the views of the Central African Bantu groups thus: "Ill will is the same as an evil deed. It has an effect in the same way as the sun's warming rays or the poisons of plants and animals." According to the Lobedu of the Transvaal, a mother who is so displeased with her daughter that she leaves the house risks ruining her fertility.

– Evil looks and words. The latter make uneasy feelings audible, while the former bore into their target and can cause illness, impotence, infertility, and even death.

– Damaging sorcery and witchcraft, either using various magic practices or an innate gift, as described above.

– Influence by spirits. This can cause serious psychological problems. An evil spirit might enter a person and take possession of his soul, perhaps at night when it is outside the body, then mislead it, hold it captive, and torment it in one way or another; this can lead to fainting fits, hallucinations, short-term madness, severe psychoses, or even death. In West Africa (according to the Kusasi of Ghana, for example), if large trees (or tree spirits) are harmed, they avenge themselves by inflicting skin diseases or joint complaints.

– Punishment by the powers of the other world; ancestors and deities take action against the crimes of sinners.

The cause can usually be recognized by the nature of the problem, but in more complex, disputed cases a more precise diagnosis can be made by experienced old men and women, healers, and priests, who might analyze dreams or refer to oracles. The Lugbara of Uganda explained to the English ethnologist John Middleton: "While Europeans visit doctors in their hospitals, we seek advice from our oracles to obtain information about the cause, nature, and treatment of illness."

Therapeutic measures depend on the findings. In less serious cases herbal remedies are usually used. Contamination must be removed by washing, smoking out, self-chastisement, or vomiting; social discord is improved by public confession; damages are put right by restoration rituals; sins must be atoned for. Touching, rubbing in, or consuming mineral, herbal or organic substances help to renew strength and effect a cure.

In order to be successful it is essential that traditional healing methods be undertaken in the presence and with the active participation of the next of kin, and in some cases the whole group. Among the Kaguru of Tanzania, the parents of newly circumcised boys take care to do nothing which might impair the healing process. They follow the normal rules of behavior even more strictly than usual and especially avoid arguments or marital infidelity, in order not to weaken the family sense of togetherness. A person who commits adultery while his or her spouse is seriously ill puts their own lives in jeopardy. The spiritual is always part of the social relationship.

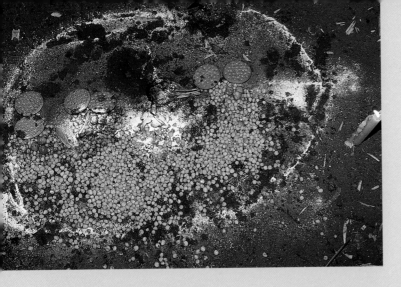

Left: A protective circle of food offerings for a sick child.

Health problems were always of great concern to the "primitive races." Many ethnologists refer to this as an obsessive hypochondria. In the 1940s South African ethnologists Eileen and John Krige wrote about the Lobedu: "Every sign of a problem, every change in life is treated as if it were a serious threat. Any European would be amazed at the number of remedies which are tried out, rejected, or changed when someone thinks h ill." One could take the view that the wish shown by traditional r societies to preserve the accepted order is actually a concern to uph and, if necessary, restore the health of the individual as well as tha the whole community.

Below: Screened by a wickerwork fence, preparations are made for a protective ceremony for the young man wearing the blue loincloth.

Far left: To protect the young man gunpowder is lit next to a pot of herbal water.

Left: For the protection to be effective, the young man has to stand over the smoking gunpowder.

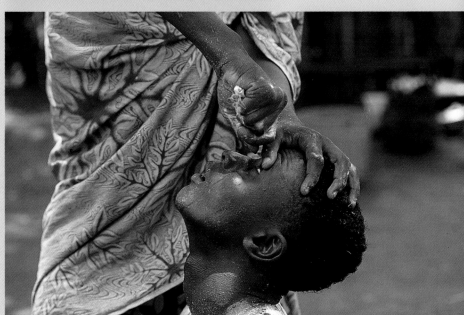

Left: The young man washes thoroughly in order to purify himself.

Above: The eyes are washed out with a herbal extract. This extract acts as a protection in that it enables the young man to see better and so recognize danger.

Healing rituals of gods and spirits

A young woman is dogged by misfortune. Childless, disowned by her husband, and penniless, she pins all her hopes on divine help. She is ritually cleansed and wrapped in white cloth in a vodun convent. The two white doves and the chicken that she is holding have been chosen as sacrificial animals.

A procession leads her to the entrance gate, where the priest cuts the chicken's throat. This will tell him what is in store for the young woman. If the chicken ends up on its back, she will remain unlucky. If it falls onto its breast, she may hope for better times. Only a sideways position means release from misfortune.

Where religion and medicine are but different aspects of one and the same thing – illness being attributed to incorrect religious conduct and recovery generally seen as regaining salvation – the difference between the two is only very slight. That is why in many parts of Africa priests are also healers. This applies to representatives of the old earth and river deities as well as to the heads of later cultural communities, although existing differences do, of course, have an effect on methods of treatment. Differences are wide-ranging, focusing on prediction – usually in a possessed state – followed by healing rituals. Spirits and deities reveal the cause of the medium's suffering and give instructions on what to do.

Plants play an important part in all healing rituals. A therapist trained in the vodun tradition might know about 1,000 and use about 500 plants in everyday practice. Belief in their effectiveness (the placebo effect) is even more important than the plants' healing substances. As early as 1955 a number of studies proved what African healers had been taking advantage of: treatment with so-called sham medication showed, across all illnesses, a clear improvement of the symptoms in 35 percent of patients, and this was not based on subjective feelings. It has been proved that measurable aspects – such as blood pressure and hormone levels, for example – can be influenced by placebos. If one believes in the soothing effect of a medicament or ritual, relief can be obtained by stimulating the production of the body's own "opiates," endorphins which have an analgesic effect.

In addition, successful treatment depends very much on the healer's personality. The more confident and determined his manner, the more incontestable his authority and the more certain his chances of success. Priest healers treat their patients according to holistic therapy concepts. They take the patient's special environment and circumstances into account and from it draw conclusions about the person and his illness. In the course of lengthy ceremonies they familiarize themselves with his case history and his life. If there is disruption in the patient's

The priestess Delassi leads the unfortunate woman with the sacrificial animals to the place of sacrifice. Priest healers use the principles of holistic therapy. Both the patient's environment and circumstances are taken into account. By looking beyond a single examination of the illness or misfortune, a picture of the whole person can be formed.

The young woman is led across a skillfully executed drawing on the ground. On her way she tears a thread as a sign that she has broken with the past and that her path will lead toward a better future. The drawing shows the change which will take place in her life.

After being cured, the priest welcomes her with drumbeats.

relationship with a deity or spiritual force, with the family or neighbors, his relatives will be included in the healing process. They either take part themselves or are indirectly involved by being forbidden to eat certain foods or come into contact with the sick person.

Initiation rituals are often involved at the same time. If the illness is an unmistakable sign of a calling, the patient can only be cured if he joins the appropriate culture community and so becomes a medium. Admission rituals alone are said to have great therapeutic effect. Although initiation into one of the numerous cults is a long and costly procedure, it is the only hope of a cure in some cases.

In less serious cases, such as when someone's well-being has been impaired by a poor lifestyle, a competently administered cleansing ritual is enough to put things right. In larger towns, where so much depends on one's professional success, many people turn to priest healers to insure themselves against misfortune and failure, or to be freed of worry. Usually this involves ritual treatment with holy water and healing plants as well as sacrificial offerings to one of the many deities

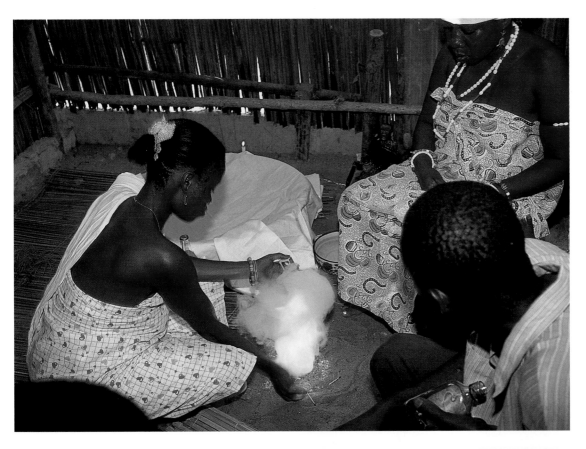

under whose special protection the person concerned then comes.

In Benin one of the best-known priestess healers is Wekenon, the "mother of the universe," because she does not serve only one god or even a number of them, but all gods. Before practicing on her own, she spent eight years in a vodun convent in Lakossa. Since then she has incorporated various worlds within herself. She is a typical phenomenon of modern life.

Special treatment is required for mental illnesses, which are often attributed to confusing encounters with spirits. The Bambara of Mali wash people with such disabilities with kuhurin (cleaning) and beat them on the back (exorcism) with the young twigs of a particular tree (Caltropis procera) that grows in the bush. Another effective cleansing lotion is made from the bark of sacred trees that guard the villages as protective deities. Generally, admission into one of the many initiation cults is regarded as more reliable.

Priests frequently use drugs: in Africa hundreds of alkaloid-containing species with toxic, hallucinogenic, and anesthetizing qualities are

After the necessary preparations Wekenon spreads out a white cloth on the ground on which offerings are placed.

213

Sacrificial food for the water goddess Mami Wata. Objects such as a comb and powder are among the sacrificial offerings, which will please the goddess since she particularly loves all beautiful things. The market woman eats a little of the offering, so that she is dining with the goddess.

The offerings are wrapped in a white cloth and together with a white dove everything is entrusted to the sea.

known. Depending on the clinical problem, priests prescribe stimulating, sedative, or hallucinogenic drugs. This therapy does not seem to be very successful in the long term, though, as shown by the number of psychologically disturbed people to be seen all over Africa. In the big cities, before conferences and especially when visitors from abroad are expected, they are routinely rounded up by the police and the army and taken away into the country. However, a few days later they are back in town. Obviously African healers, too, have their problems with psychotic illnesses.

The sacrificial bundle with the white dove is thrown into the sea. In this way all misfortune is washed away. Then Wekenon and her helpers prepare a herbal bath from plants and sea water.

For the cleansing bath, water infused with herbs and condensed milk are poured over the market women.

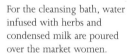

The women's eyes are washed out with herbs, so that in future they will be able to see things more clearly and recognize their enemies better. The cost of this ceremony is very high.

Leaves, roots, and ritual dying

Plants are chopped up and dried.

Right: A mixture of different parts of plants are burned and then administered in the form of powder.

Far right: Preparation of an ointment for the treatment of skin diseases.

All plants can be used for medical purposes if one knows how. Some, of course, are more powerful than others. Even one and the same plant can be more concentrated in certain parts than in others – especially in the roots, bark, and leaves. You can often tell just by looking at a plant. The roots and leaves exude a special fragrance, or the wood of a tree might prove to be very hard and tough. Generally speaking, many parts of woody plants

have healing properties, but leaves, fruit, seeds, and the skin of roots and the bark of trunks are mainly used. Every part of herbaceous plants, or sometimes only the green parts, are used.

Traditional medicine mostly works on the similia-similibus principle, according to which like is treated with like. In Burkina Faso jaundice is thus treated with the yellow roots of Cochlospermum tinctorium and Cochlospermum planchonii, as well as other yellow, flowering plants; bindweed (for example, Cuscuta sp.) is used as a remedy for tapeworm.

The way a medicine is prepared depends on the type of illness that is being treated and the specific part of the plant that is being used. Soft substances are crushed or mashed so that their juice can be applied to the affected area of the body. This treatment is particularly suitable for wounds, abscesses, and skin infections. When purified, the liquid is also used for eye infections. Decoctions and other liquid medicines are most frequently used. For internal diseases the medicine is often drunk, and for external complaints it is put on the skin. Often two or more plants are cooked in water and the stock used as a drink and an ointment, as well as for washing, enemas, mouth rinses, and vaginal douches. In African healing practices great significance is attached to food: often the method of preparation is the only thing that makes a dish different from a medicine. Millet gruel, rice, or

216

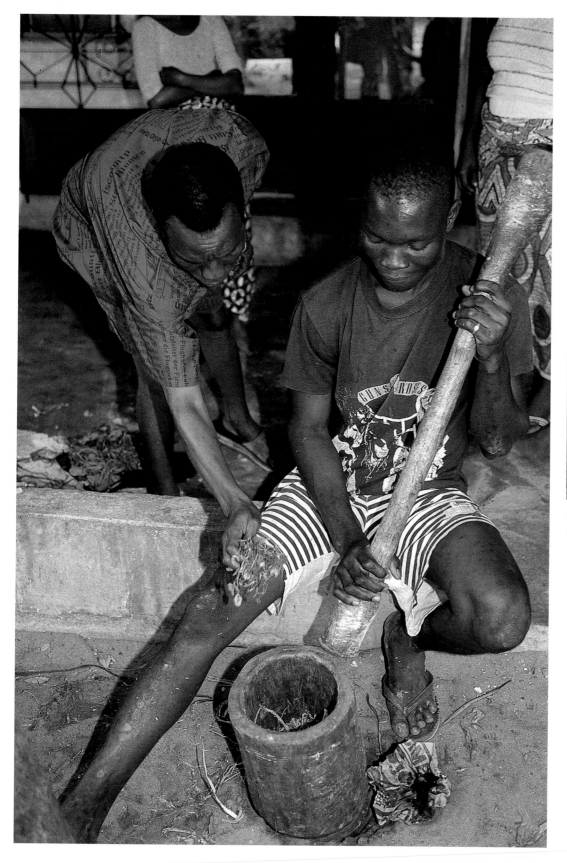

Here the plants are pounded in a mortar.

The plant powder is sieved until it is as fine as dust.

217

A witch has cursed a young woman, who is now in mortal danger. The ceremony at which the curse is to be lifted is very secret. Before it starts, an oracle is consulted as to who is in danger of becoming cursed during the exorcism. The priest himself is in danger of becoming a victim of the curse. The priest's son is chosen to carry out the ritual. During the ceremony all the villagers shut themselves in their huts for fear of being seized by the curse of death. As the ceremony begins, the outline of a grave is drawn on the ground.

meat broth, for example, are cooked with sap rather than water, and are then eaten.

Another form of preparation is the cold extract (or maceration). To make this, roots, bark, fruit, or leaves are soaked in water for some time. The liquid is then drunk or rubbed in, or often given as an enema. Calabashes and wooden pipes are used for enemas. With small children the mother usually uses her mouth to blow the medicine into the child's anus. In many places newborn babies and infants undergo such "washings" daily. They clean both externally and internally and are supposed to help evacuate the bowels and prevent stomachache, indigestion, diarrhea, and other common childhood illnesses. It is also believed that they give strength and aid growth. Babies are fed with the decoction of various plants, as well as being washed in it and given an enema of it. Older children are given this treatment only occasionally, mainly for stomachache or diarrhea. Orthodox medicine does not

recommend it, since the decoction contains strong substances which can harm babies' intestines and stop their bowels working naturally. But this warning has fallen on deaf ears among the rural population.

Externally, when for example treating wounds and rheumatism, plant ash is often used. The necessary plant parts are chopped up, roasted in an earthenware vessel and crushed in a mortar. The powder, which keeps very well, is either painted on directly or is made into an ointment by adding fat (shea butter, for example). As a kind of serum it can be introduced into the body by way of incisions, preferably at the points of inflammation and also the limbs. For skin infections the affected parts are rubbed with the leaves. Plant sap, especially latex, is used for the treatment of eyes and ears. For respiratory problems, confusion, and headaches, the smoke of burning plants is inhaled or the plants are smoked. Chewing certain types of bark helps to stop toothache and can stimulate the appetite.

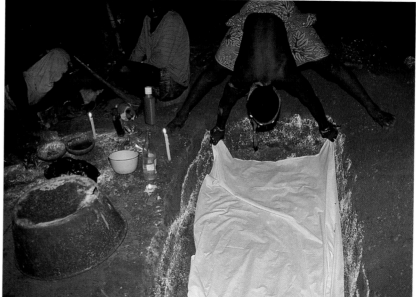

In order to pacify the earth for the disturbance caused, an offering of spirits is made.

All these possible applications are based on the belief that the prescribed medicine develops its healing power in or on the patient's body. In addition, patients try to free themselves from an illness by using magic and transferring the disease to a tree or an animal.

The Adja of the Mono region in Benin practice a healing ceremony which includes a rebirth ritual. This is often staged very dramatically; for example, a sick man or woman is buried alive and medicinal plants are put in his or her "grave."

In the case of a girl who was being hounded by witches, an oracle decided that another life had to be sacrificed for hers. This was the only way in which her life could be saved. The ritual is intended for an emergency case when someone is in mortal danger and everything has to be done to save that person from imminent death. It is about the most powerful defensive magic, feared even by the priests themselves. The oracle chose his 16-year old son to carry out the ritual.

Burials take place at night, because it is not good for people to come into contact with death. The "grave" is dug at midnight, the turning point between the two days when the girl's fate will be decided. Animals are used, and through them her life is extinguished and the witches' lust for blood satisfied.

Above right: The grave is lined with a white cloth.

Right: A wooden pole is cut to approximately the young woman's size. It represents the sick young woman or her "dead body". To turn it into flesh and blood, a ram is tied to it. The young woman touches it with her hand to make contact.

More animals are tied to the pole, one after the other: a goat, dog, chicken, guinea fowl, cat, and duck.

The young woman is "cooled" with the blood of the guinea fowl; this animal has a special status because it can be both wild and domesticated, and therefore ranks between nature and culture.

The guinea fowl is also tied to the pole.

A small black cat is added.

The pole and animals are put in the grave.

A sacrificial liquid is poured over the animals, and powder is scattered over them. Now everything has been prepared and the grave can be closed.

The grave is filled in.

The scared animals are covered with a white linen cloth. They try desperately to free themselves, making it look as if a human being was moving beneath the cloth.

Above the grave the "rising star" is drawn, as a symbol of new life beyond the grave. When the animals have perished, the young woman will rise from the dead to a new life and the curse will have been lifted.

The young woman snatched from the jaws of death pours powder in the sacrificial bowls.

The animals' grave with sacrificial gifts.

Spirit healers and orthodox medicine

The concept by which health is seen as a fundamental expression of an intact relationship with one's natural, social, and spiritual surroundings and by which illness and other problems are seen as a disruption of this relationship, can only work as long as the healer and the patient share the same view of the world.

Recent far-reaching changes have meant that there is a stark difference in attitude between urban and rural populations. Many towns have a hospital, and cities have specialist clinics; for most villagers, however, it is a long way to the nearest hospital. This means that they rarely have a choice between a modern clinic, on the one hand, and traditional

Just as the town is full of different types of people, Louis Aguidamo of Cotonou uses a wide variety of treatments and practices. He specializes in spirit healing. Here he summons the spirits to help a man who has been plagued by misfortune.

Louis Aguidamo has put up a cloth, which is printed with the sacred signs of the Fa oracle. Louis presses his forehead against the sacred signs in order to receive strength and inspiration.

Healer and patient both eat a plant powder which will release a protective power within their bodies.

Louis makes a sign of blessing on the young man's forehead.

healers, on the other. Even if there is a first-aid post in the vicinity, it is likely not to be equipped even with essentials, and the staff are often temporary workers. In regions with better facilities treatment is usually only undertaken in emergency cases; although medical consultations are free, in Burkina Faso for example, the patient must pay for every prescription, every vaccination, and every bandage. Most of the rural population cannot afford x-rays, anesthetics, or operations. This means that traditional medicine continues to be indispensable in most villages.

Traditional medicine still has its place in towns. Town-dwellers certainly visit trained doctors more often, but if their methods fail, they still turn to traditional healers. To be on the safe side, many seek out both options. In any case, there are problems, such as enduring misfortune that, unlike African healers, Western medicine cannot treat. On the other hand, traditional methods cannot compete in biomedicine. Many believe that the two systems therefore complement each other; the one or the other may be more effective, depending on the cause of the illness.

There are also enormous differences between traditional healers, and they do not all treat the same illnesses. Deciding on which of the specialized healers to visit depends on the particular complaint. Usually only bonesetters and midwives treat people without using magic remedies. The latter are mostly old women who have passed the menopause. In order to combat high child mortality rates, special emphasis has been placed on training midwives according to Western methods in many parts of Africa.

Medicinal plants are used for everyday complaints, as they have been in African society for a very long time. Many of the so-called household remedies for common complaints such as headache and stomachache are known to most people. People know where the relevant plants are to be found, how to prepare the remedy, and the appropriate dosage. Even old women, who are normally responsible for this kind of treatment, usually have no need for magic. They collect their remedies in the bush or buy them at the market. If an illness does not respond to treatment, a more serious cause is considered and a specialist sought, who may be able to determine whether the problem has been brought on by witchcraft, magic, or a curse.

Louis keeps a number of animal skulls in a large calabash. They represent Lisa, the male part of the vodun deity Mawu-Lisa.

Sakpata the smallpox god heals the sick

This woman is possessed by Age, the god of hunting and medicinal herbs. She puts her hands on the bleeding neck of the goat in order to feel which healing ritual is indicated for a sick child.

Age bestows unknown strength on his medium: the woman swings the animal's carcass around quite easily. At the same time she calls for the gods' support.

Mediums play an important part in the cult of earth deities such as Shoponna, among the Yoruba, and Sakpata among the Fon, who are called smallpox gods. A large number of illnesses, including smallpox (or variola) and psychoses, are ascribed to clashes with these gods. The British colonial administration in Nigeria banned the practice of the cult, as it was believed that it might cause the disease to spread; it certainly appears that some cult followers were voluntarily being vaccinated with the living virus. The cult continued in secret, however, even after the ban.

The Alladahonu rulers of the kingdom of Dahomey thought little of the cult of Sakpata. Sakpata rules over the earth and makes it fertile, while Hevioso governs fire and water; both work together for people's well-being. In the Yoruba territory, Hevioso (under the name of Shango) was regarded as being closely connected to the royal dynasty of Oyo. In Dahomey, however, Sakpata claimed all power for himself, and his relationship with the ruling dynasty was therefore hostile, especially since he imposed the death penalty, which was the inviolable privilege of the king. Like the Alladahonu rulers, he also claimed the corpse of the person whom he had killed through smallpox. This meant that Sakpata was placing the kings' dynastic legitimacy in doubt, and so they regarded him and his followers as rivals for power. During the reign of King Agaja (1708–32) the ritual authority of the "lords of the earth," that is, members of lineages which had been the first to take land into ownership and had formed a sacred alliance, presented a serious threat to the rulers. They tried to win the old owners of the land to their side by making one of them their fictitious ancestor and granting them various honors, but opposition remained until the reign of Tegbesu (c. 1740–74).

The earth gods endangered the unity of the kingdom, since they gave off "heat" and destructive energy, so their shrines were moved from the towns

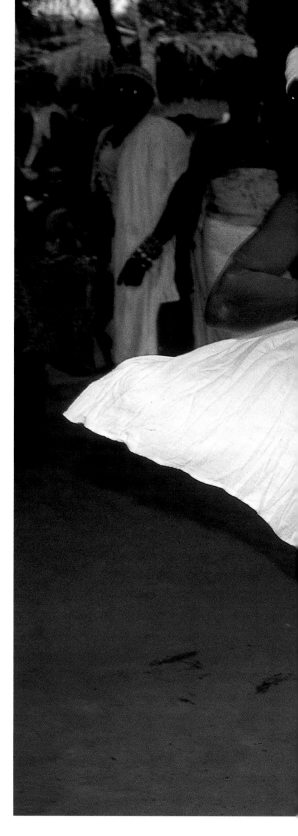

In a trance, the woman goes to the sick child and announces the will of her god to the priest. The child's parents have failed, and so the god's help is urgently needed. If the parents had been more conscientious, their love would have surrounded the child like a magic wall of protection and the witches would not have been able to touch him. Finally, the child's grandmother entrusted him to the care of Age.

into the country or bush, where they could be better controlled and reconciled. Dancing and drumming, mainly a feature of funeral ceremonies, were banned when Sakpata came to town and smallpox was rampant. His priests also had to stay away from public demonstrations of the god's ruling power. The conquering dynasties probably feared the native earth gods, and they certainly feared Sakpata. Of all the scourges inflicted on mankind, smallpox was considered the worst. In fact, it was probably brought to present-day Benin in the second half of the 18th century on slave ships. Even some of the kings of Dahomey are supposed to have fallen victim to the dread disease, though this should not be taken literally; it was probably a reference to the fact that their royal

power was under threat. More than one battle was lost because a smallpox epidemic decimated an army. The kings therefore hated the earth gods for two reasons: firstly, the gods disputed their rule and undermined their legitimacy (hence the saying "A town cannot have two kings"); and secondly, they threatened their lives and their political aims.

On the one hand, Sakpata threatens people with smallpox in order to gain the respect that is due to him; on the other hand, he gives people everything they need to live, above all millet. Anyone who scorns him, however, has the corn taken "out of his skin," resulting in the notorious red spots, blisters, and pustules.

People suffering from smallpox would be strictly isolated. The Adja would take them out into

Far left: The sick child is covered with white spots, the sign of Sakpata, in order that he be dedicated to the god and have his sickness taken away.

Left: The priest holds his hands over the child as if blessing him; this gesture shows that from now on the boy will be under the god's protection.

Left: During the ritual the boy's grandmother falls into a "short death," in which she sees what would happen to the child were he not cured.

Above: Having been brought into the healing ritual in this way, the grandmother wakes from her short period of derangement.

Right: The grandmother is brought before the god of war, who will protect her. The priest says protective words over her.

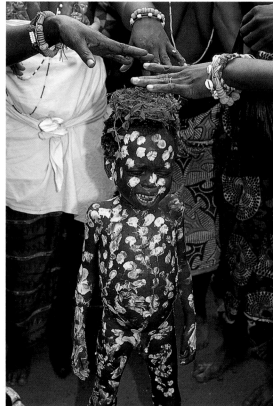

Far right: The child receives the blessing of the community.

Right: The child's head has been covered with herbs. He sits on a healing pot, while a white chalk line is drawn on the ground to make a protective circle.

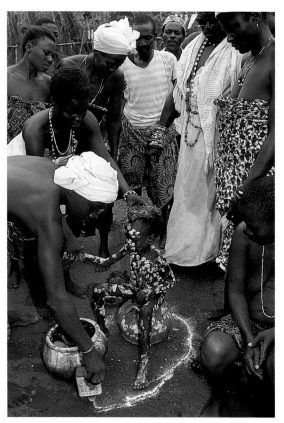

Far right: A cockerel's blood is poured over the child. Evil should drain away along with the cockerel's life.

Far left: The healing ritual is also a purification rite. The child is washed, to take all evil away from him.

Left: After the boy has been thoroughly cleaned, he is washed off with herbal water.

Far left: The boy has clearly not found the ritual pleasant, but it is almost over.

Left: Finally the boy has to cross several intertwining circles, meaning that he walks over his enemies and goes on his way to a cure.

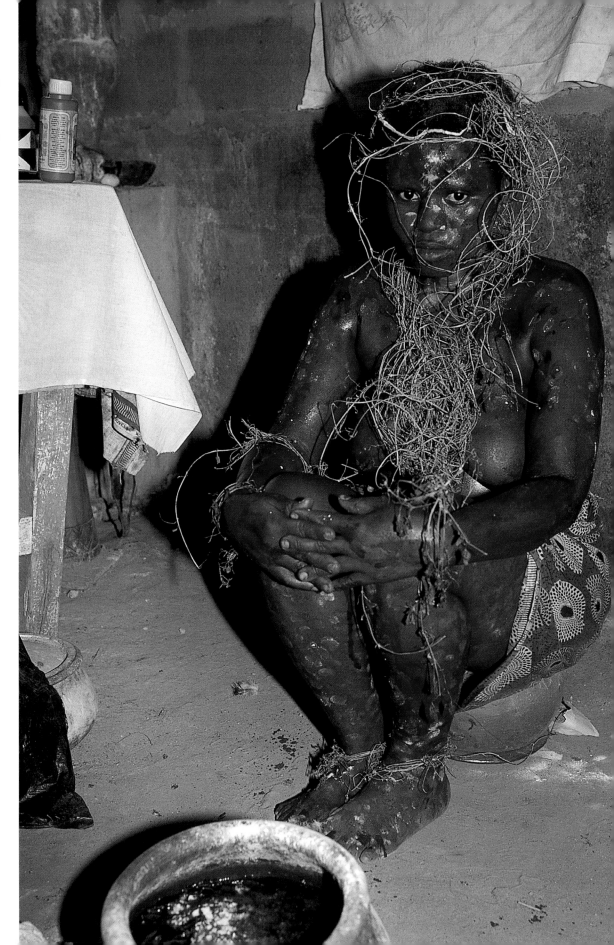

Curing a pregnant woman who cannot give birth because she has broken the rules of vodun. The oracle prescribes a Sakpata purification ceremony. The patient's body is covered in blue spots, symbolizing smallpox and therefore Sakpata. She is covered with herbs and placed next to an altar dedicated to Mami Wata, in order to be cured.

the bush, accompanied only by Sakpata's priest and anyone who had successfully survived the illness. If the patient confessed to the offense which had brought on the illness, there was hope of a cure. Otherwise the patient's body swelled up as it became covered in pustules and began to decompose. Finally, the sinner died alone in the bush; at the hour of his death all was quiet in the village; not even a cock crowed.

Since inoculation was introduced, smallpox no longer presents a serious threat to the population. Sakpata's priests have turned their attention to other illnesses, and this has resulted in the cult acquiring a higher reputation and greater popularity. One of the reasons for Sakpata's attraction is that he is one of the three deities (vodun) whom humans have to thank for their knowledge of numerous healing and magic cures; his priests are regarded as being particularly well versed in both white and black magic.

Before a duck is sacrificed for the benefit of the young woman, the priest's assistant touches her on the forehead with it.

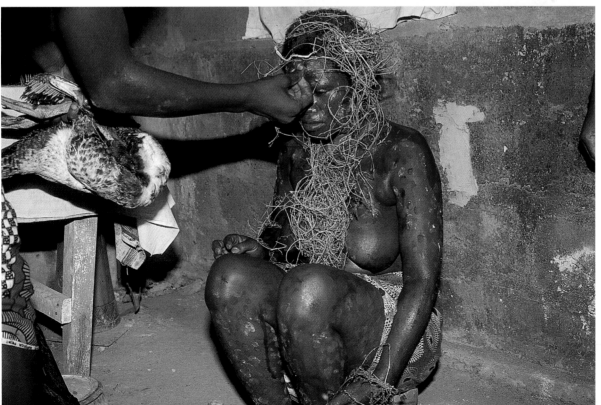

After the sacrifice, the woman's forehead is smeared with the duck's blood. This is supposed to have a cooling effect, because ducks live on water.

231

The patient is covered up so that no one will recognize her. A cloth is put over her head before she is led to the sanctuary.

In the sanctuary she sits before an altar of Shango, the god of storms and heavenly judgment, who weighs up her offense. If he exonerates her, her ritual rebirth can begin.

The young woman is bathed in milk, since a baby's food will give new strength to mother and child. She is also given medicine from one of the holy pots; this consists of water in which certain plants have been soaked.

Then her head is shaved to look like that of a newborn child, and the evil of her old life leaves her along with her contaminated hair. Her body is powdered and covered with a white cloth, which here stands for nakedness. Then the priestess leads her out of the shrine and delivers the "newborn" into the care of her family and the cult community.

Sakpata's story

A figure of Sakpata the smallpox god by the Ewe artist Moses, made in 1996.

After he had created the world, Mawu-Lisa, the bisexual creator god, wished to rest, and so he handed supervision of his work over to his sons Sakpata and Sogbo. The sons argued, however. This caused Sakpata to leave the sky and make his home on earth. As the elder son, he took his father's possessions with him as his inheritance. His younger, somewhat violent brother stayed with the gods of heaven and after a time won their absolute trust. Meanwhile Sakpata had taken up the position of a king on earth and, since he commanded great riches, people seemed very happy with his rule at first. To their horror, however, they soon realized that all rainfall had stopped. They began to complain bitterly to Sakpata, who put them off from one day to the next. A year soon passed, and

still there was no rain. Then Sakpata heard that two sky-dwellers were traveling about the country telling everyone about something called Fa. He had them brought to him and asked them why there was no rainfall. The men replied that they had no idea either, but that they could ask their Fa oracle. They threw palm kernels and announced that there had been an argument between two brothers who wanted power and that this was the cause of the problem. The solution required that the brothers be united. For this to work, it would be necessary, however, for the elder brother to appease the younger and be subordinate to him.

Then Sakpata remembered that he had brought many things with him from the sky to earth, but that he had left fire and water behind. He realized too late how much people, animals, and plants relied on water, which was now at Sogbo's disposal. When asked how the earth could be saved, the men told Sakpata to put a portion of his earthly goods together. A bird called Otutu could then fly up to heaven with the goods and deliver a message to Sogbo. As soon as the bird was in the air, he cried at the top of his voice: "Hey, Sakpata has a message for you. Can you hear me? He says he'll let you have the universe! Do you hear? He says he'll let you have houses, sons, fathers, children, mothers! Can you hear me?" To be sure that he had heard correctly and to see who brought this joyous news, Sogbo lit up the world with a flash of lightning. In the glaring light he saw Otutu, who was bringing him gifts as well as the message from his brother. Then he told the bird to tell Sakpata that as the older brother he had certainly inherited all his father's goods, but had not realized what constitutes true power: for fire and water were capable of destroying all earthly riches, which was why it was fitting that whoever possessed these was the ruler. This was how Sogbo gained victory over Sakpata.

This is a story told by priests of the storm deities, who tell it to show their superiority.

Vodunsi singing before a picture of Sakpata in a vodun convent.

Fortune-tellers' interpretation

The Fa oracle Bokonon with his chain of nutshells.

In societies with less complex pantheons of gods, premonitions and spirits take on a more important role in healing. Fortune-tellers are more than seers and priests; they are primarily healers. Fortune-tellers rarely limit themselves to prophecy. Many are also hunters, while blind fortune-tellers are often especially talented, perhaps because they can see "beyond things." Most are called by the bush spirits.

Fortune-tellers make use of various means to communicate with those on the other side. They put specific questions and receive answers by skillful handling of the objects they use, which usually involves throwing or rubbing them. A conversation with the patient is often conducted at the same time; the fortune-teller offers him or her several possible interpretations, in order to help jog his or her memory. Vague, tentative interpretations become more concrete, until at last there is a diagnosis and the fortune-teller can prescribe the appropriate remedy and required therapy, which might involve rites of atonement and sacrificial offerings.

In many societies consulting a fortune-teller is considered essential. It is not simply a question of finding out what is wrong with the patient, but why he or she – rather than someone else – has become ill. Social relationships are central to the diagnosis, and may include references to conflicts within the family, between friends, neighbors, or with spiritual powers. There is a wide range of techniques associated with fortune-telling, from the simple throwing of cowry shells, coins, or bones, to the highly specialized oracles of the Yoruba.

Fortune-tellers treat many illnesses themselves. If they are not able to do this, they refer the patient to a specialist in the immediate vicinity; this is often someone who has successfully overcome the relevant illness, showing that he or she knows the appropriate healing method.

The fortune-tellers' methods are perhaps less impressive than the striking vodun-cult ceremonies, but they are certainly just as effective. Their simple treatments include washing with medicines, inoculation, which often involves rubbing medicaments into a cut in the arm or forehead, and the production of amulets and talismans. Muslim fortune-tellers, who are also mostly Koran scholars (marabout or malam), especially use talismans.

If treatment is not successful, this is usually the fault of the patient, who has either concealed important details or not followed the advice offered.

Bokonon interprets the nutshell oracle for a man who has come to consult him due to a run of misfortune.

...okonon with a sacrificed white dove, a sign of purity.

Bokonon prepares an offering of herbs, talcum, and feathers.

...e pours gin onto a fetish to strengthen the power of the vodun ceremony.

Bokonon licks the offering from a vodun board.

...he fortune-teller prepares a fetish for the man who has suffered misfortune.

In order to be rid of his misfortune, the man buries the fetish in front of the Fa oracle, in this case the fortune-teller Bokonon.

Guarding against evil

Prevention is better than cure. True to this maxim, all healers offer means and rituals which can help people avoid illness and accidents. Many join a cult without any specific reason; they simply want to benefit from its wide-ranging protection. Whole village communities try to ward off potential trouble by taking part in a general purification ceremony at the right time, usually at the beginning of a new year. In many places this is associated with ritual rebirth.

Protective magic belongs to the realm of preventive medicine; it is used to guard against evil spirits, witches, and magicians, the evil eye, envy, and resentment. Talismans and amulets are used mostly for this purpose. These are usually small objects which are worn next to the body, and from their shape it is difficult to differentiate between them. Talismans are supposed to bring luck, while amulets ward off evil. Both are made out of all sorts of materials and are known in all societies. Most important is that people believe in their

Above: A sacrificed chicken, corn flour, and red palm oil are put on a white cloth and hung at the entrance to a village in the Mono region, to act as protection.

Right: Preparing palm branches with red and white cloths, as well as offerings of sacrificed chicken and food, to guard against evil spirits.

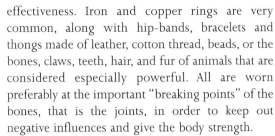

Preparing the palm branch for the entrance to the village, the priest mixes the offering for the gods who are supposed to protect the village.

The priest speaks as he holds up the sacrificed chicken.

The offerings are mixed together, and then placed on a cloth and hung up.

effectiveness. Iron and copper rings are very common, along with hip-bands, bracelets and thongs made of leather, cotton thread, beads, or the bones, claws, teeth, hair, and fur of animals that are considered especially powerful. All are worn preferably at the important "breaking points" of the bones, that is the joints, in order to keep out negative influences and give the body strength.

The Bambara call them tafo. Cotton bands are popular; the maker inserts knots at certain intervals, and before pulling them tight says a magic formula (kilisi) and spits on them. All over West Africa both Muslims and non-Muslims carry small leather bags, which are produced by fortune-telling healers as well as Koran scholars. The fortune-tellers usually fill them with a mixture of animal and plant ashes, while Muslims sew in small pieces of paper with secret signs and sayings from the Koran. Monson are also used as preventive measures; these are pellets made from the earth of termite mounds, moistened with water or shea-butter (made from the fat of nuts from the shea tree, Butyrospermum parkii).

The prophylactic can also be taken internally, mostly by swallowing the relevant medicine. Koran scholars write sacred texts on wooden boards; water is then poured over them and this can then be drunk or rubbed into the body. Priest-healers prepare magic spells for both individuals and whole village communities.

The palm branches are suspended at the entrance to the village. They are intended to prevent entry by evil spirits by offering gifts and encouraging them to move elsewhere.

Far left: During their new year's ceremony, the Ewe of the Mono region in Benin go into a grave. After their ritual death, they are purified and resurrected.

Left: They are given a stick called a kpantin, which acts as a scapegoat. Evil is transferred to the stick.

Far left: They are dusted with white powder while in the grave.

Left: When they are resurrected, it is as if they are born again and their heads are filled only with good thoughts. Then they are washed with sacred water.

Free of all sin, they can now look forward to the new year with a light heart.

After they have all been through death, the grave is filled in and all the cast-off evil is locked in.

241

Plant healers as general practitioners

Isaac Sayi, a great healer of Cotonou.

In many families both men and women are extremely knowledgeable about medicinal plants. This knowledge is usually passed on from father to son and from mother to daughter. Whereas women usually concentrate on using plants on their own, men often like to mix them with other materials such as parts of animals and aluminum oxide. Like women, men use mainly plants, however, and many of them are useful economically. Most medicinal plants are found in the bush, which means that healers must be on good terms with bush spirits and wild animals. This is, of course, the case with hunters, who are often taught the use of healing plants by bush spirits.

Many healers are particularly careful when they are out searching for medicinal plants. They often make a small offering or recite a formula before picking leaves, peeling off bark, or digging up roots; in the case of trees, they surround the trunk with a circle of ashes. It is also important that it is the right day of the week, the precise hour or phase of the moon, so that the healing power of the particular plant is at its strongest. Healers'

A woman collects medicinal plants near Sakete (Benin).

mysterious behavior out in the bush often provokes distrust as well as respect. Since there are so many poisonous plants in Africa, healers are often suspected of making up poisons. It is said that anyone who wishes someone ill can obtain substances from healers that they can then mix with food to cause a slow, painful death.

Most village healers practice as a sideline, and they once offered their services free of charge. Things have changed, and today there are many professional practitioners, especially in urban areas. They have formed professional associations which give certificates to their members to help them be taken more seriously. This says little about their suitability for the profession, though. Many of the associations have no entrance examination, and membership is often granted simply on request.

Plant healers are "general practitioners" – that is, they are experienced and knowledgeable in many areas. They know the function of the individual body organs and treat a wide variety of illnesses. In fact, they really only treat the symptoms, such as back problems, constipation, cramps, coughs, dizziness, fainting, flatulence, headache, and stomachache. They normally take a lot of time and go about treating their patients with great care. Many will suggest a remedy only after they have examined the patient thoroughly. In order

242

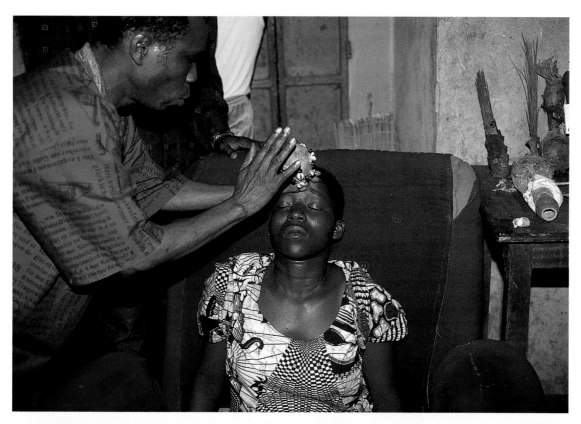

Many healers use magic along with medicinal plants. Here Antoine Tottin from Cotonou is treating a psychopathic girl.

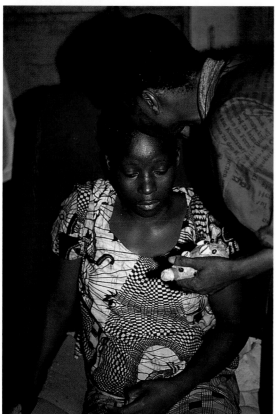

Far left: An armchair serves as a treatment chair.

Left: At the end of the ceremony the healer gives the girl some calming herbs.

Antoine Tottin treats physical as well as psychological problems with magic. Here he is trying to cure a woman of stomach pains. He is pressing crushed yam tubers and a bottle fetish against her stomach, in an attempt to draw out the pain.

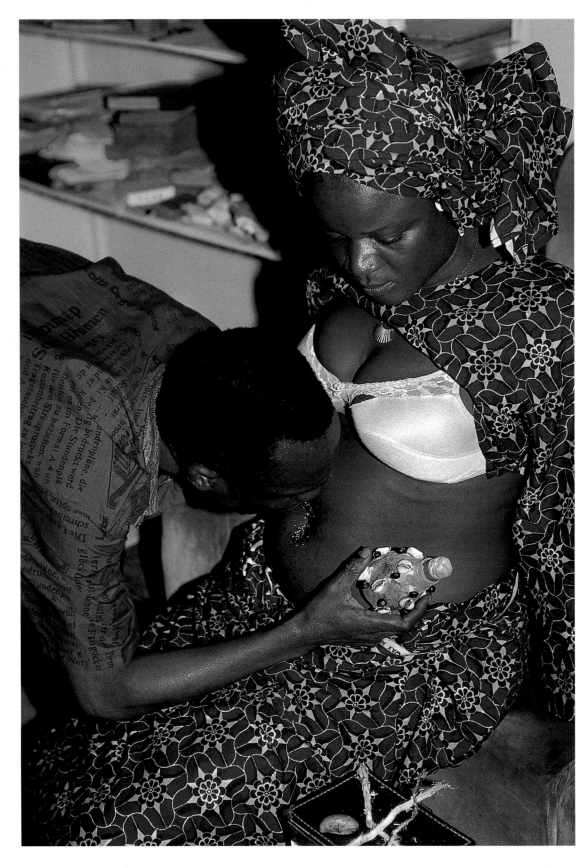

to discover the cause of an illness, healers often also use fortune-telling; the dividing line between the two practices is a thin one. Some turn to an oracle even before they have made a diagnosis. They are principally concerned with telling whether their kind of therapy has any chance of success. Only then does the healer go in search of the ingredients for the necessary medicine. Since many plants, and especially fruits and seeds, are only available at certain times of the year, they are usually dried and kept in small goatskin bags.

Healers rarely keep a large store of plants or prepared medicaments, except those used for milder, more routine complaints. Usually every case, like every patient, is unique. Every treatment therefore requires a special procedure, and every medicine must be fresh and specially prepared, often with the help of the patient or a close relative.

An enormous variety of plants is available to healers, not only across the various groups, but also within a single society. Even so, the plants themselves are seen as carriers, which only release their full effect when their "soul" has been activated or magically stimulated. In order to achieve this, the names of all those in whose possession the medicine has already been are listed, and specific magic spells are recited. The magic words have a result simply by being spoken, but they are even more effective if an animal such as a chicken is sacrificed at the same time and its blood poured over the medicine. Modern healers know many other magic processes, which they use according to the nature of the particular illness.

Given a correct diagnosis and individual treatment, nothing should stand in the way of a cure. If the treatment is not successful, it is usually assumed that another person or spirit is using a stronger countermedicine, which condemns all efforts to failure.

Top: As soon as the yam has sucked out the pain, the healer presses it against the wall, since the yam cannot harm it. Later he will drop the yam at a crossroads and, if an animal eats it, it will also have stomachache.

Above: At the end of the session the healer presses a coin to the woman's forehead. This will protect her from problems in future.

245

Drugstore in the street

Right: A typical streetside "drugstore" in Ghana. Here the druggist offers medicines for all sorts of illnesses. The placards behind the medicinal plants show the illnesses to which they are supposedly suited.

To help the illiterate, the illnesses which each plant alleviates are illustrated by the pictures.

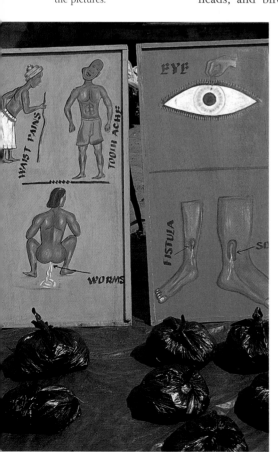

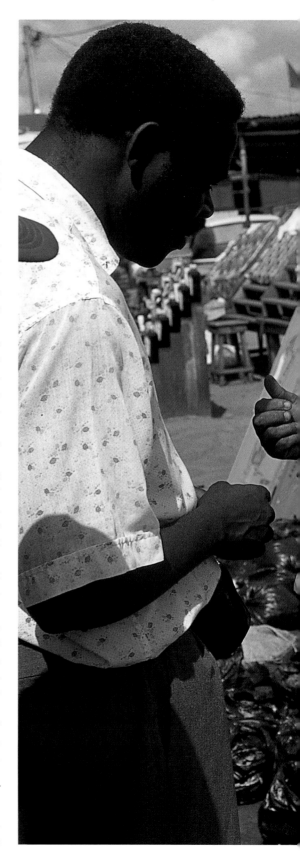

Many plant specialists, such as the dingaka tsa dichowa in Botswana, act as traders. Like traveling faith healers in the western United States, they move around the country and stop at markets. In towns and cities people are dependent on them, since they cannot themselves go out into the bush and collect roots, bark, and leaves. With their fresh and dried plants, the traders are therefore very welcome. In recent times powders have become more common. The price for these is higher, since the preparation has to be included in the price. There is a wide assortment on offer; some traders deal only in plants and plant medicines, while others offer animal parts such as snake skins, lizard heads, and bird skins. A study of the market in Mamako (Mali) revealed a typical range consisting of leaves, bark, and roots from 28 different kinds of plants.

Most market customers are women, and they are usually looking for specific plants. A minority of women seek advice about a particular illness or want a special medicine prepared. Following demand, most market traders offer their services increasingly as druggists, selling raw materials or ready-prepared medicines. This has replaced the rural method of preparing a specific medicine for each individual, and the old ways are no longer in demand in town.

Many other specialists offer their wares or services on the markets. In Burkina Faso there are more and more traveling traders from Ghana who, if what they say is to be believed, have all sorts of miracle cures on their vendor's trays; there are

A plant drugstore beside a street in Cotonou (Benin), with medicines for various complaints.

A market in Porto Novo (Benin).

Antoine Tottin mixes various plants and plant parts. His business is booming, otherwise he would not be able to feed his 13 wives and 60 children; his offspring are the best advertisement for an aphrodisiac prepared by him!

Far left: A healer called Ogunlola in front of his drugstore in Porto Novo.

Left: Inside the store. Ogunlola packs all his medicines in plastic bags and displays them neatly. Liquid medicines are sold in bottles.

Benoit D. Soudo, a healer in Abomey, behind his druggist's table.

ostensible remedies for snakebites and impotence, right through to deadly diseases such as AIDS. Although they have their customers, many people still remain understandably skeptical.

In Bamako (Mali), Hausa from northern Nigeria arrive not only to sell medicines but also to act as doctors, bleeding and scarifying patients. They claim that this helps relieve muscle and joint pains, as well as other limb complaints. Less often they perform uvulectomy, the removal of the uvula (the rear extension of the soft palate). For this they use a long, hooklike instrument with a small knife at the tip. The operation is supposed to remedy complaints of the pharynx such as pharyngitis and stammering, as well as acute and chronic laryngitis. It is certainly a dangerous operation, and subsequent bleeding and infections are common.

249

The secret healing power of plants

Plant medicine in tropical countries, sometimes referred to as the "rainforest drugstore," is being scrutinized ever more carefully by the West. Many people are looking for therapeutic alternatives to the hard medicine of the pharmaceutical industry, which itself is on the constant lookout for new substances, not least in the fervent hope of finding remedies for cancer and AIDS. Plant-hunters are sent to try and elicit from traditional healers the secrets of their medicaments, giving them hope of finding fame, recognition, and wealth.

The old wall of silence went up once again, however, when there were a few mysterious deaths among West African medicine men. In 1992, for example, the Ghanaian healer Nan Drobo died in suspicious circumstances shortly after his return from the Far East, where he had been at the invitation of a Japanese pharmaceutical company. Expertise in the therapeutic qualities of plants is part of the secret knowledge of initiated vodun priests and is passed on in confidence to pupils and initiates during a ten-year education. This does not seem such a long time considering the scope of what has to be learned; there are no textbooks and written notes are not allowed, yet there are more than 1,000 different medicinal and useful plants to be learned of, around 400 of which are used daily in phytotherapeutic practice.

But things are changing, and not only because of the brutal approaches of the plant hunters.

At the end of the 1970s the medicine men of Benin, which was then ruled by a socialist regime, were given the choice of either becoming part of the public health service or being driven out so that their activities would become illegal. Typical of representatives of vodun culture, who have always shown great adaptability, most healers reacted quickly. They naturally never gave away the ritual secrets of their healing arts, but they founded a movement named "La Feuille et non le Fétiche" – The Leaf and not the Fetish. This created a new focus for their practice, away from the embodiment of spiritual healing and toward phytotherapy, or healing through plants. The medicine men began personally to publish their first pharmacopoeia, even if they were not extensive and did not give away their deepest secrets.

They were now the subject of both public and scientific discussion. And officials in the health services of West African states were not alone in recognizing the resources that were potentially opening up. They had known for a long time that a Western style of mechanized medicine and pharmacy could not be financed or developed on a long-term basis in their countries, which came as a bitter realization to those specialists who had been educated in Europe or the United States. When they looked more closely at the publications of their traditional healer colleagues, they saw the potential of this wealth of knowledge. Not only were the characteristics of the plants described in exact detail, but also the various effects of their separate parts: roots, barks, leaves, stems, flowers, and fruits were outlined and differentiated, and their remedial and toxic effects precisely noted. Paracelsus's statement that "It is only the dose which makes a poison not a poison" is the basis of African medicine, though under more difficult conditions: since no precise scales are available to a medicine man, he has to perform a complicated series of dilutions in order to produce the right dose. He can, however, fall back on another basic of African medicine: many medicaments were formerly used as hunting poisons, especially arrow poisons, and were then diluted as the phytotherapeutic formula was developed. These formulae correspond exactly to the traditional preparation of medicines with which we are familiar: the most widespread is herbal tea, but alcoholic extracts, inhalants, powders, and ointments are also produced.

Rationally comprehensible techniques and discoveries make it possible to assess vodun medicine in a scientific way. Joy at the valuable indigenous resources is quickly followed by disillusionment, however: in some regions of West Africa the continued survival of herbs is already threatened by over-harvesting. The first development aid projects are attempting to change this situation by aiming at controlled cultivation.

The experience of healers, who know the plants' requirements in terms of soil conditions, light, and moisture, as well as exactly the best time to sow and harvest them, are crucial and are being passed on willingly.

But there are limits. An initiate will never give away the meaning of the 41 therapeutic virtues contained in every plant, just as the workings of the Dahomey, the mother tree, are not scientifically accessible. After the birth of a child, the healer buries the placenta in consecrated earth. A tree is planted on that spot. The tree grows up along with this person and for the rest of their life provides them with bark, leaves, and fruit, strengthening their physical and psychological defense.

Konrad Rippmann

Nerium oleander (Apocynaceae family). Parts used: stem, leaves (toxic), flowers, roots (antiseptic, antibiotic), milk. Uses: rashes, diarrhea, disturbances of the heart rhythm, cancer, leukemia.

Combretum micranthum (Combretaceae family). Parts used: leaves (antiseptic), fruits, bark. Uses: fever, malaria, jaundice, diarrhea, worms, wounds, incontinence, asthma.

Jatropha multifida (Euphorbiaceae family). Parts used: leaves, latex (milk). Uses: astringent, contracting tissues in complaints of the mucous membrane of the mouth and sore throat; checks bleeding of wounds.

Commiphora africana (Burseraceae family). Parts used: branches, leaves, bark, roots, milk. Uses: boils, skin diseases, for chewing (branches, bark), flatulence, strengthening the stomach and helping digestion (leaves), arthritis, gout, joint edemas, rheumatism (milk).

Bixa orellana (Bixaceae family). Parts used: leaves, fruit, seed pods. Uses: worms, fever, inflammation.

Mitracarpus scaber (Rubiaceae family). Whole plant used. Uses: fresh herb rubbed in for acne, rashes, and fungus diseases; taken internally for headache and toothache.

Lantana camara (Verbenaceae family). Parts used: stem, leaves, flowers, fruit. Uses: coughs, fever, jaundice (flowers).

Moringa oleifeira (Moringaceae family). Parts used: leaves, roots, seeds. Uses: leaves and roots for gonorrhea, typhus, diabetes, pain and inflammation, abscesses, viral hepatitis; seed oil externally for arthritis, gout, joint edemas, rheumatism.

Lawsonia inermis (Lythraceae family). Parts used: leaves (antiseptic, contain vitamin K), bark, roots. Uses: diabetes, wounds, inflammation, hastening birth contractions (abortion), menstrual problems.

Argemone mexicana (Papaveraceae family). Parts used: stem (antiseptic, antibiotic), leaves, fruits, seeds, roots, milk (toxic). Uses: pain, bacterial diarrhea, tuberculosis (caused by Mycobacteria tuberculosis), nervous conditions, insect bites, disturbance of the heartbeat, high blood pressure.

Ocimum gratissimum (Labiatae family). Parts used: whole plant, leaves, roots. Uses: colds, fever, memory problems, stimulation of the immune system (increasing body's defense), psychological stimulant, antispasmodic.

Crataeva andansonii (Capparidaceae family). Parts used: stem, bark, roots. Uses: pain, wounds, hastening birth contractions (abortion), cancer (antitumor properties), stimulation of the immune system, migraine.

The presence of spirit powers

People everywhere imagine themselves to be surrounded by a whole range of spiritual powers. Some are thought to be benevolent and helpful in people's daily lives, while others strive to do evil in one way or another, diverting people from a regular way of life and even plunging them into misfortune. The latter may be bush or wild spirits, or they may be the souls of people who died an unfortunate death and which cannot find the entrance to the kingdom of the dead; these souls rush around restlessly, as if obsessed with a desire to take revenge for their ill fortune on the living. Among the benevolent spirits are ancestors, who care for the health, welfare, and fertility of their descendants and watch over their loyalty to tradition; also personal spirits who accompany a person throughout their life, helping and protecting them, warning of danger, supporting them in critical situations, and generally giving strength, happiness, and success.

A dwarf temple dedicated to bush spirits.

How the "little creatures" came to Dahomey

"Little creatures" who lived in water were known to the people of Dahomey during the time of Akaba (1685–1708). No cult was devoted to them at that time, however, because the king feared their wildness. Akaba's successor, Agaja (1708–32), kept things that way, but the spirits took bitter revenge: during an attack by the royal army they appeared on the battlefield and destroyed all the Oyo troops in one fell swoop. Nevertheless, Agaja still refused to set up a cult for them. Agaja's son and heir, Tegbesu (c. 1740–74), also kept his distance from the spirits. Then the spirits sent a bat with a burning leaf under its wing. When it arrived over Abomey, the bat dropped the leaf and set the whole town on fire. Tegbesu fled. The toxosu ("little creatures") followed him to Kana, where he thought he was safe and where he wanted to found his capital. He soon saw that there was no escape and returned to Abomey. Shortly afterward a large number of toxosu appeared in the town; they were bearded creatures with little whips. They drove the people out, and the king only just managed to escape. For a long time he journeyed here and there with his followers; but everywhere all he found was terrible famine, for although they had planted rice, the people were harvesting stones.

A sick prince by the name of Homenuvo was the only one to remain in the town. The spirits, who by now had doubled in number, took the prince prisoner. They brought him before their chiefs, who under the leadership of Zumadunu had assembled at the place where their shrine was later to be erected. Zumadunu, who had six eyes (two extra on his forehead and two on his chin), told the prince that the whole of Dahomey was doomed to fall if he did not institute a cult for him, the son of Akaba, and all the other deformed dead. Horrified, Homenuvo agreed at once. Then the spirit leader instructed him on the right way to worship ancestors and gods: he gave him 666 different songs which were to be sung at various ceremonies. He also told him where the new shrine was to be erected and predicted various events, including the birth of 11 further toxosu who would be born to the royal house. Then he released Homenuvo, having told him that he expected the king at the same place at midnight in exactly 11 days. The prince, who was suddenly cured of his illness, reported to the king all that had happened; the king did not hesitate to take up Zumadunu's invitation.

On the said day the king heard loud singing accompanied by pumpkin rattles from a long way off. Zumadunu gave the king

Two toxosu ("little creatures" who live in water), with cigarettes stuck in their mouths and bananas in their arms. The toxosu are the "kings of the water."

seven of the rattles and instructed him as to the occasions on which each of them should be played. Then he gave him 33 cowry shells, as well as other holy objects. Tegbesu now had no choice but to dedicate a cult to the toxosu. He gave the sacred objects into the safekeeping of his mother, a woman from Adja who from then on served the toxosu as well as the heavenly gods. Later a group of them returned to tell the people of Abomey that every single toxosu insisted on having an object or shrine dedicated in his memory and to his veneration.

This was how the toxosu cult was integrated into the cult of ancestor worship. Later Dahomey kings used the cult to consolidate the expansion of their kingdom. All dependent towns and villages were urged to erect a shrine to the royal toxosu, as a sign that their sovereignty over Dahomey was recognized.

Spirit time in the bush

Laying out a new field usually requires the permission of bush spirits. Every year the inhabitants of Lakple, an Anlo-Ewe village in Ghana, hold a ceremony in honor of Arabzie, the founding father of the settlement. During the ceremony he and the other ancestors receive an offering on the road to the village.

Whereas the gods are far away, spirits live close by, and some even dwell among people. Their real home is nature – that is, the undeveloped, uncultivated land and stretches of water which seem to be in opposition to the cultural world of people and appear to threaten them. The wilderness, or bush, breathes pollution, dangerous, yet at the same time immensely effective forces, which are personified in the beings that live there. All meaningful contact with powerful spirits takes place in the wilderness, and the further away from any settlement a region is, the greater and more incalculable are the forces which live there.

In the bush things are the other way round. At night, when everything is quiet in the village, the bush is full of life. Dawn and dusk form a clear boundary between the light, active cultural time and the spirit time, which is governed by a wild irregularity. The first rays of the sun drive the spirits back into dark, hidden cracks in the earth, to the tops of high trees, into the undergrowth, caves or water; from these places they may make themselves known to people at midday, the turning point of daytime. Then they might throw stones at people, and anyone who is hit falls ill or finds their head reeling. Those who go out face this risk. The bush spirits lie in wait for them, unnoticed, ready to cast their spell over them. Very few people ever see them, however. Yet, we know what they look like and how they live. They are usually of dwarflike stature and lead an almost human life in families. Their striking characteristics are extreme hairiness, the backward position of their feet, and the extreme size of their genitals. They talk through their nose in their own whistling language, which the villagers cannot understand. Anyone who is forced to spend a night in the bush can hear how they enjoy themselves, singing, dancing, and calling to each other, though people cannot understand most of what is heard. Many people have also seen them during the day, when they are less frightening and have a more comic appearance; this has given rise to many stories of their witty playfulness and their tendency to play pranks, and people often imitate their speech in a high, nasal singsong.

Bush spirits are often subordinate to a "lord of the wild," who looks after the stock of wild animals in the same way as the earth deity looks after fields and cultivated plants. Hunters ask this spirit for good fortune, which he grants if they follow his rules of behavior, offer him a portion of their provisions and, most importantly, some of their bag. He punishes contraventions himself by removing game and by causing illness, especially madness, or he entrusts punishment to the bush spirits, his gamekeepers.

The relationship between bush spirits and people is ambivalent. The spirits behave like goblins; they are unpredictable and their actions are arbitrary. Sometimes they merely play tricks on their victims, while at other times they might take a life if they were really angry. There are precise rules for the way to behave if you suddenly meet a bush spirit and he speaks to you. They usually show themselves to be harmless, but they can hardly stop themselves from committing mischief. They seem to find great pleasure in stealing palm wine and leftovers from women, and in dipping their fingers in milk churns.

The relationship can be a positive one, however, if people actively seek contact with the spirits, turning to them and accepting them as helpful and protective. It often happens that someone comes across a striking or remarkable object in the bush or unexpectedly sees certain animals, such as chameleons, mating. A fortune-

Arabzie and the other forefathers came to the area of the settlement as hunters, following the appearance of a spirit in a human form completely covered in leaves. The spirit advised the ancestors to settle there, and then vanished as suddenly as he had appeared. He has never been seen again, and yet people still think he is present. Every year he is remembered and people put on leaf costumes and wear it.

Everyone tries to cover themselves with leaves so that even their neighbors will not recognize them.

Top: A large drum is played during the procession through the village; this beats out the rhythm for the marchers.

Above: With this disguise only the legs remain visible. The pretend spirit looks as if he had just come out of the bush.

teller on intimate terms with the bush spirits and who has gained most of his knowledge from them can then tell whether this is a sign or a gift – an indication that bush spirits want to get in direct contact with that person or, through him, with the village community. If this is followed up, it can bring help in the form of advice or deeds and can even offer privileges. In order to seal the bond for the longer term, a concrete means of caring for it must be found. Animals and bush spirits can only become the object of a cult if they are captured in something or are represented figuratively – in clay, wood, or as a mask. Such representations are found at many shrines, since in many societies – such as the Mosi and Asante, for example – the spirits are in close contact with the nature deities and are regarded as their nimble messengers; sometimes the spirits have their own centers of worship.

Because they are more intelligent, more knowledgeable, and most importantly more powerful than humans, spirits can help humans in many ways and teach them a great deal. According

Face paints are also used; white is the color of death.

Below: Togbui Nazah Kudese, priest and village chief, is thought to be a direct descendant of the founder of the village. After the costumes have been taken off at the village shrine, he purifies the people with sacred water, to keep them free of illness and evil.

Bottom: The priest bids farewell to the ancestors by pouring an offering, just as he did at the start of the ceremony.

to tradition they have been particularly helpful in the fields of cultivation, brewing, the making of musical instruments (especially xylophones), dancing, the domestication of animals, and plant medicine. Bush spirits are considered to be particularly experienced in plant medicine. Many hunters and healers have served an apprenticeship with the spirits.

Conversely, the spirits often show their darker side. People who come too close to them are sometimes struck down with illness, mental derangement, sleeplessness, or blindness. Others become so confused that they never find their way back to their village. The victims sometimes undergo a transformation, becoming wild, moving and behaving strangely, seeing and hearing things which they never noticed before, understanding the language of animals, and seeing the spirits themselves. This ruins their reason, and they become victims of the spirits rather than employing their services.

The spirits are just as real as natural phenomena. Every society has a wealth of names for their various forms; they are very often compared to the wind, which is also invisible but leaves traces behind. "The spirits," so it is said, "are wind, for we do not see them; we recognize them only by what they do."

Water spirits, rulers of the water

Carver Sallah Moses at work on a statue of the water goddess Mami Wata.

He continues the work in his hut.

Many spirits appear to be driven by an urge to enter the human world. As well as nighttime, market days offer them a good opportunity: they can mix with visitors to the market by pretending to be strangers. They rarely succeed in hiding their true nature, however. Children who are born with visible abnormalities, for example, act as if they are spirits in human form and are seen as changelings. The Fon believe that children born with too many fingers or toes are connected with Lisa, the sky deity associated with the chameleon and the sun. They are regarded as relatively harmless and if the extra digits are removed, they can develop into regular people. It is more difficult if children are born with too few digits, however. Then the parents turn to a priest of the toxosu, or "water kings," as the Fon call these spirits of deformed children. The priest asks an oracle whether the child will bring its parents wealth or poverty, which in earlier times decided the child's fate.

The birth of such a child can have positive as well as negative consequences for the family. In most cases the parents bring the child up, even if somewhat reluctantly. In earlier times, however, the children were often "sent back." Since they were abnormal, they were not accepted into human society and were returned to where they belonged: many took them into the bush, while the Fon placed them on a riverbank after a brief ceremony. Many of the children resisted: they cried as loudly as they could and even protested in words – some were said to have been able to talk at birth – until they were finally taken back to the village.

This was only done in certain cases, however, such as if a child had four fingers on one hand or was born with hair or teeth. Other physical irregularities made people feel certain that the children were messengers of evil spirits. This was certainly the case with hermaphrodites and children with hydrocephalus. Just like stillborn, aborted, or illegitimate children, they were always taken to the river, because it was thought that was

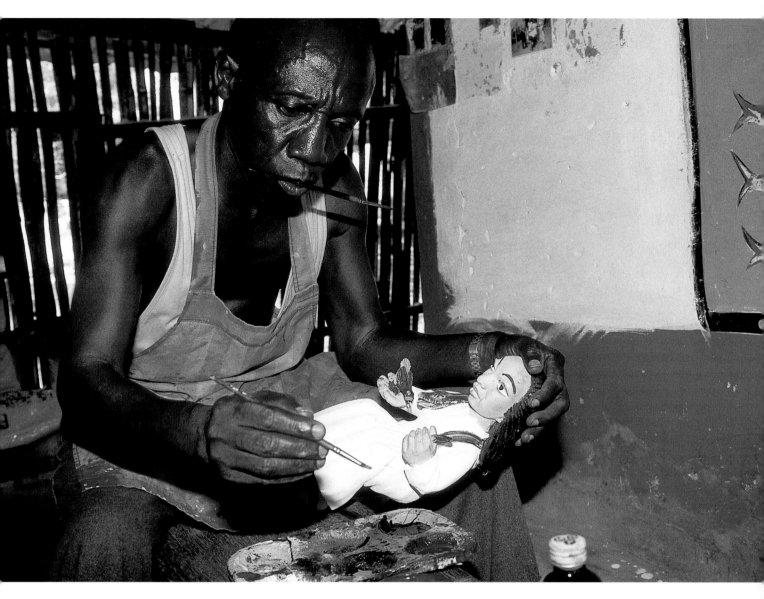

The carved goddess is carefully painted.

where they belonged. This meant that they were not allowed to enter the kingdom of the dead, but were condemned to wander the earth or water for ever. These outcast, restless souls are still feared more than any other spirits, especially since they go around in large groups. They are driven to take revenge on the living, pursuing, frightening, and molesting them, as well as wreaking havoc all over the country. They are also seen as guardians of the rivers which all those who have died a proper death have to cross in order to reach the kingdom of the dead. If they are not sufficiently reconciled, they do not let the deceased across and condemn them to a fate like their own. The living then feel the revenge of these disappointed and cheated spirits.

The toxosu cult became famous in the old kingdom of Dahomey. Just as kings ruled over the Fon, the toxosu were governed by Zumadunu, a deformed son of King Akaba (1685–1708). All future rulers of Dahomey were supposed to have had at least one deformed child, who then took up a leading position in the spirit world. The wild, uncontrolled power of rivers and their spirits has always presented a challenge to social order. Just like the element in which they live, water spirits are seen as malicious and unpredictable. Using their services is risky, and it is imperative that their demands are followed to the letter. If they are well disposed toward someone, they will display extraordinary abilities. They can appear on the

Left: In order that it can become active and show its power, the figure must be brought to life by Abidjan Mami Wata, the priest of the shrine.

Center and below: The priest dedicates the cult image. A rite or series of rites, in which certain substances are offered, magic words are spoken, and sacrifices are made, enables the figure to become an effective sacral object. Without these measures it would remain a carved piece of wood.

battlefield and destroy the enemy without playing a single trick, or they might simply watch as the kingdom is destroyed. When the French conquered Dahomey, King Behanzin (1889–94) is said by tradition to have been 45 miles away from Abomey. The French victory was apparently only possible because Zumadunu was angry. So the people sacrificed a bull to him during the night and asked him for urgent assistance. Next morning the animal's carcass had disappeared, and it was found the following day in front of the king's door, a clear sign that Zumadunu had rejected the sacrificial offering and that Dahomey's fate was sealed.

In Abomey the toxosu had shrines near the royal palace, and in August some of the most important ceremonies of the royal ancestor cult took place there. For deformed children of the royal family there were special shrines, where sacrifices were made during ancestral remembrance ceremonies. The rites for the royal toxosu are very similar to the cult ceremonies held for the great gods. They all had their own cult houses, priests, and novices, who went through an initiation period in which they were dedicated to the cult of the toxosu. In this way the toxosu are no different from deities at all.

Today the toxosu are closely associated with the cult of Mami Wata, especially among the Ewe and the Minah. They belong to the spirits or gods who shape the personalities of their priests and followers.

The wooden figure now possesses its full
sacral power as a goddess.

The hierarchy of the gods

The dividing line between spirits and gods is blurred. One significant difference is that deities are close to the creator god; they are often thought to be his younger siblings, or children, and have a greater range of influence than spirits. Some, though not all, gods exist further away from the earth than spirits, who live separately from people but still in their immediate vicinity.

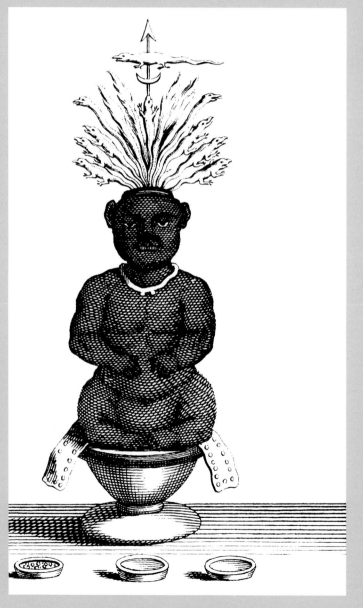

West African deities may be divided roughly into three groups. Firstly, there are those associated with natural phenomena such as the earth, sky, storms, and water, and these are worshiped everywhere. Secondly, there are those that are connected with a specific place, such as a town, or a particular related group, such as a clan or lineage; in these cases the priesthood is inherited by the eldest member of the family. Thirdly, there are those deities who have been introduced from outside; many of these newcomers were originally simply magic powers which were used on witch-hunts; their priesthood may be bought.

In societies with a long and checkered history, war, trade, and migration usually led to the fusion of various belief systems, with specific selection processes and a hierarchical structure. This is particularly true of the expanding empires of the Yoruba and the Fon. Typical for them was a characteristic microcosmic-macrocosmic parallel between the structure of the earthly and godly worlds, as in the ancient cultures of the Middle East. The earthly world acquired its inviolable religiosity as a reflection of the world of the gods. In Dahomey, for example, the king stood at the top of a pyramid of officials, the structure of which mirrored that of the gods; as the American ethnologist Melville J. Herskovits put it, "Just as every chieftain of a region had subordinate chiefs who were responsible to him, every superior god had subordinate deities who were answerable to him."

Since deities have a greater range of influence than spirits and ancestors, they are much further removed from people. They still affect the destinies of mortals, however. As personifications of individual aspects of life, such as fertility, they act as important mediators for people.

Agoye, god of the council assembly, in the house of great sacrifice in Whydah, Benin. Made of black clay, the figure of the god sits on a rostrum made of red clay above a piece of red cloth. He wears a scarlet band around his neck, from which hang four cowry shells; snakes, lizards, and red feathers crown his head, and at the very top an arrow pierces a silver crescent and a large lizard. Engraving of 1746.

The cosmos of the vodun gods

"In the beginning only Olorun, god of the sky, existed. He ruled over the sun. There was no earth then. Beneath him everything was water. Olorun sent his son Obatala down with a large sphere – the earth – which Obatala put down on the sea, where it broke into chunks which formed mountains and islands. The first living thing that sprang up there was Agbon, the palm tree, from which Obatala made palm wine. He drank the wine and fell asleep. Outraged at this, Olorun sent his daughter Odudua to put things in order. She was accompanied by Aje, the goddess of wealth and abundance in the form

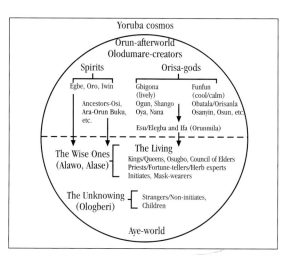

of a turkey, who pushed the ground apart so that it covered a greater area and became inhabitable. Olorun gave Odudua a basket of millet, which she scattered with other seeds so that plants and trees soon grew everywhere. Then Olorun (who is often identified with Olodumare, the creator god) went down to earth and settled near the palm tree, which is where the old town of Ife now stands and which is the center of the earth." So says a legend of the Yoruba.

Although most Yoruba in Nigeria and Benin are either Christian or Muslim, their traditional religion has by no means died out; indeed, during the time of the slave trade it even spread to the New

Above left: Diagram showing some of the main elements of the Yoruba cosmos. It is made up of two separate but interactive spheres – aye, the tangible world of the living, and orun, the invisible region of spiritual powers such as gods, ancestors, and spirits. All beings, whether living or spiritual, possess vital energy, or ase. Wise individuals such as priests, initiates, and fortune-tellers are known as alase or alawo.

Above: The Ivi River in Dahomey, a region of lush, varied vegetation. From *Malerische Studien*, Neuchâtel, undated.

An ancient representation of a bocio (Dassa, Benin). A bocio gives power a human form. The abstract concept of power thereby becomes tangible. The concept itself consists of an activating object, the power (bo), and the shape of the human body, or more precisely a cadaver (cio). Bocio are seen as instruments of great power.

Right: Representation of the rainbow god Dan, with offerings of alcohol and cigarettes. Such items should not be offered to any god, since they are considered to have a heating effect. They should be particularly avoided as gifts to the storm god Shango.

World. It is based on a four-stage hierarchical pyramid of spiritual powers. Olodumare, who is also called Olorun, "owner of the sky," is ranked highest in the hierarchy of the gods. He is seen as immortal, unique, and just. The Yoruba do not erect shrines for him, but call upon him in an emergency. His helpers, the Orisha, form the second rank. They have their own shrines and priests. The most important among them is Obatala. The third level is occupied by the deified ancestors, such as Shango. The fourth rank is occupied by the spirits, who are often associated with natural phenomena such as rivers, mountains, and trees.

The Fon, who have long been in close contact with the Yoruba, have a similar picture of the world and its gods. The double or twin deity Mawu-Lisa – Mawu attributed to the female moon, Lisa to the male sun – created the earth. According to the Fon also, creation meant putting the world in order. Land and water had to be distributed and connected to each other correctly. In this Dan acted as the right hand of the creator. It is said that his power still lives in rainbows. He stretched himself around the earth as a python and pressed it together. Since then all the gods have made use of him. He never acts automatically, but nothing can move without him. In this way he guarantees continuity, serving everyone.

Mawu-Lisa is a typical West African supreme god of the sky, far removed from humans and their cares. Myths tell of a time long ago when Mawu-Lisa lived with people, but he/she was disappointed and returned to the sky. In order to keep up contact with people, however, Mawu-Lisa created the vodun, who in future would govern the earth and communicate between the god and humans. The three eldest of these 14 "children" of Mawu-Lisa – Sakpata, Sogbo, and Agbe – each arranged their own pantheon. In the world of Mawu-Lisa, Ogun (or Gu), the god of iron, holds the highest position. Just as Dan had helped with creation, Ogun was the supreme god's right hand when it came to arranging the world, and he gave it the power which people use to control nature. He therefore has a central position in all shrines to the sky gods.

It is the task of the vodun to help maintain the world. They look after health, fertility, and happiness. Mawu equipped them with great powers to do this. Hevioso (or Sogbo), who guides atmospheric phenomena, and Sakpata, who rules over the earth and smallpox, are especially popular. With the growing complexity of existence, the vodun are granted an ever-increasing number of new, special tasks.

How the vodun came to Abomey

For a long time the vodun gods were unknown in Dahomey. According to legend, they were brought to the country by a woman named Wandjele in the time of Agaja (1708–32), the fourth king of Dahomey. During his reign there were many wars, and town and country sank into chaos: pregnant women bore goats, and goats bore human children. Wandjele, who sold indigo on the market, often saw men mounting goats and goats mounting women.

The king had a wife named Naye Adono, but he was not happy with her. One day when she

returned from the market, she told her husband that she had met a woman who knew the right sacrifices to bring order back to the country. The king had the woman brought to him. Wandjele, for it was she, said: "In our village women bear human children and animals bear animals. This is taken care of by the vodun, which you do not have here." Then Agaja asked her to bring these wonderful gods to Abomey. Wandjele agreed to do so and told the king what would be needed to worship the gods. When everything had been properly prepared, she went back to her homeland and returned with Mawu-Lisa, Sakpata, Hevioso, Ogun (Gu), Dan, and many other vodun. Then the king took her as his wife, and from then on life in Abomey went on in a well-ordered fashion.

Representation of the rainbow and snake god Dan. Snakes live on land and in water, and in the form of rainbows they are also involved in the sky. Dan is the god of traders and merchants; he stands for wealth which can be gained and lost, for money and gold, pearls and gemstones. The upturned pots are symbols of the god Sakpata, who brings and takes away illness. The gods have very human traits. If they are not properly looked after, they can cause harm. Gifts encourage them to have a positive effect.

Arranging a war god. He is placed on an asen (ancestral altar), which will increase his power.

Legba, the unpredictable deity

Offerings to the Saint Michelle Legba in Dantokba market in Cotonou. This figure of Legba is one of the oldest in Benin. Beneath it lie the bones of humans who were sacrificed to the god when the figure was created.

The Yoruba and the Fon believe that a person's fate is fixed from birth. This is the responsibility of the deity called Fa, who was created when Mawu's words gained independence. One is not tied inescapably to one's lot; one can change it with the help of a god – Eshu, according to the Yoruba, and Legba according to the Fon. There is a special story behind the involvement of these gods. Although they occupy a high position – Legba is the youngest child of the twin god Mawu-Lisa, and Eshu the first servant of the Yoruba supreme god Olodumare – they are closer to human beings, both in their passions and their weaknesses. In stark contrast to the strict Fa, Legba (like Eshu) is a typical trickster, full of capricious ideas and devoted more to chance than to fate. Sly, compulsive, and selfish, he plays the most terrible pranks on gods and people. To the Christian missionaries he was the devil personified, which was unjust since he does good as well as evil. He has the power to reward and to punish; he can be helpful to people and he can make life difficult for them, especially those who do not get things straightened out with him. Most people, however, are clever enough to worship him more than any other god. Because he moves between two worlds, one of his legs is shorter than the other: one of his feet is in the realm of the gods, the other on earth. In both worlds he causes total confusion. Even the most powerful gods are not spared, and he is quite prepared to modify instructions given by Mawu, or Olodumare, at his own discretion.

People are dependent on him because it is through him that they have to get the ear of the other deities, which is why all priests can also perform his service. Petitions to the gods are usually accompanied by an offering to Legba, so that he too will help if required. Anyone who thinks that this is not so important can very quickly have reason to regret his mistake: how a message arrives is entirely in Legba's hands.

Portrayals of Legba can be found in front of many rural houses and villages, either in the form of a human or a dog, always facing outward. Dogs are sacred to Legba (and Eshu), and they are therefore given food offerings for the god. If the dog eats the food, the god accepts it and thereby expresses that he is well disposed. Dogs are also indicative of the god's guardian aspect. Like them, he deters strangers and enemies, without biting the hand which feeds him. He cannot be totally trusted, though. He even deceives Mawu and remains a shady, unreliable character, who can nevertheless set changes in motion.

Why Mawu, the mother of all gods, lives in the sky

In the beginning Legba was always near his mother Mawu, following her instructions and doing nothing without her approval. If he did something disastrous on Mawu's behalf and people turned to her, she said Legba was responsible. Whenever he did good, however, she accepted people's thanks. People therefore began to hate Legba. He asked his mother why evil always fell to him, to which Mawu replied that it was all right for rulers to accept responsibility for their subjects' good deeds, while all trouble was seen as the responsibility of their henchmen. "Very well," said Legba as he left.

Mawu had a garden in which she grew yams. Legba informed her that thieves wanted to steal the yams. At that Mawu called her subjects together and warned them, "If anyone so much as touches my yams, he will die."

The following night it rained. Legba crept into Mawu's house, put on her sandals and removed all the yams from the garden. Next morning, when Mawu saw what had happened, Legba advised her to call everyone to her so that she could determine whose feet had made the clear footprints in the damp soil. One after another, all her subjects placed their feet in the footprints, but none fitted. Then Legba asked, "Could it be that Mawu herself was in her garden during the night and has forgotten?" Mawu replied, "What? Me? Legba, I don't like you for saying such a thing. But I will submit to the test." Of course she failed the test, and the people were surprised, "Ha, imagine stealing your own yams!" In her anger Mawu cried that her own son had obviously played a trick on her, and that she would therefore leave earth and go and live in the sky. In future Legba would have to appear before her every evening and report on what had happened on earth during the day. That is how it came about that Mawu lives in the sky.

A depiction of Legba in in front of the royal palace in Abomey. It has the typical characteristics of the clay sculptures that stand at entrances to villages, courtyards and houses in the region – an overlarge head on a rough, stocky body, with enormous feet.

Ogun, god of iron, has many faces

The original shrine of the iron god Ogun (Gu to the Fon) is supposed to have been erected on the exact spot where the hunter, who carried him, disappeared into the earth. Many say that Ogun does not have such a sensitive nature as the other gods, but has great strength, with a body of steel and a head of iron. Among the Fon, Gu is one of the highest-ranking gods.

Among the 201 to 401 (or even more) named vodun deities, some are revered locally, while others stand in high regard throughout the whole country. Ogun is one of the latter among the Yoruba, and Ogun Gu is the supreme sky god within the group around Mawu-Lisa. From time immemorial he has had the task of making the world inhabitable, and he still does this today. According to tradition he cut a path for the gods with his bush knife when they came to earth for the first time. Because of his skill with iron and his great strength, he rose to become the god of hunters and warriors, blacksmiths and goldsmiths, butchers, soldiers, and barbers. With increasing social and commercial complexity, his field of influence also expanded: today his domain encompasses everything in modern technology to do with metal, danger, and transport, including road safety. He is specially worshiped by craftsmen who use metal tools, by truck and taxi drivers, by mechanics, and by hairdressers, in fact all those who deal with metal. His followers belong to the most mobile social groups. He is the patron god of engineers who build roads, bridges, and settlements, and who stand for change and renewal.

Ogun (Gu) is a violent, bloodthirsty god. Blood, the juice of life, is seen as the holiest offering that can be made to him.

Above and right: The sculpture of Ogun (Gu) is rubbed with the fresh blood, the vital life-juice, of a slaughtered ram.

Ogun combines the most varied characteristics and tendencies. On the one hand, he is thought to be wild and unrestrained and is portrayed as a heavily armed warrior festooned with deadly "medicines." On the other hand, he also represents the "ideal man": extremely potent, feeding and protecting his own with a strong arm, acting justly and always with good manners. He faithfully watches over contracts and agreements, and when a follower of the old Yoruba religion appears before a court, rather than choosing the Bible or the Koran he swears on iron, which is filled with Ogun's powerful essence. "He has many faces," as his followers say. When he shows his destructive side, he takes on the features of a lonely, isolated outsider; when he does good, it is the creative force which drives him to bring about something new.

The basis of his power is his special ability to smelt iron. Blacksmiths hold a similarly extraordinary position in African society. Their special talents bring them great awe, sometimes esteem, and at other times contempt. As well as producing useful farming tools, smiths make weapons which are used for hunting and making war, which exercise power and destroy lives. Hunting and soldiering used to be closely associated with each other; in many West African empires hunters formed the advance guard in war. Hunters and warriors who were polluted by death

had to be "cooled down" by water from the forge before they could return to society. This is one reason why forges are sacred places, which can have a purifying and healing effect.

The first mention of Ogun being worshiped as the god of iron dates from the 16th century. The need for iron grew at that time in the eastern Yoruba territory, and many wars were fought. Both here and in the old Benin empire there were ritual duels between rulers and village chiefs as part of the demonstrations in honor of the god. Tournaments, which were actually supposed to demonstrate Ogun's victorious power, also played a part in royal ceremonies in Dahomey and are still held in a smaller way by followers. Swords or other iron weapons with sharp blades are usually used. The god's destructive nature is revealed when his followers are in a trance; fits of rage, effectively demonstrated, are marked by extreme violence. Even this side of Ogun has some good: rulers, warriors, and hunters all kill with good intent; their higher aim is to look after their people and to expand the empire. Destruction takes place for the sake of preservation, as well as making way for new

things: Ogun destroys the old in order to make room for the new; when hunting, he over-exploits nature in order to safeguard the continuation of culture.

In cosmogony, in which Ogun plays a central role, destruction and creation are closely associated; destructive acts always possess creative potencies. Ogun, who taught people how to use fire and produce iron, and showed them how to build cities and found empires on the ruins of others, is a symbol of creative will and change. The wisdom hidden behind his features comes from the knowledge that passing away and coming into being are irreconcilably connected with each other. Ogun teaches people that every action can develop its own dynamic, get out of control, and have unforeseen consequences.

His lonely remoteness stands for this. In a well-known legend, of which many variations are told and which is about civil war, rebellion, and bloody conflict, warlike Ogun condemns himself to eternal isolation; in some versions he even commits suicide after butchering his own people, or after a bloody battle he simply vanishes down into the earth. According to tradition, he helped his mother Odudua in a battle against her enemies and showed so much courage that he was rewarded with the kingdom of Ire, whose rulers claim to be descended from him. He was last seen in Ire as he sank into the earth with his sword. A shrine was erected at that very spot.

In Dassa (formerly Ida-Cha), in present-day central Benin and one of the first Yoruba settlements in the region, Ogun lived on with other old Yoruba gods. It was from there that the gods came to the Fon. Ogun became Gu, whose original shrine is in Dassa. It is said that for a long time a man named Gu lived on a mountain thereabout. Every five days when the market was held (the Fon took their five-day market week from the Yoruba), the man came down from his mountain in order to catch men and castrate them. The king was worried by this and sent a messenger to bring him to his palace, where he commanded him to stop these atrocities. Gu appeared to be deaf, for he continued to hunt men; armed with a spear, he would sit on a huntsman's shoulders and never leave him. After he had carried Gu for a long time, the huntsman disappeared in the mountains, leaving only his spear behind. It is said that he is still up on the mountain today, in the

hands of the people of Dassa. Since then the ruler of Dassa has been Gu's guard.

The story makes clear that the first inhabitants of Dassa were hunters who already knew how to smelt iron, and that the Fon must have taken over the craft of smelting from them.

Top: Ogun's followers also emerge from the ceremony strengthened: they drink the ram's blood.

Above: The urge to drink blood is prompted by the fact that Ogun's followers are possessed by his spirit and so have the same desires as the god. Others stay close to the possessed, to ensure that they do no harm to themselves or others.

271

Nana Tongo, the god who came from far away

The priest brings from the shrine two sacral objects which possess the great power of the god Nana Tongo. Cult members spend money on equipping the deity properly, with clothes, spears, gongs, talismans, and other things typical of the north – especially spears, which the god uses to strike down his followers' enemies.

A number of deities are not native to their land. They were brought from the north, in the hope that they would offer effective help, especially in catching witches.

Nana Tongo is such a god. He was brought to the Volta region by Charles Adowo, a priest from Gbedzekope who spent three years (the classic period of training for a traditional priest) in the Tong region around Zuarungu. Like most gods imported from the north, Nana Tongo is employed mostly in the pursuit of witches who were not known in his homeland. There he was known as Ton-nab (Chief of Tongo); his responsibilities included ensuring that crops thrived, that there was sufficient rainfall, and that people and animals suffered no famine and were blessed with offspring. He was extremely important. By the 1920s his fame had spread as far as the coast. He received his power directly from god (Na Yin). The chief (*tendan*) of the Tallensi who lived in the region was entrusted with

Top left: The priest's assistants carry Tong fetishes and spears. The fetishes are covered with layers of old, dried sacrificial blood.

Top right: The "medicines" are placed on sheepskins. Nana Tongo protects against witchcraft, which accounts for the two owls, or "witch birds," which have been tied before him.

Above, left and right: Nana Tongo's cult members and mediums are mostly women, who go into a trance when the god enters them.

Right: The possessed women adopt the god's thirst for blood; they want to drink sacrificial blood with him.

Nana Tongo feeds on blood. The ritual begins with the sacrifice of a duck.

The priest pours sacrificial blood over cult utensils, and then shares the blood with the god by drinking some himself.

A medium in a state of trance carries the duck in her mouth, in order to taste its blood.

Gin is given to a ram before it is sacrificed. In the north, water is used to see by the animal's reactions whether the ancestor, god, or spirit is willing to accept the offering.

The priest licks and bites the ram's raw flesh.

The priest's assistants carry the ram in their mouths; both they and the priest wish to get as much of the animal's blood as they can.

274

serving him. The center of the cult was originally in the wilderness of the Tong mountains, whose former inhabitants had been forced to move down to the plains during the course of a punitive expedition by the British. Ton-nab was worshiped in a large cave, and his altar was kept in another cave nearby. In 1928 Captain Robert Sutherland Rattray, the British ethnologist and colonial official, met people who had come a long way to ask the god for favors. Visitors left their clothes at the foot of the mountain, since the shrine could be entered only by those wearing a loincloth, and it had to be entered backward. One after another people put their requests to the god, and according to Rattray's notes these were mainly of a pecuniary nature. The chief repeated each request in the local language. After each petition a long, drawn-out wailing came from the back of the cave and all present clapped their hands. After all the requests had been heard, everyone left the cave and followed the chief to the entrance of the second cave. There offerings were made on the cone-shaped altar. Encrusted blood and a huge pile of chicken feathers on the floor testified to the age of the custom. The chief introduced each offering to the god by banging on the altar with a round stone. Then he made the offering. When all the offerings had been made, the petitioners returned in silence to the foot of the mountain. Finally, they all had a line drawn in red clay on both cheeks, as well as on their arms, legs, chest, and back.

The priest and his two assistants lie next to the sacrificed ram in a state of total exhaustion.

Mami Wata, the beautiful water nymph

Mami Wata, goddess of water, is a more recent, highly successful deity within the vodun pantheon. Very different ideas are combined within her. The cult that the Ewe of southern Togo and southeastern Ghana dedicate to her shares many characteristics of both old and new cults of water spirits, but is very different from traditional views with regard to modern consumer goods. Mami Wata is not concerned with morals, group solidarity, or public spirit, but with the happiness or unhappiness of the individual. Those who are possessed by her experience a kind of split personality. The goddess seems to attract people who have problems of self-discovery and who fluctuate between old traditions and new, foreign goods. She combines elements of water worship with nonindigenous features, and her cult represents an amalgam of African, Indian, and European traditions.

The first Europeans appeared on the coast of Guinea as if their ships had suddenly risen from the sea. Their skin was the color of a drowned person, and their tools could only have been created by

A shrine of water goddess Mami Wata in the Volta region of Ghana. She is represented in all sorts of different ways, but often as a nymph. This cement figure shows clearly the Hindu influences: each of the seven heads carries the sign of an Indian caste. A figure of Christ stands in the water next to the goddess. Christ revealed himself to the priest Abidjan Mami Wata, and the priest commissioned an artist who also had a vision of Christ to make the figure.

Abidjan Mami Wata at prayer. Priests form the most important link between people and the deity. They call up the gods, present human cares and worries to them, and try to negotiate the most advantageous conditions and compromises. The priest and other cult followers gather around the statue and sing songs of praise to the goddess.

precious stones, and pearls. She is also known as the wife of the god Ablo, who by the beginning of the 20th century was associated with the "riches of the sea." She is also worshiped as the spirit of a drowned person or as "mistress of water" and drowned people. A whole series of the "old" deities (including Mami Toxosu, Mami Ablo, and Mami Densu) appear in her retinue, having been given some of the attributes of modern life. She is also accompanied by Hindu deities such as Mami Rama and Mami Vishnu. Christian Ewe identify her with the Virgin Mary, Mami Jesuvi, and Mami Joseph. Over time this resulted in a pantheon of gods that was extremely mixed but always characterized by worship of the spiritual powers of water.

A cult follower becomes possessed.

The cult follower kneels before the image of the goddess. Mami Wata has greater power than Christ, which is why the priest puts the figure of Christ beneath that of the goddess. The integration of Christ into the Mami Wata pantheon is limited to only a few cultures.

strange water spirits. European culture and its wealth became associated with the sea. A whole range of different water spirits were given the pidgin title Mami Wata, or Mammy Water, and at the same time they acquired new, surprisingly similar characteristics.

The Ewe managed to fit the cult of Mami Wata into the older vodun cults by associating her with various traditional deities. This was especially the case with Dan, the vodun of money, merchants,

The first northern sea goddesses of the Guinea Coast clearly developed from the figureheads of sailing ships. A new type arose when European prints appeared in African markets and were copied by wall-painters, woodcarvers, and sculptors. At first these were popular representations of nymphs, and shortly before World War I a German showman's poster entitled *The Snake Charmer*, which had probably been printed in Hamburg between 1880 and 1887, spread throughout the markets of West Africa. The motif, milieu, and facial features are reminiscent of India.

In the 1940s and 1950s the picture was so enormously popular that Indian traders copied and printed it. The wealth of reproductions caused the picture to become even better known throughout West Africa. It soon decorated the walls of many houses in which the followers of Mami Wata met. Fortune-tellers and healers used representations made of plastic, wood, or cement as advertising and cult figures.

In the same context there was a growing African interest in various Hindu gods and goddesses. The presence of Indian merchants and their obvious commercial success gave new impulse to the cult. A Yoruba merchant who sold popular Hindu pictures in Togo explains: "We already had the pictures in colonial times, but their meaning was foreign to us. People liked them and decorated their rooms and houses with them. Then Africans began to study them and to wonder why Indians put candles, lights, and incense sticks in front of the pictures. I believe they used them to get our money. We made friends with them in order to discover the secret behind the pictures."

This statement makes a direct connection between the Indian pictures and their financial success, similar to the connection between the earlier mermaid and European wealth and power. Today, Mami Wata has developed into a highly complex cult, which blends together traditional, Christian, Hindu, Buddhist, and even astrological elements.

Abidjan clearly enjoys the power that his important position affords him. He is head of a whole Mami Wata village and is the leader of a cult group with hundreds of members and followers.

Possession – souls in the hands of the gods

In a world in which gods make up a small number, humans a larger part, and ancestors and spirits the overwhelming proportion of higher beings, contact between them is unavoidable. The effect of the gods can be seen in the rule of nature – in the radiance of the sun, the cyclical waxing and waning of the moon, in rain, wind, and the force of storms. The gods show themselves directly to very few. Ancestors and spirits, on the other hand, often appear to people or show themselves through signs, such as special events, illness, or an abundant harvest. Direct contact, however, is possible only via a peculiarity which is common to all.

Gods and spirits have spiritual natures only. People also share in this, thanks to their soul, which does not pass away with death but goes on living as an ancestor and after a time is reincarnated among the living. The soul, which gives people consciousness, the ability to think, willpower, and judgment, also allows people to be in contact with the powers beyond. Unlike the mind, which is responsible for the organic functioning of the body, the spirit is independent and capable of freeing itself from the body. Anyone can convince themselves of this during sleep at night when the body is physically at rest and the soul's bodily "supports" relax; the soul can then leave the body and journey into the immaterial afterworld which is open to spirits. What the soul sees and experiences there forms the content of dreams.

While in a trance, a medium seizes a child and carries her away.

Very early on people obviously knew how to make use of this opportunity. All they had to do was subject the body to a situation that was similar to sleep. This was made possible – and still is in many parts of the world – by strict fasting and other forms of self-denial, by rhythmic movements, dancing, singing, or by taking consciousness-enhancing (hallucinogenic) drugs; these can lead to a trancelike state in which the soul leaves the body and comes into contact with ancestors, spirits, or gods, just as the person concerned wishes. This is a form of ecstasy (from the Greek *ekstasis*, meaning "standing outside oneself"). The masters of this technique were the shamans. They used it to bring back souls which had lost their way or had been stolen by spirits (the cause of psychoses), to present people's wishes to ancestors and gods, to locate wild game, and to see into the future.

Contact is, of course, also possible in the opposite direction. Spirits and gods who want to communicate with people or whose advice has been sought choose a particular individual in order to use his or her voice. When they do this, they possess the spiritual part of his or her personality, namely the soul, which is in keeping with their nature.

During a trance the medium's face is covered with white powder and marked with blue stripes. Both colors protect him from disaster and give him the ability to detect witches' intrigues and foresee future events.

This has certain consequences. The "possessed" subject must be subdued before the medium goes into a trance. If the incorporation of the spirit is consciously sought, the same preparations as for ecstasy are then required: seclusion, fasting, self-denial, concentration exercises, prayer, rhythmic movement, dance, and sometimes the use of drugs. Once he or she has been possessed, the medium's voice and behavior change in a characteristic way depending on the nature and gender of the spiritual powers. Ancestors and protective spirits express themselves differently from evil spirits; fertility goddesses are different from war or storm deities. In order to intensify fusion with the approaching identity, mediums often try to adopt the external features of the spiritual power which is taking possession of them; they may put on special clothes and carry typical tools or weapons.

Possession occurs almost without exception in settled agrarian and urban societies in which social problems are on the increase; this means that people in difficult situations seek advice more often from higher powers, as well as seeking judgments on disputes. Possession can then be used to discover the will of the ancestors, to obtain information about the cause of an illness or some other misfortune, or to seek clarification in problematic situations. Possession can also serve prophecy.

Possession cults

Like ecstasy, possession is often an individual phenomenon, but can also work collectively. When several people come together to practice religion, the spirit may come over one of them, and this may act as a catalyst for the others, especially if they are all in a sensitized, receptive mood. Since the people who come together are very often neighbors, there is always the tendency to integrate common religious experience into an organization. This resulted in so-called possession cults, which were known in antiquity among the ancient Israelites and early Christian communities. Today they are increasingly common in Third World countries, especially in cities. Again, this is a result of increasing social problems and especially inequality between the sexes; in many cults, such as the Candomblé in Brazil and the Zar in northeastern African, women play a leading role. In Nigeria the Islamization of the Hausa developed in such a way that women were practically excluded from public life, so they formed their own autonomous world of the Bori cult.

Spiritual communities sometimes take the form of a "church." They lay down rules for their members beyond those of their religious meetings, concerning behavior that is appropriate to specific moral ideas, such as moderation, helpfulness, and self-sacrifice; they have strict conditions of admittance, special customs and rituals, their own cult centers and costumes, as well as priestesses or priests who sometimes form a hierarchical clergy.

A person is called to be a medium usually by the spirits themselves. He or she senses this on falling ill in a certain way. This may involve skin complaints, leprosy, stomach problems, impotence, infertility, and above all mental confusion. If someone accepts the call and is initiated into a cult, he or she is cured of the specific illness.

The initiation follows a traditional pattern: novices learn to convert their suffering into a positive force, which they can later use to help themselves as well as others. The initiation is the beginning of a lasting relationship. The spiritual power is captured in an altar, so that during celebration of the cult people may be possessed by it. At first the circumstances of altered

consciousness are uncontrollable, but they gradually subside to a typical pattern: cult members learn how to master the technique of the trance. Novices learn this during initiation. They learn more about the spiritual power which has called them, and are instructed in the language and typical behavior of individual spirits and gods, their songs of praise, drum rhythms, dances, and particular way of moving. Then they have all the necessary prerequisites for their future activities as a medium.

With lay people and beginners the transition from normality to a state of trance is more abrupt and violent than it is with experienced mediums. Cult members know this and adjust to it, since no trance is exactly the same as another. Trances vary according to the experience, age, and routine of the medium.

Some external aids play an important role in entering into a trance. These vary from cult to cult, but there are basic similarities between them. The acceptance of the spiritual powers is eased by earlier fasting and staying awake, followed by rhythmic singing to a drumbeat and persistent, gradually more energetic dancing. Another effective means is concentration on certain parts of the

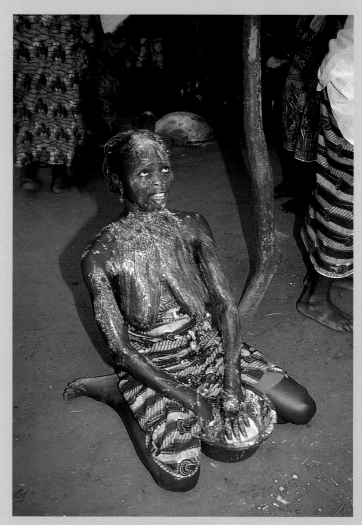

Possession rituals among the Minah usually begin early in the afternoon and end during the night or early the following morning. Here we see a medium of Jagli, a powerful god from the north who causes strong trances and encourages his mediums to particularly wild dancing.

A Minah initiate of water goddess Mami Wata in a state of trance.

body or movements, in order to prevent the thoughts wandering. During the course of a cult meeting it is often known for various spirits to take possession of the mediums one after another. Those present can easily tell the difference between affected and genuine possession. The latter results in a rise in body temperature: a medium's body becomes hot, and an outbreak of sweat is one of the clearest signs of the presence of a spiritual power. As soon as a medium is possessed, his or her behavior changes. Above all, their sensitivity appears to be dimmed. Mediums act in an abnormal way: they kill animals, drink the blood or cover themselves in it. They show no reaction to being injured by pieces of glass or even weapons, or to being burned. It is therefore important that their actions do not get out of control, and the cult sees to this. Experienced members watch over the course of the trance. If the self-renunciation of a medium should become threatening, they take appropriate measures and bring him or her back to reality. The state of possession is followed by complete amnesia: the medium has no memory whatsoever of anything that was said or done during the trance.

Bori – horse and rider

One of the periodic dances of the bori cult takes place in a square in front of the sponsor's house in a side street of Dogon-Doutchi (Niger). Musicians clear the way for the wind spirits (*bori*) with the rhythm of their large calabash drums; this could not happen without the music.

A prostitute starts to dance. The dance leads her into a possessed state. The relationship between spirit and medium is expressed by the symbols "horse" (medium) and "rider" (spirit); male mediums are known as *doki* (stallion), and female as *godiya* (mare).

"A long time ago," according to a legend of the Hausa, "Allah ordered the first couple, Adamu and Adama, to bring him their children. The woman advised her husband not to show all their children to God, but to hide some, in case God wanted to keep them. Allah saw through her and said, 'The others are hidden there; they are hidden people; they will remain hidden people forever.' These hidden beings, to whom we are still bound today by mutual obligations, are the spirits."

The roles played in the legend by Allah, Adam, and Eve show that the myth is relatively recent. Possession by spirits, however, was part of the pre-Islamic Hausa religion (Maguzawa), to which a small number of people in rural areas have remained loyal; the old cult was once closely bound to the state religion, but it was forced to the periphery of Islam. Today spiritual mediums, musicians, and followers of the bori cult (cult of the wind spirits) form a kind of marginalized subculture.

As is often the case in the Islamic world, the bori cult is mainly women's business; it is followed mostly within the farmstead. Respectable women rarely attend public bori rites where there is a mixed attendance. The men, who are mostly strict Muslims, behave in a reserved way toward followers of the bori cult; those who join are often defamed as being impotent or homosexual.

Hausa society is divided into a strict hierarchy according to sex, age, origin, status, number of children, social success, and wealth. In this system, which turns a girl into an adult, marriage is a natural condition for women. Any woman of an appropriate age who is divorced and has not remarried or who has remained single is known as *karuwa* (*karuwai* in the plural; from *karuvanci*, meaning "prostitution"). People keep their distance from karuwai. During the fasting month of Ramadan children make fun of them in public. Many members of the bori cult are stereotyped as being karuwai.

Musicians, mediums, and followers of the bori cult belong to despised professions (butchers, fishermen, ferrymen, woodworkers, canoe-builders, potters, dyers, blacksmiths and metalworkers, showmen, farmers, and servants), or they are social deviants and outsiders (such as prostitutes, homosexuals, and transvestites).

The bori cult of the urban Hausa is rightly known as an association of outsiders, degraded and ostracized people – with all the necessary experience to stand by all recent sufferers. Cult followers and their sympathizers are people of ambiguous origin; their identity is split because of specific characteristics (such as homosexuality, transvestism, or nymphomania); their career prospects are minimal. Divorce or illness caused many of them to become solitary and secluded. They all use the bori cult to redefine their social position. By joining the cult they at least gain some status and a precise role. The fact that a spiritual power is responsible for their deviation makes it easier for society to understand the abnormality, which is accepted after initiation into the cult. Membership of the cult turns a rootless outsider into a "horse of the spirits" with his specific mediumistic tasks. In this way the cult fulfills a definite function of social integration. The bori cult offers those on the margins of Hausa society a meaningful existence in their own world of mutual responsibilities and gives them the opportunity collectively to defy stigmatization or at least to escape from it.

In future they must be of service to the wind spirits (bori). In order to maintain or improve his or her status within the cult community, any member must voluntarily take part in all events. These mainly comprise healing and initiation rituals (girka), as well as periodic dances (wasan bori, meaning "playing bori"), which take place at the invitation of followers or sympathizers to weddings or Islamic naming ceremonies. It is the duty of cult dancers and musicians to attend, but the events also serve as entertainment.

Just like the mediums, bori cult musicians have a low status. They are seen as lazy, dirty, wasteful, and groveling; their activities are a despised trade (sana'a) and are known as begging (roko). They are not usually initiated into the cult and play for money. It is their job to pass on the oral tradition,

songs, and customs of the bori cult. During cult ceremonies their songs and rhythms make a connection with the spirits, who could not "ride" without their music. They therefore have considerable influence.

The spirits, which are tolerated by Islam, are attracted by the music. They move as if they were floating on the wind, which is why they are called iskoki (iska in the singular; meaning "wind"), or in

The trance has begun and the medium grabs one of the men present. A cult follower, or "daughter of the bori" (yar bori) helps the medium to climb on a man's back. In this way she imitates the wind spirit, which has entered the medium and is now "riding" her in her state of trance.

The woman, and therefore the spirit, rides the man. When dancing with the priest, prostitutes use lascivious movements to attract customers.

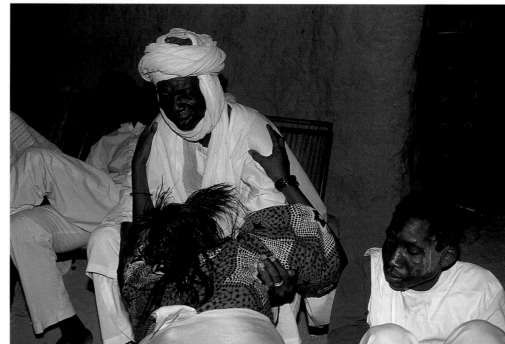

Finally, the medium sinks to the floor before the priest (*sarkim bori*, "chief of the bori"). In order to rise to this office, the priest must be experienced as a medium and have the support of the local cult followers. He organizes cult ceremonies and presents gifts and invitations to the various performers. For this he receives a large part of the cult's income.

A transvestite starts to dance in a "womanish" way. The yan dauda have high, soft voices, which are appropriate to the way they move. Their transvestism is quite noticeable, and as a rule they make no attempt to hide it. There is a price to pay for this openness: they are often caricatured, both within the cult and also in public.

urban areas often *aljanu* (*aljani* in the singular, from the Arabic *jinn*) or *bori*. People believe that the spirits live in families in the mythical city of Jangare, where they are ruled by a king (Sarkin Aljan, the chief of all spirits) with a large court. One role of the spirits is to mediate between Allah and people, which is why one finds them everywhere. Cult followers recognize between 125 and 275 named gods, and they know all their favorite locations and sacrificial offerings. Each spirit has one or several names, its own piece of music or song of praise, its own typical way of talking, as well as its own costume and dance. A number of spirits share the same features, and these are considered to be related to each other within the same family of spirits. During cult ceremonies the spirits stay among people for a limited period. Each one is greeted with proper respect. If a spirit's medium has to sneeze, this is a sign that the spirit has to leave, in which case it is bidden farewell.

Spirits are classified as "black" or "white," mainly according to location. The former live in the bush, in trees and water, and are known as heathens to Muslims. White spirits, on the other hand, are known as believers, since they live in towns. If you make offerings to white spirits, they will bring wealth; if they are neglected, they will take revenge by bringing illness. Black spirits are almost exclusively responsible for suffering, and each one has its own specific kind. If the spirits are accepted, people are cured: the illness changes into a "professional" possession. The distinctions between groups of spirits are not always strictly held. A Muslim spirit can turn black if it does evil or wears dark clothing. Any spirit can appear white to one medium, black to another.

Below: The medium goes into a trance. The arrival of the spirits and the onset of possession are often very theatrical: the medium starts to moan, falls to the ground, and foams at the mouth, while her body trembles all over. She covers herself with dirt to show her low social standing.

The medium breaks down in a state of exhaustion. She is brought round by a "soldier."

287

Hauka – dance of the European spirits

Many European spirits (*iskokin turawa*) are found within the bori cult (cult of the wind spirits). Unlike the Songhay, the Hausa, an Islamic society, do not devote a cult to them. In Baboule (Niger) mediums are led by a priest as they march to the dancing area.

There are also numerous European spirits (*iskokin turawa*) within the bori cult. They belong to foreign spirits whose mediums represent foreign cultures in various rituals and often demand exotic sacrificial offerings. In the bori cult of the Hausa and in the hauka cult of the Songhay in Niger and Mali this role is often taken by European colonials and soldiers.

In both the Hausa- and Songhay-speaking groups in Niger the roots of possession cults go much deeper, possibly back to the time of Islamization in the 15th century. The holey cult, for example, is very similar to the bori. It is known that the Songhay took their hauka spirits from the Hausa. *Hauka* is a Hausa word meaning "madman" or "maniac." The holey spirits are divided into various families, each of which is associated with certain natural phenomena and neighboring peoples, allowing them to be assigned to certain times in history. For example, the tooru, or spirits of rivers and the sky, are associated with great ancestors, the founders of the first Songhay dynasty. The *genji kwaan*, or "white spirits," represent the Tuareg and Koran scholars who gained in

The chief priest of the hauka cult in his hut.

A woman is possessed by the bori spirit Dumboro and gives a loud groan. As soon as the spirit enters human society, the medium reacts by changing her behavior.

The medium's head is covered with a cloth so that the spirit can "ride" its "horse" undisturbed.

Below: The woman is possessed by the bori spirit and groans loudly.

She is comforted by other women of the group.

influence after Islamization of the region, while the *genji bi*, or "black spirits," represent the early landowners, including the "lords of the earth," who were later enslaved. The *doguwa*, or Hausa spirits, on the other hand, are relatively young; they entered the native world of spirits when large Hausa-speaking groups arrived in 1911. Even more recent are the hauka, the "spirits of madness" from the European cultural world. They made their first appearance in a small village near Filingue in the Kurfey region in 1925, just three years after Niger became a French colony. There had been unrest in this region, which was inhabited by both Hausa- and Songhay-speaking groups. When a foreign spiritual power suddenly took possession of a woman, she was asked the name of the spirit and replied that it was Gomno Malia, the "governor of the Red Sea." Soon afterward other women and men were possessed by unknown spirits. These "daughters and sons" of Biladi, the African friend of the prophet Mohammed, came with the harmattan, a dry desert wind, and introduced themselves as hauka, guests of the violent storm god Dongo. They appeared in a country occupied by white men, where the military burned villages like Dongo, as well as killing people, seizing animals and grain, imposing taxes and dragging men off into forced labor. Anyone who resisted was fined or put in prison; the power of the whites bordered on the supernatural. The Europeans drew people's attention not just through the pale color of their skin but because of their martial conduct. As a result, the spirits saluted and drilled with great energy. They even demanded burning torches, which they used to set about the bodies of their mediums.

Soon after its introduction this form of possession spread well beyond the boundaries of Filingue. It met with stubborn resistance from the traditional holey and bori cults, however, not least because of its violent nature, and so the mediums formed smaller groups and founded their own villages. They called upon the local people to refuse to pay taxes and endure forced labor. In 1927 they even declared that they had the power to turn the Europeans' bullets into water. To the French colonial administration this meant open rebellion. Anyone who imitated their affected behavior was simply a thorn in their flesh. Since they knew little about the basis of Hausa and Songhay possession cults, they saw the movement as a political revolt and reacted with severe penalties. The French colonial official

Croccichia ordered that the first dancers be taken to Niamey and imprisoned. When they were released three days later, they began to dance again at once. Croccichia then demanded that they confess that it was all a fraud and that the hauka spirits did not in fact exist. The dancers did as he said, but it was not long before the betrayed spirits made themselves heard. The cult was then banned and its followers were forced into exile, which resulted in the possession ritual developing increasingly complex forms.

The movement had its religious as well as its political aspects. Besides giving it ammunition, the colonial regime created a breeding ground for the movement. The old village chiefs were relegated to the status of puppets of the colonial masters; people were forced by the heavy burden of taxes to go elsewhere in search of work or be obliged to work on plantations that produced cash crops for the global market; and they lost their former independence, becoming subject to the arbitrary power of administrators. These conditions enabled the movement to overcome family ties, membership of groups and villages, and even language barriers to create a higher form of community and develop into an international phenomenon. Using their detailed imitation of colonial masters in a highly creative, subtle, and complex way, the hauka spirits turned conflict into a form of grotesque theater.

Most European spirits portray soldiers and carry military titles. Armed with wooden rifles, they demand discipline and the immediate execution of their orders. Their clothing and equipment are a visible expression of their foreign nature.

The mediums stamp on the sand as they groan, yell, and beat their chests with their fists. Their eyes blaze while they foam at the mouth and stammer.

The spirit called Kabrana ("Corporal") seizes a medium and puts her in a trance.

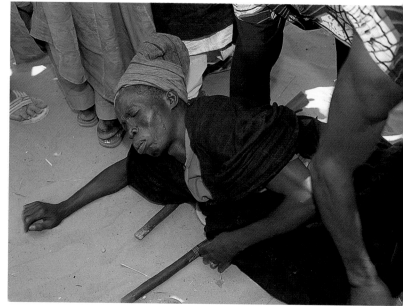

Right: The medium falls to the ground in a state of exhaustion.

In the 1930s Songhay emigrant workers introduced the hauka cult to the Gold Coast, where it blossomed in the 1940s and 1950s. Cult followers swung burning bushes around in their hands, ate poisonous plants, sacrificed dogs, and banged their heads against walls. In 1954 Jean Rouche, the famous French ethnologist and moviemaker, showed the annual festival of a hauka cult group in Accra in *Les Maîtres fous*. The movie shocked the Parisian public. Protests rained in from African intellectuals as well as ethnologists; Marcel Griaule even wanted it banned.

Since the end of the colonial period the hauka have disappeared from Ghana, but not from Nigeria and Niger. One wonders why the European spirits of the bori and hauka cults still play a part in countries where colonial administrators and soldiers left after independence was declared in 1960. Why do followers of the cult continue to imitate the colonial rulers and their institutions in a way which certainly amuses the public but at the same time fills them with fear? One reason could be that since those days conditions have only really improved for a small section of the society. Most of the rural population continues to suffer from poverty and misery, and there is a huge gulf between rich and poor. Perhaps the possession cult offers the needy the opportunity to caricature their recent experiences of changing military regimes and those who wield power in general. In the ritual this is presented in a highly dramatic yet tragic way. The "dance of the European gods" describes a current reality and for a few hours turns it into a grotesque unreality. Judges, doctors, lawyers, truck drivers, generals, majors, even the president set about local problems as they dance. A Songhay told the American ethnologist Paul Stoller in 1987, "We need the hauka more than ever today; they do good work for us."

The European spirits mime demonstrations of power. In a trance the mediums wave burning torches over their arms and bodies. During this "fire purification" (*wankan wuta*) they conquer the heat of the flames and demonstrate their complete fearlessness and powers of resistance. This shows them to be superior to other Africans as well as to the Europeans.

The bizarre appearance of the foreign spirits brings back both comic and terrible memories. Here a medium captures a child in the same way that his forefathers were taken off to forced labor. History lives on in the spirit rituals.

"Soldiers" escort two girls who are about to be initiated into the cult. The spirits are seen as unrelenting authority figures who insist that everything be done quickly and efficiently, just like earlier soldiers in the French colonial army.

The priest spreads the wings of a chicken that he has sacrificed to the gods as protection for the girls.

The priest washes the girls' hands in chicken's blood and water.

The priests know how to prepare magic potions and "cakes," which promise both to protect and to heal. Here a priest unrolls a cloth to reveal a small portion of hashish.

The girls are put together with the other initiates.

The power of the witch-hunters

Tuesdays and Fridays are sacred to Akonedi, and it is usually on these days that she takes possession of her priestess. The priestess dances on white squares that are meant only for mediums.

Other gods can also enter the priestesses and others present on the days when Akonedi appears. A young man foams at the mouth, which is a sure sign that he is possessed by a god. In this case it is a deity from the north, whose specialty is supporting its mediums in hunting witches.

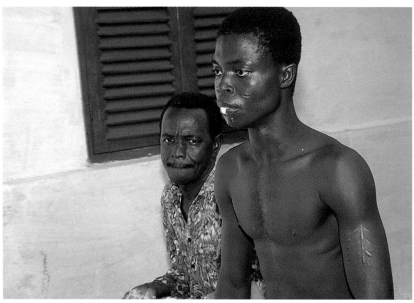

Cults often expand into neighboring groups and over great distances from the place where they originally formed. In Ghana and southwestern Burkina Faso cults are experiencing a boom; they can be acquired and then disposed of again like goods. There is a brisk trade in "medicines" that can be used to catch and combat witches. This has resulted in numerous religious changes both on the coast and inland. New cults are often integrated with existing ones, as in the case of the Akonedi, or they become part of community life in the same way as the old male societies; this is particularly the case in communities with existing developed cults, such as the cult of Wara among the Senufo.

By the end of the 19th century a possession cult had established itself in Late, a town in Akuapem, and this has since spread throughout the whole of Ghana. The famous shrine of this cult's

Top: The young man is given a warrior's outfit, which he will wear on the witch-hunt.

Center: He wanders through the narrow streets in search of witches.

Below: He regularly whips himself into a wild dance.

goddess is visited by many people. According to legend, Nedi was the daughter of a man named Ako who lived in the Kubease district. She was pregnant but died in the bush, where she turned into an anthill. Soon after her death her spirit possessed a woman from Kubease, who then became chief priestess for the shrine erected to Akonedi. Since then all leading priestesses have belonged to this family. Today women from all over the country undergo training in Late, so that when they return to their home village they can erect a new shrine or join an already existing group.

Akonedi's tasks are many and various. People come a long way to put all sorts of requests to her: infertile women ask to be blessed with children; mothers whose children always die ask to be released from a supposed curse; sick people ask to be healed; people facing a journey, school exams, or an important business transaction ask for her divine support. Those who have been cheated out of possessions or whose spouse has been unfaithful ask for the guilty parties to be punished. Many do not have a specific request, but simply wish to be in the goddess's care in order to ward off any potential misfortune.

Before the goddess appears, the priestess prepares herself for the visit. From the day before she refrains from sexual contact and certain foods, in order to become a pure vessel for the deity. During the night she cuts her hair short. Before daybreak cult members and visitors wait for the arrival of Akonedi. Her appearance is announced when the priestess becomes sleepy. Shortly before this many mediums experience a short, unusual period of peace and relaxation; they yawn and stretch their limbs. The transition to a state of possession happens quickly and dramatically. At once there is a great deal of activity. Since Akonedi avoids light, all the lamps in the sanctuary are extinguished. Drummers call the cult members to assemble in the court outside the priestess's room. There is a lot of noise: the medium cries out, sings,

Below: People living nearby are asked whether they have seen witches or could themselves be one.

Below: Toward the end of the ceremony priests make a liquid offering to Akonedi.

mumbles, jumps about, and dances around, while assistants dress her in white, hang beads round her neck, and put sandals on her feet. She comes out into the courtyard as Akonedi, with a ritual dagger in one hand and a brush in the other. Her clothes and her pale face shine in the darkness. Nana – a title given to the priestess when she is possessed – seems tense yet in high spirits, and she speaks in an old-fashioned Guan, the language of the original population of the region. The assistants give her bottles of spirits, which she pours liberally over cult objects, as well as her own head and shoulders. Soon she will be ready to listen to the many petitioners. But first there are domestic matters to be dealt with. She speaks in an aggrieved tone of a lack of discipline among the cult members and reprimands novices who have broken the rule of abstinence. After she has put her own house in order, she turns to the visitors. One after another they put their petitions to the goddess. Akonedi makes appropriate remarks to each one, making judgments and giving instructions. She discovers the causes of various complaints and prescribes the relevant cures.

For some considerable time, however, other deities besides Akonedi have appeared. She always appears first, but then other deities enter the priestess and other cult members. It may be Kwaa Asou Gyebi, a rather tentative god who speaks Twi (the language of the Akon) with a northern Ghanaian accent and asks for Scotch whisky, or other deities from the north, who specialize in supporting their mediums on a witch-hunt.

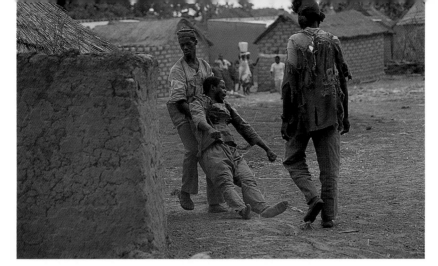

The Wara cult (a witch-hunting cult) in the Senufo village of Kankalaba is of recent origin. Previously the Senufo knew nothing of this kind. Masks or bush spirits would seize possession of a villager now and then, but they usually merely confused him or her. To them, seeing a strange power such as *Wara* (which means "as strong as a lion") in this role is a novelty.

Like the hunting and masked societies, Wara plays an important part in the memorial ritual of the cult, during which dancers honor a deceased member. This always includes "playing with fire," which demonstrates Wara's immeasurable power. The flames symbolize the god's "heated" nature, as well as showing the invulnerability of his mediums.

Only cult members are immune to the flames. They feel no pain, and no burn marks appear on their bodies.

When the gods speak

The Ewe of the Mono region have adopted a range of cults originating with the Minah. The gods of these cults – Koku, Jagli, and Ganbada ("wild iron") – can cause particularly intensive trances, during which mediums often inflict injury on themselves. At a cult ritual in Dogbo Zafi (Benin), a follower smashes a bottle against his head to demonstrate the strength of his god.

Ganbada's strength is contained in various objects (bo), notably iron bracelets and the horns of some wild animals. These objects are placed on cult robes worn by the mediums, enabling Ganbada's strength to transfer to both fabric and medium.

In Ghana, and also in Togo and Benin, possession of the human spirit is a distinctly regional phenomenon. Among the northern populations possession is a rare occurrence, unleashed only by the gods and spirits of other communities; the old, native spiritual powers of these regions do not possess people. In the south, however, virtually all the spiritual powers may periodically take possession of certain people. This is particularly the case among the Ewe and Minah, two ethnic communities whose language and culture are closely related.

In the 19th century, the Ewe broke up into numerous, mostly politically autonomous, chiefdoms and princedoms, established by those who had previously fled the old kingdom of Notsie. The Minah, on the other hand, are descendants from the region of Accra, where the modern capital Ghana is located. But they soon mixed with Ewe from Anlo and Deta, with Portuguese, with slave descendants returned from the New World, and with Fante refugees from the Elmina region – which is why the Ewe called them Minah (Ge was the name they gave to themselves). This community, already an ethnic melting pot, has, in practically all the larger settlements, been joined by Hausa, Yoruba, Fon, Anlo, Adja, Kabye, and other newcomer groups. The complexity of this ethnic mix is reflected in the highly complex world of spirits and gods and in the frequent occurrence of possessive trances such as can often be observed in communities with a myriad of different ethnic backgrounds and a high population density, and which have been subjected to accelerated social change. It is not surprising, therefore, that not only their ancestors, but also countless spiritual powers play an important role in the Ewe and the Minah conception of life. These spirits dwell at specific natural sites, usually choosing to appear in animal form, most notably that of a python or crocodile. But there are also those spirits of the deceased who suffered a violent death, who were buried without any form of ritual outside the village (as slaves of foreign origin had been in the past), and who incessantly seek to wreak vengeance on the living for their own wretched fortunes.

The more complex a community became, the greater the number of spiritual powers that existed within it. Today, these powers have each achieved an individual status in accordance with their origin. The Ewes distinguish between dependent and free spirits. All spirits are able to enter the free cult and even be promoted in status. For dependent spirits, however, both of these options are linked to their affiliation with specific local and descendant groups. Spirits are further distinguished on the basis of being "old" or "new." Ancestors had brought the old, or hereditary, gods with them from their original territory, while acquaintance with the new gods was made only later, on resettlement. Just as the free spirits and the new, or nomad, gods are often one and the same, so the old and the dependent gods are identical. There are, however, always exceptions to this rule as well as considerable regional distinctions. The Minah practice a similar form of differentiation between their gods. They refer to the divinities of their original settlement as *kotavoduwo* ("sound gods") or *gevoduwo* ("gods of the Ge"), while the new gods, generally worshiped by individuals, are *adjavoduwo* ("gods of the Adja").

Like other groups in West Africa, the Ewe and Minah believe in a preexisting world (*amedzofe*) – an exact replica of the visible world. In the preexisting world, humans live as child spirits (*nolimewivo*) in various families before they are born into this world. Before a child spirit (*nolimevi*) descends to

Right and following pages: When violent gods such as Ganbada enter their mediums, it is all but impossible to restrain them. Ganbada's presence first becomes apparent in the form of violent cramps, rolling eyeballs, and fierce yelling; the body appears to be convulsed in a struggle to resist the alien power.

Possession cults involve a range of spiritual powers. Here a medium is seized by the crocodile god Adzakpa, causing her gestures and mimicry to change. The crocodile is a being that lives both in water and on land, thus transcending borders.

Generally, onlookers are initially unaware of the identity of the spiritual power possessing a medium. Followers bring a medium who has fallen into a trance to the spirit's "house" – the sacred shrine – where he or she is appropriately dressed. Some mediums are clothed in unfamiliar costumes or have their faces painted.

By the various costumes that they wear and the ways in which they act, mediums are able to communicate certain messages to onlookers. Each dance forms part of a "dance story" in which several spiritual powers each stage their own "performance."

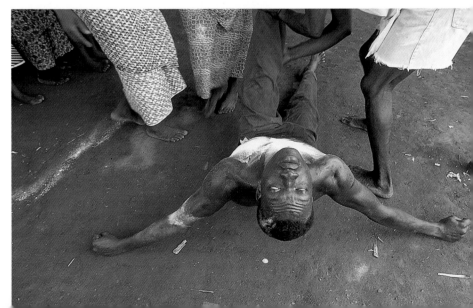

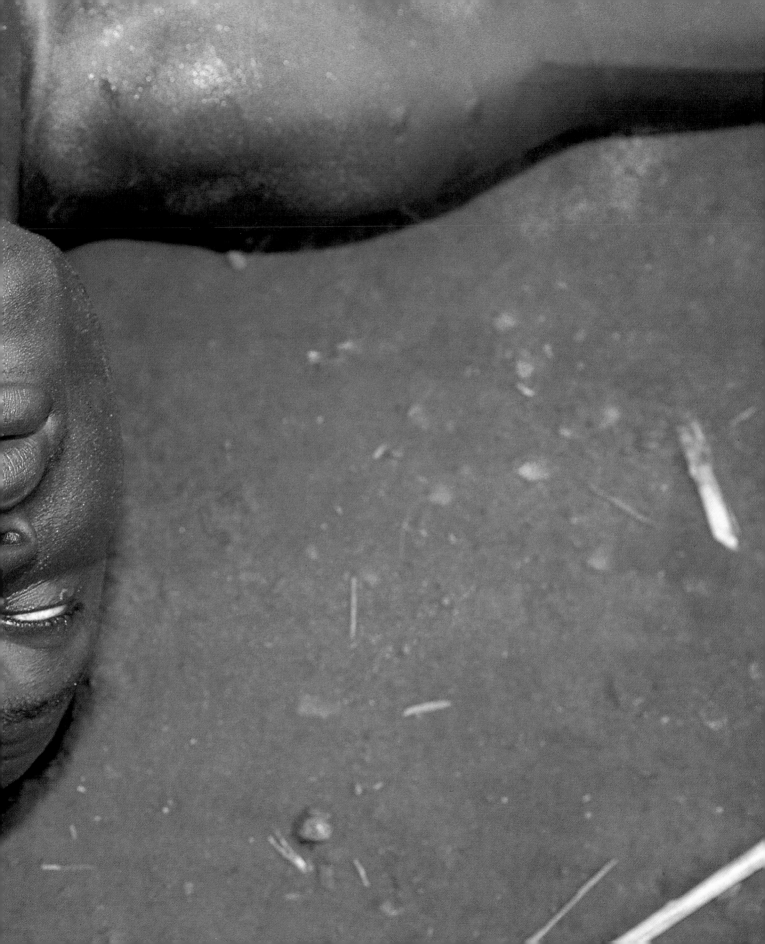

Ganbada unmistakably influences the way mediums behave. They act wildly, violently, and bloodthirstily. Those possessed by him will stop at nothing, not even at tearing the head off a chicken and drinking its blood.

One of the characteristics of the tempestuous slave gods is causing their mediums to climb onto roofs and up trees or compelling them to bang their heads against walls.

Onlookers identify the spiritual power by the medium's costumes and emblems – at once a sign of recognition, a verification of legitimacy, and a means of gaining respect. Plant fibers around his head and the animal's tail in his hand indicate that the god originates from the northern region.

This medium demonstrates his exceptional strength by igniting gunpowder on the palm of his hand.

Ganbada enables his mediums to take exceptionally high leaps into the air.

The invulnerability that Ganbada lends his followers is demonstrated here by the ability of a medium to crush glass with his bare feet. Other followers of Ganbada will then consume the pulverized remains in an attempt to gain some of that power and to achieve invulnerability.

In a state of possession, mediums often convey valuable information or medicinal remedies. This medium leans over an afflicted member of the community, explaining how the woman can be helped.

earth, a meeting is held in amedzofe at which God (Mawu-Lisa) and the spirit mother will assign a personality, a life duration, the entire fate of the child, in fact. The departing soul is given appropriate rules of conduct, committing itself to adhere to those rules. Souls that make this vow will achieve wealth, while those that depart secretly or leave in anger will be afflicted by poverty and misfortune.

On their often hazardous journey to earth, child spirits lose memory of their previous existence and their commitment. An ancestor is assigned to accompany and protect them on their dangerous journey, influencing the child spirit's personality (*dzodome*) which also harbors its personal relationship with the free divinities. All humans have such ties, but not in everyone do they reveal themselves. While some live a life in full harmony with their spiritual powers, others suffer illness under them. Such illness need not necessarily be caused by the defectiveness of one's own relationship, but may just as easily be the result of ties maintained by an ancestor and then transferred to that individual. A person's specific relationship with a spiritual power, therefore, is determined either by their previously assigned fate

He then loses consciousness and collapses. He is taken to a more secluded resting place and is covered with cloths.

When the medium regains consciousness, after several minutes or possibly even hours, he feels as though he has been relieved of a weighty burden.

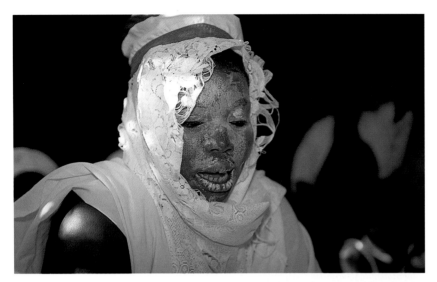

A medium in the costume of Mama Tsamba (the Muslim war god). The emblem of divinity is an Arabic men's headscarf (*hatta*) such as was often worn by slave hunters and traders. Tsamba is the name of a city in central Togo which in previous centuries was a flourishing slave market where wealthy Ewe and Minah families procured their "wares," either reselling them to Europeans or keeping them for their own purposes.

or by their family lineage. Hence, the quest to "find oneself" is possible only for those who do not harm the relationships and who acknowledge the spiritual powers that determine their character, should such powers reveal themselves.

There are also powers and spirits that may be acquired by one's own initiative – through physical intake, for example – that is, by eating their medicine (*atikedudu*). Such spiritual powers also possess their sanctuaries and communities displaying structures similar to those of other cult groups. Some mediums have multiple relationships, first appearing at cult ceremonies as the personification of one spirit and then as that of another. Almost no one, however, is possessed by a spirit to whom they are not related by the power of their initiation. The powers worshiped by cults normally appear in the form of a human or an animal. They are discernible by the attire, by the hairstyle, and paint with which their medium is adorned. Each spiritual power also has a unique way of behaving and speaking and has its favorite special foods and drinks. Their characters, too, are individual. While some may be reserved and possess a noble manner, others are wild and brutal. Among the latter are Koku, Tsamba, and Ganbada, on the one hand the dead spirits of slaves, but also representing beings with whom the slaves themselves had relationships and thus originating from their home regions in the north. It is believed that these relationships, too, are determined before birth and that the reincarnation of a slave will cause his or her relationships to be transferred to the new being. The fact that such spirits are slave gods is discernible on the grounds of the lined face tattoo with which the medium is adorned. This custom was formerly widespread in the northern regions of the West African savannas, but was one that the Ewe and Minah, however, rejected, as did the Asante. The metal chains used to bind slaves in former times also play an important part in these cults.

A medium seeks contact with the figure representing his god, one that belongs to the Tsamba group. These are not gods who actually dwell in the northern regions; they merely represent the experiences of the Ewe. The connection to the northern region is illustrated by the red headdress (reminiscent of the fez) and by the white robe.

As part of the ceremony for water goddess Mami Wata, a war god enters one of the women.

A possessed woman dancing. Every individual has different tutelary gods who can enter them. During a ceremony for Mami Wata, therefore, other gods may very well take possession of those present. Any of the tutelary gods of those attending the ceremony may enter the scene.

Mami Wata generally prefers to make her appearance donning the Western clothes of foreign women. Her mediums wear strapless white dresses, wigs, or hairpieces braided into their own hair, thus assuming the appearance of conceited European women.

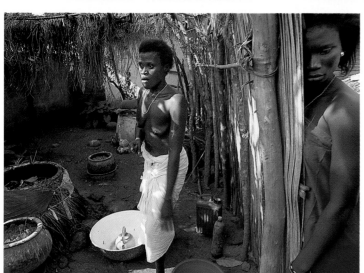

Calm has been restored. The pots and bowls contain the various cult medicines concocted according to secret formulas, the basis of which is mostly leaves and roots to which animal blood is often added. Mami Wata formulas also include powder, perfume, and fizzy lemonade.

A medium is induced out of her trance and back to consciousness. This requires trained helpers. In this case a mixture of certain herbs has been used. Occasionally, however, helpers use perfumes to induce a return to consciousness.

Lydwin's death and reincarnation

Lydwin has not recovered from a malaria attack despite all attempts to help her using regular medicine. The young woman's mother has sent her to Hounon Djalé, a healer and vodun priest. To protect her from the curse upon her, she is to be consecrated to a mighty war god. The procedure begins with the young woman going into a trance. She bends her back as though something is clinging to her, then writhes like someone being thrown about, now trying to balance, now straddling her legs and stamping her feet to the rhythm of the drums.

In an abrupt, partly defensive and partly submissive gesture, Lydwin throws both arms up to her head. The whites of her eyes becomes fixed; the trance begins.

In August 1997, a team of ethnologists and physicians traveled to southern Benin. Commissioned by a development aid organization, they researched and assessed the importance of traditional medicine in the region. They focused on the credibility of healers and plant therapists, the medical potential of their treatment methods and remedies, and the conditions under which the medicinal herbs used could ideally be cultivated.

One member of the team, a clinical physician, examined the ethnomedicinal significance of the state of trance. He had previously published work on this phenomenon, focusing on the medical, psychological, and social aspects affecting the people of Haiti, in the West Indies, where vodun is also an integral part of the culture.

This field trip provided the opportunity to observe states of trance in a village in the tribal region of the Minah, close to the Togo border. The research also explained the ethnomedicinal and psychological correlation involved in each healing procedure, the puzzling, even shocking, gifts of language, and the intensity of the experience, which nonetheless constitutes an effective therapy.

The healer and vodun priest of the village, Hounon Djalé, introduced his patient. In early March 1997, shortly after her 18th birthday, Lydwin unexpectedly collapsed. Unconscious and suffering intense fever, she was taken to Cotonou University Clinic. The diagnosis was malaria. Having been given medication, the patient regained consciousness and was responsive. The fever fell. She did not, however, recover from the disease. Continuing to suffer pain throughout her body, bouts of unconsciousness, and disturbed sleep, she was forced to quit her secretarial job. After their initial success, the attending physicians in Cotonou were unable to arrest the continuing deterioration of their young patient's health.

By then Lydwin had been suffering for six months, and Djalé, the vodun priest who had made a name for himself well beyond the confines of his own home village, was her mother's last resort. Disregarding the wishes of her husband's strict Catholic family, she took Lydwin to the priest. After only a brief consultation, Djalé diagnosed a *crise de prépossession*, a *vodún d'asi* ("vodun takes woman"), a condition of trance in which the afflicted person almost inevitably enters a phase of initiation. Two vodun adepts then took the apathetic and emaciated Lydwin to the priest's cloister area.

Three months later, Lydwin's mother was notified that her daughter had recovered. Lydwin had not only regained her strength and weight, she also appeared changed, matured. The experience of having endured the disease seemed only to have emphasized her beauty. Lydwin the patient had become Lydwin the adept, and after weeks of

Djalé hands to Lydwin two wooden poles covered in palm leaves. She grasps them and he proceeds to pull her into the sand, all the while persistently talking to her in a quiet tone. He then motions for a *vodunsi* (a female adept of the vodun gods) to come to them. The vodunsi feeds her a revitalizing mixture of palm wine and water from a clay bowl.

cloistered seclusion, she was to be consecrated to her tutelary god in a final *grande cérémonie*.

Djalé had diagnosed a range of conflicts as having been responsible for her state of ill health. These conflicts were brought on by an unfortunate love relationship which the patient had had and which had ended in a *maladie malfaiteur*, a disease caused by a curse. This pathogenesis (the manner of development of a disease) is one of particular significance in vodun and requires elaborate healing treatment. The conflicts and the parties involved must first be precisely identified, after which the issue is placed into the jurisdiction of the village. Inner and outer balance is regained through a process called *rachat*, a "promising action." Finally, Lydwin had to subject herself to one such action. Because the curse under which she had suffered was a particularly evil one, she was to be assigned a powerful tutelary spirit: Danou-Woto, war god in the cult of Mami Wata.

On her last day in seclusion, Lydwin was subjected to painstaking preparation for the event. This consisted of alternating relaxation in aromatic baths of leaves and rhythmic tensing through drums and chanting. Thus an erstwhile somnambulistic, dazed state turned to excitement, and rigidity turned to dance. The involuntary and agonizing *crise de prépossession* of the past months had been overcome and replaced by states of trance which the adept was increasingly able to bring on intentionally and which were almost controllable.

The *crise de possession* – "the vodun that rides her" – is the final act of initiation. First, however, the "old" Lydwin had to die. In a spiritual burial, she underwent "vodun death." During the night in her ritual grave, Lydwin's state of rigidity coupled with heightened concentration reinforced itself further. She had reached the phase of utmost vulnerability of the soul and of ideal receptiveness. The next morning, Djalé brought her "back to life" and led

Her elbows bent and fists clenched, she appears to be filled with new strength. With a movement of her arms reminiscent of a bird flapping its wings, she takes long, unerring strides back to the circle of dancers and bows deep before the altar of her tutelary god Danou-Woto.

311

She pulls the sacrificial chicken over her forehead as if it were a feathered cap and, in a single, violent move, tears it apart. From the mangled body of the chicken, the blood runs down her head and her upper body.

her to the circle of vodun dancers and drummers that had gathered around Danou-Woto's altar. She reached the group – taking small, uncertain steps – and a change occurred. Eyes wide open, she was hit by the increasing intensity of the rhythmic drumming.

Djalé, earnest and concentrated, watched the scene from an armchair not far from the drums. He directed the intensity and rhythm of the instruments through occasional movements of his fingers. He was aware that Lydwin's strength was gradually waning. Suddenly, he raised both hands. The hectic staccato changed to deeper, steady beats.

The priest carefully approached his adept. Breathing heavily, she dropped to her knees before him. To revive her energy, Djalé decided to enlist even more potent spiritual help: Sakpata, god of illness and disease, was called upon.

Lydwin's expression now underwent the most momentous change of all. Her distorted face adopted totally alien features, her left leg became

lame, and with her right leg she stamped into the clayey ground. She had reached the *vodún djó me ta* ("saints in my head") phase of the trance. In a baritone voice and an alien tongue – one, however, which the villagers recognized as that of the tutelary god Danou-Woto – Lydwin yelled short phrases at Djalé. He understood her commands and motioned for her to be given a live chicken. Silence immediately descended upon the followers. The drums now sounded a solemn, syncopated rhythm.

The sacrificial animal, the whirling movements, the guttural shouts – every one of the adept's gestures was familiar to the onlookers, be they the initiated or simple villagers. Everyone present recognized the unmistakable pattern of the proceedings – the form of the trance and the course it took, the patterns of movement that the dances contained. As he had done in the past, the tutelary god whom they had called upon now appeared in their midst, in archetypical clarity – through Lydwin, his intermediary.

Gradually her movements slowed down. Her left leg once more became lame, appearing to be fixed to the ground, as had been the case at the beginning of the trance. The spirit which had taken possession of Lydwin was obviously about to let go – a sign for the priest to intervene.

Djalé approached Lydwin, speaking loudly. The white of the adept's eyes was replaced by a tired, yet radiant, glance. He intercepted her final nervous movements by embracing her, and entrusted the exhausted woman to his servant, who led her back to the temple district.

He had successfully recalled her from the trance, but the ceremony did not end there. An hour later, Lydwin returned, a steaming bowl in her arms. By offering the sacrificial meal, she brought the ritual contact with the god to a close.

The reward for the mental and physical exertion of trance and initiation would be lifelong spiritual protection, prestige within the village community, and visibly apparent mental and physical recovery. Djalé, too, was content. The ceremony had given him an opportunity of demonstrating before the community and before the European observers his ability to control and implement the techniques of rite, trance, and healing. He returned Lydwin, healed and in restored harmony with her spiritual and social environment, to her relieved mother. And he smiled at the thought of having introduced a vodun spirit into the midst of an urban Catholic family.

The utility of possessive trances is variously judged by the scientific world – from trance as a therapeutic system to trance as an instrument of power in the hands of vodun priests. In the case described above, it appeared primarily to be an instrument with which to overcome situations of conflict and alleviate mental tensions, a therapy which also possibly has a stabilizing and stimulating effect on the body's own defense response.

According to the vodun understanding of health and disease, well-being is a state of being in harmony with the gods, with one's ancestors (the spiritual heritage), and with one's social environment. The spiritual element, however, must be comprehensible to those concerned and to the assisting village community.

This means that the spiritual element must be incorporated into the treatment in such a way that the senses can experience it. This was observed in

Lydwin has prepared a meal using the sacrificial fowl. She now wants to offer it to Danou-Woto, her tutelary god.

Approaching the altar, she once more falls into a trance. The rhythmic drumming which, up until then had controlled the scene, now ceases. Lydwin's prayers are all that can be heard.

the case we have portrayed – initiation through ritualized contact between the afflicted and Danou-Woto, the tutelary spirit.

The mechanisms of trance induction have been scientifically examined. Normal thought processes, for example, may be suppressed by intense concentration on certain bodily movements. Obsessively increased breathing (hyperventilation) and the production of the body's own, stimulating hormones (release of endorphins) together with a condition of exhaustion such as can occur after excessive dancing, and influence bodily functions in a complex way. The heart rate changes, as does cerebral efficiency. Biochemical and bioelectrical factors also undergo change. The outward signs are a dazed composure, perspiration, dilation of the pupils, impairment of vision, and even visual cramps (when only the white of the eyes is visible).

However, rhythm is what principally triggers a state of trance. The sound of drums and chanting at a certain frequency directly activates the central nervous system by stimulating the acoustic center of the brain. The signs of such stimulation are a sensation of light-weightedness, dizziness, an itchy-tingly feeling, and finger cramps. Changes in rhythm and tempo can influence the intensity and duration of a trance.

From a psychological point of view, such a moment may cause a patient's identification with himself or herself to be temporarily replaced by a spiritual principle – in our case the tutelary spirit. "Her spirit had given way to the god," namely, from a psychoanalytical perspective, in a ritualized dissociation in which religious acts led to a split in personality, albeit temporarily and controlled by an experienced healer.

This process is diversely assessed. Some observers consider it to be a behavioral disorder (psychopathological behavior) influenced by fear and depression. Ethnopsychoanalysis describes it as a suppressed part of one's self (the id, according to Sigmund Freud) that is acted out during the trance. All the explanatory options offered do, however, have one thing in common: they acknowledge the effectiveness of trance as a form of mental hygiene.

From a medical point of view, it can be described as a mood-changing therapy, having a stabilizing effect on mental and physical health. But

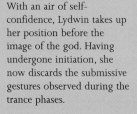

With an air of self-confidence, Lydwin takes up her position before the image of the god. Having undergone initiation, she now discards the submissive gestures observed during the trance phases.

it also has an effect that goes beyond what is medically definable. It allows patients to reassert their position within the village community, also stabilizing their status within the social structure of their family and tribe. This aspect, however, is realized through the *grande cérémonie*, the only ceremony that offers the individual healing, and the community moral direction and an experience of the senses, and priests an opportunity to demonstrate their power.

Performing such rituals before an audience enables methods such as hypnosis, suggestion, and trance to be instigated far more potently. It is a practice that is found not only in African rituals. The phenomenon is apparent in other cultures, too: for example, in the ceremonies of Native American shamans, the seances performed by European mesmerizers, the ecstatic trance dances of the dervishes of the Middle East, or the mass healings performed by Asian gurus. Common to all is the fact that rituals are staged both before a large audience and as a special happening – a fact emphasized by the location selected, by decorations and adornments, and by ritual objects and actions.

The healing expectations of those present – both observers and patients – coupled with the extraordinary experience such rituals offer when well orchestrated by the therapist, culminate in the anticipated effect.

Modern trance therapists and hypnotherapists whose work has a scientific basis (for example, those who operate according to the principles of the international Milton Erickson Association) generally do not stage their sessions in a big way, choosing instead to keep them small but intense. Creating heightened excitement and inspiring a willingness to respond through targeted provocation, and just the right amount of confusion are contributing factors in achieving states of hypnosis and trance.

Despite the existence of defined standards of therapy and quality controls, the personality of a physician or psychologist, their manner, and the healing atmosphere that they consciously create will always lend an air of mysticism. Paracelsus commented on this aspect, "A practitioner's treatment entails the notion that it will be effective."

Konrad Rippmann

In a final gesture, Lydwin pours the meal into the sacrificial bowl on the altar. Steam immediately rises from the bowl. The vodunsi see this as a sign that Danou-Woto is prepared to accept the sacrifice. This last gesture constitutes the close of the ceremony. Lydwin has now been liberated from the curse which had prevented her recovering from her illness. She has also now become a vodun adept.

Cult – a stage for sacred acts

Fetish worshipers, and in the background a fetish grove and temple, in the town of Pram pram in Ghana (between La and Niingo). Seated to the right, in a colorful floral robe, is the town chieftain. From: *Im Lande des Fetischs*, Basel, 1890.

If they are to be lasting, relationships need to be fed and fostered. We take particular care with our marriages, our families, and superior beings, because a breakup in these relationships would prove to be very painful, possibly even disastrous. People who belong to cults turn to their ancestors and to gods, and sometimes to influential spirits. The term "cult" is derived from the Latin noun *cultus*, which, in turn, comes from the verb *colere* (to care, maintain, serve). Cults serve as a means of fostering the relationships that humans have with their ancestors, and with certain spirits and gods.

In contrast to individual, less complex rites and ceremonies with only limited impact, cults are fixed institutions whose rituals have set locations, times, and formalities. They bring together a well-organized corpus of diverse rituals and ritual sequences. While rituals and ceremonies – that is, a series of connected ritual acts – may be conducted by individuals or specific groups of individuals (as in a wedding party), a cult is generally upheld by an entire community, and outsiders are normally not granted access. Only in some cases, such as esoteric, secret cults (a subject dealt with in greater detail below), membership is restricted to selected individuals of the group and access dependent on particular prerequisites (age, sex, status, profession).

Cult events, similar to rites and ceremonies of smaller dimension, are only performed on special occasions. For cults, however, such occasions must have significance for the entire community. Because they serve to maintain relationships with powers beyond this world, upon whose benevolence human existence depends, cults are employed both constantly to foster such relationships and to ward off all things that pose a threat to those good bonds. Unlike rites and ceremonies that are performed irregularly in response to certain events such as personal misconduct, a drought, a wedding, or a death, cult practices are (ideally) always performed according to the same patterns. Their purpose, therefore, is to act in prevention of all possible hazards, rather than to act upon a given circumstance.

The threats posed to traditional communities chiefly concerned their food sources, the ability of the group to procreate, and the maintenance of the order of creation. Cults therefore focused on times of seasonal or cosmic change that were seen as turning points, when things could go wrong or an unwelcome change could take place if the appropriate preventive measures were not taken. This fear was most discernible at the end of one year and the beginning of a new. Thus, most cults deal with these particular basic issues: fertility cults at the start of the crop-growing season to ensure fertile earth, strong seed stocks and good growth; cults of the dead, performed after harvesting, that is, at the change of the season, in remembrance of the dead and inviting them to partake in the harvest, giving thanks to them for the yields, celebrating with them, sharing their foods, and showering them with gifts in order to be assured of continued benevolence and, above all, the fertility of men and women – a benevolence which the gods may bestow or refuse at their discretion; renewal cults at the close of the year (the season) which reach a climax on the first day of the new year, a day on which everything – houses, clothing, tools, and even the community itself – is cleansed, on which offenses are confessed and sins atoned for, on which thanks is given and sacrifices are made to the gods, on which gifts are exchanged among the members of the community in order to strengthen anew people's existing ties, on which invigorating foods are communally consumed and the myth of creation is recited in order verbally and magically to renew and restrengthen the world order, thus ensuring the community's well-being during the coming year.

The advent of crop cultivation and a settled way of life, with an increasing number of people settling together within a confined area, caused growing tension and social conflict, as a consequence of which crises and awareness of problems among those peoples also grew. While cults among hunting societies existed only to a limited extent (for example, annual rituals ensuring the plentiful supply of plants and game), they were rapidly and prominently established in agricultural and, to an even greater extent, in urban communities. The more omnipresent a threat appeared to be, the more excessive the cult events were. Christian worship services are just one example of this.

The celebration of a cult always has several prerequisites. Because of the highly sacred nature of cults, their rituals can be performed only in certain sacred locations, clearly defined and distinctly separated from their profane surroundings – for example, on the village's central meeting and festival grounds, under which the founder of the settlement is often buried; in a "natural shrine" on a hilltop; under a large, old tree; at a waterhole; in a cave; in a sacred grove (in which, once selected as a place of worship, no tree may be felled or anything changed); in the men's house; or in a cult dwelling (a temple).

A Kamma sorcerer.
From: *Westafrika. Vom Senegal bis Benguela*, Leipzig, 1878.

Depending on its specific purpose, a cult is practiced only on the occasion of the major seasonal or cosmic turning points relevant to the community as a whole: universally at the turn of the year or at the advent of the new year; at the time of the solstice and at new moon; at midday, when the sun is at its peak; or at dusk, the time when the beyond becomes the here-and-now and ancestors, spirits, and gods appear. Cults should be conducted only by those who, because of their age, their social position, or their training, possess the necessary knowledge and are familiar with the powers of the world beyond. This could be the elders (who will themselves soon join the ancestors), the head of a clan or village, the king, or the priests or priestesses. Only certain tools and objects – those dedicated specifically to the cult – should be used: sacred bowls and drinking vessels, sacrificial knives, ancestral objects, idols, symbols of the gods, special musical instruments (flutes, bone trumpets, drums). The outward appearance of the participants, especially those directly involved in performing the sacred rituals, should also differ markedly from their everyday appearance. This applies to their body paints, costumes, masks (if ancestors, spirits, and gods are represented and mimicked), movements, gestures, and language. Finally, the ritual itself, the liturgy, must have comprehensive relevance as an act of sacral significance for the community: that is, through a central feature of the cult itself (for example, Holy Communion in the Christian Church), through a particularly important sacrifice, or through the defeat of a primeval monster that threatened the world order soon after its

Sacred islands in the Lake Jonanga, in a sketch by Griffon du Bellay. From: *Westafrika. Vom Senegal bis Benguela*, Leipzig, 1878.

creation. The myth relating this tale will first be ceremoniously recited, while enactment of the events – for example, through a procession of masks, pantomime, battle scenes, sacrifices, and a final communal meal – is accompanied by sacral chanting, recitations, music, and dance.

Because cults address powers that reign over mankind, the behavior of cult participants displays appropriate reverence. Worshipers prepare themselves before appearing before the worshiped. This involves sexual abstinence, fasting or special dietary restrictions, and most especially thorough cleansing. During cult events, while prayers are being said and contact is being made, worshipers bow their heads, kneel down, or even throw themselves to the ground before the object of their worship. They use deferential language, much the same as the language normally used in the presence of kings and other high-ranking people. "Court cult" has always included adherence to a specific etiquette, most importantly the use of a submissive form of conduct and a special, strictly conventionalized formal language. As it is predominantly those in a position of power who have no interest in seeing the relationship between themselves and their subjects changed, such conventions tend to remain constant. Thus, court ceremony, with its dress code, language, protocol, and so on, will always retain a particularly stilted and antiquated air. This

Fetish rock at the mouth of the Congo. From: *Westafrika. Vom Senegal bis Benguela*, Leipzig, 1878.

they are infinitely old and because of the sustained continuity of their traditions.

This exceptionally formal archaism is the key to the magical power of cults. Placing a pot on the fire or throwing a stone at a donkey would be a spontaneous act of no particular meaning: the pot would heat up, the donkey would – probably – leap to one side. These acts would have no impact on the future, and certainly none on the powers beyond. But by conventionalizing and ritualizing an act, it is stripped of its everyday character and, instead, is veiled in the air of the supernormal, and designated magical and sacred powers.

Cults make use of a combination of such instruments, making them highly melodramatic. They present the proceedings on a quasi-levitated stage, bestowing upon them a kind of dramatic tension by the buildup of individual acts, systematically leading worshipers to the climax: the sacrifice and the communal meal. The actors in this drama don costume and mask, as in the theater, and are accompanied by the play of light and shadow from the fire and torches, amid the sounds of flutes and drums. The whole performance takes on an air of celebration, has a highly theatrical expression, and leaves its deep impression on all.

This act of consecration is staged once a year. It confirms the validity of the order bestowed upon the community by the gods and upheld by their ancestors of old. It also renews both the guarantee of unity within the cult following and the bond that followers maintain with their ancestors and gods. The holy act obliterates all evil, cleanses and bestows new life upon the worshipers, and reassures them of the promise of salvation. Constant repetition provides the assurance that the future will continue to hold that which has always been. Cults offer salvation, strength, and hope.

Human sacrifice for Ogun, God of Iron.
From: *Fetichism and Fetich Worshipers*, New York, 1885.

applies even more to religious cults. Just as ancestors acknowledged traditions, so gods acknowledge with inexorable severity the order of the world as created by them. Permitting a breach of the rules would be questioning their own power. Traditional cults, passed down through the generations and therefore mostly cults of central significance, are therefore exceptionally archaic in character. Their costumes, requisites, chants, dance, and foods are in keeping with age-old customs generally obsolete in modern life. The language of their myths and the liturgical formularies of their worshipers are often no longer comprehensible to present generations. However, cults thrive on the impression that such practices have seen no change since the days of their inauguration. Their potency would otherwise be reduced, and the higher beings with whom they make contact would no longer understand what those residing in this world ask of them. Cults persist both because of the idea that

Dance of the fetish priestesses. Backdrop: a tree with bats and the king's execution ground. From: *Westafrika.Vom Senegal bis Benguela*, Leipzig 1878.

Home of the ancestral spirits

A place of ancestral worship for the Dogon (Mori, Mali). The shrine of the ancestor Damada Ketubile is a cave, the entrance to which is closed off by a wooden door.

The keeper of the shrine is 82-year-old priest (*hogon*) Barokomo, the only village member who practices his forefathers' religion. Dogons from other villages often come to offer the ancestor a sacrificial lamb or cow.

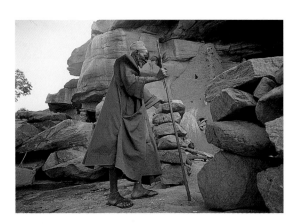

The priest shows the photographer the rusted key to the door and a ring belonging to the ancestor. Leaving the cave, he bids farewell with the words, "My journey is coming to an end. I hope we will see each other again in a better world."

Cult rituals are performed at sacred sites, at the preferred natural dwellings of spiritual powers – notably the earth god, but also ancestors and bush spirits. Many local gods are associated with an earth cult. Local gods often maintain close ancestral ties. In some cases it is virtually impossible to differentiate between gods and ancestors. Vodun or orisha, for example, can sometimes be deified ancestors. Spiritual powers first reveal themselves by appearing in visions or dreams, occasionally in the form of an animal, or by giving a sign. Once a cult for a spiritual power has been established, it will protect its followers, blessing their farming activities, nurturing their well-being, and mediating between them and the god, but also punishing insubordinate behavior with a bad harvest, disease, or other misfortune. Thus, there is a close inter-relationship between local divinities and a village community. The villagers worship and offer sacrifices to the spiritual powers, for which they, in turn, are rewarded with success and well-being.

Shrines are often located on a hilltop or at a river, or they may take the form of a cave or an old tree. The ground in their immediate surrounds is sacrosanct. Trees and other forms of vegetation therefore flourish and spread unhindered by humans. Some sites become sacred groves in which the souls of ancestors are believed to dwell. A stone or a conical clay altar marks the site as the "navel of the world." In former times, wooden statues of ancestors or clay sculptures of animals (such as crocodiles) were often placed at the site, as worshipers believed themselves to have ties with both their ancestors and the local earth gods, a belief based on the fact that an animal of that species had once come to the aid of an ancestor or that it was the animal believed to be the one favored by the earth god or local deity for his or her personal incarnation. Just as plants are touched only in special circumstances – if they are needed for their healing properties, for instance – likewise no animal that appears in the proximity of the shrine is killed. In some of these groves, animals (quite often crocodiles, as was the case in ancient Egypt) were actually tended to – they were fed and highly honored. Both symbolically and in reality, the sacred grove is a site of refreshing coolness, peace, and harmony, where dispute and discord have no place.

Pressure on land for cultivation that inevitably accompanies population growth has left its mark on sacred groves. Today, many of these sites (like those of the Mosi) have been reduced to no more than small groups of trees, while others (like those of the Senufo) have retained a tree population spanning four or five acres. From afar, such sites appear to be veritable islands of virgin forest in the midst of the savanna. The diversity of species and the size and age of the trees indicate that these wooded islands are, in fact, vestiges of primeval forests.

Even though they are mostly located in the immediate proximity of villages, such groves are considered to be shrouded in mystery and to be the sites of strange occurrences, particularly at night. Access is normally granted only to a small group of initiated worshipers. Foreigners (Europeans, for example) are not permitted entry to the sites. Members of secret societies (such as those to be found among the Yoruba) use these shrines as a meeting place and as a place where masks, cult objects, and musical instruments are kept. However, since the number of incidents in which such items have been stolen (for the purpose of selling them) has increased, villagers no longer risk leaving these objects unguarded.

All the village community's important cult activities, particularly at sowing and harvesting time, take place in the sacred grove, as do meetings

A priest from Nombori before his temple at Bandiagara Table Mountain.

Before entering the sacred grove, vodun priestess Wekenon, naked from the midriff upward, summons the gods. The sacrificial gift that she holds is a bottle filled with liquor.

She pours the sacrificial drink for her ancestors and divinities into the grove where they dwell.

She gathers leaves from a variety of plants. As a woman, she was permitted to enter the sacred grove only by virtue of being a powerful vodun priestess.

Yet, she is not permitted to go near the actual sanctuary, where only one of the elders may bring the sacrificial drink to the ancestral statue.

of community leaders to take political decisions, administer laws, and initiate their youth.

Unlike natural shrines in rural areas, the erection of cult shrines in cities or townships, with their mixed populations and countless gods, involves not only considerable funds, but also adaptation to suit the different circumstances. Urban shrines must incorporate altars for a range of divinities, a consultation room (for consulting oracles, and so on), and a courtyard in which cult ritual can be performed. Urban shrines rarely contain the simple clay cones of former times. Modern gods are often cast in cement or concrete.

Shrines generally reflect a cult community's size and its financial capacity. Those of smaller groups, of around five to 20 members, tend to be no more than simple huts or small rooms. Medium-sized cult groups, comprising 20 to 100 people, possess a complete farmstead, including several shrines and living quarters. Only few cults, however, can boast multiple, connected farmsteads or whole villages (such as that of the priest Abidjan Mami Wata). Whether modest or large, the shrines are the site of all the major cult ceremonies. The most important celebration is the yearly festival attended by the whole community, both the initiated and lay members, and by many cult followers. The entire congregation crowds into the shrine area, which at all other times is accessible only to priests and certain novices.

An oversized and colorfully painted image of Dan, the rainbow and snake god (from the Mono region in Benin), to whom a sacrifice is being offered. Dan is also worshiped in regions beyond Mono. The shrine also contains images of local divinities.

Dan is surrounded by red, oversized war gods who guard the shrine. All the statues are of cast concrete.

They serve as temple slaves

In precolonial times, cult groups also played an important role in politics. Depending on their position and the ranking of their gods, they supported kings in times of war or took part in otherwise dangerous undertakings. They also provided asylum. Those who placed themselves under the protection of a priest made themselves safe from others, but they also forfeited their civil rights and were required to be initiated into the cult. Once initiated, they worked in the fields kept by the priest. Their status was in fact that of a slave. Such "slaves to the gods" no longer exist in West Africa. According to the Anti-Slavery Society, however, thousands of women still lead lives of slavery. The society estimates that around 8,000 girls and young women are not only slaves in the

A fetish bowl, filled with red palm oil, has been placed to protect the entrance to the convent.

Temple slaves in a convent dedicated to the gods Hevioso, Sakpata, and Dan, and situated in the Comdji-Wougba district (on the Benin-Togo border). The young women are not permitted to leave the cult farmstead. They are sustained by the priest. They may not wash their garment. The cloth, worn constantly, becomes soiled stiff in time, indicating how long the temple slaves have been in the convent.

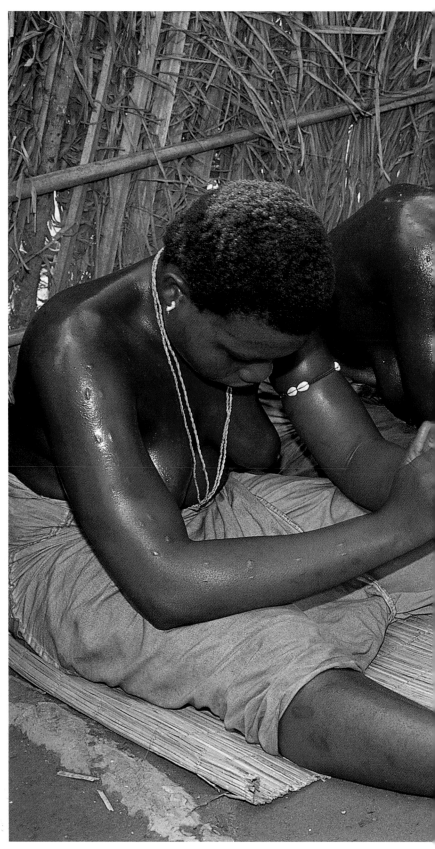

Temple slaves at prayer on a mat within the confines of a cult center. During the time of their seclusion, these women are introduced to the secrets of vodun and are taught the sacral language and dances.

houses and fields of their masters, the vodun priests, but are also often beaten and raped. Girls are sometimes handed over to the priests at no more than four years of age and then consecrated to serve as temple slaves. The Volta region is considered to be among the notorious centers of this kind of temple slavery. Since 1996, the Anti-Slavery Society has managed to buy freedom for more than 500 girls, in most cases for a low fee, but in the face of sometimes fierce opposition by the priests. However, such liberation is of little help to the girls, since they have neither training nor family support to fall back on, making it extremely difficult to reintegrate them into society. The relationship entered into with the divinity severs their links with their families.

According to legend passed down orally, temple slaves were once sacrificed to the gods,

ensuring their divine support in times of war. The girls were consecrated to the gods and subsequently thrown to the sacred crocodiles. Today's temple slaves are mostly children, offered to a divinity because of an offense committed by a family member, possibly even generations ago. The family offering is a sacrifice for atonement, an attempt to make amends with the gods.

In a wider context, the term "slave" is applicable to all those girls and women who, until their initiation, live in the cult precincts of the priests. The period of their sojourn there may be of considerable length, especially if they are in the process of being ordained priestesses. Normally, however, this period constitutes the transition phase between entry to the cult and full membership – that is, the attainment of the status of "wife of the gods." Because the initiation and, even more so, the final ceremony are very costly affairs, the women are often subjected to such slavery for a very long period of time. Not all the women devote their service to the divinity of their own free will. Some vodun priests (Amegnindu Dangnigbe, for example) recruit their slaves among their former patients. If a patient or her family is unable to meet the cost of treatment, the priest keeps her in slavery until her family can produce the funds to buy her back and, additionally, to pay for the costs of the initiation ceremony. These girls and women are predominantly slaves to the priests, rather than to the gods.

Right and below: Novices practising dance moves. During the time of their initiation, specific designs are carved into their shoulders and upper arms. A black powder is then rubbed into the wounds, infecting them and leaving the women scarred.

From novice to adept

Ama's final day as a slave to the gods begins. Today, she will be ordained a priestess of water goddess Mami Wata. She is still seated on the mat on which she slept during the past year of her term of training. Two of the figures to her left represent deceased twins in her family for whom she is responsible and from whom, in return, she will receive support.

An initiation is an important event, as it represents both a turning point in the initiate's life and a radical change in their personality. The object of the initiation is to create a close tie with the ancestral beings and the spiritual powers. Initiation rituals vary not only according to region; in some cases they even vary from one novice to the next within a single cult group. The common focus of such practices, however, is on the ordination of new members and priests. The time taken to prepare for ordination (the training time) may also vary tremendously. Urban communities have even introduced shortcut or weekend initiations.

Once all their former social ties have been broken and they have entered the cult establishment, those being trained for initiation are virtually stripped of their original personality. They undergo a ritual death, from which they arise only during the final initiation act. The reintegration ceremony at the end of the initiation period is an important event, if only for the fact that, apart from the annual festival, it marks the only gathering of cult members. This ritual ends the novices' seclusion, allowing them to reappear as newborn

Ama has ties to deities other than Mami Wata: Papa Densu (the name of the river and its god), husband to Mami Wata; Ogun (Gu), god of war and iron; Adela, god of hunters; and Tsamba, a violent vodun of the north. Ama's wrists and ankles are adorned with beads. An enamel bowl filled with fortune-bringing beans has been placed in front of her.

Far left: Ama is clothed like a princess for this celebration. Her attire includes a wig, a new garment, chains, glass and porcelain beads, and white paint applied in bands to her upper body, arms, and legs. A final adornment is a crown placed on top of her wig. All these elements of her attire hint at Mami Wata's European features.

Left: Ama receives her ordination.

Far left: The path that she will take to the ceremonial precinct is first swept.

Left: Ama and the priestesses dance in a procession to the ceremonial precinct.

Far left: A mat and a whitewashed stool have been placed in the dance area. The stool was commissioned especially for this occasion. The "stool ceremony" is one of the ritual highlights of the festivity. Ama sits majestically on her stool, her twin figures beside her.

Left: She greets the other adepts.

Far left: She dances in honor of the goddess, finally falling into a trance.

Left: She returns to the convent accompanied by the other priestesses and adepts.

329

This woman had previously been initiated into the vodun cult, but no longer properly heeded the rules of the gods, whereupon she began to suffer severe headaches. The oracle was consulted and instruction given that the woman must return to the gods of her grandfather. Thus she needed to be reinitiated. Her body is painted with red palm oil (the color of Hevioso, god of thunder) symbolizing the slime and blood of the newborn.

Above: The spots of Sakpata, god of chickenpox, and the colored dots of Dan, the snake god, are painted onto her body.
Below: Ritual cleansing is an important element of initiation ceremonies.

Above: In a bowed posture, representing a small child, she is led from the shrine to the bath place.
Below: She imparts her secret wishes to a duck, which is then sacrificed.

When the animal has been killed, its blood is poured over the woman's head.

Blood, eggs, evaporated milk, and soda water have been poured over her body. She now falls into a trance and dances one round for each of the gods into whose cult she is being initiated.

She is then cleansed of the vodun meals and the other liquid sacrifices. Her cleanliness is thus re-established.

Left: In the next stage she is painted white and adorned with beads. The beads are predominantly placed around her hips (as is done with newborn babies), symbolizing her renewed cleanliness and her incarnation as "wife of the gods" (*vodunsi*). In this new capacity, she is once more coated with white powder.

Above right: A procession now forms, headed by the priest and his assistants, and followed by the novices and cult adepts. The procession enters the ceremony precinct.

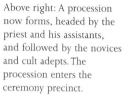

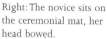

Right: The novice sits on the ceremonial mat, her head bowed.

In Koudohouhoue (in the Togo-Benin border area), the priest Mahounon Koudjega consults the Fa oracle as to whether the ceremony in which an adept of Legba is to be ordained can proceed.

He takes hold of the buffalo horn (*okpe*) containing his "medicine" and touches it with his tongue – an act which bestows protection upon the novice.

individuals – the dramatic climax of the overall initiation – and is celebrated accordingly.

This festival is a very costly affair. Few initiation candidates are able to provide the necessary funds themselves. Parents and relatives are usually asked to contribute. However, they often have other financial priorities, such as a funeral celebration for an elder. Initiations are likely to be postponed, unless the individuals themselves can find other sources of funding. Only when the financial means have been secured and a priest has been commissioned to head the initiation is a date set for the final festivities. The initiation candidate then receives a list from the priest containing the sacrificial offerings and requisites for the festival. All cult groups and priests from neighboring communities must be invited to attend and usually offered food and accommodation for one night and one day. The head priest expects payment, and material and monetary gifts must be arranged for the musicians and notable guests. Thus, total expenditure is quite considerable.

The festivities often take place over a weekend. Starting late on Saturday afternoon, they continue through the night, finally ending at dusk on Sunday evening. As with all rituals, the preliminary act in this initiation is a sacrifice to Legba. At dusk the priest and his assistants proceed to a statue of Legba located in the border area between the village and the wilderness to inform the god of the ritual about to commence. He is offered a meal of chicken, mush, red palm oil, and liquor. This act signifies the start of the ritual festivities, during the course of which the novice will become a fully-fledged member of the cult community.

The new initiate presents herself to the god Legba in the festive robe that identifies her as an adept. She does not fall into trance, since Legba does not enter his followers.

The adept of Legba is surrounded by the followers of other gods.

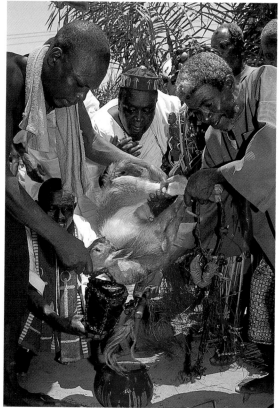

Left: The gods are offered a sacrificial goat.

Above: The shrine is fed with the blood of the sacrificial goat.

Food for the gods

In the Mono region of Benin, a sacrifice of kaolin is made to Lisa, the male personality of the principal vodun god Mawu-Lisa.

The occasional gift can do wonders for a friendship! But only, of course, if both parties do their bit. The friendship would otherwise become a one-sided relationship of dependency. This piece of wisdom is the basis of an age-old rule for social harmony, a rule as elementary as it is universal. It is a practice observed to this day in smaller village communities. The principle implies that a gift should always be reciprocated with another of corresponding value, or a service rewarded with a similar one. Ethnologists refer to this as reciprocity. In traditional societies, this rule applied not only to proper conduct within a group, particularly among family members, but also to the relationship with ancestors and the gods. It was indeed the core principle of sacrificial customs.

Just as people in industrialized societies often "sacrifice" a part of their income to foster relationships or support social causes, members of traditional hunting societies – for instance the Bushmen, or Hadza, of East Africa – always sacrifice a portion of their hunting "income" to the god of heaven or lord of the animals. Sacrificial animal flesh is thrown into the bush; this sharing of the meal with the gods symbolizes their communal relationship. In return, the Hazda expect continued contribution on the part of the gods toward their food supply. In agricultural societies, priority is given to sharing with deceased family members and relatives – the ancestors. At main meals, the

Women offer a sacrificial meal of kola nuts in a temple in the Mono region of Benin.

head of the household consigns a portion of the food and drink which is about to be consumed to the fire and then sprinkles or pours flour, tobacco, or other savories over the family's ancestral altar. On special occasions, such as festivals commemorating the dead, the offerings are more profuse. A lamb, a goat, or even a cow is slaughtered and its blood, believed to contain vital energy, is offered to the ancestors in a sacrifice. The animal's flesh is consumed by the living. The meal thus reunites all family members. A similar practice applies to sacrifices made to the earth gods. The gods of heaven (notably the High God), on the other hand, are predominantly offered burned sacrifices. Entire animals or animal parts are burned; the smoke, the "spiritual essence," of the meat, rises up to the gods. The world over, gods and spirits are considered to have a keen sense of smell. Just as they feast on the aroma of sacrificial meals, so they loathe rude stenches. For this reason worshipers often burn scented woods for them during a cult act or pour aromatic oils (known as myrrh in the ancient Orient) onto their altars. Nowadays, perfume is sometimes used, for instance in the cult of Mami Wata.

Sharing food is one of the most direct and intimate ways of expressing solidarity. This is why the communal meal is a core element of all cults. However, relationships can also be nurtured and reinforced through a range of other reciprocal expressions of devotion. The exchange of gifts is particularly common. Those on whom a blessing has been bestowed express thanks by offering a reciprocal gift or by making a sacrifice – for instance, in gratitude for hunting success, a plentiful harvest, or recovery from an acute illness. Such gifts are placed on the graves of ancestors or on ancestral altars near the house. Gifts to the gods are placed in the shrine of the relevant god. If the occasion for making a gift is a more serious one, the sacrifice will again be an animal but in this case a domesticated animal, since it is a personal

Left: A cow is sacrificed as part of a vodun ceremony in the Mono region of Benin.

Below: The sight of the blood puts the cult followers in a possessed trance.

Bottom: Possessed worshipers dance around the dead cow, in the blood into which they will later dip their heads.

Right and below: The Dogon sacrifice a goat to the gods; its blood is offered to a fetish.

possession and thus a true sacrifice. When someone has committed a sin and upset the relationship with the spirits of the world beyond, an atonement is required to restore order. Here, too, an animal may be sacrificed. As always, the blood is sacrificed to the ancestors and earth gods, and the smoke to the gods of heaven, while the living eat the meat. Thus is the relationship restored.

The most intimate of personal "possessions" includes one's own relatives. Extreme situations are therefore conceivable in which gods insist on being offered a human sacrifice (ancestral spirits generally do not). Sacrifices of this kind have been made virtually all over the world, though solely within advanced or highly developed civilizations: in the ancient Orient; in South East Asia and Oceania; among the Celts, the Germanic and Slav people; among the Aztec, Maya, and Inca peoples; and not least among the ancient Egyptians and in some of the advanced civilizations of Africa, notably in the western part of the continent.

Plant cultivation deprives the earth, and thus the earth goddess, of energy. In a kind of advanced system of remuneration, many African cultures offered the earth a human sacrifice when they began sowing. In the kingdom of Matamba (Angola), a man and a woman would be clubbed to death with a rake (that is, with a field tool) and buried beneath the earth. Such was the observation of Cavazzi de Montecuccolo, a 17th-century traveler. The Wandjis in Tanzania attacked outsiders passing through their territory, choked them, and then prepared medicines from their blood and bodily parts. Such medicines were then used to enhance the fertility of their fields. The Tswana in South Africa, on the other hand, would burn the blood, brains, and parts of the corpse of the

sacrificial victim, subsequently sprinkling the ashes onto the freshly tilled earth. Similar practices had also been previously observed in western Sudan.

So-called building sacrifices were based on a similar concept. Buildings that made demands on the earth because of their size and weight, or which needed to remain intact (bridges, protecting walls, defensive structures, or palaces, for example) often required a human sacrifice to be made (as was once the case throughout Western Europe). The sacrificed humans, preferably young, were generally buried alive, embedded in the building's foundation. Their vital energy was intended to vitalize the ground and to reinforce the construction itself. Also, the local spirit, displeased at the erection of the building, would thus be appeased.

It was also often believed that if someone had committed a grave offense against divine law, nothing could be offered to atone for it but the sinner's own life. He or she would be executed – offered to the god as a means of compensation for the marred relationship. In other cases, an angry god might withhold rain or some other crucial necessity, yet the people could not identify the exact cause of the divine indignation or who the individual perpetrator was, since the sin had been concealed from them. The gravity of such circumstances also appeared to call for a human sacrifice. In times of continued drought, therefore, there seemed no other way out of the predicament. The Lugbara in Uganda still upheld this practice until the late 1920s, although they did not sacrifice their own people but prisoners of war or other outsiders. In earlier times, however, as they explained to ethnologist John Middleton, their offering would have been in the form of a child from their own community. The rainmaker was responsible for performing the sacrifice. The British managed to put an end to this practice in 1930, since when rams have been sacrificed instead.

In many agricultural societies (before the spread of Christianity) the principal fruit of cultivation was considered to be the child of the heavenly father and the earth mother. It was believed that both celebrated their marriage at the beginning of every year. In subtropical regions, this was the time of the onset of the rainy season. The first rainfall was seen to be the semen with which the heavenly god inseminated the earth goddess. Once the godly child was ripened, it must be killed brutally in order for mankind to be sustained. This was seen as an absolute necessity, but also as a great sin against the "earth parents," one which was accordingly lamented in reaper chants. To offer some form of atonement for this unavoidable crime, a child from within that society would be sacrificed to the earth goddess, either during or at the end of harvesting time. This custom still existed in some parts of Africa at the beginning of the 20th century; for instance, among the Tswana in South Africa, the Wamegi in Tanzania, the Bobo in Burkina Faso, the Ekoi in southern Nigeria/Cameroon, and the Asante, who poured the sacrificial blood into the holes left when new yams had been extracted.

Another very common form of human sacrifice was companion death. On the death of an important tribal chief or, in monarchies, of a noble person, a sovereign of high status, or the ruler himself, often hundreds of slaves and prisoners, or even servants, friends, wives, and high-ranking court officials were killed with the aim of further pleasing the deceased as he resided in the realm of death. As an ancestor belonging to the ruling class, he was entitled to keep court in his new abode just as he had in life. Occasionally, village communities also practiced ritual companion death – for instance the Lele on the central Kasai in the southern Democratic Republic of Congo (formerly Zaire), but predominantly within the monarchical cultures of East, Central, and West Africa. When a king (an asantehene) died in Ghana, and until his successor was enthroned, veritable hecatombs of people were killed. In Dahomey, it was the bravest of female warriors (the "Amazons of Dahomey") who would follow their sovereign to the grave.

Akin to the concept of following a powerful being to his grave in order to serve him in death as in life is the solemn pledge or the willingness of people (be it free or forced) to devote their lives to the services of a deity. These men and, more often than not, women renounce the world, retreat to the shrine of their deity, and fully sacrifice their lives to service. In some cases they even enter into a kind of marriage with their god, pledging lifelong chastity. Such forms of heavenly bondage – although they are not freely entered into – are often encountered in the vodun cults of West Africa, particularly in the Volta region. It is always girls who make this sacrifice, who are required to commit themselves to temple slavery.

In a ceremony among the Minah tribe in Benin, sacral items are dipped into the blood of the sacrificial goat in order that they be "recharged."

The vodun priest holds up a goat to be sacrificed.

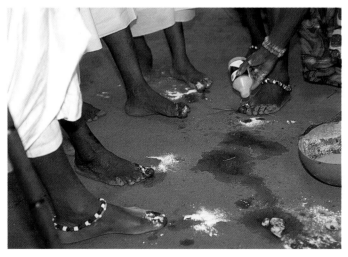

The blood of the sacrificed goat, powder and perfume are applied to one of the big toes of each adept to provide protection. Minah tribe, Benin.

Oracles – answers for those who seek

"Only those who never cease to ask questions will not lose their way." The constant search for the right path is an essential aspect of life. Consulting oracles is one of many forms of fortune-telling or divination. In all cultures and at all times in history, divination has played an important role in finding solutions to life's problems. In Africa no society exists that is not familiar with at least one such technique, if not more.

A fundamental prerequisite of divination is the conviction that there is a close connection between humans, the environment, and the cosmos, so that whatever is triggered in one of these spheres can lead to visible or tangible interactions in others. An impulse of this kind could, for example, be the committing of a sin, which then causes disease; alternatively, it could constitute a question put to the ancestors or the gods in response to which a sign is accordingly received. Divination offers help in times of uncertainty, doubt, or indecisiveness.

The techniques and methods employed in divination are extraordinarily varied. Every culture has its own system of signs, often even multiple systems, one of which may be of particular significance (such as Ifa, which is deeply ingrained in Yoruba culture). Some systems are commonly used across large regions or have been adopted by neighboring groups.

Scientific terminology differentiates between "inductive," "art-based," or "technical" forms of divination on the one hand, and "intuitive" or "natural" forms on the other. The former are based on the observation and interpretation of signs (omina), the latter on inspiration such as may come upon privileged individuals (priests or mediums, for example) on certain occasions. Oracles are "experimentally inductive" methods of divination, in which specific questions are expected to generate specific answers. This may be achieved by mechanical means (for example, by throwing for lots) or through an animal medium (mice and foxes are the favored animals in West Africa).

Because it has so much in common and virtually cohabits with humans, the mouse is a typical West African oracle animal. It feeds on grains, as do humans, even consuming the scraps of their meals. Mice are also extremely fertile, an attribute considered to be a sign of being blessed. It is these traits that often qualify mice for divination. The tracks that they leave are read or they are put in baskets or pots to discern the way in which they change the order of the contents; during this process, Kirdi fortune-tellers play a one-stringed fiddle as a means of offering encouragement to the mice.

Fortune-telling, however, is never a purely mechanical procedure, but a type of intensive, direct or indirect dialog with ancestors, spirits, and gods. A fortune-teller is generally aware of the difficulties and tensions within his own community – circumstances which he can therefore take into account when consulting his oracles. During such a session, a fortune-teller will offer those seeking

counsel the opportunity of talking about their troubles, worries, fears, sufferings, humiliations, and own misdemeanors. They will then be given advice on ways of freeing themselves from their own predicaments.

He provides an initial proof of his ability by divining the reason his client has turned to him. The quicker he is able to do so, the more his reputation will be endorsed. In any event – be it with the aid of bones, stones, seeds, or other means of consulting the oracle – he attempts to induce his client to talk (in much the same way that psychotherapists in Western society do). His task is to make a diagnosis, to identify the problem and what has caused it, and to point out possible and practicable solutions.

Oracles summon ancestors and spiritual support

"We go to a fortune-teller when we fear something and do not know what to do," the Lobi explain in justification of their frequent visits to the fortune-teller. Lobi fortune-tellers seek "spiritual support" from the thila (spirits), while the Nankanse rely on ancestors, particularly on deceased fortune-tellers themselves. It is assumed that both are present during such sessions.

The tools of the trade of Nankanse fortune-tellers include a pumpkin rattle, a strong forked stick with a metal section at the end, and a leather sack containing a selection of obejcts apparently collected at random. This array of objects – some found, others fabricated – includes cowry shells, animal bones and teeth, coins, rings, and bracelets – all core tokens of Nankanse life. For fortune-tellers they serve as a veritable system of coordinates, references, and codes for interpretations. Fortune-telling consultations are all conducted according to a standard pattern, comprising a dramatic dialog accompanied by highly animated gesticulations.

A Nankanse fortune-teller at work. He uses his rattle to summon the ancestors of his predecessor. The consultation itself is performed using a stick, the forked ends of which are held by the fortune-teller, while his client takes hold of the lower, metal-coated part. The two grooves in the metal spout serve to provide alternative answers. This technique, involving the use of an inanimate object – in this case a stick – thus appears to be a totally objective means of providing answers.

Clients first enter the fortune-teller's premises and pay a fee, the amount being left to their own discretion, which the fortune-teller, regardless of how low that fee may be, is obliged to accept. The fortune-teller then sits on a bench or a stool, and his client positions himself, in respectful posture, cross-legged on the floor in front of him. The fortune-teller summons the ancestors of his predecessors by beating the leather sack with his right hand, all the while rhythmically shaking the rattle with his left hand. He then spills out the contents of the sack and adds to the items two stones or pieces of metal. Continuing to shake his rattle, he implores the ancestors to make their appearance. He then takes two flat "test stones," spits on one side of each, presses these two surfaces together, and forcefully throws the two stones onto the ground. All adult Nankanse men are able to interpret the result now before them, which may entail one of three possibilities: if both dry surfaces of the stones face upward, this implies rejection (the ancestors have not appeared); if both moistened sides face upward, this means laughter (they will not commit themselves, are possibly even laughing at him in mockery); and if one moistened side and one dry side face upward, it signifies acceptance (he has their wholehearted support).

Two throws of the stones must be performed with a successful outcome before questioning can begin. Only then, the fortune-teller will take hold of the forked end of his stick with one hand, continuing to shake the rattle with his left hand, and thus urge the ancestors to remain present and alert. Beating the prophetic stick this way and that, he touches one or more of the items spread out before him, bringing his diagnosis to a close. Depending on the degree of difficulty inherent in any given issue before him, his findings may take one, two, or even five or ten minutes.

As soon as he strikes one of the two stones, his client takes hold of the other end of the stick. Repeating the procedure as the fortune-teller had done, the client swings the rod back and forth, pointing in various directions to one or another of the objects and to certain parts of the body. Each of the items spilled from the sack has a fixed meaning or stands for a certain notion. An animal horn refers to a particular ancestral shrine; cowry shells may stand for wealth or money; the hooves of a goat or sheep, or the claws of a chicken may mean sacrifice. The same applies to various gestures. If the stick points to the abdomen, this heralds a future pregnancy or refers to an existing child; if it points to the side of the body, it refers to in-law relations; if it touches the hand, this refers to money or possession. It is now the fortune-teller's task to apply the general meaning these references contain to the client's concrete situation. He takes extreme care in doing so, examining each step of the procedure through a test with his throwing stones. He will formulate his questions as alternatives, indicating either of the flat stones once he has named the possible options. If the answer is correct, the stick will move to the relevant stone. If a question does not correspond with the core of the issue at hand, the stick will remain suspended in the air.

The following dialog could ensue. The issue involves a woman. Is she dead or alive? The answer is "dead." Is she a mother or a wife? Answer "mother." The woman who gave birth to me or another mother? No answer: Is she the mother of my mother? Positive answer. Meaning what? The stick swings to indicate a sheep's hoof. Is a sheep involved? Positive answer. Has this sheep already been sacrificed or does it still need to be sacrificed? Answer "needs to be sacrificed." Why does it need to be sacrificed? The stick points to the abdomen. Is the child alive or not yet born? Answer "alive." Is it my own child or that of my "brother"?, and so on.

Each solution to a problem presents yet another problem, and the fortune-teller must ultimately find the correct answer among the countless options. Questions are often repeated several times and answers cross-checked by putting the question in another form or interchanging the meaning of the stones. Once the result is clear, the client takes the test stones, requesting of them confirmation of the validity of that result. He then hands them back to the fortune-teller, who once more spits on them and suspends them over his prophetic sack before throwing them anew. If the answer is "rejection" or "laughter," then some obstacle still exists, in which

case the consultation will enter a second, third, fourth, or even further round. The problem will be "discussed" as long as it takes to reach unanimity between the throwing stones and the test stones.

Lobi divination sessions are conducted according to similar criteria. The fortune-teller and his client are seated next to one another, holding hands. In this procedure the fortune-teller puts to the spirits at his disposal an array of questions in quick succession. The answers (yes or no) that he receives are expressed by slaps on his thighs. If both hands slap the fortune-teller's thighs palms down, this indicates "yes," if they tilt to the side, the answer is "no." The first set of questions that the fortune-teller asks are of a very general kind – whether someone has had bad dreams, whether there has been an accident, or whether someone intends to embark on a journey, for example. If such questioning generates no positive information, he will question the thila: "What is it that I cannot find?" The fortune-teller's and the client's hands will be led to make signs in the air, providing certain indications.

When performing divinations, the Nankanse and the Lobi operate according to the rules of induction pertinent to the notions and the form of discourse inherent in their lives. Their method of consulting oracles is based on uniform codes. Everyone can learn and command such codes and thus, theoretically, learn the art of fortune-telling.

The fox is never wrong

Every evening, at sunset, Dogon men leave their village and make for a rocky terrain, in the proximity of which they mark large rectangles in the sand. They place thorny acacia branches around the border of their "fortune slate" (*yurugu goro*) in order to ward off wild animals that could destroy the markings. Having removed all stones and fragments of wood from the surface, they sweep the sand within its bounds using an acacia branch. Only then do they distinguish their various "houses." The questions that they pose – for instance, on the condition of a child's health, on how a particular relative is faring, or on the success of a courting endeavor – are coded using lines, grooves, piles of sand, or stalks of millet stuck into the sand. Lastly, they shell and crush a handful of peanuts and scatter them indiscriminately across their slate, thus luring the fox onto its surface during the coming night. The men return to their village before the sun has set. On their way back they mumble words for the fox to bear in mind when linking the future and the present.

Early the next morning, often before dawn, they return to their slate and study the messages that the fox has left for them. All traces have their particular meaning: if the fox has knocked down a millet stalk, this indicates illness or death; if it moved back and forth, an undertaking will start out well, but end badly. The fox is never wrong. In the event that its predictions do not materialize, it is thought that the track readers themselves must have erred. If the messages that the fox leaves behind can be construed to mean more than one thing, a neighbor or friend (preferably two) is asked to put the same question anew. If the answers are the same, there is certainty on the issue.

The meaning of the objects and animals used in consulting an oracle is often rooted in mythology and traditional symbolism. The Ḍogon name their oracle after their trickster, the large-eared fox Yurugu (a god who can appear in a multitude of guises). This nocturnal creature leaves its tracks on designated surfaces. The tracks are read and interpreted the next day.

The Ifa oracle speaks in riddles

"Ifa speaks in riddles, but wise men understand its words," goes an old Yoruba saying. Ifa, the Fa method of oracle consultation used by the Fon, is an order-inspiring power and the personification of divine wisdom. The highly complex system upon which this method is based entails recording or analyzing signs, given by scattering palm seeds, that provide insight into the will of the gods and help prevent ill-fate. Ifa is also considered to be a god in his own right and is celebrated as a cult that includes a range of other gods, most notably Eshu. Since Ifa shares the wisdom of the god of creation, all seek his favor in order to be spared from evil.

Ifa is considered to have been founded by Orunmila of Ife, a skilled healer who gained a deep insight into the workings of the gods. Despite his wisdom, he remained poor, which is why Olorun took pity on him, on his death promoting him to the rank of lower orisha, below the gods. From this time onward she made use of his gifts and assigned him to fortune-telling. As a way of expressing thanks, according to one of the numerous Ifa creation myths, Orunmila incited humans to make plentiful sacrifices to the gods.

Because of the complexity that Ifa entails, its practice requires special training that can take up to seven years. During such training, a master introduces his pupils not only to the techniques and meaning of Ifa, but also to the medicinal knowledge and the political-cum-social aspects involved. Only those who have undergone this training can achieve the status of *babalawo*, "father of the secrets."

The basic instruments of classical Ifa include a square, round, or semicircular oracle board, the central part of which is decorated with carved reliefs depicting symbols and the countenance of Eshu, ruler over fate. Ifa priests take their board to the grave with them. Other objects include a pointer rod, small guardian figures made of bone,

A priest in Cotonou consults the Fa oracle. This is a highly complex procedure that requires lengthy training.

He repeatedly throws an oracle chain made of eight nutshells or cowry shells to the ground. Every time he does so, depending on the number of shell openings facing upward, he is given one of 256 signs, each of which, in turn, is linked to a swathe of mythical stories.

a bowl containing palm seeds, kola nuts, stones, seeds or the like, a metal rattle rod depicting two birds, and a bell carved with ivory figures and used to summon the gods. During lengthy questioning, the priest shakes the seeds and throws them onto the board, which has been covered with flour. The priest reads the message of the gods by determining the position of the seeds on the board and the marks that they leave in the flour, and by employing the 256 basic sacred texts (with all variations, more than 4,000) or oracle verses that make up the core of Ifa and that supposedly contain all human experience. Priests must study these verses thoroughly during their training. A priest does not necessarily need to use an oracle board to seek out the relevant text; other methods are also at his disposal. All priests, however, operate using certain obligatory items such as palm nuts, cowry shells, pieces of clay, and so on. Such items are normally thrown to the ground and numerical values thus ascertained which are then separated according to even and odd figures. An example of a common variation is throwing to the ground an oracle chain made of eight nutshells and then examining how many shell openings lie face upward. This number or the positioning of other objects thrown to the ground supplies the sacred text's mystic codes (the Yoruba call them odo, the Fons afadu), which the priest then combines freely in order to achieve an initial, rough frame of reference on the issue of interest to his client. This initial result must then be

further defined in a second run-through, for which the priest often uses a certain assemblage of items, each related to particular spiritual powers and situations in life: tree seeds, bones, peppercorns, pieces of metal, beads, stones, and the like, uncovered in a second procedure and linked to a mystical framework story. If, for example, the result achieved is the number 168, meaning "If a bird swoops through the clouds, bright light will descend upon a number of destinies," this could be interpreted in a positive way to indicate that something will take a favorable turn. Conversely, it could signify an unfavorable turn of events, since a certain problem is brought into public light (as is the bird). The priest must then decide exactly what is meant, discussing with his client the possible meaning of the bird symbolism, the obstacle (clouds), or the light. Often, however, the priest will leave his client none the wiser about the problem, if all that his client is interested in knowing is whether a certain undertaking is seen as favorable by the gods.

The answers that Ifa gives have absolute validity, yet offering sacrifices may nonetheless contribute to winning the favor of the gods for a given undertaking. The oracle will provide precise information about the kind of sacrifices necessary. Subsequent requestioning – again, using one of the object-throwing variations – will then clarify whether or not the gods have accepted the sacrifice and therefore blessed the client's undertaking.

345

Secrecy and the manipulation of power

There are things in life that should not be disclosed to others. We keep such things to ourselves or as secrets. However expressed, it amounts to the same. When our secrets are revealed, we feel exposed, possibly even subjected to the mercy of others.

The fear of exposing ourselves to others, especially to strangers and those who do not belong to our intimate social environment, is deep-rooted. In many traditional societies it was wise to ensure that one's fingernails, toenails, or hair did not fall into the hands of others. Such bodily waste would be hidden or buried. This was based on the notion that it contained a great amount of our vital energy, since it continued to grow even once the overall bodily process of growing had ceased. Others, it was believed, could use a person's nails or hair to gain magical power over their life. Genitals are kept covered for the same reason. It is even common practice in some cultures to keep hair, eyes, and mouth veiled. The ill-will of others, chiefly concentrated in the evil eye, could pass into the genital region, damaging our procreativity and fertility, poison our breath, or enter our eyes and scorch our innermost parts. In ancient cultures, in which clothing constituted nothing more than a body strap or certain adornments, a subtle form of etiquette offset the absence of clothes. Physical encounters, for instance, required that each person's gaze was directed away from the other's, that one's hands covered the genitals, or that legs were crossed when seated. Also, it has always been disapproved of to talk of love and intimacy in public. At best, the subject would be circumscribed through the use of paraphrases – for even words, moist with spittle and conveyed by breath, could be a means of applying magic spells.

Names are particularly susceptible to magic – if they are known, that is – for names are considered part of our personality. In contrast to clothing, names are our constant "garment," therefore endowed with even more vital energy, and are considered to be the intimate possession of their bearer. Our personal name is generally disclosed only to our more intimate contacts. In our public life, we use another name, even a nickname, in its place. Hence, the true names of unholy powers or predatory animals are often not spoken, but circumscriptions such as "may God be with us" or "the tailed one" (farkas: Hungarian for "wolf"), used instead – in the same way as it could present a danger to one's life if one's own name should be spoken for the beast to hear. The names of sovereigns have remained especially secret. In West Africa, kings adopt a new, official name on being enthroned; to name a king by his old name would be tantamount to a verbal form of magic deposition.

Our social intercourse is more relaxed within our own family circle. Words spoken and things that happen in this environment are meant to remain within its confines. The protection necessary to ensure that this remains so depends, in turn, on strictly observed custom. If a villager approaches someone's hut, he or she will clear their throat in a gesture audible to those within and signaling their approach. They will then wait until somebody comes out to greet them.

They will rarely be invited to enter; visitors are usually received and entertained outside the (generally one-roomed) huts, for instance on the veranda. Visitors are prevented from seeing a family's private sphere and the women's area. Close relatives, however, are allowed access at any time. "A man who reveals his secrets to the whole world," say the Gola of Liberia, "enables his rivals to cause him harm." It is inconceivable, therefore, that anyone not among the closest relatives, or who does not have the status of dignitary or personal servant, should have access to the private quarters of a king. His person stands for the welfare and well-being of all his people. His private life thus remains a state secret.

Secrecy is a form of manipulation of power. To rob a person of his or her intimacy, to expose them, would be to humiliate them. Keeping someone's secret to oneself, a secret which, revealed, would be to the disadvantage of that person, means retaining the power to harm and blackmail that person. If we possess powerfully effective magic, we hold power over others and would be foolish to disclose our knowledge. Intellectual property, such as magic formulas, recipes for magic medicine, knowledge of healing plants and cures, is also something that we like to keep to ourselves. These are the types of secrets, as the Golas say, "that make a family strong and that others would like to possess in order to be able to weaken them." This pertains likewise to professional secrets. Blacksmiths, weavers, dyers, hunters, healers, and rainmakers keep their knowledge to themselves. For one thing, this assures them of a monopoly of sorts, for another, the revelation of their knowledge could lead to a kind of inflationary effect. In Tenkodogo (Burkina Faso), the magic of the court's professional rain priest has lost most of its value because a predecessor had shared his knowledge with far too many others. People therefore tend to place their confidence

To chase away an illness afflicting a child, a pot has been turned upside down and a chicken placed on top of it. The chicken is cut open and blown apart with gunpowder; palm oil is poured over the remains.

in the abilities of the king (the Tenkodogo-naaba), who kept secret the rain magic that he commands in his capacity as king.

Such specialized knowledge – power-supporting and even lucrative in nature – may be the possession of a secret or cult society. The information is mostly of a medical or religious nature; for instance, magic formulas and rituals for enhancing the fertility of fields, animal stocks, or people. Those entering societies of this kind must fulfill certain prerequisites and will only partake of the secret knowledge in a gradual process within the framework of an initiation. If any information is divulged to others, the culprit is liable to be punished with death.

To some degree, a local community of any sort could be perceived as being a kind of secret society as far as its relationship to the neighboring community and to outsiders in general is concerned. Certain, predominantly central, religious knowledge (myths, sacred chants, magic formulas, rituals) – knowledge essential for the community's continued existence – is strictly guarded by the elders and passed on only to younger men during their initiation (the rule of exogamy means that the women are from outside groups and daughters will marry into outside groups). The secrecy in which the groups are shrouded has always been a difficult issue for ethnographers, even during colonial times. At the end of the 1920s, for example, a young French ethnographer wanted to establish the connection between chicken sacrifices and circumcision among a people in western Sudan. To make sure of receiving the information that he needed, he engaged the help of a regional commander. All his attempts,

however, were met with unyielding resistance on the part of the elders. They argued that they could divulge such information only to those who had undergone the circumcision themselves – something that a European would hardly be willing to subject himself to. Astutely, the elders came to an agreement, saying: "Alright, we will just keep him out of our hair by giving him a nice little show, without his ever knowing it was a pretense." This approach, to "throw sand in someone's eyes and simply serve him a fabricated story, if they were not prepared to reveal the truth," is summed up by the African writer Amadou Hampaté Bâ, who was present on the occasion, as "an idea born of the time when the colonial powers sent their agents and representatives to carry out ethnographic studies, but were not prepared to live with the people they were studying under the necessary conditions." Such was more often the case than ethnologists were willing to admit – and some did not even realize they had been misled. Africans would evade unseemly questions, would conceal the truth behind polite but empty statements, providing nothing more than insinuations and vague circumscriptions, or simply lying outright.

That which is considered private, be it in the context of family or society, which is the carrier of a group's vital energy, and which, in certain situations, is at risk, is protected, veiled, or even kept a total secret. Secrets need to be safeguarded: public disclosure would render them commonplace. However, secrets only have special value when they are linked to sacred sites and to powerful, religious figures. Both elements are ultimately interdependent.

The Dangme's secret objects

For the annual kpledzo festival, held in honor of the gods, participants paint their bodies in a mud color.

Below: In elaborate festival costumes and body paint, the Dangme honor their gods.

Below right: The ritual dress of priests and priestesses is held to be the costume of their ancestors.

"You learn to keep knowledge not in your head, but in your kneecap, safe from poison and the lure of women." The importance of keeping special knowledge and all that goes with it secret could not be more typically described. The Dangme of the eastern Accra plains – a people who, culturally, have much in common with their neighbors, the Ga – have been able to maintain to this day some of the traditional theocratic structure inherent in their culture. Their traditional form of religion, especially their faith in ancestors, has endured.

The Dangme have both major and minor spiritual powers. The former are the old divinities, the *dzemawoi* (*dzemawo* in the singular; *dzemi* meaning "in the world," *wo* meaning "guardians"). Only few of them – the Kple and Klama gods, the latter being the original, first local divinities – were adopted by the Dangme from the autochthonous inhabitants of the Accra plains, the Guan. Both kinds of gods are relevant to the origins of villages. Each god is considered to be the patron of a particular settlement. Specific objects are assigned to them and kept at their shrines. These objects are publicly exhibited only on such occasions as the annual festival, at which remembrance of the past is celebrated and at which the emblems of hierarchy – symbols with specifically fixed meanings – are also displayed. The annual festival is a celebration of the principal gods. Myths are presented in animated and condensed form. Even on these occasions, however, not all relics are displayed. Some secrets remain concealed. Stools of

state, for instance, are never publicly exhibited – contrary to practice among the Asante. Each Kple or Klama god is allotted his own shrine and own body of priests.

Dangme religion also incorporates the belief that secrecy is a means of power (*hewam*), an invisible force that, concealed, acts from within. Those who possess this force can use it for either positive or negative ends. The secrets thus veiled serve to ensure the continued existence of the community. They are called agbaa, a comprehensive term describing traditional ritual practices such as oaths, expertise in areas such as knowledge of plants, secret knowledge about the emblems of ancestors, and local priesthood. The local priesthood is very influential in that it protects state secrets (its namesake) and oversees the annual ceremonies. It is competent in dealing with the spiritual powers, has knowledge of sacred plants, and watches over ancestral relics. Agbaa is the pivot of the human and the cosmic world; no Dangme settlement could survive without agbaa.

Such esoteric knowledge is accessible only through acceptance into agbaa society, something for which not everyone is eligible. An essential element of the agbaa society's overall secret knowledge is its specific knowledge of botany and herbs. It is primarily the leaves of plants that have central significance in contact with the spiritual world. Plant medicines are an effective means of influencing both the environment and people, endowing warriors with strength and generally

This priestess is possessed by a minor spiritual power. The *abodo* (bush spirits) were adopted by the Dangme from the neighboring Akan. Religious body-cosmetic applications (*he dra mo*) have a symbolic meaning that depends on the combination of individual motifs. The special characteristics of minor spiritual powers in Prampram include linear patterns applied to the upper body and to the lower legs of the priestesses.

Priestesses walk in procession to the shrine of Digble, god of water, honored as patron of the town. The beads that they wear are signs of wealth and symbolize ritual cleanliness – the wearer of beads draws the blessing of the gods upon herself. Beads are essential attributes of priesthood. Servants of the Kple god (the local deity) wear beads made of fish bone or ivory (*nyoli*).

Men take the sacred drum, the central object of this festival, from the shrine honoring the ocean god. During the rest of the year, this instrument may only be viewed by six individuals. The sight of it would cause others to go mad. Like all the relics in the Digble shrine, this object is adorned with double-line motifs for the festival. They symbolize the god of water.

Women carrying "medicines" to the ceremonial precinct.

protecting people against evil. The capability to exploit plants and leaves is therefore the vital prerequisite for acquiring power (hewam), a force considered to be inherent in every human, but one that can only be effectively activated through contact with "medicines."

People are taught how to deal with hewam by an agbaa master or through introduction to a political office. Hewam comprises plants and herbs (baa), medicines or magic potions (tsupa) made from plants and other natural materials such as alumina earth and animal parts, and secrets. A whole variety of prohibitions prevents the disclosure of these secrets and protects group emblems, which determine the fate and success of the society, those in power, and the witnesses of its history. The expectations of the ancestors rest within them; oaths are sworn, formulas for curses and blessings are uttered on them. The possession of hewam ensures the political authority of rulers. The secret has been kept because its origin is linked to the history of the monarchs – though, not kept well enough for a rough knowledge of what is involved not to have been disclosed. Knowledge of the existence of the secret is part of its stabilizing prerequisite.

The statue of Oluwedoku, meant to endow the new sowing season with the gift of fertility (clearly symbolized by the figure's oversized phallus), is adorned with green leaves. Knowledge of sacred plants is an essential part of the overall secret knowledge in Dangme society. An adept places the statue on his head, whereupon the power inherent in the figure takes possession of him. The white markings on the carrier's lips are a symbol of his discretion: his mouth remains closed – he keeps his knowledge to himself.

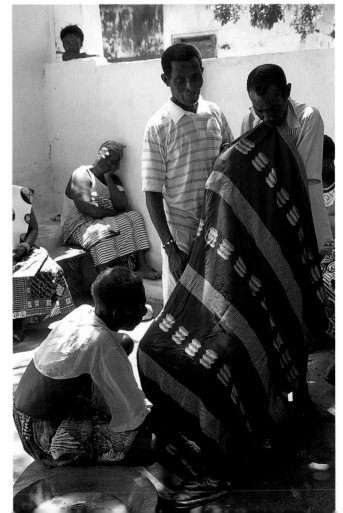

Above: Women carrying pots containing herbal mixtures and secret objects covered in white cotton cloths to the ceremonial grounds. Many objects, particularly ancestral stools, are kept from public view even during the ceremony.

Right: Inside the shrine of the god of water, a woman is drawn out of a trance. She has been covered with a large cloth to allow the god to exit without suffering desecration. The god bids farewell before withdrawing.

Men's secret societies

Secrets that are of any significance to a society and that are carefully safeguarded by selected members of that society are a valuable asset, being respected or inspiring fear. Possession of such secrets may confer not only prestige, but also power. For this reason it is in the interests of high-ranking individuals to gain control of such secrets. This also applies, however, to groups in a society attempting to gain influence over others, or perhaps even a degree of political power which, in turn, would enable them to rival official authorities, elders, chiefs, or kings.

Even in the village communities of traditional tribal societies, power was something quite often striven for. In many parts of the world, especially in Oceania and Africa male societies, secret societies, and cult cooperatives were a widespread phenomenon.

In Africa secret societies were predominant in western Sudan, from Sierra Leone to Ghana, and from Nigeria and Cameroon into the neighboring Congo region. There were inclusive and exclusive societies. The former generally comprise all the initiated men of a group. Admittance to such a society is automatically granted once initiation is completed. Apart from their sex and their status as adults, common to all members is their knowledge of certain secrets, primarily those of a traditional religious nature – concerning myths, prayers, chants, liturgical texts, important rituals, magic practices, ingredients for potent medical remedies, and the art of carving idols and playing certain ceremonial musical instruments (drums, flutes, bone trumpets, and so on). None of their knowledge may be imparted to outsiders – in this case meaning children, women, and anyone outside the community. Meetings and cult events are generally held in the men's house or club house in which the "temple

A member of the Egungun secret society; ancestors assume his guise. Sketch by Azokus, 1996.

treasures" of that society (such objects are also secret) are kept: the aforementioned musical instruments, the skulls and bones of important ancestors, collected spoils, traditionally valuable items, tools, costumes, and masks used in major ceremonial events. Children, and especially women, are not permitted even to come near the men's house. In former times they could expect harsh punishment (possibly even the death penalty) if they did.

The king of the Egungun secret society, of the Yoruba. Sketch by Azokus, 1996.

In almost all traditional agricultural societies women, marrying into the community as outsiders, are of a lower, less privileged status than men. According to the myths and legends of the region, men were the original inhabitants. Numerous generations of male ancestors thus rest beneath the ground. Men are familiar with every inch of the ground, with the spirits and gods, and with the rites that make survival in their environment possible. It is their country; they are its rulers. It is therefore incumbent upon them to pass on the knowledge and the wealth of experience inherent in their existence to their sons only and to keep such knowledge and experience concealed from others – women, for instance – so as not to endow outsiders with any power over them. This is the mission and purpose of men's societies. Women may do the greatest share of all work in the fields (the purely "profane" tasks); this fact, however, is of no real relevance. Access to ancestors and knowledge about dealing with the spirits and gods is of far greater importance, ensuring that the fields are fertile, harvests are plentiful, and the group well cared for. Viewed from this angle, men, thanks to the knowledge they possess, bear the chief responsibility for the continued existence of the group.

Exclusive male societies, on the other hand, are secret societies in the strict meaning of the term. Not every initiated male adult is automatically accepted into them. Although, in some cases, membership can be bought, in most it must be painstakingly earned. Candidates undergo a lengthy and demanding process of initiation, during which they are only gradually introduced to the society's most revered sources of knowledge, step by step in a procedure of ritual reincarnation. Lastly, they are given a new name and will duly celebrate the end of initiation together with the other members in a ceremony in the society's cult house. The festivities reach their climax in the customary communal meal.

Such men's secret societies were common among many of the Native American cultures of North and, to some extent, Central America, in Melanesia and in West Africa, where they continue to exist to this day. The specific knowledge that they monopolize and keep strictly secret is not principally of a religious nature, but rather concerns specific expertise – for example, on healing plants, special therapeutic methods, magic and fertility rituals, the maintenance of certain religious traditions (myths, chants, dances), relations with sacred animals, or various spiritual cults. All the knowledge and requisites are generally in the possession of the secret society.

Such societies normally legitimize themselves through a myth of creation or constitution, thus certifying their age-old existence or even a divine origin. The fact that deception and "melodramatic show" contribute to maintaining a society's force and influence is revealed in a Kulere myth – in a way that is as disarming as it is naive. The Kulere are a tribe of some 7,000 to 8,000 people who live on the southwestern edge of the central Nigerian tablelands and who until recently maintained a range of cult societies. The following describes the origins of Rai.

Once, there was both a men's and a women's society. It was to be decided which of the two was more powerful. Each society was to contribute a cow; the victorious side would win both cows. The men dug a trench and, when several of them had hidden themselves in it, it was covered over so as to conceal them from view. The women were asked to demonstrate proof of their power; they had nothing to offer. When the men were asked to do so, their leader played a horn pipe. The men in the trench answered his call by playing their own horn pipes and yelling. The women were frightened and ran away. It is by this story that Rai is considered supernatural and that men legitimize their superior position.

The special power of secret societies can sometimes induce terror, but it can also be used to mediate between various groups or between the people and their leaders. The Poro society, for instance, won certain notoriety among several ethnic groups in Sierra Leone and Liberia. Thus it came about that this society developed a role as arbitrator in interethnic disputes. If, for example, a tribal war erupted, the society assembled its highest-ranking representatives in a tribunal that examined the causes of the dispute, subsequently subjecting the group that had brought the situation to a head to a four-day period of looting by the warriors of those tribes who had remained neutral. Wearing masks and bearing flaming torches and daggers, the executors killed anyone who did not retreat to their houses in time, and stole whatever they could get their hands on. Half of the loot was then passed to the assaulted tribe, the tribunal awarding the other half to the looters by way of reward. The society was also responsible for examining and providing retribution for everyday offenses. As is the case in many other countries, this secret society also had policing powers. That was not all. It administered social justice too. If Poro members found individual families to have become excessively wealthy and powerful, orders might be given to subject them to looting. It was pointless to oppose such rulings; anyone who went as far as to complain was immediately punished with death.

The Poro society proved to be a skillful mediation force, as prudent as it was resolute. It was exceptionally successful. Not only did its authority come to be universally recognized, it also achieved a position of considerable power throughout the region and beyond. This situation did not, however, worry the British colonial authorities in Sierra Leone. On the contrary, they saw an opportunity to use it and, on the basis of the doctrine of indirect

A Yoruba Gelede mask. Sketch by Azokus, 1996.

The Yoruba Zangbeto (police of the night) secret society. Sketch by Azokus, 1996.

rule, assigned administrative and policing tasks to the authority of the society. This enabled the British to maintain a background position and to keep their hands clean.

Although women's societies and women's secret societies exist, they are far rarer. In Africa, they are found mainly in western Sudan, and most prominently in Sierra Leone and Liberia. Little is known about their structure and functions, since men (including European ethnographers) are not permitted access. Their main purpose appears to involve giving assistance in childbearing, and practicing medical and agricultural magic or corresponding cult rituals. Many such societies exist among the aforementioned Kulere, mostly, it would seem, devoted to promoting the growth of fruit-bearing plants. During the main festival event of the most powerful of these societies, the women will visit particular caves to receive field fruits from unnamed water spirits, which they then use as a magical fortifier to strengthen the growing properties of their plant stocks.

At least women here were once in a position to use their solidarity to achieve a position of influence and to counter men's claim to dominance and general male attitudes with some degree of success. In some cases, they even assumed responsibility for enforcing public order. Women's societies, however, were founded on previously established privileges. For example, among the Ibo, or Igbo, in Nigeria, if the men should issue a ruling which the women considered unacceptable, they would form a committee and decide on appropriate countermeasures. Such countermeasures could be the public ridicule of all, putting a deadly curse on individual men, or even a concentrated mass boycott. Yet another popular way of bringing disagreeable males back to their senses involves the women congregating and settling on their farmsteads, dancing and singing disrespectful and derisive songs, and possibly even beating against the men's houses with pestles or smearing mud on their walls. This behavior is maintained until the men finally capitulate and apologetically admit to their lapse in good judgement. The secret societies themselves, however, take disciplinary measures within the seclusion of their own ranks. The members of the Njembe society of the Mpongwe in Gabon, for example, have certain magical powers which allow them not only to expose previously unidentified culprits, but also to reveal secret male intrigues directed against the interests of the women. Societies in Sierra Leone concoct potent "medicines" with which they can harm the health of those men whom the women deem have done them wrong. They can even go so far as to deprive a man of his virility. Since their abilities remain secret and the solidarity of the society members intact, they are able to exercise their power.

An Egungun gown for Olohunde, the Egungun bringer of peace and tolerance.

An Egungun gown for Tnama, who acts as a fool and causes unrest.

Secret Yoruba societies

The Yoruba (originally a Hausa term for the kingdom of Oyo) live mostly in Nigeria, where they number about 15 million. Smaller groups are also found in Benin. They speak several dialects, not all mutually comprehensible, and originally belonged to a total of five independent kingdoms. In times of war, these kingdoms entered temporary and varying alliances with one another. The only lasting common attribute of all the kingdoms, however, was the fact that their kings all traced their origins back to Odudua, the god who descended from heaven to Ife to create the world. In other myths, Odudua is considered to be either the wife of Obatala, a particularly significant god, or the earth in the form of its prime matter. In many of the world's mythologies, the earth divinity is androgynous and has the ability to give birth to all living creatures without insemination.

Among the Yoruba there have existed many societies of varying degrees of exclusivity. As secret societies, they would maintain a thoroughly terrorist-like regimen. In practical terms, control was often held not by the king or the elders but by the powerful secret societies whose messengers, shielded by masks, had the power to demand and command as they pleased. Other societies, for instance the Gelede, have a more profane role, such

Above left: An Egungun gown for Olohunde.
Above right: An Egungun gown for Odé, the hunter who often seeks prey to crush. The costume is finished with a piece of wood depicting a monkey's skull.

as providing entertainment. These societies are also centered on their religious orientation, but they are less exclusive than others.

How Oro and Egungun came to be possessed by men

Olodumare, the god of creation, endowed the first woman, Odu, with the ability to bear life. However, she abused this power, and anyone who looked at her face risked becoming blind. Odu asked Obatala to come and live with her. One day, Obatala sacrificed several snails. He ate the slime of one, offering Odu to partake. The snail slime softened her heart, so that she revealed all her secrets to Obatala, including those of the Oro and Egungun societies. Since then these secrets have been possessed by men. Odu did, however, recommend seeking the consent and the cooperation of the women, since they are all mothers. And so it passed that men had power over women, yet the women retained control over life. Without women nobody would be born.

Oro, society of whirring plates

Oro's shrine is in the bush, where there are sacred groves (*igbo oro*). In the past, anyone who was not initiated was prohibited from entering them on pain of death. Initiation ceremonies are carried out every three or seven years in secret bush camps erected by members of the society. In the past, these ceremonies spanned three months. Wearing palm-leaf skirts, their faces painted white, initiates are led to the sacred grove by a "being" whose face is concealed.

Of Yoruba secret societies a particularly influential one is Oro, a men's society. Its political power among the Oyo and Egba people (whose capital is Abeokuta) even surpassed its claim to religious authority. For these people, Oro had the right to monitor whether sovereigns acted in faithful adherence to the divine moral code. It was in charge of upholding traditional order, and ruled over knowledge and the maintenance of myths, folklore, and heritage. In precolonial times, it commanded the right to impose death sentences in secret jurisdiction and ultimately to execute those whom it sentenced. It was not least on account of this that the society's considerable power was

guaranteed. Those pronounced guilty were brought to the society's sacred groves and thus beheaded. Their corpses were rarely seen again; it was said that Oro came to "take" them. Pieces of clothing were sometimes found hanging from a tree. It was claimed that the cloth had been caught on its branches as Oro carried off his victims through the air.

Oro also fulfills a variety of social functions. For example, its members ensure that the deceased are properly laid to rest and their souls conveyed to the realm of the dead; this includes those who suffered a bad death – who died in childhood or as the result of an accident, for example.

Initiates stand in humility before Oro's shrine. Oro serves mainly the death spirits and so appears only at night. His emblem is a piece of metal or wood attached to a pole with string – a whirring plate. These whirring plates make a noise which is said to kill witches.

Oro serves mainly the death spirits and appears only at night. His emblem is a flat piece of metal or wood (usually óbó or camwood, which witches may neither see nor smell) attached to a pole with string, making an instrument that produces a whirring sound. Each society often has two instruments of this kind. The smaller, known as an *ise* ("disruption"), could once be heard most nights. It generates a high-pitched sound known as *aja oro* ("Oro's dog"). The larger version, known as *agbe* ("sword"), produces a humming sound considered to be the voice of Oro, announcing an impending death. Oro conveys the voice of the dead, so it is said to be the dead calling. He must be kept concealed from women; witches especially fear him. The whirring sound kills witch birds and witches. It may even destroy trees on which witch birds are perched and drive those who have committed a condemnable act out of their minds.

In the past, seven, or in some places nine, days of the year around the new moon were dedicated to the worship of Oro. Even during the day, women would only leave their houses to procure essential foods. On the final day, however, they were not even permitted to go on these errands. At night, Oro's voice would be clearly audible. Any inquisitive woman who laid eyes on Oro or his emblem and thus discovered the secret was killed by magic means. It would be claimed that Oro had killed her.

Although the belief in witches is still widespread today, the Oro society has lost much of its former significance. Often, Oro's calling is heard only on the death of important members of the society. The members of this secret society often wear neither costume nor masks. The only exception is the wooden masks worn in Abeokuta; they do not, however, cover the wearer entirely, as do those of the death-cult society Egungun.

A ram is sacrificed to Oro. The initiates will drink the ram's blood.

357

The blood of the ram is dripped onto Oro's shrine.

The initiates dance wildly around Oro's shrine until they reach a state of total exhaustion.

The initiates throw themselves to the ground as if they were dead. They will then be "resurrected" as new members of the Oro society.

Opposite page: Such threatening gestures are part of the ritual. The young man leading the initiation tries to intimidate the youths with the bloody head of the sacrificed animal.

358

The death cult and Egungun

In June, a festival is held at which those who have recently died are mourned. Members of the Egungun society travel from village to village to collect money for the festival. The colorfully clothed individual at the head of the procession represents an ancestral spirit. Masks keep alive the memory of the deceased and maintain their relationship with the living.

Egungun member in a swirling dance. Guardians with long rods ensure that onlookers show respect to the ancestors. It is important that the costumes do not slip and that nobody touches them. This had grave consequences in the past. If the costume slipped, the mask-wearer and every woman in attendance were sentenced to death. If the costume was touched, death was imposed on the mask-wearer and on the person who touched it. Today the Egungun dance is merely an entertaining spectacle.

Right: A relative of the deceased is marked by the ancestors as punishment. The Egunguns take on the guise of ancestors.

Egun means "bone," "skeleton," or the spirit of a dead person who has returned to earth. The secret society maintains strict role allotment. In Oyo, the alapini, one of the seven "distinguished people" of the town, holds the highest rank. In individual districts, leadership rests with high priests, or alagbâ, from whose ranks a kind of president is chosen. A part of his farm is reserved for society members, who assemble and store masks and costumes there. At the society's public appearances, its high-ranking members, always older men, tend to remain in the background, leaving costumes, adornments, and dancing to younger members. However, they make all important decisions and keep most of the society's income.

Egungun is centered around ancestor worship, so that the principal duty of its members and mask-bearers is attendance at funeral rituals. A mask-bearer, for instance, becomes possessed by the spirit of the deceased, which uses him as a means of consoling the bereaved family and to decide issues of dispute. His word carries weight, especially in family disagreements and issues of inheritance. The society once had a great deal of political influence as well. If a village chief acted in too independent a manner, for instance, or too often sought to serve his own interests, he was summoned to appear before the society. The society's tribunal, representing the ancestors on earth, would meet at a sacred grove (igbole), reprimand the culprit, and specify the punishment. If his offense was serious, he risked being removed from office or being ostracized from the village community. Today, the

society's authority is limited, and its power curtailed. The fear that it once evoked is greatly diminished, yet it is still shrouded in secrecy. Boys are now initiated into the cult when they are five or six. Women, still excluded, readily uphold their belief that the Egungun come from the spirit world.

Apart from attendance at funerals, members of Egungun appear only once a year, before the start of sowing in May or June, when the Yoruba turn to their ancestors to request their blessing on the community and the fruits of the field. In every district there is a four-week period during which the Egungun appear. This is why sowing times vary from place to place. Once roads and village areas have been swept and any disrepair to houses and granaries made good, the living and dead prepare to celebrate together. This is a festival to which people (including the deceased) will travel over great distances. During the short time that the Egungun are involved, the community celebrates the triumph of the (free) spirit over death. The past and the present merge, thus generating optimism for the future.

Performance of the first ritual acts begins in darkness, in the time of the spirits, when the houses are closed and the villagers sleeping. In the town or village center, at the intersection between this world and that beyond, a spirit named Agan inaugurates the festival. His arrival is as indeterminable and enigmatic as is the coming of the first rain after the dry season. No one is allowed to see this mysterious spiritual power; its presence is discernible to humans only through certain sounds. On the eve of the first day of festivities, the society's members assemble in the sacred grove. They spend the night there kneeling and praying for the blessing and mercy of the ancestors. Countless chickens and goats are sacrificed on their graves, their blood soaking the earth. Invigorated by the blood, the ancestors appear in public on the following morning in the guise of younger members of the society who lend them physical form and through whom they speak. In a sepulchral voice or in high-pitched, trembling, whistling or nasal tones, they give advice or issue instructions. Their voices are reminiscent of the sounds made by a species of monkey called ijimeme.

Accompanied by the alagbâ and by low-ranking priests, the Egungun proceed to the house of the village chief, all the while drumming and dancing. He offers them an abundance of gifts, in return for which they promise to support him and the whole community. After some three hours of exuberant celebrations, including the exchange of gifts, wild dancing, and carousing, the Egungun take their leave, each headed for a different part of the village, each mask normally going to the house of the person wearing it. An important task now is to expose any recent misconduct, and to reprove and avenge it. The women's conduct is examined most closely. Today this mainly involves subjecting those accused of objectionable behavior to public reproach. Formerly, punishment was meted out to women suspected of witchcraft, murder, fomenting unrest, or committing other capital offenses.

It is the responsibility of the ancestors to settle issues of discord and thus give renewed strength to the community's solidarity. Villagers are then able to devote their energy to working in the fields and to

The ju-ju man, or magician, is a special figure, a kind of executioner who appears only on special occasions. This expert on all deadly poisons, black magic, and hypnosis drapes himself in drab sackcloth, his face concealed by a red hood. He carries the tools of his magic trade in a sack tied around his neck. In his hands he holds a severed gorilla paw.

begin the new year in a spirit of unity and harmony. This is the mission of the mask-bearing reprimanders – to cleanse and reconcile the community and liberate it from burden. It is also a means of ensuring that the elders maintain total control over the activities and conduct of the women and youths.

The mask performances take place over seven days, culminating in displays of sport and games, some of which are daringly acrobatic. Particularly popular are the magical tricks with which some Egungun also fascinate their audience.

Finally, on the eighth day, all Egungun assemble in the house of the first alagbâ. The festival then ends as abruptly and unexpectedly as it started. A spirit by the name of Aranta or Oludungbodu ("Owner of the Fire") "carries it away" into the other world.

Gelede – the magic of the spectacle

In the palace of the Yoruba king of Sakete (Benin), old women greet the Gelede masks. They are honorary guests at the festival. One society members remarks, "We call the old women together so they can laugh and be happy. Without food (a synonym for sexual intercourse) the world is no longer sweet." Providing entertainment is the Gelede society's foremost aim; the religion is often of secondary importance.

The youngest dancers appear first. As soon as the drumming begins, the children appear, half-clad in costumes, often wearing old masks, and moving with a halting, uncertain gait. They have not yet mastered the accuracy of experienced dancers and use their hands to keep the masks firmly on their heads.

According to a poem by the renowned Yoruba scholar Adeboye Babalola, "Two things delight the human eye. One is the performance of magic, the other is beauty." Gelede attempts to merge both. Demonstrations of acrobatic feats, the performance of mythical themes, and the statuesque elegance of dancing masks delight people and gods alike. The purpose of Gelede ceremonies, held most prominently by the Yoruba, is to bring people and spiritual powers closer together by means of the magic of drama (irun). "If many outsiders attend the performance, this means that our prayers have been heard and our contact with the world beyond has been successful," a king explains.

The individual elements of each performance vary from one place to another. What always remains the same is the purpose of the mask performances, which are chiefly of a comical nature: this is to use art to take the sting out of witchcraft. While Oro and Egungun endorse the power of violence, Gelede applies a milder means of placation. Witches (aje) – the Yoruba use the flattering term "mother" – are a threat to everyone's life and well-being. Those who are successful in life and who have been abundantly blessed with children presume that they must fear the jealousy of those less fortunate, especially that of aging women who are generally suspected of practicing witchcraft. Those joining the Gelede society hope to be invulnerable to the assault of witches.

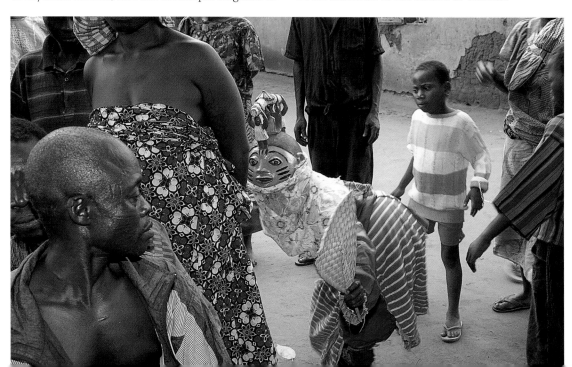

In Yoruba towns and villages in Benin, the annual festival of the Gelede society (*odun gelede*) is held during the dry season – the season of the spirits, when most work in the fields ceases. Although it is the major event and the most popular entertainment of the whole year, the expense of staging it means that not every community can celebrate it every year. It is often held only every two or three years. When a community does stage the Gelede festival, this makes it all the more fascinating, titillating the senses with a multifaceted combination of painting, sculpture, textiles, music, and dance that is not only a feast to the eyes and ears, but also serves the higher purpose of balancing and maintaining the order of the world and of life. Universal energy draws both on the artful dancing of the masked performers, who to the accompaniment of drumming, enact scenes from everyday life, and on the complex masks, themselves a feature of the performance and donned by otherwise inexpressive wearers. The

performance appeals to witches, who as members of society are themselves afflicted by tensions, and to their sense of discernment and solidarity. By enacting conflicts, it fulfills the purpose of resolving them, to the benefit of all.

Gelede performances are structured in two parts. The festival is ritually inaugurated at nighttime by two masks personifying Eshu and Ogun, after which the Efe singers perform. Efe appears only in the darkness of night. The importance of his appearing, however, is exceeded by the importance of his message. Most communities have only one leading impersonator of Efe; he entertains his audience with witty songs, poems, and satire, and with the exaltation of the *orisha* (the gods) and "mother" – in whose honor the festival is staged – and of past and present performers. All the events of the past year – theft, love affairs, corruption, abuse of official office, political despotism – are brought to light. His performance, spiced with sarcastic remarks,

Pairs of Gelede dancers traditionally perform in the same costumes. The dances are held in the market square. This is the women's arena: Yoruba women are skilled traders who often earn more than the men. Gelede have an educational function. If, for example, a villager is infected with Aids, the Gelede are called upon to teach the community how to avoid contracting the disease.

reprimand, and wit, serves to relieve existing tensions. Flitting from the trivial to the earnest, from the sacred to the profane, he intersperses his performance with acts of homage to the dignitaries in attendance and to the high-ranking dead. This alleviates the pain of the bereaved, while flattering the deceased, who will thus be more willing to bestow their blessing upon the community. Efe songs are probably the most important part of the whole festival. All other elements only lead up to or adorn their presentation.

The night's events are followed the next day by a Gelede dance that appeals to the eyes rather than to the ears, which is why it is said that "the deaf do not attend only the Efe ceremony, the blind not only the Gelede dance." Even though the mask dances are performed by men, the ceremony is supervised by the women and a female cult head, Iyalase. "Gelede," its members claim, "is the secret of the women to whom we are slaves. We dance in order to appease our mothers." In essence, therefore, this is a reconciliation ritual (etutu) meant to "cool" the "heated" powers of witches.

The mask protects the dancer both from and through the "mother." This is illustrated by the myth about the journey made by Orunmila, god of prophecy, to the secret grove of the "mother." When Orunmila entered the women's domain, he wore a mask (aworan), a headscarf (oja), and ankle rattles (iku) – the basic items that make up Efe and Gelede costumes. He ventured into the proverbial lion's den, subjecting himself to great risk. Yet he escaped death, for he was cautious and did not anger the powerful "mother," but appeased her. Dressed in his bizarre attire, he entertained her with song and dance and returned in safety. The Gelede performance enacts this scene as an example of conciliation and good sense.

There are many different types of Gelede masks. Those who carve them virtually have a free creative hand. The masks can personify animals, plants, people, or gods, depict erotic motifs, or even take the form of airplanes, automobiles, chains, and locks, and a range of other subjects. Movement brings the masks to life. For a fleeting moment, their eyes appear to take in their surroundings, while the face remains a picture of statuesque dignity, almost as though it were able to sense the spirits presiding among the onlookers and critically assessing their performance.

The bobbing movements of the dancers echo the rhythm of the accompanying drumbeats, their steps keeping time with the instruments. The performances are staged in quick succession, and each pair of dancers strives to outdo the others as the rhythms set by the drums become more demanding.

The dancers all appear together once more before heading for the sacred grove.

The festivities end with a dance before the sacred shrine (ase), home of the Gelede where Iya Nlá, the "big mother," is worshiped. She is the source of all life, but is also able to cause death and infertility.

Masks – the spirits rule

Most of us wear a "mask." Our gestures, our way of speaking, our haircut, and our clothes are perpetual imitation, be it conscious or not. Our "mask" is based on a combination of other people's traits. This tendency is given free rein at carnivals, during which participants openly masquerade in the guise of others. There are two aspects that are most predominantly linked to traditional carnivals. Firstly, carnivals (such as Mardi Gras) have always taken place during a time of transition – during the "time of the spirits," before the arrival of spring and, therefore, between the close of the old and beginning of the new year. Secondly, carnival has a burlesque character; people behave in an exaggerated boisterous way, adopt a role that contrasts to their everyday one,

indulge in clownery and buffoonery, and are unabashedly critical of public authorities. Both these elements are features of carnival that originate from mask-wearing customs.

The word "mask" can be traced back to the Arabic term *maskara*, meaning both mockery and clownery, as well as describing the person who performed such clownery. The universal, and probably the original, significance of masks, whether they cover the face, head, or entire body, is that they give concrete form to the powers of the world beyond, as is generally suggested by the names that they are given. They may represent spirits of nature or the spirits of the dead (ancestors). Significantly, masks of such original form make their appearance only at times of cosmic change or at important life stages: at night, in winter, during the days around the close of the old and commencement of the new year, at harvest and new year festivals, at the climax of initiations, at funerals, and ceremonies held in memory of the dead – that is, whenever the spirits reign. When, for example, the spirits of ancestors appear at the close of the year, they are represented by the senior members of society, who always see that traditions are upheld by the younger generations. Thus, they will probably take the opportunity to publicly cite and denounce, and possibly even make rulings and pass sentence on the offenses committed during the recent past, much the same as secret societies do.

Masks often have an extremely bizarre, repulsive, fearful, or grotesque appearance, with unusual, distorted, or ugly features. They may portray dwarfs with overlarge heads, animals, or fantastic monsters. Yet, this is not necessarily the work of an overactive imagination or the expression of visions of horror. It is, in fact, quite a realistic portrayal, for this is just what the bush and natural spirits are presumed to look like. They are seldom a pretty sight. Should such spirits ever appear as a seductive-looking or charming figure, anyone confronted by it must be especially alert, since this is likely to be nothing more than a crafty deception. Once the spirit has beguiled its victim, its handsome guise will soon become horribly distorted. When the spirit masks appear at festivals or cult ceremonies, the way they act is in keeping with their looks: their movements are jerky and uncoordinated, they jump this way and that in a bizarre motion,

A Loniaken plank mask, Tusyan, Burkina Faso. These masks are linked to the do or lo cults to which all youths are introduced. The masks were made especially for this purpose and appear only on this occasion.

Opposite page: A Bamun mask from the Cameroon savanna. The nakang mask is worn by the mask group leader who heads the ceremony and determines the style of dance. The mask portrays a typical male face.

Baga, a Guinean mask. Nimba masks are among the most impressive masks in Africa. They appeared at funerals, wedding ceremonies, and harvesting rites, and symbolized human fertility and the fertility of the fields.

dancing in a frenzy, attacking onlookers, groaning and wheezing, and speaking in a hissing, staccato, and often completely incomprehensible voice.

The people wearing the masks and thus impersonating the spirits are perpetually on the verge of moving from the status of performer into the actual world of the spirits. The ritual that they perform can have such a forceful impact on their emotions that they may ultimately identify with the spiritual power. It will take possession of them, amalgamating their two identities. At such times, those possessed will take on masklike features – the features of the spirit possessing them. There is but a fine line between wearing a spirit mask and entering a state of spiritual possession.

Myths of origin surrounding spirit masks can sometimes show that a mask precisely replicates the spirit that it represents. According to a myth current among the Nuna culture (in Burkina Faso), for example, a hunter from his raised hunting stand "once saw strange beings dancing about." Fearing what he saw, he hurried back home and reported the incident to his father, who ordered him to capture some of them. The son thus stalked his

way back to the spot where they danced and then ran at them. They immediately sank into the ground. The hunter was only just able to catch hold of one of the being's heads – a mask – to bring back to his father. The father asked his son whether he had paid attention to their dancing and could therefore imitate it. The son confirmed that he had, whereupon his father decided to make the masks himself and hold mask dances, since this would "be a good thing." The hunter was made leader of the mask dancers, and he taught the younger generations what he knew.

A mask cult had thus been established. Why is it deemed important to impersonate the spirits in the form of masks and, with their help, to imitate them or even become one with them? Ancestors and spirits are more powerful than humans. Whereas ancestors need only be feared in the event of human sin, spirits are moody, unpredictable, and generally spiteful. If a person unexpectedly happens upon a spirit, he or she can only hope to escape with nothing more serious than a fright. Often, however, during times of seasonal change and transition, spirits appear among humans with uncanny regularity. In order not to give them free rein and thus have to fear the worst possible consequences, people restrain them by assuming their appearance and character. This enables people to maintain control over their activities. There is a risk involved, however: a spirit may easily take control of a human and assume his or her guise. This risk is what has caused possession to be ritualized – that is, spiritual possession has become a feature of cults. Secret cults, and to an even greater extent possession cults, focus on critical situations of this kind and through their playful approach attempt to overcome the dangers of possession, masks being a central element in the procedure as the most important means of identifying spirits.

The story of a mask

A young man was on his way to the river to fish. While walking through the bush, his foot hit the blade of an old iron hoe. He continued on his way, only to stumble across the iron blade again several yards further on. On the third encounter, he became alarmed. He picked the hoe up off the ground and returned to his father's house. Father and son then went off to seek the advice of a fortune-teller, to whom they told the story. The fortune-teller explained that a bush spirit (niblé), intent on protecting the young man and his family, had wanted to make his presence known. The young man would need to carve a mask in which the spirit could live and through which it could communicate. The fortune-teller then proceeded to spread an array of small cast-brass replicas of a variety of masks onto the floor; he took a hooked wooden stick and held it over the brass masks. The young man also took hold of the stick, and both men waved the stick back and forth over

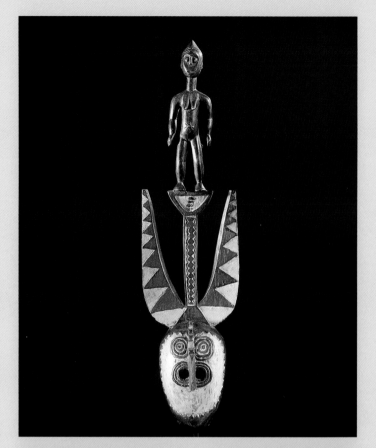

the brass masks. The stick suddenly lashed out and touched one of the models. The form for the new mask was thus decided on, and the young man ordered it to be made by the smiths. The mask first danced at the ceremonies held to dispel the evil spirits at the end of the dry season.

(Christopher Roy, from *Art of the Upper Volta Rivers*.)

Introduction of the dama

Before the dama, the ritual commemorating the dead, was known to people, the souls of the dead dwelt among the living. The original sin of mythical ancestors caused death to spread quickly, and numerous stricken souls thus contaminated the villages and troubled their inhabitants. Since they did not want to remain alone, they sought others to take into their midst. This situation of perpetually hovering threat needed to be brought to an end, whatever the cost. The sigui rite in memory of the first incidence of death proved to be useless. No solution was found until, one day, a man returning home from his work in the fields became aware that the soul of his dead father was dwelling in his house. He sought the advice of an old fortune-teller, who advised him to put on a mask and climb onto the roof of his house in order to dispel his dead father's soul. The force (*nyama*) inherent in the red color of the fibers would do its deed, he was assured. So it was that, from that day on, men would don the red fiber weaves (aprons and skirts) and the hoods that they had adopted from the andambulu, the dwarf former inhabitants of their country. In this attire of warriors, they climbed onto the roofs of the houses, for it was here that the souls of the dead liked to dwell and vessels containing libations were left for them. Swinging their hoes, knives, spears, and sabers, and accompanied by the rhythmic drumming, they rushed into battle with their invisible foe. This dance (*gyemu*) has since been the central element of the ritual commemorating the dead.

Right: An Ibo mask from Nigeria. This mask is called "The Spirit of a Beautiful Girl" and is crowned with representations of an antelope, a leopard, and two snakes.

Dogon festivities

Having been circumcised at about 15 years of age, Dogon youths begin performing dances in which they wear masks, only ceasing to do so once their facial hair turns white. The mask society (*awa*) is a unity of all village men, with the exception of those who belong to a caste (such as the smiths). Membership is obligatory and joining is followed by a communal youth initiation ceremony. Isolated in the bush school (the initiation camp), novices are taught the beliefs, myths, and traditions of the group and are prepared for their life ahead. The masks serve as an indispensable requisite for the often very dramatic enactment of the great mystery of death and reincarnation to which the initiates are physically subjected and which they painfully

Below: The masks emerge from the bush. When not in use, they are stored in a cave west of the village, in the direction of the sunset and the realm of the dead. An occasion for their use might be a festivity celebrating the dead. The wearers of the woven pull-on masks, walking on high stilts, each appear separately. A march in procession would be too slow, and they would risk losing their balance.

Right: As they enter the village, the masks keep a certain order. *Bede* and *yagule* (both personifying young girls) appear first, followed by *walu* (an antelope) and *kanaga* (a bird). Only those on stilts (*tene dana*) and the comedians may move freely. Mask wearers who are still very young are led by older men who often direct the drum rhythms by means of an iron bell.

Above: The mask in the foreground represents walu, the oryx antelope that plays an important role in mythology. Walu masks are distinguishable by their extreme abstraction. The box-shaped face of the mask consists only of two broad, deep incisions, inside which the triangular eyes are set, and a small slit for the mouth.

Left: Research has uncovered a wide range of meanings for the symbols that adorn the masks. This is particularly true for the kanaga mask topped with a symbol reminiscent of the Lotharingian Cross. To outsiders it appears to be a bird of prey (*kommolo tebu*) with red talons and beak, white wings, and a black head. Others see a lizard or crocodile, on the back of which the ancestors once crossed a river, or a person, arms reaching for the sky and legs for the ground. To the most highly initiated, it represents the balance between heaven and earth, a symbol of the sacred world order, or even a likeness of the creator himself.

endure when "the big wood devours them." The first ancestors were not afflicted by death, but metamorphosed and were rejuvenated, becoming snakes. During such times, they – and likewise the initiates – were not allowed to speak. An ancestor once broke this rule and thus faced death. Since the time that this taboo was broken, death has been the inevitable fate of all humans. A grand mask festival (*sigui*) is held every 60 years in memory of this mythical ancestor. The purpose of the sigui cycle is to renew the great mask, mainstay of the mythical ancestor's soul. To dance it means to beg forgiveness for the sin that will in time lead to death.

Awa is the collective term used to describe not only the men of a certain age group who participate in the ritual, but also the masks that they wear and the fibers of the mask costumes. Members of the society are divided by age into various ranks. The highest echelon within the hierarchy is that of the very old who in their life have experienced two sigui. The elder of this group has overall command of the society. Ranked below this group are all those who have seen one sigui. Women, with a few exceptions, are refused admittance. The precise roles of masks and times that many of them appear are predefined. They are often an important element in particular rites relating to the fertility of fields or hunting and fishing success. Mask dances are held at sowing and harvesting times to obtain blessings on both these seasons. The powers that they generate are used as much in times of need and affliction as in times of transition from one life stage to the next or in the event of death. They serve to re-establish the destabilized or shaken order of things. They can even stop famine and plague.

Left: Mask dancing in the village square. Each of the different masks – about 80 and a variety representing the diversity of the world – requires a specific dance movement. A kanaga dance performance is an exceptionally wild event. The swirling dance reminds the initiated of the inner vibrations of matter and of the creator of the world who, at the dawn of history, standing tall, "danced the world by making all four corners of the earth spin."

Because mask societies are closely linked to the cult of the ancestors, one of their most important functions is to dance at funeral ceremonies for prominent members. The festivities celebrating the dead are an occasion for making new masks, a task which, because of the carving and weaving involved, can be very time-consuming. Most Dogon masks are made of wood; some are woven and worn with a short, usually red fiber skirt fitted with baldrics made of cowry shells. Decorative collars, ankle adornments, and girdles are also made. Some mask costumes include breastplates made of gourds or the fruits of the baobab tree, halved and painted black. Because these ceremonies are costly affairs, they are often jointly held by several families.

Elaborate ceremonies for the dead (*dama*) generally take place every two or three years. In colloquial language, dama means "forbidden" or "dangerous," referring either to the principles governing food or to gestures, or possibly to sites that it is advisable to avoid. Because death imposes an array of prohibitions upon family members, the ceremonies for the dead are also known as dama. How elaborately an individual festivity is staged depends on the status of the deceased and on the number of deaths being commemorated. The event may last several hours, but can also continue for up

Apart from their wooden masks, the Dogon also use woven pull-on masks that portray members of their own group (religious leaders, young girls, the deaf and mute, smiths, drummers, thieves, healers, hunters, and so on) as well as those of other groups (the Fulbe, Marabut, Tuareg, Europeans) in a schematized way. This mask, called pulloyana, personifies a Fulbe girl.

to six days. The object of the event is to convey the soul of the deceased safely to the realm of the dead. Because the masks illustrate the diversity of the world, the Dogon have a great variety of them, and the wealth of religious symbolism they display is rooted in the Dogons' profound mythology.

Costumes made of dyed red fiber and cowry shells are worn with masks that cover the heads of wearers like helmets and often have artful hair designs. The skirts are knee-length; elbows, wrists, and ankles are adorned with colorful fibers.

The Winiama's dance of the bush spirits

This wooden mask represents a spirit that has no natural image. The mask is known as *mitchi* (mosque), because the towering section represents a mosque. Winiama masks appear during the dry season on a whole range of occasions. They dance to keep the evil powers away from the village during the course of the new sowing season, but also appear for entertainment during market days, and during the funeral ceremonies held for all those who have died throughout the year and who are thus honored and escorted into the world of the ancestors.

"Disease is our enemy" and "Suffering is a warning" are names that the Winiama give masks that express wisdom and human experience and whose mission it is to impart such wisdom and experience both to the initiated and to the community as a whole.

The Winiama, a small Gur-speaking group of around 25,000 people (including the related Nunuma), originally came from northern Ghana. They crossed the Black Volta River and occupied empty territory in the Bwaba region east of Bagassi. Their most important townships are Boromo and Ouri. The Winiama have much in common with their neighbors, the Nunuma and Bwaba, both with respect to their conception of life and to their mask culture. All three groups have stylistically similar masks. For instance, they often portray images of the same animals – predominantly buffalos, warthogs, rhinoceros bird, and snakes. This has led to the Winiama sometimes being thought of as belonging to the Nunuma or Bwaba. All their masks have large round eyes within concentric circles. Animal masks often have a short snout, and those of bush spirits a projecting mouth. They are decorated with various combinations of geometric design in black, red, and white. The heads are covered with a full wig made of vegetable materials and attached to the edges of the mask. Geometric and abstract designs are a dominant feature of Winiama masks, particularly those representing spirits neither related to animals nor in any other way figurative. The Winiama are also the only group that does not repaint its masks every year. After repeated use they are often coated in dirt, so that the original colors and designs become difficult to make out. It has been said that these "black" masks represent evil

The Hiengo mask, with diamond-shaped mouth, gapped teeth, and feminine headdress, portrays young girls and, even more, fertility. The geometric patterns carved into the mask probably indicate scar tattoos such as were customary among men and women in the past.

Because the Winiama do not paint their masks every year, as do neighboring groups, they tend to become soiled and black over time, so that the painting on them is no longer easy to make out.

This smaller mask is known as *kalé*. The various shapes and styles of masks are part of a complex system of symbols. Each element generally has its own specific meaning, though that meaning varies from one group to another.

and unpredictable bush spirits which are assumed to be unkempt and dirty in the way that the mentally deranged are. However, most masks portray protective bush spirits who guard the family, the clan, and the village and who will bestow fertility, health, and wealth on their owners, on the condition that they receive the worship rightly due to them.

Numerous stories tell the tale of an encounter with a spirit in the bush, something most often experienced by hunters in pursuit of game or farmers clearing land for cultivation. Both hunters and farmers, therefore, have a special affinity with masks portraying bush spirits or spirits that appear in the guise of animals. Ultimately, however, all these masks embody the spirit Su, considered to be a kind of aspect of the highest being. Su is resident in all masks and often in carved wooden figures. The oldest and most sacred mask of any community constitutes a kind of shrine. Su is feared, yet if duly worshiped he will bestow well-being, ensure the fertility of all women and, if so requested, harm enemies.

The various forms and styles of masks, the combinations of their colors, their designs and ornamentation are part of a complex system of symbols. Each element generally has a fixed meaning. Of course, such meanings can vary between groups or even between clans. The message that they communicate – their language – is not immediately comprehensible to everyone. For the non-initiated or the newly initiated, the masks portray bush spirits who mediate between humans and the supreme god. On the esoteric level of initiated male elders, their designs have social, political, economic, and religious significance – the geometric characters of a language that only the initiated can comprehend. Their meaning changes

or is augmented according to a given level of initiation. A triangle construed by a newly initiated person to represent the footprint of a kobus antelope is interpreted by the more highly initiated as representing a man, while those who have undergone the highest possible level of initiation know the symbol to represent Su. Each of the geometric patterns on the masks is part of an overall statement which describes the meaning and the significance of the mask. While all symbols together make up the identity of the mask, they also constitute a lesson in correct and pious conduct.

The kêduneh mask, with its curved horn, is a typical Winiama mask. It is rarely found among the Nunuma, and never among the Bwaba. It portrays a wild and uncontrolled bush spirit. The dancer often falls into a trance, takes high leaps, or staggers about.

Left: Masks that show signs of wear or that are damaged are put aside and sold. This does not apply to the fiber costumes, however, which are meticulously cared for by their owners. During dancing, they become soaked with the wearer's perspiration – that is, with his life energies. If someone else were to gain possession of it, he or she could use detrimental magical influence on those life energies. The next time he performed, the dancer would fear losing his balance and falling or even suffering a much worse misfortune.

Far left: Inspired by the masks, youths succumb to the pleasure of dancing.

Left: Honbue, the buffalo mask, performs. Buffalo are among the animals most frequently represented by the masks. They symbolize the untamed.

375

Vagla – the bush cow dances for the dead hunter

Jentilepe, a Vagla village in northern Ghana, has two mask societies who are responsible for rainmaking, among other things. First a chicken is sacrificed, dying by being held suspended over a calabash bottle that contains the rain medicine. The rain medicine has great powers; it can even bring lightning down from the sky.

Masks appear only in the dry season, the time of harvest. Their most important function is to appear at ceremonies for the deceased who led an exemplary life and who had a good death. Although the Vagla live mostly from the fields that they cultivate, hunting is still an important element of their culture. Sigma masks are also in some sense related to the art of hunting. On the final day of the funeral festivities for Ayai, the great hunter, the skulls of the animals that he killed are gathered around a stake.

Adults know that there are things that have lethal power, which is why children must not come into contact with them. If they hear the flute that accompanies a funeral or the bells of the mask bearers, they run to their houses as fast as they can and hide. This was so in the past at least, when Sigma (the name of the Vagla secret society and its various masks) killed anyone who dared to venture onto forbidden ground – which may have meant either visiting certain sites within the village and in the bush or practicing magic and witchcraft. Those who ignore the taboo bring the wrath of Sigma on themselves. In the past, the culprits would be punished by mutilation, "taking their breath away" and thus causing bronchitis or asthma-like symptoms. Others would face death in the bush in some other cruel way.

The Vagla dwell in 13 villages in the Bole district of northern Ghana. Like the Winiama, their language is Gur. Bole was formerly the capital of the kingdom of Gonja, founded by Mande immigrants in the 16th century. Its peoples belong to three groups. The Ngbanya are the ruling elite, descendants of Ndewura Jakpa, the non-Muslim conqueror and founder of the kingdom. A second group, Muslims or Karamos, comprise Mande clans that trace their origins back to a Koran

scholar (mallam) who endowed Jakpa with magic support for his conquering mission. The Nyamase are third-class citizens – the original inhabitants as well as immigrants, some of whom migrated to the region in the wake of the Mande conquerors. The sovereign, Bolewura, a direct descendant of the fifth son of Jakpa, reigns over a number of the Ngbanya elite, who in turn reign over a collection of villages.

However, even the Bolewura did not possess total power over the mask society, so that their traditional judicial practices remained untouched. The people – the subjects – were thus able to maintain a certain degree of autonomy. Yet, not all Vagla villages have Sigma shrines and masks, and even fewer have both.

The Sigma society consists of three levels. Being admitted into the ranks of the first level is akin to entering adulthood. Boys and girls are led to the initiation grounds blindfolded. There they are confronted unawares with the masks that had previously instilled so much fear in them. Their introduction to the essence and function of the mask is only superficial. They are taught that the Sigma is made up of costumed villagers and that the fear-evoking voices of the spirits are nothing more than the sounds made by wooden whirring plates. During the further course of their training they receive a black medicine (tagdunna) that will kill anyone who subscribes to witchcraft. It is impressed upon them that they must disclose none of what they are being shown on pain of death. An elder will rip out the tongue of a sacrificial chicken and lay it in the mouth of a mask.

The "society career" of most women ends there. Very few, mostly the sisters (seldom the wives) of Sigma elders, are initiated into the ranks of the second level at the onset of menopause. Those who are, are generally only assigned to the task of brewing millet-seed beer for the nightly meetings of the men. This second-level ranking, the "Night Sigma," is generally only open to adult men. Their privilege constitutes being permitted nightly access

Villagers enacting a hunting scene in honor of the deceased.

to the presence of this, the most powerful religious object of the society – one far more dangerous than any of the masks. When these men proceed through the village, a fearsome whirring sound is audible. The sound drives women and children into the darkest corners of their houses, and men interrupt their conversations to listen in solemn attention. The next morning, stones and pieces of wood can often be found in the village, items that will disappear as mystically as they appeared. The initiated know that this was the work of Sigma. Tales do the rounds – of strangers who inadvertently crossed the Night Sigma's path and were later found mutilated. During daylight hours, the Night Sigma lies in wait for the women on the outskirts of the village, instilling fear in them with his horrible rattling calls.

Only very few of the elders have power over the death-bringing Night Sigma. To those who do, this is not only a source of personal satisfaction; it also earns them the admiration of the villagers. If the Night Sigma reigns, such elders climb onto the roofs of their houses and call down "Nothing bad is coming out of the bush, you fools! It's just a

Sumbenali Adae, the village chief (koru), is equipped with a red headdress and an elaborately carved wooden pole – both are emblems of honor that testify to his status.

Mask dancers waiting to begin their performance. The flat helmet masks pulled over their foreheads vary between villages. They are worn like caps. Because they have no eyeholes, the dancers have to peek through the undersides. The masks, with their geometric designs in contrasting black, white, and red, are topped with elegantly curved horns.

Masks that portray animals (often bush cows) are worn with a black fiber costume. They dance the kpana dance in honor of important figures. If the honors are directed at death spirits, the dance continues throughout the night until early the next morning.

Right: The dancer bows at the end of his performance.

young man who has been eating and drinking (so he's a human)! And you, son of a bitch, leave the village alone. Don't you realize you are frightening women and children? Beat it!" In so doing, they actually reveal the secret of Sigma. Very few, however, can understand what they have said, since they speak in sigu, the secret language understood by only a few core members among the initiated.

This third, and highest, level can be aspired to by any male adult previously initiated into the ranks of the Night Sigma. The admittance ritual, however, is conducted – only after long intervals and sometimes even according to specific cycles of about 20 years. It is carried out only by a few traditional villages. Candidates spend a period of seclusion in the bush, learning Sigma myths and chants and the secret language of sigu, and also how to make costumes and cult items. They learn the meaning of secret symbols, the advanced art of dancing and playing drums and the flute, and receive instruction on the moral codes that will accompany their new status. They are taught about the powers of the masks, the activities of the society, and the characteristics of the spiritual powers with whom Sigma will bring them into contact.

This third level (the highest of all) is a central element in funeral ceremonies for the society's leading figures and this is, in fact, their most important task (sigma kuma). A funeral in which the masks take part and at which sigu chants are

Far left: Masks dance for the well-being of the community on a variety of occasions. Their home is the bush. A hunter received them from the spirits that he observed dancing and who allowed him to bring them and their dance to the village. This hunter is considered to be the master of the mask dancers' ancestors.

sung is the ultimate climax to the successful life of an elder. It ensures his admittance to the realm of the ancestors. The voice of the Night Sigma is replete with the lamentation of the community in its time of bereavement for a dead friend. But Sigma also passes judgment on the fate of a deceased person. Should it be concluded through divination that his death was a punishment for practicing witchcraft, the masks will drag him out of the house by his feet, bash his corpse, and throw him into the bush where he will remain unburied. However, those who are found to be without fault and who have died a good death are honored by respectful greetings and by repeated dancing around their corpse. Festivities that crown the existence of a deceased person in this way and confirm his acceptance into the ranks of the ancestors are attended by members of the society from all villages.

Left: At the end of the dance, the masks, the geometric patterns of which are clearly discernible, are laid before the *Vagla-koru* (the Vagla religious leader).

A close-up view of the bush cow with its highly geometric head, a design further emphasized by the black-and-white squares and rectangles.

379

The rulers of Africa

In August 1995, Otumfuo ("The Mighty") Opoku Ware II, principal ruler of the Asante, celebrated the 25th anniversary of his rule. This was the occasion of many celebrations in honor of the history of his kingdom and of the king himself. The pageantry of those festivities, their polished ceremonial, and the exhibition

A king and his chieftain.
From: *Im Lande des Fetischs*, Basel, 1890.

of the symbols of evident power with which African kings surround themselves in public remain impressive to this day. This effect is further emphasized by the sovereigns generally remaining secluded from the public eye, only periodically appearing in public on occasions such as an audience or the administration of justice; when new members are introduced to the royal court; in the past, before the start of battle campaigns as well as upon the return of the warriors; and, above all, on the occasion of fertility and cleansing rites. Even at these times kings remained unapproachable, their detachment making their sanctity all the more apparent.

Despite the fact that the power of the monarchies has been curtailed – initially by colonial regimes, later by modern heads of state – this institution has survived. In many regions, kings remain the symbolic figures of cosmic order and stability. They continue to stand for the cultural values of their communities, for the kingdom and its heritage. They are spoken of in familiar figurative terms, variously described as a "father" of their people, as guarding their flock, as defending it like a lion or leopard, or as being firmly embedded in the land like old trees.

Monarchies can generally be traced back to supernatural origins. A sovereign possesses great magical powers that can guarantee growth-enhancing rains and plentiful harvests. Evident proof of his vital energies are his numerous offspring. In the past important victories in battle also testified to such energies. This special endowment is bestowed upon kings by virtue of their ancestors and by the divine protecting powers. The charisma that they possess is due on the one hand to their lineage and on the other to the power of the enthronement rites. During such rites kings are subjected to a range of secret ceremonies that bestow upon them "the power." Heirs to the throne "die" to be "resurrected" as rulers. On his enthronement the sovereign relinquishes his old name and assumes a new one. Upon his becoming king, or Asantehene, Kwaku Adusei, alias Jacob Matthew Poku, became Opoku Ware II. Like the descendants of other African rulers, he has the blood of royal master ancestors in his veins, which is why various kings sometimes bear the same name (the kings in Luapula Valley, the border region between Zimbabwe and Congo, being one example). The death of a king only constitutes the death of his person, not of the institution. The institution is eternal. A sovereign may die; the monarchy will not.

Dedjazmatch Aialeu, one of the great sovereigns of Ethiopia, in his state robes, holding a pistol in his hands, and seated on his throne. His vassals are paying respect to his sovereignty. Photograph taken 1927.

Only on taking office will a new king be presented with his sacred insignia – spears, sabers, swords, animal horns, footstools, and so on – which are imbued with the mystic powers of his ancestors. Later, he will periodically be brought into contact with them, especially in times of crisis, during the sowing season, and at harvest times. This contact will enable him to "revitalize" his "spent" energy. Such religious insignia often stand in contrast to the ostentatious emblems with which sovereigns surround themselves in public. They are withheld from the community at large and shrouded in secrecy – which is why they are so intensely feared by the people.

To this day, traditional potentates retain the status of central, parentlike figures. One of their most essential tasks is to bring together different worlds. They act as mediators between various social groups, tribes, and clans. In the past this even extended to mediating between free people and slaves, and (in the context of ancestral cults) between the living and the dead. This is why it is important that their position should not only be elevated above the rest of the community, but ultimately that it should also be that of an outsider. Their special status is founded on the fact that, in many cases and according to tradition, the first king – whose blood they carry – migrated to the region as a foreign conqueror or that they are descendants of mystical strangers – hunters, for instance.

Men's mission is to rule. This notion underpins the common status quo of the sexes and the common social structure which gives men the role of leader within the family clan, in politics, and in other community offices. Thus, it seems only logical that the king is referred to as "father of the people." Yet, women are not without influence. In some monarchies, for example in the kingdoms of the Asante and Lunda, a woman of high status (the *ohemmea* or *lukokashi*) has a share of the royal power. She makes proposals regarding the candidate for the throne and is endowed with the office of virtually monitoring the king. Her status allows her publicly to correct or reprimand him for his behavior, and to supplement, moderate, or even change the decisions he makes. In

The king of Ifanhim, Dahomey, and his entourage.
From: *Malerische Studien*, Neuchâtel, undated.

some (albeit exceptional) cases, women actually came to hold absolute power as queens or regents, ruling their kingdom on behalf of their underage sons.

Some of these women were remarkable figures. Among them was Queen Njinga Mbandi Ana de Sousa (c. 1582–1663), who temporarily ruled the kingdoms of Ndongo and Matamba (in present-day Angola) and who was successful in resisting the intruding Portuguese. However, their high office required of them that they relinquish all femininity. Their lovers, for example, had to wear women's clothes. Similar rules applied in other communities. The queens of Sakalava and Merina in Madagascar, for example, who were established in their offices only in colonial times, were masculinized. They were endowed with masculine attributes, wearing men's costumes, and even enabled to marry women, but not allowed to have children of their own.

Female sovereigns were, however, rare. Only very few incidences are known in which female rule was an institutionalized phenomenon. The most prominent example was in the small kingdom of Lobedu in the South African Transvaal, where Mujaji ruled as Queen of the Rain. But even Mujaji I came to the throne, around 1800, only as the heir of her grandfather. She and her female successors had little political authority. Their power was derived from their control over rain medicine: Mujaji could cause clouds to turn into rain. The queens owed their mystical powers to an incidence of incest among their ancestors. Mujaji I was a child of the relationship that the king, her grandfather, had with his own daughter. This concept of incest-induced powers is found throughout Africa.

Colonialism caused momentous change. Many kings were forced to look on impotently as Europeans took possession of their country and their rule came to an end. Those willing to collaborate were able to assume subordinate positions within the colonial administration. Only very few were able to salvage a share of their traditional authority, carrying it into the modern day, as could the emirs of northern Nigeria.

Not even eventual independence restored these rulers to their former positions of power. In fact, independence tended to create new problems. Many of the revolutionary leaders and heads of state who came to power in the 1960s as leaders of their fledgling nation states greatly feared such former kings, confronting them with open distrust and even absolute rejection. Fearing that the traditional ruler Mwami Moshesh II (of the Tutsi minority of the day) would rise to renewed power, the government of the former Belgian colony of Rwanda sent him into exile once the country achieved independence. In neighboring Burundi, a constitutional monarchy modeled on the Belgian system was initially maintained – until such time that the military formally imposed republican rule in 1966. In 1972, when Mwami Ntare V attempted to regain control of the throne, he was murdered by the army. The ancient Christian empire of Ethiopia, having survived colonialization relatively unscathed, came to an end with the revolution of 1974.

Elsewhere, political rulers came to realize that they would have a difficult time without the support of the kings. Judicious leaders thus took a more conciliatory stance, cooperating with the monarchs and, in doing so, fortifying their own position and gaining the support of voters. In Ghana, for instance, the influence of traditional sovereigns continues to be acknowledged, albeit only at a local and regional level and although the extent of their former powers has been curtailed.

During the first euphoric continent-wide movement for independence in the 1960s, the constitutional monarchies of Lesotho and Swaziland in southern Africa were considered archaic and in need of a transformation, but they ultimately proved to be stable systems. Apart from these, there are no more officially autonomous kingdoms in Africa. However, although it is only in these regions that kings still officially reign, many more enjoy a de facto status of king. The traditional potentates of the Asante and Yoruba – of the former city-state in northern Nigeria – continue to be revered and worshiped by their people and thus respected and consulted by the political elite. They have lost a considerable amount of their former authority, but have nevertheless survived as figureheads, who serve to strengthen national identity and personify the cultural unity and heritage of their people. The rituals, ceremonies, palace cultures, ideologies, and myths that accompany traditional monarchies have retained a cultural significance that secular states are hardly in a position to offer.

Moro-Naba, king of Upper Volta, sets out on his journey to pay an official visit to the French governor of the region. The king is a powerful figure in his land and maintains good relations with the French administration. His personal entourage includes princes and chieftains. Photo c. 1930.

The art of the kings

For people who did not know the art of writing, other forms of art were important in expressing religious, political, and social ideas. Court art tends to take the form of statues, and can express subtle distinctions. "Power," claims Nigerian writer Chinua Achebe, "flows through many channels." Decorative and graphic art, choreography, and theater are all important forms of royal art. Festivals are a means of displaying sovereigns in the glow of their power. Seating, marching procedures, and the order of food consumption all adhere to strict rules and are used to mark distinctions in social status. Dress, jewelry and other personal adornments, and symbols of rank are a further means of indicating age, status, office, or wealth. Everything with which a king surrounded himself, demonstrated splendor and marked the distinction between him and the common people. Such splendor tended to reflect upon high-ranking individuals, who also enjoyed the privilege, albeit to a lesser extent, of bearing specific parade objects – axes, crowns, scepters and stately rods, the furs and feathers of certain animals, fans, and long pipes. They also directed the rhythms of the drums and sat on thrones. Their glory in turn

Right: A sovereign of the Ga tribe in full regalia. His head is adorned with gold stars and moons. Gold chains cover his upper body.

Below: The ceremonial robes and heavy gold jewelry of an asantehene. The jewelry can be so heavy that the wearer's arms need to rest on his legs or be supported by an aide.

reflected back on the king in their midst, whose grandeur was even further illuminated by it.

The majesty of the king was thus visible, but not necessarily comprehensible, to all: anything that is too understandable appears controllable and therefore loses its sacrosanct character. Power and knowledge are closely intertwined. Court art is comprehensible only to those versed in matters of heritage. Certain objects, notably those of a simple nature, are endowed with great spiritual power, of which only few initiated individuals possess knowledge. The naamtiibo, for instance, combines plant and animal materials. Mosi rulers derive their powers from the possession of this object. Such sacred objects are only ever seen by a small group of people close to the sovereign. Specific interrelationships often exist between the secret

and the publicly exhibited symbols of power. One example, in the Akan kingdoms, is the blackened stools of royal ancestors that remain concealed from the community, whereas the partially gold-coated chairs of reigning kings are exhibited in a very demonstrative fashion. Both objects are facets of the same system. They bestow upon the sovereign an aura of mystery and grandeur. A showing of court art to the whole community usually takes place when the king appears in public. On such occasions, there is a stark contrast between his attire and symbols of supremacy and his face, the appearance of his person: while the former are a conspicuously emphasized, the latter is often hidden by a parasol, veil, or drape.

In kingdoms, where a system of central rule operates, the king stands at the apex of a pyramidal hierarchy, the individual echelons of which are assigned to groups of dignitaries and court officials, each identifiable by the symbols that mark their rank. Such symbolism is a reminder of when sovereigns still maintained control over the administration of their kingdom, rewarding loyal supporters with fiefdoms and generous gifts. Kings had power over life and death, waged wars, and distributed the spoils. Many also determined the artistic culture of their people, deciding who would be assigned to particular artistic tasks, remunerating artists and thus influencing the character of their work. The king would have teams of artists working exclusively for him, making beads or casting precious metals, and so on. Art was a means of self-glorification and of increasing his personal renown. The community at large benefited from this only to the extent that their sovereign was a figure that represented salvation. Such art did not, therefore, develop and flourish as an integral aspect of a community's culture. Then, as now, it served to enhance the public show of power. The settings for ceremonial events and the melodramatic elements of such festivals combine to create an overall work of art that puts the majesty of the king in an appropriate light. Great ancestors and significant historical events are brought to life through dramatic re-enactment, the roles of historical figures who helped establish the kingdom are celebrated, and ancestry is invoked to highlight the sovereign's powers. On such occasions, the king not only takes a physical position of superiority (central and elevated), but also sets himself amid the most

An ivory mask in the form of a leopard's head, from the kingdom of Benin (Nigeria) and dating from the 17th or 18th century.

In Benin, the leopard was a symbol of royal power. As the representative of his people and a descendant of his royal predecessors, the king (*oba*) possessed great and exceptional powers. This cast bronze figure of a leopard dates from the 18th century.

magnificent works of art. While the nobility presents itself in a somewhat less regal way, they still adorn and surround themselves with symbols of obvious distinction.

One impressive example of how court art was instrumentalized in the power game was the annual huetanu spring festival celebrated in the kingdom

of Dahomey in the 19th century. People would pour into Abomey, the capital, from all over the kingdom. The king, enthroned beneath a high tentlike pavilion, was surrounded by sovereigns of lesser rank, all positioned under magnificent parasols. The parasols and a number of ostentatious banners were adorned with pictures that portrayed the greatness and the invincibility of the kingdom and its leader. The Dahomey state treasure, comprising silverwork and other imported items, would be carried on the heads of several thousand people in a colorful procession through the streets. The onlookers, dazzled by the magnificent sight, thus glimpsed the power and glory of court life. A small portion of this wealth was then distributed among the soldiers and other loyal followers. Some rather dramatic sequences were also added to the event. Human sacrifices would be made (mostly prisoners who, because of their poor physical condition, could not be sold), instilling terror and generating feelings of both disgust and loyalty. Kings and their counsel knew which instruments would be most effective in stirring up feelings of veneration and pride, fear and obedience.

Elsewhere, similar objectives were achieved using royal art. This is attested by the portrayals on bronze statues from Benin and carvings from Cameroon. The terracotta portrait heads, excavated in 1910 in Ife, the sacred city of the Yoruba, by Leo Frobenius (1853–1938), next to which the famous crowned bronze head and other objects were found, caused a sensation among academics in this field. A number of other bronze statues were soon discovered. Even by 1897, when Ife fell victim to a British expedition of retribution and was torched, the English had already stolen 3,000 bronze relief plaques. They depicted 16th-century Portuguese figures, with uniform and arms, sentries, and fan-bearers, as well as gods and god kings (oni or oba). These bronze works, as well as ivory objects of comparable value, are now in European museums. They quickly achieved worldwide renown and are today acknowledged as exemplifying the greatest treasures of African art.

Conversely, other forms of art were used as political currency to reinforce existing alliances or commit new partners to them. It was common practice for kings to present certain objects, or grant the right to wear them, to deserving supporters or new vassals. The fact that weapons outnumbered other items is an indication of the underlying priorities. Whether in rituals or in art, the military aspect of a sovereign's power always had primary significance. Art from the 15th to the 19th centuries remained, for the most part, unchanged; this is especially true of iconographic art depicting high dignitaries and kings. Warlike motifs are the most prominent designs on plaques, often depicting the king as an unconquerable, superhuman figure.

The same can be said for the court art of Cuba (Bushong), in the Democratic Republic of Congo. Here, too, the image of kings (ndop) was used as a propaganda tool. Even

Opposite page: A depiction of battle from a royal palace in Benin, Nigeria.

Below: Stool of honor for an asantehene (Asante king). Only kings were permitted to sit on elephant stools, since elephants represent the mightiest of animals.

though such works of art were made during a king's lifetime, his individual features were quite deliberately not depicted. Each of the portraits shows the king as a relatively corpulent but youthful figure seated on a simple throne. Every one of these images, be they a work of the past or present, emits a sense of permanency and power.

Court art included not only statues and portrayals, but also ornamental artwork. Magnificent textiles, jewelry, and prestige objects were specially made for the royal residence. Such items were often adorned with geometric designs. The use of certain materials – because they were rare or exceptionally valuable – was often the privilege of the king. These precious items included leopard and lion skins, ivory, the feathers of certain birds, and ostrich eggs. For the Akan people, who lived in a region rich in gold fields, this particular precious metal was considered "the king's material" and only he was permitted to use or assign it.

Court art thus had a dual function within the societies of sacred kingdoms. It depicted, and thus kept alive, images portraying important aspects of a dynasty or heritage, and exhibited and eternalized the mission, significance, and power of the king. Since the ruling institutions have had to forfeit power and influence, their art has become less expressive and has lost some of its content. In many cases it has diminished to no more than a reflection of former glory.

The kingdom of Ashanti

The Asante king Otumfuo Opoku Ware II holding an audience on the occasion of his 25th anniversary of his accession to the throne.

"Asante porcupine, beat a thousand to death, and a thousand rise anew." Royal musicians would beat this message on drums after signaling for an attack to commence. A porcupine also adorned the chairs on which court representatives sat when making decisions on important issues.

Because of their long, sharp spines, porcupines cannot be harmed, even by large, dangerous animals. The Asante say that they use this armor not only to defend themselves, but also to attack their assailants. As soon as one spine has been shot off, another will grow in its place, which is why the Asante use this image as a metaphor for their own numerical, physical, and moral superiority over their enemies. Porcupines became synonymous with the kingdom of Ashanti.

In the 19th century, Ashanti, in modern-day Ghana, was one of the most powerful kingdoms in Africa. In contrast to many other important kingdoms in West Africa, it was situated not in savanna, but in wooded country. Edward Bowdich, who came to the court of the Asante ruler, the asantehene Osei Bonsu, as head of a British delegation in 1817, was impressed by the pomp surrounding the king. The massive wealth of the Asante people was due mainly to the rich deposits of gold in their territory. The kingdom of Ashanti was the last of the larger kingdoms to be established in the territory of the Akan, in present-day Ghana, Togo, and Ivory Coast. The kingdom of Ashanti evolved from a long history of social and political development in which both trading and the knowledge of specialized techniques played an important part. The Asante were skilled in working iron, brass, and gold. They also produced exquisite textiles using treadle looms. Their textiles were elaborately bordered and trimmed. What made them politically and militarily strong was their rigidly centralized form of leadership under the control of a highly organized administration.

The kingdom of Ashanti was established in 1660 as an alliance of clans that had settled north of the coast and which, at the time, were independent and equal in status. Their union was initially created to defend its people against demands for tribute and attacks by the neighboring kingdom of Denkyera. The long-term objectives of the union also included obtaining access to the coast and thus to trading opportunities with Europeans. The new kingdom received the support of the kingdom of Akwamu, the direct adversary of Denkyera for predominance over southern Ghana which, around 1675, had developed to become the supreme power in the eastern hinterland of the coast. In the context of this alliance, Osei Tutu, later appointed leader of the combined individual principalities and given the title of asantehene, learned of numerous military innovations and familiarized himself with effective army organization and the use of European firearms. Thanks to the increased efficiency achieved by reforming its army, the union was able to defeat Denkyera near Feyase in 1701. This victory marked the beginning of the ascent of Ashanti to become the undisputed

unifying power on the Gold Coast. By the mid 18th century, it ruled over most of the Akan groups.

During the course of disputes between the Ashanti union and the Denkyera, the political balance within the union itself had undergone change. Once Denkyera and its vassals had yielded to it, the Asante elders, incorporated as part of the military command, elevated their victorious military leader Osei Tutu to the position of first king of the Asante (the asantehene) and thus officially founded the kingdom of Ashanti. Osei Tutu was from the Oyoko clan of Kwaman, a region which would later become the town of Kumasi and which was rich in gold deposits. His becoming king is

A servant walks ahead of every procession in which the asantehene takes part. On his head he carries a metal vessel containing an array of plants, amulets, talismans, and other sources of energy. A "medicine" called *samanka* (*saman* meaning "death spirit") is meant to ward off harmful powers and clear the way for the king.

The asantehene's personal guards. In the past, their leader, the ankobeahene, would join them in battle. He was also responsible for the construction and maintenance of the royal dining room and, more importantly, the stool room (*barim dan*) in which the blackened chairs of royal ancestors are kept.

Left: The ohemmea, a high-ranking woman of respected authority, represents the link connecting the community to its maternal ancestors. She is not, however, the "mother" of the king, although she might be his sister. Despite the fact that she possesses no formal powers, she has a procession of her own. It follows that of the asantehene. Her procession is also headed by people carrying chairs and other valuables, while horn blowers and drummers bring up the rear. In contrast to the king and to the princes, whose supremacy is shown by parasols, she is both cooled and adorned by two large fans made of palm leaves.

Below: Dignitaries dressed in the kente robe always worn on joyful, festive occasions, and adorned with gold jewelry. Yellow, the color of kings, is the dominating color. The sovereign is surrounded by the bearers of the gold-coated swords of the kingdom. These objects are among the masterpieces of Asante and Akan goldsmiths.

shrouded in myths. It is said, for example, that his companion in life and battle, the legendary priest (*okomfo*) Anokye, had kum-tree (*Lannea accidissima*) cuttings planted at three sites and proclaimed that the site at which the tree took root would be the future center of the kingdom. This, of course, was Kwaman, renamed Kumasi (*kum ase* meaning "under the kum tree").

Under the rule of Osei Tutu's descendants, the kingdom of Ashanti continued to expand, until most of the Gold Coast and parts of Ivory Coast had either been incorporated into the kingdom or made to pay tribute. The Asante soon controlled the important trade with the north where, at the end of the 18th century, Dagomba became a vassal. By now, the region over which they reigned had become very extensive, and was further extended through treaties of protection and friendship. To rule effectively over such a large territory required a centralized system of administration and the implementation of elaborate means of control. The army was important in this system, not least as an organizational role model for the people, who virtually merged into the corpus of soldiers and thus made things simple for the ruling class. Every citizen was fully aware of his or her precise function. Strict regulation ruled people's lives. Custom and ceremony had utmost priority; they marked and lent emphasis to the new social order.

The sovereigns of precolonial Ashanti were not only warlords; they also played a leading role in legislative and judicial institutions. They administered their territory, but also worked toward increasing the legacy of their ancestors. The demands placed on every member of this system were high. The aim was to leave to their descendants more than they had received from their own ancestors. Wealth was important in Asante life. But people were also encouraged to achieve distinguished standing through exemplary conduct and by gaining a knowledge of adages and wisdom through experience and understanding. Those who mastered this gained the prerequisites needed to be a skilled speaker, a judge, and an aspirant to the status of elder.

In the 19th century, Asante culture was at the pinnacle of its power. Roads led from Kumasi to all parts of the kingdom. The fact that its southern border was 40 miles from the coastline meant that the Asante had no direct access to the ports there

and to highly desirable European arms and goods. Access was cut off by a number of kingdoms in the coastal regions, notably that of the Fante, who had secured their position using British protection. Attempts by the asantehene Kwame Bonsu to reach a trade agreement with the British were unsuccessful. During the 19th century, seven wars were fought between these parties. Although the Asante fiercely resisted their much stronger opponent, ultimately they lost. In 1896, the asantehene Osei Agyeman Prempeh I was banished; and Ashanti was declared a crown colony in 1901.

Economic developments and modernization during the past hundred years have changed the life of the people in many ways. They have nonetheless maintained many of their traditions – not least the monarchy. They continue to uphold the self-image of a people with a glorious past. Ghana, the first African colony to be granted independence in 1957, allowed the asantehene to retain the status of a traditional sovereign. The old capital of the kingdom, Kumasi, with its population of over 800,000, is now the country's second largest city. Its huge central marketplace attracts thousands of visitors daily from all over West Africa. The reigning asantehene studied law in England and was a practicing lawyer before succeeding his uncle, his mother's brother, in office. The Asante follow matrilineal descent, so that the line of succession runs from the brother of the mother to the son of

Like many hierarchical societies in Africa, the Asante use dancing to mark distinctions of status. Subordinate sovereigns and women thus express both their own status and the reverence and worship that they extend to the king.

At a funeral ceremony, the high-ranking regional chieftain of the Konongo performs a war dance in honor of the ancestors.

the sister (the nephew). The present-day sovereign respects the cultural and religious diversity of his country as did his predecessors. During festivities held to commemorate the 25th anniversary of his accession to the throne, he granted audience to the traditional ancestral priests, wearing a robe adorned with Arabic characters and designs. He wore this in recognition of a centuries-old relationship between the monarchy and the Muslims, a relationship based on economic cooperation, mutual respect, and political understanding. Other public ceremonies included attending an Anglican mass, prayers in the central mosque, the opening of an art exhibition, the staging of a banquet, and the opening of a new museum in the Manhiya Palace. The climax of the celebrations, however, was the traditional adae ceremony, normally held in the courtyard of the old residence of the Asante king. For this silver jubilee celebration, the ceremony had to be staged in the football stadium in order to accommodate the numerous guests invited to attend. The order of seating was precisely organized and printed on the tickets. The country's president, Air Lieutenant J. J. Rawlings, was seated on the broad side of the stadium, opposite the asantehene seated on the other side. Certain sections of the stadium were reserved for the royal family, others for foreign ambassadors, the representatives of other African countries, and for government officials. Even the Asante colony in the United States was assigned a special section. The dignitaries within the palace hierarchy and sovereigns from other Asante regions automatically seated themselves according to rank, with no need to consult the printed seating plan.

Drums and ivory horns finally announced the arrival of the asantehene and his royal retinue. Amid the loud jubilation of some 100,000 guests, the king, majestically lounging in a sedan chair and sheltered by large parasols, entered the stadium. Along with the king entered his golden chair, on a special footstool and likewise shaded by its own parasol. This was a very rare public showing of the royal chair, and probably the last in the millennium.

Below: In the reception hall, the prince sits amid his subjects. The leopard man in the royal retinue keeps order and chases away evil spirits.

Right: Speakers as well as rifle carriers and sword bearers accompany the high-ranking chieftain as he enters the reception hall.

Insignia of power

A ceremonial stool, the artfully designed central section of which is the statue of an elephant, the largest animal in the jungle. In the past, the use of this motif was the sole privilege of the asantehene. Chairs came to be used only at a later date, when the shape of European thrones – as first seen when the British colonial forces entered the country – was copied.

Power should be conspicuous. The pomp and glory that surrounds kings – such as the meaningful assemblage of items that accompanies a sovereign on his public appearances and serves to certify the foundation and heritage of the kingdom – are a time-honored means of exhibiting power.

The most important insignia of the kingdom of Ashanti are the Golden Elephant's Tail (Sika mmara) and the Golden Friday Chair (Sika Dwa Kofi). The former personifies wealth and power, and the latter houses the soul (sunsum) of the kingdom. It symbolizes the union of related and neighboring clans in the 17th century, whose aim was to increase their strength through unity and thus be able to go into battle against the powerful kingdom of Denkyera. In addition to these two major symbols of the monarchy, special drums and arms (swords) recall past deeds of glory. They are retrieved from the palace treasure vault and publicly exhibited on ceremonial occasions. The battle drum, for instance, recalls the Battle of Feyase (1701) in which Denkyera warriors suffered grave defeat, and in which their king lost his life. The Asante beheaded him, coated his head in gold, and attached it to their battle drum as a symbol of their triumph. In so doing, they not only endowed the drum with additional energy, but also kept alive the memory of this event for future generations.

Numerous royal swords (afena) are also adorned with solid gold images of human heads, a motif known as worosahire ("head of Worosa"), though these images do not always portray the same person. Only in Kumasi and Nsuta does this image actually portray the head of Worosa, a past sovereign from the Banda kingdom on Ivory Coast. The asantehene Osei Kwadwo (c. 1752–81) declared war on him in retribution for the murder of Asante traders. Once defeated, he had him decapitated. In other areas of Asante culture, this motif is based on similar incidences. In Kumasu, such images personify the adage that "One head alone does not make decisions," meaning that a ruler should always consult his advisors. Other insignia of power do not necessarily relate to memorable historic events, their image alluding instead to various aspects of the monarchy.

Chairs and stools

In the life of the Asante and other Akan people, chairs and stools of various forms play an important role. Their meaning and function can be wide-ranging. They may be an article of everyday use, such as is found in every household. They could represent a ceremonial chair (adanu dwa), the possession of which was once the privilege of the king and other high-ranking individuals. Alternatively, they could be the spiritual center of a community or a nation – like the Asante Golden Chair. The traditional stools of the elders (dwa or nkonnua), reported by early travelers, are all identical in their basic form, but the design details differ. Stools are carved from a single block of white osese or Nyame dua (Alstonia boonei) wood and consist of one central column set on a flat rectangular base. The seat itself is fashioned in an upward curve, reminiscent of a crescent moon. The Asante have added to this basic shape a multitude of designs, as they have done with other objects inherent in their culture. In 1929, British colonial officers and the ethnologist Robert Sutherland Rattray (1881–1938) compiled a list of 30 different types. The pillarlike central section is generally adorned with a variety of geometric or figurative designs and images of certain animals – most commonly elephants (*esono*) or leopards (*osebo*). These animals represent greatness and savagery respectively. The asantehene were the sole owners of such meaningful and artfully designed items. The use of cross motifs (*mmaremu*) was also the sole privilege of the king.

Since the time of Osei Tutu, the first asantehene, each of his successors has had his personal stool. Such ceremonial stools were not only larger and more elaborately crafted than those of common people, they were also covered with embossed gold foil. The "queen mother" and important dignitaries also possess their own stools which, in the past, were covered with silver foil and

profusely adorned with small bells, beads, clips, and amulets. The simplest of these decorations is a small round piece of metal at the center of the seat. It is called *otadee* ("like a pond") and its purpose is to defend the stool and its owner from attack by evil powers. A variety of amulets and talismans attached to the stool's central column serve the same purpose. These attachments are generally of Muslim origin and inscribed with verses from the Koran. They are sewn into leather or enclosed in metal casings in order further to empower the energies inherent in the stool.

The central section of the stool often includes the inscription of an adage that epitomizes the characteristics and the importance of its owner. The motif chosen by the asantehene Osei Agyeman Prempeh II (1931–70) was a complex knot that appears to be impossible to untie.

This image was intended to indicate that a judicious ruler will reign with wisdom rather than force. The ceremonial stool of the asantehene Kofi Kakari (1867–74) was adorned with a circular

The asantehene's throne chair and other symbolic seats are modeled on European forms. The chair seen here is the most famous of the chairs known as *akonkromfi* ("praying mantis"). Its name is *kodie* ("eagle").

A procession in honor of the Asante king in which the chairs of each and everyone of the chieftains present at the ceremony are displayed.

rainbow (*okontonkorowi mpenu*) symbolizing the adage that "A rainbow will coil around the necks of the rich," meaning that the Asante union incorporates many links.

Neither the feet and buttocks of the duly enthroned owners of the ceremonial stools nor the stools themselves may touch the ground. Every direct form of contact with the earth would lead to the contamination of the sovereign and a diminution of his energy, which in turn would lead to grave misfortune for his people (such as starvation or disease). When, in the past, anyone wanted to rid himself of a rival, he only needed to remove that person's sandals and place his feet on the ground. The ceremonial stools stood on leopard or elephant skins, which themselves were a further show of sovereignty and power. When it appears in public, each stool has its own bearer. Bearers were once recognizable from a distance by their hairstyle: a tonsure in the form of a bare strip that ran across the pate. The stools rest on the backs of their necks, the seat of the stools always facing forward. Some ceremonial stools, such as the little golden stool from Mampong and Akuapem, are passed on from one sovereign to the next. In such cases the stool does not represent one king, but rather the entire kingdom. In other parts of the former Asante union, for example in central Kumasi, a new stool is made for each ruler prior to his taking up office. On the death of their owner, these personal ceremonial stools are blackened and kept in the stool house. There they continue to be worshiped like idols, with regular sacrifices being made to them. The number of stools that a community stores is equivalent to the number of its former rulers. However, any monarch found to be unworthy and thus deposed or punished by the ancestors through a bad death was dropped from the line of ancestral descent and his stool accordingly excluded from the "stool archive."

The stools continue to be objects of great significance for the Asante. However, rulers no longer have exclusive right to the use of certain materials and designs, and there is no longer any strict distinction made between stools for men and for women.

In addition to ceremonial stools, the Asante also have chairs that lack any ritual meaning, but that do have representational significance. These chairs were purely objects of ostentatious show. Even until modern times, they were owned by the ruling classes only. Such prestigious stools are of three varieties that can all be traced back to European prototypes. The one most commonly used is called *asipim* ("fixed"), a name which, in a figurative sense, expresses the stability of the monarchy. Asipim chairs have a timber frame and an integrated leather seat. They are about three feet high. While lower-ranking sovereigns possess one or two of these chairs, higher-ranking potentates

such as the Ejisuhene have more than 14. They are all covered with brass and serve as the representational chairs of dignitaries during their negotiations in matters of state. Together with other objects of grandeur, they are publicly exhibited during ritual processions. Sometimes, they are even kept in the stool rooms and sacred shrines, although no sacrifices are made to them nor is it believed that they are linked to the souls of their owners. The form of the *hwedom* chair ("to look the enemy in the eye") is similar to that of the asipim. However, it is larger, blackened, and adorned with silver pins and knobs. Hwedom chairs are modeled most closely on European originals. In the past, they were chiefly used on portentous occasions such as the declaration of war or judicial proceedings. A third variety of chair, called *akonkromfi* ("praying mantis"), is more carefully crafted and used on festive occasions. The asantehene and lesser sovereigns use these chairs to present themselves to their community. They seat themselves on the chairs which, in turn, are set on elevated platforms (*sumpi* or *sumpene*) in front of their palaces. Talismans are often attached to the undersides of the seat sections in order to endow these chairs with a certain amount of energy.

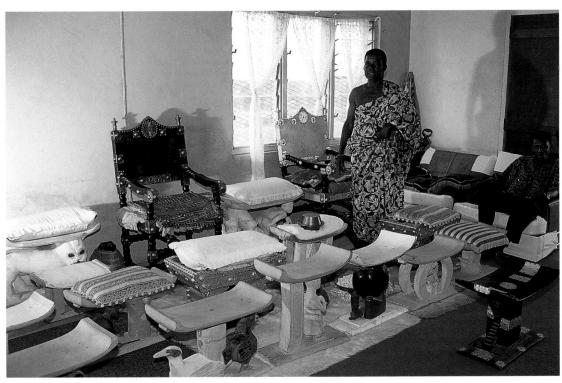

A modern showroom in which a variety of stools and chairs are displayed. The salesman, a Ewe, sells them, and other items of symbolic import, to kings, sovereigns, and village chiefs who no longer employ their own court craftsmen.

The Gold Chair: myth, meaning, and history

Once the kingdom of Denkyera had been conquered (in 1701), the task was to prevent the Asante union from disintegrating. Each clan chief in the alliance now had his sights set on gaining dominance, so the legendary priest (okomfo) Anokye left the issue to be decided by God. According to legend, he called for a grand meeting to be held in Kumasi, inviting all the male and female elders of the various clans to attend. Osei Tutu, who had led the war against Denkyera, hosted the assembly under a kum tree before the gates of the city. Suddenly, things turned dark, thunder roared, and lightning flashed. In a dense cloud of dust, a wooden, gold-covered stool descended from heaven directly onto Osei Tutu's lap. There was no mistaking the sign. The god of heaven himself had chosen Osei Tutu to be the supreme ruler. As a means of firmly cementing the union, the priest Anokye called upon each of those assembled to contribute tufts of head and pubic hair and pieces of nail from their forefingers. He then mixed these carriers of vital energy with a powdered "medicine" and poured water onto the mixture. He smeared some of the mixture onto the stool and handed the rest to the men and women of the assembly to drink. In so doing, they pledged their loyalty and assured Osei Tutu – ordained to become their supreme leader (the asantehene) and hold the destiny of their nation in his hands – of their allegiance and unconditional support. This mixture of vital body hair and nails had caused all their souls to become one (sunsum), subsumed into the Gold Chair, and the formerly independent territories to become a single kingdom. Previous autonomies and alliances were null and void; all latent rivalries were settled. Any future attempt to rebel against the central leadership in Kumasi would be akin to revolting against the god of heaven who had personally elected Osei Tutu as their leader.

From this day on, the Gold Chair was the Asante's holiest sacred object. As long as it remained unscathed and in the possession of the monarchy, the nation could prosper and achieve wealth and renown. Conversely, losing the chair would mean its doom. So, it is claimed, was the wise prediction of Anokye.

Okomfo Anokye, about whom many tales are told, is a figure of some fame in the annals of Asante history. Documentary information is available on the first asantehene, Osei Tutu. He had already been maintaining relations with the early Dutch trading posts on the coast, receiving firearms and gunpowder in exchange for gold. It is therefore claimed by some that he actually staged the descent of the Gold Chair in an act that was as clever as it was calculated. Of course, this in no way alters the fact that the Gold Chair became an object of exceptional significance for the Asante and has remained so to this day. Although it is not blackened, it is considered to be the ancestral chair of Osei Tutu. It is kept closely guarded in the chair house at Manhyia Palace, together with the stools of succeeding Asante potentates.

Over the years, it was embellished with a number of precious items – mostly with a variety of bells, some of which had been bought from the Europeans on the coast and others which were copies. Each bell has a different purpose. One is used to assemble the people, another to announce the approach of the chair. Others, for which there is no mallet, are decorated with images of enemy rulers thus degraded to act as servants (nkoa) of the Gold Chair. They constitute a public demonstration of the ultimate fate of those who oppose the Asante. These cast portraits include one depicting a former king from Ivory Coast. He had had the audacity to have a replica of the Gold Chair made for himself. This so angered the reigning asantehene, Osei Bonsu, that he sent his army to punish the miscreant. He was killed and his gold chair brought back to Kumasi, where it was melted down. The gold was used to make two portraits of the king, each of which was attached to the sides of the Asante Gold Chair. Yet another servant of the chair is the image of British governor Sir Charles

MacCarthy, who was killed by the Asante in 1820. The increasing influence that Muslim scholars had on the monarchy led to the attachment of numerous Islamic amulets and talismans, most of which adorn the central column. All these objects added even greater spiritual power to the chair.

Its sacred powers were never questioned, not even when the British, in their sixth war against the Asante, captured and ransacked Kumasi in 1874. The Asante later blamed their decline on their renunciation of the directives and commandments of Anokye. For prior to this loss of independence some members had turned their backs on the Asante. The kingdom, riddled with internal power struggles, was powerless in the face of this decline. The end of the Asante nation was sealed in 1896 when the British deposed the asantehene Osei Agyeman Prempeh I, expelling him and some of the country's other important dignitaries first to Sierra Leone and finally to the Seychelles.

In 1900, British governor Sir Frederick Hodgson took up office in Kumasi. He not only made extremely high reparation demands, but was also said to have insisted on the surrender of the Gold Chair. As the representative of his queen, Victoria, he planned to seat himself on it – an unimaginable sacrilege considering that not even the asantehene is permitted to do so. In an announcement consisting of just three phrases, he committed no less than six errors so grave that, under Asante law, each and every one of them would have caused him to be sentenced him to death. The most serious were that he demanded the Gold Chair be surrendered to a woman (Queen Victoria) and that he himself wanted to sit on it. He obviously saw the chair as a particularly magnificent type of throne rather than the sacred symbol of Asante unity that it was. Speechless, onlookers listened to him. Returning to their homes, they donned mourning attire and prepared themselves anew for war. This war was led by one of the most famous Asante women, the queen mother Yaa Ashantewa from Ejisu, a smaller territory within the Asante confederation. The Asante lost this war, too. The British, however, were yet again unable to take possession of the Gold Chair, which went missing until, in 1920, street workers happened upon it and stripped it of its gold adornments. Once more the Asante were stricken. The people demanded the blood of the

culprits as the only possible means of atoning for the sin and warding off the threat of disaster. To prevent the incensed community decapitating the felons, the colonial administration sent them into exile.

The bared skeleton of the Gold Chair was committed to the mausoleum of the Asante kings. Several years later, in 1924, Osei Agyeman Prempeh I returned from exile. He was not, however, recognized by the British as the ruler of the Asante, as asantehene, but merely as the sovereign of Kumasi, as Kumasihene. In spite of this situation, reconstruction of the Gold Chair was now a matter of urgency. The exact form of the original chair was no longer known. But in 1925 Osei Bonsu carved a small wooden model of the chair based on a description given by the chief chair bearer. Nana Osei Bonsu (1900–77), grandson of the asantehene Mensah Bonsu (1874–83), was the foremost Ghanaian carver of the 20th century. He was responsible for creating many of the symbolic objects used today by the court of the asantehene. Working from his wooden model, two goldsmiths produced a new Gold Chair, incorporating into it the core remains of the desecrated original. Today's chair would thus appear to be a faithful copy of the old one. Today, the Gold Chair radiates its new splendor. It not only represents the noble history of the Asante, but also has come to be a symbol of their tough resistance to British colonial rule.

The Gold Chair – Sika Dwa Kofi – houses the soul (sunsum), or spirit of the nation. It is the most sacred of symbols representing the alliance of related and neighboring groups who joined forces with the Asante in the 17th century. Only on rare occasions – such as the celebration of the 25th anniversary of the asantehene's accession to the throne – is it displayed in public, accompanied by bearers of the courier sword (esonfofena).

Parasols and palanquins

In times gone by, when the tumult of battle was reaching a climax, or in modern times, as people fight their way through the crowded streets of Kumasi, the great parasols that shield kings and lesser rulers can always be seen from afar. Rising high above the heads of the crowds, they announce the presence of nobility. The sounds of horns and drums accompany the asantehene. His honorary titles are called out, his deeds praised. In keeping with this rhythm, the parasol bearers "dance" the canopy, raising, lowering, and turning it, making its frills flutter and sway in a play of colors. Reclining in comfort, too, can create an air of superiority; the parasol itself, plus various fans (such as those made of elephant tail) with which servants constantly cool the monarch, subdue the light and moderate the heat.

The colored parasols (kyinie) symbolize the sovereignty of African kings and have probably long been among the requisites of Asante rulers. The Arab traveler Ibn Battuta reported the use of a parasol in the kingdom of Mali around the time of the Middle Ages. The object that he documented had a bird at its tip. Asantehene are shielded by a parasol whenever they leave their residence or go from one part of their palace to another. An asantehene will even be seated under one during nighttime audiences. This is meant not only to provide cooling (dwo), but also to lend him an air of aloofness. And just as his sandals serve to isolate the soles of his feet from the ground, so the canopy provides a shield in the opposite direction. A proverb claims: "God must not see the crown on the king's head," possibly to prevent him envying the king's high status. Kings are the link between heaven and earth. They ensure that the rain – the

God of Heaven's sperm – makes its way to the folds of the earth and provides fertility.

Asante parasols of the 19th century were predominantly circular. Only a few were square or rectangular. Making the parasols required skilled craftsmanship. The parasol makers would reside in a village of their own before the gates of Kumasi. Today, all the greater Akan sovereigns have their own craftsmen. The structure that bears the canopy is made of hard twafoyeda wood (Harrisonia occidentalis). The fabric used tends to be extravagant and ostentatious – often imported. Red is favored, but this base material may also be interspersed with yellow velvet or other fabric. A few exceptionally grand parasols were made with thick, multicolored nsaa cloth, a textile woven from sheep's and goat's wool. Such cloth is a product of the stock-breeding Ful people from the north. One member of this community, the "coverer of the nation" (Katamanso), is responsible for the canopy adorning the Gold Chair during its public appearances. Another mark of distinction is the tip (ntuahire) of the parasol.

The imperial treasure of the sovereigns of larger territories always includes a number of parasols, each used on particular occasions. Their main function is to symbolize the special traits of the ruler whom they adorn. Many refer to a proverb, others feature animals (often birds) with whom the ruler has mythical ties. One most prominent motif is the babadua (Thalia geniculata), a robust bamboo that towers over most other plants. It stands for the supremacy and military potency of sovereigns. In the past, before entering battle, the Asante constructed a marching route made of this bamboo. As many warriors would cross it as it took to crush the material. This number would then denote the force to be sent into battle. At the same time, the act ensured that the special energy of the plant entered the bodies of the warriors. To this day this bamboo is said to ward off evil spirits or at least to neutralize them. The babadua parasol tips of lower-ranking territorial rulers (amanhene) were made of silver; only the Juabenhene, the sovereign of Juaben whose family belonged to the Oyoko clan of the asantehene, had a parasol with a gold tip – the use of which is an ancient privilege of the asantehene.

Two other frequent images are also botanical motifs. The pinnate leaf of a fern, aya, is considered

The parasol that towers above the crowds announces the appearance of the king of the Asante. His arrival is also heralded by horns and drums.

to be exceptionally beautiful because of its symmetrical form. This motif is also associated with a play on words. Given a slightly different intonation, the word aya means "malevolence" or even "insult," expressing both the fearless indifference with which the ruler faces threats and a warning not to talk badly of him. The second plant, prekese (Tetrapleura tetraptera), emits an aromatic, sweet scent, and symbolizes the ruler's omnipresence, a presence felt at all times, even when he is physically absent.

Another popular item used to decorate parasol tips is the battle horn (akoben), which is linked to the proverb: "If the army is defeated, no horn should be blown in its honor." The battle horn, too, symbolizes confidence of victory. The less warlike elements of a monarchy are symbolized by a hen guarding her chicks or a mother breastfeeding her child.

Parasols provide a canopy for the ruler seated beneath them. They also protect the shrines of the gods of a kingdom, which are paraded in royal processions. A shrine was dedicated to Tano, a river in Asante country that is worshiped as the son of the god of heaven and the great god of war. As a god concerned with the well-being of the king and the community at large, he is closely linked to the royal cult. Like the shrines of numerous divinities of the kingdom, Tano's shrine is a brass vessel which is kept in a sacred room. Local sovereigns each possess not only their own parasols, but also their own chairs. Their parasols are made of white fabric, the tips adorned with a gong (odawura).

The deliberate show of royal pomp makes regional sovereigns and kings the center of public attention. Veritable living works of art, they intentionally aestheticize their being and their surroundings to produce a concentrated demonstration of power. Elevation is an effective means of creating such an aura. At audiences they sit above those in attendance; if they leave their residence, they do so on horseback. In the wooded regions of Ashanti in which the tsetse fly makes it impossible to keep horses, potentates are carried on palanquins (apakan) when they appear in public. These are a type of sedan chair carried by four men. Borne thus a ruler is elevated high above those around him. In the past, palanquins were fashioned from a single tree trunk just large enough for the king or ruler. Today, they are simple, unadorned cane or timber litters that can hardly be called significant works of art. Some are lined with animal skins or cloth. One of the lining materials considered to be more valuable is the woolen nsaa cloth produced by the Ful.

401

Swords

Until the end of the 19th century, imperial swords (*afena*) were among the honorary gifts with which the representatives of the border provinces were usually distinguished in return for, and to further strengthen, their loyalty. Other such gifts were stools and palanquins. Both the number of swords that an individual possessed and the especially artful design of particular objects emphasized his honor and power. From the 18th century until the early colonial period, swords evolved from weapons of combat to parade objects that were increasingly adorned with gold trinkets. Before the introduction of firearms, spears and swords (*domfena*) were the armaments of all warriors. As the process of centralization continued, swords developed to become symbols of the authority that asantehene

bestowed upon the dignitaries of their community. The essential significance of the sword was now as a symbol of the royal delegation of power.

Legend links the use of swords as a symbol of authority to early Asante history: one of the envoys of the ruler of Denkyera, as a sign of his royal assignment, carried a long sword (*afatene*) that legitimized his authority to collect due gold tribute in Kwaman, the core region of the Asante. In Ashanti, "courier swords" (*asomfofena*) of this kind were just as numerous in the 19th century as were war swords (*domfena*), which were part of the armament of military leaders. In the ceremony with which such leaders were appointed to office, the asantehene would thrice gently strike the head of the appointee with a gold-handled sword; the latter would then swear over the sword that he would depart that night and return to Kumasi with the heads of the enemy (normally the Fante). Even local

Mourning ceremonies in Konogo, Ghana. The leopard mask dispels evil spirits.

sovereigns and the king himself swear allegiance on the sword at their inauguration ceremony. From the time of his enthronement, swords always accompany a potentate. While they are of particular importance in critical situations, their magical significance is what counts the most. Ritual swords (*bosomfena* and *akrafena*) are considered to be profusely endowed with energy. Oaths are sworn on bosomfena. Akrafena are used in cleansing ceremonies for the king's soul (*kra*) and those of his ancestors, who periodically take up residence in the blackened stools. Ritual swords are among the essential items in stool houses. They are also among the objects in the shrines dedicated to the divinities of the kingdom, and they are linked to the spiritual well-being of the king. To lend him protection as he sleeps, they are placed on the framework surrounding his bed. After his death, they are leaned against his elaborate catafalque.

At a king's public appearances, swords also glitter in the hands of the escorts who permanently surround him. If a king sits on his throne amid his retinue, his sword bearers position themselves to his rear; if he is being conveyed in a palanquin, they let the shaft of their weapons rest on the litter.

Each sword has its own name. The most important swords of all those an asantehene possesses is called Mponponsuo ("responsibility"). Its shaft and scabbard are covered in leopard skin interspersed with gold. The scabbard is further adorned with a variety of silver and gold talismans and a large gold emblem in the form of a fish holding a small antelope in its jaws. This sword is said to have been that of Opoku Ware I, successor to Osei Tutu. It is claimed that his mother endured a pregnancy of three years and was in labor for 14 days before she gave birth to him. At birth, his right hand quivered. Anokye, the long-lived priest, took this to be a sign that even in the cradle he was anticipating future deeds of war. Thus, he made the Mponponsua sword for the child. Having reached adulthood, the child gave his life and the sword to the service of the people. The king apparently won no less than 16 great victories with his sword in battle. Later, the leaders and important dignitaries of the individual territories of the kingdom swore on this sword their absolute allegiance to the asantehene. Today's Mponponsuo, however, is a reproduction of the original: the original sword was stolen by the British when they pillaged the king's palace in 1874 and is now on display at the British Museum in London.

Once firearms were introduced, swords took on increasingly ornamental forms. Ceremonial swords had elaborately crafted, elongated, wafer-thin blades, some of which even displayed intricately intertwined or wrought designs. These swords often have several blades and specially formed gold-plated hilts. Large cast gold emblems (*abosodee*), some of the most skillfully designed works of Arkan goldsmith craftsmanship, are adorned with scabbards made of antelope hide, leopard skin, and the skin of ocean rays attached with strips of leather. The sword bearers themselves often wear elaborate headdresses such as tight-fitting caps made of antelope hide. The sheaths of the most distinguished sword bearers (those who bear the Mponponsuo) are covered by a cap made of eagle feathers (*ntakerakye*) and adorned with a solid gold ram's horn.

While the evolution of ceremonial swords ended in the 20th century, other insignia, most notably rods, developed to become increasingly more elaborate.

Imperial swords, dating from the 17th century, express the power and honor of their owners. From: *The Arts of Ghana*, Museum of Cultural History, University of California at Los Angeles, 1977.

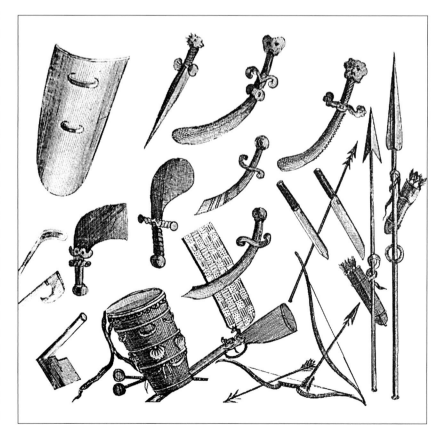

403

Official rods

As a symbol of recognition and dignity, the speaker (*okyeame*) carries a speaker's rod (*okyeame poma*), 4 ft 6 in to 6 ft 6 in long. Important potentates have several such rods, often coated in gold foil, sometimes in silver, and generally kept in the palace as part of the imperial treasure. A feature of many modern, gold-encased rods is the variety of exquisite, often representational or figurative, knobs that adorn them.

In public, rulers exercise noble restraint. In the past, their spokesmen, known as speakers (*akyeame*; *okyeame* in the singular), would conduct negotiations and hold court in the name of their sovereign. This high office is occupied by men who do not belong to the ruling family. The leading representative of this office, the senior speaker (*okyeamehene*) or advisor, would bear great responsibility. He was not only a kind of premier or foreign minister, but also the special royal envoy entrusted with important or sensitive assignments. In addition to such tasks, he also fulfilled the duties of a priest, leading public prayers and offering drink sacrifices. Because he was the only male dignitary who had the right to disturb the king during sleep, he was called the "wife" of the king.

All dealings with the king must be conducted in the presence of the speaker, who acts as a mediator. He is thus witness to everything the king and his contacts say. No ruler was able to make decisions without his advisors being informed. An okyeame repeats everything spoken by any party, while reformulating the most essential contents of what is being said in a witty and skillful way. His eloquence also sweetens the king's words by moderating the formulation of commands and omitting or paraphrasing insults. He is required to memorize important decisions, so must be an expert on tradition and a faultless chronicler. A new ruler is always introduced to his office by the speaker, who ensures the potentate is not subject to danger or impurity.

The recognition and honor of an okyeame is expressed by his rod (*okyeame poma*). The more elaborate rods probably evolved in the late 19th century. The asantehenes' speakers began using rods with ornamental knobs only on the return of Osei Agyeman Prempeh I from exile in 1924. They copied forms in use in the territories of lower-ranking sovereigns – notably among the Fante – where such development was already under way by the end of the 19th century. Initially, these were probably replicas of European walking sticks of the kind in use in coastal regions at least since the 17th century. In Europe of the day, walking sticks were popular status symbols. For this reason they were issued to local rulers on the Gold Coast, who were thus endowed with the status of having access to valuable European goods and of being equal in rank to the Europeans.

Asante tradition throws some light on the history of the rods. According to Asante tales, the office of the speaker and the traditional black rods used in Asante and other Akan regions of the hinterland were introduced to court by a woman. People who needed to discuss certain matters with the king turned to Nana Amoah, a woman already marked by age. Although she could only walk with the aid of crutches or walking sticks, she would stand before the sovereign and eloquently represent her client. This made the king more compassionate, increasing his willingness to listen to the requests put to him. On her death, her no less articulate son continued the tradition. In memory of his mother, he too used her walking sticks. The king of the day, Oti Akenten (c. 1630–60), is said to have been so impressed by his eloquence that he assigned him to speak in his stead at all official events. This story explains very clearly the early origins of both the office of the speaker and his status object.

What is certain is that the traditional rods common among the Asante were simple, cylindrical, sacrificially blackened poles. They had no knobs and were partly covered with gold or silver. Some of these rods were coated in the skin of the monitor lizard (mampam, meaning peacemaker") – an obvious reference to the most essential function of a speaker. The lizard skin design was introduced by Obiri Yeboah, successor to Oti Akenten, at the end of the 17th century. The black rods, initially used predominantly in judicial proceedings, have a purely ritual significance, and they are generally not shown to strangers. The more ornamental akyeame poma, on the other hand, are publicly exhibited. Ever more artfully designed rods of this kind appeared in the 1940s. The motifs of the knobs of these more recent rods were sometimes modeled on the designs used for parasol tips. Both objects emphasize similar aspects of the monarchy: the power of the sovereign and the upholding of the unity of the kingdom. It seems somewhat ironic that rod designs should have reached their most creative heights after the office of speaker had lost its significance and the kingdom of Ashanti had long disintegrated.

The knobs on speakers' rods, like the tips on parasols, express an aphorism or proverb (ebe), represent royal power, or symbolize the unity of a community. Snails and tortoises, for example, are an expression of peace, since they are not aggressive, but simply retreat into their shell at the first sign of danger. If these motifs appeared on the rod of a hunter, however, they would symbolize the adage, "If nothing other than tortoises and snails existed, not a shot would be heard in the forest." But in this case the image could also mean, "If someone wants to carry you, do not say 'I want to walk.'"

Costumes and jewelry

Costumes and jewelry are a further indication of status and regional origin. Today they also serve to mark differences between men and women and between people of various age groups or professions. In the past, they indicated whether someone was a refined person, a common person, or a slave. A system of symbols made it possible to categorize individuals. Occasion, color, and design combined to make a statement. Blue sections of cloth on a light-colored background are an expression of innocence, joy, and justification. Leaders don such robes after they have made a sacrifice to the ancestral stools: the lower-ranking wear them when they first present a child to the community or when they have won a legal dispute.

Kings and sovereigns dress in ostentatious attire. The glamour that their many robes reflect, the richness of their headdress, their footwear and jewelry all underscore kings' sovereignty. The Akan have particularly refined the art of body symbolism. High-ranking officials wear different robes according to specific occasions. When a ruler is appointed to office, he makes additions to the existing stately attire. He may add robes, fans, rings, or sandals to his wardrobe, items with which his name will be associated in future. He will also receive such items as gifts from other sovereigns or from the people. (In the past this was a form of tribute.) Public appearances by sovereigns are a prime opportunity to display wealth and opulence. Ornamental clothing and jewelry are as much an expression of power as of great wisdom and immeasurable wealth. One rule of attire is that an individual of inferior rank must never outdo someone of superior status. Although this would be no more than a blunder today, such conduct was once subject to punishment.

Only the asantehene is entitled to wear the richest robes. On certain occasions he will wear no jewelry – as is mandatory, for instance, when he enters the stool house or appears before the ancestors, who are superior in ranking. In public, however, rulers and their entourage reflect all the glory of their standing. The size and individual makeup of a king's retinue is an indication of the status of his kingdom. The asantehene has by far the largest entourage in all of Ghana, reflecting the economic, military, and imperial strength of Kumasi as the former center of the kingdom. In processions more than 12 different retinue groups are likely to appear: speakers, criers, bodyguards, sword and shield bearers, and so on. Each group is identifiable by their costume, headdress, or hairstyle. Subtler distinctions often exist within individual groups, for example the distinction between the headdress of sword bearers and chair carriers. Other positions have special attributes: the soul cleansers have gold disks (*akrafokonnu*), the

A Ewe sovereign in a full costume of colorful robes and royal adornments. The rather unusual heart-shaped necklace was personally fashioned for him. This is not a traditional form.

guards have ammunition belts, and speakers have distinctive rods.

The most exquisite pieces of Asante attire are large shawl-like wraps made of fine imported silk. Many thin strips of silk are sewn together to make a large piece of material. The majority of wraps, however, are not made of silk but of a cotton textile with silk thread woven into it. A characteristic design comprises small geometric patterns – diamonds, cubes, triangles, meanders, and so on. Typically of Asante culture, each design is linked to certain proverbs. A wide range of pattern combinations lends variety to the designs and also expresses different meanings. These cloths are called *kente*, originally a Fante term but now commonly used throughout Ghana. Some kente have names of their own, usually those of sovereigns, while others are named after animals, plants, or objects. In former times, the asantehene controlled the use of certain designs and would himself commission the majority of weaves. The most elaborate textiles were reserved for the asantehene or for members of his family. Others he would issue to members of his entourage whom he wished to reward or on whom he wished to bestow special distinction.

In stark contrast to the kente textiles, with their myriad of light colors, the attire worn to indicate mourning called, *adinkra*, is somber. Many of the designs, it seems, were originally imported from the north. The fabric is first dyed a dark color, then printed using stamps or color-drenched timber combs. The printed designs may be based on Arabic characters. The Asante claim this technique was introduced only after the war with Gyaman in 1818 (whose king, Kofi Adinkra, had had a replica of the Gold Chair made for himself) – even though Edward Bowdich had purchased an adinkra textile in Kumasi in 1817. After Gyaman had lost the war, and Kofi Adinkra his head, these textiles were named after the dead king. They stand for the link between the living and the dead and are an expression of mourning and loss. There are, however, also lighter-colored "Sunday adinkra" worn on festive occasions or even as everyday attire.

Influences from the north are also apparent in war costumes – the batakari tunic and the fabric cap worn with it. The Asante have long believed that people from faraway places could provide powerful protective magic. Such people, it was thought, were well versed in sorcery. Muslims, for example,

provided the amulets sewn into leather or fabric sachets – or even inserted in gold or silver capsules for the use of high-ranking individuals – and attached to war tunics. They made warriors invincible, paralyzing the arms of the enemy or making them quiver, so their bullets would miss their targets. The largest of these tunics, *batakari kese* ("big batakari"), are owned only by the asantehene, who inherited them from his ancestor Katakyie Opoku Ware (thus from the year 1731) and other influential rulers. Each asantehene wears the batakari kese twice in his life: on his ritual enthronement and during the aye-kese ceremony at the close of the funeral festivities for his predecessor. On the former occasion, this item of costume emphasizes his role as military leader; on the latter, it is an expression of the untamed force freed on the death of a sovereign.

By contrast, the traditional bark clothes (*kyenkyen*) made from the bark of the tree of the same name (Antiaris sp.) and commonly worn by hunters up until about 1920, are no longer worn at all. While they were, it was also customary for the asantehene to wear kyenkyen during particular phases of the odwira festival. This attire was in stark contrast to the magnificent robes that made up the rest of his festive dress.

The unbroken strength of royal tradition is evident in the fact that traditional costumes have changed very little over the last centuries.

The gold jewelry that a sovereign wears on festive occasions is so heavy that a servant needs to support his hand.

Griots, drummers, and trumpeters

A Hausa praise singer, one of those known as griots, whose profession has lost much of its former significance. Griots can nonetheless still be found in some cities. For a fee, they will sing their client's song of praise, flattering and celebrating him.

"Awaken, Adu, descendant of the Korobea Asante. Osei Tutu, allow me to call upon you. Who would not like to be Owusu Panin, the child of Edweso and Akua Bakoma, famed for their treasure of gold? If anyone were so privileged, he would greet his fate. Dommirefa holds nightwatch. O child of Atie Difie (Manu, the mother of Osei Tutu), awaken." With these words and similar phrases court singers (*kwadwomfo*) reawaken the founder of the nation and his great descendants. This text was recorded during the reign of Prempeh II (1931–70), which is why this ruler and his noble lineage – Owusu Panin and Akua Bakoma were his parents – is especially emphasized in it. Two professional storytellers sing in the service of the court. Their song is interspersed by the sound of talking drums, followed by "talking trumpets." They, too, repeat "texts" based on historical passages of the song or ones that praise the monarch. The instruments keep time with the intonation and cadence of the songs. This is possible because the language used is a tone language that not only consists of vowels and consonants, but in which words are also made up of a variety of pitches.

Music was a very important part of the court culture of African kings. It even had political significance. Music accompanied both the daily routine of sovereigns and, more importantly, festival events. It required specialists with the ability to improvise texts, to compose spur-of-the-moment melodies using new or certain words, and to memorize orally conveyed texts. For the most part, these "songs of the old" contain allusions to significant events or give genealogical accounts. Thus, they are understood only by those with a good knowledge of tradition. In the genealogies, the ruler is put at the head of his illustrious line of ancestors, thereby reinforcing his authority and the legitimacy of his claim to power. The songs exhort the king to follow the example set by his predecessors, but also to learn from their mistakes. In praise songs such as genealogies, the past is invoked as a supportive foundation for the present; past heroes and the heroic deeds of former rulers, great battles and victories are revived in song. Memorial Sundays (*akwasidae*) serve as a special occasion for performance by Asante court musicians. As the guardians of orally transmitted tradition and professionals with a true command of the art of committing texts to memory, these musicians serve their sovereigns as spokesmen who convey the official versions of national heritage.

As in the former French colonies of West Africa, the specialist literature uses the term "griots" to describe not only the praise singers, but often all musicians. The etymology of the word is controversial. It may possibly have originated from the Portuguese word *criado* (servant). Griots do indeed have a special status. In many parts of West Africa they make up a separate caste, their status being similar to that of smiths – though highly valued, they are also held in contempt and feared. Some griots will, of their own accord, attend funerals, memorial festivities, name-giving ceremonies, initiations, weddings, and annual festivals, and then expect their tribute to be remunerated in cash. Often, however, they are part of the entourage of a king or lesser sovereign. In some societies they even mimic the court jester and public clown. Only in the former British colonies is the term "griot" part of neither the official nor of the colloquial language. The people of these regions use their respective local term.

In many African societies, legend and music are closely connected. Music serves to raise people's spirits and to create an atmosphere. Instruments

"A man fights; a man does not walk away." It is this adage and similar ones that drummers beat on their drums with both sticks. The instruments they use, either placed on the ground or held on their head (*fontofrom*), are Asante talking drums. The syllables of each word are beaten on the drum in precise order. The drummers take the utmost care to express precisely the correct rhythm and intonation.

and the sounds that they make have special meaning, serving as a form of dialog between the living, the ancestors, and the spiritual powers. This is particularly true of drums. Originally, it seems, they were used to transmit signals: rulers would let their will be known to their people through "drum language." An example of this are the "talking drums," of which the Asante have at least two kinds. Atumpan drums are most noteworthy. They are made in pairs, one serving as an instrument for "feminine" beats and the other for "masculine" beats. The cylinder is made of the wood of the tweneboa tree (Cordia millenii), considered both to be exceptionally strong and to have a "not so good" (nye kora) "soul" (sunsum). The membrane is made of elephant-ear hide (preferably from female elephants) and is attached to the sides of the

Apart from drums, an important ritual musical instrument used in many ceremonies is the cross horn. It often has a richly decorated mouthpiece.

Opposite page, above: Music has a social function. It accompanies many important phases in the life both of an individual and of society as a whole. Drums are undisputedly the chief instruments of sub-Saharan Africa. All local sovereigns have a range of drums of various kinds and in various forms. One of the eternal mysteries of the art of African drumming is the ease and grace with which drummers can create an atmosphere of communal harmony.

Opposite page, below: The cup-shaped atumpan, always played in pairs, are talking drums. The female drum (in this case, the more resonant of the two) has a sound-modulating metal section attached to it. The atumpan is wrapped in a white cloth (*nwira*). The "divine drummers" (*odomankoma kyerema*) are not permitted to carry the instruments themselves, for if they did, they would lose their mind.

cylinder with strings and pins. The bent drumsticks (*konta*) are made of forked branches of ofema wood (Microdesmis zenkeri). In the past, it was only those of the status of an omanhene, ohene, or asafohene who were permitted to own them. They were, and are still today, stored in a room at the palace. At public parades, the drummers walk in procession following the ruler. When he sits, they are seated behind him. Women are not permitted to touch drums, much less own them – a rule which even applies to the "queen mother." But there are also other taboos associated with atumpan drums, predominantly that which dictates they are not to be brought into contact with blood, jaws, or a skull – quite contrary to the rules which apply to the aperede, which are said to have special contact with ancestors. These drums were painted with the blood of killed foe and adorned with trophies of the enemy's jaws, skullcaps, or whole skulls. When a king dies, atumpan drums resound over a period of eight days and nights. They generally also accompany the blackened stools on their way from the stool house to the royal mausoleum (*barim*).

Atumpan and aperede are only two of the many drums that are made in all shapes and sizes. Each drum has its specific meaning, a meaning which also reflects the social standing of the musician playing it. Aperede drummers, for example, have the same status as chair carriers, while atumpan drummers are equivalent in ranking to the ivory-horn blowers. Of secondary rank is the group of cross-horn musicians. Cross-horns also exist in a variety of shapes and serve varying purposes. In Ashanti, they are made of the tusks of young elephants. Most of them have a rectangular mouth hole on the inner side of the point. The right to own elephant tusks is normally the privilege of sovereigns. Accordingly, the ivory trumpets used by the Arkan, Ewe, and Ga are not only royal instruments, but often great works of art. This valuable material and the motifs engraved on it symbolize majesty and power. Ivory trumpets begin to "speak" when a practiced player brings to life a resounding sequence of words by intoning the praised names of the king or words of certain proverbs, or even "telling" whole stories.

Gold

"The treasurer further augmented the splendor of his office by spreading out all his wares; bowls, boxes, scalepans, and weights were all made of pure gold," wrote Edward Bowdich describing his reception by the King of Ashanti in 1817.

The kingdom's treasure (*sanaa*), kept in state coffers, once consisted mainly of gold. During major festivities, gold and other valuable items are put on public display. At other times the treasure remains locked in the stool house, along with the asantehene's heaviest gold weights and the ancestral stools. Regular offerings would traditionally be made to the gold. "Unscheduled" sacrifices were made whenever a sovereign planned to "attack" the gold. To escape being blinded upon opening the receptacle in which it was kept, he would donate a sheep or a drink sacrifice to the treasure.

In Ashanti, gold and especially gold dust served various cult purposes. In the receptacle that contained the weights dwelt a part of the soul of their owner – which is why he was included in the soul-cleansing ceremony. Once the owner of the gold – on the anniversary of his birth – had donned white attire and painted himself white, he would position the receptacle and soul vessel opposite his bedstead and sacrifice a chicken or sheep as well as eggs and yams to both. Shrines were equipped with gold dust. At court, it was predominantly used during transition rites. It was rubbed onto the children of local sovereigns to make them strong. On their deathbeds sovereigns were fed it mixed with alcohol. Once death had come upon them, it was rubbed onto their corpses, after which pure dust was strewn on them. Elsewhere, the mouth and ears of a dead sovereign would be filled with it, or a paste of gold dust and shea butter was applied to his eyes. In a parting gesture, his hand would once more be thrust into the receptacle filled with gold. Because gold dust was the recognized currency in Ashanti and a certain amount,

Gold weights in geometric shapes with smooth undersides and decorated upper sides. Recurring motifs include bars, comb designs, waves, lines, and zigzags, arches, crosses, spirals, and swastikas. The currency used for trading was gold dust, which was weighed using these gold weights.

previously weighed and poured into a cloth pouch, would accompany people on their journeys, it was also given to the dead to take with them on their travels. The pouch was attached to the deceased's loincloth – a custom still practiced to this day. However, as most families no longer own any gold dust, this custom has been adapted. When the pouch containing gold dust was attached in the past, the act was accompanied by the words "so you can buy water to drink." Nowadays, gold dust has been replaced by coins and the words changed to "so you can pay to ride on the lorry."

Before the discovery of the New World, West Africa was the principal supplier of gold to Europe. Until the end of the 19th century, it was extracted by the indigenous people, using simple methods. At times, heavy rainfall would wash it free ("wash gold"), so that it need only be collected. On other occasions, people would find gold while hoeing the fields. It is not clear when gold mining began in Ghana (in pits deeper than the height of a man) or when the practice of washing gold in riverbeds and

on riverbanks started. However, it is known that men would set out either alone or in groups to look for certain plants, or by observing the color of the ground or of the water would identify the existence of deposits. At such sites, they would carry out some trial washing. This was quite successful. When, at the end of the 19th century, the first European prospectors began to scour the country, they discovered that all the sites rich in gold were already excavated, in a kind of honeycomb. Since the walls of the shafts were not planked and there was no known method of draining water out of the mines, gold was extracted only near the surface of the ground. Today, modern mining techniques dig deep into the earth's crust. Accordingly, the gold now being extracted is of an extremely high quality.

Before mining was controlled by large companies, permission to extract gold was issued by the local sovereigns, who ordered that all finds of nuggets be handed to them – unless they weighed more than 8 lb, in which case the asantehene was entitled to them. The finders would

This map of the Gold Coast from 1729 shows places with rich gold deposits and the rulers of the individual regions. For example, one finds the entry "country of Akanni: formerly very powerful and rich in gold." The political organizations of a few kingdoms and regions are also mentioned. The country of Adom, for example, is described as "powerful and a kind of a republick."

413

The profound significance of gold dust currency in Akan culture is emphasized by the many adages that are visually symbolized by the weights. Because of growing demand for these pieces in the international art market, quantities have been sold and goldsmiths have for some time been producing small replicas of the originals. Although they are often good copies, they have lost all value as a measure of weight.

the people of Sudan), with its extensive gold deposits. The often imaginative reports of Arab geographers included accounts of "plant gold." In the 9th and 10th centuries Ibn al Fakih wrote, "In the Ganalands (the old gold country of Gana, founded by the Berbers and people of mixed Berber descent in western Sudan around AD 300), gold grows like beets in the sand and is harvested at sunrise."

receive no more than one third of the value of their spoils. Gold dust, on the other hand, was not subject to any tribute. However, if gold dust was spilled onto the ground during trading in the marketplace in Kumasi, it would forthwith be considered the property of the king. In times of hardship, the king would even have guards scanning the marketplace for this purpose.

The many rules concerning gold mining testify to the fact that it was a risky ordeal. Before digging the pit, the owner of the land or the diggers themselves would sacrifice a chicken and liquor to the ancestors, pledging to offer a further large sacrifice in the event of a major find. When washing gold at a river, a sheep, eggs, yam mush, and gin were provided for the god of that river. Upon discovering gold, a second sacrifice of rum or another alcoholic drink was due. If a digger broke a taboo or otherwise brought the wrath of the powers of beyond upon himself, the gold could take on the appearance of an animal and flee, thus depleting the site of any deposits, or a golden dog would appear, barking loudly and coughing up nuggets. This meant that there was a risk of the pit caving in, and everyone fled in a state of frenzy.

For many years, the gold of West Africa was a major trading commodity. Thanks to this commodity, sovereigns and kings achieved their legendary wealth. As far back as the 8th and 9th centuries, Arab invasions were directly targeted at conquering the Land of the Black People (meaning

Initially, in fact, the Arabs knew very little about the gold deposits, and Africans saw no reason to help them broaden their knowledge. Once gold trading had become a matter for the Portuguese and Dutch rather than the Arabs, trading was relocated to the coast, a situation from which the inhabitants of the coastal regions profited.

The intercontinental gold trade brought foreign influences to traditional regions of West Africa, one of which was the introduction of scales and measures of weight. Weights, today among the most fascinating objects of Akan art, eloquently testify to the exceptional artistic creativity and talent inherent in this particular culture. At the beginning of the 18th century, possibly even earlier, gold dust was the sole currency in Ashanti. It may, however, have been preceded by a legal tender based on iron. Except on the coast, where, before the introduction of gold dust, small pieces of inferior gold (kakra) were being used as a means of exchange, gold was never cast into any form of fixed-value coin. Special devices were in use during the time that gold dust was the Ashanti currency. These included: an equal-armed bar scale (nsania) and a set of weight measures (mbrammo; abrammoo in the singular); a brass spoon (saawa) with a small bowl head and a long handle often embossed or fashioned in such a way as to move easily between the cords of the scale; a "blowing spade" (famfa) with a broad-headed, deep-bowled spoon form, worked using a brass plate, with a circular ornamental design, and useful for blowing away other materials mixed into the gold; sieves, feathers, and brushes; small cloths in which to wrap the dust required; and boxes (*abamprawa*). Together with the weights and a quantum of gold dust, these objects were stored in a receptacle (*fotoo*) made of leather, skins, or cloth.

Precisely when gold weights were introduced to Ashanti is unknown. They are often said to have been invented by their direct neighbors, the Denkyera and Techiman. Osei Tutu apparently distributed copies of the weights looted during the war with the kingdom of Denkyera among his military leaders after their victory. Metal weights are predominantly geometric, but can sometimes also take figurative forms; "natural weights" may take the form of seeds, shells, or bones. Glass beads and buttons are often used as supplementary weights in small weight sets and used when dealing with small amounts. The acquisition of metal weights and expensive accessories accordingly increased the income and standing of goldsmiths. At the courts of Akan rulers, they created a kind of brotherhood (a trade guild), passing down their knowledge and talents to family members only. Their privileged status was demonstrated by the fact that they were permitted to wear gold jewelry outside the confines of the court.

During a transaction, both parties' weights were first compared using a scale. If they were equal, the buyer weighed out on his own scale gold dust to the value of the agreed price. The seller then compared this result with that given by his own weights. Even though incidences of fraud were subject to severe punishment, the use of trickery at times became an issue of serious concern – both in trading among the Asante and in their dealings with Europeans. This could involve using nonstandard weights, manipulating scales, or adding other substances to gold dust (most often brass dust – *dutu* – which was hard to distinguish from gold).

When the Akuroponhene Gyamfi Kwadwo died in the late 1820s, his wealth of gold dust was appraised, and the majority of it was found to be counterfeit dust. Thereupon, the asantehene Osei Yaw (1824–34) had his corpse exhumed. Brought to a judicial hearing and found to be guilty, it was decapitated. A goldsmith from Kumasi who was convicted of fraud in 1867, had his ears cut off. The process of introducing coins as a sole currency was nonetheless not readily accepted (especially in inland regions). On 1 June 1912, the colonial powers issued a bill forbidding the use of any currency other than British within the entire region of present-day Ghana (formerly the Gold Coast Colony, Ashanti, and the Northern Territories).

Figurative gold weights depict plants, animals (often fish and crocodiles), and humans as well as objects of material culture. Thus they are valuable documents of West African culture.

Dahomey and Oyo – the kingdoms of "Black Ivory"

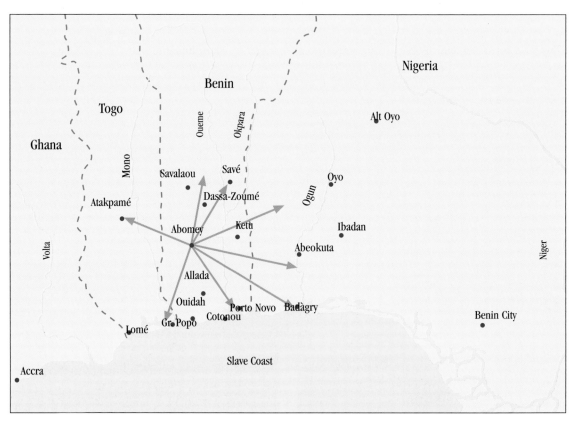

A map of Dahomey showing the direction of the kingdom's military campaigns. By maintaining strict centralized control through its monarchy, the kingdom of Dahomey was able to assert itself, despite continuous trading with Oyo, its powerful northeastern neighbor, and even gained control over other kingdoms.

Gold and ivory decided the names given to several sections of the coast of Guinea. "Black Ivory" was one such name: European demand for slaves had redirected trade from inland regions to the coastal areas. Lucrative opportunities abounded for rulers and traders alike. The coastal strip between the Volta and Niger rivers hence developed to become the "Slave Coast." The African dealers in this trade included kingdoms such as that of Dahomey, whose territory was no more than 30 miles wide and which, in the second half of the 18th century, stretched all of 90 miles in a northerly direction inland. This territory was very densely populated: the port town of Ouidah (Glehwe) was said to have 8,000 inhabitants and the capital Abomey as many as 24,000 to 30,000.

The kings of Dahomey were not exactly devoted fathers of their people. The image that they evoked was that of a water pot riddled with holes. To prevent even the smallest drops escaping from this pot, citizens were obliged to hold their proverbial finger to a hole. Thus, the citizens of Dahomey became the veritable stoppers in a leaking society. Based on the requisites of centralization, this notion did, in fact, aptly reflect reality. Its strictly centralized monarchy was the prominent feature of Dahomey society. This system contributed to the ability of the small kingdom not only to assert itself in spite of the ongoing extraction of its people for the slave trade and trading with its larger neighbor, Oyo, in the northeast, but even to gain control over other kingdoms.

The Europeans appeared on the coast inhabited by Adja groups around the end of the 15th century. The Portuguese were followed by the Dutch,

French, British, and Brandenburg regimes, each of whom erected forts and trading posts at strategic sites. This not only led to economic tensions and rivalries among local sovereigns; the new circumstances also gradually resulted in the disintegration of traditional ties between the kingdoms of the region. At around the same time, the sons of kings from the Allada or Ardra kingdoms had established a new power base and dynasty that was preparing to fill the existing political vacuum. This was in Kana and Bohicon (in present-day southern Benin), a region beyond the reach of European control. King Wegbaja (c. 1645–85) relocated the royal residence to a site northwest of Bohicon and surrounded it with a defensive wall – which gave the settlement its name, Abomey (Agbome), meaning "within a protective wall." European visitors would later describe the residence as a veritable town, with wide streets and squares, and shaded by huge trees. The name Dahomey (locally spelt Daxome or Danhome, Dan being a proper name and home meaning "body") alludes to

the legend that Wegbaja founded the kingdom on the body of his enemy, Dan.

Wegbaja, like other groups from the south, probably found it easy to overpower the Fon, who were later to become the "state people" and who at the time lived in a village community on the site known today as the Dahomey Plateau. Their settlement lay exposed between Oyo and the kingdoms of Allada and Ouidah (both active in the slave trade). Thus they had previously been the victim of slave hunters, a situation which was not about to change. Oyo's cavalry was a source of constant anxiety and had actually ravaged Abomey several times over and put its inhabitants to flight. In the years 1724–27, Wegbaja's son, Agaja (c. 1708–32) conquered a number of kingdoms on the coast. Most historians presume that in his fight for access to the ocean he exploited the conflicts that existed between Allada and Ouidah and that had been provoked by the Europeans. His objective was to eliminate the middlemen involved in the transatlantic slave trade and himself take part in this

A stone lion guards the royal palace in Abomey. It stands in memory of King Glélé (1858–84), whose priest name means "No animal that shows its anger as distinctly as a lion." The figure of Lebga to the right is protected from the elements by an iron structure. In the center is a shrine dedicated to Ogun (also called Gu), god of iron and blacksmiths and also standing for the battle victories of kings. As here, he is often portrayed by rusty metal splinters encased in a block of stone. This combination is meant to dispel dangers and ensure blessing for the king.

The exterior of the palace of King Ghézô in Dahomey. It was built in about 1820. At the time that this photograph was taken, in 1911, it was one of the few constructions of the entire palace complex that remained intact.
From: *Les Bas-Reliefs des Bâtiment royaux d'Abomey (Dahomey)*, Paris, 1926.

Statues of the kings of Dahomey in the Musée d'Ethnographie du Trocadéro. These figures are assumed to represent the kings Ghéyo, Gbéhanzin, and Glélé (respectively, from left to right). The images are not based on the kings themselves, but symbolize their power as defined by a consulted oracle. The description given may be of an animal such as a lion or fish, but it can also have the appearance of a human.
From: *Les Bas-Reliefs des Bâtiment royaux d'Abomey (Dahomey)*, Paris, 1926.

lucrative business. Though he was probably aware of the opportunities open to him (primarily through the defeat of Ouidah, which brought him into direct contact with European traders), this was his sole ambition. He did provoke Oyo, a kingdom that saw itself as the protector of small territories and that was unlikely to relinquish its control of the coast to the Fon. Numerous uprisings, incited both by Oyo and by foreign traders, ultimately forced Agaja to accept the superior strength of Oyo and its leading influence on both slave and foreign trade with the Europeans on the coast.

This new tie to Oyo followed another, older, one. The ancestors of the Adja (of which the Fon are a subgroup) came from Tado (on the Mono River in present-day Togo), a town founded by migrants from Ile-Ife, the Yoruba sacred center. According to legend, the progenitor of the rulers of Dahomey, or onidada from the Alladahonu clan (the Side of Allada) or Agasuvi (the Children of Agusa), was half man, half wildcat – the child of a leopard and a princess from Tado. His sons, in whose veins flowed the blood of predators, killed the successor to the throne, broke the king's calabash, and fled to Allada, where, in 1575, they united the territories of southern Adja into a kingdom. Allada thus has a significance for Fon similar to that of Ile-Ife for the Yoruba. The sons of kings had set out from both centers to establish their own kingdoms.

Dahomey is often portrayed as an autonomous kingdom that hunted slaves and participated in the

slave trade for its own profits. In reality, however, it was also commercially dependent on Oyo, which over time had successfully expanded from its center in the open savanna to the north and south. It conquered the Nupe (on the Niger) in the north and, in the port towns of the south, established trade contacts with the Europeans. This development began in 1550, after the ruler of Oyo first purchased horses from the Hausa in the north. At the height of its power, Oyo reigned over the entire savanna corridor all the way to the coast. Oyo's kings bore the title of alafin. Their lineage traced them back to Odua, the creator of the earth and king of the holy town of Ife. Accordingly, the hierarchy of Yoruba kings was based on genealogical proximity to the sons of Odua.

Despite their divine ancestry, the earthly existence of the alafin required them to face the power of the local sovereigns, who themselves had cavalry at their disposal. The kings attempted to neutralize them by recruiting members of their retinue from the ranks of former slaves. All the same, the kingdom of Oyo's main strength – its efficient cavalry – was particularly volatile. Because of the tsetse fly, it was impossible to breed horses. Instead, the animals and their carers had to be brought down from the north on a regular basis.

This was either extremely expensive or required that reciprocal services be rendered.

After the arrival of the white man, imported European goods became the most sought-after trade commodities. The procurement of such wares required a payment of slaves. Oyo thus became a major purchaser of slaves. It was only when the slave trade declined around the end of the 19th century that this traffic came to a standstill, which in turn soon led to the old conflicts between kings and sovereigns being intensified.

Until that time, Oyo met its demand for slaves predominantly by using the tribute received from the kingdoms under its control. One such kingdom was Dahomey, which made contact with the international trade network via Oyo. In addition to slaves, compulsory tribute included the delivery of some 1,700 firearms every year (a tribute paid annually over a period of close to 100 years). Were its demands not met, Oyo pressurized its debtors through repeated brutal attacks on Abomey.

In 1743, after the town had again been destroyed, Agaja's son Tegbesu (c. 1740–74) reconstructed it. Tegbesu was an exceptional king in several ways. During his youth, his father sent him to Oyo as part of an annual tribute obligation. Evidently, he managed to flee, because he returned to Abomey to depose from the throne his influential mother, Naye Wandjele (who already played a part in the myth surrounding the introduction of vodun), in the face of fierce opposition from his brothers. He then had his oldest brother drowned (possibly one reason he introduced the torhosu cult) and had other rivals killed or sold into slavery overseas – even though the latter solution ran counter to the ban against selling free citizens. He reorganized his court based on the Oyo model. A number of dignitaries were given increased administrative responsibility; cults based on newer divinities were introduced. Yet the proverbial sword of Damocles perpetually hung over the kingdom, so that in 1748 Tegbesu was obliged to enter into a new contract with Oyo, according to which Dahomey subjected itself to full political and military dependence. Dahomey's people would have to pay regular tributes, and were not permitted to fight wars without Oyo's consent. The supremacy and invincibility of Oyo's mounted troops had a paralyzing affect. Since Agaja had conquered the coast, Dahomey had experienced no

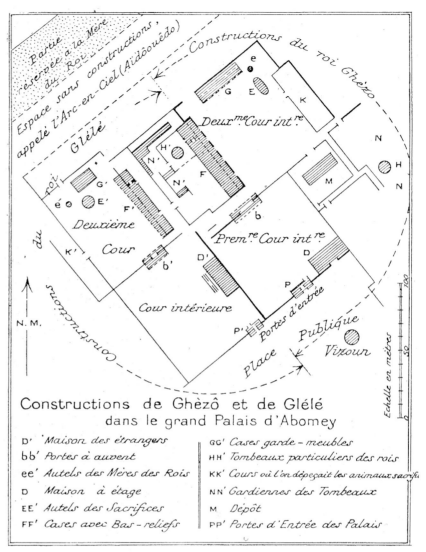

Constructions de Ghèzô et de Glélé
dans le grand Palais d'Abomey

D' Maison des étrangers
bb' Portes à auvent
ee' Autels des Mères des Rois
D Maison à étage
EE' Autels des Sacrifices
FF' Cases avec Bas-reliefs

GG' Cases garde-meubles
HH' Tombeaux particuliers des rois
KK' Cours où l'on dépeçait les animaux sacrifi
NN' Gardiennes des Tombeaux
M Dépôt
PP' Portes d'Entrée des Palais

significant military successes. Then Geyo (1818–58), having deposed his brother, Adandozan, led the kingdom to new, glorious heights. For the first time, Dahomey achieved political autonomy. Geyo, who profited from the disintegration of Oyo and the ongoing wars in Yoruba territory, now concentrated on the slave trade.

Strict centralization and the organized nature of the society proved to be its special strength. The kingdom consisted of a highly stratified, extremely hierarchical society, with an elaborate system of services, a well-developed agricultural system and economy, high-quality craftsmanship, and wide-ranging, flourishing trade links. Its religious practices were based on several gods – the vodun – to whom plentiful sacrifices were made, including human ones. The royal cult was headed by priests

A plan of the royal palaces of kings Ghézô and Glélé in Dahomey. The entire palace complex is made up of the buildings of ten rulers, each of whom erected his own palace.
From: *Les Bas-Reliefs des Bâtiment royaux d'Abomey (Dahomey)*, Paris, 1926.

who were also responsible for initiation ceremonies. Secret societies, common in the forest belt of West Africa, were banned, so as to suppress from the outset any opposition to the king. The king kept all rivals within his own ranks in a state of material dependency. Relatives lived at court, had no independent income, and were kept by the king. Thus, any aspirants to the throne were in no position to gather supporters. The rule of succession excluded sons born of women with royal blood from succession to the throne. Since these women enjoyed the privilege of being allowed sexual relations with other men, the king could always raise doubts about the legitimacy of a child. High offices were never occupied by members of the royal clan – "common" people filled these positions. Because their position excluded any hereditary succession, they had no means whatsoever of establishing any kind of clan authority. The royal household also included 2,000 to 3,000 women formally married to the king, who either worked within the administration, or were farmers, craftswomen, or soldiers. Together with a number of eunuchs, these women (*gbeto*), who came to be known as the Amazons of Dahomey, made up the king's personal guard. They are known to have fulfilled this function since 1720. It was not until the 19th century, however, that they received training as a standing army, ultimately winning a higher degree of respect and being more feared than the army's male warriors.

The origin of this institution is a matter of dispute. One possible explanation could lie in the organizational structure of the kingdom, since for every male official, there was a female counterpart who lived at the palace. It was their duty to ensure that the men were working, to review their performance, and to monitor their expenditures – all in the interests of the king. Likewise, the army's firearms unit comprised both male and female soldiers and officers. In early times, the army consisted of around 3,000 warriors, a number which doubled during the years 1725 to 1820 and doubled again by 1845 (women accounting for approximately one third of the troops). When more fighters were needed, women would be recruited from the ranks of other citizens. In times of war, military service was compulsory. Kings would also employ sections of the army for slave hunting. Whole villages were assaulted, their inhabitants killed, sold, or forced to join the army and their possessions confiscated. In cases of leniency, death penalties could be commuted to a sentence of enslavement – as a consequence of which that person might be sold overseas. Yet another lucrative source of income was the internal system of taxation. A basic tax (a payment in kind) was fixed for each of the villages, above and beyond which levies were made on livestock, salt, the products of craftsmen, and the goods sold at markets. The

members of this society were sometimes under the total control of the authorities.

Soon after the interests of the Germans, French, and English were negotiated at the Berlin Conference held on the coast of Guinea in 1884/85 and Dahomey was declared to be a French dominion, war broke out between Dahomey and France (in 1890). With the exception of some spells of peace, the war continued until 1894 and ended with victory for the French, who banished King Behanzins first to Martinique and then to Algeria. His brother, Agoli Agbo (1894–1900), was named successor to the throne. However, he was nothing more than a monarch at the mercy of France. In 1900, he too was deposed and the monarchy thus abolished. On gaining independence in 1960, the new rulers named their fledgling nation Dahomey and the old kingdom was once more remembered in a short-lived revival. Three years after the coup d'état of 1972, however, it was renamed the People's Republic of Benin, after the famous advanced civilization of the kingdom of Benin, in southern Nigeria.

Dahomey and the slave trade

The image that 18th-century Europeans had of the kingdom of Dahomey embodies many false conceptions and misunderstandings, since it is based on the accounts of three writers who were actively involved in the slave trade and who thus saw only positive aspects of the phenomenon. Their attention was focused on the violent elements of African society, such as the practice of human sacrifice and the despotism of regimes. According to their portrayals, wars repeatedly destroyed the land, generating excessive numbers of prisoners, who, left to the devices of their captors and not bought by Europeans, were doomed to be sacrificed to the gods. The kingdom's subjects themselves fared no better than slaves. The shipment of slaves to overseas destinations, therefore, had no more significance in their lives than a change of continent. Views of this kind provided the

The king of Dahomey orders several prisoners to be beheaded in an act of sacrifice, a scene here depicted on the Slave Coast. From: *Fetichism and Fetich Worshipers*, New York, Cincinnati, St. Louis, 1885.

TOMBEAUX des ROYS de GUINÉE tirés de BRY.
GRAFSTEDEN der GUINÉESSE KONINGEN, uit de BRY.

"Graves of the Kings of Guinea," an illustration of 1749 by the Bry brothers that accompanied a text about the Gold Coast by Dutchman Pieter de Marees, who journeyed through the Gold Coast and Ivory Coast between about 1598 and 1601. This copperplate print, repeatedly used to illustrate a variety of travel reports, contains many elements that are not based on fact. It aims to bear out the unjustified ideas that readers had with respect to cannibalism, human sacrifice, and the extremely bloodthirsty nature of Africans. This illustration was accordingly made to match the attitudes of the day.

supporters of slavery with valuable arguments in its favor. Indeed, they even entered into the accounts of several 20th-century historians. For these chroniclers, Dahomey was a perfect example of the extent to which European influence and the great demand for slaves contributed to the establishment and development of African kingdoms. Dahomey was confirmation of the "Atlantic theory," according to which a causal cycle existed between firearms and slaves, in which firearms were purported to be the decisive factor. Slaves were hunted using these weapons and new weapons were bought with the proceeds from the sale of the slaves on the coast; yet more slaves were hunted down using the newly purchased weapons. This seemingly endless cycle led to the expansion of the kingdoms: it sustained absolutist monarchies by ensuring the king the possession of firearms and a profitable monopoly on the slave trade. The economy of the kingdom thus rested entirely on this trade. Annual military campaigns served as a means of procuring prisoners. Some would be condemned to slavery in their own country, others would be sacrificed (predominantly at huetanu festivals), and still others sold to the white man by the king's agents. This cycle is claimed to have caused as many as 100 million young people (even from their own ranks) to be killed or enslaved. The king himself, it is said, profited more than anyone. He had slaves hunted down and sold to the Europeans; he was the main beneficiary, coming into possession of highly desirable imported goods such as firearms. He controlled trading, but transferred responsibility for the Atlantic slave trade to the provincial governor of Ouidah, the yovogun (gun meaning "master" and yovo "white man"). The governor's task was to greet the captains of all incoming ships and to assign local bearers to bring the valuable freight to the town's ammunition stores. It was the king, however, who determined prices for the slaves and for firearms. The Europeans were permitted to leave Ouidah only with the king's consent. Conversely, slave traders from the north were forbidden access to the town. They were forced to sell their prisoners to local middlemen. The fate of the slaves was ultimately left to the discretion of the king. Nobody was allowed to keep or trade slaves without his permission. On the payment of a tax, some of his officials were allowed to go on slave hunts, using an assembly of troops of their own, and to keep those that they caught.

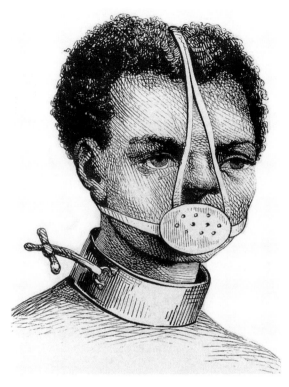

rulers were ever attempting to gain such control and to restrict private trading. They never quite managed to achieve it, however. Any partial successes were short-lived and the status quo soon restored. At most times, therefore, foreign traders were able to sell their slaves freely in Dahomey. But they were forbidden to make direct contact with the Europeans. Accordingly, many decided to turn to other ports. Generally, these findings clearly refute the notion of a monopoly and the causal link between firearms and slaves, and instead support the idea of an overall economic order and "peaceful" inner-African trading in an otherwise unpeaceful and inhumane business.

Left: Portrait of a slave. From Jacques Etienne Victor Arago's *Souvenirs d'un Aveugle: Voyage autour du Monde*, Paris, 1839.

Below: The grave of a king of Dahomey, showing people sacrificed on his death.

This roughly summarizes the idea that people had of Dahomey. More recent research has refuted these notions, especially the central premise – "Atlantic theory" – according to which, first, the history of Dahomey was determined by the slave trade and, secondly, it was based on an archaic economy, whose outside trade was monopolized by the king and whose internal trade did not adhere to market-economy rules. It is now clear that outside trading was mainly in the hands of smaller traders, while the king himself held a stake of less than 20 percent. The Atlantic slave trade actually contributed no more than 2 percent to the overall turnover. Furthermore, slaves and firearms were by no means the main trade commodities. Tobacco from Brazil, for instance, was a far more significant import.

The question arises as to where and by what means slaves were procured. In principle, the only viable sources were the "peaceful" inner-African trade, the compulsory recruitment of one's own people, self-sale with the intention of freeing oneself and one's family from the burden of debt, and the taking of slave prisoners in battle. The last of these was long mistakenly held to be the rule. War, however, actually disrupted trade. The concept of a royal monopoly on slave trading cannot be proven either, even though it must be said that

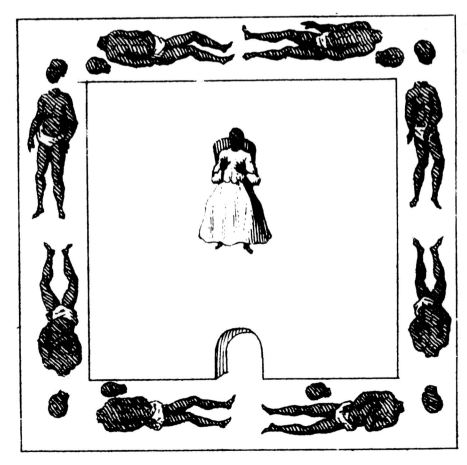

Foreigners in black Africa

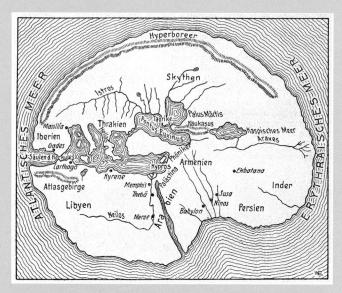

A map of the world, after Herodotus. From: *Das grosse Wagnis*, Berlin, 1936.

Exploration in the "Heart of Darkness"

In his *Histories*, Herodotus (c. 490–430 BC), the "Father of History and Ethnology," gave an account of a remarkable incident: the Egyptian pharaoh Nekau II (610–595 BC) had ordered Phoenician seafarers to sail around "Libya" (Africa). They set sail from Egypt, heading through the Red Sea. When autumn came, they broke their journey, going on land to plant grains and cereals and await the harvest, and then they continued on their journey. After three years they reached the Strait of Gibraltar and soon returned to Egypt "and they reported how the sun had suddenly moved to the other side of them. Thus it was proven for the first time that Libya is surrounded by the sea."

By then the Phoenicians had been sailing the seas for around 1,000 years, and so had gained much knowledge. At the time of this event, they controlled all trade activities in the Mediterranean and parts of the Atlantic (as far as the coast of England). They had also been the first to learn the art of

Henry Stanley's first contact with the Mazamboni. View from Nzera Kum hill. From: *In Darkest Africa*, New York, 1890.

orientation by the stars. This enabled them to sail at night, to travel away from the coastline, and thus to enter previously unknown waters. Herodotus's report is therefore considered credible.

A generation later, a North African Phoenician, that is, a Carthaginian, attempted a similar expedition. In about 500 BC Hanno, a military leader of royal lineage, was instructed to sail to the Strait of Gibraltar and then travel southward, both on a tour of exploration and to establish colonies. The Carthaginians were already trading in ivory, gold, and slaves from Africa. Their aim may have been to avoid expensive caravan trading expeditions through the Sahara. Hanno's fleet comprised of 60 50-oar galleys, carrying at least 30,000 men and women. Part of the travel log of this journey still exists. The land, it states, "was inhabited by Ethiopians everywhere, who fled from us and avoided all contact with us." After numerous adventures, setbacks, and losses, the remaining ships did at least manage to reach Sierra Leone, maybe even Cameroon, where the travelers were awestruck by continual nocturnal drumming and cymbals. Later (2 BC), the Greek Eudoxos of Kyzikos was twice unsuccessful in circumnavigating Africa from the port of Gade (Cadiz). Both times his endeavor ended on the southern coast of Mauritania.

The Romans, discouraged by the Sahara, took little interest in Africa. The Mediterranean region and its European hinterland, from Spain to eastern Europe, had far more significance for them. But around AD 100, a Roman corps led by Septimius Flaccus did cross the Sahara and reached the edge of the Sudan. Soon after, a merchant by the name of Julius Maternus, accompanying the king of the Garaments (roughly equivalent to present-day Libya) on a

424

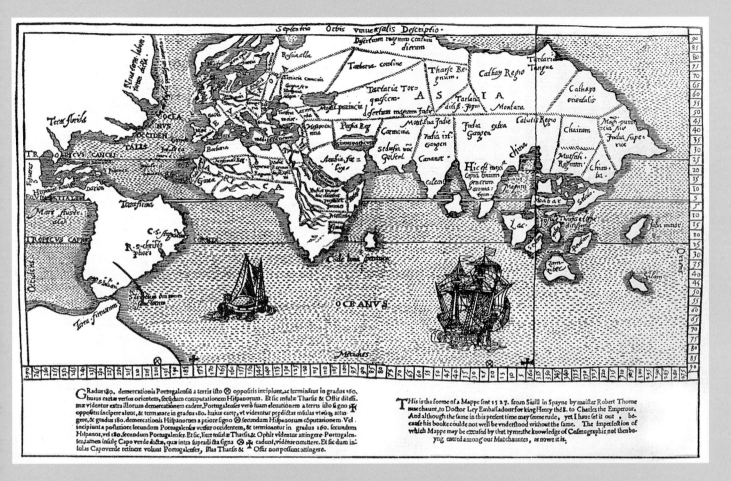

Orbis vniuersalis Descriptio.

A map of the world by Robert Thornes dating from 1527, with lines of demarcation that divide the world into Spanish and Portuguese territories. From: *Das grosse Wagnis*, Berlin, 1936.

military campaign, reached the Lake Chad area. Nero (AD 54–68) even dispatched an expedition to discover the source of the Nile – something that remained one of the chief objectives of European researchers on Africa right into the 19th century. The Byzantine empire, successor of the Eastern Roman Empire, was far too concerned about its restless neighbors on the plains of southern Russia and interior Asia, and too interested in trading with them and with the Chinese, to pay much attention to far-away Africa. However, like the Carthaginians and Romans, Byzantium maintained trade links with the African continent, especially with the Sudan and the coastal countries of northeastern Africa. Here again, the main commodity was fine timber, ivory, gold, and slaves.

It was these very goods that aroused the interest of the Arabs. With the rise of the Abbasid caliphate (750–1258) to a major power, trade soon began to flourish along the ancient routes through the Sudan (which in Arabic means "Land of the Black People") – a development closely followed by Islamization. The fact that reports about a wealth of gold in Africa seemed to be true was impressively confirmed when high-ranking African pilgrims visited Mecca. Mansu Musa, the ruler of the kingdom of Mali (or Malli) in western Sudan, spent such huge amounts of

gold on his journey through Egypt in 1324 that the price of this precious metal actually fell.

The Sudan thus attracted the attention of Arab geographers. In the second half of the 10th century, Ibn Haukal, one of the earliest, ventured all the way to western Sudan, but found nothing truly worth reporting, "For how could I, a lover of wisdom, intelligence, religion, justice, and an orderly government, take notice of people like these or even honor them with the privilege of being written about?" Idrisi (c. 1100–65) traveled further, at times advancing deep into the south of the continent. Ibn Battuta (1304–68) crossed the Sahara to Mali, where he saw armed warriors whose weapons were coated with silver and gold. He traveled along the Niger River in a dugout canoe, dealing in slaves on the return journey.

As demonstrated by Ibn Battuta's reports and the accounts of other explorers, the geographical expertise of the Arabs was far superior to that of their European contemporaries. This situation remained basically unchanged until the end of the 18th century. The emergence of merchant shipping initially affected the coastal

Mungo Park. From: *Westafrika.Vom Senegal bis Benguela*, Leipzig, 1878.

regions only. In 1291, the Genoans Vadino and Ugolina Vivaldi made a further attempt to circumnavigate Africa in order to gain insight into the spice trade. They failed. It was not until 100 years later that the Portuguese brought about a decisive change. This was essentially the achievement of Henry the Navigator (1394–1460), who, like Hanno before him, was of royal lineage, but who, despite his epithet, had never traveled. He developed a clear, forward-looking policy for Portuguese merchant shipping, while simultaneously creating the conditions that would support his plan. He had captains and officers systematically trained and taught the most up-to-date geography and astronomy. His plan also focused on tapping the wealth of gold in western Sudan and on creating a direct trade route to South East Asia and its wealth of spices.

In 1415, the Portuguese set foot on African soil for the very first time. They conquered Ceuta (on the coast opposite Gibraltar), thereby taking control of one of the major centers of caravan trading. In 1441, Antão Gonçalves reached Cape Nouadhibou (in northern Mauritania), returning with gold dust and slaves. In 1456, Alvise da Cadamosto led a major expedition that successfully traveled all the way to the Gold Coast (Ghana), where a first trading post was established. In 1471 the gold mines of Aprobi were seized and a fortification for their protection was erected. In 1488, Bartolomeo Dìaz was the first European to sail around the Cape of Good Hope.

The Portuguese did not venture much further inland. Attempts to travel up the major rivers were thwarted by shallow water. For the time being, therefore, only the coastal regions were

The first expeditions through West Africa. From: *Westafrika.Vom Senegal bis Benguela*, Leipzig, 1878.

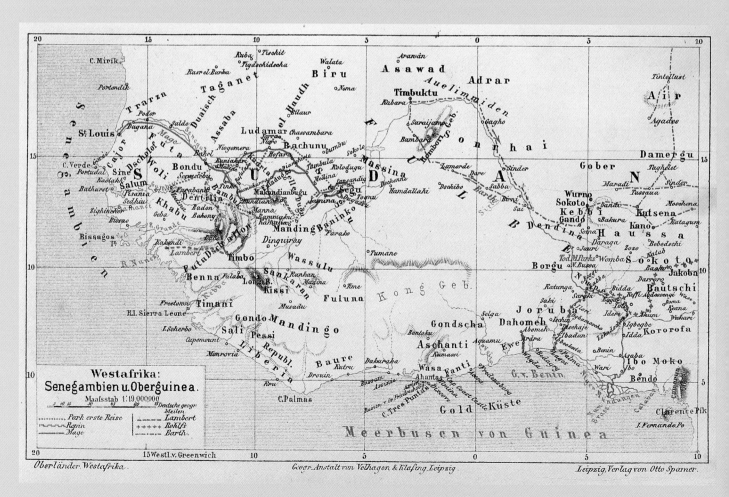

Dr. David Livingstone. From: *Into the Heart of Africa*, Toronto, 1989.

explored. The Portuguese contented themselves with establishing bases to service shipping to and from South East Asia. These also became trading posts for the slave trade.

Little changed until the end of the 17th century, when the French, Dutch, and British began to challenge the Portuguese. They, too, were primarily interested in gold and slaves. In 1697, the French managed to settle on the upper Senegal River. This was their only inroad, however. The Europeans remained otherwise restricted to setting up bases, soon to be numerous along the west coast of Africa. The major turning point came in 1788 when the African Association, later known as the Royal Geographical Society, was established in London.

It was founded with a particular purpose. Five years earlier, the independence of the colonies in North America had meant the loss of major markets for British goods. It was hoped that the losses could be compensated for in Africa. The society was an essential feature of the plan to launch a more detailed and comprehensive exploration of the continent. The aim was to foster "the expansion of trade and the promotion of British industry."

Expeditions were sent into Africa overland from the north and east of the continent. But the best way to gain access to the interior appeared to be via the large river systems in the west. Although advances were made, overall progress was slow. Most explorers were not equal to the enormous strain of such endeavors. Only the Dutch were initially successful in conquering a larger piece of territory in the 17th century. They founded the Cape Colony, which soon, however, fell into the hands of the British. The

Henry M. Stanley. From: *In Darkest Africa*, New York, 1890.

society owed its more measurable successes to a handful of men who were as fearless and callous as they were fortunate.

Mungo Park (1771–1806) was commissioned to explore the Niger region. He went further than any European before him – though he came close to starvation, constantly fell ill, and almost lost his life several times. On his return, he gave a shocking account of the unimaginable horrors of slave hunting, which ultimately led to the slave trade being abolished in 1815. David Livingstone

A page from Henry M. Stanley's notebook. From: *In Darkest Africa*, New York, 1890.

(1813–73) also undertook several expeditions, the first of which he set out on in 1849. His starting point was South Africa, where he had previously worked as a missionary. He traveled along the upper course of the Zambezi River, then to the Atlantic coast, and across the entire continent back to the east coast. Among the things he encountered during this leg of travels were the waterfalls of the Zambezi, which he named the Victoria Falls in honor of his queen. He then headed back west, discovered the Njassa, Mweru, and Bangweolo lakes, then set his sights on the north, the upper Congo region. Often ill or suffering from total exhaustion, he had to be carried along some stretches of the journey, several times suffering life-threatening conditions. He eventually went missing, presumed dead like so many before him, whereupon the *New York Herald* sent its best reporter, Henry Morton Stanley, to Africa to look for him. He was successful: on 28 October 1871, he entered the scientist's camp, greeting him with the famous words "Dr. Livingstone, I presume?" Livingstone set out on one last trip. This time, however, he was defeated by exhaustion and died. He, too, had spared no effort to inform the world about the atrocities of slave hunting. His African escorts thanked him for it. They carried his body all the way to Zanzibar to be received by his son, who had him transported to London where he was ceremoniously buried in Westminster Abbey.

German explorers, some commissioned by the Royal Geographical Society, also made a contribution to shedding light on the inner regions of the African continent. Heinrich Barth (1821–65) traveled across the Sahara (from 1850 to 1855), through Timbuktu, and on to Chad (dressed as a Muslim). Gerhard Rohlfs (1831–96) was the first European to cross

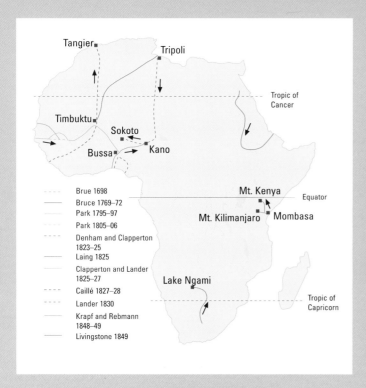

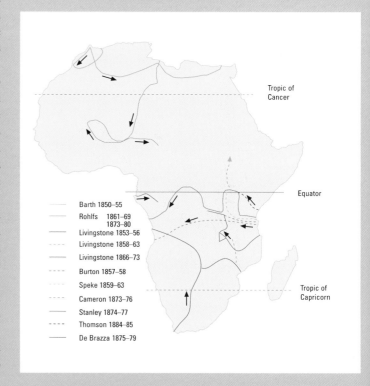

The European exploration of Africa before 1850.
From: *Cultural Atlas of Africa*, Augsburg, 1998.

incarcerate a soul in such a black and repulsive Negro body." His contemporary, Voltaire (1694–1778), a leading philosopher of the Age of Enlightenment, was certain that "The black race is a human species as different from ours as spaniels are in comparison to greyhounds [...] Even if the mental faculties of Blacks should prove to be comparable with ours, they are certainly considerably inferior. They are not in any way capable of operating by thought or creating patterns of linked thought."

It was only due to ethnographical research on Africa, which began around the end of the 1920s, that this image very gradually began to change. Ethnologists, too, were out to find "treasures," but theirs was an interest in the cultural wealth of the African people. Much of what they found has long since perished in the regions where it formerly thrived, but it continues to live on in the museums of Europe. Museum-goers are thus provided with a different and more adequate portrayal of the creative energy, originality, and magnificence of African culture.

Even more significant is the ethnological research which has uncovered the continent's true "gold" – the communal life, social morality, religion, and spirituality of the African people. This book is widely based on the findings of ethnologists. Just two of the numerous scientists and explorers who deserve mention are Leo Frobenius (1873–1938), whom African thinkers to this day acclaim for restoring the dignity of the peoples of Africa, and Marcel Griaule (1898–1956). The latter undertook several

The routes taken by European explorers in the interior of the African continent, 1850–80. From: *Cultural Atlas of Africa*, Augsburg, 1998.

northern Africa (from 1865 to 1867), from Tripoli via Bornu to Lagos. Gustav Nachtigal (1834–85) also set out on his journey from Tripoli, heading (from 1869 to 1875) through the Fessan and the largely unexplored Tibesti to the sultanate of Bornu southwest of Lake Chad. From there he continued through the kingdoms of Bagirmi, Wadai, and Darfur and on to Cairo. His reports are among the most valuable accounts of those times.

Hence, Europeans were only more precisely introduced to the geography of the continent – albeit to no more than its rough contours – toward the end of the 19th century. Excepting the slaves, however, not much attention had been given its inhabitants. This had not least been the fault of Arabian and European thinkers. The scholar and writer al-Dschahiz (c. 776–868), himself probably of African origin, compared the black people to ravens, describing them as "the worst of people, the worst of beings with respect to their constitution and temperament." The jurist and philosopher Ibn Khaldun (1332–1406) was hardly willing to accept that they even had "human traits." "They are much like animals," he claimed. He nevertheless considered it wiser to acquaint them with useful work – such as carrying loads – than to leave them to their own dull animal devices or wage costly war against them. Charles Montesquieu (1689–1755), French philosopher and jurist, questioned in astonishment whether it was conceivable "that God, who personifies all things good, could have decided to expidions in the 1930s, primarily to Dogon in Mali, and impressively demonstrated that traditional societies certainly do have ideological systems which, as in the case of the Dogon, entail no less differentiation, complexity, and depth of thought than those of ancient pre-Socratic philosophers.

When the Dogon learned of Griaule's death, they conducted their own, complementary funeral ceremony in which a lead pencil represented his body. The funeral address of the priest included the words: "The Dogon know neither decorations nor titles with which to honor their kinsmen; but without exception we are all convinced that Griaule was one of us."

Right: Constructing a steel boat. The multiple sections made it easier to transport.
From *In Darkest Africa*, New York, 1890.
Below: *Mission in Africa*: after an arduous march through the bush, the assembled boat is floated. From *In Darkest Africa*, New York, 1890.

The Muslim holy war

The history of regions and continents is governed essentially by geographical conditions and by geopolitical location. To the north Africa is bordered by the Mediterranean, from the eastern side of which emerged the first early civilizations about 6,000 years ago. The eastern coast of Africa was an ideal starting point for sea journeys to India and South East Asia – Indian and Asian immigrants had, in fact, already settled in Madagascar by the end of the first millennium. Both the northern and eastern regions of Africa had therefore always been important entry points for foreign cultures and ideas. The first known urban and monarchic cultures evolved on the east coast. While some were in the interior, most were located in the northeast (in Nubia and Ethiopia) and throughout the Sudan – immediately south of the Sahara on the final posts of the great caravan routes.

Mtesas residence. From: *Westafrika. Vom Senegal bis Benguela*, Leipzig, 1878.

Two further influences of an entirely different nature reached Africa via the same channels. They, too, had their origins in the eastern Mediterranean and possibly had an even more far-reaching impact on the history of Africa. They were the advent of Christianity and of Islam (in the first half of the 7th century).

Mtesas and his dignitaries. From: *Die Völker der Erde*, Wurzburg and Vienna, 1891.

Both were world religions with a declared missionary agenda. Having each found political support, they evolved to become extraordinarily dynamic in their expansion. However, the missionary aims of the early Nestorian Church and, later, Orthodox Byzantine Church were directed more toward the countries of the eastern Mediterranean, inner Asia, China, and India rather than Africa. At first, Christianity was successfully introduced only to Egypt, which at the time was part of the Byzantine empire, and to Nubia and Ethiopia, where several Christian kingdoms were established.

The rise of Islam quickly and decidedly changed this situation. In the crusades of 622 to 750, Byzantium was forced back to the Anatolian region of its origin as Muslim armies conquered Persia, Afghanistan, parts of Central Asia (Chorasan), Egypt, northern Africa, and Spain. Unlike the Romans and Byzantines before them, the Islamic rulers of the various southern and southeastern Mediterranean territories of the Umayyad and, later, Abbasid caliphates (750–1258) had their sights equally set on the African interior. For many centuries, the Arabs had maintained thriving trade relations with African coastal towns and had even settled in the region; trade along the Saharan caravan routes had also been going on for at least as long. Gold, ivory, fine timbers, and slaves continued to be sought-after commodities. New trade momentum was to add important impetus to the Islamization of the continent.

There were other contributory factors. One was the wanderings of Bedouins around the time of the Early and High Middle Ages; their travels spanned northeastern Africa from the region of the upper Nile through into eastern Sudan and across northern Africa to Mauritania in the west. Other factors were the expansionist policies of various Maghreb states which spread into the region of western Sudan; the advances made into the Sudan (via Egypt) by the Mamelukes and, from 1517, by the Ottoman empire; and the enterprising missionary activities of Islamic Sufi brotherhoods. A final

King Ahmadu. From: *Westafrika. Vom Senegal bis Benguela*, Leipzig, 1878.

factor was the outstanding leadership qualities and thirst for conquest of individual local rulers and religious leaders.

Trading towns on the northeastern coast of Africa were the proverbial bridgeheads of Islam. For centuries, this region had been home to colonies of Arab merchants. Over time, the intermixing of Arabs and indigenous people produced the Swahilis (from the Arabic *sawahil*, meaning "coasts") of the coastal regions between Somalia and Mozambique. Both the Arabs and the Swahilis contributed to the Islamization of eastern Africa. The old port town of Mogadishu played an important part in this development. It was from there that the new faith spread into the Somalian hinterland during the 9th and 10th centuries. Smaller sultanates emerged throughout the region (initially, for instance, in southern Eritrea and northeastern Ethiopia). They maintained sometimes loose alliances with towns and neighboring ethnic groups. By the Middle Ages, Zanzibar, the coastal regions, and Somalia were fully Islamized. Further south, this development influenced only those inland regions situated along the trade routes. Excepting the Yao, who controlled all

goods traffic between the Njassa region and the coast, Islam did not assert itself here in any sweeping fashion (as in Somalia) before the arrival of the Europeans. Moreover, groups in other non-coastal regions were far too intensively plagued by Arab slave hunters to develop any inclination toward the religion of their tormentors.

Since the 8th century, trade towns in the Sudan, at the end of important caravan routes directly south of the Sahara, had long proven to be receptive to Islam. Timbuktu in particular played a leading role, since it was an early center of Islamic learning. Egypt was a primary accessory in introducing Islam to inner Africa. The decisive breakthrough, however, came only after the Christian kingdoms in Nubia were destroyed in the 14th century, to be replaced by the Islamic Funj kingdoms.

From the north, across the Sahara, and in the east, from the region of the upper Nile, pressure increased on the large

The Great Mosque in Djenne, Mali, after Friday prayers. Like all monumental buildings in the arid zones of West Africa, this mosque is built of sun-dried mud bricks.

The imam prays in the Great Mosque at Djenne, Mali.

A youth studies the surahs of the Koran outside the Koran school in Djenne.

432

kingdoms of the Sudan. In the 11th century, the first Islamic centers evolved in Ghana, Mali, Songhai, and Bornu-Kanem. They, in turn, influenced neighboring groups within their immediate environment – primarily the Fulbe and Mosi. However, they also influenced Hausa city states such as Kano, which experienced an early Islamic boom under Muhammad Rumfa (1453–99).

At first, the situation everywhere was much the same as it is today in some towns and kingdoms of western Sudan. Muslim merchants and Koran scholars settled in a separate part of their village or town, maintaining mosques, Koran schools, and Islamic centers of higher education. Their knowledge of writing and their learnedness earned them the respect of "heathen" and Muslim leaders alike, and led them to take up influential positions or even ministerial office. They remained strictly endogamous, avoiding marriages with "unbelievers". Thus, a mixed culture gradually evolved among the urban upper classes and at court. While many of the traditional ceremonial customs were upheld, education, diplomacy, and everyday life were subjected to strong Islamic influence.

Another turning point came in the 18th century, when Islam was firmly established not only in urban areas, but also within individual ethnic groups, thus setting off a kind of local self-perpetuating trend. Possibly as a result of a distant echo of the Wahhabi fundamentalist reform movement in Arabia, a series of revolutionary uprisings broke out in the Sudan. They were directed both at "heathen" rulers and Islamic followers. The main instigators of these movements were the Fulbe who, in the 14th

century, set out from the Senegal to conduct a *djihad* (Muslim holy war) in the east. The overall movement led to a series of processes by which old systems were newly aligned and theocratic states created. Bagirmi and Wadai thus fell in the 16th century, Adamaua was ultimately subjected to Islam in the 18th century. Yet again, it was predominantly the urban populations that were affected. The djihad gave impetus to the process of Islamization – albeit with sometimes brutal force – so that its influence ultimately reached as far as the Yorubas in southern Nigeria.

Students at an Islamic seminary (a *madresah*) for aspiring imams (theologians who lead prayers in the mosques) in Bamako, Mali.

An Islamic scholar reads the Koran at the Great Mosque of Bamako.

New heights were reached by the rigorous fundamentalist movement led by the great reformer Osman Dan Fodio (1754–1817). Born into a scholarly family from southern Nigeria, at a young age he received instruction from a variety of teachers until, in 1775, he himself began to teach. He had already made a name for himself as a religious poet and for this reason more readily attracted an audience. In his sermons he attacked the luxurious lifestyle of the ruling and influential classes, especially that practiced at the courts of Muslim leaders in the Sudan with their exaggerated etiquette, countless offices and titles, pomp, art, and other forms of worldly pageantry. He called on his followers to take up arms and declared a djihad against all holders of power in the land. Ethnic affiliation was not an issue. Himself of Fulbe origin, he made no concessions to spare the Fulbe ruler, although he was defeated in the east when he tried to attack Bornu. One of his major successes was his battle against the Hausa states in the south, whose kings he accused of paying no more than lip service to the Muslim religion. He ultimately Islamized large expanses of western Sudan, from Senegambia to deep into southern Nigeria.

The increasing rigidity of the religion was also due to another factor, one still relevant today: Muslim brotherhoods. They were an early and essential phenomenon of Islamization. The most prominent brotherhoods in the sub-Saharan region were the Qadiriya (established 1165), Tidjaniya (1781), Rahmaniya (1793), and Sanusiya (1837). Their success, especially among the rural population, was based on their tolerance of regional traditions. They appeared also to have certain things in common with people's traditional faith. They practiced fortune-telling and the interpretation of dreams. The masters of their orders, the sheiks, had special blessing powers (*baraka* in Arabic) – as did their African counterparts – bestowed upon them by the Prophet himself, to whose lineage some (in Somalia, for instance) traced themselves directly via their ancestors. If it became necessary, they would go to war, but generally only as helpers, healers, spiritual advisors, and miracle-workers. Some of the brotherhoods sent their members on missionary assignments,

A marabut and his followers travel through Dogon territory, Mali.

A Dogon village in Mali with its mosque and forecourt, typically built of sun-dried mud bricks.

A marabut teaches the Koran to the Dogon in Mali.

so that many Africans were not only Muslims, but also members (or followers) of a brotherhood. It was thanks to these Islamic orders that the religion was able, in some cases, to penetrate deep into the forest regions.

The Sanusiya brotherhood made a name for itself in this respect. It was very popular among "heathen" groups. By the late 1880s it already had more than six million followers in central Sudan – despite its austere, puritanical tendency. Like the Wahhabi in Arabia and other religious brotherhoods in the Sudan, the Sanusi had set their sights on restoring Islam to its original form. These brotherhoods also caused a new element in the Islamic mission to become increasingly important. They systematically stirred up a feeling of hatred for the European colonial powers, thus adding permanent strength to their own standing among the Africans and also to that of Islam itself. Moreover, having been taught by native Africans for centuries, Islam was by now considered to be a somehow authentically African religion. Muslims did not, in fact, live very differently from their "heathen" neighbors. Their skin was of the same color and the men had up to four wives. It was therefore easy to link Islam with the movement opposing the colonial powers. Certain groups that had rejected Islam in the past flocked to be converted to it in

A marabut places a grigrí on the head of a circumcized girl. In Dogan, Mali.

colonial times. This was a way of expressing their protest. Islam provided the motivation and drive for more than a handful of nationalistic movements (in Dahomey and Senegal, for example). It is easy to see that Christianity, by contrast, appeared to be a religion of oppression. The uprisings that multiplied during the 19th century were mostly spearheaded by the leaders of religious orders (sheiks or marabuts). Because the French and English had superior weaponry at their disposal they easily suppressed most

of these incidents. The only opponent who proved to be a serious threat was Muhammad Ahmad ibn Abdallah (1843–85). In 1881 he declared himself to be Mahdi, the Islamic Messiah who would appear at the end of time to renew the world. His goal was to establish a "kingdom of God on earth." He embarked on his mission in the upper Nile region. By 1885, he had command over all of Egyptian Sudan, which at the time was still under Turkish Ottoman rule. When Khartoum fell, he relocated his headquarters to Omdurman. He died there the same year. His successor continued the djihad, but was defeated when he attempted to conquer Egypt (in 1889). The end of the Mahdi state was sealed by the English through several campaigns led by Lord Kitchener (later Field Marshal), the last of which took place in 1899. "Anglo-Egyptian Sudan" was in the hands of the "unbelievers."

In some ways, the Islamic movement also benefited from colonialism. An improved infrastructure and the boom in trade that ensued because of it gave unprecedented momentum to the spread of Islam in Africa. Today, this religion has over 50 million followers in black Africa, two thirds of whom live in West Africa, notably in Nigeria, Senegal, Guinea, Mali, and Niger. Other centuries-old centers of Islam include the Republic of Sudan, Eritrea, Somalia, Zanzibar, and, to a lesser extent, Kenya, Uganda, and Malawi. Islam is an established feature of modern Africa.

Praying muslims at the market for livestock in Fatoma, Mali.

Veiled Wahhabi women and an animist woman in a Dogon village.

The call for evening prayer in a Dogon village in Mali.

Soldiers of God

For Europeans, the "discovery" of the New World represented not only the tempting prospect of supposedly immeasurable wealth and new lands. It also posed a delicate problem: they encountered beings that, despite looking rather different from themselves and seeming to lack any form of civilization, did unmistakably possess signs of being human. Could these people be descendants of Adam and Eve? If so, how had they reached faraway America? The issue was not only one of academic interest, for if they truly were human beings, they would need to be treated as such. This posed problems of a legal nature. Furthermore, the affirmative would imply that they were far beyond the historical reach of God's salvation, bestowed only upon those who had been endowed with and professed to the true Israelite/Jewish and Christian Revelation. Was it permissible to leave them to their fate?

This issue preoccupied the Spanish jurists of the day, the overriding majority of whom were members of religious orders (mostly Dominicans and Jesuits). The controversy was eventually clarified by a bull issued by Pope Paul III (1534–1549) on 2 July 1537 proclaiming the indigenous inhabitants of the New World to be "real humans" and thus "capable of accepting the Catholic faith and the Sacrament" ("veri homines et fidei catholicae et sacramentorum capaces"). They were, however, refused any form

The arrival of the Portuguese before the king in Congo. "Upon hearing about the religion of the Portuguese, the king of Congo desired to be given instruction on the Christian faith. He dispatched a written appeal to John, king of Portugal, to send him priests that would Christianize his people. His request was met. The king of Congo received the king's emissaries and priests with great joy. He also thankfully accepted the church fittings, vestments, pictures, and crucifixes that he was given. His people demonstrated their humility by thrice falling before the king of Congo."
From: *Warhaffte und Eigentliche Beschreibung des Königreichs Congo in Africa* by Lòpez Odorado, Frankfurt am Main, 1597.

David Livingstone discovers Lake Nyasa.
From: *Into the Heart of Africa*, Toronto, 1989.

among other things, their scanty dress, belief in the spirits, practice of human sacrifice, and cannibalism. There could be no salvation for them "without the commitment and leadership of foreigners." This referred primarily to work in God's vineyard – for "every schoolchild knows that, wherever the Apostles did tread, the face of the earth was renewed, and from the quagmire of heathen depravity rose the blossoms of lillies of chastity."

This aspect of Christianity can thus be seen as the religious manifestation of the Europeans' missionary zeal to civilize others. Attempts to introduce religion and the desire to civilize have in fact always been closely connected. This does not, however, necessarily mean that the missionaries saw themselves as the accomplices of colonialism. Many of them saw only positive aspects in it. David Livingstone who can undoubtedly be described as having been a sincere friend of the Africans, was convinced that "civilization and Christianity are so closely linked that the one cannot be promoted in the absence of the other." He meant this in the sense that civilization and Christianization of the Africans would help to create the requisite equality of status between Africans and Europeans which was ultimately the precondition for their freedom and independence.

"Conveying the Gospel to the heathens must involve doing far more than is generally associated with the work of a missionary. First, special consideration must be given to the fostering of trade, since trade and change will bring the awareness to the tribes that they are inter-dependent on and that they can reciprocally benefit one another. My observations in this area instill in me the keen desire to promote a situation

of concession for more than a hundred years thence. But at least the Holy Sacrament ensured them salvation at the end of time. They could now rely on the fact that the Church, true to the teachings of Jesus to "Therefore go and make disciples of all nations, baptizing them in the name of the Father and of the Son and of the Holy Spirit" (Matthew 28, verse 19), would take care of them.

The task appeared difficult enough, as these heathens were considered to be "people gone astray" and caught up in the most abominable of vices. Even a well-meaning late 19th-century missionary writer who sharply denounced the degrading and cruel treatment of colonial peoples concluded that "Properly illuminated from all sides, these 'cheerful, harmless, sweet children of nature' do not seldom reveal themselves to be highly intelligent and perceptive beasts, tarnished through and through with the most horrid of passions and vices, capable of any vile and sacrilegious deed." His accusation addressed,

Congolese children attend reading lessons at the Kwango missionary school. They are being taught to read and write in their mother tongue.

439

Missionary Johann Ludwig Krapf. From: *Land und Leute von Abessinien*, Leipzig, 1869.

whereby Africans will generate and prepare the raw materials used in European factories, for in doing so, we can not only offer future objectives for slave traders, but also introduce Negroes into the universal family of peoples in which not a single member can suffer without the others partaking in his suffering."

White immigrants would establish farms and build factories, later to turn them over to the Africans. They would live among them as brothers and sisters, epitomizing good Christian conduct. Livingstone dreamed of a free Africa that would work solely to meet its own needs.

While his views were shared by many, they certainly did not represent majority opinion. "Disbelief" and "barbarism" were considered to be as much interrelated as were Christianity and civilization. If, therefore, all efforts of insistent persuasion were to no avail, it was believed the higher nature of the aim justified the use of more vigorous means. The apostles of harsher measures would legitimize their stance by quoting the word of Jesus, "Go out on the roads and country lanes and make them come in, so that my house will be filled" (Luke 14, verse 23). Missionary publications abetted this position with warlike encouragement by reporting – in a style reminiscent of military accounts – on the "Advance of the Mission in the Heathen World" or the "Triumphant March of the Gospel." Islam, however, proved to be an obstacle in this battle for heathen souls. It was making inroads

far more easily and expediently. Christian zealots such as the missionary Johann Ludwig Krapf (1810–81), "discoverer" of Mount Kilimanjaro, believed the devices of evil to be inherent in the Islamic faith. "My opinion," he confided in a Basel newspaper, in 1854, "is that Muhammedanism is a masterpiece from hell. As long as the Devil has such hold on the earth, he will not fall into the abyss and cannot be put on the great chain. I have disputed with Muslims a hundred and a thousand times and have always found that this religion can be dissolved by nothing other than the sword by which it was created."

Monseigneur de Marion Bresillac, founder of the Society of African Missionaries. From: *Fetichism and Fetich Worshipers*, New York, 1885.

The Protestant mission, to which the majority of disciples working in Africa in the mid-19th century belonged, was essentially financed by the English Church Missionary Society which, at the end of the 18th century, had been established first in Britain and then in other countries on the European continent. Any layperson was eligible for membership if he or she was prepared to support the "heathen mission" by paying fees and making further donations. Members would receive a regular issue of the society's newsletter containing reports about the activities and successes of the society out in the bush. The most successful of these missions were the Baptist Missionary Society (established 1792), the London Missionary Society (1795), the Higher Church Missionary Society (1799), the Basel Mission (1813), the Berlin Mission (1824), and the Rhineland Missionary Society (1928). It was imperative, of course, that the holy scriptures be translated into the languages current in the regions of missionary activity and that they be as widely distributed as possible. In order to procure the sizeable funds that were needed to do so, additional Bible societies were founded.

The Catholic Church was surprisingly hesitant about engaging in missionary activities in Africa, adding momentum to their operations only in the second half of the 19th century when the French colonial empire began to emerge. Missionary orders had long since been established. Long-standing French missions

Johann Ludwig Krapf is taken prisoner by Adara Billde, as described in Krapf's travel journal. From: *Land und Leute von Abessinien*, Leipzig, 1869.

included the Congregation of the Holiest Hearts of Jesus and Mary (the Picpus Fathers), established in 1805, and the Sisters of Joseph of Cluny (1807), whose founder, Mère Javouhey, is not only considered to be the pioneer of the Catholic mission in Africa, but also that of female disciples working overseas. In 1868 Archbishop Lavigerie founded the Society of Missionaries in Africa, better known as the White Fathers (Pères Blancs), an association of priests and brothers specifically focused on African missions. In 1869, he supplemented this society with the order of the White Sisters (Sœurs Blanches). The "White Fathers" society was soon the mainstay of the Catholic missionary assignment in Africa. During the 19th century, in addition to the orders themselves, many missionary associations were founded to support the formers' activities in Africa. They were established in quick succession in a number of western European countries. These orders and institutions answered to the central administration of the Vatican's Missionary Congregation in Rome.

Despite all the organizational effort and expenditure, success was minimal for some time. The missionaries were, after all, European, so their message was not readily accepted, but viewed with suspicion. It would, however, seem more than fitting to see their role as being that of colonialism's fifth column. Many, if not the majority, of them felt called to or destined for the work that they did. They invested heart and soul, attempting to alleviate the suffering of degraded and exploited native people and perpetually mediating between the people and officialdom. Many of them fared badly under the unaccustomed strains, paying for their dedication with their lives. Their work in the area of education deserves particular mention. In Rhodesia (today Zimbabwe) and Nyassaland (Malawi) they alone ran 90 percent of all schools. These schools taught their students more than general curricular subject matter; where possible they also instructed pupils on modern farming and agricultural methods and the state-of-the-art techniques of craftsmanship. A list of the first 100 Basel missionaries who were sent to the Gold Coast includes a remarkably high number of trained craftsmen. In addition to 13 merchants, it contains the names of ten farmers, 11 joiners, ten weavers, and six shoemakers, as well as several bakers, potters, locksmiths, glaziers, ropemakers, furriers, and blacksmiths. For many years afterward their workshops were highly renowned throughout the west coast of Africa. Had the goodwill and the merits of these missionaries not been a recognized fact, they would hardly have been allowed to stay on after independence and continue with their work.

As in Europe and other parts of the world, Christianity in Africa incorporated some of the local traditions. Community life was thus more deep-rooted, more colorful, and enjoyed a more creative variety than that of Christian communities at the time of the Apostles in the ancient Mediterranean countries. In some cases this led to the establishment of syncretistic churches.

René Grosseau celebrates mass before a figure of the Mother of God in Lac Nkoúe, Benin. He has worked as a missionary among the Tofinu for many years.

A Catholic cemetery, with the graves of colonial officials, in Grande Popo, Benin.

A Polish missionary celebrates mass in a church in Cameroon.

441

Christian missions and spiritual alienation

The northern and eastern parts of Africa were areas of advanced civilizations such as those of Egypt and of the city of Meroë, in Ethiopia. Access to the Mediterranean and to Asia was a contributing factor in this development. These complex cultural systems – societies in which much more occurred than just the cultivation of fields, hunting, and basic craftsmanship – had long ceased being governed by the whims of nature. The social inequalities between these cultures and those of neighboring regions led to war and subjugation, and later to the introduction of culture, religion, and the start of missionary-like activities.

The first Catholic mission in Lagos. From *Fetichism and Fetich Worshipers*, New York, 1885.

In these advanced civilizations, slavery was widespread and an acute awareness of the value of work and social status had already evolved – there was an institutionalized comprehension of superior and inferior status. The nature-oriented ways of less "developed" African societies was likely to be their downfall, as they were considered primitive. Exploitation, slavery, and impoverishment soon ensued. Christian missions later established themselves at the sensitive centers of power and religion, thus dissimulating the problem and achieving notable, if questionable, successes.

Power and the proliferation of power through the suppression of weaker communities are an inevitable aspect of patriarchal rule. This type of power is expressed by the brute force of the sword, and rhetoric is its ideological pendant. All documented religions (notably Judaism, Islam, and Christianity) have therefore been ideal tools with which to educate and discipline the subjects of a society in matters of citizenship and to firmly establish religious dogma. This approach would prove to be fatal for the true soul of Africa.

A fetish doctor shows Father Baudin his diploma. From: *Fetichism and Fetich Worshipers*, New York, 1885.

During the first century AD, Paul — on the path of righteousness since his experience on the road to Damascus — spread the word of Jesus of Nazareth. His popular teachings flourished in a heretical environment of rabbinical lateral thinkers and Essenian gnostics. Citing earlier gospels, Paul set out on the first missionary journey of early Christianity at the time of the Apostles. His teachings soon spread to North Africa. The Gospel was the word of God, good tidings for all who desired to abide by the principle of hope and the promise of deliverance and salvation that it contained. Many early Christians were people who, at a time of apocalyptic beliefs, no longer had anything to lose. In practical terms, this (in Paul's day) meant the promise of deliverance from Roman dominance. It was only in a second phase that the first advocates of this new salvation discovered the practicality of the prospect of salvation for fortifying communal morals. The notion of the hereafter – introduced in its initial form in Zoroastrian Persia in the 8th century BC and polarized into good and evil – required focusing on one's own path. At the end of such a road, judgment would be made on one's conduct. This notion was unfamiliar to nature-based religions, for they acted in response to natural phenomena. In contrast, Christianity is based on the prophetic word that prognosticates, warns, punishes, and tempts – with eternal salvation. For the first time, a religion speculated on "a good and a bad conscience," thus instilling into the minds of faithful souls a concept of guilt. This notion was closely linked to an important and easily extorted basic need of mankind: his sexuality.

The thing that made the Gospel so flexible right from the start was that it did not

A mission chapel. From: *Im Lande des Fetischs*, Basel, 1890.

require a code of authoritative law. Its followers were not meant to feel forced to do or refrain from doing anything. Many states thus did not consider their established systems of legal order to be in any way threatened, but felt at ease with the religion.

Shortly after he had negotiated an edict of tolerance in Milan in 313, Constantine the Great declared the teachings of the Christians to be the state religion of the Roman Empire, thus making it superfluous to undertake any further missionary assignment in many parts of the Near East and North Africa. It was these regions, Christianized under Byzantine dictate, that were converted to the teachings of Mohammed in an Islamic campaign of conversion in the mid-7th century. The Koran not only provides a religious basis, but also the basis for state law. It never differentiated between Church and State.

In contrast to Muslims, Christians did not officially see their mission as a holy war – with the exception of the seven Crusades launched by the Catholic Church in the West between 1096 and 1270. There did, however, always exist an official (and fatal) link between power, brutality, and missionary zeal.

The "discovery" of America in 1492 opened up new opportunities for the spread of Christianity. In an act of extraordinary arrogance, Christian conquistadors repressed and exploited the people, environment, and culture of the continent. They imposed the "new faith" through cruel punishment of those who resisted it. Having decimated the indigenous population, they established a slave trade, something that figures among history's greatest crimes against humanity, the primary scene of which became black Africa. The coasts of Africa (mainly West Africa) had been prepared by the Portuguese for overseas trading. They now served as a loading platform for hundreds of thousands of black people. North Africa played an important part in this era of slave trading. The Europeans found

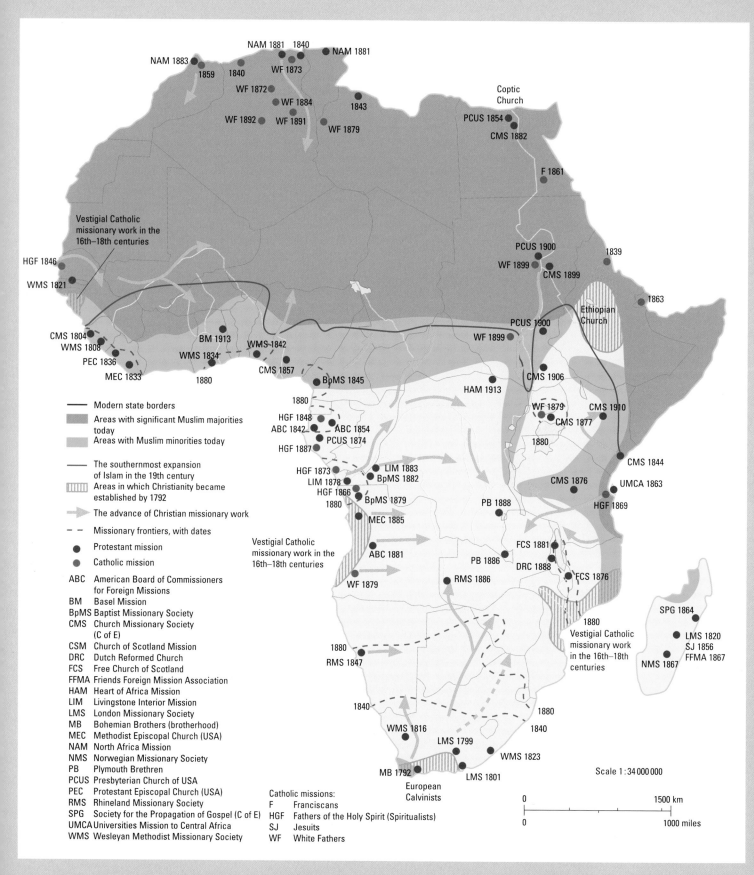

NAM 1881 1840
NAM 1883   NAM 1881
    1859   1840   WF 1873
            WF 1872
                   WF 1884   1843
        WF 1892   WF 1891
                    WF 1879

Coptic
Church

PCUS 1854
CMS 1882

F 1861

Vestigial Catholic
missionary work in the
16th–18th centuries

HGF 1846
WMS 1821

PCUS 1900   1839
WF 1899
    CMS 1899   1863

Ethiopian
Church

CMS 1804   BM 1913   PCUS 1900
WMS 1808   WMS 1842   WF 1899
PEC 1836   WMS 1834   CMS 1906
MEC 1833   CMS 1857   CMS 1910
        1880   BpMS 1845   HAM 1913   WF 1879
                   1880   CMS 1877
            HGF 1848   1880
            ABC 1842   ABC 1854   CMS 1844
                   PCUS 1874
            HGF 1887   CMS 1876
        HGF 1873   LIM 1883   UMCA 1863
        LIM 1878   BpMS 1882   PB 1888   HGF 1869
        HGF 1866
        1880   BpMS 1879
            MEC 1885   PB 1886   FCS 1881
                                              DRC 1888
Vestigial Catholic   RMS 1886   FCS 1876
missionary work in the   ABC 1881
16th–18th centuries   1880
        WF 1879   Vestigial Catholic
                                       missionary work
                                       in the 16th–18th
        1880   centuries
        RMS 1847

        1840   1880
                              1840

                    WMS 1816
                         LMS 1799
            MB 1792   WMS 1823
                    LMS 1801
            European
            Calvinists

SPG 1864
LMS 1820
SJ 1856
FFMA 1867
NMS 1867

Scale 1:34 000 000

0   1500 km
0   1000 miles

— Modern state borders

Areas with significant Muslim majorities
today

Areas with Muslim minorities today

— The southernmost expansion
of Islam in the 19th century

Areas in which Christianity became
established by 1792

⟶ The advance of Christian missionary work

‑ ‑ Missionary frontiers, with dates

● Protestant mission

● Catholic mission

ABC   American Board of Commissioners
      for Foreign Missions
BM   Basel Mission
BpMS Baptist Missionary Society
CMS   Church Missionary Society
      (C of E)
CSM   Church of Scotland Mission
DRC   Dutch Reformed Church
FCS   Free Church of Scotland
FFMA Friends Foreign Mission Association
HAM   Heart of Africa Mission
LIM   Livingstone Interior Mission
LMS   London Missionary Society
MB   Bohemian Brothers (brotherhood)
MEC   Methodist Episcopal Church (USA)
NAM   North Africa Mission
NMS   Norwegian Missionary Society
PB   Plymouth Brethren
PCUS Presbyterian Church of USA
PEC   Protestant Episcopal Church (USA)
RMS   Rhineland Missionary Society
SPG   Society for the Propagation of Gospel (C of E)
UMCA Universities Mission to Central Africa
WMS   Wesleyan Methodist Missionary Society

Catholic missions:
F   Franciscans
HGF   Fathers of the Holy Spirit (Spiritualists)
SJ   Jesuits
WF   White Fathers

the North Africans, who had a background of slave trading, to be willing and capable suppliers of slaves. Slaves were hunted down like animals; sometimes whole families were captured. The Portuguese, English, and Dutch would pick them up, pay badly for them, and ship them in huge numbers chiefly to Brazil and the United States. This continued for centuries. Yet the indescribable suffering of black people was becoming known to an ever-increasing number of people. A new era in humanitarian thinking prompted strong opposition among Christians in Europe. It was also to reform the missionary idea. The philosophy of the 18th-century English, French, and German Enlightenment as well as the strong influence of religious groups were the deciding factors in support of such change. These societal reforms led to the Bill of Rights, the French Revolution, and ultimately to the secularization of central Europe. Slave trading was considered dubious and was stigmatized. Thus pressurized, European governments banned the trade in humans, without, however, actually stopping slavery as such. In the midst of Napoleonic expansion, a fundamental change in the Catholic landscape came in 1803. The separation of Church and State in a secularized Europe had repercussions for black Africa's future.

The Church saw itself materially and ideologically deprived of its influence in central Europe and recognized the opportunities of the emerging enthusiasm for Africa. It quoted Rousseau, who had laid the foundation for a new "veneration of the primitive" by redefining man and nature and thus also helping to create an emancipated attitude toward children. Gotthold Lessing (1729–81) developed new views on child-raising. Africa became an environment for fieldwork and the target of missionaries. But Africa was a virgin continent that had not even been mapped, let alone made accessible. The North American pioneering spirit would now prove to be a fillip for the Old World. New theories of statehood as well as the Industrial Revolution brought forth colonialism, the impact of which had yet to be borne by the maltreated and yet endlessly rich continent of Africa.

European religious culture that Christian missions attempted to instill in them stood in stark contrast to the traditions of the African people. Thus it was that, in the name of Christianity, exploitation and aid, the uprooting of religion, and cultural alienation combined to produce tragedy on a continental scale. At the beginning of the 19th century, the established churches had merged the promise of salvation with the concept of charity. Civil and academic education as well as medical care now constituted the main part of their mission. A network of Christian facilities spread out over black Africa and continued to dictate Western values, irrespective of the actual needs of black Africans. The Congo, Burundi, and Rwanda were almost entirely Catholicized. What the missionaries were unable to accomplish was achieved by those now returning home, "liberated," mainly from Brazil, where they had been living for generations as converted Christians and whose beliefs were deeply engrained. Generally, it was easier for them to reach the black peoples, despite the fact that, here too, a rift had developed due to cultural alienation. This often led to conflict, for many of those who returned vaunted an air of superiority, thus laying themselves open to inescapable comparison with the white man and his supremacist attitude.

The Anglican Church, predominantly represented by the English Church Missionary Society, which had been active since 1806, had established itself in the British colonies as had the Dutch Reformed Church in South Africa. In 1787, English abolitionists, decided opponents of slavery, proclaimed a kind of state in the region of present-day Sierra Leone, in which liberated slaves from the New World would find refuge.

In the German colonies, Catholic and Lutheran influence reigned. But independent churches had also extended their influence throughout the colonies. In Ghana, Nigeria, the Congo, Kenya, and Zimbabwe, they mixed established Christian religions with folkloric tradition. The unremitting efforts of the missions to instill into Africans the fear of God, diligence, humility, and gratitude served the purposes of those who saw in Africa a land of exploitable resources. The industrialization of European societies had brought with it structural change. These societies now focused on the natural resources Africa had to offer: tin, copper, and oil. A new form of slavery emerged, and Christian missions provided the ideological basis. Together with corrupt regimes and with a functioning infrastructure at their disposal, they constituted an important cog in the system of exploitation. Huge railway and canal projects, mining, and oil drilling exhausted thousands of black workers and destroyed their homes and environments. The Christian missions, with their assignment to educate, could not, or would not halt this development. Most African states, demarcated by arbitrarily drawn borders, increasingly focused on attaining self-determination and independence. Education, vocational training, and medical care were put under state control and the influence of missionary institutions reduced. By the 1960s most African states had achieved independence.

One of the fundamental, postcolonial objectives of black Africa was to rediscover its roots, by then reduced to no more than mere folklore. This did not, however, imply that all things white were to be thrown overboard. The people wanted to revive their cultural identity, their true soul, which had suffered immensely but which had not been forgotten. Those who fully accept nature and its conditions will live a pleasurable and harmonious life: this was their philosophy of life. Their concept of matter and of the spirits with which their souls are endowed is part of a spiritual communication network that required neither the written nor the spoken word. Ritual thinking determined their everyday lives. The notion of salvation was, is, and will likely continue to be a strange concept for Africans.

Herbert Köhler

Black slaves for the New World

To separate people from their families by force, rob them of their freedom, hold them captive like animals, and then further exploit their labor with no form of remuneration, is a crime against humanity that is as old as it is cruel. Even traditional societies might capture members of neighboring tribes in order to compensate for losses within their own group. This fate, however, only ever came upon a few, who were then used as house slaves. Larger numbers would have required not only space and feeding, but also adequate monitoring. Generally speaking, house slaves were not badly off. They were kept within the home, or at least close to it; they ate and worked as did their masters; they could even marry (although normally only within their own ranks) and have families of their own. They simply remained in bondage – with the occasional exception of those youths who were adopted by families who had no sons of their own or had lost their sons in battle (a practice common among Native Americans).

This was in stark contrast to what regularly occurred in the vicinity of advanced civilizations. In these regions, there had always been great demand for slave labor. Even in modern times, there are transitional regions of this kind (for example on the Indian subcontinent and South East Asia) where a relatively harmless form of house slavery has been known to turn into open slave trading. Prisoners, or even members of a community who have committed a crime or have otherwise fallen from grace, were sold to traders. This was, however, something only men in powerful positions could afford to do. Slave trading generally required the existence of local suppliers.

In all early developed civilizations, slaves were an important economic factor. They were used for house and field work, as court servants, and palace guards. Their main use, however, was to provide building labor (for channels, fortifications, roads, palaces, and pyramids). Slaves were obtained chiefly through war and conquest, although trade also played a role. Even in early times it was said that the Carthaginians and Romans used the Sahara trade belt to procure not only precious African timbers,

Slaves were used to carry loads.
From *Westafrika. Vom Senegal bis Benguela*, Leipzig, 1878.

ivory, and gold, but also slaves. Wealthy Romans used slaves on their estates (*latifundia*), the advantage being that they were not liable to serve in war. Greek slaves were used as home teachers and secretaries. The practice of slave-keeping continued in Western Europe through the Middle Ages. The victims were often Welsh, Irish, and Scandinavian. Most, however, were taken prisoner during wars with eastern neighbors – Turks and predominantly Slavs who were then sold to the Islamic kingdoms in the eastern Mediterranean and North Africa. Many a port town profited considerably from the slave trade. The origins of the word "slave" (from Slav, meaning "captive") in all European languages is no coincidence. Slaves made up 15 percent of the overall population of approximately 22.6 million Europeans.

A similar situation existed in Byzantium and Islamic lands during the Middle Ages, and among the Ottoman Turks. Mass slavery was also a traditional part of life in the ancient Arabian kingdoms. Like the Romans, the Arabs distinguished between house slaves and field slaves. Some were assigned privileged duties as cooks, servants, doormen, guards, secretaries, or teachers. Female slaves might join a harem as concubines or

In a slave caravan, slaves were kept chained together day and night covering long distances on foot. From: *Die Völker der Erde*, Würzburg and Vienna, 1891.

Weak slaves who would slow down the caravan are massacred. From: *Die Völker der Erde*, Würzburg and Vienna, 1891.

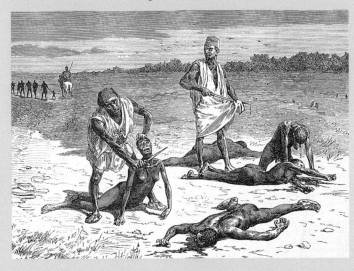

Cover page of the account of the life of Captain Canot who dealt in gold, ivory, and slaves.

When, in the mid-15th century, the Portuguese began to travel along the coast of West Africa in search of gold, they soon set up a scheme that would richly reward them but that was to have grave consequences. On the stretch of coastline between the deltas of the Volta and Niger – that is, on the Slave Coast – they bought slaves from the hinterland of what is today Nigeria, shipped them to the ports of modern day Ghana, and traded them in for gold on the Gold Coast. Not all of them, though. Some they kept with the intention of selling them to the owners of the sugar cane plantations on the Canary Islands or to European aristocrats as curiosities. Several decades later, at the end of the 15th century, when they reached the east coast of Africa, they encountered the Arabs' flourishing slave trade. Quickly able to bring the coastal towns under their control, they took over this highly profitable business. Moreover, it seemed that their timing had been perfect. The "discovery" of the New World meant that the demand for slaves as well as their sale price were perpetually increasing. African labor was urgently needed in the silver mines of Mexico and Peru and the cotton, tobacco, and sugar cane plantations of European planters in North, Central, and

secondary wives. Again, house slaves in particular were not necessarily maltreated. They could marry (within their own ranks); their children, although remaining unfree, grew up together with those of their masters. Several sections in the Koran even warn Muslims to treat their slaves well; their release was considered a creditable deed. Yet slave trading as it was practiced by Arab merchants – at first chiefly in the eastern part of Africa – was anything but pious.

South America. The Portuguese were hard put to keep up with demand. Around 200 years later, the sultan of Oman, with the support of the Swahili, managed to drive them from the central eastern coast of Africa and to regain control of the slave trade. Their clientele, however, remained unchanged. In 1770 alone, around 1,000 slaves were shipped overseas.

But the Portuguese did have another iron in the fire. They now intensified slave trading on the Angolan coast. Luanda (founded in 1575) and Benguela (founded in 1617) soon developed into prosperous towns. Countless slaves were dispatched to the New World from there, notably to Brazil. During the 18th century approximately 1.4 million people were "exported" in this way.

The biggest sacrifice was probably made by the countries of West Africa, although trading was vigorously supported by local potentates who made no small profit from their involvement. Both coastal towns and hinterland kingdoms soon enjoyed an enormous economic boom. Dahomey was one of the kingdoms at the forefront of this era of prosperity. Between 1687 and 1702, an average of 15,000 slaves a year were shipped out from the ports of the Slave Coast. Having achieved wealth, local rulers could now themselves afford to keep larger numbers of slaves. Veritable armies of them were used to work the plantations, and were given to noblemen as gifts or to officers as a reward for their services. "Crown slaves" served in the army, worked as bodyguards or in administrative positions, or were even used

Slave ship. From: *Westafrika. Vom Senegal bis Benguela*, Leipzig, 1878.

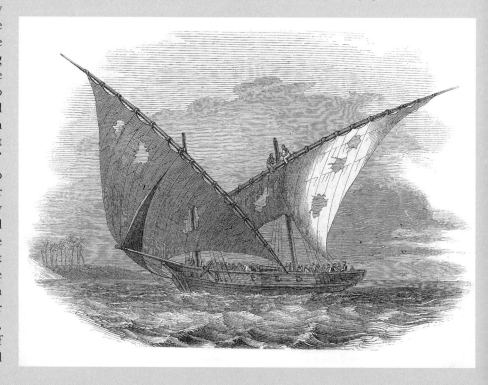

Slaves in the 'tween deck.
From: *Westafrika. Vom Senegal bis Benguela*, Leipzig, 1878.

as diplomatic messengers – that is, they were often given positions of exceptional responsibility, though without relinquishing their status as slaves. Again, they were permitted to marry only other slaves, and their children remained the possession of their masters.

The transatlantic slave trade had its heyday in the second half of the 18th century – one of the most abysmal eras of atrocity in the history of mankind. The fact that a slave had no rights whatsoever was a circumstance resulting from social uprooting. Stripped of all family ties, slaves had neither status nor protection, became total strangers, mere commodities offered and traded at markets like farm animals. In Dahomey in 1788, the price of a male slave was 11 ounces of gold. By comparison 36 bottles of liquor were worth three ounces; 16 pieces of fine linen, two ounces; two pieces of jewelry, 40 lb of cowry shells, 16 ells of silk, one piece of cotton fabric, eight bars of iron, and one roll of Brazilian tobacco, one ounce each. From 1740 to 1797, 77 percent of slaves from Dahomey were traded for tobacco, liquor, and textiles, 21.4 percent for cowry snails, gold, coral, and silk, 1.1 percent for bars of metal, and only 0.5 percent for weapons

and gunpowder. The total number of slaves exported from Africa to the New World is estimated at just under 12 million – an abstract figure that gives no hint of the countless individual fates, the unimaginable suffering, and the atrocities involved. This is no doubt the largest-scale crime against humanity ever recorded.

Criticism did, however, begin to rise in 1800. The English Free Church of the Quakers, Methodists, and Baptists played an essential role in the opposition movement. They, and other philanthropists along with them, regularly met with like-minded parliamentarians at the Clapham Sect, a kind of club that was to achieve a position of central importance within the British movement for the abolition of slavery. In 1787, Britain had already founded the colony of Freetown in Sierra Leone, a settlement where liberated slaves of African origin found refuge. The establishment of this colony cost Britain the proud sum of £20 million. The hinterland became a British protectorate in 1896. Today, the descendants of former slaves make up around

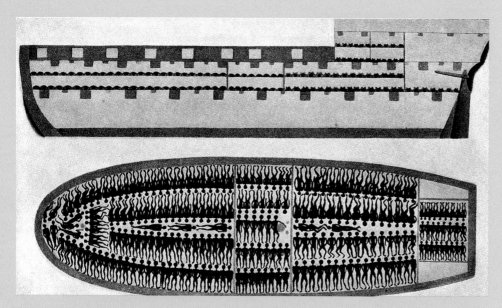

Accommodation plan for "black freight" on a slave ship destined for overseas. From: *Adventures of an African Slaver*, London, 1928.

apprenticeship, labor, and adoption contracts, until 1949.

Meanwhile, it was not until the mid-19th century that a true picture of circumstances in the African interior was revealed to ordinary people around the world, by Scottish missionary and explorer David Livingstone. Many were shocked by his deeply moving accounts of Arab and Portuguese slave hunting, in which native groups and local potentates were often involved (as a means of procuring guns). Livingstone wrote about slaves who were left to die when they could no longer do what was demanded of them: they were tied to trees or abandoned in the dirt by the wayside. In 1866, he visited the slave market of Zanzibar. "The adults," he noted in his diary, "all appear to feel shameful about being displayed for sale like livestock. Their teeth are examined, clothing lifted up to examine their lower limbs, and sticks thrown for them to retrieve so that potential buyers can be given an exhibit of their gait. Some are taken by the hand and pulled through the crowds, their price called out over and over. The buyers were mostly Arabs from the north or Persians."

When, several decades later, slavery had been curbed and considerably reduced, it reemerged in another form. The decline of the business of human trafficking had initially plunged the

two percent of the total population. The British parliament was not, however, inclined to support the cause of abolition until Britain had lost its colonies in North America and English planters were no longer directly affected. In North America itself, slavery was an issue of decided controversy, despite the fact that the Declaration of Independence of 1776 had made much of equality and the inalienable rights of all people. But black people were not really considered "true" specimens of mankind. Denmark – a country with the least to loose – set the course of abolition in motion by banning slave trading in 1789. England followed suit in 1807, and France in 1830. Slavery itself, however, was not banned in England until 1834 and in France not until 1848.

Of course, neither slave trading nor the holding of slaves was actually stopped altogether. The Arabs did not feel bound by resolutions passed by Europeans, and the Portuguese simply ignored them. The French likewise continued with the business until the Catholic Church, in the person of Cardinal Lavigerie (1824–92), supported by Pope Leo XIII (1878–1903), stepped in and finally, toward the end of the 19th century, managed to enforce the ban on slave trading – at least within the confines of French national territories. Soon after this achievement, Brazil also abolished both slave trading and the holding of slaves (in 1888) – at least according to law. While slavery was officially abolished in China in 1911, it continued to exist, in the guise of

The trade routes for slaves, sugar, tobacco, and cheap goods. From: *A History of West Africa, 1000–1800*, Harlob, U.K., 1965.

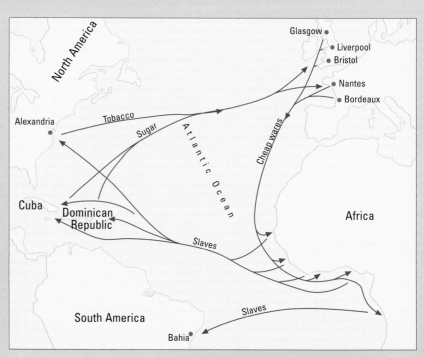

450

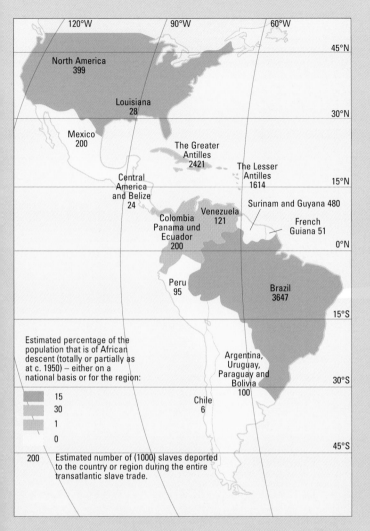

The African diaspora in the New World (after Curtin).
From: *Cultural Atlas of Africa*, Augsburg, 1998.

In the map:

North America 399
Louisiana 28
Mexico 200
The Greater Antilles 2421
The Lesser Antilles 1614
Central America and Belize 24
Surinam and Guyana 480
Colombia Panama und Ecuador 200
Venezuela 121
French Guiana 51
Peru 95
Brazil 3647
Argentina, Uruguay, Paraguay and Bolivia 100
Chile 6

Estimated percentage of the population that is of African descent (totally or partially as at c. 1950) – either on a national basis or for the region:

15
30
1
0

200 Estimated number of (1000) slaves deported to the country or region during the entire transatlantic slave trade.

In some cases the results were devastating. Large regions of western Sudan were forced to make a rapid change from their old subsistence economy, which supported nothing more than local needs, to money-based market economies, which forced them to become dependent on world market trends. Thousands of seasonal workers left the interior to work on plantations located in coastal regions. Others were forcibly recruited by the colonial powers (sometimes with brutal ruthlessness) – for example, by press gangs consisting of police or military units that virtually snatched people away and set them to work on public projects in faraway locations. In all cases, the work performed by the indigenous population was extremely hard labor, at times even a danger to life (in the mines, for instance), and the pay they received abominably low. During the construction of the railroad connecting Brazzaville to the coast in the years 1925 to 1932, thousands of forced laborers – some of them brought down from the north – lost their lives. In the Portuguese colonies of Angola and Mozambique, where the colonies' "own" labor forces were put to the services of Rhodesia (now Zimbabwe) and South Africa, the mortality rate was approximately 40 percent. Again, these are abstract figures that veil the terrible fate of all those laborers and the families they left behind. "Classic" slavery had now given way to "domestic" slavery.

When those African countries eventually gained independence, their people became neither freer nor richer. Still today, many people literally take themselves to market. They make up veritable armies of day laborers, working immigrants, seamen, mercenaries, and prostitutes.

coastal countries of West Africa into an economic crisis, albeit one that would prove to be short-lived. The progressive industrialization of Europe meant there was a growing demand for raw materials. First, palm oil was in high demand for the production of soap. Then, when a process for manufacturing margarine was developed in France in 1870, palm seeds (or rather the fat contained in them) became the object of desire. Peanut, coffee bean, and cacao crops were increasingly being cultivated in the coastal regions so that the Gold Coast (Ghana) went on to become the world's largest producer of cacao. Mining became increasingly significant. Tin was mined in Nigeria (on the Jos Plateau); diamonds in Angola; diamonds and manganese on the Gold Coast; copper, gold, diamonds, and cobalt in Katanga. The Congo experienced a boom in demand for rubber. Fine timbers, which had been traded since ancient times, were now being mechanically extracted in large numbers. These mining, felling, and cultivation operations made it necessary to improve the infrastructure in the regions concerned. Roads, ports, and, above all, railroads, were built.

The slave fort at Cape Coast Castle, Ghana, was the most important British stronghold on the Gold Coast. It was built on the foundations of the former Swedish Carlsberg during the second half of the 17th century.

"Tell Daddy, we are all happy under British rule"

The "discovery" of Africa was, from the outset, driven by commercial interests rather than by the curiosity to explore. For hundreds of years, gold, fine timbers, ivory, and slaves were brought to the Mediterranean and northern Europe. Their conveyance was complicated, involving many stages and pushing prices to ever-greater heights. When, during the 15th century, advances in shipbuilding produced vessels better able to withstand the rigors of the high seas, this was an additional incentive to make straight for the country producing the desirable goods. Thus the seafaring nations of Europe, led by Portugal, began to establish trading posts at suitable coastal locations. Where necessary, these were fortified by small armies of watchmen.

A turning point came when the industrialization of Europe increased during the late 19th century. The demand for raw materials grew, competition increased, and opportunities to trade outside Europe were sought. Overseas resources, including those of Africa, became the object of competition. Networks of national trading posts evolved, contracts were drawn up with native rulers to safeguard individual interests in the face of competition, troop stations were built to guard trading posts and their trading connections, and individual trading facilities merged to form large trading conglomerates. Among the more prominent of these were the South Africa

Cape Coast Castle. From: *Westafrika. Vom Senegal bis Benguela*, Leipzig, 1878.

Company, the British East African Company, and the Niger Company on the British side; the German Deutsch-Ostafrikanische Gesellschaft; the Portuguese Companhia do Nyassa and Companhia de Moçambique; and the French Compagnie Française de l'Afrique Equatoriale, Compagnie Française de l'Afrique Occidentale, and Société de l'Ouest Africain. These companies were granted the necessary rights of utilization and sovereignty by their respective governments. The African people themselves were not consulted.

A bird's eye view of the European trade fort and the king's palace in Xavier, Sabi. J. von Schley, 1760.

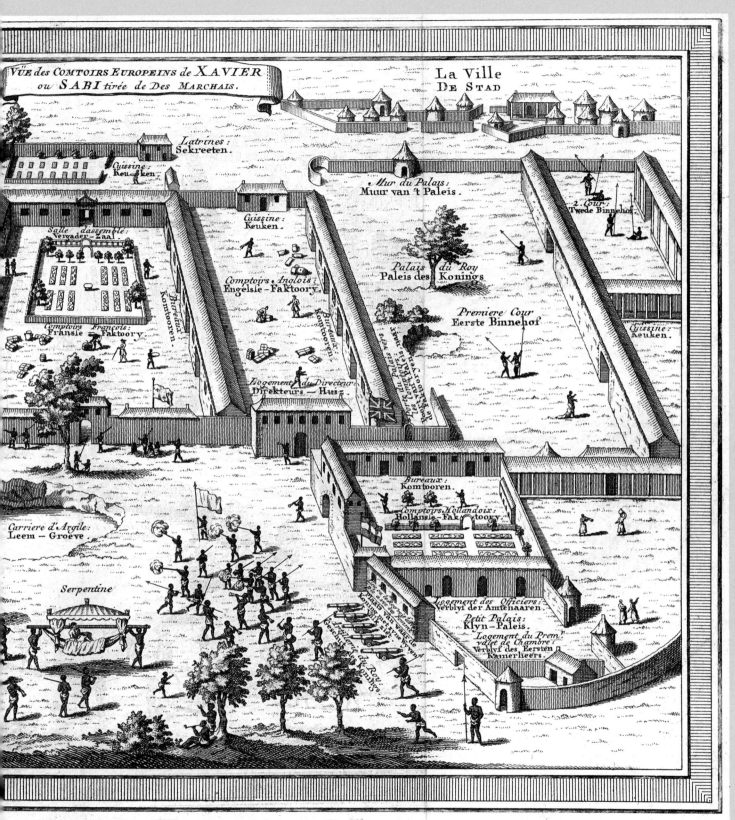

Vüe des Comtoirs Europeins de XAVIER ou SABI tirée de Des Marchais.

La Ville DE STAD

Latrines: Sekreeten.

Cuissine: Keuken.

Cuissine: Keuken.

Mur du Palais: Muur van 't Paleis.

2. Cour Twede Binnehof

Salle d'assemble: Verrader-Zaal.

Comptoirs Anglois: Engelsche-Faktoory.

Bureau Komtooren

Palais du Roy Paleis des Konings

Cuissine: Keuken.

Comptoirs François: Fransie-Faktoory.

Bureaux Komtooren

Première Cour Eerste Binnehof

Logement du Directeur: Direkteurs-Huis.

Carriere d'Argile: Leem-Groeve.

Serpentine

Bureaux: Komtooren.

Comptoirs Hollandois: Hollanse-Faktoory.

Logement des Officiers: Verblyf der Amtenaaren.

Petit Palais: Klyn-Paleis.

Logement du Prem.r valet de Chambre: Verblyf des Eersten Kamerheers.

TOORYEN, te XAVIER of SABI, uit Des Marchais.

453

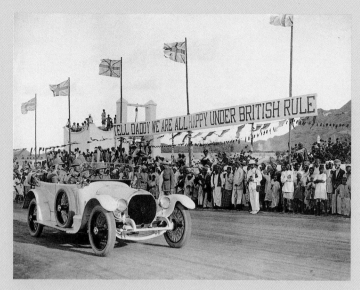

The Prince of Wales is driven past a huge banner. The message asked him to tell his father, King George VI, that the people were happy under British rule.

These companies aimed to make maximum profits with minimum investment and in the shortest possible time. This resulted in overexploitation of the land and its people. Inevitably, conflicts with the local population ensued – particularly as these companies often intruded into the interior by force. In other cases, disputes between firms and the authorities, or inner-African wars would interfere with commercial operations. Consuls – who often introduced customs systems of their own and who kept mercenary guards for their protection – could occasionally mediate in such conflicts. However, in more serious cases, such as uprisings, they could not. Their own countries were increasingly called upon to provide military intervention to protect the merchant groups. This led to the establishment of protectorates in which regular colonial troops were stationed to keep the peace and ensure order.

The tendency to expand these regions so as to beat off rival European competition for territory, and also to create and lay claim to new settlement zones, was to be expected. Officially, land designated part of a colonial territory was claimed to be "unowned." Thus a German "Introduction to Colonial Policy" issued in 1908 claimed that "No further proof is required for the fact that securing suitable locations for the settlement of excess populations from the booming developing nations of Europe while maintaining the nationality of settlers would remain an important policy factor." For a small country such as Portugal, this step was of deciding importance.

The Prince of Wales is driven past a huge banner. The message asked him to tell his father, King George VI, that the people were happy under British rule.

Those who could afford to joined in the race; smaller nations such as Denmark and Holland withdrew from Africa. Uprisings were an ideal excuse to step in and take command of a region. In 1874, for example, the Asante on the Gold Coast challenged the British; they were defeated and their land declared a British protectorate that same year. When the British requested that the Gold Chair – the most sacred symbol of the kingdom – be handed over, this incited a rebellion that ultimately led to the annexation of the territory, henceforth considered a crown colony. In 1897, the city of Benin, capital of the old kingdom of Benin in southern Nigeria, was subjected to war and pillage on the grounds of similar acts of "unfriendliness."

The French could not idly watch English expansion. The military was keen to establish a mighty colonial empire modeled on British India. Since the old warehouses on the coast were already under the control of the ministry of naval affairs in Paris, it made sense to place the new strategy of imperial rule in the hands of the navy. In two simultaneous campaigns, the French advanced into the Congo and, from Senegal, into inner Sudan. Before their victory in Sudan, however, they suffered several defeats. Guinea became an autonomous colony in 1891, Ivory Coast in 1893, and the Sudan in 1899. These countries united to form the federations of French West Africa (AOF) and Equatorial Africa (AEF). France now reigned over a colonial empire that

At the market in Lagos in 1956, women crowd around a portrait of Queen Elizabeth II, who had arrived to tour Nigeria.

The white colonial rulers feared getting wet because of the probable worm infections. Therefore, they let themselves be carried through the water by the so-called native "taxi-service." Photo 1930.

rule over the other, less endowed peoples of the world. Cecil Rhodes (1853–1902), who was Prime Minister of the Cape Colony from 1890 to 1896 and who expanded British "colonial ownership" in southeastern Africa from Bechuanaland to the land later to be given his name (Rhodesia), once said, "I contend that we are the finest race in the world and that the more of the world we inhabit the better it is for the human race. What a dream! And yet the realization of it is possible." This conviction even had repercussions on Britain's kinsmen in the United States. An American senator, Albert J. Beveridge, offered the maxim that "We are a conquering race. We must follow what our blood dictates." He also stated the true aims of colonialism as being "to take into possession new markets and, where necessary, new lands." Doubtless mindful of the circumstances in his own country, he further explained that "Our cleverness in the art of governing is a God-given skill with which to administer over wild and servile peoples." The Germans and French were similarly convinced of their own position in the universal scheme of things – the former making reference to the Supreme Being himself, the latter deeming themselves to be destined to carry the banner of enlightenment, social reform, liberty, humanity, and the advancement of civilization.

In practice, however, these countries went their separate ways. Britain adhered to the principle of indirect rule. Although not implemented in India, this was applied in Nigeria and then

Preparing for a visit by the Prince of Wales: students of the Kericho School in Kenya wash themselves.

spanned in a powerful arch from Dakar to Chad and all the way to the mouth of the Congo.

The Portuguese also had ambitious plans. Angola was to become a second Brazil, since the latter had "fallen away" in 1822. However, the rewards for their efforts were meager. Only a few coffee planters settled in the central highlands. Commercial activity was dominated by traders. Conferences held subsequent to the Berlin Conference of 1884/85 aimed to mark the boundaries of each European power's sovereign territory. Portugal, economically flagging and ridden with internal crises, was lucky to be spared any loss. It remained largely unscathed which was due mainly to the disunity and conflict apparent among its rivals.

Colonialism did not, however, thrive on economic and power-based motives alone. It also had more noble aims. The larger European powers, at least, were imbued with a sort of national religious missionary zeal. In England, this tendency became apparent in 17th- and 18th-century literature. The English motherland was glorified as a stronghold of freedom. Its Protestant religion was deemed free of fault and devoid of superstition; its people considered themselves to have been elected by heaven to

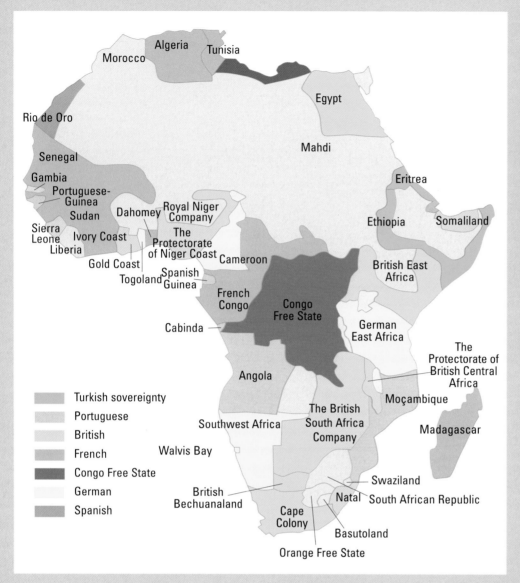

Map of the colonial territories in Africa at the end of the 19th century.

colonies than within the British. Small hamlets, for instance, were combined to form larger settlements so as to make them more easy to administrate and to increase production. Individual villages, each represented by a *chef de village*, were united to form cantons with *chefs de canton* (either local native people or sometimes people from other parts). These were in turn united to form *cercles* (districts) headed by French administrative officers. The Portuguese governed in much the same way. Their administration was overseen by the *governador*. He ruled over *administradores*, the highest administrative officials, who were granted all powers of sovereignty (military, administrative, and judicial), and who imposed taxes, assigned public work, conducted censuses, and monitored local native leaders.

These administrations were by no means easy to run. The imposition of taxes in particular (either in kind or in currency), but also the growing obligation to use forced labor were constant sources of conflict, even of rebellion and uprising, that regularly necessitated punitive expeditions against individual communities. Entire villages and their harvests would be reduced to ashes or widespread suppression would be enforced by way of a concentrated military effort. In an attempt to prevent incidents of this kind occurring, the colonial powers implemented a policy of assimilation. In the British colonies, this constituted offering apparently "suitable" native individuals a chance to receive vocational training and be employed within the administration. The idea was to provide the prerequisites for self-administration and to create political awareness. In contrast, the Portuguese and the French understood this policy to mean administrative integration and acquainting local populations with their respective forms of society. The Portuguese maintained the most open approach. Those able to achieve the status of an *assimilado* were granted all the privileges of Portuguese citizenship. This, of

throughout West and East Africa. There could be no other way of governing such vast expanses of territory and millions of people of varying linguistic and cultural background, while keeping expenditure and staffing to a minimum. For purely pragmatic reasons it was advisable not to dismantle existing structures and forms of rule, but to build on local systems. The deciding rights of sovereignty – in particular police powers and systems of taxation – did, however, remain in the hands of British residents. "There are no two sets of rulers – British and native – but a single government," it was declared. The French, on the other hand, favored an administration based on their tried-and-tested form of home rule – the centralized principle of direct administration. According to the French constitution, the French parliament in Paris was the only body permitted to make laws for the colonies. Restructuring was undertaken on a larger scale within the French

course, entailed forfeiting all traditional ties, converting to Christianity, being fluent in Portuguese, adopting a European lifestyle, and having served a term of impeccable military service. In view of the state of the education system in the colonies (even in Portugal itself illiteracy was still high) and the costs associated with any form of continuing education and training, only a handful of individuals were ever in a position to achieve this goal. In the 20th century, when conflicts began to intensify and World War I weighed heavy on the nations of Europe, the "policy of association" was introduced. Based on an element of additional autonomy for the colonized peoples, this left them to follow their traditional culture, that is, bound them to the colonial powers by nothing more than association. However, the policy aroused suspicion among the colonized populations, who felt they were to be kept in a state of underdevelopment so they could be further suppressed and exploited. The change did, in fact, mean legalizing racial apartheid and maintaining the status quo with forced labor and the relentless exploitation of natural resources.

Tensions grew. There was also, by now, a marked increase in the number of Africans who had received a Western education. The members of this social group were aware of their common interests and began to organize themselves. These educated Africans worked mostly as government officials and clerks, teachers, journalists, and businessmen, and freelance in the larger, mostly seaport, towns. They saw their adversaries not only in the colonial powers, but equally in the representatives of their own traditional elite who had little ambition to change things. To some extent this ruling class even worked hand in hand with the colonial powers, profiting well, but by the same token losing authority among their own people. Those who began to oppose this state of affairs assembled in small groups, where ethnic affiliation was of little relevance. Initially, their aims went no further than demanding moderate reforms that would improve living conditions and provide better education and training, and make higher offices more generally accessible. Colonial rule itself was not yet questioned.

When these groups received little response to their proposals, this soon changed. The huge disparities between black people and whites with regard to the distribution of wealth and to rights encouraged the view that colonial rule was a capitalistic system used purely to exploit the peoples over which it ruled. The urban intelligentsia formed transregional parties with political agendas. The echelons of leadership within these parties became more rigidly organized, often reflecting socialist models. Youth societies and women's associations, professional bodies and trade unions issued increasingly tougher demands; the call for independence grew louder. Demonstrations, strikes, and boycotts were organized and met with severe resistance. But the developments set in motion could no longer be halted. In the end, the colonial powers had no choice but to yield to them.

Colonialism did have some positive effects. It paved the way for the colonized nations to enter modern times, albeit by the implementation of objectionable means and despite the fact that such an outcome was unintended. Pacification contributed to the development of national infrastructures. Administrative bodies, schools, sanitary services, and modern communications systems were created, and even remote areas enjoyed economic development. The colonial powers showed no interest in industrializing their colonies since this, it was assumed, would mean losing markets to which they could sell their goods in future. Their reasoning failed to consider the fact that such economic interaction could only evolve if future consumers had a use for Western industrial goods – and this in turn required that they be sufficiently assimilated. Yet the doctrine of association forbade this.

The newly independent states were built on the foundations of a promising practical infrastructure. Real and lasting damage had, however, been done by the humiliation the people had suffered – wounds cut deep into the flesh of the people of colonial Africa by racism. Africa suffered more harshly from this phenomenon than any other region of the world. A huge debt has yet to be settled.

Above and below: Stock shares in French and Belgian colonial trading companies.

A notice of the "Types of Mankind"

It was not necessarily the bodily features of black Africans that Caucasians from Europe often considered to be repulsively ugly, but their facial features, as they were so very different from their own. To white men, these features seemed "animal-like," even "ape-like." At best, they were willing to concede that some of the women were exceptionally well proportioned, with a statuesque beauty and the lithe movements of a big cat. Their black-as-night outward features were thought to conceal a deeper darkness of the spirit. Discouraged missionaries lamented these people's "irresistible urge to steal and tell lies," their "lack of any sense of

But for the color of their skin, these figures of a British officer and his wife, made in about 1914, are exact replicas of the colon figures of the Ewe (Ghana). The pith helmet and tight-fitting uniform of the colonial European are symbols of power and are characteristic of most of these figures. European women are far less frequently portrayed than men. The name colon (colonist) was somewhat disrespectfully given to French immigrants who settled in the African colonies by their countrymen in France.

shame," and their "perpetual willingness to indulge in any form of instinct-driven pleasure," namely their "laxity in the sexual arena." Even in their textbook *The Types of Mankind*, published in 1854, American anthropologists J. C. Nott and G. R. Gliddon found that Africa was populated by a people "whose mind is as dark as their skin, and whose skull formation lets any hope of future improvement appear to be mere utopian reverie." It was irritating, however, to find that the palms of their hands and the soles of their feet were so strangely light-colored. Luis Bernado Honwana is an African writer from Mozambique. Born in 1942, he attended a school in Lisbon, Lourenço Marques (today Maputo), studied law, and went on to become a reporter and short-story writer. He recalls how many Portuguese attempted to explain this astonishing phenomenon. One of his teachers speculated that but a few centuries ago Africans were still

A more recent colon figure from Benin, made in 1998. It was placed on top of a Mami Wata altar so as to guard it. This broad-shouldered figure, with black facial features, tie and pith helmet stands to attention, in an attitude unfamiliar among Africans, his hands against the seams of his trousers – just like a well-drilled European colonial soldier. His gaze looks beyond the visible world; witches and malevolent spirits of which humans are unaware are likely to approach at any time. The divinities of the cult community protect their followers against these evils.

A colon figure from Togo, made in about 1930. It is used to guard an altar dedicated to Mami Wata, goddess of water.

crawling on all fours like wild animals, which accounted for the fact their palms and soles had been protected from the effects of the sun. Then there was a woman who was convinced that God had made the palms of the black man's hands white so that they would not soil the food that they had to prepare for their white masters. One Senhor Frias considered all this to be utter nonsense. In his opinion, the following was true: "When God had finished creating mankind, he invited man to bathe in a heavenly lake. After this bath, all men were beautiful and white. The Blacks, however, had been created in the early hours of the morning. Because the water in the lake was very cold at this time of day, they only washed the palms of their hands and the soles of their feet before dressing and descending to earth."

Caught up in their complacency, Europeans did not consider that Africans might think them just as strange. Henry Morton Stanley (1841–1904), who "found" the missing explorer Dr. David Livingstone in 1871, experienced this himself, but evidently did not draw any conclusions from it. In his travel log he noted: "Looking at this row of faces, I could only quietly remark to myself: ugly, uglier, and the ugliest of all. Then I look at their dirty, naked bodies, at the enormously large, udderlike, low-hanging breasts of the womenfolk and their indecent overall nakedness and I summarize everything decorum would allow me

to say and which would sufficiently describe it with a single cry of 'horrid'! And how strange they smell, these odd, barely humanlike creatures that are gathered about me staring at me!" Stanley was surprised that they did not do so in silence, but that they displayed excited curiosity about his own person and where he might come from. This led to a discussion that ended with the exclamation: "Humans! They are truly humans!" Stanley replied, "Just think of it! While we whites arrogantly discuss amongst ourselves whether the beings standing before us are in fact human, they have just as much doubt as to whether we white men are actually part of the human race!"

Ethnology has presented enough evidence of the fact that all ethnic groups and peoples with an intact awareness of their identity respectively consider themselves to be the crown of creation. One's own people are not only deemed to be more skilled, more intelligent, and simply better than the rest, but they are also seen as being the most beautiful people on earth. Depending on the given degree that their features differ from ours, others who do not meet our ideal appear to be conclusively less intelligent, less skilled, less civilized, less good and less beautiful. Europeans were – and still are – considered by non-Europeans to be shady, without morals or culture, and ugly: just as we likewise consider them to be unattractive. The Guaikuru of the Chaco, in South America, thought that the Spaniards, in

Colon figures from Baule (Ivory Coast), made in the 1950s. The short pants and extremely short legs of the male figure, and the slightly bent elbows and straight hair of the female figure are typical features. The fixed gaze of both figures appears to focus on nothing at all and does not meet the eye of the beholder. Their posture is tense, their facial expression vigilant.

A concrete soldier used as a guard at various warrior temples in Ghana. The figure has the distinctive posture of the British military officer. In addition to their stiffness and their uniform, Europeans were often depicted wearing a beard and holding a bottle of gin. One ethnologist especially wore a full beard and partook liberally of the beer that he was offered so as not to be mistaken for a colonial officer or a missionary: the image of colonial officers was that of beardless drinkers, whereas missionaries were known for their temperance and full beard.

Europeans, however, were frowned upon for their pungent body odor, their linguistic inelegance, their unattractive facial features, and their bizarre costumes and habits. In a word, they could be nothing other than uncivilized savages! In the 1940s, English ethnologist Mary Douglas worked among the Lele in southern Zaire (now Democratic Republic of Congo). Until that time, these people had had little contact with whites. One of the women of the group explained how much she appreciated Ms. Douglas' presence, since it gave her an opportunity to get a realistic impression of whites. Her people had been doubtful as to whether Douglas would even have teeth and eyebrows.

Like all peoples who dwelt in places far from Europe, Africans deemed Europeans to be cannibals. Occasionally they were even comparison to themselves, were deformed, awkward in their movements, and feeble; on the whole, they considered Europeans to be members of an underdeveloped race. The Trobriand Islanders in Melanesia were convinced that they were all albinos; and to them, their noses were comparable to the sharpened blade of an axe, their eyes like pools of water. Almost all colonial subjects judged Europeans to be undisciplined, unstable, and as foolish as animals.

Their attention was focused on the features that contrasted strongly with their own familiar ones. African colon figures often depicted Europeans as stiff-postured, in uniform, bearded, and with a bottle of gin in their hand. During his field studies in Uganda, English ethnologist John Beattie took care to wear a full beard and partook liberally of the beer he was offered so as not to be mistaken for a colonial officer or a missionary – for the image of colonial officers was that of beardless drinkers, whereas missionaries were known for their temperance and full beard. All

A concrete soldier used as a guard in a posuban (warrior temple) in Ghana.

The asafo (warrior groups) of the Fante have erected many *posuban* (monuments). The architecture of these memorials is similar to that of the forts built by the former colonial powers. Their military character is emphasized by the inclusion of objects such as cannons and soldiers.

thought to be the legendary monster creatures – half-human, half-animal – that all the world's cultures were inclined to think lived at the end of the earth. Even as late as the 1950s, the Lugbara in Uganda assured English ethnologist John Middleton that "the British walked on their heads, covering great distances in this fashion. The moment they think they are being watched, they will suddenly change to walking on their feet. If they are threatened, they disappear underground, only to reappear some distance away and continue walking on their heads." Less significant mannerisms had also been observed. One African, for example, recalled: "The whites are incredibly devout believers in the alphabet. I do not expect that they can keep anything in their heads if they have not previously written it down. I have often done business with them. Every time I came, they had to take down notes before considering my requests."

Unpleasant, ugly, pushy, tactless, clumsy, easily disappointed, and lacking manners – that is basically the memory most Africans continue to have of the colonists. To this day, unfortunately, this image is often confirmed. The overall impression Africans have of Europeans is based on a disastrous combination of prejudices and actual experience, and one that is decidedly difficult to dismiss. But at least Africans have found a way of incorporating the European presence into their own culture: by typifying Europeans in stylized portraits, the colon figures. In so doing they were able to gain a certain amount of magic power over Europeans, since the element of caricature in these figures gave them an air of inferiority.

Strictly speaking, the term colon applies only to those African pieces of art that were created in the context of modern cults during colonial times and that expressed the ongoing conflict with colonialism. For a long time, ethnologists and art collectors scorned these naive portrayals as the hardly original, inferior waste product of African art – until, that is, German ethnologist Julius Lips, exiled in America, "discovered" them as an artifact of interest to science. In his opinion, it was not the intention of "primitive artists" to create lifelike replicas of whites. Their skill was rather to draw "from the great storehouse that is our imagination," while underscoring those attributes that are both typical and significant. It is in doing so that they accurately relay the essential nature of modern civilization.

Colon figures do, in fact, often reflect the shock that the artists experienced at the sight of a European. The physiognomy of a figure may be alluded to only through a symbol – for example, a mustache or goatee, a large nose, or straight hair – and at other times may be concisely detailed, at least with respect to its basic features. Early colon figures portrayed the people with whom either the artist or the person commissioning the work had had direct contact: soldiers, traders, and missionaries. Like many objects of traditional West African statuary, colon figures are often placed in shrines or on altars dedicated to gods or spirits, but not to the ancestors. Like so many other cultural elements of Western origin, colon figures thus used were incorporated into traditional concepts and fundamentally reinterpreted to suit the purpose of the creators.

The warrior groups of the Fante

"A dead lion is worth more than a live leopard," meaning "Even at the best of times, a rival company will never achieve the status of our own," is the proud assessment of their own strength that the emblems on asafo flags and shrines are meant to communicate to others, particularly to their rivals.

All Akan kingdoms have warrior groups, or *asafo* companies (*sa* meaning "war", and *fo* "people"). They were the defense troops of the kingdoms. In the 19th century, many an invasion from the hinterlands was quashed by them, especially attempts by the Asante to gain access to the coast. In the 20th century, the groups even fought among themselves until British colonial rulers stripped them of their powers and replaced them with mercenaries. But being deprived of their combat assignment did not necessarily weaken the asafo. They made the most of the situation, developing highly expressive art forms, the essential visual elements of which include costumes, flags, and shrines. Ever since, they have competed with one another on an artistic level.

Asafo groups are basically democratic. They constitute a counterweight to the aristocratic bureaucracy of the matrilineal Akan, whose titles are passed down through the maternal lineage. Ancestors, officially worshiped, belong to the matriarchal family. "A woman who belongs to a particular clan will always bear a descendant of the same clan." In contrast, membership of an asafo group is achieved by virtue of one's descent on the male side of the family (*ntoro*). The ntoro is a life soul that is the legacy of the father and is responsible for mental capabilities and for certain characteristics of an individual's personality – especially courage and fearlessness. These traits are always attributed to the father, "since," so claims an adage, "a crab does not give life to a bird." The various ntoro originated in the natural environment – from the waters, rocks, and trees – and are closely tied to gods of nature (*abosom*; *obosom* in the singular) that not only provide vigilance and promote fertility, but also once controlled war campaigns. When someone dies, the ntoro does not enter the beyond, but unites with its obosom or supports other individuals with the same ntoro.

The company's religious center and parade ground is a shrine at which the ntoro groups make sacrifices to their gods and young men are ordained warriors. Once they have passed puberty and reached a marriageable age (about 18), young men pledge loyalty to the company of their father and thus become full members. Their commitment to their father and to the paternal military company now takes precedence over all other bonds. In the past, this might even have entailed going to war against maternal relatives.

Originally, the ntoro shrine was a simple "medicine mound" (*esiw* or *siw*, meaning "earth mound") about 12–15 inches high and made of clay mixed with water and occasionally vegetable substances to harden it. A tortoiseshell covering protected it against all weather. A mound was built either on the grave of an important member of the company or on a significant battleground. It was consecrated by burying into it a medicine (*edur*) or sometimes even the severed heads of the enemy, giving it additional potency. A sacred tree (*dua ese*) was situated close to the site. The tree was the residence of the ntoro group's nature god (*obosom*), and was surrounded by a fence. The local god was "assisted" by other spiritual powers in the area. This divine unity of forces was at the disposal of the company. Soon after their contact with the British, the obosom was also referred to as a *posuban* – probably a combination of the English term "post" (a military post) and the Fante word *iban* (fortification). The shrine also included a hut (*buw*) in which the company stored possessions, armaments, and cult requisites.

During the late 19th century, asafo companies in coastal regions began to lavish creativity on decorating these "posts." Their commitment to war was replaced by a new kind of rivalry. They were now intent on outdoing each other in artful pomp, ostentatious parades, and new buildings, the architectural extravagance of which had little in common with traditional monuments. The visual demonstration of a group's superiority reduced the standing of its foe.

This tendency took root around 1880. Numerous new shrines have since been erected. In

Flags are the mobile equivalent of the posuban, often adorned with the same motifs. From their earliest contact with Africans, white men honored local rulers by presenting them with European flags. Flags have therefore probably been used in coastal regions of Africa for over 300 years. The upper part of an asafo flag is almost always decorated with either a Union Jack or the national flag of Ghana, making it easy to differentiate between older flags, predating independence (i.e. pre-1957), and more recent ones.

Wealthy asafo companies have flags over 300 yards long. They illustrate the proverbial sayings and aphorisms that are commonly expressed in all forms of Akan art, and also depict the history of the company. At the celebrations held during the great annual festival they are carried through the streets in a long procession.

1977, 71 such sites were to be found throughout the Fante region. Some of these cement structures are as much as 30 feet high and up to 13 feet wide. The posuban are richly decorated and adorned with both traditional symbols of power (such as lions and leopards) and modern, Western ones (such as airplanes and canons). The canons are either real ones taken from 17th-century European forts on the coast of Ghana or representations painted on the walls of the shrines. Some posuban are stylized replicas of European forts; more often they replicate warships.

While the sacred tree traditionally located near the posuban has remained an unchanged symbol, the huts of earlier times have been replaced by monumental structures. Like the huts, the buildings serve as ammunition stores, places of assembly, and cult sites.

Individual Fante kingdoms and Fante towns each have several asafo companies whose names were often chosen in remembrance of an important

battle or of a location of historical significance to its members. Traditionally, the companies represented the defensive powers of a kingdom. Since colonial times, they bear not only a name, but also a number. The British, in their attempt to prevent trading activities among the various units, ordered them to be registered. The twafo company (*twa* meaning "to sever"), former vanguard of the town of Anomabu, has since been known as Company No. 1, the *adonten* company ("main body") in the center as No. 3, and so on.

The influence of the asafo is considerable. Because they represent their members' interests before the ruling class, membership of one of these groups gives ordinary people an indirect voice. At least this is true with respect to traditional matters – for, nominally, the asafo companies rank immediately below the local sovereign (*omanhene*) who, in turn, requires their support in order to rule. His appointment is considered effective only once the warrior groups have taken part in it. If they have not, the legitimacy of his status remains doubtful. Their absence from the festivals of the kingdom – most notably at the path-cleansing festival (akwambo), the most important festival of the year – can be used to put pressure on the omanhene. Without their participation, the festival – held to ensure the benevolence of the gods and ancestors – cannot be celebrated. Their open opposition could even lead to a sovereign being removed from office.

Asafo companies also fulfill a range of other public and social functions. They build roads, market squares, and community facilities, and undertake rescue operations, such as searching for people missing in the bush, recovering the bodies of the drowned, or putting out fires. They assist any members in need. In the past they would also guard the virtue of their comrades' wives. Suspicion was only ever aroused, however, when a member died, in which case his widow was subjected to a "test of truth." To this day, they have maintained a judicial system of their own, albeit one which generally metes out punishment only in the event of unexcused absence from important ceremonies by its members. In rare cases, it might also deal with offenses connected with witchcraft.

Apart from participating in the annual festivals, the only significant religious role that warrior groups play is in funeral ceremonies for their members. They also remember their dead on certain days. In fishing communities the designated day is Tuesday, the day dedicated to the god of the sea; in farming communities Friday is the remembrance day, for this is the day dedicated to the earth goddess. On these days, the company assembles at the "post" and proceeds to the house of the host lineage (abusua), where they spend the afternoon playing drums, firing guns, singing battle songs, and generally socializing. This honor is reserved for members, an exception being made only of the omanhene. All companies participate in the funeral ceremony held for the omanhene.

Each company (etsiku, meaning "group of heads"; etsikuw in the plural) has its own hierarchical structure. Certain positions within this structure are inherited, but most are elected. Leadership of the company falls to the elders, under a commander or commander in chief, the supi or asafohen. This position is generally held by the oldest officer, but another person can be voted into office. Prior to taking up office, the designated commander "flees" and must be "captured." He then undergoes a series of initiation rituals, on the eighth day of which he takes his vows and supplies plentiful drink for the company as part of the final festivities. A newly appointed asafohen is obliged to pay for a new flag to be sewn, which is then turned over to the company. He will henceforth have control of all the company's flags, its supply of gunpowder, and war drum, and about ten to 40 men comprising officers of varying rank, flag bearers, drummers, and priests.

A company's flags are an extremely important possession. They depict key moments in the memory of their commanders and special events in the history of their group – for example, the inauguration of a new posuban. To lose a flag is a great disgrace. In the past, if this occurred in battle, it was considered a sure sign of imminent defeat. Flags therefore need to be strictly guarded, a task entrusted to the "first scout" (asikamaten), who neither in times of war nor of peace ever leaves the side of the flag bearer (frankakitsanyi; franka meaning "flag," kitaa "to hold," and nyi "person"). In the past,

With sleight of hand, the flag is repeatedly concealed from the eyes of the onlookers. The bearer wraps it around his body or passes it on, folded, to the next member of the company to hold. To the sound of loud drumming and gong beats, it is once more triumphantly waved.

The flag bearer's performance is a choreographic and spiritual expression of a company's superiority, its strength, the defense mission of its members, and its readiness to enter into combat against its enemies. The dancing is a playful enactment of past battle scenes. In a typical scene, the flag is presented, then the bearer lies down on it to show that he can be so sure of his company's victory, that he is able to lie down peacefully and sleep. In yet another display, he describes imaginary traps, or "witches' holes," on the ground into which the enemy will fall and be taken prisoner.

For members of an asafo company, flags are the most important means of expressing their honor. In the past, it was common practice to "slaughter" the enemy by depicting insulting motifs on one's own flags. Even as far back as 1860, all companies in the Cape Coast territory were required to present their flags to the governor before exhibiting them in public. The depictions on them had to be granted approval and were required to be registered. If a company exhibited flags not previously approved, those responsible were liable to be punished. Even today, each new motif must be approved by the sovereign, the chief commander (tufohen), and the asafo's elders.

the bearer would carry the flag into battle. Today, his job is to dance, holding the flag, on all ceremonial occasions, including Christian celebrations such as Easter. Even so, he is still guarded by 12 scouts (asikamafo), their gaze firmly set on the flag. His raffia costume, adorned with numerous bells, beads, and amulets, is a reminder of the priestly functions he once fulfilled in the past.

The drummer (akyerema) also enjoys a high-ranking position. Whereas in the past he would have been responsible for passing on the commands of leaders during battle, he now uses his drum to summon members to meetings. The company drum (asafo kyen) is considered to be sacred. It is carved from the wood of the odum tree (Erythophleum guineense). In this tree dwells a nature god (obosom) that reveals itself mostly to hunters. Before one of these trees is felled, a sacrifice is made to it. Later, sacrifices of eggs and chickens are also constantly made to the drum.

Each company has its own priest (komfo or osofo), whose responsibility it is to persuade the gods to support their side, to make them well disposed toward the company, and to concoct "medicines" (edur) that will render the warriors invincible. Since women, too, are members of their father's companies, some of these groups have

female auxiliary troops led by one or two female officers. In the past, some of these women accompanied the men into battle to cook and take care of them. Today, they still accompany the men at important ceremonies, where they dance and fire guns in praise of the warriors.

Finally, all the subunits (etsikuw) of the company answer to a chief commander (tufohen, "chief of the riflemen") whose main job it is to settle disputes between the various divisions. In this capacity, it is essential that the chief commander be impartial. On being elected to office, he therefore relinquishes all ties to his company.

Despite the fact that there is an enormous number of symbols on the flag, they all relay essentially the same message by alluding to the all-conquering power and shining glory of the company. Old and tattered flags can either be updated or replaced. Even when no longer in use, they are always kept as a memento of ancestors and past events.

For the asafo companies, flags are an extremely important possession. To lose a flag is an act of great disgrace. Flags therefore need to be strictly guarded, a duty entrusted to the "first scout." He is also the one who dances with the flag on all ceremonial occasions, including Christian celebrations such as Easter.

The repertoire of the flag-bearers includes some highly athletic displays.

Posuban, temple of the warriors

Asafo companies have erected shrines along the coast between Winneba and Takoradi. This "man-of-war" shrine is located in downtown Anomabu (Ghana), and is the site of the great annual festival at which the company's flags are displayed.

The Fante variously refer to the sites on which their warrior groups have erected monuments to themselves as forts, castellums, posuban, posts, or shrines. The main feature of these sites is a central post that is obviously a replica of the flagpoles of European forts. Many posuban also display a style of architecture that resembles the forts that were built between the 15th and the 18th centuries in the coastal regions of Ghana. In some cases they are reproductions of churches or, more often, of

warships. The military character of warrior groups is additionally underscored by displays of cannons and ammunition and by the typical sculptures that adorn the posuban: soldiers dressed either in their traditional war costume (batakari) or in European uniform; policemen, preachers, or severed heads; and lions and leopards, an expression of the "savagery" of the groups. The variety inherent in the motifs is truly impressive; the traditional is very liberally combined with the modern.

468

Above: A posuban shrine with warriors, demons, and animals in Mankessim (Ghana). This warrior temple is considered to be the most handsome Fante posuban in all Ghana.

Far left and left: Details of two posuban figures: a bull with a snake and a dove on its head, and a lion, open-mouthed and bleeding.

The Celestial Church of Christ

A bishop of the Celestial Church of Christ in Lac Nokoué (Benin). The church's display of splendor – such as the robes of the church sovereigns – is modeled on Catholic Church symbolism. Religious content and practices, however, are based on Yoruba doctrines.

Opposite page, above: Members of the Celestial Church of Christ on their way to a service.

Opposite page, below: On the banks of the dam at Lac Nokoué (Benin), two women receive the divine blessing after their christening.

"The Celestial Church of Christ is the final rescue vessel. Those who fail to board it will drown in deep waters." This is the central message contained in the sermons and hymns of this religious community. The Celestial Church of Christ (CCC) was founded in 1947 on the initiative of a Yoruba carpenter, Samuel Bilehou Oschoffa (b. 1909). His profession led him to spend much time alone in the forest. One day, as he was deeply absorbed in prayer near Toffin, a village situated in the midst of the mangrove swamps of Garvié, he heard a voice utter "Luli, Luli, Luli" and then translate it as "The mercy of Jesus Christ." It was 23 May 1947. A second encounter followed on 29 September this time coinciding with a visual manifestation. It called upon him to found a church:

"While I was praying with friends in my house there came upon me a ray of brilliant light similar to the headlights of a car. At its rear stood a winged being with a body like fire and whose tiny eyes flew towards me. The ray of light became increasingly shorter, until the being came to stand about a yard in front of me. Thereupon it spoke: 'God has conferred upon you a mission to preach to the world. Many Christians who are troubled or in need of help still seek the counsel of fetish priests and other dark powers. They die believing themselves to be Christians, although they have long ceased to be, since Satan has put his mark on them. Therefore they cannot meet Christ after their death. God has assigned you to preach to the world and to warn the people. In order that they shall believe you and listen to you and follow you, you will perform healing miracles in the name of Jesus Christ. These deeds will bear witness to the fact that God has sent you.'"

The prophet Oschoffa was successful, for he had extremely charismatic ways. In a matter of only three years following his calling, the movement had spread across extensive areas of Dahomey and Nigeria. Today, branches of the Church have been founded not only in Togo, Ghana, Senegal, and Ivory Coast, but also in Europe, the United States, and Canada. The originally small flock of believers has meanwhile grown to a huge community; there are more than 10 million Celestial Church Christians in Africa alone.

Since the death of the prophet in a car accident in 1985, a veritable bouquet of legends has blossomed around his life, especially concerning his healing successes. It is said, for example, that when he went missing in the bush, he was kept alive by a bird and an ape who fed him wild honey.

Members of the Celestial Church of Christ during Sunday prayers at the cult site on Lac Nokoué. The cult community has drawn many of its followers from the area around the lake. Thousands of people in the area now wear the cult's white tunic and matching ballooned headdress.

The cult of this new church is centered around prayers, confessions, and prophecies. Dreams, visions, trances, and speaking in tongues are all considered manifestations of the Holy Spirit or of guardian angels. The mission of the prophet Oschoffa – like that of many charismatic African movements – is to oppose Satan, the fetish priests, and other powers of darkness that have always managed to captivate people by means of fortune-telling, amulets, talismans, and fetishes. The Sovereign of Hell is backed by a massive army of demons who vigorously support his evil efforts. The members of the Celestial Church of Christ believe that their church already existed in heaven before it was sent down to create a "heavenly kingdom" on earth. This notion is even inherent in its original name, *Le Christianisme Céleste* (Celestial Christianity). This name was revealed to Alexander Yanga (an apostle who had entrusted himself to Oschoffa to be mentally healed) at the end of a seven-day session of self-communion. The Church sees itself not only as a worldly branch of the Mother Church in heaven and as a "rescue vessel," but also as a bridge between heaven and earth.

The beliefs of the CCC are based on those of Yoruba culture, according to which the world consists of heaven (*orun*), the residence of spiritual beings, and earth (*aye*), the home of mankind. The former is populated by the gods (*orisha*) and the "masters of war" (*ajogun*). The orisha are well disposed toward humans, bestowing blessing upon them provided that they abide by their rules. The ajogun, on the other hand, strive to destroy humans. Their most feared representatives are Iku, Arun, Ofo, Egba, Epe, Ewon, Oran, and Ese – personifying death, disease, loss, paralysis, the curse, jail, "great trouble," and all forms of suffering, respectively. Protection can only be given to those who duly worship the benevolent powers. Evil is also brought upon humans by witches (*aje*) and sorcerers (*oso*), water spirits (*emere*), and the souls of children who died prematurely (*abiku*).

The earth is the stage on which people must stand their ground between the forces of darkness and light and on which their fate (ori) may take a good or an evil turn.

It is before this backdrop that the efforts of the prophet Oschoffa and his community unfold. Inexplicable or incurable diseases, infertility, premature death, unemployment, in fact all forms of suffering that afflict humankind, are still the doings of malevolent powers. The only thing that has changed is the way in which people defend themselves against them. In traditional Yoruba society those who suffered sought the advice and help of the oracle priests (babalawo), who generally recommend making sacrifices (ebo) to the spiritual powers to placate them and prevent impending disaster. The new Church, however, combats evil with celestial help. During prayer, believers receive messages in the form of prophecies, visions, audible revelations, and dreams. Intense prayer brings them closer to heaven and opens their eyes to the deeds of God (Jehovah), Jesus Christ (Jesu Kristi), the Holy Spirit (Emi Mimo), and the angels (maleka or angeli) as well as to evil forces and the power of temptation.

The Army of Heaven is led by four archangels (maleka). The first of them, Michael, bears the spiritual sword (ida) against the enemies of belief (ajogun, aje, and oso). As the Angel of Victory and Guardian of the Church, he is ranked directly below Jesus Christ. Most prayers thus begin by calling upon "Jehovah, Jesus Christ, Michael Mimo, Oga Ogun" ("Jehovah, Jesus Christ, Holy Michael, our captain"). He, who assigns the other angels their various tasks, resides in the east and is the head of the Church. Gabriel, the Guardian Angel and the Angel of Blessing, who is responsible for healing – especially infertility – and who stands for humility, rules over the west. In the south, on the ocean side, resides Raphael, who combats suffering and disease. Finally, there is Uriel, the Endower of Gifts, who rules the north. The archangels preside over numerous other angels, only two of whom are actually represented by name: Jimata, Angel of the Waterworld, and Jerimo Yamah, who spreads the light and glory of God. The Bible, which contains the word of God, is a forceful weapon against the powers of evil (ajogun, aje, and oso). It instills fear into them and makes them quiver. They are refused access to the rescue vessel.

Above: The Celestial Church of Christ has a rigidly hierarchical structure, which is clearly illustrated by dress. For example, blue sashes identify visionaries, upon whom revelations and prophecies are imparted during prayer.

Left: An assistant writes an account of a follower's visions.

Left: The visionary is overcome by a state of rapture. She begins to speak in tongues, now uttering inarticulate sounds, now individual words and fragmented sentences.

The cult of the heavenly powers requires a suitable setting. CCC followers worship God in ceremonial rooms that they call Ile Esin ("home of devotion"), Ile Adura ("home of prayer"), or "heavenly town," the "new Jerusalem." The measures they take to perpetually strengthen their spiritual being serve to protect them from evil powers. Such measures include, above all else, sprinkling holy water, which has the power to

Members of the Celestial Church of Christ occasionally retreat to their holy rooms to fast and pray, but also to avoid the assaults of demons, witches, and sorcerers. The phase of "spiritual incubation" (abe abo) that they undergo there is often prescribed by the prophets (both male and female) as part of a healing ritual. The young man seen here is a student whose fellow students are said to have jinxed him. Surrounded by consecrated foods and white candles, he submits to healing sleep; he will be awakened to new life with holy water.

cleanse and to bless. At the church entrance, before they enter the building, worshipers dip their fingers into a basin of water and mark a cross on their foreheads. Clouds of incense, candlelight, ringing bells, pious hymns, and incessant cries of "hallelujah" add force to the Christian defense against evil powers. A cross placed diagonally across the entrance to the church during services is yet another defensive measure in the effort to guard "heaven on earth" against the profane world.

Church services are held by leaders who preach the word of God. During religious awakenings it often occurs that individual followers appear before the congregation and publicly confess to the fact that they practiced witchcraft or sorcery before discovering the path that ultimately led them to the Celestial Church of Christ. They subsequently undergo a cleansing ritual and are entrusted to the care of spiritual supervisors so as to ensure that their bonds to the powers of evil are severed.

"Visionaries" receive heavenly instruction as to how purification can be achieved in any given case.

Every church should have a "Mercy Land" (Ile Aanu). This very special place, enclosed by surrounding wall, fence, or simple stone markings, is a sacred area; here ocean or river sand is usually heaped up into a mound and here the well that is the source of holy water is located (although tap water is sometimes used). Because it is deemed to be particularly rich in energy, it is also used for therapeutic purposes. A variety of rituals and cult acts are performed at the well – including foot cleansings and Holy Communion. For prophets, fortune-dreamers, and visionaries alike it is a spiritual reservoir of energy, since it is believed that the angels assemble there in great number.

The heavenly powers not only provide personal protection, but can also protect personal possessions. Hymns are sung in honor of these powers at weddings and important ceremonies, and at the blessings for houses and vehicles. These deeds, it is hoped, will protect worshipers – especially in the case of vehicle-blessing – against theft, but also against assault by the evil powers. In urban communities, cars are additionally protected by being parked on church grounds, in which case they are considered to be well and truly out of harm's way, for "The power of the Church makes witches shudder, bewilders sorcerers, and even brings the Devil himself to his knees."

A highly important position within the Church hierarchy is that of the "evangelists." They administer Holy Communion and perform the christening ritual – in this case an "immersion christening" at Lac Nokoué. The ritual ends with the evangelist blessing the christened person.

The white fairy-tale kings of Ghana

"King" Marcel, alias Marcel Bauer (53) from Belgium, at his inauguration. In acknowledgment of his superiority, his "subjects" carry him on their shoulders through the Fante town of Krofu.

In complete contrast to the situation that existed in colonial times, when the defeated Africans were often forced to adapt to the ways of their European masters, there are now white men who happily adopt the lifestyle of Africans, albeit only temporarily. Significantly, it is not so much street life and everyday reality as traditional court life that attracts these foreigners.

Like people anywhere in the world, Africans honor those who make special contributions to their community. The Akan award not medals or certificates, but an office, something akin to awarding the status of an elder. This occurs not only with their own people, but may also be bestowed upon outsiders. So it was, for example, that Nana Osei Agyeman Prempeh II, uncle and predecessor of the reigning asantehene, awarded a chair to German theologist Eugen Rapp (1904–77) in the 1930s. This distinction was based on the fact that, having been commissioned by the Basel Mission to translate the Bible and to record a series of dialects, Rapp had created an indigenous literary language. Possession of the chair gave him the right to appear before and address the court at any time. It was an object that permitted him privileges that no ordinary mortal would ever enjoy.

The "king" is dressed. In the past, social differences were marked chiefly by dress. Rulers donned magnificent kente cloths, worn in the style of Roman togas, and much gold jewelry, including that worn on their headdress.

The new dignitary, henceforth responsible for the development of "his village," is flanked by the village chief and his wife. He swears an oath of allegiance on the state sword, pledging to risk even his life for the wellbeing of his people.

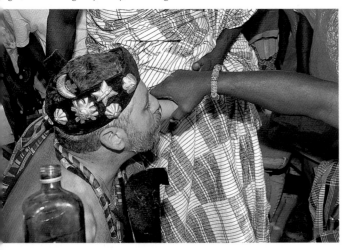

The oath is substantiated by a swig of liquor. Rulers are expected to be able to express their ultimate dignity by dancing.

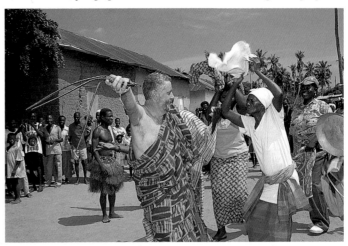

Should a ruler be unable to meet this expectation, he may seriously lose prestige. He will, however, remain dependent on the gods and ancestors, an understanding which he expresses by pointing the sword toward heaven and earth.

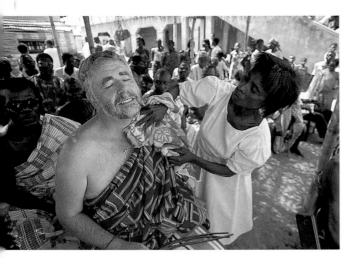

Courtiers express their approval of the "king's" dance performance and pledge their loyalty to him through special formalized gestures. All the while, a servant wipes sweat from his neck and forehead.

The asafo companies, who play a major role in all community festivities, take part in the inauguration ceremony. This important event is documented on a flag that has been specially made for this occasion.

"Siggi," Siegfried Kaufmann (48), a nuclear physicist and management consultant from Würselen near Aachen, Germany, is minister for development in Ntoroso. He is shown here seated next to "his sovereign."

This, a very rare distinction indeed in the past, is no longer such an uncommon occurrence. The difference, however, is that many of those honored in this way today tend to be aristocrats in the financial sense rather than individuals who achieved their position through personal merit, as in the past. Local potentates use such offices and the

insignia that go with them (chair, costume, etc.) to commit whites to their community. The whites do not of course become black men, and the whole procedure is a masquerade, but who could resist being the recipient of so much distinction and being made a "fairy-tale king"? There are, however, obligations that are inseparable from the privileges. White dignitaries so honored bear real responsibility for the wellbeing, more accurately for the wealth, of their community, meaning that they are expected to provide substantial financial and technical aid. It is their concern to ensure that development funds regularly flow into their "territory." Nana Akuoko Sarpong, official advisor on tradition to the Ghanaian president, sums it up when he says "White kings are a way of providing support to individual village communities."

In 1996, there were already 20 such "rulers" in Ghana. They regularly visit their "kingdoms" – and never with empty coffers. Money is collected through fundraising campaigns back home. "King Fritz" of Konongo, for example, has raised development funds totaling DM 100,000 within five years. He has accomplished this feat by giving approximately 150 lectures a year about "his

Right: "King Fritz," alias Fritz Pawelzik (69), formerly a mineworker from Germany, and now a dignitary in Konongo, during a visit to the capital.

Far right: Leaves are stuffed into his mouth in order to prevent him from speaking. This act signifies that he must refrain from publicly disclosing state secrets.

Right: "King Fritz" presents himself as a mighty warrior. His war dress (batakari) is covered in amulets that protect him from danger.

Far right: "King Fritz" dances among his "subjects." He has his own "palace" in Konongo – an atrium building with a corrugated iron roof – and a "throne," a wooden chair covered in rivets.

"King Klaus," alias Klaus Thüsig (57) from Germany, is the head of the German Development Service's presence in Ghana. He is also the "king" of two kingdoms, and has refused yet a third "request." In one of these kingdoms, the wife of the Indian ambassador is his "co-ruler". Here he is on his way to the festival precinct. A rod-bearing speaker goes before him.

kingdom" to school students, religious groups, and women's clubs. Thanks to his commitment, his African community has made considerable additions to its library and has built toilet facilities. A kindergarten is presently being built. The next item on the request list is a school bus.

The whites are enthusiastically celebrated for their commitment and application – if, that is, they meet expectations. But views are divided as to how wisely donated funds are actually spent. Often enough, they do not go toward fulfilling the basic needs of a community, but are used to satisfy the consumer desires of the already well off – to

purchase items claimed by the media to represent a "modern" Western lifestyle.

Both sides, of course, profit by the deal. The Africans acquire funds they would otherwise never have been able to raise. The whites gain the satisfaction of being important and of being needed. The natural warmth with which village people treat their new kings and the exalted status these kings enjoy are more than enough compensation for the money that they invest. "King Fritz" is even considering being buried in Konongo, for here he will not be forgotten, but will live on in people's memories long after he has died.

The responsibilities of a sovereign include paying his respects to the asantehene in Kumasi on the occasion of special events. Here, "King Richard," alias Richard Sattler (57), a scrap dealer from Germany, who deals in used cars in Ghana, enters the city on the occasion of the 25th anniversary of the asantehene's accession to the throne in August 1995.

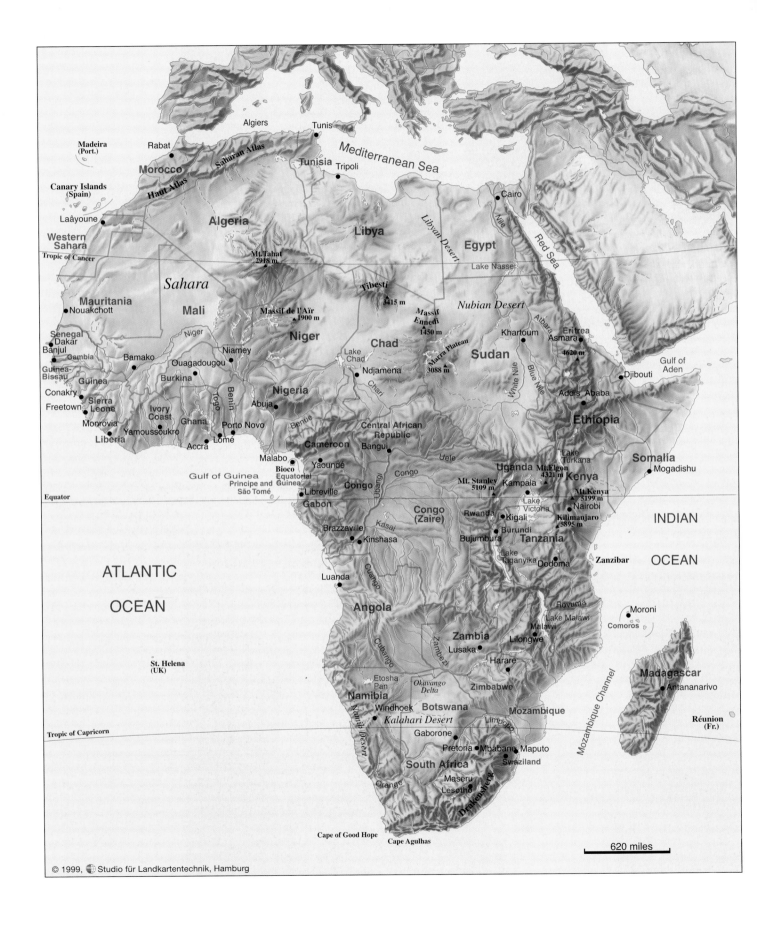

GLOSSARY

Affinal relationship (from Latin affinis, "bordering on something" or "related by marriage"). Relationship created through marriage; primarily between a spouse and his/her relatives (genealogical family or blood relatives), i.e. brother-in-law, sister-in-law, and parents-in-law; and secondarily between the spouses of one's own close relatives and, in turn, the relatives of those spouses.

Akan. Groups from the forest belt of West Africa – between the Volta river (Ghana) and the Bandama river (Ivory Coast) – who speak the Kwa languages and dialects. They are linguistically and historically related to the Ewe, Fon, and other groups who settled in East Africa. The Akan include the Asante (the largest and politically most influential group); the Fante on the coast; the Akim, Swahu, Akuapem, and Guan (all in Ghana); the Baule and Anyi in the dense jungles of Ivory Coast. The Akan are known for their artistic skills, particularly for their metalwork (copper and gold in particular), and their fine textiles (kente and adinkfa). From the 16th to the 19th centuries, the Akan experienced momentous social, political, and economic change. This period saw a final wave of immigration by the Matri clans to the regions that they subsequently settled, some of which were rich in gold deposits. The trade routes that crossed the Sahara soon extended beyond the savanna (where they had originally ended), reaching further south so as to exploit the gold mines of the Black Volta, and into the rainforest. There was an increase in trade to the north (to the Niger belt and Hausa territory). Gold and wild kola nuts were exchanged primarily for textiles, leather goods, and copper items. Mande traders (known as Dyula) ventured south and established trading posts (including Begho, a post of great significance during the 15th and 16th centuries, situated on the border between savanna and forest country). Kingdoms were also founded further south. These included Bono, Adanse, Denkyera, Akwamu, and finally Ashanti, which soon predominated over the others and controlled trading with the north. The economic and political development of the Akan was further promoted by the arrival of the Portuguese on the coast (in 1471), followed in the 16th century by the French, Dutch, and British, and in the 17th century by influxes from Denmark, Sweden, and Brandenburg. Between 1487 and 1800, these European nations erected more than 60 forts and bases on the Gold Coast.

Amoah. According to legend, Nana (grandmother) Amoah was an old woman who was said to have introduced the use of speakers' rods (akyeama poma) in Kumasi. They are used to this day (albeit in modified form) to symbolize the officialdom and authority of a certain group of court dignitaries. All verbal contact with the asantehene and other local sovereigns is conducted both in the presence, and using the mediation services, of a "speaker" (akyeame).

Ancestors. The spirits of dead relatives (free spirits) play an important role in many of the religions of non-nomadic cultures in Africa, South East Asia, and Oceania. Together with other spirits and gods, they are one of the powers of the beyond. Generally, their authority increases with age. Thus, those ancestors who are most closely descended from the original ancestor, or master ancestor and founder of a people, are usually highly revered, enjoying a higher status than the eldest of their descendants, but ranking below the gods and especially the creator and supreme god himself, who is the oldest of all. Like living elders, ancestral spirits counsel their people (in their dreams), ensure their wellbeing, bestow fertility on them, their animals, and their fields, and ensure that their descendants uphold the traditional order. While they warn negligent descendants through signs and minor incidents of misfortune, conscious offenders are punished through disease, accident, material loss, or death. Everyone therefore has a vital interest in maintaining good relations with ancestral spirits. Ancestral relationships are fostered through prayer and the regular sacrifice of food and drink, but also by inviting ancestors to smaller family and larger communal festivities, at which they are praised, lavishly fed, entertained with song and dance, and offered gifts.

Medallion depicting William Wilberforce
From: *Westafrika. Vom Senegal bis Benguela*, Leipzig, 1878.

Antislavery movement. Organized opposition to the inhumane business of slave trading first arose in England as part of the Evangelical movement. This movement of enlightened Protestants did more than the traditional Church did to appeal to people's moral sense. It represented a humanitarian, philanthropic tendency rather than a specifically religious one. Its ultimate aspiration was to mobilize the masses in favor of abolishing slavery. William Wilberforce (1759–1833) became the main advocate for the abolition first of slave trading and then of slave keeping, a cause for which he was awarded honorary French citizenship by the National Assembly in Paris. Wilberforce became leader of a philanthropic party which, because of his residence in Clapham, now in south London, was also known as the Clapham Sect. The philanthropy practiced by the Evangelicals brought about several humanitarian reforms (including the abolition of corporal punishment for women in 1820). Its greatest and most spectacular achievement was the fight against slave trading. Wilberforce first brought the issue before the House of Commons in 1788. When little was achieved through parliament, the Anti-Slavery Society was founded (in 1790) and through it public opinion was mobilized. The abolitionists were forced to make great sacrifices for their cause. The law banning slave trading (passed in 1807) was an initial success for the Anti-Slavery Association, but slavery itself was only abolished throughout the kingdom in 1833.

Asantehene. The supreme ruler of about a million Asante in central Ghana. He resided in the political, cultural, and economic center of Kumasi. The first asantehene was Osei Tutu (1688?–1717), the ruler or sovereign (ohene) of Kumasi. In the 17th century he managed to create a confederation of various clans who, until then, had each had their own sovereign ruler (all of equal ranking). His immediate predecessors, Oki Akenten and Obiri Yeboah, had not held the title of asantehene. It was only after their victory over the kingdom of Denkyera at the Battle of Feyase (1701) that the Oyoko clan, to which Osei Tutu belonged, gained a position of supremacy over the various subgroups of the union and that Osei Tutu was endowed with the title of asantehene (ohene of Ashanti). The Gold Chair became the symbol of the kingdom he had created and which he represented. Its ritual significance has been maintained to the present day. The chair embraces both the memory of an eventful past and the kingdom's fierce opposition to the British colonial powers. Ashanti underwent further expansion under Osei Tutu's successors. This was especially so under the reign of Opoku Ware (1731–41), of whom it is said that he introduced both the symbolic Sword of the Kingdom

(Mponponsuo) and the Big War Shirt (Batakiri Kese) that every asantehene wears at his inauguration. With each new conquest, Asante rulers were able to enlarge their political power. One of the factors that fostered their political ascendancy was that many of them controlled regions rich in gold deposits. This gold, and the kola nuts that grew wild in the territory, meant they were sought-after trade partners who soon controlled trading with the north and with the coastal regions. Gold and kola nuts were traded with one region in exchange for textiles and slaves, and European goods were traded with another. Inter-family conflicts at the end of the 18th century were one of the factors that led to a number of satellite kingdoms breaking away from the union. Asantehene Osei Kwame (1777–1803) was forced to abdicate; his successor Opoku Fofie died after only several weeks in office. Only Osei Tutu Kwame Asibe Bonsu (1804–23) was able to reestablish real stability. It was during his reign that a selection of oft-cited descriptions about the kingdom of Ashanti were documented. Edward T. Bowdich, author of *Mission from Cape Coast Castle to Ashantee* (London, 1819), came to the court of the asantehene in 1817 as head of a British delegation and closed a contract with him on September 7. The contract was ultimately broken, as were subsequent ones (each side broke some contracts). During the 19th century seven wars erupted between contracted parties. But the military superiority of the British forces led to their ultimate victory over the native people, and in 1896 the reigning asantehene, Osei Agyeman Prempeh I, and other important dignitaries were exiled to the Seychelles. On his return from exile in 1924, the British colonial regime no longer recognized him as an asantehene in the true sense of the term. His status was now that of a Kumasihene, a rank which put him in the company of all other merely regional sovereigns. This also applied to his successor, Osei Agyeman Prempeh II (1931–70), during whose reign the modern state of Ghana was founded (in 1957). The Ghanaian regime did, however, allow the asantehene to retain the status of traditional ruler.

Balanchine (from Sanskrit *paljanka*, bed). Usual term in India for a sedan or litter with sunroof and curtains, carried on long poles by four to six people. In their colony on Africa's Gold Coast the British applied the term to a type of sedan (apakam in Twi) in which the king and his courtiers made their public appearances.

Bantu. A linguistic group (rather than an ethnic group) with about 800 distinct languages, including a number of mostly unresearched dialects, in sub-Saharan Africa. The term is derived from the Zulu word *ba-ntu* (people), which occurs in similar form in many other Bantu languages. Bantu is a classed language, one

in which terms that have the same form (e.g. singular, plural) or meaning (e.g. living beings) are ordered in classes by prefixes or suffixes attached to the word stem.

Baobab. African tree (Adansonia digitata) of the Bombacea family, of which there are about 15 varieties, found in Africa, Madagascar, and northern Australia. The baobab, which grows up to about 65 feet high, is characterized by a pillar- or bottle-shaped trunk, in which the tree stores water. The trunk can reach up to 130 feet in circumference and usually has horizontal branches. The baobab is the characteristic tree of the African savanna. During the rainy season it has large, finger-shaped leaves, which are eaten as vegetables and which fall at the beginning of the dry season. Pollinated by bats, the large, white, beautifully shaped blossoms develop into lightweight, cucumber-shaped fruit about 8 inches long. Inside the wooden husk is an edible fruit, which is sweet and acidic, and which contains edible, oil-rich seeds. The soft, easily rotting wood and bast of the trunk are used to make rope and have other uses as raw materials.

Heinrich Barth.
From: *Das große Wagnis*, Berlin, 1936.

Barth, Heinrich (1821–65). German traveler in Africa who studied classical philology in Berlin and later took up geography. In Tripoli, after a Mediterranean journey, Barth joined the British African expedition (1850–55) led by J. Richardson. The journey led him via Mursuk, Katsina, and Kano to Kuka. Barth, the only European survivor of the expedition, reached Adamaua, Yale, the Benue, and finally, in September 1853, Timbuktu. In 1863 he became professor of geography and president of the Geographical Society in Berlin. He carried out not only geographical and linguistic research (he conducted his interviews in Arabic but is said to have been fluent in six African languages) but also ethnographic studies based on meticulous observation.

Bedouin (in Arabic, *badw*, people not living in one place, as opposed to *hadar*, people who are settled). The term describes fully nomadic, or more precisely camel-herding, groups who inhabit the deserts and semideserts of Arabia. Apart from the single-humped dromedary (Camelus dromedarius), the Bedouin also always keep sheep and goats. The first Arabian Bedouin are known to have reached Africa in the 1st century BC: in 46 BC the Romans obtained 22

dromedaries from them in Numidia (northern Tunisia). About 400 years later nomadic camel riders presented a constant and serious threat to the Roman provinces in Africa. However, only with the expansion of Islam, in which they played an important part, did the Bedouin gain a firm foothold in large parts of northeastern and northern Africa. The first advance, in the 7th century, was followed by a decisive conquest under the Beni Sulaim and Beni Hilal in the 11th and 12th centuries. Extensive tracts of land then still used for agriculture were devastated and turned into steppe. Since then the Sahara has been dominated by nomadic camel herding, shared in almost equal parts by the Bedouin and the Tuareg, a people of Berber origin.

Belief in power. Every movement, every change in life and in nature is driven by powers which must be recognized and controlled by anyone who wants to exist successfully. According to traditional views there are three kinds of power: the power of life, manifest in plants, animals, and humans as fertility and growth (and therefore found particularly in sexual organs, seeds, fruit, eggs, and so on); the powers of nature, especially strong in waterfalls, fire, wind, and hard rock; and the spiritual powers, which are identical to spiritual beings or free souls (q.v.), ancestors, spirits, and gods. The powers of life and nature can directly transfer to spiritual powers, strengthening minerals, plants, and locations (e.g. ancestral graves) also human life power; blood, bones, hair, nails and other carriers of organic power can be used as fertilizers and therefore contribute to the yields of crops. Powers do not work at random. Unless their transmittal is blocked or misdirected by magic (q.v.) or spirits, they are bound (as they have been since creation) to maintain the order of society, nature, and the cosmos: the power of life (vital soul) keeps organic functions (breath, blood circulation) working, the sun rises and sets, free souls become embodied over and over, and the gods rule the world. Power can be transmitted through immediate contact (touching, consuming), by radiation (such as smell, heat, or a look), or through strong or sick people. Adhering to traditions ensures that power can be harnessed and controlled; transgression is the abuse of power. Magic (q.v.) is a way of using vital, natural, or spiritual powers to an unusually high degree.

Benin. A kingdom (distinct from the modern state of Benin) founded by the Edo (Bini) possibly as early as the 12th century. It lay in the tropical rainforest west of the Niger (southwest of what is today Nigeria), about 170 km south of Ife. Benin is particularly famous for its high artistic achievements in bronze, ivory, and wood. The Edo, close relatives of the Yoruba, were ruled by a

Baobab tree.
From: *Die Völker der Erde*, Würzburg and Vienna, 1891.

religious king (oba) who was both their worldly and their spiritual leader. He was supported by a succession of princes (uzuma), representatives of the most important lineages. According to oral tradition, the ruling dynasty traces its origins to the king (oni) of Ife, who in response to an urgent request for a chief sent his son Oranmyan to Benin. With a local woman Oranmyan fathered a son, to whom he transferred his powers. He himself returned to Ife and later founded the kingdom of Oyo. The close links between the Edo and the Yoruba recognized the religious superiority of the oni of Ife, who dispensed royal insignia to every oba. At the death of an oba, a bronze head of the dead king was sent to Ife. The bronze heads of conquered princes were kept in Benin. The first written documentation of Benin dates from the 15th century, when trade, first with the Portuguese, then also with the Dutch and the British, began. In 1897, when Benin had long passed its cultural apogee, the kingdom fell victim to a British penal expedition. The British took away about 2000 bronze, ivory, and wooden sculptures – valuable works of art now found in museums all over Europe.

Berber. Generic term for the non-Arabic-speaking people of North Africa, a population that today numbers 6 to 7 million. Before the Arab-Islamic expansion in the 7th century, the Berber were densely spread from the Canary Islands (Guanchen) to the western border of Egypt. Today most Berbers (about 45 percent of the total population) live in Morocco; they also inhabit Algeria, the Sahara southward to Mali, the Niger, and Chad (Tuareg). They are found in small numbers in Tunisia and Libya, and in a few oases in lower Egypt (from Ghadames via Sokra and Kufra to Siwa). Like the Caucasian languages, the closely related languages spoken by the Berber are part of the remaining pre-Indo-European and pre-Turkic languages of the central and western Mediterranean. Apart from the nomadic camel-herding Tuareg, the Berber are agriculturalists. In spite of their strong resistance

to the colonial powers – the Rif-Kabyls under Abd el-Krim were not defeated until the 1920s with the use of airplanes and poison gas – the Berber do not even have minority status in their home countries, so that their languages are not taught in schools.

Black magic. Magic (q.v.) by which harm is caused to others through physical or emotional injury or by damaging material goods (e.g. making pots crack in the kiln), crops, animals, or social reputation (e.g. sowing suspicion or jealousy). A typical example of black magic known the world over is binding, in which straps, belts, or strings are tied or knotted so tightly that impotence is caused in the man one intends to harm. The extreme application of black magic results in death. As with all magic, black magic encompasses a wide variety of methods. One can push or hurl a stick in the victim's direction, saying his or her name out loud and adding an appropriate curse, such as "May your heart burst!" Another method is to obtain a personal object owned by the victim and place it next to a corpse in a coffin. Often the magician makes a "revenge" doll (see Fetish) and then pierces its heart with a needle or smashes it. It is important to name the victim and to state the intention clearly. There are proven cases of people who were aware that black magic was being used against them, and in which the effect could have been caused by autosuggestion. Autopsies showed that the cause of death was exactly like receiving a strong shock: a general collapse leads to a rapid slowdown of blood circulation and a drastic fall in blood pressure, with fatal consequences for the organs' ability to function.

Blacksmiths. Artisans who work with metal (copper, gold, silver, and most especially iron). In agrarian societies blacksmiths were very important, as they manufactured essential tools for farming, and, in expanding societies, weaponry as well. Blacksmiths were the object of ambivalent feelings: sometimes they enjoyed high status, sometimes they were looked down upon, but they were always feared. Their exceptional place in society is often a theme in mythology. According to the Dogon, Amma, the god of creation, made the first blacksmith (djemene) from the blood and umbilical cord of the nommo that he had sacrificed. The father of all blacksmiths therefore belongs to the pre-ancestral generation, the reason for the important and influential position of Dogon blacksmiths. They formed a socially limited, endogamous group who were forbidden to marry members of the second generation, descendants of the Lebe. As the blacksmiths were not involved in working the fields they lived a life of constant dependency.

Blood-brotherhood. Bond between two unrelated, usually young, men, created either through a mutual exchange of blood (by drinking, or mingling through cuts), or through adoption, in which one youth touches the breast of the other's mother with his mouth, or in which the mother simulates the birth of her adopted son. Blood brothers have the same rights and obligations toward each other as real brothers. Instances of blood-sisterhood, as among the Ziba in the small kingdom of Kiziba near Lake Victoria, in East Africa, seem to be rare.

Bush school. A somewhat inaccurate term for the camp, usually lying outside a settlement, where youths live together during their initiation. This custom is common among many African and other peoples. Initiation involves not only deprivations, tests of courage, the passing down of secret religious information known only to men, and the central ritual of rebirth, but also a course of teaching, although this plays a rather subordinate part.

Calabash. Dried and hollowed-out shell of the bottle pumpkin (Lagenaria vulgaris) and other types of gourd, used mostly as a container but also as a vessel for food, drink, and sacrifices. Calabashes are often decorated with paintings, engravings, patterns made by cutting away the skin, applied decoration, or carving. As household items they belong to women, who often wrap them in a net to carry or hang them. These calabash nets are schematically represented in the chevrons which decorate the walls of certain

Calabashes used as containers in northern Cameroon.

Nankana houses and which serve to represent an ordered household.

Carrier of soul or life power. Body fluids or parts of people or animals as well as parts of plants carrying a particularly high amount of vitality. Most societies differentiate between a vital soul (or life power) and a free soul. The latter comes from the beyond (such as the land of the dead) and is similar to a spirit; the former manifests itself in humans (and similarly in animals and plants) and its purpose it to maintain the living organism. According to universal belief, its main carrier substances are blood, bones, and teeth, as well as all bodily secretions such as sperm, mucus, breast milk, sweat, saliva, tears, and less frequently, urine (but never feces). Also seen as bodily secretions in the wider sense, and regarded as having a high concentration of soul or life power, are fingernails and toenails, hair, breath, the spoken or sung word, a look, and one's shadow. All these substances either have to do with movement (= life) or have a level of resistance. Blood flows, breath is exhaled, sperm and sweat are secreted, saliva increases with chewing, tears are the result of moving emotions, and nail and hair continue to grow after the maturing process is finished. Indeed, both of these as well as teeth and bones are less affected by the passing of time than any other part of the organism.

Circumcision. Operation in which parts of the external genitalia of children or adults of both sexes are removed or altered. The ethnological explanation for circumcision lies in the following facts and their central significance. Circumcision always concerns the genital organs; it is usually carried out at puberty, as part of the process of initiation; it occurs mostly in settled or partly settled societies. In settled communities, stronger social tensions arise, including around the transition period between one life stage and another. The fundamental purpose of life-stage rituals is to avoid conflict in these times of transition, particularly in the passage from child to adult, which is marked by various procedures, including circumcision. Widespread opinion holds that children are born bisexual (since they were produced by both parents). Outer signs of bisexuality are seen as the foreskin (believed to be a kind of vulva) and nipples in boys, and the clitoris and inner vulva (believed to be a kind of penis and foreskin) in girls. To mark the difference between their sexes, thereby making them fully fertile and able to reproduce, these secondary attributes of the opposite sex must be removed. In Africa male circumcision mostly takes two forms: circumcision (especially among the southeastern Bantu, in Central and West Africa, and in Madagascar), in which the entire foreskin (preputium) is removed by a cut around the penis, and incision (mostly practiced in central East Africa; for example, among the Maasai), in which the foreskin is merely cut from the collum glans to the end along one line. The two parts of skin initially hang down but soon grow together into a bulge which gradually reduces considerably in size. Through the spread of Islam many families and communities who had not previously practiced circumcision (*bitan* in Arabic) adopted this practice, as it served the purpose of religious purity. Female circumcision (more properly termed clitoridectomy or excision), which is carried out in Egypt and in nearly all of sub-Saharan Africa, involves the removal either of the labia or the labia and the clitoris, sometimes also the inner vulva, and very rarely also the upper part of the larger labia. The operation can take place just after birth, a few months or years later, or at the onset of puberty, and is carried out by older women, men not being allowed to attend. The Western media rightly attacks the practice of infibulation (also called pharaonic circumcision) carried out in Nubia and the Republic of Sudan, but also in parts of Eritrea, Somalia, Chad, northern Nigeria, and Mali. This is the process of closing or sewing up the vagina, always carried out together with excision on girls between two and eight years old. The labia majora, and sometimes also parts of the labia minora, are totally removed and an opening the size of a finger is left to allow urine and menstrual blood to flow out. Shortly before a girl's wedding an experienced woman or the bridegroom performs defibulation, cutting open the scar. Before the birth of the first child the scar is again cut open further, only to be closed up again after delivery, leaving an opening just large enough for sexual intercourse. Some men also request a total refibulation before going away on long journeys. These repeated operations often result in serious psychological and physical disorders (especially hemorrhages as well as acute or chronic infection of the urethra and genitalia) which can lead not only to infertility but also to death. Even so, 80 to 90 percent of girls and women in Nubia and the Sudan probably still undergo infibulation.

Clan. Originally a Scottish term describing larger groups of relatives with unilineal, that is either matrilineal or patrilineal, descent. A clan possesses its own territory; its members, who may number several hundred, tend to live in several villages, forming a series of smaller subclans or lineages.

Climbing tree. A tree trunk cut with notches serving as steps in the manner of a ladder, and forked at the upper end. Devices of this kind are used particularly in villages the West African savannas for reaching storehouses and climbing up to roof terraces.

Colon. Term applied to a certain type of African sculpture which appeared during colonial times in connection with cults and which is an expression of life under colonial rule. Colon figures depict people such as colonial bureaucrats, soldiers, merchants, and missionaries, with which the artists or those commissioning had dealings on a daily basis. The term originates with French emigrants who settled in the colonies, usually forced by economic hardship, and were called *colons* (colonists, with the derogatory meaning of peasants) by their more fortunate countrymen.

Consanguineous relationships (from Latin *consanguineus*, blood-related). Familial relationships based on common ancestry. In almost all traditional societies, consanguineity is restricted to paternal or maternal relations, as only unilineal (patrilineal or matrilineal) genealogies are acceptable. Therefore only patrilineal or matrilineal relatives are consanguine, or blood-related, though not the mother in the former case or the father in the latter.

Cosmogony (from Greek *kosmogonia*, the creation or beginning of the world). Mythical account of the creation of the world. The creators are usually the original supreme god and a kind of counter-god, a trickster (q.v.) who seeks to destroy or at least to damage the work of creation. Generally there are two different cosmogonies. One maintains that in the beginning there was a whole, usually in the shape of an egg, which the creator burst open from the inside to create heaven from the upper half, and the earth from the lower half. The second, more frequent (and probably the older) conception is based on a motionless mass of fluid over which the creator floats in the shape of a bird. Out of "boredom" he dives down into this original ocean, picks up a little mud with his beak, and makes the earth out of this, a flat disk which he lays exactly in the middle of the cosmos on the surface of the water and somehow anchors down. All cosmogonies have in common the principles of differentiation and evolution. Creation is a series of steps separating the solid from the fluid, light from dark, the formed from the shapeless, the earth from the ocean, even the here-and-now from the beyond. It follows the pattern of shaping the cosmos from the original chaos, the creation of the earth and the stars and planets, the subordinate deities, the spirits, plants, animals, and finally humans, who are taught how to live appropriately, their culture being brought by semidivine cultural heroes. All this happens through magic, as at the beginning the gods had neither tools nor technical knowledge, but did possess infinite magical powers. Often only a thought or a word is enough for something to happen. This is why so many myths now appear strange, bizarre, and often simply unbelievable.

Cowry. The highly-polished shell of the small sea snail Cyprea annulus, which is used as currency in Africa. Imported from the Maldives, cowry shells were used as small coins. They were recognized as currency throughout the Sudan, although their low value – in 1850 one English penny was worth 300 shells – forced merchants to carry them in huge amounts. Today they are used as decoration (for example on masks), in various rituals, and in divination (often in oracles).

Cult house. A building or space dedicated to religion or ritual. With regard to religion, cult houses, or sites, cover a broad spectrum, including not only natural sites, ancestral shrines, and sacrificial places, but also areas deliberately separated from the secular world. Important sacred objects of a community (family, village, association, or cult) are kept there. Cult houses also serve religious or cult assemblies. They often reflect the society's particular conception of the world, or at least embody hints of it.

Dahomey (also Dahome, Danhome, or Daxome). The second most important West African coastal kingdom after Ashanti. Possessing no gold, it became known in Europe mainly through the role it played in the slave trade. In the late 15th century Allada (Ardra) and Ouidah (Whydah) were the largest political communities of the Ewe, in what today is the Bay of Benin. Dahomey was a realm in the back country and had begun as an outpost of Allada in the 17th century. In 1724 Dahomey conquered Allada and became the dominating local power, although it had to pay tributes to the kingdom of Oyo. The power of the king, resident in the capital Abomey (Abome), was limited by the most important princes, who countered absolutism with their more down-to-earth communities. Even so, Dahomey was a more strictly authoritarian kingdom than its predecessors. Succession fell to the firstborn, and as a result there were only ten kings of Dahomey between 1650 and 1899. While Dahomey did make raids into neighboring territories, it never established a great empire, always remaining a small kingdom ruled by local chiefs and the royal court. Religion was strictly controlled by the king. Dahomey's army consisted mainly of regular soldiers armed with muskets. The famous army of Amazons, probably initially the royal bodyguards, was one of several ways in which the king gave women important official responsibilities. There was a strict order of rank, severe etiquette and rigorous militarism, and slaves were the king's property. The last king of Dahomey, appointed by the French, was deposed in 1900, when the monarchy was abandoned. When Madagascar (colonized in 1896) became a French protectorate, France connected the lands surrounding its various support points and also gained new territory. France finally gained control of the colonies of Senegal, French Guinea, Ivory Coast, and Dahomey, which came to be collectively referred to as French West Africa.

Digging stick. Basic tool in nearly all traditional agrarian cultures of America, Oceania, South East Asia, northeastern and southwestern India, and northeastern, eastern, and central Africa (in other areas the ax was used). It is usually a bamboo or wooden pole, 3 to 6 feet long, sharpened at one end, either all the way round or on one side only so as to give it a wider, rudder- or lance-shaped working point. To make the stick more effective a rock is often fastened to it and there may also be a "pedal" at the lower end. The tool is used for digging holes for seeds or plants, for breaking up the soil, and also partly for raking. Digging sticks were used from very early times in hunter-gatherer societies for extracting roots, truffles, and bulbs lying beneath the ground; thus it is one of the oldest implements.

Duodecimal realm (from the Latin *duodecim*, meaning twelve, or a dozen). Derogatory term for a state consisting of tiny, or "dozens of," countries. Originally used to describe Germany's situation in the 18th and 19th centuries in particular, when a number of small and tiny near-autonomous principalities ruled by counts, princes, and dukes shattered the old country's unity.

Earth-chief. The chief, the "eldest" of the local "founding clan," in many traditional agrarian cultures around the world, particularly in Indonesia and West Africa. Agrarian cultures commonly maintain a legend according to which their ancestors were the first to set foot on the land and civilize it; thus it belongs to them, which is why they also have the closest links to it, particularly to the ancestors and the various nature spirits of nature and earth deities. The head of the founding clan, the earth-chief, is therefore responsible for the main priestly functions by which the ancestors and the earth are honored. He works to maintain good relations between people and the earth, so as to ensure fertility, health, and prosperity for all, performs the main rituals at sowing and harvesting times, offers sacrifices to the earth, and holds ultimate powers of decision in the distribution of, and disputes over, land.

Ethnology. The term is a combination of the Greek words *ethnos* (nation) and *logos* (teachings), and it was created in Europe toward the end of the 18th century. Ethnology is the study of the culture and history of "traditional" peoples (so called because they live closely bound to traditions), mostly tribal peoples but now also certain sectors of modern society (groups of children, people grouped by profession or area of residence, communities, societies, minorities, businesses, and so on). An analogous term is "cultural anthropology." In contrast, "ethnography," formed from the Greek words *ethnos* and *graphein* (to write), writing, is understood to mean the description of a people, that is, the depiction of the culture of a single ethnic group (local community, tribe, or population) based on research on location. Because it is such a wide field, ethnology has now divided into several subdisciplines, such as ethnobotanics, ethnogerontology, ethnomedicine, ethnopedagogics, and ethnophilosophy, which concerns the foundations of wisdom and conceptual systems in traditional societies.

A fetish priest of Dahomey.
From: *Malerische Studien*, Neuchâtel, undated.

Fetish. Originally a term for the amulets (*feitico*) carried by Portuguese sailors in the early days of European exploration, and later used by Europeans for any object that they saw being used by the inhabitants of the African coasts in connection with magic or cult practices. With no exact definition, a fetish is usually a manufactured object that is entered by spirits or impersonal powers after the appropriate rituals. The European concept of fetishism (belied in fetishes) dates largely from the 19th century, when the ethnology of religion regarded fetishism as the precursor of religion. In European parlance, fetishism now carries negative connotations. The power of fetishes can be activated through sacrifices and are magically used for protection, causing harm, or increasing wealth or fertility. In West Africa the term *ju-ju* (a corruption of the

French word *jouet*, toy) is synonymous with fetish. Particularly well known are the fetishes of the Ewe and Fon (the local population refers to an inanimate object as *bo*, a humanlike figure as *bocio*). Even better known are the sculptures from the Bantu area, also described as mirror or nail fetishes, whose energy is located in a bulge or fold in the belly area. These are similar to shrines but also act as "revenge" dolls. Like the dolls used in Europe in the past, they are pierced with nails and can cause harm to an enemy, depending on the type of magic used. Most fetishes, however, are collections of energy-giving substances, often including certain stones, horns, claws, teeth, bones, hair, animal skin, and so on, but also pieces of material, dirt, menstrual blood, and other similar "unclean" but effective things.

Fetishes from the temple at Toffoa (after Repin). From: *Westafrika. Vom Senegal bis Benguela*, Leipzig, 1878.

Founding family. In settled, agrarian societies a local or tribal community usually consists of several families (lineages or clans); all have a single common ancestor but only one is directly descended from that ancestor, while the others are descendants of different, younger side branches. The founder of the family is said be the first to have taken possession of the territory and cultivated it, as he was created there, stepped out of the earth there, or came to that particular place. His direct descendants are the members of the founding family. As priority and seniority automatically confer greater authority in traditional societies, direct descendants always enjoy certain privileges: they "own" the land, their huts are at the center of the settlement, their eldest, the "earth-chief" (q.v.), plays a leading part in ancestor and earth cults, acts as judge in land disputes, and carries the main responsibility for maintaining tradition, especially in religion. All members of the founding family are said to have special mental powers (for instance in interpreting dreams and divination) as well as greater effectiveness in working magic. Often they

are seen as more virtuous, more upright, and even more beautiful than others. They are the equivalent of the community's aristocracy.

Free soul. Up until the Middle Ages, and even later in some rural communities, people in Europe, as in most of the rest of the world, believed not in the theologically correct "unitary soul" but that a person has two souls: the vital or life soul, which maintains his or her organic functions (breathing, blood circulation, etc.) and which is responsible for body warmth and mobility, and the free soul, which is usually located under the skull and is the seat of consciousness and the powers of understanding, decision, and will. While the life soul is indissolubly linked to the organism, the free soul is regarded simply as a spiritual being independent of the body, similar to spirits and gods. Whenever the functions of the organism are suspended, such as during sleep, a fainting spell, in delirium, etc., the free soul can escape its physical bonds and journey into the beyond. Whatever it sees and experiences there is communicated to the person in dreams. Many tribes believe that after death the free soul enters the underworld of the ancestors, to reappear as a reincarnation three to five generations later. From this point of view people are not immortal but their free souls are.

Frobenius, Leo (1853–1938). German cultural philosopher and explorer of Africa. From 1904 until his death Frobenius and his colleagues from the Research Institute for Cultural Morphology (which he founded and which is now known as the Frobenius Institute) organized 22 research explorations around the world, mainly to Africa. Frobenius himself went on the following: Congo-Kasai (1904–06); western Sudan (Mali, Burkina Faso, Togo; 1907–09); northwestern Africa (Morocco, Algeria, Tunisia; 1910); Nigeria, Kanem (1910–12); Cordovan (1912); Saharan Atlas (Algeria; 1912–14); Red Sea (Eritrea; 1915); Nubian desert (1926); southern Africa (Zimbabwe, Botswana, Lesotho, Mozambique, Namibia, Zambia; 1928–30); Fezzan (1932); Libyan desert (1933). His interest lay in culture as a whole, in the "being" of cultures, defined by each one's immanent soul (paideuma). For Frobenius every culture was a living organism in the biological sense, independent of the human being, to whom he merely ascribed the role of

Leo Frobenius.

"carrier." A culture's history therefore also follows the rules of the natural world, marked by birth, growth, and decay. He drew an analogous lifeline for cultures, comprising "capture" (youth), "expression" (maturity), and "experience" (old age). As controversial in his lifetime as now, Frobenius is the best-known and the most famous German ethnologist. His respect for Africans and their culture won him the admiration of African intellectuals (particularly Léopold S. Senghor and Aimé Césaire). They enthusiastically took up Frobenius' ideas of the fundamental equivalence of all cultures and valued him as someone who saw Africa as a cultured and civilized continent and who had restored to Africans the dignity of which they had been robbed by colonialism.

Gana (Ghana). Trading kingdom at the southern end of the caravan routes, located between Senegal and the Niger bend (approximately corresponding to the border region between what are today Mauritania and Mali). It was founded in AD 300, probably by Berbers, and conquered by Soninke c. 790. It reached its apogee c. 900 as the main trading point between North Africa and the Sudan. (It is not to be confused with today's Ghana, with which it shares only the name.) The trading metropolis Gana (Ganata) was one of the largest and most densely populated cities in the world of its time; there gold and slaves were exchanged for salt, copper, textiles, brassware, coral, glass beads, cowry shells, dates, figs, and horses. Early Arab scholars called Gana the "land of gold": it was estimated that the country produced 9 tons of pure gold a year, and the king owned a lump weighing 1 ton which he tied his horse to. In the 11th century Gana was plundered by the Almoravids; in 1240 it was conquered by neighboring Mali, situated south of the upper Niger, and assimilated into the realm.

Gonja empire. Empire founded in the mid-16th century in what is today northern Ghana, between the Volta and Oti rivers in the Nta region. Traders (wangara) and mounted warriors from the old Mali empire were crucial to Gonja's emergence. Traders had advanced from the Niger belt in the southeast into the gold reserves of the Akan as part of Mande expansion or to obtain kola nuts in the southwestern forests; warriors were in control of the gold trade. The economy of the Gonja empire was based mostly on trade. On the border between savanna and rainforest, gold was exchanged for slaves who had been acquired by raiding local populations and who were intended for labor in the forests. The reputation of Mali, from where the strangers originally came, was so high among the local population (of whom the Guan are a relatively closed group) that even the rulers of Gonja, who did not speak Mande, traced their origins to Malinke horsemen. Ready to accept any power that proved effective, the local population revered the Muslims as great sorcerers.

Griaule, Marcel (1898–1956). French ethnologist, one of the most important African scholars of his time. He undertook several long research expeditions, first to Ethiopia, then to western Sudan, most notably to the Dogon in Mali, to whom he subsequently devoted much of his interest. For Griaule ethnological fieldwork was less valid than dialog. He understood how to listen and respected the culture, conceptions, and dignity of the people to whom he spoke. A committed defender of cultural relativism, he believed that every culture has its own unique and valid greatness, and that it always represents a coherent, regulated whole that is explained and legitimized by its mythology alone. He expounded this in his most famous work, *Dieu d'eau: Entretiens avec Ogotemmêli* (1948; *God of Water: Discussions with Ogotemmêli*), a monument to his great Dogon teacher, the blind seer and wise man Ogotemmêli.

Griot. Term used mostly in francophone West Africa to describe professional singers or musicians who recite historical texts and genealogies at festivities and ceremonies. Griots frequently have special status (especially among Mande speakers) and are considered to be a distinctive group, or caste, in society (much like certain artisans, such as blacksmiths). While griots attached to royal courts are considered to be courtly dignitaries, those without fixed patronage, who beg for custom, have a low status.

Guardian deities, guardian spirits. Spiritual beings associated with a place, an individual, or a group, which they protect from danger and from damaging influences, on the condition that appropriate rituals and codes of conduct are observed. Personal guardian deities, who are often found by young men during a long period of searching isolation, are particularly recognized by Native Americans as well as by shamans. In Africa people acknowledge not only personal but also territorial guardian spirits, from the spiritual owner of a field, forest, or village, to the divine guardians of whole regions, who, mirroring human society, stand in hierarchical relationships to each other. The most influential among them often act in legitimizing the power held by the current political leader by delegating some of their authority to him, their highest priest. Elaborate annual ceremonies are dedicated to these important deities; lesser guardians receive sacrificial gifts before a field is used, while a house is being built, or before hunting.

Guinea coast. The West African coast between the Senegal and Kunene rivers, on either side of the Gulf of Guinea, divided into northern Upper Guinea and southern Lower Guinea by Mount Cameroon. In spite of the hot, humid tropical climate of the lowlands (where temperatures exceed 100° F in summer, and rainfall is more than 60 inches a year), a high risk of fever, and a strong tide (Kalema), the Guinea coast attracted Europeans, who were successful traders, especially in the western part. The old names of Pepper Coast (the coast of Sierra Leone and Liberia), Ivory or Tooth Coast (Ivory Coast), Gold Coast (Ghana), and Slave Coast (Benin, Nigeria) are indicative of this mercantile importance. In the 17th century, the initial traders, Portugal and Spain, were joined by England, France, Denmark, and the Netherlands. They all sought to establish themselves on the Guinea coast, where they ran factories protected by forts. They initially had no interest in venturing into the interior.

Gyaman. Province and one-time vassal state of Ashanti in Ivory Coast. Kofi Adinkra, king of Gyaman, broke the unwritten rule that only the asantehene is allowed to decorate his stool with gold and to own a gold elephant's tail. Any transgression of this fundamental rule counted as treason, a challenge to the asantehene's singular authority. In 1811 Kumasi received the news that the ruler of Gyaman had ordered a gold stool to be made for him. In response the asantahene sent out a delegation to demand that the stool be handed over. However, the negotiations brought no success, and the rebellion was only suppressed in 1818 by a military invasion, in which Kofi Adinkra was killed.

Herskovits, Melville Jean (1895–1963). American ethnologist (a student of Franz Boas). In the 1920s Herskovits also worked in physical anthropology, and later only in regional and comparative ethnology. He led field research in West Africa (his two-volume work *Dahomey. An Ancient West African Kingdom* appeared in 1938), as well as in North, South, and particularly Central America. He is seen as the founder of Afro-American studies in the United States. In 1941 he declared syncretism to be fundamental to the assimilation process of blacks in America; he therefore acknowledged the existence of a separate Afro-American culture, which had previously been denied. Questions of comparative and changing culture comprise the main thrust of Herskovits' work. He is regarded as the founder of the methodology and philosophy of cultural relativism. According to cultural relativism, law, justice, ideals of beauty, and so on vary between cultures, although there are certain similarities; more significant are universal human experiences. Herskovits' theory of cultural relativism made a significant contribution to the possibility of developing a better understanding between peoples.

Hierodules God's handmaidens (from Greek *hieros*, sacred, and *doule*, maid). In various countries of the ancient Orient and Asia Minor, girls and women could either voluntarily commit themselves or were given by their relatives as an offering to work in the temple of a (usually female) deity. The tasks of the hierodules usually included prostitution; as representatives of the goddess they received either all visitors or only particular priests.

Hogon. Priest of the Lebe cult and also the highest religious authority among the Dogon. Everyday

The hogon of Nombori.

matters are settled by the eldest of the patrilineal lineages, but beyond that the responsibility for every village lies with a hogon, who is assisted by a number of people who help with particular rituals and secular functions. There is a chief hogon, but his authority is weak and imprecisely determined. Basically a religious leader, the hogon is mainly responsible for general wellbeing, and especially for the earth's fertility and, as rain priest, for sufficient rainfall. In Sanga he is elected from among the elders; in other villages a younger man "full of the power of life," who must also descend from a particular lineage, is chosen. The hogon's office is explained in myth. The original ancestor (Lebe) in the land of the Mande (q.v.) had two sons. The elder of them fathered three sons, each with different woman, and these became the founders of the Dogon subgroups Dyon, Dono, and Oro. The second child of the younger son is regarded as the original ancestor of the Aru. After Lebe, the original ancestor, died, the Dogon carried earth from his grave to their new settlements, where they built altars with that earth.

Hourglass drum. Membraphone named for its shape, wide at either extremity and narrow in the center. The type is particularly common in East and West Africa. In East Africa the drum often has only one membrane and is played in a different way from that in West Africa, where the drummer changes the tension of the membrane while playing. He does this by tightening or loosening the strings running between the two membranes, either with his hand or, if he is holding the instrument under his arm, by compressing them. He beats the skins with a bent stick.

Hunon. Ewe term for priest. Like *tro* and *vodun*, hu (blood) describes a deity, but it is almost always used in connection with other words, such as hunon, owner of the *hu*, and *hukpame* (*houmfo* in the Haitian voodoo cult), the deity's home or the cult house. *Bokonon*, owner of the *bo*, is a similar formation describing the owner of magic means (*bo*) or magic figures (*bocio*).

Hunter's initiation. A form of individual initiation of boys, carried out until quite recently

After killing a lion as part of his initiation, a youth becomes a hunter.

in hunter-gatherer societies in Siberia, North America (among the Inuit), and Africa. The underlying reason for the ritual was a belief in close similarities, even a familial relationship, between humans and animals, typical of hunter-gatherer societies. A young hunter had to confront the problem of learning how to kill a "relative," which constituted a cardinal sin. The hunter's initiation was a preparation for this

intended to strengthen the bond between hunter and animals, in particular his prey, through magic and a kind of blood-brotherhood. Among the Bushmen the elders rubbed ashes from the burned meat of the main hunted animals into cuts between the initiate's eyes and on his upper right arm, which would also help him see the animal from afar and aid the accuracy of his aim. Among the Pygmies, the initiate's weapons were anointed with the blood of the animal that he killed during a trial hunt, and the hunter given the animal's stock to drink or made to hold and press important organs such as the heart in his hand. This connected the vital energy of both and established the desired relationship between hunter and hunted animal. The belief that killing was only possible with the prior agreement of the "lord of the wild," and that the animal would be reincarnated if its skeleton remained whole (great care was taken in this), greatly assuaged feelings of guilt. In addition every animal received apologies after it was killed, and a ritual of reconciliation followed.

Hunters' society. Association of hunters with characteristics similar to a secret society. Knowledge is passed on only to initiated members, and the society has its own secret language, often also owns masks, and fulfills an important role on the death of a member. For instance, during funerals and mourning ceremonies members of the society appear in masks, disguised as the most important hunting animals, so that the rituals for the dead man are observed correctly and his soul safely reaches the world beyond.

Initiation (from Latin *initiare*, to start, to introduce, and *initiatio*, celebration of a secret religious service). A partly sacred, partly profane ceremony carried out in many traditional societies at the onset of puberty to carry adolescents into adulthood, which, in comparison with childhood, is considered to be a new and qualitatively different phase because it brings sexual and moral maturity as well as social responsibilities. Girls' initiations differ from those of boys in that the former are mostly individual initiations, whereas the latter are usually collective. However, the form is similar for both. First, the initiates are separated from their families and taken to a bush school (q.v.) outside the settlement (a house of seclusion in the case of an individual initiation). Here the leading older men or women make them undergo certain physical hardships (beatings, torture, food and sleep deprivation, tests of their resistance) to strengthen their physical and moral fortitude, and teach them about important cultural issues such as social and sexual mores and religious traditions. As this is a marked change in their existence, the ritual rebirth lies at the core of the initiation. The

separation from their family is like dying; in the bush camp, representing the land of the dead, they are "killed" by the "ancestors" (the masked elders) and then, as "dead," they may not eat or speak, are hardly allowed to move, neglect bodily hygiene, and are painted white. During this central phase their transformation takes place: they are circumcised and marked with their tribe's signs – a mutilated lip, nose, or ear, deformed teeth, or a specific tattoo. Thereafter the rules of behavior are gradually loosened, the initiates receive a new name and new clothing and are painted red. Returned to life, they leave the bush school, which is then destroyed, and triumphantly return to the village, where a great feast awaits them. They are now allowed to marry. While individual initiations for girls take place nearly everywhere, collective initiations for both sexes occur mainly in the tropical agrarian cultures of South America, Melanesia, and Indonesia as well as Africa. Individual boys' initiations were customary only as hunters' initiations (q.v.) in some hunter-gatherer societies.

Jihad (from the Arabic *djahada*, meaning "trying for something"). Fight or war against "unbelievers," that is, non-Muslims and those who pretend to be Muslims, as well as those who have abandoned the faith; also an Islamic "rule of virtue" (not a duty of faith). According to several passages in the Koran, participating in the jihad guarantees not only the benefits of looting but also entry into paradise after death. The "holy war" is meant to spread the "true faith" and therefore will end only when Islam has become the world's dominant religion.

Kaolin. A thick, white earthy clay, named for Kaoling, the mountain in China, which feels fine to the touch because of its specific mineral content (mostly kaolinite), and which becomes malleable when water is added. In Africa, particularly in eastern and western Sudan, kaolin is painted on the body, the white color symbolizing either ritual purity (for instance, of priests) or ritual death and entry into a new life during initiation.

Kola nut. Fruit of the trees of the genus Steruliacea, of which there are more than 100 varieties). The tree grows up to 50 feet tall in the West African rainforest. The fruits grow as star-shaped clusters of woody pods, each about 6 inches long. A single pod contains five to ten plum-sized seeds (wrongly described as nuts) coated with a thick, white mucous substance. The thick, hard casing around the seed is yellowish-brown to red in color, which as it dries changes to reddish-brown. In spite of its bitter taste, the kola nut is a highly valued food in many parts of West Africa. It is a high-energy food that satisfies both hunger and thirst.

Land of the Mande. Region claimed as their original homeland by several groups spread widely across West Africa. Today there are about 20 million speakers of Mande languages and dialects living between the upper Niger and the Atlantic coast. The differences between the "central" and the "peripheral" Mande are defined in geographical and historical terms. The former live in Mali and on the Niger bend; the latter left the core area many centuries ago and are today spread over Senegal, Gambia, Guinea, Sierra Leone, Liberia, Ivory Coast, and Burkina Faso. The central Mande area may have been settled as early as 5000–4000 BC, where Mande's ancestors grew grains and vegetables (including millet, different types of beans, sesame, and okra). It was here that the two empires of the West African savanna – Gana (9th to 11th centuries) and Mali (12th to 15th) – developed, controlling trade across the Sahara between the gold-producing lands in the forests to the south and the Mediterranean countries. When Mali declined, its position was taken by the smaller Bambara, or Bamana, empires in the south. Today the Soninke, Malinke, and Bambara, altogether about 5 million, make up the majority of the population of present-day Mali, while other smaller Mande groups live in the south and west of the country.

Law. The norms and rules by which the life of a community goes on without conflict. In contrast to the codified law that has existed in highly sophisticated civilizations since ancient times, law in nonliterate societies is a "law of customs" (e.g. the Adat law in Indonesia). It is validated by the passing down of an all-inclusive, traditional order of life which was established by the gods in the very beginning and repeatedly affirmed by the ancestors. From this point of view there is only one law, although there are of course certain focal points: the protection of body and life, the maintenance of harmony within the household or family and in the society, and of good relations with the powers beyond. In traditional societies there is also a difference between law relating to material property, claims of ownership of all material objects, and the law relating to immaterial goods such as intellectual property (songs, poems, magic spells, decorative patterns, etc.). There is collective ownership (of wild animals, land, pasture, and use of water) as well as individual ownership. Generally valid is the rule that anything which someone finds or discovers outside the settlement, makes or invents themself, has acquired through an exchange of his or her own goods (or purchase), and what has been given to him or her personally, such as a name, jewelry, or a guardian spirit, belongs to that person. The law prevents transgressions, protects goods, and punishes offenses. The instruments of the law are public opinion, gossip, mockery and outright criticism, social isolation, physical

punishment according to the principle of "an eye for an eye, a tooth for a tooth," and finally, exile or execution. In serious cases, such as theft, black magic, witchcraft, sexual offenses, murder, or severe transgressions against ancestors or gods, a judiciary usually consisting of the heads of families, the elders of the resident lineages or clans, and the village chief assemble. Trials involve questioning the accuser and defendant, witness statements, direct evidence, oaths from those questioned, and the judges' experience, based on their knowledge of the society and previous cases. In cases of persistent doubt the parties involved must undergo an ordeal – i.e. trial by poison, fire, or water, which is really handing the decision to the ancestors or gods. If offenses are committed in secret, the sinners must expect justice from the ancestors or gods: their good fortune disappears, their harvest fails, they fall sick, suffer an accident, or are struck by lightning. Traditional justice was highly effective, and the crime rate was frequently observed to be extremely low.

Legba. Divine trickster figure of the Ewe and Fon, very similar to Eshu (Exu), a Yoruba deity. The Fon regard Legba as the youngest but highly talented child of the creator couple Mawu-Lisa to whom people owe their knowledge of healing and magic. Legba straddles the border between the two worlds: he acts as messenger between humans and gods, and as guardian of entrances to houses, villages, and estates. Although there are no cults specifically dedicated to him, he is the first god to whom people turn. He richly rewards those who venerate him; those who neglect him are punished, as he upsets all their plans and activities and spins intrigues against them.

Lineage. Ethnological term referring to a sideline or subgroup of the common unilineal (patrilineal or matrilineal) genealogy of a clan (q.v.). Lineages cover only a few generations, so that the name of the originating father (or mother, in the case of matrilineal lineage) is known. Members of a lineage usually number no more than 80 and all therefore inhabit one village or, in towns and cities, a single street or quarter. They are much more closely bound together than a clan, a larger grouping.

Livingstone, David (1813–73). Scottish doctor, missionary, and explorer of Africa. In the first of his 28 years in Africa, Livingstone worked for the London Missionary Society, mostly among the

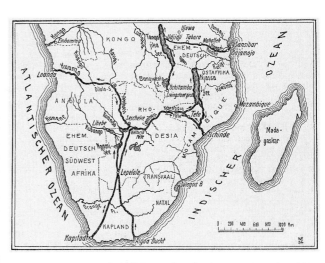

David Livingstone's exploration routes in southern Africa. From: *Das große Wagnis*, Berlin, 1936.

Tswana in southern Africa. From 1849 he embarked on a plan to push further into areas of the interior as yet unknown to Europeans, thereby preparing the way for God's word. Rather than saving a few souls in a small area, he considered it more useful in the long term for missionary work to be supported by the development of world trade. On his travels through the interior he discovered Lake Ngami in 1849. His great expedition (1853–56) led him from Linyanti to Luanda and from there eastward through the continent to the Zambesi estuary. In 1859 he reached Lake Nyasa (Lake Malawi), and from 1858 to 1864 he was the official leader of the British Zambesi expedition, whose declared aim was to find raw materials which could be sold profitably and would therefore provide an alternative to the increasingly controversial slave trade. He researched and reported on the slave trade in the African interior mostly when he was traveling through what is today Zambia and Tanzania in 1865–73, where he also refused to be "saved" by the journalist Henry Morton Stanley in 1871. He died during his search for the source of the Nile, which he mistakenly assumed to be at the upper Congo, near Lake Bangweulu. His African servants carried his body all the way to the coast so that it could be brought to England and buried in Westminster Abbey, London. Livingstone was greatly admired for his exploration and description of large parts of the African interior and its population, but especially for his tireless work against the slave trade (particularly as conducted by the Arabs), the abolition of which he wanted to aid by opening up Africa to world trade.

Magic. Term derived from the word for the Zoroastrian priests (magoi) in ancient Persia who were reputed to be great sorcerers, a phenomenon registered by the Greek word *mageia*.

Sorcerers from Urna.
From: *Die Völker der Erde*, Würzburg and Vienna, 1891.

The Latin form of the word – *magia* – is legacy of the Romans. Magic is always used at times of crisis (in sickness, hardship, or before risky undertakings) which are considered to be unusually problematic and which can therefore only be mastered by unusual methods. Unlike witchcraft (q.v.), magic requires no innate talent, only a technique, which can be learned. The greater someone's knowledge, experience, and skill with the necessary means and methods, the more likely his or her success. But this alone does not suffice: the underlying basis of all magic is the belief in power (q.v.). In order to influence something, to move, shape, change, or destroy, the practitioner of magic must be able to recognize and harness the one or more powers required. Traditionally there are three basic powers: organic life power (identical to the vital soul), the power of nature (working in moving water, fire, wind, hard rock, and so on), and spiritual power (found in the free soul, ancestors, spirits, and gods). Through mental concentration ("wishing"), particular spells, and rituals, magical acts bring these powers via carrier substances to their target, where they effect the desired outcome. This can generally be made to happen in three ways: by immediate transmission, or contact magic, either by bringing someone in touch with a powerful material (a root, ointment, or relic) or consuming a strengthening or healing potion; by targeted radiation across medium distances, transferring powers through words, song, shouts, looks, or gestures; or by transfer from afar. In the last case, the target, such as someone not present, an ancestor, or a spirit, and his or her reaction cannot be registered. Therefore transmission can be effected only by means of spiritual powers – the free soul (mental concentration, willpower) or a spirit called for this purpose – and requires sign language to clarify its intentions. The practitioner of magic expresses himself or herself by analogy (analogous magic) by miming, or pictorially displaying, his or her intent, for instance by making a doll out of wax and stabbing it in the heart area with needle, with the intention of removing a hated rival. In anthropological terms magic is a universal phenomenon; it is known and practiced in all cultures, even prehistoric ones. It appears to be infallible, as success is proof of its effectiveness and failure can always be ascribed to incorrect preparation or application. For this reason magic continues to be used in present-day industrial societies, even if less obviously: it plays a part in questions of love, sport, gambling, in sickness and other hardships, during war, in advertising, and in political propaganda.

Mahdi (from Arabic *al-Mahdi*, one led by God). Initially an honorific for great figures in Islamic history (such as Abraham, Mohammed, the first four caliphs), later a kind of messiah, similar to the Jewish-Christian messiah, who, at the end of time, when evil, depravity, and tyranny have triumphed, would appear as the "last caliph" of the prophet, hold judgment, and restore Islam to its original form. In the course of history, especially during times of hardship, many claimed to be the awaited Mahdi. Particularly well known was the Sudanese Mohammed Ahmad ibn Abdallah (1843–85), who made the claim in 1881 and assumed leadership of the revolt against Ottoman rule. Four years later he had taken control of almost all of eastern Sudan. Only in 1889, when his successor Khalifa Abdallah was in power, were the English under Lord Kitchener able to reconquer the land.

Mami Wata. In Central and West African pidgin, the name of a female water deity, generally also for extraordinarily beautiful women who are believed to embody qualities of Mami Wata. The Mami Wata cult probably began in the early 20th century in the river area of southern Nigeria and spread from there over the whole of West Africa. Today Mami Wata is an independent goddess with specific shrines and cult practices dedicated to her. She is characterized as a beautiful, seductive river goddess with long, flowing hair and light skin. She is believed to help her followers to unexpected riches, but also punishes those who anger her with terrible poverty or madness. To emphasize her connection with water and its inhabitants, she is often depicted with a fish's tail. Both men and women are initiated into her cult for various reasons (physical and psychological sufferings are often cited). Sometimes her followers are rumored to have sexual intercourse with her in the spirit world, a relationship which she guards with jealousy and vengefulness. Apart from the connection between money and sex, the goddess embodies other phenomena of the modern world. Full of irresistible charms, independent and self-reliant, but also unreliable in her moods, she reflects urban life and its impermanence. As foreign people and ways of life come together in large urban areas, so the Mami Wata cult is an amalgam of African, Western, and Indian traditions and images. The altars dedicated to the goddess are covered with a variety of objects: lemonade, sweet foods, perfume, baby powder, and similar objects seen to be an urban woman's essentials are some of her preferred sacrificial gifts.

Marabout. In North Africa a god-fearing man or woman, or even a saint or his or her descendants, from the Arabic term *murabit*, which reached European languages via Portuguese *marabuto*. In Morocco *wali* and especially *saiyid* are more widely used terms with the same meaning. More than others, marabouts dedicate themselves to ascetic trials and religious contemplation often tinged with mysticism. To achieve this they would often withdraw to live as hermits or retreat to the isolation of a monastery, a community of the like-minded. Prominent marabouts are often revered as saints after their death and sometimes become the guardians of villages and cities, even of entire regions. Their graves, with their characteristic chalk-white domes, become the focus of shrines. Believers from the local area make pilgrimages to the site, and at certain times of the year the saint's descendants organize great celebrations there. The head of the family collects the often considerable donations and distributes them among the other family members. It is believed that a marabout's power (baraka) still works through his descendants, so that they are often asked for help and advice. Even at the end of the 19th century marabouts and their families still had considerable influence in North Africa, and their members were often called to mediate in local and ethnic disputes.

Mask (from the Arabic *mashara*, practical joker, thence from Italian *maschera* and French *masque*). Whether covering only the head or the whole body (a costume mask), whether a naturalistic image or a strongly stylized form, masks are originally and universally regarded as representations of the greater powers. These are often ancestral spirits (ghosts), but can also be nature spirits and demons of sickness, such as giants or dwarves. Those wearing such masks do not merely act out the part of a spirit, but identify with the power to such an extent, especially in rituals, that the spirit takes possession of them, and they are turned into the spirit to whom they have lent their bodies. Masks usually appear at times of transition, at night, at the arrival of the new year, at harvest celebrations, and at initiations, funeral ceremonies, and commemorations of the dead. The ancestors in particular take this opportunity to name miscreants and admonish them for transgressions that they have committed over the period of time just ended, to administer justice if necessary, and to mete out punishments. Communicating with the spirits, and coming into direct contact with the masks, are the prerogatives of men. Often men formed mask societies, secret associations from which those not initiated, especially women and children, were strictly debarred. The uninitiated were usually not permitted to know on pain of death which men were behind which masks. There are myths telling of a time when women were in possession of the mystery of masks, until the men snatched it from them.

Mawu-Lisa. Twin deity of the Fon, embodying the female Mawu and the male Lisa (broadly equivalent with Mawu-Sodza and Mawu-Sogble

A masked dancer at a mourning ceremony among the Winima.

of the Ewe). As the divine couple, Mawu-Lisa stands at the head of the heaven's pantheon, to which, among many others, Gu, the god of iron, and Age or Adela, lord of the bush and wild animals, also belong. The three eldest children of a total of 14, Sakpata, Sogbo, and Agbe, founded their own pantheons. The cult of Mawu-Lisa and her "children" (voduwo) was introduced in Dahomey by the mother of King Tegbesu, an Aja woman and initiated priestess. The cult replaced that of Nana Buruku, an older androgynous deity which created the world out of itself. Efforts to harmonize "foreign" conceptions and names of gods with local ones have resulted in the assumption that Nana Buruku gave birth to the twin couple Mawu-Lisa. Many of the "new" deities are regarded as different manifestations of already established powers (e.g. among the various thunder deities). In many parts of West Africa Mawu-Lisa is linked with the conception of a creator god associated with the heavens who is of little importance in people's everyday life. Numerous myths tell of a time when the deity lived close to its creations, but it suffered disappointment and retreated into heaven. To maintain contact it created the voduwo to look after the earth and communicate between the earth and the heavens. Early Christian missionaries believed that in the heavenly couple Mawu-Lisa they could recognize divine concepts similar to their own and interpreted Mawu as God the father, Lisa as Jesus.

Medicine. Substance or combination of substances of various kinds, usually organic and of plant origin (in many African languages the words for "medicine" and "tree" are identical), used for healing. As it is not always possible to differentiate between the empirical and magical effects of a medicine, the meaning of the term extends to any means or objects which support the efforts or benefit the intentions and aims of the owner, or protect him or her from harmful influences. This is often a combination of several carriers of power, which are activated through particular rituals and sacrifices and greatly influence the result of human endeavors as well as human fate in general. As long as he or she knows the recipe, any adult can prepare medicines, most of which are taken orally, or rubbed into or carried on the body. A well-known example of the latter are the "medicine bunches" or "medicine bags" of Native Americans such as the Sioux or the Iroquois. These are bunches or bags containing feathers, stones, bones, birds' claws, lighters, pipes, rattles, small figures, healing herbs, and more, which were reputed to possess special magical powers. The owner had put them together following instructions received from his or her guardian spirit in a dream. Their effectiveness could be applied to fishing, hunting, the harvest, and the weather as well as to the healing of sickness, protection from danger, and the general wellbeing of the carrier and his or her family. In Africa, medicines protecting the individual from bad luck mostly take the form of amulets or talismans (constructed from animal parts, metals, various plants bound in leather, or sayings from the Koran) or of "medicine shrines," vessels, often clay pots, containing a mixture of several plants and materials that protect a person, a family, or a whole group from danger, especially witchcraft.

Men's societies. In contrast to the exclusive men's secret societies (q.v.), these are institutionalized associations to which virtually all initiated adult men in a community belong. Admission therefore automatically follows the completion of initiation. Some societies, like those in Melanesia, have a hierarchical structure. In such cases a rise to the next level in the hierarchy is bought (for instance with pigs) or obtained by holding a great feast. All members own and are responsible for certain esoteric knowledge, in particular religious traditions, as well as for sacred musical instruments (drums, flutes, bone trumpets, whirring rattles), whose sounds reproduce the voice of the beyond. None of this must reach the ears of women and boys who have not undergone initiation. In the past women who came into possession of such secret knowledge faced death or rape. The meeting place of these societies is usually either the men's house or a club house, where the above-mentioned instruments as well as other cult objects, masks, ceremonial clothing, and relics (e.g. ancestral bones) are kept. Such men's societies are found particularly in Melanesia as well as in other parts of Oceania, and in Central and West Africa.

Milking effigy. In order to maintain the flow of milk from the mother animal, nomads often stuff the fur of a young animal that has died with grass, straw, or other material, rub its urine over it and place it next to the mother when milking. The custom is particularly common among African nomadic herdsmen, but is also found in other nomadic cultures such as the yak-herding nomads of eastern Tibet.

Millet. Collective term for all types of cereal grain with small, round seeds up to $\frac{1}{5}$ inch in size and without a vertical furrow. The cultivation of millet has played, and partly continues to play, an important role in self-sufficiency in tropical and subtropical countries (in East Africa and the Sudan, India, and parts of China). Since ancient times the most important varieties have been proso, or broomcorn, millet (Panicum miliaceum), the foxtail varieties (Setaria italica), sorghum, known as durrha in most of Africa (Andropogon sorghum), finger or koracan millet, also known as raggee (Eleusine corocana), and pearl millet (Pennisetum spicatum), which is found particularly in the Sudan and grows to 9 feet tall. Tef (Eragrostis abessinica) is grown only in Ethiopia. Sorghum, raggee, and pearl millet are assumed to have been cultivated in Africa first. The grains are eaten cooked and are also made into flour or bread. Millet beer, brewed from fermented millet gruel, is a highly nutritious drink. It is usually made by women and is widely popular in Africa.

Nachtigal, Gustav (1834–85). German explorer of Africa. Nachtigal went to Algeria in 1861 as a doctor and in 1863 to Tunis. In 1863 he traveled

from Tripoli via Mursuk to the relatively unknown mountain country of Tibesti, presenting the sultan of Bornu with gifts from the king of Prussia. From 1870 to 1873 he explored the Sudan from Kuka and described the local population. He stayed in Bagirmi in 1872, Wardai in 1873, and Darfur in 1874, and returned to Germany via Cairo in 1875. In 1879 he became the German consul general in Tunis. As imperial commissar he raised the German flag over Togo and Cameroon in 1879.

Njembe society. Women's secret society (q.v.) among the Mpongwe in the Ogowe estuary (Gabon). Admission to the society usually occurs around the age of 12, with the performance of various initiation rites in the cult's ceremonial huts in the bush. Members of the Njembe society were said to possess special magical powers, including the ability to uncover thieves. It acted as a counterbalance to the Nda, the men's secret society whose focus was a kind of spirit of the forest. At various times the spirit would make a masked appearance in the villages to frighten the women and youngsters. Through their association in the Njembe society the women of this area were to a large extent able to free themselves of the men's violent domination.

Ogun. Yoruba god of iron and war (identical to Gu among the Ewe and Fon). Ogun is the god of blacksmiths and generally every metal, and the god of all workers and artisans who use metal implements and tools (such as butchers and hunters) as well as of soldiers, who used to make sacrifices to him before every battle to ask for his protection against death and injury. Today the god is revered mainly by truck and taxi drivers, mechanics, and hairdressers.

Ontology (from Latin *ontologia*, from Greek *ta onta*, the really existing, and *logos*, teaching). Fundamental philosophical discipline dealing with being, or more precisely with concrete appearance (peculiarities, aspects, and kinds), and with structures and rules of reality (principles, logical terms, and sentences) appreciated through experience (material/formal ontology). In ethnophilosophy the term is used to refer to the concept of being, represented, usually implicitly, in custom and proverb.

Oracle. Form of divination. For all peoples and at all times the oracle has played an important part in solving a variety of problems. Unlike omens and most dreams, oracles are not concerned with the interpretation of unexpected, random signs. Instead, contact with various unearthly powers (ancestors, spirits, or gods) is actively sought. An oracle is not only able to uncover the hidden, it also offers help with decisions in times of crisis. The methods and techniques used are extremely diverse, but are always bound to the particular culture's system of codes or signs. The Ifa oracle of the Yoruba is particularly well known: by casting lots (palm kernels, for example), a number is elicited. This number corresponds with a ritual text, which is then interpreted by the oracle priest (babalawo).

Orisha (Orisa). Humanlike deities, of which there are a very large number, among the Yoruba. The first orisha and highest deity is Olorun, the "owner of the heavens" and the creator of the world. However, no altars or priests are dedicated to him; he is a god removed from the people (deus otiosus). Subordinate orisha are much closer to humans, for instance, the thunder god Shango (mythical king of Oyo), the trickster god Eshu, whose practical jokes stir up confusion, and Ogun, god of war and iron. In the cities those who honor the orisha make up between 6 and 20 percent of the population, but Christians and Muslims often also participate enthusiastically in certain rituals, especially in the annual celebrations dedicated to them.

Osei Bonsu (1900–77). Ghanaian woodcarver, regarded as the most important of the 20th century. He created many of the emblems and symbols for the court of the asantehene, most notably the wooden model for a new version of the Gold Chair after street workers had desecrated the original in 1920.

Oyo. First city of Ife, the original Yoruba area, founded by Prince Oranmyan around the 14th century, in what is today southwestern Nigeria. Later Oyo was the seat of a profane ruler (alafin); but the king (oni) of Oyo remained as religious leader and is still recognized as such by the Yoruba today. Political conflict both abroad and at home forced the new kingdom to move its capital to Igboho. Only two centuries later, after the return from Igboho, was Oyo able to strengthen its position and, thanks to its cavalry, expand successfully. At the height of its power Oyo made great profits from the slave trade. From the 18th century onward internal troubles increased. Rebellions by vassals and slaves were followed by attacks from Muslim groups set off by the Sokoto jihad. In the late 1820s Oyo was sacked, and as a result it was moved to its current site (190 km further south). In 1895 the British conquered Oyo; they allowed the alafin to remain in office but placed him under their overall authority. Today Oyo is a predominantly Muslim city.

Palm oil. Oil from the oil palm (Elaeis guinenensis), the most productive of all oil-giving palms, which include the coconut palm (Cocos nucifera). Found in tropical West Africa from Guinea to Angola, the oil palm was originally only grown and used there. Traditionally it is planted in groves. The oil is extracted mainly from the flesh of the fruit, which contains up to 70 percent oil. This is done by heating the plants in water and pounding them in large troughs or mortars to press out the oil, which is then poured through sieves to remove impurities.

Polygamy, sororal (from Greek *polloi*, many, *gamos*, marriage, and Latin *soror*, sister). The marriage of a man to two sisters, rarely more. He marries them simultaneously or in succession, for instance, when the first wife does not produce any children. Although not very common, this custom is known the world over. It serves to strengthen both relations with in-laws and the wives' position in the household.

Poro society. Men's secret society, membership of which crosses ethnic lines, and which is very prominent in West Africa (Sierra Leone and Liberia). Like other secret societies (q.v.), before independence the Poro acted both as mediator in community and ethnic disputes and as an immediate police and judiciary authority that investigated and punished all kinds of offenses. In cases of war, a tribunal of the highest representatives of the society assembled to examine and assess the reasons for the conflict. The group found to be responsible was then handed over to the warriors of neutral tribes, who were free to plunder the community for four days, which they did without mercy. Wearing masks, they killed anyone who was not inside his or her house, and made off with everything they could lay their hands on. They were allowed to keep half of what they had pillaged, the other half being given to the party who had suffered the original attack. The Poro acted as a judiciary in other ways, too. Families judged to have become too rich and powerful were also subjected to plundering. Objection was useless, as the society had means of murdering or ruining anyone who resisted. The system found favor with the British colonial authorities, who saw its advantages and granted it official administrative and policing powers.

Possession. State of altered consciousness, which usually manifests itself somatically as a trance in which ancestors, spirits, or deities temporarily take over a person's free soul or consciousness, communicating through them, sometimes with a changed voice (sometimes also in a foreign language or in sounds incomprehensible to the uninitiated), and directing the person's behavior and actions according to their will. Possession can be individual or collective, unwanted or desired. Some mediums maintain a lifelong "marriage" or relationship with their spirit partners. Entry into this state requires certain preparations such as isolation, fasting and other deprivations, concentration exercises, the consumption of certain consciousness-altering drugs or hallucinogens, rhythmical body movements, music, dance, and so on. The particular person then falls into a trance and is now able to make contact with the spirit.

Possession cults. Forms of collective religious worship found the world over, practiced mostly in agrarian cultures, in which possession as a method of communicating with certain spiritual powers (ancestors, spirits, or deities) plays a central role. The better-known cults include Bori (among the Hausa), Zar (in Egypt, Ethiopia, Sudan, and other parts of Africa), vodun or voodoo (in West Africa and Haiti), Kromanti (in Jamaica), and Candomblé (in Brazil). These often prescribe a special social behavior for their members along the lines of their moral ideas, and have strict rules concerning admittance and membership, specific rituals, their own shrines, clothing, and priests (often in a carefully set out hierarchy) who lead the cult's activities as experienced mediums. Cult members usually belong to specific ethnic or social groups and are often also marginalized in terms of the official religion of their culture (as, for example, women, homosexual men, or transvestites may be). They meet regularly for trance dances, sacrifices, or to initiate new adepts into the cult. These have usually received a "calling" from the appropriate spirits through certain "signs," mostly sickness. Initiation into the cult enables them to overcome the disease; in return they pledge the use of their bodies by the spirits during possession trances. Possession cults have proliferated in farming and urban communities where colonialism and missions, as well as industrialization, urbanization, and great pressure to adapt have led to serious economic problems and crises of identity. Religious syncretism always plays a large part in the development of cults.

Praying mantis (Mantis religiosa). Type of locust (Mantodea) found in dry, warm environments worldwide, and so called because when it lies in wait for prey it holds its front legs like hands folded in prayer. It also has a real religious meaning for some peoples. The Bushmen regard it as the creator or the trickster (q.v.). It is said to speak the human language; its dreams are fulfilled; it can change into other animals; and when it dies it is always resurrected.

Praying mantis.

Queen mother. Originally the oldest woman in a royal or aristocratic lineage and later a high-ranking woman at African royal courts. The queen mother (ohemmea) is especially well known among the Asante and other matrilineal Akan peoples. The term is misleading and ethnologists disagree as to the nature of the position. The European term "mother" is inaccurate, but a "sister" of the king could hold the position. Contrary to some authors' opinion, the ohemmea was definitely not a priestess of a moon-related cult. She did not have sufficient power to be a ruler, but her authority was respected. In spite of her gender-specific title (consisting of the female suffix mea added to the male title ohene, meaning chief or prince), she was not simply a female chief. Her status was more like that of a man (she also wore male clothing), and if she was married she was allowed to have extramarital relationships. She had her own courtiers and was the only woman who could issue orders. Her importance was great; unlike the king, however, she did not symbolize the kingdom, but rather embodied the ideal of motherhood (regardless of whether she had children herself) and was the emotional link with the matrilineal ancestors. One of her main tasks, at cleansing rituals, was to lead the mourning for those who had died in the past year. Her word counted for much in disputes, and she had the power to resolve difficult questions. She held her own judicial court of which she was the only female member. Among some Akan she also participated in certain female rituals such as the girls' puberty rites (bragoro), and name-giving and cleansing ceremonies. Her political importance stemmed from the fact that, as the representative of the royal lineage, she

possessed exact knowledge of the genealogy. Therefore she had the casting vote at the election of a new ruler, who would only come to power if she had declared him legitimate. Once he was in office she had the absolute right to advise and criticize him. If he died or was deposed she remained in office and was closely involved in the choice of a successor.

Rainmakers, rain priests. Specialists who can summon or prevent precipitation at will. Particularly in areas short of water (e.g. in the West African savanna) the population depends strongly on rain. Even so, depending on the season, rain can be welcome or not, and it is therefore essential to be able to influence it. Usually this responsibility lies with the chiefs, who in a request for rain offer sacrifices (mostly black animals) in the ancestors' house or over graves, and who claim their legitimacy through their ancestors, a close relationship with water, or the ownership of certain sacred objects. For example, the Alur of northwestern Uganda recognize the ruler of Ukuru as the highest rain priest because he is in possession of rain stones and metal rain spears. When placed in a river, these can summon rain; turned toward the sky and moved back and forth, they prevent rain from falling. Elsewhere there are specialists who own "rain medicine," which enables them to send rain to their enemies at the wrong time, but also to "bind" it and therefore keep it away from the fields if necessary. In both cases they use magic by analogy. Because of their close connection with rainfall, often linked to thunderstorms, they are also able to direct a "heavenly" thunderstorm to those who have committed an offense (especially theft) against the community.

Rattray, Robert Sutherland (1881–1938). British colonial civil servant, linguist, and ethnologist (a student of R. R. Marett). In 1907, he joined the Gold Coast custom service and in 1911 was appointed Assistant District Commissioner in Ejura (in Asante territory). As a captain during World War I, he took part in the campaign against the Germans in Toho. In 1921, after holding different posts within the colonial administration, Rattray became the first and only director (and member) of the newly founded Anthropological Department in Ashanti. His pioneering works in West African ethnology appeared over the next years: *Ashanti* (1923); *Religion and Art in Ashanti* (1927); *Ashanti Law and Constitution* (1929), and the two-volume *The Tribes of the Ashanti Hinterland* (1932). Rattray's works show him to be an excellent field researcher but also a hopeless romantic.

Religious kingdoms. In traditional agrarian cultures, the fertility of land, animals, and people is a matter of survival, as it guarantees both food and future existence. Anyone who is strong and healthy, brings in rich harvests, has an impressive herd, several wives, and many children, and is generally fortunate in everything enjoys high social standing. In some instances he may take up a position of leadership, although this could bring him less power and more responsibility, as it is expected of him that he will use his particular powers for the benefit of the group by personally carrying out all the important public agrarian and fertility rituals. This person may be the eldest of a clan, the village chief, or the settlement's wealthiest farmer. A particularly typical figure is the earth-chief (q.v.), who ideally has all the above-mentioned attributes. Toward the end of the 5th century BC, the early civilizations of the eastern Mediterranean emerged, influencing at the edges of their realms the development of a particular type of kingdom. In these tropical zones people lived in agrarian societies, but conditions did not favor the development of highly hierarchical states. The kingdoms that arose there can be understood as more highly evolved versions of the old earth-chiefdoms. These religious kingdoms, as they are known, were found even until recently in Polynesia, parts of India, and especially in Africa. The king, even more than the earth-chief, was regarded as the carrier of fertility for soil and subject alike, and therefore his existence was a guarantee of the life and prosperity of the community. He had to carry out all important agricultural rituals or at least initiate them (e.g. at sowing and harvesting ceremonies), ensure sufficient rainfall, and maintain peace in his realm. In order to carry out his duties he had to be not only healthy and strong but also free of any physical defect (hence rivals for the throne were always blinded or mutilated) and live strictly according to tradition. This in turn meant taking many protective safety measures. Religious kings were often not allowed to leave their residence, eat or drink anything foreign, and could not be touched or looked at by anyone except their personal servants, closest relatives, and highest dignitaries. They therefore often wore a thick veil or sat behind a screen during public appearances. They were not so much rulers as prisoners of their people, too precious to be exposed to anything that might take away even the tiniest amount of strength or health from them, because this would affect everyone in the whole realm. If there were droughts, bad harvests, plagues, or other disasters, the blame lay with the king: either he had fallen sick, or he had broken a serious taboo. As he now presented a threat to everyone, he was either deposed or killed (ritual murder) and replaced by another. Religious kings bore heavy responsibility while possessing practically no political power, for that too would have been profane. The business of ruling was carried out by regents or a council of ministers or nobles.

Rites of passage. Literal translation of the phrase *rites de passage*, introduced by the French ethnologist Arnold van Gennep (1873–1957). These protect the process of change in spatial, time, biographical, social, and cosmic systems. These kinds of passages – overstepping of borders and limits, births, initiations, marriages, seasonal or status changes, death – are experienced as risky and dangerous. They are breaks between two phases of life, where the old order is no longer valid but the new has not yet been established. The rituals follow the procedural model, which can be separated into three phases: departing from the life lived previously, marked by ritual farewells or killing (separation rites), the actual passage in between, marked by isolation from society and everyday life, with a transformation to

Waterfall on the Ntambunah.
From: *Westafrika. Vom Senegal bis Benguela*, Leipzig, 1878.

prepare for the next life phase, and the transfer into a new existence, ritually accompanied by ritual resurrection, greeting, and acceptance into society (assimilation rites). The core is the middle phase, the metamorphosis. The form and intensity of the ritual alter according to the occasion (initiation, marriage, death). However, usually the aim is to dramatize the current borderline state and the necessary transformation. Postulants, bride-and-groom-to-be, or princes not yet in power must for instance not be seen, retreat in seclusion to a place outside the settlement, exist there in a death-like state, fast or eat only raw foods, hardly speak or move, neglect decoration and hygiene, are painted white, must undergo trials of courage and repulsion. In fact, they pass

through, as does the whole population in extreme cases (at new year, or the death of a king), an anarchic and disorderly phase (see ritual anarchy), like the dead in the underworld, a life turned upside down. Toward the end assimilation starts up again: the baby, postulant, future couple, or next king are cleansed, fed or covered with strengthening, nutritious foods (e.g. grains or flour), painted red, given new clothes and often a new name, and, having come back to life, they return to their society. They may appear uncertain there, cannot walk or talk properly, and do not recognize even their relatives. However, the assimilation rites in the third phase soon put an end to this, re-familiarizing the "newborns" with all they had forgotten during "death." This is crowned by a communal celebration. Rites of passage ensure that any instability during the transferring phase remains under control and does not lead to undesirable developments for those involved or the whole community, i.e. that the new order reflects the old. This happens by making the process a ritual one, keeping it in place through dramatization.

Ritual anarchy. Extreme instance of a rite of passage (q.v.). No society could last without stable rules of life and law. However, social order is constantly under threat from enemies within and without, and at particular life stages and times of social or cosmic transition; at those times the two sections of a cyclical whole briefly come apart, making it possible for dangerous alien influences and malicious spirits to enter and bring evil, even cause chaos. In traditional societies, major breaks of this kind occur with death, initiation, the transition between seasons or around the new year (the "days between the years"), and the time between the death of an old king and the enthronement of his successor. To resist the potential dangers in such special "open times," when the old order is no longer valid but the new one is not yet established, people turn impending chaos into a tangible object through dramatization, playing out the chaos and, with magical protection, keeping everything under control. Depending on the calendar and resources of the particular culture, order is ritually turned upside down, and anarchy reigns for the duration of the time of transition. Children can scold their parents, throw dirt at them, even beat them, and the same goes for wives against their husbands. Men and women swap sexes by wearing each other's clothes (ritual transvestitism). The socially low, such as beggars, take the position of high-ranking officials and dignitaries. Kings must give way to jesters from the lower classes. The rules that normally control life are no longer valid. Prison gates open, alcohol flows freely, and forbidden games, even sexual liberties up to incest, are allowed until the end of the "mad" days. Then the old order returns, impending chaos is banished through controlled prevention, and it has once again become clear to everyone that an existence without rules and order can only lead to depravity and decay.

Ritual rebirth. Certain life stages or temporal events, such as birth, puberty, marriage, adoption, appointment to office, evening and morning, or seasonal changes, are generally, but especially in traditional societies, regarded as "risky processes of passage." They are temporary states of limbo between two life stages, when the rules of the past (e.g. of childhood) no longer apply and those of the new life (adulthood) are not yet valid. Two connecting parts of a cycle temporarily separate, leaving a gap through which harmful influences and malicious spirits can reach those affected. Light and dark, order and chaos spill over into each other like night and day at dawn or dusk, so that everything is unstable and evil impulses can easily lead to unwanted developments. Rites of passage (q.v.) act as defenses. Whether a young woman is becoming a mother, a grown man assuming council membership, a visitor turning into a guest, or a living person dying, all the according rituals follow the life model. The three phases – separation, transformation, and reassimilation – are regarded respectively in terms of death, preparation for a new birth, and rebirth itself. This ritual change takes place in a very obvious way. Those affected are isolated, quite often violently, from their community, sometimes even ritually "killed." In their seclusion, which stands for the realm of the ancestors, they behave like the dead. They wear no clothes or different clothes, hardly eat or speak, use their left hand instead of their right, are painted white to appear like dead souls, and communicate with their dead ancestors (in the form of masked carers). After a certain time, often three days, they are "brought back to life" and return to the community. At first they are like newborns, unable to feed themselves or to walk properly, much less speak. In this way critical changes in the natural life cycle are "bound together" and therefore protected from dangerous mistakes.

Rohlfs, Gerhard (1831–96). German traveler in Africa who took part in the French campaigns in Algeria as a doctor (1855–61) and member of the Foreign Legion. As a converted Muslim he traveled through North Africa (mostly Morocco) and was the first European to reach the Tuat oasis. In 1865–67 he was again the first European to cross Africa from the Mediterranean, traveling from Tripoli via Bornu to Lagos on the Gulf of Guinea. Later he traveled through the Libyan desert (Cyrenaica, Kufra oasis) and became German consul general in Zanzibar in 1884.

Rouch, Jean (b. 1917). French engineer, ethnologist (a student of Marcel Griaule and Marcel Mauss) and moviemaker. In 1952 he and ethnologist A. Leroi-Gourhan founded the Committee for Ethnographic Film in Paris and he has since made more than 120 movies.

Secret societies. Institutionalized associations of certain men (less frequently women) who possess a particular knowledge that must strictly be kept from outsiders, and who perform certain special tasks. Although membership can be bought, it usually has to be won through hard work and is valid for life. The candidate must undergo a series of demanding initiations (q.v.) which, if he passes, allow him to rise to a higher rank. Depending on its purpose, each society has particular specialisms and knowledge; for example, of healing plants, specific therapies, the communication and maintenance of sacred traditions (myths, magic formulas, and dances), and special arts and handicrafts (such as woodcarving). This often gives the societies great influence and power. Although these are sometimes abused, societies usually use them in a mediating capacity, so that they tend to hold judiciary and policing powers. Secret societies were, and to some extent still are, found in traditional cultures in North and South America, southeastern Australia, and in many parts of Oceania, as well as in Africa, in western Sudan and in the belt from the coast of Guinea to Tanzania.

Shango. Mythical king (alafin) of Oyo and thunder god of the Yoruba. Like the thunderstorm he causes and embodies, he is regarded with ambivalence. People fear his destructive powers (threatening crops, for instance), although they are also seen as a blessing, bringing fertility to the earth. Shango resides in the heavens; he hurls thunderbolts and lightning, made by his blacksmith brother Ogun, down to earth to punish offenders. The Fon and Ewe have similar gods, Xeviésó (also So or Sogbo) and Mawu-Sogbla respectively.

The Sacred Axe of Shango.

Sacred ax of Shango. From: *Faith, Fancies and Fetich*, London, 1924.

Shea butter. Edible oil obtained from the seed of the shea butter tree (Butyrospermum parkii, B. paradoxum, Vitellaria paradoxa), which is found in the West African savanna, both wild and cultivated. It has yellowish-green fruit, about the size of an apricot; the thin, soft, and very sweet pulp surrounds a chestnut-shaped seed about 1 to 1½ inches across which contains a nutritious oil with a mild, cocoa-like taste. The fruit is collected and through elaborate and laborious processes the women of the West African savanna extract the oil.

Sheik. Arabic title of honor, originally given to the eldest, so that a sheik can be the head chief of a family, lineage, clan, or tribe. A sheik enjoys high status and commands authority, but also has corresponding responsibilities. Among the Bedouin (q.v.) a sheik's particular tasks include ensuring that traditional order is upheld, mediating in cases of conflict, and settling legal disputes. Generosity is considered an obligatory virtue. A sheik must keep open house to all guests and must support the impoverished or help them with gifts. He possesses no real political, much less executive, power. Always dependent on the agreement of all other elders of the group in matters of decision-making, his position is approximately that of *primus inter pares* (first among equals). With the rise of Islam the title was soon used for state dignitaries (such as city administrators, governors, and viziers), notable scholars, religious authorities, and founders and officials in Muslim brotherhoods.

Shrine (1). A sacred object of any kind. Initially it referred to wooden containers or closets ("shrine altars"), sometimes also triptychs, whose central part is usually filled with figures and which can be closed up. Its meaning was expanded, mostly in the literature about Africa in English, to refer to not only buildings or containers holding ancestral figures (ancestor shrines) or other dedicated cult objects, but also any object imbued with special powers.

(2). Place always or sometimes dedicated to religious activities, within or outside the settlement. In the latter case these are often natural shrines, such as particular mounds or hills (especially if these rise above an otherwise flat landscape), clearings and sacred groves, springs, stones, rock formations, trees (especially very old or tall ones) and caves. Built shrines may either be constructed for that purpose or be existing structures declared shrines. They include hearths, a certain house on the estate, the central village square, cult houses, etc. Shrines are often connected with the origin or history of a family, village, society, or empire, and the presence of spirits can be felt in their vicinity – by the whispering of the trees, the murmur of a stream, or the crackling of the fire. Sacred sites serve only positive purposes of the cult: prayers are said here, sacrifices offered, and fertility rituals, marriages, initiations, and other important ceremonies carried out. Buildings (also in sacred groves) act as storage for the necessary cult paraphernalia (musical instruments, masks, medicines, etc.), figures of great ancestors, totem animals, guardian spirits and gods, and the temple treasure (such as votive gifts, relics, the skulls and bones of ancestors, chiefs, and certain animals, old weapons, rare stones, and other objects, as well as war trophies). These assemblages of objects increase the shrine's sacredness and make protection against sacrilege essential. Shrines are often surrounded by ditches, walls, or palisades, but are more usually protected by an invisible circle. The uninitiated or unclean, women, and especially strangers are not allowed to approach the shrine, much less enter it. However, within a shrine there is an obligation to keep the peace, so that shrines were often sought by refugees and even those sentenced to death.

Sigui, sigi. Elaborate ceremony and dance of the Dogon, held every sixty years to commemorate Dyongu Seru, the mythological ancestor and direct founding father of the Aru. Dyongu Seru had to die, even when he had already changed himself into a snake so that he could come back to life as a spirit. He was also the first healer and initiator of the mask society (awa). As no funeral ritual was held for him, his soul remained in this world and has since lived in the snake-shaped Great Mask (imina na), which is always carved anew at each sigui. When the old and new masks are placed close together the soul can change its place of residence. On this occasion men of a certain age are initiated into the secrets of the Great Mask and the language of the Sigui (sigui-so). They spend three months in the Sigui cave, where the Sigui mask is kept, finally coming back to life as "sons of the Great Mask" and, splendidly dressed, returning to the village with undulating, snakelike movements. The whole ceremony lasts seven to eight years, starting in the villages around Yougou, moving westward from community to community until it completes its circle in Yougou.

Sororate (from Latin *soror*, sister). Marriage of a man to two (rarely more) sisters. In contrast to sororal polygamy (see polygamy, sororal), sororate is usually understood as a secondary marriage, the man marrying one of his wife's sisters only after her death. For clarity, the latter meaning of this term is sometimes qualified as "postmortal sororate."

Soul boy (okra). Term used by the Asante and other Akan peoples for a child born on the same day of the week as the ruler. For this reason the child was regarded as the carrier of the king's soul and was responsible for protecting him from danger. The boy lived in the king's immediate vicinity in the palace and tasted all his food and drink in case of attempts to poison him. In the past the soul boy was usually a slave who was sacrificed at the king's death so that he could continue to be his servant in the world beyond.

Even today a soul boy accompanies the ruler on ceremonies and sits in front of him in the balanchine (q.v.) when the ruler appears in public.

Stanley, Henry Morton (alias John Rowlands; 1841–1904). British writer and explorer of Africa. Raised in England, Rowlands went to New Orleans in 1859 where he befriended the trader Henry Stanley, later taking his name and adding "Morton." Stanley's life was marked by instability. For a while he fought on both sides in the American Civil War, then he became a sailor. Later he worked as a reporter on the battles with the Native Americans, and then as a correspondent for the *New York Herald* in Ethiopia and the Gold Coast. Only in 1871, when he had found David Livingstone in Central Africa, did he become an explorer. When Stanley heard of Livingstone's death on his return from Ashanti, he decided to continue the older man's work. From 1874 to 1877 he crossed the African continent from east to west. From Bagamojo he traveled across Lake Victoria (which he recognized as the source of the Nile) and Lake Tanganyika to Njangwe, and from there down the Congo to its mouth on the Atlantic coast. From 1879 to 1884 he was in the service of the Belgian king, Leopold II, who had practically taken possession of the Congo valley. In 1887–89 he crossed the continent from west to east, from the mouth of the Congo to Zanzibar, to rescue Eduard Schnitzer (Emin Pascha). He left Africa in 1890 and was elected to the British parliament in 1895.

Henry Morton Stanley and his officers.
From: *In Darkest Africa*, New York, 1890.

Sun lizard. Relief decoration in the shape of a lizard, applied particularly to the doors and locks of Dogon storehouses. The lizard is artistically portrayed in many parts of the world, especially in Australia, Oceania, and Indonesia, but also in Africa. In African mythology it often brings the news of death to people, instead of the intended message of eternal life from God. Worn on the body as a metal amulet, or used as decoration on vessels or buildings, the depiction of the lizard is

Sun lizard on the outside wall of a Dogon men's house.

regarded as possessing great magical powers of protection. With the Dogon it also symbolizes the "female" foreskin on the male penis, which is cut off during initiation as part of the "death" suffered by the boys, to be reborn as adults.

Swahili. A people living along the coast of East Africa from Somalia to Mozambique and also on the islands Zanzibar, Penba, and the Comores. They were named Swahili (coast people) from the Arabic rulers of the sultanate of Zanzibar when the latter conquered the East African coast in the early 18th century (and thereby became "swahili" themselves). Their population currently stands at about 400,000. Their language, Kiswahili, is a Bantu language containing many Arabic words; often in abridged form, it serves as the lingua franca in wide parts of East Africa. Many Swahili, who name themselves after the city they live in, were merchants and town dwellers, with a more global outlook than other African peoples. They were middlemen in intercontinental trade between Asia and Africa. At their cultural apogee (between the 12th and the 16th centuries) their standard of life hardly differed from that in Europe. The Swahili lived in stone houses in cities and distinguished themselves by their fine clothing as well as their high level of education and exalted poetry. The noble Swahili families recognized no superior political authority and never formed an association but always lived in cities independent of each other.

Syncretic churches. Churches in which two or more religions are merged. The term applies particularly to the more recent churches set up mostly in Latin America and Africa, and initially often linked to anticolonial interests. Religious images and concepts of differing origins are merged or reinterpreted. In the Catholic churches of Latin American countries Christian saints were often identified with deities of African or, less frequently, Native American origin. Many of the new African churches have clearly syncretic attributes. In spite of intensive efforts by missionaries, some societies or social groups only partly accepted the Christian message and chose those passages which fitted into their world conception. The basis for many syncretic churches, orientating themselves along the lines of Christianity, is mastery of a "chaotic" world and freedom from earthly suffering. This manifests itself especially through sickness and other misfortunes (such as the effects of black magic and witchcraft), concerns which lie at the core of traditional African religions. Healing, often accompanied by a complex liturgy, is therefore central to most syncretic churches. In spite of many hospitals and medical stations, the supply of medical care, particularly to rural populations, is still insufficient. In addition, scientific explanations of illness stand in stark contrast to the concepts held by uneducated people. Self-appointed prophets who also appear as (miracle) healers find it easy to attract followers.

Tattoo (from Samoan *tatau*, fitting or appropriate). Decoration of human skin with motifs such as rows of dots, wavy or circular lines, stars, spirals, and less frequently figures. Four techniques are used. In point-tattooing, or needle-tattooing (practiced in Oceania), patterns are drawn by making a series of pinpricks which are then filled with color. In cut-tattooing (also practiced in Oceania), shallow cuts are made and filled with dye. Tattooing by sewing (practiced in Siberia and northwestern North America), involves pulling a blackened thread through the skin. Tattooing by scar, or scarification, is especially common among dark-skinned people (in Africa and Melanesia); serial, ornamental, or figurative cuts are made in the skin, and either medicinal powders for magical strengthening or dyes (e.g. mixtures of indigo, ash, and charcoal) are rubbed in. The healing process is often deliberately delayed so that the scars stand out more. Universally the most frequently used color is black (obtained from ashes mixed with plant juices), which changes to blue once under the skin. Tattoos providing magical protection are often made only near openings in the body (eyes, mouth, navel, vagina), while others, such as decorations or signs of status or ethnicity, are made on the hand, women's breasts, or even on the whole, or at least the visible parts of, the body. Oceanic peoples, particular the Marquesas Islanders, Samoans, and Japanese were the true masters of the art. The type and design of the patterns are dictated by clan or tribal traditions. Another reason often cited is that tattoos help the ancestors to identify a new arrival in the land of the dead as one of their own.

Trance (from Latin *transire*, to go over). A state of altered consciousness, resembling hypnotic or sleeplike state. The expression "falling into a trance" describes a psychosomatic process by which a person becomes extremely receptive and gives way to internal as well as external powers. Trance phenomena are said to be part of religious and therapeutic practices in 90 percent of societies worldwide. Some societies accept the presence of spirits and their possession of the medium's body. Such cases are described as "possession trance." Another kind of trance is the experience of ecstasy, "stepping out of one's self." Here the free soul leaves the body and travels to other places, sometimes to the other world (classic examples of this are the journeys of shamans), to communicate visions or messages from there. The numerous methods of inducing a trance or easing the passage into the trance require psychological stimuli and certain physical techniques, such as monotonous rhythmical drumming, dancing, breathing techniques (e.g. hyperventilation), and meditation or concentration exercises, as well as the consumption of stimulants (e.g. smoke) or plant-based drugs such as toadstools. Once a state of trance is reached, conditions for communicating with the spirits are set.

Tribe. Political association of linguistically and culturally related groups with a common ancestry – that is, of several clans who, usually, inhabit a single territory and are connected by marriage, bartering, and other associations. Because of the autonomy of each clan, and even of lineages, in traditional societies, these connections are quite loose. However, when danger threatens them all, the bonds of which they have been only vaguely conscious are immediately revived: people help each other through shortages of prey, natural disasters, and large-scale loss of domesticated animals, and close ranks in resistance to hostile attacks. Problems that arise in such crises and in conflicts within the tribe are collectively resolved by the leading representatives of each group, who gather in the tribal council. In recent times the term "tribe" has been discredited. Adherents of postmodern ethnology in particular find the term too imprecise, given the loose structure of the tribe and their few mutual obligations, and the fact that it is partly the construct of colonial

Chinchua, on the Ramboëh River.
From: *Westafrika. Vom Senegal bis Benguela*, Leipzig, 1878.

powers, who exaggerated its importance for administrative reasons. It has also gained a rather derogatory meaning through its use in adventure books. "Ethnicity" is increasingly used as an alternative term: although no more precise, it carries fewer connotations.

Trickster. Mythical being attempting to act as a kind of counterforce in creation but finally only able to disturb the creator's works with tricks, the basic element of his actions. Of dubious character, he is blindly led by his moods and passions, and indulges in hair-raising obscenities and food orgies. He is unsteady, sly, and cunning but also continually falls victim to his own shortsighted haste and greed. He is frequently malicious, but sometimes foolishly generous. His ventures are the subject of countless comical tales that are full of wit and bawdiness. True to his split nature the trickster already appeared in the earliest days not only as a malicious troublemaker, but also as a helper to humans, a cultural hero who taught people how to make tools and how to use them, who led them to hunting prey, and instructed them in healing sickness. However, he did these things not with the thoroughness of the gods, whose actions were planned, but on whims that suddenly overcame him. A mood swing, and only a moment later he was back to hatching nasty schemes and thinking of evil, which is why his doings could affect people both positively and negatively. Although a master of disguise and transformations, he prefers the guise of black or night animals (e.g. the spider among the Akan, the fox among the Dogon and in many European tales, and the raven or coyote among many Native Americans).

Tro (plural trowo). Among the western Ewe (Anlo, Ho, Abutia) an anthropomorphic, male or female spirit sent into the world by the heavenly god to guard over humans and to help them in their daily troubles. Trowo are also regarded as guarantors of fertility, health, and good fortune. They punish neglect, inflicting plague and drought on societies, and sickness and lasting misfortune, even death, on individuals, depending on the offense. People must keep the trowo in a good mood by obeying their rules and through regular or occasional sacrifices. The sick and those dogged by misfortune often enter the service of a tro and become initiated into a dedicated cult. There are trowo for individuals, families, and social groups, standing in hierarchical relation to each other. Those trowo close to oneself, one's family, or group are generally considered benevolent, "strangers" as malevolent. Some trowo possess great powers, others are clearly limited in their effectiveness. The former include especially the great nature deities who are revered across regions, such as Hevieso (or So), the god of thunderstorms; Dan, a snake and rainbow deity; Sakpata, the god of the earth and infectious diseases, especially smallpox; Ogun, god of iron and patron of blacksmiths; and Adela, the god of hunting. Those limited in their effectiveness are local or family deities with weak powers of influence. Although trowo prefer certain natural locations, people build residences for them, or honor them in objects that they have made. Nyigbla, who used to support soldiers, can be found in a piece of iron; Legba, who guards cities, city districts, villages, and entrances, is represented as a human figure in stone or wooden sculptures.

Tsetse fly (from a Bantu word). African fly of the genus Glossina, belonging to the Muscidae, the family of two-winged insects. Tsetse flies can reach a size of ½ inch long and survive only in areas of high humidity, that is, on the border between wet and dry savanna. Among the 20 known kinds, the most common transmitters of sleeping sickness and tsetse sickness (nagana plague), which affects cattle and horses, are Glossina morsitans and Glossina palpalis. Typical symptoms include fever, anemia, weight loss, and paralysis, finally leading to the animal's death. For this reason cattleherding in Africa is mainly limited to the dry savannas.

Urban cultures. Urban settlements appeared toward the end of the 5th century BC in the great early civilizations. They were not made up of growing villages but were princely residences encircled by extensive fortification, which provided the surrounding rural population with protection against enemy attacks. The more intensive agriculture of sophisticated societies, based on grain crops complemented by animal farming, more efficient tools, such as the hoe, and more developed irrigation techniques, resulted in greater surpluses which could be stored over several years. This meant that larger parts of the population were able to abandon agriculture and dedicate themselves to artisanship and manufacture. The need for such skills had arisen through court life, with its many requirements (for cooks, stately robes, and court officials), warfare, and the ever-developing techniques of agriculture itself. This led to increasing specialization, and such specialists as weavers, dyers, rope-makers, chariot-builders moved into the cities. Not only could these craftsmen work more closely together and therefore more cost-effectively, they also had better access to raw materials. Trade began to flourish in parallel with their own work and cities became business centers. Their population therefore consisted of a great variety of social and professional groups: slaves, day-laborers, porters, artisans, merchants, servants, artists, musicians, administrative officers, priests, military staff, and finally members of the aristocratic class. This was reflected by a variety of material possessions, houses and buildings, and valuable and luxury objects. On the other hand, urban life caused the importance of old familial connections to decrease. People were now grouped by profession and status: the day-laborers' huts stood at the edge of the city, then there were the artisans' quarters, with streets of carpenters, blacksmiths, basketweavers, or butchers; further toward the center were the wealthy merchants and higher officials of the city who lived near the palace and the temple precincts. This in turn led to the formation of communities united on the basis of their members' professional standing. Society fragmented into a number of strictly separated groups, classes, and strata that developed their own subcultures – in guilds and temples, in the army, among singers and musicians, at court – with their appropriate tools and equipment, customs, legends, and forms of religion. Every group had a full view only of its own way of life and therefore became dependent on all others. Strictly centralized governing powers were required to maintain the ability of the whole to function effectively, and these became increasingly removed from the society's lower levels. The opaque circumstances, conflicting interests of different social groups, their mutual dependence, tensions and hostilities, conflicts and fears, suppression and misery after military failure expressed themselves not through the ruling temple theology but through a lower-class populist religion. With its flourishing beliefs in magic and witchcraft, sacrifice, and malevolent spirits, it served populations that had been susceptible to apocalyptic predictions and salvationist religions since antiquity. Little changed until the beginning of the modern era, and populist religions still exist in the less prominent cities of Asia, Africa, and Latin America. The urban cultures of Asia Minor in ancient times, those in Europe and the Islamic

Fan drummer and hand-ja player.
From: Westafrika. Vom Senegal bis Benguela, Leipzig, 1878.

world during the Middle Ages, and those to be found in certain parts of the Third World today have certain qualities in common: highly complex, often multiethnic, always multicultural, very colorful, lively, and creative on the one hand, confusing, full of conflict, and frightening, even self-destructive on the other. Urban culture is a microcosm of a city's surrounding regions.

Virilocality (from Latin vir, man, and localis, place). In traditional village societies a newly married couple can generally not decide freely where they will live, their choice of residence being strictly defined by rules of descendancy. As exogamy is the norm, i.e. the spouse must come from a different group, the woman moves in with the man in patrilineal societies (see clan), the man with the woman in matrilineal ones, although this is often not permanent, only for "visits." The former case is virilocality, the latter uxorolocality (from Latin uxor, wife).

Vodun (vodu, vodou, voodoo). General term among the Fon and the eastern Ewe (Watyi, Ge, and Be) for anthropomorphic deities (see tro and orisha) with particular areas of responsibility and the cults dedicated to them. Anyone wishing to be accepted into the cult as a full member (vodunsi) must spend a certain period of time in a shrine (vodun monastery) isolated from society. Here, under the supervision of a priest, he suffers a ritual death and is reborn. Originating in different African traditions, these religious conceptions were brought to the New World by slaves from Dahomey, so that today many different syncretic cults exist in the Caribbean and in South America under the name of voodoo. Its main features are rituals and sacrifices, accompanied by singing and dancing, through which people place themselves under the protection of a certain deity; in turn, they "lend" their body to the deity during rituals. One of the Afro-American religions in which possession trance plays a central part is the Candomblé in Brazil (its center being in Salvador de Bahia), which is based especially on the religious traditions of the Yoruba.

Whirring rattle. An instrument consisting of wooden, leaf- or dagger-shaped blades attached to string. Made to rotate steadily, it produces a humming sound, which is interpreted as the voice of the spirit powers, especially the ancestors. Whirling rattles are always owned by men, and are sometimes the possession of mask or other secret societies. They are usually heard during the night at funerals or mourning ceremonies. They also play an important part in initiation, and announce the appearance of masks (e.g. the Great Mask of the Dogon).

Witchcraft. The use of magic, usually for evil ends. There is an idea held all over the world that certain people (witches) have the ability to cause harm to other people, crops, animals, and even the natural environment. Every kind of misfortune – whether sickness, sterility, disagreement, poverty, early death, or natural disaster – is blamed on a witch's doings, especially if cases of bad luck accumulate. Witches owe their ability to harm to an innate quality, "witch power," which is often passed down in certain families and becomes stronger with increasing age: witches are mostly adult women who harm their closest relatives above all. They act by instinct, sometimes unconsciously, but always in secret, often in association with other witches whom they join on the witches' sabbath for orgiastic dancing. Greedy, with an insatiable sexual appetite, they embody not only antisocial behavior in general but also the reverse of all duties and values approved by society. Their appearance and their behavior turns everything upside down: they are naked; they walk with their feet pointing upward or they fly; they practice incest or other forbidden sexual acts, and eat human flesh (that is, not the body itself but people's life soul). They carry out their evil deeds at night, often accompanied by animals (e.g. hyenas) or birds (often owls). Witchcraft is often stimulated by jealousy or competition. In many societies affected by witchcraft there are specialists (witch doctors) responsible for uncovering witches and healing their victims as well as protecting the other members of the community from witchcraft.

Women's societies. Institutionalized associations usually of certain (rather than all) women in a community. In traditional cultures women's societies are much rarer than men's societies (q.v.). This is because of exogamy, which operates in patrilineal societies (far more numerous than matrilineal societies) and by which women, on marriage, move to their husband's house. Exogamy splits women into two groups with different interests, limiting the possibilities for

solidarity; mothers and sisters stand on one side, wives on the other. Women's societies are very much secret societies (q.v.). Possessing specific esoteric knowledge (e.g. magic), they perform certain special tasks, such as carrying out economic or educational work, representing women's interests, sometimes defending these through word and action, and enjoying the privilege of carrying out particular rituals, usually related to fertility or agrarian magic. Women's societies are hierarchical. Joining involves an initial payment or undergoing an initiation ceremony; this may be followed by further payments or initiations as the member rises through the hierarchy. Women's societies are found mostly in simple agrarian cultures in America, Oceania, and Africa. There are

The Zambesi waterfalls.
From: *Die Völker der Erde*, Würzburg and Vienna, 1891.

particularly numerous in West Africa; they include the Sande in Sierra Leone and Liberia, the Djengu in the coastal areas of Cameroon, and the Njembe in southern Cameroon and Gabon.

Yams ("dioscorea", from the Senegalese *nyami*, to eat). Genus of yams (dioscoreaceae) with about 600 kinds. An edible tuber, one of the most important cultivated foods in tropical rainforest and wet savanna areas, alongside other bulbous plants such as taro (Colocasia esculenta), manioc (Manihot utilissima), and sweet potato (Ipomoea batatas), and tree fruit (bananas, baobab, and palms). The usual agricultural tools in this area are the digging stick (q.v.) or the ax (in Africa, inland

India, the Philippines, and parts of Indonesia), used in slash-and-burn agriculture, as tubers quickly exhaust the soil. Yams are planted as small bulbs or parts of a larger tuber and harvested with the digging stick. The maturing bulbs take about a year to mature. They can reach a length of 27 inches and a weight of over 4 lb. Like the potato, they contain 72 percent water, 23 percent carbohydrates, 1.8 percent protein, and 1 percent minerals; they are thus low in protein but high in starch. In nutritional terms this is a serious disadvantage as a diet based mainly on yams – or other tubers – is deficient in protein, potentially resulting in physical weakness, weight loss, anemia, inability to form antibodies, slower healing of wounds, and poor breastmilk production. The cultivation of tubers seems to be an ancient practice. Recent archeological discoveries have shown that it may reach back to the 14th century BC, with its origins probably in Melanesia (and New Guinea).

Zebu or hump-backed cattle (Bos zebu). Economically important domestic cattle, with many different breeds, found in tropical Asia (India's sacred cow), Africa, and recently introduced into South America. Zebu are considered valuable work animals because of their great mobility; the volume of their milk production, however, is far below that of European cows. It is assumed that its wild form is the Indian aurochs (Bos primigenius nomadicus). The zebu came from Asia to Africa in the time of Ancient Egypt. Crossbreeding with domestic cattle, especially longhorn cattle (Bos africanus), resulted in the hybrids kept by many of today's cattleherding nomads. However, the zebu type, which began to win the upper hand over the longhorn from the early Middle Ages onward, has remained dominant.

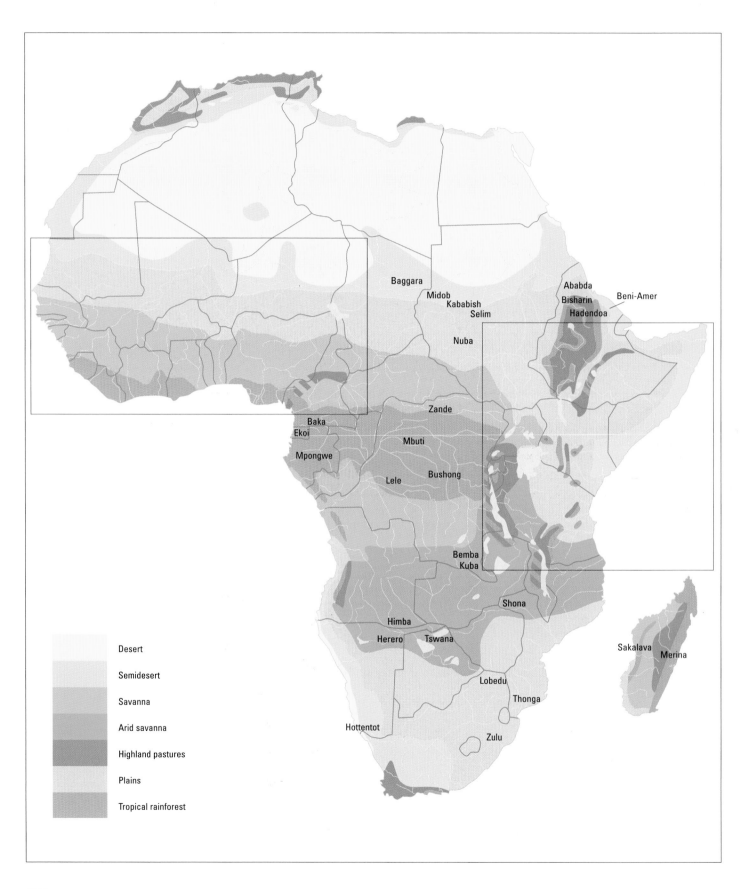

Baggara

Midob
Kababish
Selim

Ababda
Bisharin
Hadendoa

Beni-Amer

Nuba

Zande

Baka
Ekoi

Mbuti

Mpongwe

Lele   Bushong

Bemba
Kuba

Shona

Himba

Herero   Tswana

Sakalava
Merina

Lobedu

Thonga

Hottentot

Zulu

Desert

Semidesert

Savanna

Arid savanna

Highland pastures

Plains

Tropical rainforest

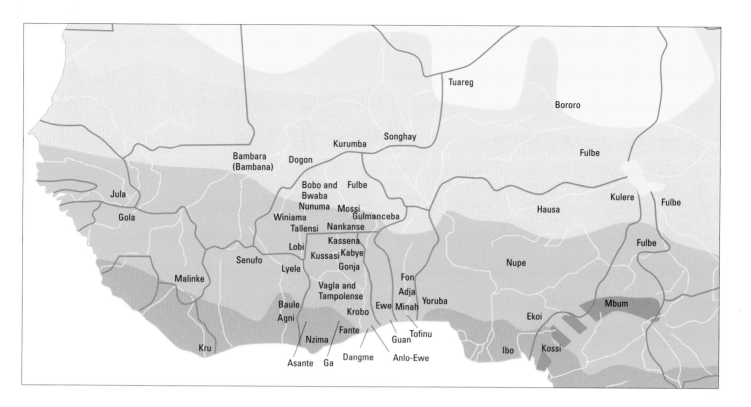

Opposite page: The tribes of Africa, showing their distribution across geographical zones. Climate and topography have been, and still are, of major importance to the development of distinct cultures.

Above and right: The tribes and topography of West and East Africa.

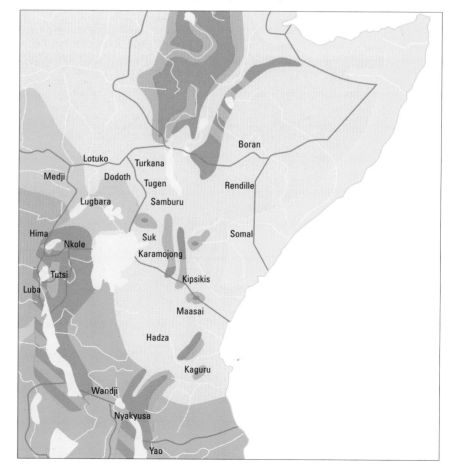

BIBLIOGRAPHY

Abélès, Marc & Chantal Collard (ed.): Age pouvoir et société en Afrique Noire. Paris, 1985.

Adventures of an African Slaver. London, 1928.

Ammah, Charles Nii: Homowo and other Ga-Adangme festivals. Accra, 1982.

Andree, Richard: Abessinien, das Alpenland unter den Tropen und seine Grenzländer. Leipzig, 1869.

Aus Erde geformt: Lehmbauten in West- und Nordafrika. Mainz, 1990.

Baudin, P.: Fetichism and Fetich Worshipers. New York, Cincinnati, St. Louis, 1885.

Baumann, Hermann (Ed.): Die Völker Afrikas und ihre traditionellen Kulturen. 2 Vols., Wiesbaden, 1975–79.

Bay, Edna G.: Wives of the leopard: gender, politics, and culture in the kingdom of Dahomey. Charlottesville, 1998.

Boddy, Janice: Wombs and spirits: Women, men and the Zar cult in northern Sudan. Madison, 1990.

Bohner, Heinrich: Im Lande des Fetischs. Ein Lebensbild als Spiegel des Volkslebens. Basel, 1890.

Cannadine, David & Simon Price (Eds.): Rituals of royalty: power and ceremonial in traditional societies. Cambridge, 1987.

Center of African Art, New York: Yoruba. Nine Centuries of African Art and Thought. Exhibition catalog, New York, 1989.

Chesi, Gert: Voodoo, Africa's secret power. Wörgl, Austria: Perlinger, 1980.

Christoph, Henning & Hans Oberländer: Voodoo. Geheime Macht in Afrika. Cologne, 1995.

Cole, Herbert M. & Doran H. Ross: The arts of Ghana. Los Angeles, 1977.

Conneau, Théophile: Adventures of an African slaver. A. & C. Boni, 1928.

Davidson, Basil: The Growth of African Civilisation. A History of West Africa 1000–1800. Harlow, Essex, 1965.

Drewal, Henry J. & Margaret Thompson Drewal: Gelede: art and female power among the Yoruba. Bloomington, 1990.

Elwert-Kretschmer, Karola: Religion und Angst. Soziologie der Voodoo-Kulte. Frankfurt/New York, 1995.

Evans-Pritchard, Edward E.: Hexerei, Orakel und Magie bei den Zande. Frankfurt am Main, 1978.

Field, M. J.: Religion and medicine of the Ga people. Accra, 1961.

Gann, L. H. & P. Duignan (ed.): Colonialism in Africa, 1870–1960. London, 1969–70.

Garrard, Timothy F.: Akan weights and the gold trade. London, 1980.

Griaule, Marcel: Masques dogons. Paris, 1938.

Griaule, Marcel: Conversations with Ogotemmêli. An Introduction to Dogon Religious Ideas. London, Oxford, New York, 1965.

Griaule, Marcel: Schwarze Genesis: ein afrikanischer Schöpfungsbericht. Frankfurt am Main, 1980.

Harding, Leonhard & Brigitte Reinwald (ed.): Afrika – Mutter und Modell der europäischen Zivilisation? Die Rehabilitierung des Schwarzen Kontinents durch Cheikh Anta Diop. Berlin, 1990.

Herrmann, Paul: Das große Wagnis. 6000 Jahre Kampf um den Erdball. Berlin, 1936.

Herskovits, Melville J.: Dahomey: an ancient West African kingdom. 2 Vols. New York, 1938.

Heusch, Luc de: Sacrifice in Africa: a structural approach. Manchester, 1985.

Heusch, Luc de (ed.): Chefs et rois sacrés. Paris, 1990.

Hirschberg, Walter: Die Kulturen Afrikas. Wiesbaden, 1974.

Horton, Robin: Patterns of thought in Africa and the west: essays on magic, religion and science. Cambridge, 1993.

Huber, Hugo: The Krobo: traditional social and religious life of a West African people. St. Augustin, 1963.

Hull, Richard W.: African cities and towns before the European conquest. New York, 1976.

Imperato, Pascal J.: African folk medicine. Baltimore, 1977.

Iwu, Maurice M.: Handbook of African medical plants. Boca Raton, 1993.

Jacob, Ernst G.: Grundzüge der Geschichte Afrikas. Darmstadt, 1966.

Jules-Rosette, Bennetta (ed.): The new religions of Africa. Norwood, 1979.

Kagame, Alexis: La philosophie bantu comparée. Paris, 1976.

Kimmerle, Heinz: Philosophie in Afrika – afrikanische Philosophie. Frankfurt am Main, 1991.

Ki-Zerbo, Joseph: Die Geschichte Schwarz-Afrikas. Wuppertal, 1979.

Lawal, Babatunde: The Gèlèdè spectacle: art, gender, and social harmony in an African culture. Seattle, 1996.

Malerische Studien. Eine Reise um die Welt in 200 farbigen Photographien nach Naturaufnahmen. Neuchâtel, undated.

Maurier, Henri: Philosophie de l'Afrique Noire. St. Augustin, 1976.

Mbiti, John S.: African religions and philosophy. London, Heinemann, 1998.

McLeod, M. D.: The Asante. London, 1981.

Meiss, Ortwin: Suggestionen ohne Trance? Gedächtnispsychologische Aspekte. Hamburg, 1998.

Meyer, Piet: Kunst und Religion der Lobi. Zürich, 1981.

Middleton, John (ed.): Witchcraft and curing. Garden City, 1967.

Middleton, John (ed.): Encyclopedia of Africa south of the Sahara. 4 Vols. New York, 1997.

Murray, Jocelyn (ed.): Cultural Atlas of Africa. New York: Facts on File, 1998.

Nooter, Mary H. (ed.): Secrecy: African art that conceals and reveals. New York, 1993.

Nyamiti, Charles: Christ as our ancestor: Christology from an African perspective. Gweru, 1984.

Nyerere, Julius K.: Freedom and development. Uhuru na Maendeleo. A selection from writings and speeches 1968–1973. London, New York, Oxford University Press, 1974, c. 1973.

Oberländer, Richard (ed.): Westafrika, vom Senegal bis Benguela. Leipzig, 1878.

Okere, Theophilus: African philosophy: a historico-hermeneutical investigation of the conditions of ist possibility. Lanham, 1983.

Platz, B.: Die Völker der Erde. Würzburg and Vienna, 1891.

Preston Blier, Suzanne: African Vodun. Art, Psychology, and Power. Chicago und London, 1995.

Rattray, Robert S.: Ashanti. London, 1923.

Rattray, Robert S.: Religion and art in Ashanti. London, 1927.

Rattray, Robert S.: The tribes of the Ashanti hinterland. 2 Vols. London, 1932.

Ray, Benjamin C.: African religions: symbol, ritual, and community. Englewood Cliffs, 1976.

Rippmann, Konrad: Vodou-Medizin in Haiti, in: Hexerei, Magie und Volksmedizin. Ed. Bernd Schmelz, Bonn 1997.

Roy, Christopher: Art of the Upper Volta Rivers. Meudon, 1987.

Senghor, Léopold Sédar: Afrika und die Deutschen. Tübingen, 1968.

Spieth, Jacob: Die Ewe-Stämme: Material zur Kunde des Ewe-Volkes in Deutsch-Togo. Berlin, 1906.

Spieth, Jacob: Die Religion der Eweer in Süd-Togo. Leipzig, 1911.

Stanley, Henry M.: In Darkest Africa, or Quest, Rescue, and Retreat of Emin Governor of Eyuatoria. 2 Vols., New York, 1890.

Stoller, Paul: Embodying colonial memories: spirit possession, power, and the Hauka in West Africa. New York, 1995.

Sundermeier, Theo: The individual and community in African traditional religions. Hamburg: Lit; Piscataway, NJ: Distributed in North America by Transaction Publishers, 1988.

Thomas, Louis-Vincent & René Luneau: La terre africaine et ses religions: traditions et changements. Paris, 1980.

Waterlot, G.: Les Bas-Reliefs des Bâtiments royaux d'Abomey (Dahomey). Paris, 1926.

Wanono, Nadine: Les Dogon. Paris, 1996.

Wendl, Tobias: Mami Wata oder ein Kult zwischen den Kulturen. Münster, 1991.

Wilks, Ivor: Forests of gold: essays on the Akan and the kingdom of Asante. Athens, Ohio, 1993.

Wright, Richard A. (ed.): African philosophy: an introduction. Lanham, 1984.

Zahan, Dominique: The religion, spirituality, and thought of traditional Africa. Chicago: University of Chicago Press, 1979.

ACKNOWLEDGMENTS

The publisher wishes to thank the museums, collections, archives, and photographers for granting permission to reproduce illustrations and for their support in the publication of this book. The publisher has made every effort to locate all other owners of reproduction rights. Copyright holders who have not been contacted are asked to notify the publisher.

All color photographs by Henning Christoph, Essen.

© P. Baudin: *Fetichism and Fetich Worshipers*, New York, Cincinnati, St. Louis, 1885: endpaper

© Black Star/Photo-archive: 86, 87 top, 89, 91 (top right), 97, 98, 99, 100, 101

© Photo-archive. Henning Christoph collection:
Photographs by Markus Matzel: 121, 152, 167, 168, 234, 354, 355, 366, 367, 385 (bottom), 386, 458, 459
Photograph by Henning Christoph: 166
Photograph by Yavuz Arslan: 124
Photograph by Daniel Kölsche: 385 (top), 412, 414, 415

© Center of African Art, New York: *Yoruba. Nine Centuries of African Art and Thought*. Exhibition catalog, New York, 1898: 263

© Basil Davidson: *The Growth of African Civilisation. A History of West Africa 1000–1800*. Harlow, Essex, 1965: 450 (bottom)

© Griaule, Marcel: *Conversations with Oggotemmêli. An Introduction to Dogon Religious Ideas*. London, Oxford, New York, 1965: 74

© Könemann Verlagsgesellschaft mbH/Graphics: Rolli Arts, Essen: 12 (top), 75, 80, 81, 84, 500, 501

© Murray, Jocelyn (ed.): *Afrika, Bildatlas der Weltkulturen*, Augsburg, 1998: 428, 444, 456

© Preston Blier, Suzanne: *African Vodun. Art, Psychology, and Power*. Chicago and London, 1995: 416

© Henning Christoph collection: 89, 126, 127, 262, 352, 353, 413, 422, 423, 452 (right), 453, 457

© Studio für Landkartentechnik, Nordstedt: 480

© SVT Bild/Photo-archive: 11, 41, 42, 43, 83, 85, 88, 102, 103, 107, 122, 128, 129, 381, 383, 439 (bottom), 454, 455, 488

© Völkerkundemuseum der Universität Zürich/Photo: Peter Nebel: 387